Gathering for Goddess

A Complete Manual for Priestessing Women's Circles,

B. Melusine Mihaltses

ISBN#978-0-9851384-4-8
Publisher: Feminine Divine Works
Schertz, Texas 78154-0114, U.S.A
©B. Melusine Mihaltses
Year: 2012

Gathering for Goddess
A Complete Manual for Priestessing Women's Circles,
B. Melusine Mihaltses

ISBN#978-0-9851384-4-8
Publisher: Feminine Divine Works
Schertz, Texas 78154-0114, U.S.A
©B. Melusine Mihaltses
Year: 2012

Gathering for Goddess,
a Complete Manual for Priestessing Women's Circles
© 2012 by B. Melusine Mihaltses.
Published by

Feminine Divine Works
P.O.Box 114
Schertz, Texas 78154-0114
Femininedivineworks@gmail.com

©B. Melusine Mihaltses 2012
B. Melusine Mihaltses asserts the moral right to be identified as the author of this work.

Library of Congress Cataloging- in- Publication Data
Mihaltses, B. Melusine, 1970-
      Gathering for Goddess, a Complete Manual for Priestessing Women's Circles

      1.Goddess, 2. Women Studies 3.Spirituality, 4. Feminism, 5. Mythology 6. Paganism, I. title

Includes bibliographical references
ISBN: 978-0-9851384-4-8
LCCN: 2012933200

Gathering for Goddess, a Complete Manual for Priestessing Women's Circles © 2012 by B. Melusine Mihaltses
All rights reserved. No part of this book may be used, reproduced, nor transmitted in any form or by any means, electronically or mechanically, including photocopying, recording or by any information storage or retrieval system, whatsoever without written permission from Publisher; Feminine DivineWorks, except in the case of brief quotations embodied in critical articles and reviews.

Although the author and publisher have made every effort to ensure accuracy and completeness of information contained in this book. We assume no responsibility for errors, inaccuracies, omissions, or any inconsistency herein. Any slights of people, places, or organizations are Unintentional.

First edition
First printing, 2012
Cover Art: B. Melusine Mihaltses
Interior Illustration and original art by: B. Melusine Mihaltses

Printed and bound in the U.S.A.

20129332000

Gathering for Goddess

A complete manual for Priestessing Women's Circles

B. Melusine Mihaltses

*For The Greatest Loves of my life;
Demetrios, Milo and Ethan-John*
May you always know "Her"magick, love, protection and gentle guidance.

Gathering for Goddess

A complete manual for Priestessing Women's Circles,
B. Melusine Mihaltses

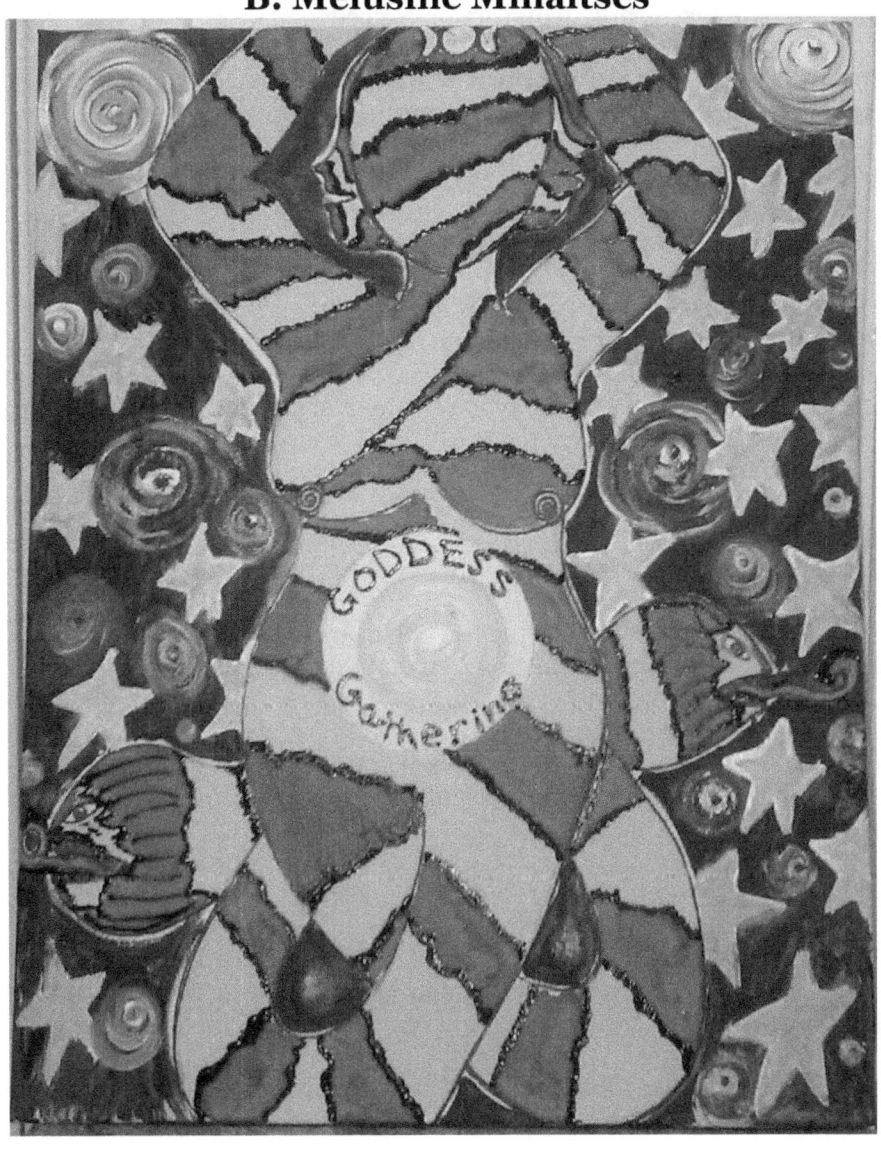

DEDICATION

Thank you Goddess, Beloved Feminine Divine, for giving me Hope, Vision, Guidance, Wings, Purpose, Inspiration, Strength, Courage and Breath...
I Dedicate this book to "She" of over Ten Thousand Names...

In the name of Amaterasu, for giving me truth and honor, bringing me out of hiding and for reflecting back at me, through my Sisters and her sacred mirror, my own self-worth and brilliant inner light.

In the name of Athena, who lovingly bestows her wisdom and warns me not to fear the battle and inspires me to fearlessly embrace the powers of my mind.

In the name of Nike, whose wings guarantee my success and in her arms, I am already victorious.

In the name of Skadi who teaches me to honor my physique and stand in my truth and with courage, dare to take action, when action is needed.

In the name of Brigit, who is my transformer and inspirer, encouraging me to use my hands and voice to birth new miracles, forged from those fires in my soul.

In the name of Oya, who feeds me courage to lead, strength for battle (when at times I want to run and hide) and who serves as a reminder of my debt to my beloved ancestry and those who paved the way before me.

In the name of Pele, who stirs and awakens great passion and encourages me to embrace my emotions and with fiery ambition, pursue my heart's desire.

In the name of Artemis, who breathes empowerment and feminism in my veins and awakens me to Sisterhood - connecting me to a much larger lineage than I could possibly fathom alone.

In the name of Aphrodite, who is forever the teacher of love, most importantly self love....and awakens my powers of beauty and attraction.

In the name of Ix Chel, who connects me to the ebb and flow of life, ancient powers of water and my gender's strong connection to the Moon and the cosmos.

In the name of Hathor, who reminds me to fill my life with wonderful joy and pleasure, who lavishes me with all the things that make me happy to be alive; dance, music, art, merriment, cosmetics, wine, gems, sex, beauty, love.... all the many splendors that bring delight to my senses...

In the name of Baubo, who shows me the healing powers of liberation in a good belly laugh and the great value of my "fabulous" yoni.

In the name of Saraswati, who awakens my spiritual connection to the Divine, the written word, and the value and power of my voice and inherented creative gifts.

In the name of Aine, who teaches me the art of an Enchantress and the right, as a Divine womyn, to protect myself from harm.

In the name of <u>Erzulie,</u> who teaches me its okay to want more, and supports my pursuit for love, abundance and the finer things in life.

In the name of <u>Demeter,</u> who supports me in the role of nurturer, mother and who teaches me to honor the cycles of life and the changes each season brings.

In the name of <u>Persephone,</u> who models living in two worlds, and shows the way life sometimes must be lived within certain confinements but always in perfect balance.

In the name of <u>Selu, Corn Mother</u>, who teaches me the power in the Corn, proper balance and how to find inner nourishment for both my body and my heart and consequently awakens in me the gifts of forgiveness and sacrifice.

In the name of <u>Aradia,</u> my teacher of the craft, who supports and uplifts me, encourages my work as Priestess... who in my moments of weakness instills in me confidence and generously teaches me to trust my instincts because all the knowledge I seek already lies within me.

In the name of <u>Hekate,</u> forever my mother, great grand-mother, ancestress and beloved teacher, Divine protector, who always holds the sacred lantern for me, guiding my way so that I may navigate better in moments of darkness.

In the name of <u>Grand Maman Brigitte</u>, who mothered me to the very edge and taught me to honor the sacred threshold of life and death, my ancestors and my beautiful bones; which now hold the imprint, the memories, of all I've experienced and endured on this earthly plane.

In the name of <u>Hina</u>, who is the Moon and my spiritual safe haven, where I am allowed to repose, regenerate, heal, realign and connect with the Divine and teaches me the value of spiritual sanctuaries.

In the name of <u>Hestia,</u> whose core fires I hold dearly, forever providing me with a much appreciated Hearth and Home to call my own....lending me a Sacred Space and temples to be born out of my hearth fires, teaching me the sacredness of hearth and home.

In the name of <u>Gaia,</u> who is fertile, nurturing immortal mother of all and thus imparts in me the importance of self nurturing and birthing those tiny fragile (seemingly insignificant) seeds of hope- that lay planted deep in the recesses of dark, yet fearsome human minds. Gaia, guardian of those fragile seedlings taking root into the most magnificent of towering strength-filled trunks of unwavering miraculous trees- a beautiful reflections of your Divine powers working through us and manifesting itself upon the earth. You are forever a gentle reminder of my lineage, the power of hope and the sacred roots connecting us to one another in this journey we call life.

Blessed Be for each Wommin and every Goddess present in my life and here in this book offering...

TABLE OF CONTENTS

Dedication	6
This Table of Content*	8
Preface	11
Images	13
Goddess preview short synopsis	14
Traditions and Acknowledgment	16
Introduction	19
Organization of this Manual	21
Organizations of Goddess Workshops	22
Goddess Themes and Symbols	24
Information on Eight Wiccan Sabbats	26
The wheel of the Year with Goddess	30

1. December Month Lore   35
Amaterasu Page and Altar Set Up   36

Illustration and Goddess Image	37
Amaterasu Lecture	39
Second part of lecture	42
Goddess Workshop Day	43
Ritual Outline	45
Japan Ritual II Offering	48
Amaterasu and Susano-O	50
Amaterasu Mirror Musing I	52
Amaterasu Mirror Musing II	53
Invocations, Evocations, Quarter calls and Prose	55
Spells of the Month	56
Personal Priestess Journaling	57
Song Text Sheet	58

2. Athena Page and Altar Set Up   59

Illustrations & Goddess images	60
Athena Lecture	62
Goddess Workshop Day	65
Ritual Outline	67
Meditation	69
Invocation of Athena	72
Aspecting Athena	73
Homeric Hymn to Athena	74
Spells of the Month	75
Song Text Sheet	77

3. Living Deity Image   78

Getting to know your Goddess wkshp	80
Goddess Workshop Day	81
Creating our Living Goddess	82
Name Changes Within Craft	84
New Name Blessing prose	85
Personal Priestess Journaling	86
Song Text Sheet	87

4. January Month Lore   88
Skadi Page and Altar Set Up   89

Illustrations and Goddess images	90
Lecture on Skadi	92
Goddess Workshop Day	96
Ritual Outline	99
Meditation	101
Energy spell	105
Dream Sharing, Giants Arrive	106
Skadi Invocation	108
Song Text Sheet	109

5. Nike Page and Altar Set Up   110

Illustrations and Goddess images	111
Lecture on Nike	113
Goddess Workshop Day	114
Ritual Outline	116
Meditation	118
Aspecting Nike	120
Homeric Hymn to Nike	121
Spell of the Month	122
Personal Priestessing Journaling	123
Song Text Sheet	125

6. February Month Lore   126
Brigit Page and Altar Set Up   127

Illustrations and Goddess images	128
Lecture on Goddess	130
Goddess Workshops	132
Ritual Outline	134
Imbolc Ritual II	136
Invocation to Brigit	138
Baking Recipe for Wkshp	139
Meditation	140
Personal Priestess Journaling	142
Spell of the Month	145
Song Text Sheet	147

7. Oya Page and Altar Set Up   148

Illustrations and Goddess images	149
Lecture on Goddess	151
Goddess Workshops	155
Ritual Outline	157
Oya Invocation	159
Devocation	160
Personal Ritual prayer to Oya	161
The Tower card, Musing as she arrives	163
Summer Amidst Change	165
Personal Priestessing Journaling	167
Spell of the Month	168
Song Text Sheet	169

8. March Month Lore   170
Pele Page and Altar Set Up   171

Illustrations and Goddess images	172
Lecture on Goddess Pele	174
Goddess Workshop Day	177
Ritual Outline	179
Invocations, Evocations, Quarter calls and Prose	181
Spell of the Month	182
Sharing a Dream	183
Song Text Sheet	185

9. Artemis Page and Altar Set Up   186

Illustrations and Goddess images	187
Lecture on Artemis	190
Goddess Workshop Day	194
Ritual Outline	196
Meditation	199
Invocations, Evocations, Quarter calls and Prose	202
Sharing Artemis Dreams	205
Spell of the Month	207
Song Text Sheet	211

10. April Month Lore   213
Aphrodite Page and Altar Set Up   214

Illustrations and Goddess images	215
Lecture on Aphrodite	217
Goddess Workshop Day	220
Ritual Outline	222

Alternate Goddess Wksp Day	225
Beltane II Ritual Outline	226
Invocations & Prose	228
Spell for the month	230
Sharing Dreams of Aphrodite	234
Song Text Sheet	236

11. Ix Chel Page and Altar Set Up — 237

Illustrations and Goddess images	238
Lecture on Ix Chel	240
Goddess Workshop Days	243
Ritual Outline	245
Ritual II Outline	247
Invocations, Evocations, Quarter calls and Prose	248
Meditation	250
Element of Water	251
Relinquishing Poem	252
Release- a Spiritual Transmission	253
Personal Priestess Journaling	255
Song Text Sheet	257

12. May Month Lore — 258

Hathor Page and Altar Set Up — 259

Illustrations and Goddess images	260
Lecture on Hathor	263
Goddess Workshop Day	265
Ritual Outline	267
Hathor Meditative Questioning	269
Invocations, Evocations, Quarter calls and Prose	270
Spell of the Month	272
Personal Priestess Journaling	273
Song Text Sheet	275

13. Baubo Page and Altar Set Up — 276

Illustrations and Goddess images	277
Lecture on Baubo	280
Baubo's Gift	281
Goddess Workshop Day	283
What brings you joy	285
Ritual Outline	286
Yoni Lecture	288
Spell of the Month	290
Personal Priestess Journaling	293
Song Text Sheet	295

14. June Month Lore — 296

Saraswati Page and Altar Set Up — 297

Illustrations and Goddess images	298
Lecture on Saraswati	300
Goddess Workshop Day	302
Ritual Outline	304
Meditation	306
Mantras and Chants	309
Mandalas Essay	310
Mudras Essay	311
Thoughts on Creativity	312
Spells of the Month	313
Song Text Sheet	315

15. Aine Page and Altar Set Up — 316

Illustrations and Goddess images	317
Lecture on Aine	319
Goddess Workshop Day	322
Reflections on Aine	324
Ritual Outline	325
Invocations, Evocations, Quarter calls and Prose	327
Spell of the Month	328
Personal Priestess Journaling	329
Song Text Sheet	330

16. July Month Lore — 331

Erzulie -Freda Page and Altar Set Up — 332

Illustrations and Goddess images	333
Lecture on Erzulie-Freda	336
Goddess Workshop Day	339
Ritual Outline	341
Meditation	343
Spell of the Month	345
Authentic Voodoo Chants	346
Song Text Sheet	347

17. Gaia Page and Altar Set Up — 348

Illustrations and Goddess images	349
Lecture on Gaia	351
Goddess Workshop Day	353
Ritual Outline	355
Orphic Hymn to Gaia	357
Invocations, Poetry and Proses	358
Personification of Gaia	361
Tapping into Mother Archetype	363
Personal Priestess Journaling	365
Song Text Sheet	367

18. August Month Lore — 368

Demeter Page and Altar Set Up — 370

Illustrations and Goddess images	371
Lecture on Demeter	373
Goddess Workshop Day	375
Musing on Demeter	377
Ritual Outline	379
Invocations, Evocations, Quarter calls and Prose	382
Spell of the Month	383
Personal Priestess Journaling	384
Song Text Sheet	387

19. Persephone Page & Altar SetUp — 388

Illustrations and Goddess images	389
Lecture on Persephone	391
Goddess Workshop Day	395
Persephone Speaks	397
Ritual Outline	398
Solitary Ritual	400
Invocations, Evocations, Quarter calls and Prose	401
Spell of the Month	402
Song Text Sheet	404

20. September Month Lore — 406

Selu Page and Altar Set Up — 407

Illustrations and Goddess images	409
Lecture on Selu -Corn Mother	411
Goddess Workshop Day	414
Ritual Outline	416
Corn Mother Invocation	418
Personal Priestess Journaling	420
Final thoughts	422
Song Text Sheet	423

21. Aradia Page and Altar Set Up — 424

Illustrations and Goddess images	425
Lecture on Aradia	427
Goddess Workshop Day	430
Ritual Outline	432
Stregheria	435
Charge of the Goddess	438
Components of a Spell	439
Chart of Planetary Hours	440
Aspecting thoughts	441

Polarities and Shades of Magick	442
Spell of the Month	444
Personal Priestess Journaling	445
Song Text Sheet	447

22. October Month Lore — 448
Hekate Page and Altar Set Up — 449

Illustrations and Goddess images	450
Lecture on Hekate	452
Goddess Workshop Day	456
Ritual Outline	458
Death Tarot Card Reflections	460
Ancestress Meditation	463
Orphic Hymn to Hekate	464
Invocations, Evocations, Quarter calls and Prose	465
Spells of the Month	468
Personal Priestess Journaling	471
Hekate Dreams	473
Song Text Sheet	475

23. Maman Brigitte Page & Altar Set Up — 477

Illustrations and Goddess images	478
Lecture on Goddess	480
Goddess Workshop Day	483
Meditation	485
Ritual Outline	487
Invocations, Evocations, Quarter calls and Prose	490
Personal Priestess Journaling & Dream	491
After thoughts	494
Song Text Sheet	495

24. November Month Lore — 496
Hina Page and Altar Set Up — 498

Illustrations and Goddess images	499
Lecture on Hina	501
Hina Musing on Sanctuaries	502
Goddess Workshop Day	504
Ritual Outline	506
Meditation	509
Invocations, Evocations and Prose	511
Polynesian Prose	512
Spells of the Month	513
Creating Altars	515
The Moon	517
Song Text Sheet	519

25. Hestia Page and Altar Set Up — 520

Illustrations and Goddess images	521
Lecture on Hestia	523
Goddess Workshop Day	525
Ritual Outline	526
Homeric Hymns to Hestia	529
Spells of the Month	531
Sprit of Gratitude	534
Song Text Sheet	535

26. DEDICATION Month

Goddess images	536
Welcome to our Group	**538**
Group's Registration form	539
Group's Agreements	540
Solitary Priestess Ritual	541
Ritual Outline for Group's Dedication	542
End of year Group Questionnaire	545
Ways of Connecting with the Divine	546
Personal thoughts on Aspecting	548
Things to Consider with Group Rituals	550
Invocations	552
Song Text Sheet	556

27. OTHER

Images	557
Advise and Observations	559
Check-In Questions for Check ins	564
Goddess Workshop Craft activities	565
List of Craft activities	566
Elemental Attribute Table	567
The Elements	568
Circle Casting Suggestions	569
Chakra and Gemstone workings	570
Alchemist Oil Recipes	571
"She Who"	572
Bardic Ritual Chant Text Sheet	573
Author's additional Song Text Sheet	574

References & Bibliography	577
Author Bio	586
Photographs	587
FeminineDivineWorks Order Form	589

PREFACE

"A Woman is the Full Circle, within her is the Power to create, nurture and transform..." Diane Mariechild

For anyone on a spiritual path, in particular one that encourages self-mastery, knowledge and empowerment; like Wicca and Goddess Spirituality, there comes a point, after intense solitary studies, when we begin to peer out and seek our like-minded brethren and sisters, craving a little spiritual companionship, also known as- Fellowship. And this is a fundamentally natural progression for anyone endeavoring to grow, as fellowship enhances our learning experience and provides a uniquely important aspect to our spiritual path. Yet, it is not often that such desired communities are readily distinguishable by open advertisement or even available in some parts of this world for many novice Wiccans and Goddess worshippers alike. Thus the need to fill a void and formulate one's own community becomes almost compulsory, as we aspire to grow and build a stronger relationship to the Divine and her many (human and non-human) creations.

The book you hold in your hands manifested out of a strong need to delve deeper into my own Goddess spirituality and an even stronger need to gather other like-minded people who were also on a similar spiritual journey -like so many of us, seeking fellowship. When I could not find a community one had to be created and this book documents the process, some of my very personal experiences and reveals every step for creating, priestessing and facilitating a Goddess Group. This special book is a complete manual that will help you create fellowship for yourself and others, strengthen and expand your knowledge of the Divine and finally, birth your own monthly Goddess gatherings.

Herein, you will find many valuable monthly Goddess lessons, advice and a very well organized book on how to create and maintain a Goddess group. Over Twenty-three Goddesses from different pantheons are highlighted with lectures, relevant articles, engaging communal workshops, path workings, craft and spells and meditations. You will also find for every Goddess offered, a detailed Ritual outline with suggested invocations, quarter calls and circle castings. And every chapter also offers song text sheets of traditional and brand new Pagan chants, which are excellent to incorporate during your day filled with the Goddess.

In this book I also share my own journey with personal journal entries of my first year as a Priestess for the group I created, "Grove of the Feminine Divine." Throughout the years I have found that journaling, musing, as well as recording my dreams, has always contributed greatly to my own spiritual growth and, recognizing its importance for future priestesses, it is shared in this Goddess Gathering manual in the hopes that it may add an element of support and further insight for you.

With ***"Gathering for Goddess, a complete manual for Priestessing Women's Circles,"*** you hold in your hand a clear concise manual to create for yourself and your neighborhood a special place for people to honor the Divine Feminine. And most importantly, via this book, you hold the great seed to proliferate the importance of Goddess Gatherings to strengthen and expand Feminist Wicca and Goddess Spirituality.

I'd like to wish you Brightest Blessings on your journey and thank you in advance. In the spirit of service and love this book is offered to the Universe, may it be well received and placed in the hands of women (womyn, wommin, wombmyn), her future Priestesses as an invaluable resource to sustain and contribute to the permanence of our Goddess Spirituality.

Hail to She of Ten-Thousand Names,
Hail to her Daughters and Priestesses, immortally chanting "Her" name...)o(Blessings.

*****

Gathering for Goddess…

GATHERING FOR GODDESS, *a complete manual for Priestessing Women's Circles by B. Melusine Mihaltses*

I. DECEMBER-Awakening to our Power

Amaterasu	The Sun, our Divine Light, Order and Truth, our reflections in the mirror, coming out of hiding, Our self-worth.
Athena	Honoring our Intellect, strategizing, education and the unique skills of the warrior. Honoring our creative skills that our competent hands exemplify with the blessings of the Goddess.
Dedications:	Creating our own modern day Deity and dedicating ourselves for a year and a day to the Goddess that calls us now.

II. JANUARY – Victory Embodied

Skadi	Winter, healthy Physique, fitness goals, the warrior, courage and honoring our truth and our sacred body.
Nike	Victory, projection of Success, Self Confidence of a winner. Goals.

III. FEBRUARY – Fires of Transformations

Brigit	Transformative Fire, Forge of creativity in its many manifestations, healing waters of her sacred Well.
Oya	Change, time to assess, courageously severing that which no longer serves us well, starting anew, welcoming the cathartic powers of drastic change.

IV. MARCH – Feminine Empowerment

Pele	Anger, Effective use of such powerful emotions like, passion and anger, re-direction of our emotions (like anger) in a positive way and unearthing the impetus to move to action.
Artemis	Sisterhood, Feminism and the important gifts of the Divine Archer; Will and Focus and the Maiden. Earth and the sacredness found in the Wild, Animal magick.

V. APRIL – Water Healing

Aphrodite	Beauty, embracing our own powers of attraction, self- blessing and acknowledging our own individualized beauty from within and without.
Ix Chel	Healing Waters, and the Moon, our intimate connection to the element of Water and the numerous ways it can positively effect our mundane and magickal lives.

VI. MAY- Earthly Delights

Hathor	Pleasure, what brings you joy and ecstasy (music, dance, scents, sex, edibles, textiles etc...) Inviting more pleasure in our lives. Awakening that part of us that celebrates our physical manifestations on this Earth.
Baubo	Laughter, and the honoring of our sacred Yoni, What makes us laugh and shift us out of depressive states. Welcoming strategies for our happiness, liberation and balanced wellbeing.

VII. JUNE – Creativity

Saraswati	Rivers of creation. Spirituality practice via our creative works. Valuing and unearthing our own artistic offerings for the world.
Aine	Sun and Moon energy. Awakening the Sacred Element of Fire and how to best utilize it, invoking protection for all wommin, learning to work with Fairy Magick and the gift of the Enchantress.

VIII. JULY - Abundance

Erzulie-Freda	Manifesting the finer things in life and accepting our rights to them. Romance and prosperity, Oaths and promises to ourselves, to love and live a richly ornamented, embroidered life with style.
Gaia	Honoring our Pregnant selves, whether we are pregnant with ideas, money, creative projects, animals or actual human children. Proliferation, birthing ourselves, multiplying our blessings and sharing it outwardly, Totem magick, manifesting abundance and creativity on the earth, gems of the earth.

IX. AUGUST – Balancing our roles

Demeter	Honoring the shifts and subtle changes in season, our primary relationships and even our own selves, as the wheel turns once more… tapping into our own bargaining powers and the Mother.
Persephone	Balancing Dark and light, Learning to walk between the realms, Honoring our numerous roles and titles, and finding a delicate balance between them all. Honoring the daughter and healing our relationship to Mother….

X. SEPTEMBER - Sacrifice

Corn Mother	Sacrifices and Forgiveness, awakening to core-our heart chakra. Honoring our relationship with food and learning how to find balance in our realm.
Aradia	The Priestess, The prophetess, The art of the Strega. Embracing our natural witchy gifts, lineage and practicing our craft, creating and honoring longstanding traditions.

XI. OCTOBER – Death

Hekate	Honoring the sacred Veil between the realms, death and our sacred lineage and ourselves as future Ancestresses.
Maman Brigitte	Honoring our Bones, ancestor spirit realms, cemeteries and the process of death and rebirth.

XII. NOVEMBER - Sanctuaries

Hina	Sacred Sanctuaries, our place of safety and respite. The Moon, its insightful role and how it affects our spiritual path.
Hestia	Hearth Fires, Honoring our core Spirit, ritualized feastings with gratitude, Food-magick making, manifesting home, honoring our abodes.

XIII. Coven Dedication

Dedicating ourselves to one another, our community and our systers in the Sacred Craft and Goddess spirituality.

TRADITIONS AND ACKNOWLEDGMENTS

*My Tradition is
that All wommin are sacred Priestesses
and that Spirit will speak to us
and through us,
individually -regardless of age, race, class and education.
And if you follow your intuition
and allow yourself to be a channel for the Goddess,
you will create connections that will lead you
to proper ways to invoke, honor
and celebrate "Her,"
via rituals (personal or otherwise....)*

*My tradition is that
everyone can have a personal connection with Divinity...
That everyone has access to the Divine,
regardless of the false sense of hierarchical, erroneous proclamations made by
other religions in the past and oppressive patriarchal society.*

*And most importantly, My tradition is
that "She" can move us,
and our lives,
to be exemplary of "Her" grandeur
(within and without, for she is immanent, within us and around us)
and that our lives indeed are a
divine reflection of her magick
and her astounding Creatrix powers....* – written in a state of trance

---

    I wrote those words upon waking up from hazy dreams one morning. With pen and pad by my bedside, I am not even sure I was fully awake, as I instinctively reached out and began to write with eyes still half closed. Days later I stumbled upon my chicken scratch notes and remembered the incident. I had a hard time deciphering what and why I wrote what I did but months later I realized it needed further contemplation. Thus began my thoughts on traditions and the traditions I wish for this book to advocate.
    Perhaps one of the most important tenets I realized after reading my trance notes is that, my tradition does not discriminate based on lack of experience or coven hierarchical degrees. It is in my humblest opinion that the Goddess comes to us regardless of titles, class, culture or academic degrees. All wommin are potential vessels for the Divine, if they simply open themselves up to introspection and sincere divine connection.

*" ....for if that which you seek,
you cannot find within yourself,
you will never find without..."*
so says the Charge of the Goddess -Doreen Valiente

    It is my belief that a woman with a strong desire to learn and connect with Goddess, can do so and nothing should discourage or impeded fulfilling that need. When Goddess Calls it behooves us, as wommin, to listen and make that mystical expedition. In doing so, a whole world opens up to us that instinctively sprawls out and reverberates back into the universe, touching positively, everything and everyone that crosses our path. A womyn who honors the Feminine, honors the Goddess and a womyn who honors the Goddess, honors herself and a Womyn who honors herself is a powerful, force of nature, that becomes a greater asset to the world.

Spirituality is such a personal journey, that varies from one person to the next and thus, we all have different personal experiences connecting with the Divine. It is this diversity and respect for it, that adds value to Goddess Spirituality and, in my opinion, all of society.

Ironically, I can't say I've always seen this as the case. Even amidst Goddess Spirituality there is the occasional stench of patriarchy and old Christian doctrine still infiltrating our practices and numerous pagan groups. And while some tenets like, "*love thy neighbors...*" can be of Universal value, others (too many for me to list here and probably better left for another type of book) can be downright destructive to wommin. I take issue with anything that only seems to oppress us even further. The practice of hierarchy is reflective of this, as is the use of money to buy your placement within that hierarchy. Also negative traits that has seeped in, is a lack of respect for various views on one subject, and the "follow the leader mentality", so often proselytize by main stream religions. I sadly have seen these traits reflected in some Pagan associations and it deeply troubles me as I feel we, as wommin, have been oppressed enough. The last place I would expect to feel oppressed in, is a Pagan organization, especially if it's a wommin's group, but sadly it has happened.

Despite the feathers I might ruffle with my statement, I strongly believe every woman (womyn, wombmyn, wommin) is a daughter of the Goddess and within her is the potential to touch upon the Divine and serve her, via priestessing, regardless of garnered tittles.

"...She gathers her daughters by Moon and by Sun,
She gathers her daughters it has begun,
She gathers her daughters to mend and heal,
She gathers her daughters
to turn the Wheel..." Ruth Barrett

I started these Goddess Gatherings in a sincere effort to gather her daughters, and transverse into spiritual community. And delve deeper into the many aspects of the Divine, more than I could as a solitary, via the multitude of various sacred wommin. For every womyn presents, for me personally, a different face of the Goddess and in my genuine effort to know her, I must know her daughters.

I wanted fellowship amongst my sisters, without power struggles or hierarchical games. Somehow, in my mind, I strongly felt that wommin just gathering together simply for the purpose of honoring and celebrating the Feminine Divine, would bring radical, yet balanced, shifts to our gender as a whole and greater transformational experiences from within. I believe that for us, as wommin, these gatherings will reverberate back to us as living Goddesses, reminding us of something long forgotten... Reminding us of our own divine ancient, ancestral lineages that somehow buried itself under the rubble of patriarchy... And perhaps after a gathering, we could take this kernel of divinity, this transmissible reminder, and take it with us as we confront the numerous patriarchal nuances we face in our mundane lives and be stronger because of it...

" We all come from the Goddess....
and to her we shall return...." Z. Budapest

In conclusion, my tradition is that, if you, as a womyn, amidst the pains of injustice, political or overly Christianized, patriarchal society, are hearing the Call of the Goddess... follow your heart and seek to find others like you. For indeed there are many who are also hungry to know her, to touch upon her, to commune with her. From all parts of the large and tiny corners of the Globe, wommin are awakening to the Feminine Divine, now more than ever and this is attributed to many reasons, from interpretations of the Mayan Calendar, to cosmic shifts in our universe, but clearly the time has come. Wommin are embracing their divinity and as a result, the entire world will witness some vastly transformative, healing energy to manifest, for all beings on this planet. I encourage you to thread forward and gather with other wommin and together journey towards the Goddess... you don't need a degree or a long standing prejudice, snooty coven to give you permission. It is our Goddess given right to have community, fellowship and above all, **Sisterhood**! And it is our gender's right to seek Goddess and all that She brings (within and without)- not so much at the exclusion of men, (our beloved sons and husbands and fathers) and Gods, but as a conscious, intentional carving out a place for something that has been all too often denied, devalued and throughout the years, suppressed by our modern day society, which leans much too often towards the male. It is only in these conscientious, intentional female realm creations that we can begin to bring balance into our own personal lives and consequently into the Universe.

Acknowledging Wommin/Wombmyn/ Womyn, taking the time to commemorate the Feminine Divine, and thus your own part in that sacredness, is profoundly crucial to our gender's wellbeing and progress. And it starts with us as individuals, reaching out and coming together and utilizing, as our vehicle - the Goddess Gatherings.

All you need, initially, is the desire and the authentic love for the Goddess to guide you. Of course, this book makes it a lot easier to plan and organize the logistics and fine details to begin and, with it in hand, hopefully you will garner more confidence in yourself and the realization that IT IS doable and possible to manifest.

I would like to Thank the numerous wommin who have blessed my life with their presence every time they attended one of my Goddess Gatherings. A simple family home, once a month, would become a sacred temple for the Divine Feminine, to honor her, honor our inner Goddess and to remind ourselves to honor one another, as Sisters. Some have been with me and this vision since its inception and some have come and gone, but all are truly loved and appreciated with all my heart... Blessings of Gratitude to you all...

Thank you; Nicole, Jojo, Christina, Cynthia, Jil, Opal, Sage, Amanda, Dee, Ashlee, Kristi, Rhonnie, Dydan, the other Rhoni, Graciela, Elaine and numerous other Grove members who have touched my life...

And a special thanks now to my Husband, John and my three Children; Demetrios, Milo and Ethan, who have sacrificed so much of their own time and energy so that I could write this book. It was a labor of love for me but it could never have manifested without their patience, love and support. These four precious, and well loved, male species have sacrificed many a weekends to help me carve out a place for the Goddess Gatherings to exist and blossom the way it has. I can't thank you all enough! And to my boys, you are all amazing bright souls and I am honored to be in your light as your mom. I only hope that one day you can grasp the magnitude of what you helped me create and perhaps even see your delicate imprint lovingly scattered about on these pages. Every day I am reminded of the power of the Divine because you were all "wish manifested" and I am forever blessed to be able to embrace all four of you in this incarnation. Thank you!

And to all of you who have heeded the call for Sisterhood and have picked up this book in the hopes of beginning your own journeys towards Goddess Gatherings, I wish you a myriad of Blessings.... May the Goddess gather her daughters in groves of multitude and may "She" be immanent and eminent, reigning in all our lives, once more. Blessed Be!!!

INTRODUCTIONS

*"....If there is a book you really want to read,
but it hasn't been written yet, then you must write it..." -Toni Morrison*

They say that *"Necessity is the mother of all invention.."* and that is certainly true with the birth of this book. This book came about when I found myself before a group of women eager and desperately yearning to learn more about the Goddess, spirituality, magick, Wicca, rituals and the Feminine Divine and they looked to me to be their lecturer. Like most teachers, at first, I found myself overwhelmed, scattered, scared and somewhat insecure. I felt unsure of how to proceed and fearful that my great passion for the Goddess wouldn't translate clearly and as concisely as I felt it needed to be for a group of diverse womyn. After all, I had a collection of information and experiences in my head, but it wasn't stored up there as neatly as you'd think and no one ever told me I'd have to draw upon those cryptic shorthand notes found in the corners and crevices of my memory.

I had a somewhat eclectic pagan, feminist upbringing in which mysticism, tarot, astrology, dream analysis and the occult was regularly discussed between our circle of family and friends. Aw, the age of Aquarius! It was, after all the 70's, and it appeared everyone was asking the right questions and passionately pursuing some sort of spiritual enlightenment and divine wisdom. As a young child, I was privy to this open exchange of knowledge and radical thoughts among my adult caretakers and, like most children, I absorbed everything I heard like a sponge. As I got older, I myself, dabbled and experimented with various religious and spiritual practices, but remained a rather eclectic pagan solitary most of my youth. It wasn't until after college, when I started branching out, becoming more actively involved with various pagan communities. After numerous years being Wicca -both as a Solitary and within a small number of groups- I accumulated a vast library of internal experiences in my spiritual world that, thankfully for me, have become invaluable points of references. Attending a diversity of open circles has also added to the bulk of my internal resource and experiences, which I now draw upon to birth this creation. Coupled with the generous guidance from known and unknown energies and spirits, this book and its creation came to life.

One of my biggest concern in teaching and facilitating as a priestess was, channelling my great love and passion for the Goddess and Womyn's spirituality into cohesive, structured workshops and rituals for a very diverse group of wommin. I had acquired a lot of knowledge throughout the years, but until then it was all only for my solitary, personal use, and until that very moment, it was just stored in my psyche, my heart and mind, and not necessarily mapped out neatly in a textbook format.

Never backing out of a challenge, especially one presented to me by Goddess, I looked to my work with excitement and as an opportunity to grow. As each month would come along, I would scourer the recesses of my mind for information and inspiration - and thankfully found plenty. Any open rooms would be filled with further scholastic research to present my day long workshops. I took great pleasure in all of this, after all, I was delving intensely into the Divine and sort of creating for myself a kind of Goddess university curriculum. And I realized quite succinctly that the details of this spiritual journey I found myself on, would be of great interest to many others going through similar experiences. Quite surprisingly, I also found myself passionately wanting others to be of service to "Her" worship and sharing my journey made that more possible.

After a few months of constant research and consulting of different authors and various books and resources, I started to wonder if there was an easier way to do things. I noticed I was gathering and compiling quite a lot of important information on the Goddess and her worship and while I took great pleasure in this process, it was at times very tedious, time consuming and brought up an important question. Was there a book or a manual out there for young priestesses, like myself, who had a strong, sincere calling to teach womyn and serve the Feminine Divine? I wondered if there was One book, just one book, that had it all. One book that I could consult for all of my various needs as a Priestess conducting womyn gatherings, workshops and group rituals. My search for this ideal, imagined, book resulted in disappointment, as I could not find an all in one, inclusive, priestess guide book. And so, I slowly began to prepare for my workshops and gatherings, keeping in mind this deficiency in our community and documenting my research, creative writings, ideas and processes. The end result is in your hands now, a book I created, that literally became a Priestessing manual that any Womyn, Goddess dedicant, could pick up to successfully conduct, create and facilitate her own Goddess gatherings with ease, clarity and support.

Noticing my own special needs as a Priestess, I organized the book into monthly offerings with approximately twenty-four Deities to call upon throughout the year. Among the Goddesses featured in this book are: Nike, Skadi, Brigit, Oya, Artemis, Pele, Aphrodite, Ix Chel, Hathor, Persephone, Saraswati, Aine, Erzulie-Freda, Gaia, Demeter, Baubo, Selu, Aradia, Grande Maman Brigitte, Hekate, Hina, Hestia, Athena and Amaterasu. As you can see, the book offers a variety of Goddesses from different pantheons to work with and it can be utilized for group workings, as well as the solitary that seeks a more structured spiritual practice.

Each month, within the pages of this special book, you'll find guidance in the following topics:

1. Lesson Plans/Historical information on the specific Goddesses
2. Workshop activities that wommin can engage in, as a community to tap into the energy of specific Deities/Goddesses
3. Chants, text and Music
4. Transformational Rituals outlined with suggested prose
5. Meditation Guides and trance work
6. Artwork- Meditative Visual aids
7. Altar suggestions and decorations for each Goddess
8. And thoughts on monthly sabbats, esbats and seasonal Holidays.
9. Suggested invocations, prose, spells and evocations
10. Author's personal dream and priestessing journal entries.

It is my hope that *"Gathering for Goddess, a Complete Manual for Priestessing Women's Circles"* will fill the void in Pagan libraries and bookstores across America as well as abroad. I also hope that my book addresses the needs of women leaders, teachers, workshop facilitators and Priestesses, with personal very detailed information on how to create successful Goddess gatherings. I wrote this book in service to the Goddess, with love, gratitude and great reverence to the Feminine Divine. May it be received in the same vein with love as we gather together now on this journey to honor "She" of over TenThousand names...Goddess, Hail and Welcome!

The Organization of this Manual

MONTH AND MOON LORE

A RELEVANT INSPIRING QUOTE
GODDESS NAME
GODDESS ALTAR DESCRIPTION

ART ILLUSTRATIONS & PHOTOGRAPHS
PHOTO OF OUR GOODDESS Altar & CRAFT

GODDESS LECTURE
    HER RELEVANCE AND PURPOSE
    MUSING , THOUGHTS, HER APPEAREANCE
    GIFT OFFERINGS TO OUR GENDER

GODDESS GATHERING WORKSHOP
    WORKSHOP DAY OUTLINE
    HELPFUL TIME LINE
    THEME OF GODDESS OF THE MONTH.
    CREATION AND GODDESS CRAFTS -RELEVANT ACTIVITIES
    THOUGHTS AND DISCUSSION TOPICS
    MUSING OR MEDITATION SCRIPT

RITUAL OUTLINE
    ASPERGING, PURIFYING, ANOINTING AND WELCOMINGS
    CIRCLE CASTING
    QUARTER CALLS
    INVOCATION PROSES
    EVOCATION/ASPECTING PROSE
    MEDITATION
    RITUAL SPELL WORKINGS

JOURNAL & DREAM SHARING:
AUTHOR'S OWN PERSONAL DREAMS & EXPERIENCE OF THE DAY, WORKING WITH THE PARTICULAR DEITY.

OTHER WRITINGS:
    ESSAYS AND THOUGHTS RELEVANT TO THE PARTICULAR GODDESS OF THE MONTH.
    OTHER PROSE & RELATEABLE SPELL WORKINGS,
A PREPARED CHANTS AND TEXT SONG SHEET FOR THE MONTHLY GODDESS GATHERING THAT CAN BE SHARED WITH ALL PARTICIPANTS.

LAST SECTION OF BOOK:
GROUP & PRIESTESS DEDICATION RITUAL

ADDITIONAL WRITINGS:
Altar creations, Sabbat Lore
Ways of Connecting with Divine
Meditations and visualizations
Chakra and Aura work
Mandalas and Mudras
Gemstones
Energy work, Importance of Grounding
Purpose of Ritual , Components of Ritual
Aspecting /evoking, Elemental Calling
Circle Casting
Spell workings
Planetary Correspondences
Oils, aromatherapy, Herbs, incenses, Candle magick
Astro and Moon magick ,
Group dynamics and its politics
Spirits of Gratitude
Craft activity list, musing and check in question

BIBLIOGRAPHY AND OTHER SITED SOURCE LIST

GODDESS WORKSHOPS PRIOR TO RITUALS

The Goddess workshops can be an all-day event or simply a few hours. Generally our Grove Goddess Gatherings tend to last four to five hours and they really encapsulate what a week-long Goddess retreat would offer, but in a smaller venue. It is a chance for us to bond as spiritual wommin and strengthen our community and learn, as much as we can, from one another about our chosen deity of the month. It is a wonderful way to honor spirit and the Feminine Divine within our own selves as well. The workshops are structured in a way to allow attendants to get to know the Goddess deeper through lectures, chanting, meditation, drumming, discussions, magickal workings and various other crafting. Typically a ritual is presented towards the end of our workshops to honor and celebrate the Goddess we've devoted our month to, but we also commemorate the season and its traditional sabbat.

These workshops give the priestess and all those involved, a chance to bond, play, strengthen relationships and at the same time, offer an opportunity to delve even deeper into the power of the Divine Feminine.

Below is my suggested outline for a Goddess Workshop. It can be a workshop among many wommin or simply one womyn. It is only my suggestion and can be expanded or modified as needed. Blessed Be!

FIRST HOUR
1. Music/ Drumming/Chanting/ Raising energy through songs/Establishing sacred space. Some new songs and some traditional songs in our community are enjoyed here and we drum to gather in this sacred moment. We set the tone of the day and our Spiritual Journey begins.

2. Sharing. Passing the speaking stick, introducing ourselves and what has brought us here. We talk and share anything of relevance to the group. Personally sharing any pertinence information or new news. Each participant will have a chance to speak uninterrupted while holding the speaking stick and return this courtesy when it is her Sisters' turn. We do this in a respectful way, allowing each person the chance to be heard and speak uninterrupted. This in essence, becomes a ritual, as meditative listening can be quite powerful.

3. Next, we present our altar items, share their meaning and place it on the communal altar.

SECOND HOUR
Goddess Lecture
1. Here is an opportunity to learn about the history and lineage of the specific Goddess. Her genealogy and her myths throughout history. We delve in deeper into the psyche of the specific Deity and thus come to experience her archetype better. We also learn of what books are available for further private studies and to conclued we have an open discussion and address her relevance in today's world.

2. Open dialogue and questions are encouraged and addressed as we discuss further all the aspects of working with this Goddess, within a sacred sister circle. We share how we personally experience her energy.

3. An image of the Goddess or one of her symbols is passed around the Circle. It might be a tarot card or an art canvas or a photograph or a book. It is passed around the Circle so that all attendants can reflect and speak on what they feel regarding its value. Some

womyn will connect with one Goddess attribute, more than another, and this gives us a chance to unearth which attributes resonate more with us personally. Here too begins the act of invocation, for within the circle we see the Goddess and call out the various gifts we see emanating in her energy.

THIRD HOUR:
1. By this point we have learned about the Goddess through a lecture and an applicable discussion. After having shared, bonded, and had an opportunity to get to know one another -it's time to have more fun. In this hour we dedicate ourselves to crafting an item that is pertinent to the Goddess, the season and our upcoming ritual. This is a chance to tap into our inner creative child and access even deeper elements of the Goddess through a physical workings. Some examples are carving and charging a candle, for Aradia's month. In March, for Ostara, for example, we might work with eggs. For Hekate, during Samhain, we might work creating keys or making protective witch bottles for another month. In February, we craft communally Brigit's cross and for a Lunar Goddess, we might make Moon Clay amulets etc… On the top page of each monthly outline, I have suggested various projects for this section of the day. At this point in our day, we dedicated ourselves to witch-crafting, connecting to Goddess via something that physically connects us to the Divine energy, we are endeavoring to know better.

2. At this point in our day, this is also the time we engage in meditation or visualizations, for here too we are able to physically, psychically and emotionally connect with the Divine in this venue.

FOURTH HOUR
At this time we offer a ritual. Sometimes it can be very simple and other times it can be an extravaganza and very elaborate. Through this ritual we exemplify our full understanding of the Goddess we've held during the entire month and we endeavor to honor her and do a magickal working, as well, within sacred space. If it is near a sabbat we will also acknowledge its importance and include customary sabbat traditions in the ritual. Here you will notice that each month a ritual outline and script is provided, and these, again, are only helpful suggestions, based on what has worked for the author. You are welcome to simplify it or expand on it as you feel called.

FIFTH HOUR
Lastly, our day is brought to an end after feasting. A Potluck of various foods unfolds after the ritual, when quite naturally, we have all developed an appetite. Our potluck is also reflective of the Feminine Divine, as the culinary choice is inspired by the culture, the chosen Goddess comes from. For example when working with Amaterasu we have a potluck offering of Japanese Sushi rolls, rice and miso soup. For a Greek Deity, we would ask attendants to bring Greek salads, gyros and spanikopitas. Sometimes it can just be a meal we know the Goddess is notorious for loving, like Eggs and Garlic for Hekate or dark purple foods, like eggplants, for Oya or champagne and sweets for Hathor. As you can see our potlucks can be quite creative and fun…and just as important as the beginning of our day. Food and the act of eating among friends is a wonderful way to ground our energy, end the day, as we began it, with elevated social energy, while still tasting the last bits of morsel from the Feminine Divine.

GODDESS THEMES & SYMBOLS

DECEMBER-Awakening to our Power   WINTER SOLSTICE /YULE
Amaterasu
Themes & Symbol: The Sun, sparkling jewelry beads, Mirrors, Order, Truth, Clarity, Our value and self- worth, our light, The Sun Tarot Card
Athena
Themes & Symbol: Our Skills, Handicraft and Intellect, Strategizing, Books, Owls, Olives, Shields and Helmets,

JANUARY –Victory Embodied   NEW YEAR'S DAY
Skadi
Themes & Symbol: Oaths and Vows, Perspective, our Physical Body and Strengths, Giants, Convictions, Ice, Winter Terrain, Animal familiars, especially Wolves.
Nike
Themes & Symbol: Goals, Success, Rewards and Medals, Achievements, Laurel Wreaths, Champagne Goblet, The World Tarot card

FEBRUARY – Fires of Transformations   IMBOLC/CANDLEMASS
Brigit
Themes & Symbol: Fire, inspiration, handiworks, songs and poetry, metal crafts, crocheting, creativity expression, Celtic cross, bread, anvil, cauldron, hearths, water wells, healings, the eyes,
Oya
Themes & Symbol: Rain, Fire, Winds and Storms, transformation, Warrior's Strength, Machete, Copper, eggplants, Buffalo, Swirls of Tornadoes, Tower Tarot Card.

MARCH- Feminine Empowerment   SPRING EQUINOX
Pele
Themes & Symbol: Fire, Explosions, Volcanoes, Lava eruption, obsidian gemstone, Anger roar, wands, will power, strength and confidence, long dark hair offerings, rum, coffee.
Artemis
Themes & Symbol: the Moon, head Circlets, Archery (Bow and Arrow), laser Focus, horns, empowerment, Wommin, Amazons, Forest, Stags, wolves, hare, bears, all animals of wilderness, Wild woman, the Maiden.

APRIL- Water Healings   EASTER
Aphrodite
Themes & Symbol: Love, Self Blessings, Glamour, Beauty, Sex, Attraction, all things related to the Arts and its expression, Water, Sea Shells, Foaming Water, foaming champagne, eggs, apples, Doves
Ix Chel
Themes & Symbol: Flowing Water, The Moon, the womb, sexuality and fertility, Snakes, rainbows, woman's creativity, textile work, handicraft, healing, women's autonomy, the Hare, Dragonflies, vultures, freedom, Cozumel island, menstruation, release and flow of emotions.

MAY- Earthly Delights   BELTANE/MOTHER'S DAY
Hathor
Themes & Symbol: Joy, pleasure, sensuality, intoxication, scents, dancing, music, gemstones (Malachite and Turquoise), cosmetics, mirrors, rattles and sistrum, solar energy, priestessing
Baubo
Themes & Symbol: Laughter, Bawdiness, Jokes, Our Belly, Caverns and Labyrinths, our Yoni

JUNE- Creativity   LITHA/SUMMERSOLSTICE
Saraswati
Themes & Symbol: Rivers, water, mantras, mudras, Throat Chakras, Mala Beads, Honey, Yoga,

Artistic offerings, Altars, Inner Fires, Chakras, Sacred Words, the Power of our Voice.
Aine
Themes & Symbol: Fire energy, Red Hare, The Sun and Moon, Water, and Glamour spells, The Cloak, Faeries, vows, creativity, writings.rocks and herbs

JULY- Abundance   USA FOURTH OF JULY
Erzulie-Freda
Themes & Symbol: Love, Romantic ideals, Hearts, pinks, whites and light blues, Chattily Lace, Wine, Champagne, Chocolate sweets, Honey, Abundance, riches all things French in style, jewelry, Haiti and New Orleans, Veve, Shrine boxes, tears, ecstasy, French candies.
Gaia
Themes & Symbol: The Earth, herbs, plants and flowers, grains, the soil, globes, pro-creations, creativity, fertility, prosperity and abundance, all things in nature growing, creatures, animals, our Totems, rocks and gemstones.

AUGUST – Balancing our Roles   LAMMAS
Demeter
Themes & Symbol: Wheat and Barley, the Harvest, Change, Seasonal shifts, the Mother, Negotiations, Compromises, Nurturer, Releasing, The Empress Card in the Tarot.
Persephone
Themes & Symbol: Grains, Corn, Colorful Flowers, Pomegranate, Gemstones, the Underworld, the Daughter, Crown of a Queen, Light as healing source, Women's various Roles, Balance Mother relations

SEPTEMBER- Sacrifice   MABON/FALL EQUINOX
Corn Mother
Themes & Symbol: Corn, Harvest Grains, Baskets, Sacrifices, Trust, Forgiveness, Nourishment, our Blood, Heart Chakra.
Aradia
Themes & Symbol: All of Nature, Strega traditions, Elemental representations, The Moon, the Sun, The Stars, the Night, Forest (*Boschetto*), Tuscany, Italy, Prose, Candles, Cat, Sorcery and Magick Spells, Learning and Teaching. The Priestess.

OCTOBER- Death   SAMHAIN
Hekate
Themes & Symbol: Crossroads, Our Ancestors, Lanterns, Keys, Cemeteries, Veils, Pomegranates, Garlic, Eggs, Retsina, the Underworld, Travels, ancestral Lineage, Magick and Sorcery, Oracles, healings, Goodbyes, Midnight Darkness, Black Dogs
Maman Brigitte
Themes & Symbol: The Dead, Skulls and Bones, Tombstones and Cemeteries, our ancestors, Black Lace, purple, bridal veils, ancestors, the Mother and the guide. Death Card in the tarot.

NOVEMBER –Core Sanctuaries   USA THANKSGIVING
Hina
Themes & Symbol: The Moon, Rainbows, Hawaiian Islands, Lei, Coconuts, Feminine Spirituality, Inner and Outer Sanctuaries.
Hestia
Themes & Symbol: The Core of our Home and Spirit, Our Hearth, Spirit of our Home, wisdom, serenity, Traditions, the Chaste Virgin, Flames and Candles, Cornucopia, Feasting, Gratitude.

****

EIGHT WICCAN SABBATS

WINTER SOLSTICE   December 20-23

The Winter Solstice is the Wiccan sabbat that celebrates the slow, gentle return of the sun's power. It comes on the heels of the Christian Christmas holiday, which has retained a lot of pagan influence obscured and veiled over the years. It is at this point that the sun begins its steady climb to its zenith, which will be experienced fully by Summer. We celebrate the birth of the sun and while the sun in some cultures might be considered masculine, here we will honor Her, as the Feminine powerful source of warm light she is so often believed to be in various other cultures, like Celtic, Welsh and Shintoism. This is the shortest day and the longest night of the year and to our ancestors, surviving this night amidst community was significant.

Winter Solstice and Yule, are steeped with the influence of numerous ancient cultures and traditions. In the Germanic language the word Yule or "Jul" means, "Wheel," an embraced ancient view of the sun. Many believed this was originally a Norse holiday that commemorated the birth of the Sun and growing light. Often, it was celebrated with communal bonfires, gifts and storytelling.

For the Romans this was the time to celebrate the weeklong Saturnalia festival, a holiday in which everything was allowed to be topsy-turvy and awkward. Men would dress as women, clothing attire would be worn inside out and parades of such silliness were held out on the streets for all to enjoy.

The commemoration of Winter solstice, some believe however, began in Brittain long before Christianity infiltrated its Christ birth theory. For the Druids this was a holiday that commemorate life amidst the darkness, stillness and death of Winter. It was celebrated with a battle between the Holly king and Oak king, which was often role played by members in the community. The Oak, as their sacred tree, always attained victory at this time of the year and later, the burning of a yule log became a longstanding ritual practiced, believed to banish evil and bring light and blessings for the new year. Another symbol of life- the venerated Mistletoe, was also cut from the Oak tree and often presented as sacred gifts to the community at large.

At this time of the year, the days will slowly, quite subtly, get longer and it appears as if the sun now will slowly increase in power. We observe the longest night of the year on this sabbat and celebrate hope, rebirth and the return of light to our Wintry dark realm.

IMBOLC/CANDLEMAS February 2nd

According to some scholarly text, the Gaelic word Imbolg means, *"in the belly"*, and is a reference to the Earth's belly, holding the promise of Spring. Calves and lambs typically were born at this time in Ireland. Ewes would also lactate and this was often seen as a sign of hope, the impending end of Winter and the return of Spring. In some literature the word Imbolc itself was believed to be a reference to the lactation of ewes. It becomes evident that the word, throughout history, had various meanings but it was most heavily associated with the Mother; gestation, birthing, holding, lactation and newborns.

This is typically one of the coldest months of the year in some parts of the world and the weather can be fiercely brutal, almost deathly, as our ancestors also faced a dwindling pantry nearing the end of Winter. Amidst the wretched cold however, we begin to witness subtle signs that change is inevitable. In the U.S.A., we search for the groundhog to gives us the hopeful sign of an early Spring. In Ireland, a snake slithering out of her hole, coming down from the mountains, was the much awaited sign of the Celtic Goddess Brigit and Spring's much anticipated arrival. In ancient time, the snake was seen as the maiden Goddess herself, returning to Earth to announce Spring's advent. At this time, you may hear larks and other birds begin to make their presence known with their songs. The Earth, in some places, begins to thaw after the glacial cold months but the biggest indicator of the seasonal change is the growing strength of the sun, as we begin to experience longer days and shorter nights.

The sabbat of Candlemass (*mass of the candles*), also celebrated at this time, was a Christianized name for the feast of candles. Candles and fire were traditionally seen as tools of purification, not surprising this sabbat became a feast of purification for all, including the church. It was also traditionally the time when candles were blessed and rededicated in most churches. Also, the Virgin Mary, one of many venerated iconic images of the Feminine Divine and representative of the importance of Mother (life and light giver) at this time, was honored with candle light ceremonies and processions. Naturally for many Pagans, the element of fire, purifications and re-dedications, becomes a beloved, common theme at this time of year.

SPRING/VERNAL EQUINOX/ OSTARA March 20-23rd

Day and night are equal and balanced at this pivotal time of the year and we anticipate the first seedlings sprouting and the first buds of flowers blossoming. This Wiccan sabbat, believed to be named after the Saxon fertility Goddess, Eostre/Ostara, celebrates the arrival of Spring. For the Romans, at one point in history, this was actually considered the first month and the start of the New Year, as there was clearly a distinctive, undeniable feeling of newness upon the earth.

On this sabbat, most of our ancestors commemorated the survival of the harsh cold weather and

Winter's bleak darkness. It was and still remains a time to rejoice in the promise of fruition and the arrival of gentler weather. Many of our Spring traditions are steeped in ancient pagan folklore and this time of the year is very much associated with the earth's potential and promised fertility.

Animals of the land that best represent and mirror these fertile, frolicksome attributes of the season, were also venerated and continue to hold our adoration at this time of the year. The rabbit, best known for its fecundity, and often very visible among the land at this time, was such a powerful symbol of Spring that it continues to be exalted, even among Christians and their Easter holiday of resurrection. Among indigenous cultures, the rabbit and hare was acknowledge as an appropriate symbol of Spring and thus the Fullmoon of this month was aptly named, Hare Moon.

For most Dianic Wiccans, it is the frolicking maiden who is venerated at this time, as she is daughter, returning to her beloved earth mother from the darkness of winter and the oppressive underworld.

Eggs have always been considered a symbol of conception, motherhood and the Goddess. As a common tradition for both pagan and non pagans alike, eggs are often painted, decorated and used in numerous fertility rites, due to their strong connection, again, not only to fertility but also to the tenet of rebirth. The wheel of the year turns once more and the Earth is now ready to receive our seeds. This is the time of planting, whether it is literal planting of your actual garden of herbs and flowers, or the planting of your new hopes and dreams. This is the most ideal time for your new year's resolutions, not January, as nature itself will support the birth of new visions and goals. Though the weather, in some parts of the world, might seem unpredictable and "clingy" to the Winter, we place our seeds upon the earth and the auric field, as we continue on our journey, through the wheel of the year, with exuberance, renewed hope and the energy of the Maiden.

BELTANE April 31st -May 1st

Known as a Celtic Fire festival because of its connection to the heat and growing height of the Sun's power, Beltane, also known as Beltaine, Mayday and Walpurgisnacht (*the night before*) is one of three Wiccan fertility sabbats. Believed to be named after the Celtic healing Fire God, Bel,Belus or Belenos, it is also considered one of the four major Wiccan holy days. The name of this sabbat is also believed to be a Gaelic word, translated as, simply, the month of May. This is a time to celebrate the fertility of the Earth, as everything appears to be growing, multiplying, verdant and brightly highlighted.

All around us are signs that spring has indeed, finally, arrived and the dark, cold winters of the last few months, thankfully, seems like a distant memory. The month of May brings colorful flowers of all kinds, blooming and blessing our senses, and trees are no longer bare, but full and lush. Bright colors saturate the landscape and awaken our inner maiden. Animals, and even humans in various ways, are bringing forth their little offspring. The green lush grass has replaced the blanket of snow of winter and inspires us to relish in the warmth of the season with some frolicking. We celebrate the fruitfulness of the Earth now and our own frivolities. Traditionally at this time, lovers would make vows and betroth one another, but this was not seen as a good time to actually jump the broom-that was best done in June to receive the Blessings of the Goddess Juno.

For most Pagans this is a highly sexualize sabbat with many illustrative symbols suggesting its prominence, at this time of the year. The traditional dancing, engagement and adornment of the body, the prevalence of flower buds, the stomping of the earth with our bare feet and the traditional phallic May-pole, so often seen in Beltane celebrations, all support the erotic hue of this sabbat. The Maiden is coming into her own true self. For Dianic Wiccans she is now a young lady experiencing her first menarche and sexual awakening.

Merriment and the various expressions of fertility can manifest itself in our lives now and this is the predominant theme of this sabbat. We celebrate our own fruitfulness and our ability to procreate, by jumping the broom, spiraling with the colorful, ribbon filled, Maypole, leaping the bonfires and intermingling with our loved ones. Pleasure and the enjoyment of both our land and our earthly form are celebrated this month.

SUMMER SOLSTICE/LITHA June20-23

Summer Solstice is considered one of the four lesser sabbats of the Wiccan year. Litha or Midsummer, as it is sometimes called, marks the longest day of the year and contrast the Winter Solstice. This is the celebration of the official arrival of Summer and the height of the sun's power. It is a sabbat celebrated by many, from various cultures, since ancient times.

In some parts of the world, the Summer heat is strongest now and we might be spending a lot of time outdoors enjoying our long sunny days. Undeniably, Summer highlights the power of the sun at its zenith now, but for those who are in tuned with the Earth's cycle, you sense and realize that this sabbat actually marks the eventual decline of the sun's power. On this day, much like the Winter Solstice, the honored Sun, holds our attention, with an awareness that soon it will slowly begin its descent. It won't be experienced immediately and it's hard to imagine when we're in the midst of heat waves, but already in the cosmos the change has indeed slowly commenced here at this point, on the Summer Solstice.

The darkness will soon take over the light. Our days will, quite subtly, grow shorter and our nights will slowly begin to grow longer, but these changes will go on imperceptibly until we reach our next sabbat celebration and so, for now, this is the time to relish and enjoy the summer days and be mindful that the wheel of the year continues to go forward and brings changes. We find ourselves standing in the middle of our calendar year, reflect on what has passed and what will come to be. Day and Night stand in perfect balance, giving us an opportunity to create balance in our own personal lives.

Many ancient Litha Rites involved elaborate processions, communal bonfires, and donning crowns and floral headwreaths. This was also the ideal time for handfastings and marriage ceremonies, a tradition that continues to influence our modern world, as many elect this month to marry and June typically sees an increase in wedding ceremonies.

Celebrate, for the wheel of the year has turned once more and for most Dianic Wiccans, the Maiden has reached the maturity of womanhood. It is at this time that the Goddess communes and merges with her lover and as the Earth appears fertile, loving and ripe, we too, at this time, can exemplify these attributes in our own lives. We celebrate the Sun's height now, our own fertile juiciness and observe the turning of the sacred wheel.

LAMMAS July 31-August 1st

An important agricultural sabbat that commemorates the first fruits and the first grains, we arrive at the sabbat of gratitude. Also known as the Celtic holiday of Lughnasadh, this is one of the four major Wiccan holy days. It was named by the Druids, after the Sun God, Lugh and its celebration was well documented in various cultures, in ancient times. It is the sabbat of the first Harvest.

As the sabbat of Lammas, it was the day that church offerings were made, with baked breads, prepared from the grains of the first harvest. Thus, it became known among the church as Loaf mass day, abbreviated, it was celebrated among medieval Christians, as Lammas. This is the sabbat that celebrates the sacredness of the Grain and reflects the initial sense of gratitude, for those first fruits. We celebrate the gifts of the first harvest and naturally make our offerings to the Gods, in sincere gratitude, as our ancestors have done since ancient times.

Although amidst sweltering heat, it feels as if August is the height of the oppressive summer heat wave and the sun's unquestionable power, it actually marks the more noticeable descent of the sun and unlike the Summer Solstice, this change is more apparent at this time of the year. What began at the Summer Equinox, is now visibly and indisputably felt, as we begin to experience the days becoming shorter and the nights beginning to grow longer. The evening breezes might begin to feel slightly cooler in some parts of the world. The trees, flowers and the grass take on a slightly different hue. By the end of the month, we are saying goodbye to our summer vacations and the season of play, frolicking and fertility. We bid farewell to the Maiden and we approach the season of harvest and hard labor, as we are left standing on the threshold of a new season. Autumn looms ahead and begins to beckon us to slowly turn inward.

The maiden is now a wombmyn, ripening, pregnant and pouring forth of her first bounty. Her seeds are now producing tangible proof of her great agricultural powers and we take this time to inspect our own lives and give thanks for the first initial manifestations of our dreams via her bounty and first fruits.

AUTUNMNAL EQUINOX/ FALL/MABON September 20-23

This is the celebration of the Autumnal Equinox, when we stand in perfect balance between night and day. It is also the sabbat of the Second Harvest and a time of much anticipated hard work, as we prepare for the inevitable dark season. Traditionally, for Pagans, this is the time of our Thanksgiving (unlike the U.S.A. three day holiday dictated by our government) this is the time to reap what we've sown, evaluate our progress, save and prepare ourselves for the anticipated fallow challenges of the dark season.

It was also known as Harvest Height and Harvest Home but there is some controversy over the term Mabon for this sabbat. It appears to be a fairly new term created in the 1970's, attributed to Aidan Kelly, and not related to any documented, ancient Celtic tradition. And the name might have some connection to characters from Arthurian Welsh mythology, as their God of the Harvest is known as "Mabon ap Modron". His name translates as the divine son of the Mother. According to the Mabinogion, as an infant, Mabon, was kidnapped from his mother for three days and found himself in the underworld (Annwfn) where immortal youth was bestowed upon him, as well as the blood that intoxicates. He later would become well known as the GreenMan and also linked to Apollo, the Greek Sun God. It is a tale reminiscent of Persephone's descent into the underworld and yet another example of how our ancestors viewed this pivotal time of year. However, the Autumnal Equinox has indeed been observed since ancient times and most practicing Wiccans include it as one of the revered eight sabbats.

It is a cross quarter holy day and a time to reflect on the year and give thanks for our crops and our numerous blessings, big or small. The hopes that we held, back in December and January, were planted into seeds in February and March. By May and June we were thrilled to witness the very beginnings of our seeds taking shape. By July and August we had much to do and enjoyed those initial blossoming. Now *is* our moment to celebrate our bounty and reap what we have sown. Yet we *too* begin to take stock. At the Second

Harvest, we have much work ahead -like gathering the grapes, the apples, corn and various other grains plucked and harvested now before the first frost arrives. Our land(internally and externally) is now beginning to prepare for the change; Winter, bitter cold winds, snow, inclement weather and blistering storms in some parts of the world are inevitable after this month.

The theme of Sacrifice is also very much imbued in this sabbat, as the Grain Goddess Demeter must sacrifice her daughter, Kore and surrender her to Hades in the underworld at this time. Nothing will grow amidst the Mother's sorrow and nothing will grow when the flowering Maiden takes her fertile light away from the earth and buries it deeply, with her, in the underworld.

Traditionally, this was the time our ancestors gathered their food stock and supplies, filling their pantries before the harsh winter months. Animals and the herd were also prepared to move inward. As the sun appears to be dying and the Earth will soon lay still, barren, fruitless and nothing will grow. It behooves us to also prepare ourselves physically, mentally and emotionally for the inevitable changes the new season will bring. Remember, the maiden Persephone has now left us and her role, as maiden, to take on the role of dark Queen of the underworld and Hade's wife. She takes with her the fertile gifts of the corn and in her sad mother, the fertile green earth is temporarily, no more. We give thanks for our bounty and the fruition of our hopes and dreams, as we also prepare ourselves for the shifts in our realm and change in climate. We gather ourselves, take inventory of our work, our failures and successes and look ahead in preparation. We give thanks at this Second Harvest, for our blessings now, as the Wiccan year is soon coming to an end.

SAMHAIN/ HALLOWEEN October 31- November 1st

One of the most venerated holidays for both Pagans and non-Pagans alike, this Celtic, ancient sabbat has even infiltrated Christianity with its proselytization of honoring the dead. For most Pagans, our Wiccan year has come to an end and we come to the season of deep introspection. Samhain marks the end of our solar year and the beginning of another and thus, like all thresholds, there is magick to be found within the veil of this transition. It is considered one of the most important major holy days for most Wiccans. A time to reflect on issues of life and death, a time to visit with our ancestors and consult our inner shamans. We call on the Mistress of the Cemetery, the Dark Mother and the Goddesses of Sorcery and Magick. The Maiden has left our land to join her consort, Hades, in the underworld and She, as Queen of this realm, now inaugurated the season of Darkness. It is also considered the season of the Crone, for "She" is no longer frolicsome maiden, nor juicy bountiful Mother but rather the introspective, dark wise one.

Samhain means *"Summer's End"* and began in ancient times, as the Druid's New year. Documented and celebrated in various cultures, there was a common belief that the spirits of old would come out to play on this day and they were believed to be visibly walking, among the living. For this reason, scary costumes and Jack o Lanterns, carved in scary faces, became a tradition, to confuse and trick malevolent spirits. Thus it is believe that this is the time when the veil between the worlds is the thinnest. Our world of the living and the realm of the spirit and the dead, blurs for just one night, allowing for reconnections to our loved ones who have passed on.

A sabbat that clearly honors the sacrednesss of thresholds, darkness and the unknown, as these were the prominent themes of the month. Our ancestors, at this time of year, did not know what kind of Winter, and harsh challenges, they would face in the coming months, adding to the ambivalent, agonizing mystery of the season. Daylight hours were short, resulting in many long hours of darkness and this too added to the eerieness so often associated with this time of year. It is a month that typically reflects shadows and uncertainties and a most noticeable threshold, as it is the gateway to the approaching Winter.

There are numerous ways this special day is celebrated among various cultures. One belief they share in common is that it has become a night when we traditionally honor those who have died, reconnect with lost loved ones and acknowledge the spirit realm. Naturally, it is a most powerful night for divination, oracular and spiritual workings and, for most Earth based religions, it is indeed a Holy day; revered and celebrated, not as scary (as the mainstream media so often enjoys portraying it) but as one of the most sacred of nights of the year....

GODDESSES AND THE CYCLE OF HOPES AND MANIFESTATIONS THROUGH OUT THE YEAR

December
AMATERASU
Goddess of the Sun, of truth and light, the mirror. She asks you to bring clarity and order into your goals and life. Amidst the chaos and holiday frenzy of this time of year, she calls you to breathe, regroup and reconnect to your authentic self. Look into the mirror and do not fear your own reflection staring back at you. It will reveal truths that perhaps, you have avoided seeing. It will awaken your own self-worth -a vital component for all magick. Pause for a moment and reflect on what your next step will be as the year comes to an end and we enter, what is typically considered, the dark of the year, a time of introspection and anticipation of the growing returning light.

ATHENA
Goddess of Wisdom, competence, skills, war-craft and intelligence. At this time of year she reminds you of the power of your mind. If magick is to be defined as, changing consciousness at will, then indeed this would seem like the most appropriate place to begin, for it is in the mind that all things begin and this is Athena's realm. All things we wish to bring to fruition must first begin with a thought, an initial vision, a plan, the engagement of the mind. Altering our moods, belief, perspective, even our environment must first begin with our mind, in order to see its fruition. She comes into your life now to teach you that wishes and goals are best met first in our initial envisioning and strategizing. She beckons you to plan, strategize, organize, tap into the power of your mind for it can be much stronger than sheer brute force.

January
SKADI
Strong Giantess, Norse Goddess, who fierecely defends what is right and engages her entire body in the journey. She awaken the Amazon woman within you and offers you the gift of physical wellbeing, strength and perspective. How vastly different challenges appear when we see them through the eyes of a Giantess. How vastly different you would feel, walk and act in the armored body of a Giantess, like the Norse Goddess, Skadi. At this time you are invited to honor your body and tap into your inner and outer strengths. Unearth your right for physical wellbeing and tap into your righteousness and positive convictions. Know that you can manifest change and in every woman, the Giantess Amazon lives.

NIKE
The Laurel wreathed Goddess of Victory, rewards generously for work accomplished, this is her domain. She anxiously awaits your success and stirs within you a healthy dose of competition and ambition. Our Laurel Wreath is awaiting and she stirs in you desire for her presence –a desire for success. A new year is beginning, do we enter it victoriously, projecting a sense of ordained achievement? Or have we already failed before we have even begun? At this point we celebrate the small and large acoomplishments, knowing that this mere acknowledgement will positively influence future ones. With Nike, we celebrate the small and monumental goals achieved in our lives now and ambitiously project that victorious energy into our future goals.

February
BRIGIT
Celtic Goddess of the Forge. Deep in the dark Belly of the earth's womb, magick is awakening, slowly, unseen by the naked eye but unquestionably forthcoming. Things are manifesting themselves quietly underneath it all and the new year has only begun. Hearth fires are quite prominent now, a reminder we are in the presence of the Divine. She who warms our heart with inspirations to create and express ourselves. She who also, through her bright flames, is able to transform us inside and out. She offers us the healing gifts found in both fire and water. She enters your life now asking what needs to burn to ashes, and like the Phoenix, be trans-mutated so that healing may come to you. She brings you, self –transformations, sacred initiations and the willingness to begin the Journey....What will be Transformed in you? What do you dedicate yourself to unearthing now?

OYA
Fierce Goddess of storms, thunder, winds and soul-transformations. In her presence, drastic change is inevitable and life will never look the same. Are you ready to surrender to her will and let things go? It is only in this severing of the old and outworn, that we get to allow a new life force to enter, grow and manifest -healthier and stronger than before. This is how our most cherished wish comes to fruition. She comes like the intense windstorms and tornadoes, to sweep that which does not serve you well anymore. She comes to sweep away, with her long rainbow colored skirt, that which impedes your progress. She awakens in you the courage and strength to welcome change. Things may need to be surrendered, shattered, and fall apart,

before greater things can come to fruition. Trust in the power of rebuilding anew.

March
PELE
Welcome the volcanic, uncontrollable erupting, passionate Goddess. That gnawing feeling within, those intial stirring rumbling inside before the spewing eruption of hot lava. She awakens passion deep within you and a relentlessness to pursue that which your heart desires. She inaugurates a Fire energy sweltering from deep within. She beckons you to give credence to your feelings, validate them, give them strength and give volume to your voice. *"Speak out, roar it out,"* she says. Like the rumbling of her volcanoes, she awaken in you the ability to acknowledge the sacred cathartic emotion of passion but also anger. She invites you at this time to banish complacency and get real with your true voice. Then let it be heard, like the rumbling of her Volcanoes and the spewing of her scorching lavas, don't hold it in...it is meant to emit outwardly. Let it all out and let your passionate voice be heard.

ARTEMIS
As Spring begins to make itself known, the energy of the wild maiden begins to awaken upon the earth with it and soon enough you will feel that energy swirling around, making its way to you. It reminds you of your effervescent youth, running care free, and the power inherent in youth's fearlessness. She comes to also remind you of the gifts of supportive sisterhood and reminds you of the power inherent in your gender, when it partners with other like- minded sisters. Spring brings the potential for new seeds to be planted, the optimism of our goals coming to life. A wild and free force is driving within and it brings new hope and the pursuit of new goals with tenacity. The Huntress awakens in you the gift of a Maiden's will. The archer's pristine, intense focus begins to take hold. What do you put your mind and focus on, now? What do you aim for? What will you "will" to be?

April
APHRODITE
Sweet curvaceous watery Queen. She brings you the power of Beauty and Attraction and most importantly, the unwavering power of self-love. You say you want a new love but are you the honey and light, love so often seeks to meld and attach itself with? She is attraction, in its many guises, from a gentle stirring to an all-consuming passion. Her Venusian gifts spread into so many different areas in our lives. Even in the passion we might feel for our goal's fruition, creative projects and its unfolding sacred processes. Here she helps you cultivate your own powers of attraction. This month, she invites you to acknowledge your own beauty and the great powers of attraction, for these are her domain. Who or what do you ensnare in your life at this time? Where can you cultivate further, your Aphrosinian powers of love and attraction?

IX CHEL
Ancient Mayan Lunar Goddess, the water, the moon and our gender's emotions, she rules. At this time we begin to open ourselves up to the gifts of our gender, reflected in her watery realm and the sacred Moon. This Mayan Goddess has a story to tell and it echoes the story of so many women throughout Herstory . She awakens this connection to the Great Mother Divine and reminds you of your own fertile, luminescent gifts. No matter, if you are a maiden, mother or crone, all reside within you and all are sacred reflections of Creatrix-Goddess. Water is the healer and has much to teach us about going with the flow and honoring all, that is Feminine. In your efforts to achieve your goals, are you leaving some room for flexibility? Are you feeling parched and dry in some areas of your life or are you overly saturated? She enters your life now to connect you with balance and the healing power of water and the moon. What personal message is the element of water conveying to you now regarding your goals?

May
HATHOR
Sensual, joyful Egyptian Bovinian Goddess. She awakens the importance of pleasure in your life. Whatever you do in life, make sure it brings you joy and gratification. At this time of year, when all of the earth seems fertile, colorful and brightly adorned, when it seems as if the vibrant earth is a vision of great delight to all of our senses and we are in a state of titillation and arousal, Hathor becomes the ideal Goddess to call upon. Her message to you is to seek joy and pleasure. Amidst the doldrums of our obligations and the inescapable mundane, seek to know and honor the highly cathartic power of ecstasy. Delight in all the beauty that is surrounding you, the earth and the beauty trying to assert itself to manifest from within your being.
"...For all acts of love and pleasure are my rituals...", Dorren Valiente, -The Charge of the Goddess.

BAUBO
Cackling, supremely bawdy, ancient Goddess, immortal friend. She arrives, like an old dear playmate, bubbling with jubilee and radiating with laughter and naughty jokes. Just when you started to feel the pull of sadness and stress caving in on you, she comes with warmth, jokes, encouragement and sincere

friendship. She lightens your load at this pivotal time of the year and reminds you of your most precious weapon against feelings of defeat, sadness and depression- it is within you, your gender, your labyrinths and caverns. Have you ever looked at yourself, really looked at yourself and marveled with laughter? Have you ever heard the funny stories of an old friend echoing in your ears after a long, hard stressful day? This is Baubo's gift to you at this time of the year - awaken to the transformative powers of laughter. While intensely pursuing your goals, anticipating challenges and overriding obstacles, take the time to laugh, lighten up and allow the cathartic power of friendship an honored place in your life.

June
SARASWATI
Wisdom, Learning and the Creative River flows through her Divine energy. She arrives at this time in your life to awaken you to creativity and the value of your voice, your words and your spirit. The creative powers of the Divine lives within every being on this Earth and beyond. Do not think that anyone is immune to the swirling powers of creativity. From the time you were born, you were enthralled by artistic elements, like the colors in a crayon box- all around you and in nature. We have the ability to create various works of wonder- big or small, they are ALL of great value to the Divine. Ask yourself; "What am I actually working on?, What am I creating right now? How is my unique soul transmitting through my hands and voice? Do I have the spirit of creativity? Is it being properly honored in my goals?" She arrives in your life at this time to awaken Artistic offerings of the self to the Great Mother Divine.

AINE
Irish Red Mare, Solar and Lunar Goddess. She is the fiery enchantress who inspires the writer and the songstress. She is a Fierce Protectress of Women, especially those who have been mistreated, abused, molested or raped by men. Oath and vow guardian, She awakens in you a call to action, where action is needed. Defend yourself and unearth the confidence to utilize your own gifts of enchantment. Imbue the pursuit of your goals with her fiery energy and you are destined to succeed. Aine connects us with the energy of Fire, in her Solar aspect, although she was later similarly connected to the moon. At this time of the year, with the Summer Solstice, we hone in on the various wonderful gifts of the element of fire and how to best utilize it in our lives, channeling it into the manifestation of cherished goals.

July
ERZULIE
Voodoo Loa of Love, beauty, abundance, romance and those delightful luxuries. She who demands nothing but the best, invites you to hold the same standard for your own life. She awakens in you a desire to pursue prosperity, abundance and all that is good for you, including the right kind of love. What are some of life's luxuries you are willing to manifest in your life at this time? Is your "Love" bringing you true fulfillment? Are you approaching life from a place of lack or from the rich fertile realm of abundance? Are you imbuing the pursuit of your goals with love? She enters your life at this time to awaken a desire for the finer things in life.

GAIA
Primordial fertile Earth Goddess who is the essence of fertility, proliferation and the powers of creation. Life is full of wonderment and all around us, there are examples of her fertile creative gifts. It is encouraging and inspiring to know that her gifts are vibrantly within us as well, for her blood courses through every single one of her creations and that includes her earth children- humanity. There is much that we can create in the spirit of the Goddesses of multiplicity, propagation and abundance. She comes into your life at this time and asks you, How do you create prosperity and enjoy small and big luxuries in life? At this stage in our Goddess journey, the sacred wheel of the year supports our endeavor to multiply and tap into our own powers of fertility, whether they are used for creativity, prosperity, ideas or actual birthing of children. She awaken in you a desire to multiply and manifest your gifts on the earthly planes. How close are you to achieving your most cherished wish? Have any flowers bloomed, and come to fruition, from the seeds reverently placed within her sacred womb back at Imbolc? She invites you to enjoy the birthing process and tap into the sacred energy of the season and the earth.

August
DEMETER
Benevolent Grain Mother who supports, protects and nourishes her children. She comes into your life at this time to inaugurates the Mother within. She awakens in you a connection to all things that need nurturance and protection, including yourself. Like the immortal Goddess herself, who would not let the grain grow until her daughter's return, where are you being asked to put your foot down, care for your needs and not compromise your dignity? Where will you utilize your own bargaining power? And where will you need to make some initial sacrifices to attain your goals? As the wheel turns once more She asks, where in your life are you being called to be the Mother? This is a time of assessments and preparedness for letting Go. The

Harvest season supports this endeavor of deep consideration and taking stock of what you have done thus far and what else will need to be done to reach your goals. The change of season is upon us once more and this time of the year, we are required to let go of many things most notably, Summer. She invites us to consider our role as mother to our creative pursuits and take this brief pause in our journey to reflect, assess and review.

PERSEPHONE
Greek Maiden Goddess who directs the flowers and the corn fields to blossom and grow and gives light to a most auspiciously dark realm. She who is Queen, Wife, Daughter, Mother... She who is all of them at once and she who is every woman on the face of this earth. Our gender is constantly required to wear a multitude of hats and roles, sometimes even conflicting ones. Yet we never falter in our ability to comply and execute them flawlessly. She enters your life to offer you balance and compassion for your own self and the multitude of offices you hold. At this time, she also want to direct your attention to your origins and a dear woman, who paved the way for your existence- your very own human, birth mother. Her message is, "I am daughter but I am so much more." It's important to cultivate right relationship with our mother. We may have differences, but we also share many similarities with the woman who birth us into existence. Consider what kind of Mother would complement your own personal journey in life? Consider if you aren't a mother yet, what would make this role most challenging, to you and your offspring? New roles emerge bringing new responsibilities and through it all, we seek balance. Healing our relations with Mother and ourselves in the process. Walking in multiple worlds and in a multitude of different roles while we pursue our most cherished wish. She comes into your life to inaugurate an awareness of the necessity of balance, as we walk in various roles pursing our life's goal.

September
CORN MOTHER
Nurturing sacrificial iconic Corn Goddesss, embraced by the myriads of indigenous tribes across the Americas and abroad. She who shed her blood so that her people would strive onward and not extinct. She who willingly sacrificed her very own truncated body so that her people would never hunger again. Despite the unappreciative nature of her greedy children and her community, she understood her role and obligation in the larger scheme of life and thus she awakens the sacrificial Mother within every one of us. She calls to mind your core, your heart-chakra and asks, how do you nurture it? Step back, if you will, and consider for a moment what sacrifices are required of you at this time of the year? What is in your heart now, that requires sacrifice for the greater good of all? What symbolizes your sacred blood and where is it being required to pour forth and serve a greater good in the Universe? Consider your initial goals at the start of the year, have you abandoned them, altered their conception or achieved them? Or is there something else required of you to proceed onward? With the change of season, how can you adjust to change and manifest balance? Are initial plans working or do they need to be re-assessed, self-forgiven, released and moved into a different direction now?

ARADIA
Magick woman, the gift of the Priestess. With Summer over, life all around us appears to have returned to school and work. She comes into your life at this moment to asks, What must you do to assure you are in right balance with the earth? The dark of the year slowly approaches with the Autumnal Equinox and as we draw closer to the Wiccan year's end, we are offered the opportunity for occult knowledge, lineage, old traditions of the Craft and, with Aradia, the empowering practice of magick. Time to slowly connect with the power of the moon, and the growing strength of the night. She reminds us that nature is our ally (within us and all around) to protect us and she avails herself to whatever we may need help with. Here now we adjust those initial goals, to the changes all around and She asks us, how do you empower yourself with spirit, magick and occult knowledge? How do we reverently employ magick and the sacredness of nature to propel our wish forward?

October
HEKATE
Ancient immortal Goddess of the night, death, sorcery and witchcraft. She brings a plate offering with our lineage and ancestry and the importance of our spiritual connection. At this time of the year, when day light wanes, while the dark of night gains power, mysteries are unfolding for us. There is much wisdom to unearth in our Ancestry and our past. As the nights grow longer and the earth seems to slow down, it is time to do, as the critters of the land, and go deep within for some soul searching. Ask yourself, "Have I been on the right track?" "Is this the right path for me?" "Does my work and ultimate life goal, fit who I am and my life's greater purpose?" "Are these goals meant to be reached by me at this point?" She arrives to help you connect to spirits and your sacred ancestors for guidance. She awaken in you other realms, other sources for support and other ways of knowing. She awakens you to your sacred role as an ancestress and your intrical part in your family's lineage. Ancestress that you are already, what will you leave behind for your beloved one?

What legacies will you leave for them? This is the time to look closely at who we share this realm with and honor our Spiritual family, and the sacredness of the cycles of life and death.

MAMAN BRIGITTE
Gatekeeper, treshhold guardian, beloved Mother of Bones and the ghede - the dead. In the darkness of the unknown, on the threshold, we must all pass through, She makes herself known to us. At this time of the year, when nature itself appears to be morphing and surrendering to death, She arrives with a rather unusual sass, lightheartedness and humor about death, for she reminds us it is not a finality but a transition and one that should be approached with love, not fear or trepidation. *"What are you afraid of, death is simply a transition and if you are free of this fear, there is very little else to be afraid of in life...."* She comes and we begin to consider our very own mortality and the content of our lifetime. Amidst longer nights and the barreness of the earth, it appears as if the earth is preparing itself for its own death, as it, along with animals of the land, embarks on its hibernation. It is here where we begin to reflect on our own cycles of death and rebirth and yet it is not as frightening as some may have you think. She comes to remind you that your time here on earth is very limited, unlike your infinite spirit. And your life's purpose must be met within those mysteries time restraints. She arrives as a wake- up call, that death, with its unpredictability, is never too far away. Whether young or old, she awaits to reclaim your sacred bones when that time does come. Will you be ready to relinquish your bones to her, upon your death? Will you be ready to surrender all that you've known in this life to enter the next stage in your development, with a Mother who will lovingly and humorously guide you, into the next phase. Are you living your life mindful of the expiration of your flesh and the infinity of your spirit? How are your goals and actions reflected of this monumental realization?

November
HINA
Rainbow, Polynesian Goddess who makes the ancient Moon her home. She comes into your life to remind you of the sacredness and necessities of Sanctuaries. She arrives at this point in your life to ask you, "Do you have a personal space that nourishes and heals you and keeps you protected?" In life, among chaos and moments of stress, we all need to identify where is home.... where is our safe haven? Where can we retreat to regain ourselves? Physical vacations are common and act as our temporary escape and retreat, but, what if we have available to us, a mental and spiritual place to retreat to, whenever situations require an escape? The question now that she presents to you is, are you able to keep your sense of self and retreat as needed to sanctuary? When confronted with toxic situations or people and negative relationships, are you able to find a sacred space within, to guard and recharge yourself? While pursuing your goals and crafting the magickal life of a Goddess wommin, you must also have in place, your home, your sacred temple. As demands in life increase and as projects and work become demanding, it becomes necessary to have these astral sanctuaries in place for our own protection and wellbeing. Are you able to manifest safety, serenity and peace of mind? She enters your life at this time and beckons you to erect your core spiritual home and unearth a place of peace. How do you create your personal sanctuary?

HESTIA
Immortal Maiden Goddess of the Hearth, the flames of our spirit and the core of our very being. At this time of the year, She directs your attention to the highly esteemed core of our personhood; our heart and our spirit. Hestia comes to remind you to honor that part of yourself that is in tuned with the Feminine Divine. She arrives with the gifts of old, venerated traditions and honored family customs. At this time of the year we also are awaken to the spirit of Gratitude and the great significance of our own Hearth and Home -which vibrates with its very own unique essence and life force. Home is more than just where we sleep. Consider for a moment, the beauty and value of your own abode at this juncture, what does it reflect? Consider your relationship with this place, the land, and the many ways it feeds, protects and nurtures you. We give thanks for its spirit with Hestia at this time of the year. If you are in the market for a new apartment or home, reflect on what will your next home look like. What will be of utmost importance to you in a home then? At this time she comes quietly and serenely to inaugurate a time to give thanks for what you've manifested thus far, and the journey to pursue and attain your heart's desire. She invites you to pause and give thanks for what you've created up to this very pivotal moment in time. She arrives and we are thus open with Gratitude for life and all the many blessings (big and small) and the place we call home is one of great significance. It is here where we may start familial traditions, continue old ones and honor the spirit of gratitude for its existence. With Hestia, it is time to show reverence to your familial and spiritual traditions, the place you call home, and honor your journey thus far, while also giving thanks to all those who have added the invaluable, loving, diverse, golden threads of your strong familial tapestry. Blessings on your journey!

We Begin with the Birth of the Sun....at the Winter Solstice....

December

The twelfth month of the Gregorian calendar, December, arrives bringing the gifts of numerous festivities and holidays from Christmas, to Hanukkah, Kwanzaa, Wassailing, to Yule, Modranicht (*Mothernight*) and the Winter Solstice. It seems the ancient Pagan traditions of our ancestors have quite subtly infiltrated the celebration and practices of numerous other religions. It probably received its name from the Latin word *"Decem"* meaning "Ten" as it was considered the tenth month of the Roman calendar. Astrologically, Sagittarius (the Archer) which is ruled by generous, benevolent Jupiter (Nov.21 –Dec. 20), influences the energy of the month.

December, for most people, is unquestionably a very busy time of the year. For me personally, the month becomes a blur that goes by entirely too quickly. At a time when our ancestors probably spent a great deal of time indoors, less active, more introspective and when all of nature (even the critters of the land) seem to join in this customary retreat and hibernation, it would seem logical for us to do the same. Yet, this time of year finds many of us harried, stressed, overbooked with activities and little time to withdraw from the world.

Some parts of the world are knee deep in snow with cold weather and quite appropriately one popular name for the Full moon this month is, "Full Cold Moon". It was also known as "Longest night Moon" a reference to the longest night of the year, on the Winter Solstice (December 20-21st). Despite the cold encouraging us to stay cozily indoors and less active, the energy levels outdoor, at this time of year, seems highly charged, split and very festive.

With the inundation of commercial advertisements and storewide sales beckoning you to shop till you drop and everyone appearing to be in such a rush to get things done and get to their appointed destinations, our environment feels far from meditative and reflective. It's easy to get swept into this swirling of fast paced holiday energy, despite what our own bodies and spirit might prefer at this time of year. Perhaps the holiday decorations everywhere, the sparkling lights, tinsels and mistletoe, the trees and the landscape of glistening white snow, covering some parts of our Earth like a blanket, can beckon us to slow down and embrace the festive atmosphere. Such imagery can sometimes touch upon our most nostalgic, tender memories in its beauty. It can also bring unexpected healing to our spirit, to be amidst this wintry canvas.

December brings the Winter Solstice, which inaugurates the rebirth of our brightest star, the Sun. On the longest night of the year, when our ancestors braved the cold of the darkest night, The Goddess gives birth to her child (the bright Sun) and thus to a special part of her own self. We honor the infant born at this time of year and the healing afforded to all of us with the sun's arrival. It is a perfect time to tap into our inner child and view the world through childlike eyes, with curiosity, freshness, hope and a sense of new perspective.

The old calendar year is coming to an end and we are in the midst of celebrating the birth of the new. The much welcomed sunlight begins to grow in strength, bringing much hope for the subsequent arrival of Spring. When you are in the dead of Winter and the lack of daylight is playing havoc on your emotional and physical health, the sun's arrival is something indeed to be celebrated.

We have much reason to celebrate the growing light as it points to yet another turn of the sacred wheel. This month, among the festivities, we seek to attune ourselves to the beloved Japanese Sun Goddess-Amaterasu O- mi-Kami and tap into her gifts of self worth, truth, harmony and rebirth. We will also visit with the maiden, Greek Goddess of Wisdom and intellect, Athena, and tap into the powers of the mind and the gift of strong creative strategizing.

CHAPTER ONE

" I wish I could show you when you are lonely or in darkness the astounding light of your own being..." Hafiz of Persia

"People are like stained glass windows, they sparkle when the sun is out but when the darkness sets in, their true beauty is revealed, only if there is a light from within..." Elizabeth Kubler-Ross

WELCOME AMATERASU

OUR ALTAR

Altar cloth : White and or a second Gold altar cloth with Japanese/Asian motif or calligraphy images.

Image: Statue of the Asian Sun Goddess
Canvas art or photo of the Sun Goddess, Japanese landscape, Asian calligraphy, a map of the Japanese islands, Asian motif and images of the Brilliant Golden Sun.

Always present on the altar;
A cast iron cauldron, speaking stick, drums, bell chimes, notes, a silver pentacle, athame, elemental representations.....

Air: Smudge wands, Incense type sticks, cones, charcoal brisket and fine powdered herbs in Frankincense, myrrh, clove, orange peels.
Fire: candles; a glass enclosed candles in white or yellow and or a sun shaped candle. A Buddha shaped candle would also work nicely. Lots of votive candles as this is the season of lights.
Water: Rain stick for gentle sounds of rain, bells and chimes. Chalice or small glass bowl with Spring Lavender Water or even a mini table fountain.
Earth: Plants like, Jade, Bamboo shoots, Caladium and Dracaena. White Roses would also be appropriate, as well as a small dish of soil and or herbs.

Other items pertinent to this particular gathering
Metal Sword blade
Round mirrors
Figurines of mini Horses (they can be toy types)
Beaded sparkling jewels with glitter
Workshop items
Mini personal altar shrine Box
Silk Textile and weavings or cord
Tarot- "The Sun"
Writing paper and pen
Bell or wind chimes or singing bowl

Offering example of Japanese Culinary food; sushi, sashimi, miso soup, rice as well as dry white rice grain.
Sacred objects from members:
Notes:

Amaterasu

Amaterasu Altars

Sun Goddess Altar

AMATERASU O-MI-KAMI (Ohiru-menomuchi-no-kami)

Amaterasu, the Japanese Goddess of the Sun, whose name, in some text, is interpreted as meaning the, *"exalted deity which illuminates the Heavens."* Like Athena, she was birthed by her father. Prior to the creation of the world, according to Japanese cosmology, it was believed that there were invisible Gods in the Heavens. The first God Izanagi, translates as, *"He who invites"* and the name of the first Goddess Izanami, translates as, *"She who invites."* According to Japanese legend these two respective male and female deities were the first known Gods and they were called upon to create the island of Japan and its eight nearby islands. They were also called upon to populate the Earth with humans and thus they united, resulting in the unearthing of sex and procreation. Together they created a number of deities, before Amaterasu came to be.

There are two known stories regarding these Japanese deities. One comes from the Nihongi, an eighth century collection of Japanese myths and legends and the other from the Kojiki (712 C.E.), the oldest of the two. The Nihongi makes Amaterasu first born from white copper mirrors held by her father, Izanagi alone. According to the writings in the Kojiki, when the Goddess Izanami, gave birth to the God of Fire, she was severely hurt. As can be expected, she was horribly injured during the birthing of this scorching God and consequently, it forced Amaterasu's mother to go into the underworld. Izanami descended into the land of the dead where she began to decay. Her lover, the God Izanagi, was devastated and sought to find his love in the underworld, but when he arrived there, she refused to be visited by him in her putrefying condition and she sends him away. He returned to the land of the living, surprisingly, unharmed, but as was the tradition of this time, he underwent a purification upon his return, by bathing in the streams. In this special purification bath, came forth three Gods; Tsukiyomi, Susano-o and Amaterasu.

According to Japanese Mythology, from the left eye of Izanagi was born the first Deity, the beloved Goddess of the Sun -Amaterasu. From the right eye came forth the second Deity, Tsukiyomi, the God of the Moon. From the unfavorable nose of the God Izanagi, the God Susano-o came forth and he was to rule the Ocean and later the underworld.

Tsukiyomi, was God of the Moon and this God ruled the night. The Goddess Amaterasu, was to rule over the almighty Heavens, as the Goddess of the Sun. Susano-o, as God of the Ocean, was not a pleasant deity and thus he was not well received. His wicked, untamable, irrepressible, ego centered ways, were viewed as dangerous to a flourishing society. Some feared that the early death of his mother had affected him adversely and he was much too dysfunctional to interact in a stable, proper Japanese society. Fearing his son's unpredictable volatile ways would destroy the Earth, he was soon cast into the underworld to rule this realm and join his missed, beloved mother. Needless to say he had acquired a bad reputation. One legend reveals that he tried to endear his sister prior to going to the underworld. Somehow, he had this idea that if he aligned himself with his adoring, most popular Sister, the Goddess of the Sun, he could improve his status and make himself more appealing to the world.

One day he crawled out of his dark realm to have a word with Amaterasu. Susano-o approached his sister desperately explaining his plight and pleading his case to welcome him in the world. Always benevolent, she agreed to help him in whatever way possible and soon she found herself uniting with her brother. From this union, eight important deities were born. According to Japanese mythology, the Sun Goddess took her brother's sword, broke it into three pieces and chewed them. She then spat it out and thus three Goddesses were born from her. Susano-o, in turned, took five pieces of his sister's jewels. He chewed the jewels and like Amaterasu, he spat it out. Five Gods were born from his action. According to Japanese Lore, these Gods became direct descendants of the royal Imperial Japanese families.

It seemed all was well with Susano-o's initial honorable intentions, but quite quickly he changed his tune and was back to his old irrepressible volatile ways. As one mythology tells it, one day he entered Amaterasu's sacred temple and started haphazardly tossing excrement all over the holy sanctuary, where first fruits were often offered to the Goddess. The final act of vile disrespect took place when according to one Japanese lore, he broke into the sacred palace where all the women were weaving holy garments. The horse was considered a sacred animal to Amaterasu, yet Susano-o, in an act of unfathomable behavior, violently threw a horse unto the priestesses that were weaving. As a direct result of his wretched action one of Amaterasu's beloved priestess was killed. The myth divulges that the blow of the horse killed her, but other myths reveal that she hit her own genitalia and then killed herself after this traumatic event. The symbolic language used in this myth might be a reference to perhaps being raped or sexually assaulted by Susano-o himself and this very act thus resulted in her own suicide.

The Sun Goddess was so outraged at her brother's repulsive disregard of her sacred temple and his defilement of her worship with this vile action. Some believe that perhaps she too was a victim of Susano-o sexual assault and thus, incest, a most vile traumatic incident, would've taken place. Regardless, Amaterasu was clearly distraught beyond measure and so greatly traumatized that she could no longer shine her divine light. She took her despondency and retrieved from the world, burying herself into a cave. Amaterasu withdrew all of her glorious divine light from the world and as a result the Earth stood in darkness. Susano-o's chaos now reign on the Earth and without the Sun Goddess, discord was ever prevalent in the world. At this time, he threatened civilization and the earth's survival with his ego driven, wild untamable ways.

The pantheon of Japanese Gods were needless to say, very concern for the Earth's survival. After sometime they grew desperate and joined to collaborated on a way to disentomb Amaterasu and bring her Divine light back to the world. At first, they brought out the cocks and enticed them to crow, as this was a trusted symbol of dawn. As the sun begins to rise in the mornings, these feather creatures are usually crowing to announce the impending new day. The Gods believed this would surely bring out the Sun Goddess. Next, they hung stringed jewels, sparkling tiny reflections of her light, all around the trees by the cave she had now resigned herself to. They also decorated the trees with cloth streamers all in an effort to entice her to stay. As the mirror was one of her most prized sacred symbol, they also erected a very large, special eight sided mirror for the Goddess to catch her own reflection upon exiting the cave. The last step in their plans to bring back Amaterasu, was calling on the Goddess Ama no Uzume to come to their aid. Uzume adorned herself with plants and bamboo shoots, appearing very much like a frolicsome Spring Maiden. She was encouraged to dance by the other Gods but her dance soon became rather frenetic, lewd and an ecstatic dance where she stripped her clothes off. It caused quite a raucous of laughter and an unexpected loud commotion. From deep within the cave, Amaterasu heard this and it confused her. She had taken her divine light away from the world and, instead of silence and mourning, all she heard now, from outside her cave, was laughter and merriment. This made her very curious. Gingerly, she slid the rock, slightly opening the cave entrance, just enough to get a peak. When she saw her own brilliant reflection caught in that special eight sided mirror she was mesmerized. Then she came out a little further and caught a glimpse at all those brightly colored jewels hanging from the nearby trees. As she stepped out even further, the Gods quickly moved the boulder to close off the entrance to the cave, forcing Amaterasu to stay out longer and return to her post as Goddess of the Sun.

From this Myth we can extrapolate many facts about this beloved Goddess and her worship. We learn about some of her symbols and appreciate their value. According to Japanese lore, some of these gifts were bestowed to her Grandson, the direct descendant of the Japanese Imperial Family, and thus they take on even greater importance to the culture.

According to Japanese scriptures, to her grandson, Ninigri, she gives him three regalias - divine gifts from the Goddess herself. Amaterasu gives Ninigri the mirror, which she instruct him to assume as the Goddess herself, reflecting truth and light. She gives him the Sword, which was originally an impressive gift from her very own brother, Susano-o. Perhaps, it was seen as a powerful weapon, but we must also remember that she broke and chewed three pieces of the sword and thus three Goddesses were born. Her brother's sword, thus, played an important part in the procreation of important Japanese deities, linking the country to its future leaders. The last gift was the Imperial Jewels. They were seen as symbols of the Goddess- gifts of fertility and agricultural procreation. We must also remember that her brother took five of her jewels, chewed them and spat out Five Gods as a result. Like the Roman Goddess Diana sends Aradia to Earth as a messenger and Like the Christian Father God sends Jesus to Earth to be the messiah, so too here we have the Divine Mother sending her grandson Ninigri to Earth, to the Japanese people, to continue her laws of order and civilization.

It also becomes very apparent that Amaterasu's withdrawal from the Earth was reminiscent of an actual Solar Eclipse. It can also be linked to the season's natural cyclical rhythm, for the Sun's bright power seems to wane, almost dying during the Autumn/Winter months. Upon the Winter Solstice the Sun is reborn again and slowly regains its full power leading us into Spring and then Summer. The Goddess Ama no Uzume can be seen as a Spring, fertility, Maiden deity drawing the sun's powers out by dancing her licentious dance. Amaterasu thus takes on an important role as an agricultural Goddess, who lends her light to help Japanese crops multiply and prosper. Here she is reminiscent of Demeter the Greek Goddess of the grain.

She also appears like a warrior Goddess, in her intolerance of Susano-o's destructive, sabotaging behavior, which put Japanese Society in great danger, almost destroying Japan. She is therefore seen as Japan's defender and the country's divine protector. Interesting to note, Japan's early name was "Dai Nihon" which literally means "*Great Sun Source*," revealing Amaterasu's strong connection to her birth country.

Through-out history Amaterasu is often seen as a parental, direct ancestor of the Japanese people In school text books there are even references to Amaterasu as a universal deity directly connected to the royal Imperial family. Her divine grandson, Ninigri, married a woman from earth and they had two sons. These two sons find wives and get married as well and have children. One of these children gives birth to a son - Jimmu and He then becomes the first Japanese Emperor. Here we have that important evidence that the Imperial family is directly related to the Great Divine and can justly assert its power over its people.

Amaterasu is one of the few Goddesses still highly venerated and worshipped today. Her existence reflect a belief in Japan as a divine land with divine people as it is believed that this Sun Goddess is ancestor to all of its people. Thus, she is ancestral founder and protector of Japan. Shrines were created everywhere in her honor. During colonization many shrines were erected for her expanding worship. The most famous and largest shrine can be seen at The Ise Shrine. Here the sacred, eight sided mirror is reputed to be maintained. At these altars people might worship the Goddess with special ceremonies, invoking her powers of light & order and also with acts of purification. The Sun Goddess, Amaterasu, is seen as holy and pure and as a reflection of truth and she inspires her people to live life with the same ideals.

Amaterasu Grove Goddess Gathering
LECTURE ON THE JAPANESE SUN GODDESS.

Amaterasu: meaning, "Great Shinning Heaven". This invocation comes from Japanese Scripture by Nihongi.

> "When I look to the Royal Sky,
> I see her, tranquil Queen
> Behind a screen of Clouds,
> The Sun.
> For thousands of Ages may she Shine.
> For thousands of ages may we serve her.
> May we serve her with reverence.
> May we serve her with Love..."
>
> *(This is from "The Goddess Path" pg 70. by Patricia Mohaghan)*

Today Amaterasu is still the Primary Deity of the Shinto Religion, therefore, she is very much a living Goddess.

SHINTO: This religion is still thriving today and it is truly one of the indigenous, Pre-Buddhist religions of Japan.

*Shinto is similar to Wicca, in that it is a nature honoring religion. It also does not have a concept of evil but rather inappropriateness. Actions and manners are judged by their time and place.

*In the myth of Susano-o and Amaterasu, it is Susano-o's uncontrollable, volatile actions among her Priestesses and in her Sacred Shrine that is so unbearable for the Goddess-causing her to retreat her light from the world.

STORYTELLING OF THE MYTH

It was the gathering of Japanese deities and the shaman, Spring-maiden Deity, UZUME who helped bring back the Sun Goddess. It becomes clear that the Number **Eight** was sacred to Amaterasu. Eight in Shintoism is the number of Perfection. The scripture also notes, there were Eight Million Kami (Gods and Goddesses) who beckoned the Sun Goddess to come out of hiding. In the Japanese scriptures, it is stated that the mirror, which she gazed upon, was crafted by the Smith God, Ishikore-dome and it was an eight sided mirror. According to legends, this mirror still exist today (though you cannot directly see it) and it is believed to be kept at The **Great Shrine at Ise**, South of Nagoya, the center of Japan. Pilgrimage to the Great Shrine are numerous throughout the many pivotal, seasonal times of the years; for example; the Summer and Winter Solstice.

One of those special times of the year for a pilgrimage to the Great Shrine, falls on February 3rd - the Japanese Feast of SETSUBUN, which is the day the door of Winter is closed. It appears similar to our Wiccan Imbolc and Groundhog day. Traditionally, families would clear their homes and scatter soybeans through-out their homes, while chanting words to expel negative energy. Hinamatsuri, which falls on March third is another important day. This is a Month long Doll Festival in which girls parade their doll collections and host ritualized tea parties. Another important event is held every Twenty years to inaugurate a newly built Shrine to the Goddess. The Sacred mirror is taken out then and brought to the new Shrine as a symbol of rebirth and renewal and an ancestral lineage being passed down.

Amaterasu has **three very important symbols** as revealed by her myths; The Mirror, Necklace jewels and the Sword.

The Sword was a gift from her Brother it was probably seen as a powerful weapon then. Amaterasu was also seen as protector and defender of Japan and thus we see here her Warrior Goddess aspect, a characteristic much like the Greek Goddess Athena. The jewels and necklaces connects Amaterasu to her agricultural and fertility gifts for Japan's growth and continued prosperity.

The <u>Mirror</u> is viewed as the Goddess herself and therefore extremely sacred. In Ancient Japanese scripture it becomes clear that Amaterasu instructs her worshippers, through her Imperial grandchildren, to look at the Mirror as an embodiment of herself, for the truth is captured and revealed gazing into the mirror. Light and truth are exposed herein. Even today, upon the Japanese flag, Amaterasu is symbolized by a circle. which is seen as her symbol of the mirror.

AMATERASU GROVE GODDESS GATHERING

PURPOSE: To honor the Japanese Sun Goddess, Amaterasu and dispel chaos in our lives. To recognize our intrinsic value and our own divine light in this world. We come out of our caves and are reborn with the sun.

CHECK INS As we enter the space, we create a circle and stand side by side, to introduce ourselves and how we are presently handling the change in season.
CHANTING
"*Amaterasu Song*", "*By the Earth that is her Body,*" and "*Let it In, Let it Flow,* " (see song text sheet)
DRUMMING TRANCE: A powerful drumming (CD), musical track will be played to allow participants to truly engage and ground in the present moment. Some might sit still and trance, while others might feel a need to move and connect, with spirit, in this way. Singing bowls and bell chimes can also be incorporated at this time as well.
CHECK INS: As we sit amidst our circle, the tarot card of "The Sun" is passed from womyn to womyn, so that we can reflect on its meaning and how it relates to Amaterasu. Every participant will have a chance to share aloud, their thoughts on the image of the Goddess.

GODDESS LECTURE
Japanese Goddess, her sacred symbols, Shinto practices and
Lecture on Amaterasu and Susano-o.

GODDESS WORKSHOP

WORKSHOP I. Creating a talisman of Amaterasu, to protect our own light and remind us to be true to ourselves. When we are creating our Pendant: think upon who you are authentically or at the very least, who you hope to be, think back when you were five or so, who you believed you'd be by now, who stares back at you when you look in the mirror today. This pendant will serve to remind you of your own Divine light. To be touched and tapped into, in moments when we are amidst Susano-o's antics. We will sculpt and craft this small, mirrored Sun pendant, then oven bake our polymer clay creations -which will be worn during our ritual. It will need to be done early, baked, dried and strung up, then place in the large Cauldron ready for our ritual.

WORKSHOP II: The Magick of Mirrors, their origins and their attributes. Through - out the ages, mirrors have been mentioned in various myths and Grimoire spell workings. We will discuss their usage and their relevance, in relation to Amaterasu. We will also explore the practice of mirror scrying and create our own Scrying tool with a mirror and black acrylic paint.

WORKSHOP III. Exploring what makes us retreat and the lessons we can extrapolate from Amaterasu's myths. What hinders our light? The Chaos that needs banishing, what do we "squash" and eliminate? What is acting like Susano-o , that needs to be banished and extracted from our lives, so that the Sun, peace, harmony, vitality and ultimately, Amaterasu, can prevail. Susano-o might not have been deliberately inflicting harm and purposely making Amaterasu disappear, but, rather in him being this strong, over powering personality and as a result of these emotionally charged events, it caused Amaterasu to retreat. Susano-o - is volatile, overpowering, turbulent, emotional, the train wreck that comes into your life and topsy-turvy everything that you are and everything that you have. The storms and tornadoes that uproot us OUT of our dwellings, OUT of our roles and OUT of our true authentic selves. The person, place or situation that comes with magnanimous force and wipes your existence, your TRUE Existence out of here and into hiding. Who makes you hide?, What or who puts a cloud over your true self?, What or Who keeps you away in that cave, hiding your light? *Write it/draw it/represent it on a sheet of paper. In our upcoming ritual, it will be burned and banished to make room for our own divine light to shine through.

WORKSHOP IV: Since we are in the month of Yule and various other special, cultural Holidays, it seems fitting to include a Gift exchange within our gathering. Participants were asked ahead of time to unearth within their closets, magickal items and tools they haven't used and are ready to recycle and part with. It can be anything- small or big. The important goal is that we are recycling and acknowledging that one womyn's trash is another womyn's treasure. We can also include services in our gift giving to one another, for example; an astrologer in the group might offer a free Astrological chart, an accountant in the group might offer tax preparation services, a patient womyn might offer free babysitting etc... Gifting exchange, to our systers with thoughtful, sincere love.

REFLECTIONS ON AMATERASU

As wommin her lessons to us about our self-worth and our own, inherent, powers are invaluable. She teaches us to look in the mirror and value our unique divine light reflecting back at us. In this Goddess, we can't deny the feminine aspect of the Sun and its correlation to our own lives as modern day Empresses. Her applicable ancient myths are still relevant for us today when we continue to still see the oppression of our gender in the world and as we struggle to confidently let our light shine, despite the darkness and chaos that has ensued.

Although Feminism and womyn's rights have come a long way since the 1970's, this is a fight far from being over. Here in the U.S.A. our struggles may have taken on a different hue and may appear subtle, compared to those in the 1950's, but in foreign countries the atrocities infringed on wommin's human rights, divine light and civil liberties are criminal, to say the least. And for a womyn to unearth her beauty, competence and self-worth, in a world that would rather silence, beat, berate mutilate and eradicate her, is nearly impossible, but one of the most crucial ingredients for a thriving , stable society. For the light of wommin, as is exemplified by Amaterasu in these myths, is an integral part and requirement for humanities progress and survival.

> *"The real religion of the world comes from women*
> *much more than from men- from mothers ,*
> *most of all, who carry the*
> *key of our souls in their bossoms.."* Oliver Wendell Holmes...

Amaterasu is also an advocate for those times when we do need to temporarily retreat and regroup because we have been severely traumatized and wounded. Retreating and sitting with that darkness for a short time can sometimes be very cathartic, equipping us with the ability to come back even stronger, with one of the most powerful artillery, our Self Confidence....this is her special message to us. Within all wommin is a strong fierce light, able to pierce through and eradicate any chaos or darkness. Unearth yourself and your divine light and come back to your rightful place in this world. Look into the mirror and embrace, "She" who is reflected back at you - for indeed you are Goddess!

AMATERASU GROVE GODDESS GATHERING RITUAL

PURPOSE: To honor the Japanese Sun Goddess, Amaterasu and dispel chaos in our lives. To recognize our intrinsic value and our own divine light in this world. We come out of our caves and are reborn with the Sun.

PURIFYING: With the smoke of the sacred smudge incense, Frankincense and Myrrh.

Circle is cast *very tenderly, a light bell/chime around, a simple phrase....*
Goddesses, ancestresses,
spirits of old
Hearken now, our circle hold,
Circle around to keep us safe,
Evil at bay, far from our gate
Truth and Love invited here
Spirits and Gods we draw you near.
Contain and preserve
the energy we create
By will and word
this Circle is made.

Quarters are called
Guardians of the Watchtowers of the **East, Ye powers of Air
Place of new perspective and winds of truth and revelations,
New endeavors and conceptions swept in, by Winter's clean breeze .
We call on you to bring us your gifts,
Guard and hold our Sacred space. Hail and Welcome.

Guardians of the Watchtowers of the **South, Ye powers of Fire
Realm of Amaterasu's flaming Powers of the Sun, Immortal flames that pierce through the cosmos to awaken our own divine light, to extract us from the grip of the dark, to thaw and warm the most frigid of hearts.
We call on you to bring us your gifts,
Guard and hold our Sacred space. Hail and Welcome.

Guardians of the Watchtowers of the **West, Ye powers of Waters
Place of Healing and Emotional reconciliations, Venerated chalice of tears, mourning and lament, held in sacred wombs of great immanense.
We call on you to bring us your gifts,
Guard and hold our Sacred space. Hail and Welcome.

Guardians of the Watchtowers of the **North, Ye powers of Earth
Realm of Regeneration and transformation, Earth's soil awakening to her divine light,
Slowly thawing from under our feet, Potential rising, though hidden from sight.
We call on you to bring us your gifts,
Guard and hold our Sacred space. Hail and Welcome.

Speaker: *Announces what will unfold- why we are here,* "We seek to invite the Sun Goddess to bring her healing light into our realm"

<u>**Invocation**</u>: Singing Chant *"Amaterasu Song"*
Then One women must begin calling out Amaterasu... she encourages them all to also call out....
Silence- NOTHING HAPPENS...***Priestess starts to do her licentious dance and really get them to laugh and they all start to giggle more etc.
       Laughter brings her out...
Amaterasu timidly peaks, then, a little closer...then womyn notice and they drag her out to the center.

She covers her face with hands, peaks, then, she too starts to laugh.
****Aspecting Amaterasu appears** (see suggested prose)**

Oh My....
What Brilliance I carry within me
and all around...
What Shimmering sparkles
from the depths of my very Soul abound....

Long have I neglected to see,
Long have I forgotten me.
I failed to embrace
my own powers and light,
my own self-worth fading
From everyone's sight

In a state of hopelessness
and devastation...I needed to flee.
In the cave I remained
until wisdom came to me.

Almost swallowed by pain
And extinguished my light
Susano-O be gone from me
I banish you into the night.

You almost engulfed me..
I almost allowed you, too
I awaken to my Divine light, now,
I am Amaterasu!!!!!

Asks everyone to face & Grab their Susano-o's paper *(the one we worked on earlier to banish,)* She begins to speak :
What OPRESSES YOU?
She crushes/destroys the paper and invites them all to do the same.
***Toss it/burn in large cauldron.

II. Then she picks up ***Large mirror,** hold it before every individual womyn's face around the circle, so that participants may look into her eyes and see her own light, beauty and truth.
The Goddess asks;
"What will shine forth from you now that Susano-o cannot destroy from this point on?
For me (I will begin, looking deeply into the mirror) it is my light, courage and connection to my systers... For some it might be; ex; Beauty, Love, Education, Prosperity, a home etc...
Chant with movement: *"We All Come from the Goddess"*

Priestess will hold up the small basket/cauldron containing the clay pendants, prepare to pass it along the circle saying:
WILL you CLAIM here AMATERASU'S SYMBOL OF LIGHT AND TRUTH?
Everywoman can seek for her personal pendant and place it around her neck then turns to her syster and continue the process.

Chanting: *" We are Systers on a Journey"*
Share a final check in...*(take off regalia)* Thank & Devoke the Goddess *(see suggestion)*
Together we entered the Dark Cave with you, Amaterasu,
Allowing Susanno-o/ Darkness and Chaos to Reign briefly,
But with you and among our Systers
We exited that Dark Cavern,
To Discover our own inner Beauty and Truth,
our deep rooted Power and our own Divine Light.
May we always remember who we are
And the gifts you have blessed us with on this day.

Blessed Be Amaterasu, Receive our Gratitude,
and to all my beautiful Grove Systers...
Hail and Farewell and Thank you...

DEVOKING QUARTERS
Guardians of the Watchtowers of the **East,** Ye powers of Air, beginnings and our breath.
We thank you for clearing the ethers and allowing her breath in our ritual today.
Go if you must, stay if you will, Hail and farewell...

Guardians of the Watchtowers of the **South**, Ye powers of Fire, the Sun, truth, ambition and drive. We thank you for your fiery presence in our sacred space.
Go if you must, stay if you will, Hail and farewell.

Guardians of the Watchtowers of the **West**, Ye powers of Waters, compassion, and healing.
We thank you for the curative waters in our ritual today.
Go if you must, stay if you will, Hail and farewell.

Guardians of the Watchtowers of the **North**, Ye powers of Earth, the Creatress, her Caverns and potentiality, We thank you for grounding and guarding our sacred space.
Go if you must, stay if you will, Hail and farewell.

******

Last minute thoughts
Open circle with merry meet song..

POTLUCK *might be able to take place before the actual ritual, feel vibe, Beforehand we can also briefly plan for ritual. Japanese culinary ex; noodles, sushi, miso soup, teriaki, sashimi, salads etc...*

II. A RITUAL FOR JAPAN
AND FOR ALL THOSE EFFECTED BY THE CATASTROPHIC NATURAL DISASTER,
A 9.0 EARTH QUAKE, TSUNAMI AND NUCLEAR POWER MELT DOWN
3/11/11 incorporated into The Spring Equinox Ritual

Asperge; Smudge and incense the space and one another gently with love and true welcoming spirit... look into each other's eyes for connection

Circle cast silently with bell chimes, singing bowl, any piercing bell like vibrations. All participant are encouraged to bring their own form of bells and around the circle we will cast this sacred space by chiming and saying....
(bell intoned)"***Let peace and love be here now, I cast this sacred Circle around...***"
(Wommin can insert their own wish for our circle casting with 1-2 words replacing suggestion)
other ex: "Let compassion and protection be here now, I cast this sacred Circle around" or
"Let light and healing be here now, I cast this sacred Circle around"

ELEMENTS INVOKED BY GODDESS QUARTER CALLS
Invoking Fire-Amaterasu
Benevolent ancient Sun Goddess, yours are the sacred Islands of Japan. We invoke you here now and beseech your energy into this ritual today. Come Solar Goddess enraptured in your gifts of fire, truth, order and "will", that we as a human race, can tap into your solar gifts during a most crucial moment in our planet's history. Give unto us the will to survive, hang on, transcend, rebuild and shine on, even stronger than ever before. In your light let us not forget our worth and our role as ambassadors of the earth. When facing these dark atrocities, let us never forget the guide of our own inner divine light which has the cathartic power to heal.

Invoking Water-Kwan Yin
Compassionate Mother, you who gathers the tears of the World, more than ever now we need you. Awaken in us, and our brothers and sisters, compassion for one another and the realization that we all swim in her waters and partake of her womb of Creatrix powers. Let these tears, we are all shedding now as a nation, cleanse away the debris, stagnation and complacency that has entrapped us in negative states of paralysis and false illusions. Mother's water flow, gently through us into this space and time and bring your gifts of compassion for earth and its inhabitants.

Invoking Earth-Proserpina
Queen and Maiden. Bride, Mother and Daughter in one. You who awakens the earth from Winter's slumber, beckoning all life to spring forth at this pivotal time of the year... We call on your fertile flowering gifts of creations. In the midst of great tragedy, may we unearth the seeds you so dedicate yourself to nurturing. May we unearth the seeds of **Hope** for a brighter tomorrow...

Invoking Air- Oya
Winds of Uranus, drastic change... like it or not you have arrived and while we try to make sense of it all, with reverence and wisdom we know thy "will" serves our healing and growth as a human race. Winds have mercy on us, gently stir and sweep that which does not serve us well anymore as a human race. Help us move and transition into this luminescent era with your effortless ease and grace. Gently teach us the Lessons that will Breathe new life into our souls and inaugurate a new age of enlightenment.

Music CD Selection or CHANT: *"Mother I Feel You"* *(the extended version)*
SPELL WORKING: *Red stained, hollowed out Eggs appropriate for the Spring Equinox. We will add elemental representation in this spell, our tears, herbs, our breath, a red seed, hawthorn or tiny bud...*

Let our Global pain and mourning **tears** represented in this **water** (****), bring the gift of Compassion for more humanitarian aid, as needed, to help all those effected by the recent catastrophic events in Japan.

Let the **earth,** whole unto itself, be healthy, nurturing and supportive, be represented in this sacred herb (*****) to bring about recovery and positive transformation after such a devastating natural disaster.

Let our **breath** upon this spell, travel into the cosmic, ethereal fields to give new life to a land now saturated with corpses and senseless deaths. We breathe (****) into this egg sending forth resurrection and renewed pulse and vitality.

Fire is our living blood, and with the **color red** it is represented in this egg, the symbol of this season, the ancient symbol of renewal, vitality, life and rebirth. Within the heat of our flesh (****) we imbue this spell with living Prana *(life force and vital energy)* that it may be well received by our Mother Earth, in our humblest supplication for the wellbeing of humanity, and all her offspring.

Place eggs on altar, participants are encouraged to take them home and bury them or crush them returning them back into the earth as an offering to Goddess, sending all of our gathered, collective good energy and prayers, for the earth's wellbeing and the protection of its inhabitants.
CHANT: *"Mother Song - Mother I call you, deep within my soul you are stirring my womb"*

DEVOKING ELEMENTS/GODDESSES
AIR
Oya, Fierce Winds of change,
When called, you came to support this work
Although We bid you now adieu,
receive our thanks and gratitude.
In peace ye arrived, In peace, please return
to your realm you go, Hail and farewell................
EARTH
Proserpina, Flowering Maiden awakener of Hope
When called, you came to support this work
Although We bid you now adieu,
receive our thanks and gratitude.
In peace ye arrived,
In peace, please return
to your realm, Hail and farewell................
WATER
Kwan Yin, Embracer of the water from our tears,
When called, you came to support this work
Although We bid you now adieu,
receive our thanks and gratitude.
In peace ye arrived, In peace, please return
to your realm you go, Hail and farewell................
FIRE
Amaterasu, The heart's light that erradicates darkness
When called, you came to support this work
Although We bid you now adieu,
receive our thanks and gratitude.
In peace ye arrived, In peace, please return
to your realm you go, Hail and farewell................

Opening the Circle: From hand to hand I now release and open this sacred circle

Opening Circle with Song: *"By the earth that is her Body, by the air that is her breath, by the fire that is her bright spirit by the living waters of her womb...."*

Potluck feasting may follow afterwards.....

AMATERASU & SUSANO-O

There is much that one can surmise and speculate when we take the time to scrutinize the relationship between Amaterasu and her Brother, Susano-o. Just like our own siblings can sometimes reveal a lot about ourselves and the imprint of our lineage, I find that meditating on him, in relation to her, brought about greater understanding of this beloved Sun Goddess. It certainly helped connect me to her even further than I had initially anticipated.

In Japanese mythology, Amaterasu was the much beloved Sun Goddess. Her brother, Susano-o, garnered the reputation of being the emotional, volatile Sea and Storm God, who won no popularity contest with the people of the land . He was the brattiest, destructive, unpredictable and an uncontrollable entity that was feared and possibly abhorred in the Japanese culture, for indeed he was a threat to a thriving society.

Susano-o -was emotionally overpowering, unstable and the train wreck that comes into your life and topsy-turvy everything that you are and everything that you have. He is the storms and tornadoes that uproot us out of our familiar dwellings, out of our roles and out of our true authentic selves. The person, place or situation that comes with this brute force and wipes your existence, your TRUE Existence, out of balance and swerves you into hiding. He is that energy of the incorrigible drunk, who just comes in and smears profanity, bumping into everyone and everything with distasteful lack of boundaries. Stumbling and falling all over the place, not cognizant of the impact of his words or actions and carelessly carrying on, without regards to those around him. His energy is chaotic, irrepressible and explosive, that is the image of Susano-o, or at least how he appears to me and it is in total contrast to how Amaterasu appears. To further understand Amaterasu through Susano-o I invite you to contemplate these questions.

*Have you witness or been around someone who was severely inebriated while you were clearly sober?
_____
*How did that make you feel? _____
*Have you ever had your boundaries compromised by someone you trusted?
_____
*Who is acting like Susano-o, (the turbulent Sea/Storm God, who's volatile nature was relegated to the underworld) in your life right now? _____
_____
*What Oppresses you and Threatens your true identity?
_____
*Have you ever been confronted with a situation or person, so overwhelming, that it made you retreat, almost disappear?
_____
*What threatens your inner divine truth and light from shinning forth?
_____

As we have learned from her mythology, Amaterasu is harmony, prosperity, growth, truth, light, beauty and structure. She emits peace, order and law, which is why in ancient times and to this day, she is still very much revered and loved. Yet her benevolence was extended to all, including her dark, troublesome brother, when it appeared he had changed his ways and was now desperately beseeching her help in making amends. Against her better judgment, she joined with him and trusted that all would be well, but it didn't take long for Susano-o to quickly show his true nature.

The situation between Amaterasu and her brother escalates into a vile, most repugnant act within her sacred sanctuary, as is well documented in various Japanese scriptures. There, within her sacred Temple, a priestess is killed and many wounded. Some even speculate that sexual assault took place and there is catastrophic devastation. For the Sun Goddess, Susano-o's repulsive behavior traumatized her and dragged her into a very scary, overwhelming dark place. It catapulted a momentous shift in her own psyche that brought up such intense emotions for her, that all she could do was retreat -give up, mourn and escape into a cave. And Susano-o might not have been deliberately inflicting harm, nor purposely making Amaterasu disappear, but rather in his true nature of recklessness, was oblivious to the consequences of his volatility. As a result of these emotionally charged events and his brute, over powering force, Amaterasu is swept into his tidal wave of negative emotions, that causes her to flee and retreat for the safety of her own wellbeing.

This very act of retreating however, almost allows Susano-o to dis-empower his sister completely. Her sadness and anger are so overwhelming that she can't face them or just won't. She hangs up the towel and retreats from the world -thus allowing darkness and chaos to reign among the Earth. And by retreating from the world she took her divine light away, effecting the survival of her people and relinquishes her role as light bearer. Her very own powers and her gifts to the world are swallowed up in this highly charged emotional tragedy.

I invite you also to ponder for yourself some of these important questions to continue our Solar Journey....
***Have you ever found yourself in a place or situation or relationship, that made you retreat or act, unlike yourself?*_____

***Have you ever found yourself lost and far away from your true authentic self?,*
...far away from your gifts and talents? _____

***Have you ever asked yourself, what happened?, What happened to me? How did I get here?*

****Have you ever had a phase in your life that found you hidden, shrinking, disappearing?*

Eventually, and with the help of other divine deities, Amaterasu does gather her strength and unearths her own self-worth, brilliance and divine gifts. Reclaiming herself, she comes out of the cave to bring back order, set Susano-o in his proper place, and return the light of the Sun to the land.

I sometimes muse and consider how the most aggravating people in our lives tend to be those who are meant to reveal something monumental within our own selves and they become a catalyst for our own growth and inner journey and Amaterasu's story always reminds me of this. Those who haphazardly come into our lives, distributing great pain to our world, end up being positively manipulated by Spirit to address and teach us some of the most imperative spiritual lessons in our lives.

Clearly Amaterasu does not want to deal with the chaos that ensued by her brother's hand. She is severely hurt, emotionally traumatized and well aware that life has drastically been altered. Maybe she has to face up to her Brother's true nature and accept that he will always be toxic to her. Maybe up to that point, she really hadn't given much thought to her own powers in handling him and the situation. Maybe she was ill prepared to meet the warrior Goddess he was forcibly, carving and sculpting out of her own soul by this tragedy. Nevertheless, the painful event was so transformative, heart shattering and so shocking that she was not able to confront it for herself and she hopelessly retreats. In retreating, she ends up effecting everything around her, she takes away her light from the World and her own divine self is hidden from everyone, including herself.

**What person or situation acts like Susano-o in your life?*_____
**What person or situation dis-empowers you and makes you retreat?*

**What makes you hide from your own true self and your light?*

**What makes you shy away from your own powers and shrivel, becoming mousy, shy, timid, subordinate.. maybe even acting insignificant?*

**What makes you retreat into your cave and withhold your gifts from the world, the way Amaterasu retreated?*_____

Hold dearly the answers to these questions for they will begin to lead you to Amaterasu's essence and journey.... Peace, light and love to you...

AMATERASU MIRROR MUSING (Part I of II)

    The Mirror is a direct symbol of one of Amaterasu's most treasured, powerful gifts. Throughout her numerous Japanese myths, it is clear that the mirror, for her, is a reflection of truth, yet what does that mean to us modern day wommin? The answer becomes quite transparent when we recognize that one of the most powerful attributes of a mirror, is its reflective quality and its ability to expose the hidden. When we gaze into a mirror it will always reflect things that cannot be denied when conscientiously looked upon. Frequently, mirrors are also employed successfully by traditional witches and wizards in the art of scrying, which is a form of oracular divination.

    I often hear that people going through tumultuous situations and emotional issues, sometimes related to weight gain and obesity problems, rarely look at themselves in the mirror. And I know for a fact, that when I am going through some rough patches in my own life, the mirror (for me) is the last place I want to stand before. Yet when life is beaming with positive energy and I am feeling quite good about myself, the mirror becomes my best friend. Shamelessly, dare I say, in these rare moments, I'm even enchanted by my own reflection. Think of how often we study ourselves in the mirror when we have just had a new haircut or a new makeup application and we are feeling renewed, refreshed and positive.

    When I was a little girl, I remember being alarmed and devastated upon learning that nuns of the Catholic Church did not own mirrors in their sanctuaries and they were obviously not allowed to study, prim nor admire themselves. You can imagine how unreasonable this sounded to a little girl who practically lived in front of the mirror. As a child hearing of this, I was mortified!!! *"Why???and how cruel..."* was all I could ask. To this day, I still think upon that moment when I first learned of this customary ban on mirrors and how I wondered for days, what kind of power a mirror must hold, in order for it to be banned in a convent. Today I meditate on all the bans patriarchy has imposed on wommin throughout the ages in their efforts to dis-empower, weaken, manipulate and control wommin and consequently eradicate her Goddess given gifts. As I connect more and more with Amaterasu, I am beginning to understand, now, quite clearly the patriarchal tenet in this practice of discouraging mirror usage. Here in this musing, I reflect on the magickal powers found in mirrors and how it intimately connects us with this beloved Japanese Sun Goddess.

    Was Amaterasu saying that upon looking into a mirror, we would be gazing at our own reflection and thus our own divinity? Were Amaterasu's instructions (left to her grandchildren, the Imperial family) to view the mirror as herself, intended as a reminder that we carry within ourselves her Divine light? The thought of a mirror reminding us of our own self-worth and divinity is astoundingly provocative and perhaps even frightening for those who would rather oppress us and keep us under the shroud of ignorance. It is reminiscent of the Christianized tales of Adam and Eve and the forbidden fruit. Does the mirror reflect knowledge too dangerous for the survival of patriarchy? Does a mirror act like a sacred portal, only to be savored by a certain sect in our society? I can see how a nation of empowered wommin, reclaiming their inner divine, authentic selves, through a mirror and their own beautiful reflection, can be dangerous to a patriarchal society, that would rather keep us feeling inferior, enslaved and ignorant.

    We are indeed reflections of her Divine light and in the mirror, staring right back, is the unquestionable truth to this titanic realization. When we look deeply into our own eyes, we can't deny what is there, what reflects back at us can be quite empowering, transformative and extraordinary. I dare say that a very simple, but most empowering ritual can be performed with just you, sky clad before a mirror- try it one night. In our Grove Gathering and our Amaterasu Ritual, I hope we can experiment with this magick even further.

AMATERASU & MIRROR SCRYING (Part II of II)

In the dark of the night -during our recent new moon- I took a moment to perform a simple yet very empowering "meditation" and it resulted in this post.

Have you ever faced the mirror, seen your reflection and asked who is that staring back at you? The Sun Goddess, Amaterasu asks this question...Never having seen her own reflection in the mirror...

The last thing I want to look at when I am feeling down about myself, depressed or frustrated, is a mirror. Often in times of great inner turmoil it is very difficult to face ourselves and confront the reality facing back at us. Rather unconsciously, we appear to pass by mirrors with heads down, avoiding our own physical reflection. For myself and many wommin I know, we tend to have a difficult time looking directly at ourselves because the mirror does not lie and it offers nothing to help you hide. It exposes the truth that our minds can so easily conceal and deceive with various exuses and tricky slight of hand . The mirror serves to expose, like the swollen eyes from a night of miserable crying, the wrinkles that tell you its time to grow up, the blemishes that reveal the lack of pampering in your life or poor diet, the extra weight you've naively think is no big deal or the purple bruise from an abusive lover. Quite conversely, the mirror might also expose a gem that has yet to be truly unearth, a beautiful human being that has been stifled, silenced, unrecognized or a dimming spirit that has suffered from self-neglect. Staring back at you is the gaze within those deep eyes, that if conscientiously looked at more closely, might reveal that you are not as happy as you appear on the surface to your family, friends and coworkers and the reality does not match up to the illusions fabricated in your mind as a coping mechanism, in your life.

And Amaterasu never having been exposed to her own luminescence... never having seen her own Divine inner Brilliance was shocked and intrigued at what she saw. And then, after long contemplation, she finds herself enamored by it....

Fear keeps us from looking at ourselves. In our mind we might conjure up all kinds of distortions and lies about our reality. Sometimes things aren't as bad as they seem, yet in our head we've made them impossible to even face. Like when wommin, so often might feel ugly and undesirable and this erroneous illusion plays on in their head, keeping them away from mirrors to face the truth. Well, truth here is that if you look deeply at your own reflection, you'll realize you are a gem and not the troll you've so wrongly conjured up in your mind. Then there are those situations that are undeniably abysmal and continue to get worse as they are avoided. A lump on your body, that you continue to dismiss, undiagnoscd, and refuse to look at, can quite obviously become a greater problem than initially feared. Yet the mirror is truth, as Amaterasu has taught us, and studying your own reflection is only going to help you see what demands your attention, what is vital and imperative to acknowledge.

In an effort to get her out of the Cave and end her self-imposed exile, the Kami's (Japanese Gods) tricked Amaterasu and captured her image with the mirrors they set before the rock. For a short moment, She peeked out of the cave, only to became enthralled at the image in the mirror that came back at her. She saw her own divine reflection. She caught a glimpse into her brilliance and this significant event ended her painful confinement. Consequently it resulted in the return of her "Self" - the rebirth of the Sun.... This is indisputably, quite a powerful metaphor when we take the time to contemplate on her story and its meaning for us today.

I wondered how many of us have ever caught sight of our own reflection in the mirror, the way Amaterasu did, and shockingly, looked at ourselves to find, lo and behold, captivated... by our own inner light. I wondered how many of us have experienced a type of rebirth awakening as a result of this simple act...the way Amaterasu did.

We will be exploring this further in our efforts to touch upon the Goddess, Amaterasu, but for now, I invite you to enter your dark chamber alone, with one single candle as your only source of light, then take up the mirror and courageously, gaze into your own reflection. I invite you to look deeply into your eyes, deeply, ever beyond.... and allow yourself to go further into the sphere. Take your time, this is, after all, a journey to the core of your soul. Have you ever heard the term, *"the Eyes are the windows to your soul...?"* Journey through them... Look deeply into the core of your eyes, continue to penetrate them with your gaze, until they become like a pool; watery, lucid, formless, night sky, expanse....with no trace of boundaries. Search within them to capture a glimmer of that twinkle of light...hold it... Keep holding your gaze and study the swirling forms that appear now, see what is surrounding the blurring lines and the hazy details of your earthly form. You will begin to see layers of your astral, psychic and spiritual bodies. Let your eyes grow soft and surrender any judgment. Continue to look deeply. Gaze ever more deeply, look until without a doubt -Spirit stares back at you.
What does it reveal to you?

When you are ready, express gratitude and slowly return by blinking a few times, shutting your eyelids fully, then open them, doing this a few times. When you are fully ready, return. I suggest turning on the electrical lights and ground yourself, if necessary, by placing the palms of your hands on the earth for a minute or two. Then if you can, record and document for yourself what you experienced and what thoughts surfaced during your mirror scrying exercise.
You are loved, You are brilliance, you are Divine....
and this is the gift of Amaterasu.
Blessed Be!

*ASPECTING AMATERASU *

Oh My....
What Brilliance I carry within me
and all around...
What Shimmering sparkles
from the depths of my very Soul abound....

Long have I neglected to see,
Long have I forgotten me.
I failed to embrace
my own powers and light,
my own self-worth fading
From everyone's sight

In a state of hopelessness
and devastation...I needed to flee.
In the cave I remained
until wisdom came to me.

Almost swallowed by pain
And extinguished my light
Susano-O be gone from me
I banish you into the night.

You almost engulfed me..
I almost allowed you, too
I awaken to my Divine light, now,
I am Amaterasu!!!!!

I. Banishing Chaos: I burn this as a symbol that Susano-o is the one that will flee in my presence. In my Divine Light it is Susano-o that will melt away by the fires of my sun light.
******

II. Mirror SpellWork: As I instructed my grandson and my people, the mirror is a reflection of truth & light. Revere it as me...
What gifts will you hold steadfast and not let Susano-o overtake?

DEVOKING AMATERASU

Dearest Grove Systers,
On this Venus Day,
Night of the Full Moon,
It is a perfect time to Bid adieu
and Thank Amaterasu,
for her gifts this past Gathering.

Together we entered the Dark Cave with you, Amaterasu,
Allowing Susanno-o/ Darkness and Chaos to Reign briefly,
But with you and among our Systers
We exited that Dark Cavern,
To Discover
our own inner Beauty and Truth,
our deep rooted Power and our own Divine Light.
May we always remember who we are....
And the gifts you have blessed us with on this day.
Blessed Be Amaterasu, Receive our Gratitude,
and to all my beautiful Grove Systers...
Hail and Farewell and Thank you...

To be done the night of the Winter Solstice or the New Moon in December. Fumigate the altar area and yourself with Frankincense and mirth, both herbs are associated with solar energy. It is recommended to do a ritual cleansing bath beforehand and approach the altar, purified and dressed in white, Amaterasu's color. Place a statue or photographic image of the Sun Goddess, as well as some of her sacred symbols, like the mirror, sword, lots of colorful beaded necklaces and the Sun. You may also wish to add Asian inspired motifs on your altar.

During the holidays in December, there are many metallic fun shaped candles available and it's a good time to stock up on your "witchy" supplies for the whole year. For this spell you might consider using a round or star shaped candle, one that symbolizes the Sun. You may also use a Golden, Yellow or White candle. Carve your dedicated candle with your initials and the symbol of the sun and then charge it, with suggested "Sun oil,"(see appendix). Hold and warm your intention seeds in your hand as you envision what the new year will bring. As you Recite the incantation, light your candle and plant your seeds and welcome her Divine energy.

WINTER SOLSTICE
* In the dark I can reflect
See the future, past, present
Look inside to find my needs
On this night I'll plant my seeds

Longest night of our year
Winter Solstice is now here
To hold my dreams in its embrace
The seeds I plant will soon take place

Rooted spell upon the Earth
ground my hopes and fears and hurt
Turn this wish into blossomings,
let them manifest by the Spring.

Wishes whispered unto seeds
Draw their strength from Earth beneath
On this night of Sun's rebirth
Wishes planted on the Earth.

Hear this wish, projected far ahead
As light grows stronger
From darkness to bright Red.

This sabbat is kept,
Blessed are we,
This spell bound round,
So mote it be!

Journaling Amaterasu- Grove Gathering-
Calling on the Sun, the powers of our light

This was a Grove Gathering quite early on in the group's inception and admittedly it was after a two month break due to the frenetic holidays of November and December. Momentum for our wonderfully, growing group had been compromised with these inevitable cancellations and it was a harsh lesson for us to all learn from. There is always a fine line between pushing through obstacles, like calendar holiday events and acquiring the courage and the wisdom to know when it's okay to pull back and allow that ebb and flow to begin once more. In facilitating circle groups I have learned that ebb and flow, momentum, growth and restarting anew are a natural manifestation of the process of group formations. Perhaps like all things in life, we get better at rebuilding the more often we are called upon to do so. I am also remembering the wise words of a priestess I met a while ago (at the Z. Budapest Goddess Gathering) who warned about preparing for fallow times and being mindful of the natural cycles when forming wommin's circles. Her words I hear clearly now and they hold much truth and wisdom for me.

However, I remember this particular gathering being very powerful despite the small turn out. As usual I had my normal fears and concerns that my grand vision for our day could not come to fruition without a large group of devoted wommin, but time and time and again, the Divine points out an important lesson for me. I am taught that it is not the size but the energy and intention of those who are indeed present, whether its fifty, ten or three. This gathering served the purpose to open my eyes to this important lessons as a Priestess, for indeed the energy we manifested and the intensity of our working, that day, was astronomical. Our day together honoring Amaterasu brought healing to everyone present and that was the impetus for starting "Grove of the Feminine Divine..."

One of the things I remember most about this gathering, was the many cathartic tears by every womyn present, including myself and how all the wommin expressed the same feeling of safety, gratitude and a deep, long awaited healing in the midst of our ritual work. We had used the fires to remove and banish the Susano-o (the Chaos) in our lives. And it was so amazing how we held each other up, in loving Sisterhood, and we supported one another, as we struggled to light and burn away our troubles. Together we moved the large, heavy cast iron cauldron away from the temple gathering place, in the back-yard and came back to our circle inside the home feeling refreshed, some relief and much lighter. It did feel like an intimate coven family was in the midst of being born at that very moment and Amaterasu was strengthening us in our shadow work.

My day had started out feeling a sense of hopelessness (this is how anxiety often rears its ugly head right before any public speaking event) and insecurity about the direction of our group and my work as a Priestess all accompanied my morning tea, but by the end of our day I felt a renewed sense of purpose and conviction, as I realized the importance of bringing the Goddess, and her amazing healing powers, to as many wommin as I can. Whether it is one or a million in our group, the weight and value of this work remains the same for me. In my efforts to bring them Goddess awareness and healing, something clicked within me that I had not anticipated that day. I too found myself healing long repressed parts of me and reclaiming Amaterasu and my celestial, sacred light even further.

Blessed be for the beautiful Sisters present that day, who made this healing journey possible for all present. Hail to you beloved Goddess of the Sun!!!

AMATERASU GROVE GODDESS CHANTS

FIRE CHANT by Moving Breath
Spirits of Fire Come to us
We will kindle the Fire....
Spirits of Fire, Come to us
We will kindle the Fire...

We will kindle the fire
Dance the Magick circle round
We will kindle the Fire
Dance the Circle Around *(repeat)*

PROTECTION SONG By Lisa Thiel
I invoke the protector,
Divine Mother's embrace
I invoke the Protector
Divine mother's embrace...

With the arms of the Great Mother,
ever surround me, -With the arm of the Great
Mother ever surround me. (repeat)

SUNG & Created(?) BY Susan Weed and Robin Rose Bennet
We are sisters on a journey
Singing in- the Sun
Singing through the Darkest night.
The Journey has begun...
Begun....
The healing has Begun *(continuous repetition...3x)*

SONG TO AMATERASU by B.M.M.
Out of darkness Comes the light
Amaterasu
Slowly growing to new heights
Take away our Blues
Darkness Reign and soon will wane
As you come to rule
Sun reborn,
Hear us call, Amaterasu....
Amaterasu....Amaterasu.... AMATERASU.....*(repeat)*

***The Ocean is the beginning of the Earth**
The Ocean is the beginning of the Earth (2x)
All Life comes from the Sea
All Life comes from the Sea....
    The Sun is a reflection of her Light (2x)
    All thing grow with her love.
    All things grow with her love...
The mirror is a reflection of our heart (2X)
    See the Goddess rest in us.
    See the Goddess rest in us. *By Delaney Johnson, Starhawk and Reclaiming Collective (brooke)*

BY THE EARTH by Elaine Silver
By the Earth that is her body
By the Air that is her breath
By the Fire of her bright spirit
By the living waters of her wombs...
May the peace of the Goddess (alt: Fairies)
Be forever in your heart
The circle is open, but unbroken
Merry meet, merry part.. Repeat xx*(into a round)*

*****CANDLE LIGHT**
In the darkness of the night
Plaaaant a seed.
Magick made by candlelight
Stirring silently,
Growing... Growing
By my might...
Words I speak and charge tonight
    Cast a Circle, Raise the vibe
    With my energy,
    Magick made by candlelight
    Sing so mote it be... Sing so mote it be...
    Sing so mote it be... *(con't repeat)* by B.M.M.

*****THE SWORD (***sung like the elemental chant*)
The sword,
the jewels,
the mirror,
The sun,
Amaterasu
You bring us the truth *by B.M.M.*

CHAPTER TWO

"Art is not a handicraft. It is a transmission of a feeling which the artist has experienced..." Leo Tolstoy

"In the prison of fears and insecurities, there is no doubt the captive is always guilty. Even when the unlocked gate is open wide, the prisoner is still looking for the key..." Dodinsky

WELCOME ATHENA

OUR ALTAR

Altar cloth: Shades of blue and a second yellow altar cloth underneath.
Image: Statue of this Greek, Grey Eye Goddess, statue or image of warrioress, figures, Roman goddess Minerva is okay to use, Helmeted female figures.
Canvas art or photo of the warrior wise Goddess and or photos of Greece, the Parthenon and owls, helmet, shield, olive branch and her emblems.

Always present on the altar;
A cast iron cauldron, drums, speaking stick, a silver pentacle, athame, elemental representations.....

Air: Owl statuary, feathers and bells, Smudge wands, Incense type sticks, cones, charcoal brisket and fine powdered herbs. Most appropriate to use your Sword/Athame or large feathers to represent your Eastern element.
Fire: candles, glass enclosed candles or pillars in blues and white. You may also use an image candle found in most Occult shops.
Water: Chalice or small glass bowl with Fresh spring Water or Retsina.
Earth: a small dish of soil and or herbs of Lemon Verbena, Caraway, Bay leaves, Anise, Benzoin, or Rosemary.

Other items pertinent to this particular gathering
Figurine of an Owl
Metal Shield and Helmet
Athame or Sword Blade
Books, Grimoires and Journals
writing implements
Feathers bundles
Rubber stamps
Crochet or knitting needles
Bowls of consecrated Water
Rocks and Gemstone like Sodalite
Plate offering of Olives.....
Light blue gauzy fabric
Workshop items
Tarot -"Ace of Swords"

Offering example of Greek Culinary Olives, spanikopitas, doublas, Orzo, lemon cake
Sacred objects from members:
Notes:

Athena

Athena Altar

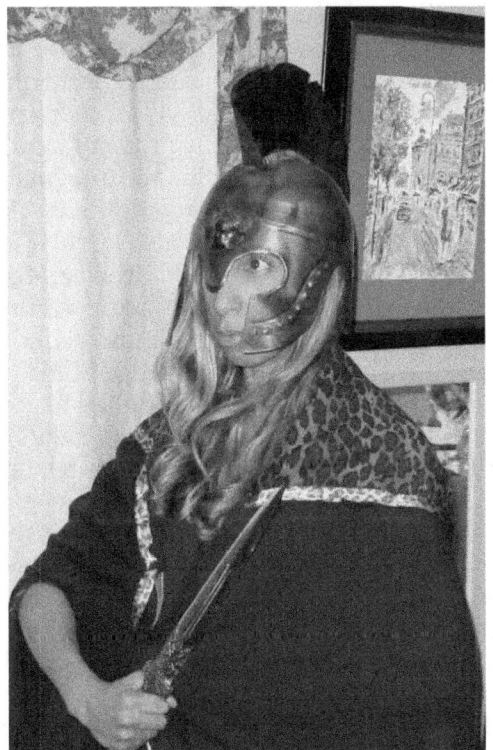
Aspecting the Helmeted One

ATHENA

The Greek, Maiden Goddess of Wisdom, intellect and war-craft was often referred to as Grey-eyed Athena in the writings of her time. She was described as bright eye, wide eye and often depicted with her totem animal, the Owl. The Owl is a perfect representation of her wisdom and this common reference to her piercing eyes. Athena was reminiscent of the Goddesses found in ancient Minoan and Mycenaean Culture, in that these earlier deities had snakes as their sacred symbols and were regarded as protectors of cities and palaces - the way Athena was regarded as the protector of the city of Athens. On the Acropolis, the olive tree was considered Athena herself because of its ability to recover quickly from any damages and thus it was seen as a perfect symbol for this resilient Goddess. Athenians believed their Greek Goddess also took the form of her many sacred totem animals; the snake, birds and the revered owl. The more we learn of this Greek beloved Goddess, the more we see her correlation to ancient deities and how her existence and her worship goes back a lot further than originally believed.

According to Greek mythology, Athena was born parthenogenesis, out of Zeus' head. As the well-known Greek mythology reveals, Zeus had been suffering from a horrible headache for days. He called on Hephaestus, the Smith God, to split his head open hoping to attain some relief from the pain. When Zeus' head was cut open, out sprang Athena. She was born fully armored, with her spear, and shield, a popular depiction of this Goddess that has survived throughout the ages. Important to note that she was born not as a child, but already as a full grown woman, ready for battle.

Athena's Mother was an ocean deity, the Goddess Metis. Not much is known about her mother for most literature connects Athena primarily with her father. We do know that Metis was the first consort of Zeus. We also know that she herself, was the Goddess of wisdom and intelligence because her name translates as such. As can be surmised, Athena's own wisdom and great intelligence can be attributed to being born from Zeus' head but most importantly, her gifts should be attributed to having the lineage of a mother who was known as the Goddess of intelligence and wisdom. It is important to note that her intellect was not of the mystical kind. Athena was not about other-worldly wisdom or spiritual knowledge. She was pragmatic and cherished practical, useful knowledge, cultural and historical knowledge. She was also a lover of all skills and art forms. In the myths of her time, we also learn of her impressive skills in handiworks, dressmaking, embroidery, pottery and needlecrafts among her many skills.

In her mythologies we learn that Zeus, after being warned by oracle seer, feared that an offspring with the Goddess Metis would produce a child more powerful than himself. He tried to remedy this situation by swallowing Metis whole. However, She was already pregnant with their child. Athena thus, continued to grow and live on (now) inside of her father, Zeus. A headache soon began to overtake Zeus and when his head was cut open, out came the strong and wise Athena. Zeus fell instantly in love with his daughter and through-out literature we also see her great devotion to her father.

Athena was the beloved Goddess of the Greek city of Athens. There she is the personification of civic law. The story of how she came to be the patron Goddess for Athens reflects her popularity and early examples of democracy. Athenians had to participate in a democratic vote to decide who would be the patron God/Goddess for the city. The choices were the God of the Sea -Poseidon or Athena, the Goddess of Wisdom and War-craft. When the ballots were counted, they discovered that all the male citizens voted for the male God, Poseidon and all the female votes were given to Athena. Because there were more female citizens at the time in Athens, Athena was the natural winner. As can be expected, the men of Athens did not like this turn of events and displayed much resistance. As a result, they imposed a series of new laws that would need to be implemented, if they were to accept a Female Deity as leader of their beloved City. The most significant new laws that manifested from this election was the replacement of matriarchal lineage by the patriarch. It meant that a child would now carry on the father's last name, instead of the traditional mother's name, according to the writings of this time. Eventually Athena was fully embraced as the patron Godddess of Athen by both, men and women.

This beloved Greek Goddess has an ancestral connection to her people through the first King of Athens -Erichthonius. This myth is very similar to the Sun Goddess, Amaterasu and the first Imperial family of Japan. According to one myth, Athena was seduced by Hephaestus. As a virgin deity, she refused him, but interestingly enough, Hephaestus' semen falls upon her thigh. In total disgust, she takes a rag and wipes it off. She throw the rag upon the Earth and from this action a child is produced. The Earth (Gaia) then gives birth to a child, which Athena then nurtures and raises as her own. In this story we see the preservation of her status as Virgin Goddess, adopted mother and teacher. She names the boy, Erichthonius and teaches him everything, including the worship of Gods. In him she creates one of Athens' first leaders. Erichthonius, fulfills her vision for Athens and succeeds in establishing civic law and governmental structure and thus Athena is directly responsible for Athens' growth and civilization as a prosperous city. There is also a direct connection between the Godddess and her ruling class descendants. Today, a trip to modern day Greece will reveal Athena is still honored and revered in her famous temple - the Parthenon in Athens, as images of her are sold in every neighboring Greek tourist kiosk.

As a Virgin deity she was never married, nor did she ever actually give birth to a child. According to Jean Shinoda Bolen, M.D. in her book "Goddess in Everywoman, A New Psychology of Women," Athena perhaps refused to be linked romantically with a man for fear this would restrict her active participation and involvement with politics, war and her public life image. However, unlike other Virgin Goddesses, she does not appear to have any animosity towards the opposite sex. Quite the contrary, she seems to have great love and adoration for men and clearly uplifts, inspires and supports numerous men throughout Greek mythology. She was born from her father and clearly had a strong bond solely with him. Through-out mythology she is always surrounded by various men and sometimes even disguises herself as one. She appears to be a defender and cheerleader of men in her efforts to empower them for battles. Through-out mythology she does not express any romantic feelings, nor sexual liaisons with men for fear it would demean her or make her seem subordinate to men. She appears to enjoy competition with men and her virginity strictly assures her independence and her status as their equal. She is almost unapproachable sexually by men and her virginity and chastity, maintain her platonic camaraderie relations with men. Reckless emotions left one vulnerable in times of war and thus she was an advocate of moderating ones' emotions... something quite difficult to do in the throes of a passionate love affair.

Athena was most concerned with order, socialization, culture and institutions - Marriages falls under this category. Though she herself never married and while she was not an advocate for romantic, nor sexual unions, she was a promoter and protector of marriages. Marriages are social institutions and promote a valued structure and order in society, according to her specific ideologies. Athena is not a Goddess to be called upon for fertility or child birthing skills, as she never actually gave birth to a child. Learning of her connection to Erichthonius, we can surmise her attributes regarding children. With children, she is more concern with education and their socialization as future citizens and leaders of her beloved city.

As a Goddess of War-craft, she was a prudent Commander and had the gift of strategizing war. She was responsible for the skills and the weapons of war.
Athena was about courage and inspiring that courage in Heroes and their companions on

the battlefield. She encourages willingness, intelligence, control of emotions, boldness and a will to victory. Athena was known for her cunningness and her ability to use words and her intellect in battles and debates. She was more about calm emotions, restraint, clear thinking, and not resorting to brute violence. Mindless killings did not appeal to her. This Goddess was not an advocate of killings just for the sake of the sport. In contrast to the other Gods of war, like Ares, who fights in an emotional frenzy and fury, Athena's approach to war in battle fields was calm, methodical and controlled and she always tempered her emotions. She despised anything crude, wild, barbaric, uncivilized. This Virgin Goddess does not use Aphrodite's physical, sexual charms to win, nor does she use the violent, brute force like Ares. She uses intellect to win all her battles. For Athena, war is more than just a battle of strength, it is part of what's necessary to attain specific goal or higher ideals. She was defender of social order and the prosperity of civilization. Anything that deviated from these ideals inspired her to battle. She represents rational, practicalities, democracy, administration of justice, rhetoric and the art of persuasion. Athena is the personification of a cultured society and she was victorious in wars because of these honorable attributes.

ATHENA GROVE GODDESS GATHERING

PURPOSE: To praise and honor the Goddess **Athena** and invoke her gifts of intelligence, strategist, protector and wisdom. Preparing and Blessing our Grimoire or journals.

CHANT :
"Athena's Chant," "Weave and Spin," "Spiraling into the Center," (see song sheets)

CHECK INS: We share our name and how we are feeling today? Speaking stick is passed around the circle so that wommin can share some of their hopes and workings for the month.

DRUMMING: A musical Drumming CD track will be played to allow participants to ground into this moment. It could be Greek flavored music with the dominant sound of the Bouzouki or inspiring Classical music, like Beethoven's symphonies.

CHECK INS II: Sharing Her Image and words. Around the circle of wommin we will connect with an image of the Goddess Athena, either from the Universal Goddess Tarot deck or any of the other numerous artistic depictions. How does she appear to us? Upon gazing at her image, what message is she whispering to us personally?

GODDESS LECTURE...
Who is Athena?
And what are the Gifts she offers us, as modern day Goddess wommin.

GODDESS WORKSHOPS:
WORKSHOP I: Breast Casting as Athena's Shield and decorating it with our own personal words of power:
With Plaster of Paris strips, attendants will be paired off to help each other create Breast Cast. This can be very messy and time consuming, but well worth the effort if allotted the right time frame. They will need to be set aside to dry overnight before painting and decorating, but this can be a wonderful weekend workshop. Another option is to ask them to create a breast casting at home and bring in the dried model so that we can decorate it together and bless our systers with our collective words of power and sigils.

WORKSHOP II: Aura Shields: how to erect an **Auric shield** of protection.
We will discuss the techniques traditionally utilized to erect a psychic Shield for ourselves. Strong creative imagery, visualizing mirrors, a warrior's armor and steel walls have often provided much psychic protection.

WORKSHOP III: Creating with Polymer **clay, an amulet** of protection, a mini version of an Athena shield. With our hands we will craft this mini shield and then bake to harden the clay.

WORKSHOP IV: Embroidery and Crocheting a **Knot Spell** Creation. The myths of Arachne and Athena reveal that this Goddess was the Queen of this art form. We will craft in her honor a chain and knot spell. *(see the End of Brigit's chapter for the Knot spell incantation)*.

WORKSHOP V: Book exchange and discussion.
Within a circle, attendants bring out and share their personal books and speak about

why their book is special to them and why they feel other wommin would benefit from it. After they speak regading their book, they donate it by placing it in the center basket. Later on there will be a book exchange so that everyone that donated a book will leave with a new one in hand.

WORKSHOP VI: Creating a hand crafted **Warrior Thinking cap** and imbuing it with Athena's energy and blessings. If time permits, with yarn and needle we will sew, knit or crochet a special head cap, imbued it with Athena's blessings, so that our minds may reflect one of her most important attributes- Intellectual Clarity.

WORKSHOP VII: LEADERSHIP, in this workshop we will briefly contemplate on the theme of leadership and communally consider the attributes that make a good leader.We also take a moment to honor a leader from our past.

1. Name 3-5 qualities you personally think a good leader should behold.
    1._____
    2._____
    3._____
    4._____
    5._____
2. Reflect on your lifetime and pinpoint who has been an example of great Leadership and why? *It could be someone in history, someone in your childhood, a teacher, a celebrity or an ancestor...*_____
_____
3.What do you think would be your best attribute as a leader? What would be your worst?
_____
_____
4.What do you think made Goddessses like, Athena and Artemis, good leaders for wommin?_____

WORKSHOP VIII: Meditation to help in Strategizing to achieve our goals
Athena's power in planning, strategizing and how can we apply that in our own lives.
Do we have a plan for our immediate goals? Do we have that Five year plan laid out? How do we break things into smaller steps so that our heart's desire can be met? Whether it is a large goal: like retirement, finding new love, writing a book, improving our physical health, leaving a bad or unhealthy relationship, quitting a bad habit, moving to a brand new state or country, switching careers. Big or small, she requires you to plan it out, step by step, and not fly off into emotional upheaval and chaos, but rather patiently plan things out. Then calmly act when appropriate, when it's strategically the right time. During the meditation questions will be asked and Attendants will have a chance to write or simply reflect on their answers. After the meditation they are invited to write their One Goal or gift, for Athena in their Grimoire and or journal. This journal will be blessed in the prepared Ritual.

Preparing for the ritual....

REFLECTIONS ON ATHENA
Above all do not let yourself get swept away by your emotions, do not let love or overwhelming feelings blur or overshadow your intellect and reason. She teaches us to value our intellect, our mind, and its capacity for great things. She teaches us to crave attention for what our minds can manifest and to crave victory in the process. She wants you to say, I am equal to any man and deserve equal pay and recognition. She teaches us to value what our hands can do and what our minds are capable of planning . She teaches us to value the (sometimes) bloodless battles fought and successfully won, in our minds...

ATHENA GROVE GODDESS GATHERING RITUAL

PURPOSE: To praise and honor the Goddess **Athena** and invoke her gifts of intelligence, strategist, protector and wisdom. Preparing and Blessing our Grimoire or journals.

Anointing/Purification by air with incense and smudge.

Circle cast with traditional sword or Athame and prose.

Quarters called

* Hail Guardians of the Watchtowers of the **East**, Ye Powers of **Air**,
Place of the Sword that cuts down the old and makes room for the new. Winds of inception stirring intellect and applications. Athena's breeze of sight and inspiration, We call on you to bring us your gifts
Guard and Hold our sacred space, Hail and Welcome
(*attendants repeat*) Hail and Welcome!!!

*Hail Guardians of the Watchtowers of the **South**, Ye Powers of **Fire**,
Place of tenacity, drive and burning ambition that sets the soul aflame with desire to succeed, We call on you to lend us your gifts
Guard and Hold our sacred circle, Hail and Welcome
(*attendants repeat*) Hail and Welcome!!!

*Hail Guardians of the Watchtowers of the **West**, Ye powers of **Water**,
Place of emotional attunement, discerment and the skill of the surfer, ridding the wave's ebb and flow. Moon realm awakening our intuition, We call on you to bring us your gifts
Guard and Hold our sacred space, Hail and Welcome
(*attendants repeat*) Hail and Welcome!!!

*Hail Guardians of the Watchtowers of the **North**, Ye powers of **Earth**,
Place of the solid dependable Earth that holds us and supports our dreams and creations. Realm of longevity , heart of our lineage, greatness in all you can produce, We call on you to bring us your gifts
Guard and Hold our sacred circle, Hail and Welcome
(*attendants repeat*) Hail and Welcome.

***********Intent Speaker:** We have spent our day learning about The Bright eye Athena, Let us honor her now in this ritual. Let us sing...

CHANT: Athena's Song

INVOKE ATHENA (*see suggested Athena invocations*)

Aspecting Prose: *Athena appears, speaks of her gifts-*
Behold your Grey eyed Goddess,
Beloved of the city of Athens
My following extends far beyond this great city.
I have been worshipped long
before the Greeks gave me the name Athena.

I rule over the mind, intellect and the skilled
I rule over the art of war and the debaters.
I rule over the hands of the weaver and handcrafter.
I am culture, art, intellect and the calm and cool.
I am civilization at its best
Will you tap into my gifts?

The gift of strategy,
and plotting out the right time to execute goals,
are all my domain.
Have you not read of my gifts through-out history?

*Have you not seen how my gifts
render success to all that invoke me?
Now that you've called me,
Will you follow my counsel as Heroes have
through-out history?*

*How can you not tap into
your immortal Goddess, Athena?
I am here to grant you order and success.*

*****She invite them to gather their journals and their meditation writings. Four rubber stamps representing the elements will be at their disposal to use upon their books. They are invited to stamp their journals while envisioning their journal filled with stories of goals attained and accomplishments of all sorts.

As they complete their)O(workings Athena will come around and give them an
Elemental blessing by saying...
With this incense and by the Powers of Air your work is blessed
With this flame and by the Powers of Fire your work is blessed
With this kiss and by the powers of Water your work is blessed
With this branch and by the Powers of Earth your work is blessed

DRUMMING/CHANT and Sharing around the Circle: what was our gift offering from the meditation.

DEVOKING & THANKING ATHENA *(see suggestion)*
Beloved Athena,
Goddess of Wisdom and the Mind,
When called you blessed us
and through the immortal plane you arrived.
Receive our gratitude,
as we bid thee adieu,
Long may we remember,
the gifts that came from you
With love and light,
Hail and farewell, Athena!

CHANT: *"Power Raising Song by Starhawk"*

Devoking Quarters
Northern realms that supports our earthly body and dreams,
Your energy was felt in this sacred moment.
With gratitude, we Thank you for Witnessing and Guarding our Sacred rites
Hail and Farewell Earth!

Western realm in your watery vessels, we let our emotions flow.
With gratitude, we Thank you for Witnessing and Guarding our Sacred rites
Hail and Farewell Water!

Southern realm with your fires, we tapped into the power of our passion and drive.
With gratitude, we Thank you for Witnessing and Guarding our Sacred rites
Hail and Farewell Fire!

Eastern realm, your sword was felt as illusions were cut and our minds were
re-awakened.With gratitude, we Thank you for Witnessing and Guarding
our Sacred rites
Hail and Farewell Air!

Opening up the Circle: *"The Circle is open, but unbroken may the Peace of the Goddess, be ever in our hearts... Merry meet and merry part and merry meet again...."*

Potluck/ Cakes and ales following

Athena the Goddess of Wisdom and intellect and strategy. Goddess of the mind and the skilled. Handcrafts like needlepoint, crocheting and knitting fell under her domain. In the famous myth with Arachne we learn that she was her first teacher of handcrafts. This was my inspiration in creating this Meditation as you will hear. This meditation requires the listener to be proactive and participate by thinking and answering the Goddess respectively.
Enjoy and blessed be!!!

ATHENA MEDITATION FOR CREATIVE STRATEGIES

Take a deep cleansing breath.... inhale and exhale, leaving the mundane stressors behind you. It does not serve you here. Inhale as you close your eyes to begin this journey. Continue to breathe. Follow my voice and it will lead you, if you allow it. Breathe.....

    Here you find yourself in a marble hall, surrounded by numerous tall sky reaching columns and all around you, are Sculptures of great deities from your ancient ancestors. There is your great grandmother, your favorite artist, your great aunt, the great philosopher and poet, your favorite composer, your favorite writers, there is even someone that looks a lot like you. Is it you?
Are you among one of the great ones? *(Pause)*

    A brilliant light bathes over you and it's so bright you must squint your eyes. You try to look for the source of this light but can't look directly at it. Still you follow this light because it appears that it is where **THEY** are all going. Yes, You are not alone on this journey. There are many others today, taking the same journey, just like you, through the white, brilliant, winding marble corridors, following this luminous light. You are among the many blessed and skilled, eager to present your offering to the Great One.

    The corridor gets narrow almost a bit claustrophobic for you and the crowd now becomes a single line procession climbing up, uphill a staircase. Climb upward on this staircase. You arrive at a platform on the top, where you see many others waiting, holding various unique items preciously in their grasp. Before you, is the sphere of soft light. You gaze upon it long enough to notice it is moving towards you. As it gets closer you begin to make out the edge of a silver sword and then you can finally see -there is also a shield.
The brilliant silver shield, the magick sword, the Divine armor of the Goddess Athena.

    You stand before her, among the others, with your gift. ...What gift do you hold so dearly in your hands now? *(Pause)*
She speaks: **"Why have you traveled here?"**
You reply over their voices *(Pause)*

Athena states, **"Before I can accept your offerings you must authenticate your work by telling me of the journey of this creation and how it arrived to my temple today. Endear me to this gift you bring to me with its history."**

You hear someone from the crowd speak. A woman's voice begins,

"I know how works of the hand are dear to your heart, Goddess, and One cold day I had this idea of creating an exquisite colorful blanket for you, showing off all of my skills and my learned stitchery...".

1. Athena turns to you and asks, **What was YOUR initial thought and inspiration?** *(Pause)*
You reply...*(Pause)*
Then the woman holding her precious hand knitted blanket continues to speak...

"I had to find just the right lamb to attain the right yarn for my creative vision. Only the best for you Goddess. I found a lamb, sheered it and carefully spun the wool for hours until I had attained just the right amount of yarn for your divine gift. I was

proud to have completed this first important step."

2. Athena turns to you and asks, **What did YOU do next after your initial thought and inspiration?** *(Pause)*
You eagerly reply *(Pause)*

The woman continues to speak now of her search for just the right pattern but when she couldn't find one, she had to create a pattern on her own.

She says, *"I searched for days for a pattern worthy of my handspun yarn. I could not find any and thus had to create my own pattern for your divine gift, Goddess."*

3. Athena turns to you and asks, **Does YOUR gift possess your own personal uniqueness**?
You answer *(Pause)*

Excitedly, the woman continues, as she reminisces about her next step.

She says, *"...Beginning that first stitch was scary and I procrastinated for days. I was concerned with this overwhelming undertaking - after all it would be an offering for the Divine. Could I live up to your expectations of me? Could I live up to mine own? Was I good enough to begin this great project? Would my skills truly be reflective in my work? Will it please you Goddess? And would it be my very best work, worthy of a Goddess?"*

4. Athena turns to you and asks, **Did YOU encounter any concerns in creating my gift**?
You reply *(Pause)*

The woman continues as she holds her masterpiece within her hands

"Goddess, every day I worked on your gift, everyday I stitched. Some days, I stitched until my fingers bled, Some days I couldn't bring myself to even look at my creation. Some days, I couldn't stop thinking about its fruition and some days I would work long endless hours."

5. Athena turns to you and asks, **What did you do daily for my gift? How did you tend and nurture this creation daily?**
You answer *(Pause)*

The woman's voice softens as she continues and now sounded a bit melancholy as she tells of what happened next....
"I made a mistake in my stitch calculations, frustrated I almost tossed the entire thing in the trash. But I couldn't let you down, I couldn't let myself down too. To continue I had to do some adjustment -Isn't that how life goes. Just when we feel we are doing okay we find ourselves having to re-adjust to something or slightly change our original plans."

6. Athena turns to you and wonders, **Did YOU encounter any regrets as you made this for me? What adjustments did you have to make to your initial hopes?** *(Pause)* reflect back on this.... *(Pause)*

The woman continued on, proudly telling the Goddess of her final days in the process of her creation and you hear her say,

"...Goddess, In the end, the gift I started to make for you became better than I originally had planned. Through patience, compassion and willingness to try something new when I encountered road blocks, I was finished with my creation and eager to present it as an offering but then... then fear crept its head once more.... What will she think of my work? (Pause) Have I put my best effort on this project?, Is it a true reflection of my abilities? Will she be proud of me? Will I be proud of myself?"

7. Athena turns to you and asks, **What were YOUR final days like with this creation? What did YOU experience upon its completion?** *(Pause)*
Ponder her words and thoughtfully reply *(Pause)*

Thrilled, The woman finally ends by handing over her gift to the Goddess and saying...

"My Queen, My Goddess, Beloved Athena, I have poured of myself into this gift, for you. I am happy with the sweat and effort I put into it. Please embrace it as a reflection of me and the gratitude I have for you." (pause)

8. Athena turns to you and says, **What do YOU have to present to me? What is your offering?** (Pause)
Bravely You come forward, present your gift, and speak ... *(Pause)*

...Athena sighs in delight as she examines your work.
She is pleased.
"What an exquisite fine work- worthy of the Divine. Worthy of me, you and everyone... I accept your gift and applaud its creation, in addition, I applaud its journey, the strategy for its fruition, as I am Queen of the strategist. You have done well, Go return to your realm and continue on your journey. When you awake, remember our visit and continue your fine work."

The light from her sword and shield begins to diminish and slowly its brightness wanes... Your eyes are now able to adjust and open wider and you notice the crowd of people scattered. The others have started to move about and go on their own respective journeys. From where you stand notice the white marble column and the staircase that started this journey for you. Approach it and with both hands free, hold the cold marble staircase railing and begin your descent. Climb down now, one step at a time, down. Follow my voice as I slowly number the ten steps you'll take to descend slowly and return to your body. 10, 9, Breathe 8, 7, and follow my voice, 6, follow as it leads you back to this room, 5, 4, breathe in and exhale audibly, 3, Follow my voice now as it lead you back to this time and place...2, and 1.

When you feel you are ready, open your eyes. Stretch your body a little and join us back in this space, join us in this room. If you need to ground more press your hands to the floor. Welcome!

INVOKING ATHENA

Hail to you Athena
illustrious daughter of Zeus
Goddess of Wisdom and Civility
Doning your (heavenly) warrior armed-suit

Immortal daughter of the Wise One
Of Divine Metis blood and womb born
A warrior of your caliber,
Through prudence, is never torn.

Beloved Grey-eyed Goddess
of the City of Athens,
We call you to transcend
all time and space
And let thyself, journey here,
That we may lay eyes upon your face.

In the magick that we weave
Empower us to see,
That your essence still lives on,
As it will for infinity.

Come to our circle
As we honor you today,
Glaukopis, Tritogeneia,
Maiden Athena, come our way

Hail to you beloved Athena!

Aspecting Athena Prose
Athena appears, speaks of her gifts
Behold your Grey eyed Goddess,
Beloved of the city of Athens
My following extends far beyond this great city.
I have been worshipped long
before the Greeks gave me the name Athena.

I rule over the mind, intellect and the skilled
I rule over the art of war and the debaters.
I rule over the hands of the weaver and handcrafter.
I am culture, art, intellect and the calm and cool.
I am civilization at its best
Will you tap into my gifts?

The gift of strategy,
and plotting out the right time to execute goals,
are all my domain.
Have you not read of my gifts through-out history?
Have you not seen how my gifts
render success to all that invoke me?
Now that you've called me,
will you follow my counsel
as Heroes have through-out history?

How can you not tap into
your immortal Goddess, Athena?
I am here to grant you order and success.

DEVOKING ATHENA
Beloved Athena,
Goddess of Wisdom and the Mind,
When called you blessed us
and through the immortal plane you arrived.
Receive our gratitude,
as we bid thee adieu,
Long may we remember,
the gifts that came from you
With love and light,
Hail and farewell, Athena

Homeric Hymn #28 to Athena

To Athena,
I begin to sing of Pallas Athena,
The glorious Goddess bright-eyed,
Inventive, unbending of heart,
Pure Virgn, saviour of cities,
Courageous, Tritogeneia.
Wise Zeus himself bare her from his awful head,
Arrayed in warlike arms of flashing gold,
And awe, seized all the Gods as they gazed,
But Athena sprang quickly from the immortal head
and stood before Zeus who holds the aegis,
Shaking a sharp spear;

Great Olympus began to reel horribly
At the might of the bright-eyes Goddess,
and the earth round about cried fearfully,
and the sea was moved and tossed with dark waves,
while foam burst forth suddenly;

The bright son of Hyperion,
Stopped his swift-footed horses a long while
until the maiden Pallas Athena
had stripped the heavenly armour,
from her immortal shoulders.
And wise Zeus was glad.

And so hail to you, daughter of Zeus, who holds the aegis!
Now I will remember you and another song as well..

Source- publc domain
http;//ancienthistory.about.com/ad/athenaminervamyth/a/072309HomericHymnto Athena.htm
http;//www.goddess-athena.org/encyclopedia/rituals/hymns/homer28.htm

Do this spell on a night of the Waxing moon and preferably on a Sunday (ruled by the benevolent Sun) or Wednesday (ruled by communicator, studious Mercury) or Tuesday (ruled by aggressive, feisty Mars). Gather artistic or sculptural images of these three Goddesses as well as their appropriate symbols. Prepare three candles, by carving and anointing with a "blessing oil", (see appendix for suggestions). Use a blue candle for Athena, Green candle for Artemis and a red candle for Brid. Place symbols connected with your goals and present them before the Goddesses. Recite incantation as you light these candles and call upon their divine energy.

FEMININE DIVINE
*Spell to invoke the Goddess in me
Athena, Artemis and Crafty Brid
Strong sense of purpose
The mind of a Queen
Clear with my goal
And the will to succeed

Athletic like Artemis
Energetic and free
Her youth and her beauty
I channel within me

Gifted creative
with money making skills
Help me to transform them
into U.S. dollar bills

Clearing the cobwebs
Of my mind
to reveal the path
that's truly mine

To you I give honor
Artemis, Athena and St. Brid
Holy Goddess of ol'
Lend your blessings to me.

On a Mercurial day, when the moon is waxing and preferably the first hour of sunrise, call upon these Goddesses. Prepare your candles (a white skull candle is highly suggested) by cleansing and anointing it with "student oil", "mercurial oil" or "get it done oil" (see appendix). Light your preferred incense stick and fumigate the altar area. Include books and any other artistic endeavor you seek their assistance with. Raise energy with drums, singing and or humming and when you are ready recite this incantation.

INTELLECTUAL CALL

****Athena and Oya
I call to bless my Brain,
Help me gain knowledge
Acquired and retained.

Help me read quicker
And absorb all I read,
Mnemosyne, memory muse
join to help me.

Sharpen the skills
And tools I need,
To write successful books,
that many will read.

Athena, Aradia,
and Oya too,
I ask that you help me
represent you

With intelligence, wisdom,
and leadership skills
I am your priestess, Goddess,
Let me do thy will.

I Read, Study,
Research, Write
Prosper as an author
and blessed with your light,

To represent my wish
This skull, I bless
Intelligence, Time,
and Writing success

This spell bound round
On mercury's night
Come Victorious one,
Help me take flight.

These things or better
An it harm none
By the power of three
it is done, done, done...... So mote it be!!!

ATHENA GROVE GODDESS GATHERING CHANTS

POWER RAISING
We are the Powers in Everyone,
We are the Dance of the moon
and the Sun.
We are the Hope that never dies,
We are the turning of the tides.
By Starhawk

ATHENA CHANT
Virgin Goddess
Sword and Shield
Lend to us the gift to yield
Come when called into our lives
Bringing wisdom
Wise, bright Eyes.

Come Athena
Come Athena
Wise one come to me, *By B.M.M.*

ELEMENTAL CHANT
Air I am
Fire I am,
Water, Earth
and Spirit I am
        By unknown

SPIRAL CHANT
Onward we go round the spiral
Touching darkness
Touching light
Twice each year we rest in balance
Make choices on this night
Make choices on this night
        By Marie Summerwood

LET IT FLOW
Let it in, Let it flow
round and round we go
Weaving the web of women
Let it in, let it flow
round and round we go
Weaving the web of life
        By Marie Summerwood

WEAVE AND SPIN
Weave and Spin,
Weave and Spin,
This is how our work begins.
Mend and Heal,
Mend and Heal,
Take the Dream and make it Real.

FIRE BIRD SONG
I align my desire
with the spirit Divine,
Dive into the coil
of the serpents mind,
I rise from the depths
My roots to my wings
I open up my head and Fire Bird Sings

WE ARE A CIRCLE
We are a Circle within a Circle
with no beginning, and never ending...
        By Rick Hamouris

CHAPTER THREE

"Nobody trips over mountains. It is the small pebbles that causes you to stumble. Pass all the pebbles in your path and you will find you have crossed the mountains..."
Unknown author

"Every piece of the Universe, even the tiniest little snow crystal, matters somehow. I have a place in the pattern and so do you..." T. A. Barron

WELCOME OUR OWN LIVING DEITY

Maiden, Mother and Crone

Goddess Dedication Altar

GODDESS WORKSHOPS:
DEDICATIONS and CREATING OUR OWN DEITIES

Our Next Gathering is the last Grove gathering of the calendar year, although it can also be scheduled as the very first of the year. This Gathering will be a little different, as each of us will introduce & share a Goddess or spiritual practice that is of great significance personally.

It will be a relaxed day, where each of us can learn from one another, in a casual, comfortable atmosphere, while simultaneously honoring our chosen Deity. If you have been dedicated to a particular deity/pantheon we'd love for you to join us this day. If there is a Goddess that calls on you today and you feel curious or compelled to devote yourself in the new year, we'd like to hear from you. If you are new to Goddess Spirituality and simply don't know, but want to learn, you are still very much welcomed to come join us and share in the festive energy of the day.

This will be a Goddess Potluck Gathering, as we will be honoring numerous Goddesses that we personally feel devoted to and the circle will come together through collaborations. There will be numerous workshop offerings and it promises to be a fascinating, fun filled day. Please Join us...

GETTING TO KNOW OUR PERSONAL LIVING GODDESS

The name of your Goddess:_____
Does she have a preferred nick name:_____
Have you opted to call yourself by her name?_____
Where is she from? Her Origins?_____
When did you meet this Deity?_____
What was going on in your life to awaken this archetype?_____
_____
How did she come to you?_____
Have you ever aspected her?_____
Could you describe what she feels like embodied?_____
_____
Have you ever felt her presence deeply in trance work? _____
_____
Have you had any significant dreams of her?_____
_____
What triggers a remembrance of her? What aligns or reminds you of her? _____
_____
What gifts do you think she has bestowed on you? _____
How do you choose to Honor and worship her today?_____
_____
What does she like? Dislike?_____
_____
Who does she get along with? Any lovers, siblings, parentage info?_____
_____
How do you hope she will manifest, move and shift your life?_____
_____
_____

GROVE OF THE FEMININE DIVINE
GODDESS GATHERING

Theme: Our Personal Deities. A Goddess Potluck Gathering

Check Ins: We gather around for **Check ins** and catching up with one another... talk about what we are looking forward to... use time to get to know each other, as we chit chat (around the kitchen counter or any other casual meeting place)creating sisterly bonds.

Altar: We take a small moment to add our personal items to the **Communal Altar** and spend time there quietly, as needed. Gentle music will play in background.

Chanting: We share songs that our souls crave to be sung amidst the circle and learn newly created chants. *(see Song text sheet)*

Drumming CD Music: Tambourine, bell ringing will initially be used to vibrate and lift the energy of the room. Afterwards, to ground us in the moment, a strong earthly drumming CD track will be prepared and played for participants.

GODDESS WORKSHOP

WORKSHOP I: Oracular Offering. We will carve out a moment in this workshop to allow wommin a chance to practice their oracular skills on one another. There will be numerous tools offered on the altar, various Tarot deck from traditional to avant garde, Goddess oracle cards, runes, astrology books and charts, Gypsy fortunetelling cards, Totem animal oracular cards and other tools. Wommin are encouraged to pair off and experiment tapping into their intuition as they read for one another. It is the ending of the calendar year and many are curious about what the new year will bring, so this is a fun, perfect workshop for this season.

WORKSHOP II: A discussion on **Energy** an open forum rapport on ideas of what happens to our energy when our physical form is no more. Ideas of after death and our own personal experiences with energy sensitivities and the experience of the Empath. The many ways "to know" and how to develop our gifts. Also touching upon the subject of energy in relation to our own personal Deities that we are dedicated to. How do we sense and utilize Goddess energy?

WORKSHOP III: Crafting and Discussion about Aboriginal Masks, the **Sacred use of Mask** and their use in indigenous cultures. How they can be a vital tool of Magick for aspecting or simply inviting the energy of our chosen Deity.

WORKSHOP IV: Mask Creation: Pre-made Plaster Masks are handed out and attendants are encouraged to decorate and paint them, while adding their own energy into them, thinking of their chosen Deity. Wommin will decorate this mask, enchant it, imbue it with the energy of the Goddess they are seeking to connect with and then wear it as a way to invoke the Goddess and touch her sacred energy even deeper still. The Masks can be decorated with words, magazine clippings, special glued objects, photos, paint colors, feathers etc... anything that will stir inspiration and connection to the Divine. On the altar it can also function as simply a representation of the Goddess. Afterwards, with music playing, we will create a masquerade party where we will show them off, recite an inspired invocation, singing of our chosen deity.

WORKSHOP V: Discussion around the room, as we each share our personal deity, our experiences and the hopes for the new year. We address who and what we dedicate ourselves to in this new calendar year and also discuss **name changes** within the craft as a form of aligning ourselves with the divine.

WORKSHOP VI: Yule Time Recycle, Gift exchange. If we didn't have a chance to do it at our last gathering, this is a perfect time to do so. After our discussion about energy it would seem appropriate to talk about the energy inherent in our inanimate objects and the Yule gifts we intend for our Systers, during this workshop. Participants can also experiment intuiting the energy they already sense from their systers' gift.

CREATING OUR OWN LIVING GODDESSES

Probably one of the earliest introductions to the idea of creating our own modern day Goddesses for me, came from a short article by Cerridwen Iris Shea in "Llewellyn 2005 Magical Almanac," titled, "Sports Goddesses" *(266-268pgs)*. She quite playfully encouraged readers to give the Goddess of ten thousand names, a new, more personal name, if necessary, to help us achieve those fitness goals we so often create for ourselves at the start of the new years. It peaked my interest then and I thought it was quite provacative but I did not delve into the practice until much later.

Then, I remembered, a few years ago, being introduced to the Wiccan author, Barbara Ardinger. She has written a number of books on Goddess Spirituality and has been an advocate for the creation of new found, modern day Goddesses. Her writings, in particular those found in her regular column to GlobalGoddess (an online Goddess Ezine), inspired me the most to investigate further this new concept.

Quite amusingly for me, in one of her online articles for Global Goddesss *(July/2008)*, she gave the example of a personal Goddess who would protect your Desktop and computer software, for in this day and age, in large contrast to ancient times when there was no need for such a thing,who doesn't need a little extra Divine protection for their beloved computers. It appears in our modern times, our entire livelihood is dependent on the wellbeing of these technologically advanced gadgets. Strangely, much like in ancient agrarian times, the wellbeing of a large field of crops was critical to the family and its neighboring community. We too place a great deal of importance on our computer's maintaining their fertileness and efficient wellbeing and as a whole are exasperatingly dependent on them to assure our own prosperity. Why wouldn't we create present day deities and special rituals to implore, honor and appease those who we've granted rule over this important realm for us in the 21st Century?

The more I contemplated on Ardinger's expanded idea of our capacity to manifest, in this present day and age, our own modern living Goddesses, the more I see its cathartic powers and its great potential for Goddess wommin in need of a shift in their lives. Although she credits Morgan Grey and Julia Penelope for first introducing this concept in their 1980's book, "Found Goddesses: Asphalta to Viscera", Barbara Ardinger has contributed a great deal to the expansion of this idea. In 2003, she wrote, "Finding New Goddesses: Reclaiming playfulness in our Spiritual Lives, published by E.C.W. Press and this book along with her numerous online articles have continued to promote the practice of birthing new found modern day deities.

Reading Ardinger's regular column for Global Goddess.org, I remember being most amused when she resurrected the modern day Goddess who rules over the Gym and our physical fitness, Buffy*(April 2009)*. How many of us can find a blessing in revering a contemporary Goddess of Fitness who understands our modern day stressors, our 21st century dilemma and fitness goals and the obstacles today that keep us from reaching them? And what an amazing concept to see this Fitness Goddess for the modern day womyn, who when called upon, assures us the energy to get fit and commit to those annual New Year resolutions and can be our source to fight the temptations of our times. I personally can connect with this one. I see her ridding the subway with me at the excruciatingly painful wee hours of the morning to get to the gym, bypassing all those strategically placed food carts and street vendors. At the office, I feel her presence helping me avoid those evil candy machines by forcing me to take a different route to the ladies lavatory. She would also be helping me just say no to the extra-large popcorn with dripping butter at the local Cineplex. Yes, I can feel this new Goddess, resembling a modern day amazon like Gabriel Reese or a Serena Williams, extending her Divine hands to my cause, reminding me of my vows to healthier living. And... maybe some might feel satisfied calling upon the immortal Ones of our past. Invoking the ancient Goddess Nike or the Maiden, Huntress Artemis or any of the other numerous wonderful deities of ancient times, might not wield the same connections or the same results for you personally, as someone who manifested in your 21st Century, who might actually share in your lifestyle, vernacular, belief system and have modern day lore and myths that you can intimately relate to.

A Goddess born of your world, as oppose to ancient Egypt, Greece, Rome, Ireland *etc.*, might appear more sensitive to your plight and daily struggles. One can only surmise this manifested modern day Deity might comprehend you more succinctly and as a result, you might therefore connect better with this energy, rather than the distant one offered to you in the Gods of ancient times. Don't get me wrong, I am a devotee of ancient Deities and see great value in the immortal Sacred Divine Feminine as she was then and as she is still today. I tend to have a strange quirk of being able to translate ancient Deities and their immeasurable attributes into our present modern times but I can see and value, Ardinger's idea and suggestion. Especially where there might be Contemporary issues, foreign to the Gods of our past, that can benefit from a newly born Deity manifested from our 21st Century visions and unique needs.

Where there is a great area in our lives or an intimately personal area of great importance that it would appear, it asks to be worshipped; we should name it, personify and claim it as our Gods. Where there is an obvious need for a power to be venerated and credited for something, we should do so and if this power/Deity does not already exist, we should feel in our right to create it. Create it from our present day needs; create it from our brilliant imaginations, create it, as so many of our indigenous brethren and sisters so often **first** did.

The torrential rainstorms heard our first thirst and parched lands… magickally it seemed, it heard our plea for water in our rain dances, and sacred rituals, She poured forth her thirst-quenching waters. This great wonderment, in the beginning, had no name, nor human comprehension, thus with great reverence we called her Mother, we called her Ix Chel, we called her Oya, we called her Goddess and so many other names of reverence. So important was the rain then that we made it one of our Gods and thus in modern times, we too should be encouraged and find comfort in being able to do the same and tap into this powerfully cathartic, ancient spiritual practice.

Blessed be to the immortal growth
of cooperative Divine beings in our Universe and
Blessed be to your living breathing
Modern day Goddesses….Long May She Live…..)O(

NAME CHANGES WITHIN THE CRAFT

I think there are many valid points why someone would elect a "magickal" name. Yes, in previous times it was a matter of life and death and indeed crucial to protect your witch identity. Taking on another name, lessen the chances of you getting burnt at the stake....and while there are no witches being burned and persecuted in the town square today, there is still something called discrimination and it is a VERY REAL threat.

In our modern day society, we are sadly, still plagued, just as we were hundreds of years ago, by overzealous religious fanatics who will kill in the name of their god and religion. Unfortunately, it is still something one needs to be mindful about and naiveté needs to be tossed out the window for our own safety. The sad fact is, there are still plenty of demented, whackoes, die hard crusaders of all religious persuasions out there (and they might just be living right next door to you) who upon hearing you are a witch will take it upon themselves to "rectify" the situation...and basically make your life, and the life of those you love, painfully challenging.

Now, I am NOT an advocate for "closet living" of any kind. I myself never leave the house without, openly, wearing around my neck, my sacred pentacle necklace. My car and my body are both adorned with statements and declaration of love for my faith and the Goddess.....but I am also very sympathetic to the other side of the coin....and those who are, rightfully so, super cautious and still in hiding.

As a side note, I will also say that in ancient times, and even in some modern pagan sects today, there was, and is, a belief that a malevolent witch, "brujo", or wizard could hex you a lot easier if they knew your actual birth-name. Again this supports the ideology that indeed names are saturated with great power and in the wrong hands, can be harmful, not just on a physically level but also on a psychic and spiritual.

On a more positive note, I think, name changes, to mark a birth or a monumental internal change, has always been a common practice through-out history. Numerous religions encourage the addition of a new name upon declaring your new faith, for example in a baptismal and the Catholic sacrament of Confirmation. When you get married, and clearly your solo identity has been slightly altered, you or your mate take on the last name of the one you are now aligning yourself with. You are given a precious birth name by your parents, but as you grow up, your family and friends might endear you with a new nickname that somehow suits you better in their eyes.... In the religion of Islam, you take on the last name of the revered prophet Mohammed, to signify entering that new family and, I hear, the same practice takes place in various gang initiations. I can go on with more examples, but I'll stop there.

Unquestionably, Names carry power and it is not surprising that upon finding our home in the Goddess we would want to honor that pivotal moment and mark that sacred stage in our life with a Special Wiccan name. Indeed, our Birth-name(s) carries their own vibrations and power, as it links us to the past, our parentage and our ancestry. Personally, I have struggled with the complete abandonment of my birth name...and for a while even refused to surrender my maiden name upon marriage- much to my husbands dismay, due to this nostalgic connection to my deceased Father and Mother. Still, after much contemplation, I moved passed this, mainly because I began to realize the monumental, psychological and spiritual effects a name can impart. I see the great validity in taking on a magickal name for safety reason yes...but mostly, for exalting the Goddess, our rebirth, and honoring our own chosen sacred path.

A new name helps align us to our new identity and inaugurates our unique spiritual journey and for this reason alone, I am in full support of those who feel the calling to change their name and adopt a Craft name.

*Blessings on your New name search....)O(

NEW NAME BLESSING

A name by Birth,
I shunned from me,
A name whose sound
Bled dissonance in its imagery...

Of Two who barely
Loved themselves,
Yet birthed a name
That offered no help.

A name, I scarcely ever upheld,
So heavy it weighted on my lapel,
So much it demanded,
Yet stole from me,
The chance to unearth
And cultivate the real Me.

It arrived to people,
Places and things,
Arriving for false introductions
As if by ethereal wings,

Introducing itself
Long before my arrival,
To mock, cage, contradict,
As thou I was its opposing rival.

As thou authentic me,
Threatened its pulse,
Veins, blood, threads
Connecting to Ghost.

A past, a name, I cannot bare,
Release you now with gentle care...
I name myself now;_____ _____

Goddess lend your Blessings,
To the name, you and I, now choose.
May this name feel like a Blessing,
And may my life be positively infused.

With Love and Magick,
Wellbeing and Peace,
With Success and Knowledge
And Creativity.

Bless this name and the path I now pursue,
With this new name,
I am blessed and filled with gratitude.

Journal- Grove of the Feminine Divine Gathering- Sharing our own Personal Deities, working with energy, honoring the ancient use & powers of Masks,

We initially gathered around the kitchen counter and surprisingly, here we did our customary **check ins**, quite casually catching up with one another. We talked about what we were looking forward to in the new year and simultaneously, proceeded to get to know each other better through our lively chit chat. It was all very cozy, sisterly and informal. Eventually, we transition into the Temple room with our personal altar items and here the womyn had a chance to sit quietly before the altar and begin to gently ground into the sacredness of our work.

Then a moment later from the CD stereo player came rhythmic drumming music to ground us into the moment and elevate the energy of the room. I must say that the Chant workshop that followed was painful for me, as I couldn't quite get this small group of wommin to commit their beautiful voices to music making - a harsh challenge I did not anticipate. They just didn't want to chant and I didn't want my frustration to ruin our day. So we moved onward and forward to our Goddess discussion.

One of the most memorable part of this Grove Goddess Gathering for me, was the lively open discussion we engaged in. There were **three main parts** to it, but it all appeared to flow imperceptibly and it was a wonderful experience to listen, share and learn from one another in this seamless way. The discussion around the room started with each of us sharing our own personal deity and what memorable experiences working with them has manifested. We shared our hopes for the new year and what or who we dedicate ourselves to in the upcoming new year. We also talked about **Energy,** Divine and human energy and ideas of what happens to our energy when our physical form is no more. We discussed different ways of working with energy, how to manifest, sense and manipulate it. For me, I shared my personal proof that energy is real- like room sensitivity and other way of knowing and discussed the experience of an empath.

As one of our craft project would involve **mask creations**, we got into a very lively discussion on the Cultural practice and traditions of Masks in occult magick and ritual ceremonies. While one woman in the group had some unusual phobias about masks, we eased her fears and talked about the Sacred use of Mask and their use in indigenous cultures. Discussing how they can be a vital tool of Magick for aspecting or simply inviting the energy of that Deity, masks were introduced as a vital part for any sabbat ceremony. I distributed Xerox copies from an article, which would give the wommin further information when they return home about the sacred use of Masks in rituals and hopefully give them inspiration to work with their own newly formed masks.

As watery music played now in the background, we crouched down to the nearby coffee table and began to craft. One beloved grove syster came prepared to share with us the art of making, inexpensive, **scrying mirrors** for our self. This was a very nice treat, as scrying mirrors can be quite expensive. When we were done, we proceeded with the final craft of the day- Sacred Mask making. I brought out a few blank plaster mask pieces and together we were encouraged to decorate and paint them, imbuing them with energy, while thinking of our chosen Deity. It was really nice and I loved the beautiful masks that were created that day.

Our day ended with a short, simple potluck and a gift exchange, since we were in the month of Yule. This particular gathering reflected a very casual atmosphere and no ritual nor sabbat was commemorated. As a priestess, the challenge for me was not to over plan this one and I purposely left room for the various energies to flow, to guide and facilitate our day. I must admit it required a lot of trust on my part to relax and let things unfold as they did but the result was a beautiful memorable day among my systers.

GROVE GODDESS GATHERING CHANTS

HEALING SONG
How could anyone ever tell you,
you were anything less than beautiful?
How could anyone ever tell you,
You were less than whole?
How could anyone fail to notice,
That your loving is a miracle?
How deeply you're
connected to my soul.... *By Libby Roderick*

POWER RAISING
We are the Powers in Everyone,
We are the Dance of the moon
and the Sun.
We are the Hope that never dies,
We are the turning of the tides.
By Starhawk

SHE GATHERS HER DAUGHTERS
by Ruth Rhiannon Barrett
She gathers her daughters by Moon and by Sun
She gathers her daughters it has begun

She gathers her daughters to turn the wheel
She gathers her daughters to learn and heal

She gathers her daughters by Night and by Day
She gathers her daughters to lead the way

(Counter Melody, higher octave and melodious)
By Moon and Sun
We have begun
To turn the wheel
to learn and Heal (*continuous repetition*)

SHE'S BEEN WAITING
She's been waiting, waiting
She's been waiting so long,
She's been waiting for her children
to remember to return.

Blessed be and Blessed are
The lovers and the Lady.
Blessed be and Blessed are
Maiden, Mother, Crone,

Blessed be and Blessed are
The ones who dance together,
Blessed be and Blessed are
The ones who dance alone... b*y Paula Walowitz.*

POWERFUL SONG
Powerful Song of radiant light,
Weave us the web that Spins the night
Web of Stars, that holds the dark,
Weave us the Earth that feeds the Spark...

DESCANT: Strand by Strand, Hand over Hand.
Thread by Thread, We Weave over Web.
by Pandora, Starhawk, Rose May Dance.

ANCIENT GODDESS
Smiling Virgin, Shinning Crescent,
Waxing Fullness, Luminescent
Maiden, Mother and Crone,
Maiden, Mother and Crone

Ancient Goddess, Daughter Moonlight,
Ancient Goddess, Mother of Stone
Ancient Goddess, Keeper of Midnight,
Maiden, Mother and Crone.
By *Abbi Spinner McBride*

WINGS
Wings wandering in the deep of night
A thousand Birds take flight
And our dreams are born
On the wings of Change,
We are weaving the World tonight .
By Suzanne Sterling and Starhawk;s Reclaiming

January

The Full moon this month is known as the Old Moon, it is also sometimes called Wolf Moon by the Native Americans who traditionally gave the thirteen full moons in a year, various reflective names. Wolves would often be heard howling in the distance at this time of the year and thus, those who were attuned to the earth, and its cycles, gave the full moon, of this month, its appropriate title. Also interesting to note, the Saxon name for January is *"Wulf-monath"* which translates as wolf month.

The weather was extremely cold in some parts of the world and thus sometimes January's full moon was also called, the Cold Moon by various tribes. This month is ruled by the astrological sign of, Capricorn. Known as the goat, it is ruled by authoritative, prudent, restrictive, Saturn (Dec 20th-Jan 20th) and its energy can be felt subtly during this month.

The first month of the Julian and Gregorian calendar, January, probably derives its name from the ancient Roman Goddess, Jana or her husband, the two faced God-Janus. Together, they were believed to rule doorways and gateways, which were considered a very sacred realm. January, being the first month in our modern day calendar year, is a good example of those precious, yet mysterious gateways. In January, we stand at the threshold of a new calendar year, while bidding adieu to the old. Most might see this as a time of new beginnings, renewed hope and thus a time to make vows and new year's resolutions. It is not surprising then, to hear of gym memberships escalating to record breaking heights at this time of the year.

With the temperatures, in some parts of the world, still very frigid outdoors, we spend most of our time indoors and thus another common theme for January is the hearth, home and handmade crafts. Before modern technology, the cold Winter forced many to slow down and retreat into their abode and the only form of entertainment was to be created within close families. The home and the creations of handmade crafts, games, storytelling and the Bardic arts, naturally became almost crucial to ones general happiness and wellbeing during the dark Wintry season.

This month, we might also find ourselves recovering from all the frenetic holiday activities of the previous month by slowing down and hibernating. It can also be a time of the unexpected slumps, and let downs, after all those highly charged festivities from the previous month. The highs of excessive shopping, partying and family gatherings are over now and we are left with a return to the mundane. It is not surprising that this month, may also find us combing through our finances, as we try to settle debts incurred from the holidays and we endeavor to start the year off with a clean slate.

Although it may feel like, after January first, there is a halt to celebrations, it can also be a time of much needed respite and a perfect time to gather up our energy for the next stage in life.

Often, works of divination at this time are appropriate to foretell what the new calendar year will bring. With the start of a new year it appears that brainstorming, fantasizing and goal commitments are the common theme for all. It is the perfect time to take advantage of the powers found in starting anew, purging and rebuilding, making goals and following them through. It is never too late to make a better choices in life and January gives us an opportunity to exercise this philosophy. It is precisely why this month, we will align ourselves with the energy of Skadi, the Norse Goddess of Winter, who reminds us to have courage and conviction and to take care of our physical bodies. We will also call upon Nike, the Goddess of Victory, as we envision our new goals being pursued and achieved with great success.

CHAPTER FOUR

"You don't start with courage and then face fears, you become courageous BECAUSE you faced your fears...." Laura Davis

"One major thing that stands in between you and the fulfillment of your dream is the willingness to start, the courage to move ahead and the faith to finish...." Stanley Anukege

WELCOME SKADI

OUR ALTAR

Altar cloth : Although black is her color, I personally love to use an all white altar cloth for Skadi, to depict that landscape of winter.

Image: Statue of the Norse Viking Warrior giantess
Canvas art or photo of the Viking Goddess, images of a Wintry Snow capped mountain landscape, Photos or images of Wolves, Eagles, Bow and arrow and Rune Symbols everywhere.

Always present on the altar;
A cast iron cauldron, speaking stick, drums, bell chimes, notes, a silver pentacle, athame, elemental representations.....

Air: Swords, Bird or Air Dragon statuaries, Incense type sticks, cones, charcoal brisket and fine powdered herbs in Frankincense, myrrh, orange peels.
Fire: candles; woman shaped candles, glass enclosed candles in white or whatever color feels right. Animal shaped candles would also work nicely.
Water: Crystal Chalice with Vodka or Spring Water or small glass bowl filled with ice cubesand or snow.
Earth: An arrangement of tree branches in a crystal vase. White Roses would also be appropriate, as well as a small dish of soil or herbs.

Other items pertinent to this particular gathering
Metal Sword blade
Runes scattered throughout altar
A small dish of snow or ice cubes
Figurines of wolves, eagles or other animals of the forest (toy figurines okay)
Beaded sparkling crystals,
Black gemstones like; Tourmaline, jet, obsidian
Workshop items: wood plaque, glue, clippings, leather round pieces. Fur, sewing needle,
Ziplock bags of Ice for ritual.
Anointing oil
Tarot- "The Ace of Sword" or "the Justice Card"
Writing paper, magazine clippings, glue and pen
Bell or chimes

Offering
Barley beer, mead, Black Russian rye bread or Pumpernickel bread, Milk or Vodka or spring water, some type of meat, horns.
Sacred objects from members:
Notes:

Skadi

Skadi Altar

Collage SpellCrafting

SKADI pronounced [SKAH-DEE]

Skadi is the Norse Goddess of Winter, mountains and wilderness. She is a Viking Goddess known by several other names like; Snowshoe Goddess, Ski Goddess, Skade, Skadhi, Skathi and Shinning Bride of the Gods. Interesting to note that her name bares a similar resemblance to the Hindu Goddess of Feminine energy, Shakti. Skadi is a Giantess and the beloved daughter of the Giant Thiassi/Thjazi and she became a Goddess through her union and marriage with the Gods of Aesir. Described as a Jotunn and a fair maiden in the Heimskringla book, Ynglinga saga. It is also widely believed that the country of Scandinavia received its name from this beloved Goddess and apparently her name, or derivations of her name, can be found throughout Scandinavia. She was also known as Ondurgodth, which means, "Ski God," and Ondurtis, which means "Ski Lady," both words come from the old Norse language.

There are numerous conflicting stories about Skadi's etymology, but her name in old High German is linked with the word, "Scato", which mean "*Shadow*". This may reflect an older, initial depiction of the Goddess as a bringer of death or a deity of the underworld. Along with the word shadow, her name has also been translated as meaning; "scathe", "damaged," or "harm".

In Norse mythology there were three known clans of Deities; the Aesir gods, who lived in Asgard and the Vanir gods, who lived in Anaheim, Eventually these two respective clans resolved their differences to join together and recognize Asgard as the hall and home of all the gods. The third clan of Norse deities was known as the Jotun, the wise, but malefic race of Giants and this is where we find Skadi's lineage. More specifically, she was believed to be part of the Frost Giant clan.

According to Norse cosmology, the sun was the first to exist in the world and from the sun came two beings; the great cow, Audhumla, and Ymir, a great giant. From the sweat of Ymir, during his sleep, his offspring were born and thus parthenogenetically, he gave birth to the race of giants. Creation of the earth and its inhabitant can be attributed to Ymir, who appears to be very much like Gaia in his role of populating the earth, as Norse cosmology reveals.

Ymir had a reputation for being extremely cruel and one day he met his fate by being killed by Odin and his brothers. The earth and its inhabitants were thus formed from pieces of his torn body. Subsequently, all giant descendants died with his blood being shed upon the earth, all except for two. Two giants, Bergelmir (mountain old) and his wife survived, by hiding in the great World-Mill. From these two giants the race of Jotnar was born and thus, here we have Skadi's Great grandparents and her ancestral lineage traced.

In Norse mythology there are the Aesir, warrior deities and agricultural gods known as Vanir, The Jotnar/Jotun or Giants were viewed as primal, primitive, existing since the beginning of time and they seemed to be losing popularity next to the cultured more sophisticated Asa-gods (combination of Aesir & Vanir gods). It is reminiscent of the Greek battle between the old primordial Titans and their new descendant, the Olympians -the old gods vs the new ruling class.

As a giantess, Skadi makes her homes in Jotunheim [JO-tune-haym] meaning a cold cliff. The threshold to this realm was the wilderness, also known as Utgard [oot-guard] and this was Skadi's beloved realm. Not much is stated about Skadi's mother, but we know of her father and how close she was to him. He was the giant known as Thiazi/Thjatsi/Thiassi. Like most Giants in Norse mythology, he had the ability to shape shift and he would often manifest himself into an eagle. In chapter 56 of the Prose Edda book "Skaldskarparmal, Bragi tells Aegir the tale of how the giant Thjazi was killed.

The story begins with Odin (father of the Gods), Hoenir (a warrior, Asa-god, who lacked wit) and Loki, (the trickster God/giant, son of the giant Farbauti -Cruel Smiter).

These three Gods were traveling through the realm of the giants. They stopped at Utgard and they failed to leave the expected traditional offering of respect as they passed into the Giant's realm. Skadi's father, Thjazi was watching the offenders very closely in his popular shape as an eagle. As the three Gods, later that day, hungrily tried to roast their dinner, Thjazi would not allow them to cook it. In the form of an eagle he kept grabbing their food and in frustration Loki tried to stop him, but ended up getting snatched up, along with the food, by the infuriated eagle. He was nearly killed but was spared upon agreeing to Thjazi's one demand. Loki agreed and was then obligated to bring the beloved Goddess of youth, Idunna and the sacred golden apple, to the realm of the Giants. He fulfilled his promised to Thjazi but as a result, the gods of Vanir soon began to lose their strength, beauty and immortality, for it was Idunna who was solely responsible for keeping the gods youthfulness alive. And the longer the Goddess Idunna stayed in Jotunheim, the more desperate the gods became. Angered, they relentlessly molested Loki and demanded that he retrieve Idunna for the sake of all the gods in Asgard. Together the Gods desperately devised a plan and it started with the Goddess Freyja, lending Loki the Falcon shape form, so that he could remake the journey to Utgard and finally retrieve Idunna. When Loki arrived however, the Giant was nowhere to be found, so Loki turned Idunna into a small nut and quickly commenced his journey, with her, back to Asgard. Unbeknownst to Loki, Thjazi was flying about as an eagle and when he saw what had transpired he quickly gave chase to stop the abduction and reclaim Idunna. The gods of Asgard, however had prepared a large fire in anticipation of this and because Thjazi was flying so recklessly fast, he flew right into the blaze of fire and was burnt to death.

    This would seem like the end of the story but it doesn't end here. From across the snow covered, crystallized landscape comes a larger than life figure, donning a warrior's helmet, suit and armor and approaching Asgard, with much purpose and speed. It was Thjazi's orphaned daughter, Skadi. Enraged, fearlessly seeking to avenge her father's death without concern for her own safety, she arrived. She wanted justice and rightfully deserved it, as Norse tradition often provide great familial compensation when a Kinship had been unjustly killed and this was the case before them when she arrived to Asgard. She enters the hall of the Gods with much anger and conviction - determined to avenge her father's death with blood. She carries with her; sword, spears, arrows and war weapons prepared for retribution. Because she is primal, she is quite capable of taking on any of the gods and perhaps this is yet another reason why the Gods at Asgard avoided a confrontation with the Giantess and quickly complied to her rightful demands. In some of the text, there is a reference to her breathtaking beauty also contributing to their compliance of her demands.

    At first, the father of all gods, Odin, tries to placate Skadi by offering her mounds of gold, but she is already full of riches, according to Norse mythology, due to all the pillaging of her clan and thus she is not interested in currency. Instead she proposes laughter (since, in her mourning, she has been grief stricken, unable to laugh and doubts anyone could make this happen) and since her kinship has been killed, she demands a spouse. Odin agrees with the stipulation that she must elect her spouse, blindfolded, looking solely at the feet of the gods to make her decision. She agrees, and the gods are lined up and covered, so that only their feet are exposed. Now, Skadi had hoped she could distinguish the feet of Baldur among the other gods, for she had secretly desired the god of Beauty and Light. When she spotted a pair of beautiful, clean white feet she automatically assumed they belonged to Baldur, but instead they belonged to the Vana God of the Sea, Njord. He was known to walk barefoot upon the sea quite often, making his feet appear supple and aesthetic pleasing. Imagine her disillusionment to learn that she would be partner with an older, wealthy, mediocre looking god. Still, oaths were sacred to her and she had agreed to the marital arrangement.

The next part of the agreement involved laughter and the trickster god, Loki, was only too eager to entertain. According to one story, Loki tied a string to his testicles and the other string to the beard of a goat (although some text state it was the horns of a live goat). The goat and Loki begin to engage in a weird dance, a tug and pull of buffoonery that ends with Loki clumsily falling backwards unto Skadi's lap. The entire hall of the gods was vibrating in their laughter, including Skadi and thus the second part of the agreed compensation had been fulfilled- they succeeded in making her laugh. Gratified, she had attained her compensation and a spouse in Njord.

Her marriage to Njord proved to be unfulfilling however and short lived, as neither could agree on a single place to live, simultaneously as husband and wife. Njord's beloved home was the seaside hall of Noatun, but after nine days of trying to adjust to this new abode, Skadi found the seaside home and the various sounds of this realm, aggravating. Together they tried Skadi's beloved home of Thrymheim, up in the snowy peak mountains of her father's old domicile. For nine nights Njord also tried to adjust to the new dwelling, but he complained of the wolf howlings and the sounds of the harsh winds. After eighteen nights they realized it was a hopeless, dreadful situation because Njord hated the mountain and the howlings and Skadi could not sleep with the sea birds screeching, thus they decided it was best to separate. Their separation, however seemed amicable and there appears to be no indication of an actual divorce but rather an understanding of their unconventional living arrangement.

It appears however, that Skadi was the model of an independent female, retaining her autonomy even in the midst of several relationships. One story tells that after Njord, she returned to her home in Thrymheim and found love with her soul mate, the God of Winter, archery and skis, Ulle. Together they appeared to share many characteristics and enjoyed their life amidst the snowy mountainous landscape- skiing and hunting . Other tales reveal that she actually married Odin, King of the Gods. Both Odin and Skadi share similar attributes, in their love of wolves and their love of fierce battles and thus their union would seem quite natural. Although she never had any children with Njord, the myth of her time tell that she did bear Odin many sons, most notably, Saeminger, the King of Norway and the first in the line of Jarls of Hladhir (this was a clan of fierce protectors of the Norse Ancient Religion).

We can learn a great deal about Skadi's character through some of her myths. Her role as one who seeks justice is reinforced when we learn of how she punished Loki for the wrongful death of two of her beloved kinsman. Loki, the trickster god of Aesir, who was also a giant and blood brother of Odin, was always causing mishap. In this tale, a mistletoe dart was thrown by the blind God, Hod, but guided by the trickster God Loki, it ends up wrongfully killing the young, beautiful son of Odin and Frigga -Baldur. Now Skadi was quite fond of Baldur, if you can recall the earlier tale, in the Prose Edda, when she secretly had hoped it was his feet she had chosen as a life mate. For Skadi, this was the second man she loved, killed by Loki and his shenanigans. Naturally, it was she who was called upon to exercise retribution for the wrongful death of Baldur. According to the tale, she bounded him and placed a venomous snake above his face, and it remained there to burn him drop by drop, making him writhe so much so, that the earth trembled, as a result we have an explanation for earthquakes. We also learn of Skadi's kind nature in Norse mythology. For example we know that despite her failed marriage to Njord, she was an extremely caring guardian and step-mother to Njord's children; Freyr and Freyja and she took great interest in their lives.

Skadi is the Norse Goddess of snow, ice, mountains, hunting, archery, justice and fairness. She is a patron Goddess to independent women and those serving the military. She invites you to reclaim the wild maiden and live your life by your own rules, in your own unique, most beneficial way. It becomes clear from the Norse writing of the time that Skadi is a strong, confident Goddess that always seems to act from a place of truth, justice and righteousness. In this aspect she is reminiscent of the Goddess Themis in her pursuit for what is right and yet her love of the wilderness, archery, wolves and her uncompromising freedom, reminds me greatly of the Greek maiden Goddess, Artemis.

     Skadi is described often as a beautiful giantess, with long flowing hair, courageous and clearly following her emotions and instincts. As a snowshoe, skiing Wintry Goddess, exploring the wilderness and delighting in the mountains, she is unquestionably a very physical Goddess who will expect you to also engage your physical body in your communion with her. She challenges you to confront fear and insecurities and is a good guide when you are ready to see how far you can go. She will test your strengths and boundaries. Don't be surprised if she, manifest herself in your body, inspiring you to take up extreme sports and a more adventuresome approach to life.

SKADI - GROVE GODDESS GATHERING

Purpose: We gather to connect with the Norse Goddess, Skadi, who teaches us about justice, fierce courage, determination and honoring our bodies.

Check Ins: Speaking stick will be passed around the room so that each womyn, while holding the stick, has a chance to be heard fully and uninterrupted, as she introduce herself and what brings her to our gathering this day.

Chant: A Song text sheet will be offered as we begin creating sacred space with our voices through singing. Songs offered that honor the season at this time, (see song text sheet).

Sharing Images: An Image of the "Ace of Swords" or "The Justice" Tarot Card will be passed around the circle of wommin as we contemplate on what this card means and its personal message to us. Each womyn will have a chance to study the Ace of Swords and say aloud one word that comes to mind while holding its image, as this card can be representative of the Giantess, Skadi.

Drumming and Dance/Movement: To connect our earthly bodies to this divine process we will each grab a percussive instrument and begin to gently raise a cone of power with sound. It can begin with a single rattle and increase with more instruments and then our voices humming, entering the sphere and through-out, we can add swinging movement, whatever feels comfortable and freeing....
Grounding the energy that we raised, we can now begin....
LECTURE ON THE NORSE GODDESS SKADI,
her myths and various attributes and how this
immortal Giantess Goddess is relevant to us today.

GODDESS WORKSHOPS
WORKSHOP I: Skadi is a Goddess most often associated with Winter, cold and ice. We will discuss briefly some ways to incorporate Ice and snow into our magickal workings. For example; there are some spells where you might need to Freeze a situation, stop it mid-track. You can write what this situation is on a piece of parchment paper with a pencil, place it in a container and freeze the whole thing in the freezer until you are ready to deal with it. Another spell incorporating Ice? Melting ice is a powerful way to melt something in your own personal life by allowing the ice to be the symbol of that which you no longer need and in a way you melt and banish it away. We can explore other ways with a communal bowl of ice and snow that we'll gather and place on our altar as an offering to the Skadi.

WORKSHOP II: Wolf as totem and what they can teach us. The Wolf is a highly regarded totem animal and indeed one of Skadi's sacred animals. There are many books on the fascinating subject of totems but in this workshop we will focus on some of the attributes of the Wolf. Wolf is the spirit of endurance, freedom, stamina, intelligence and confidence. Full Moon howlers that they are, they teach us about balance and community, as they are pack travelers, but can also survive on their own. This means their family and community is very important, but they also value their autonomy and alone time. Wolf is a highly intuitive animal and our domesticated dogs are direct descendants. In this workshop we will discuss some of the animal's attributes and how, at various pivotal times in our lives, we can connect with this energy. We will write down a list of Wolf's gifts to us. We will also introduce and explore Animal oracle cards.

WORKSHOP III: Sinking deeper, a special Skadi, Mountain and Dragon **Meditation** will be offered to help us connect with the Goddess. The Meditation script is offered in this chapter. Afterwards, we'll discuss its effectiveness and the images it conjured.

WORKSHOP IV: Rock painting. In this workshop a few plain, flat rocks will be offered so that wommin can paint or draw, with a marker, a special personal symbol of strength. It can be a rune symbol, a heart, a word, an animal even the actual word, "strength". Wommin are encourage to draw anything that will serve as a reminder of their Skadi strength and perhaps even bring forth an image given to them during the meditation.

WORKSHOP V: Vows to Physical Fitness, **blessings of our Athletic Shoes.** Skadi is very much a physically active, energetic, and athletic Deity. Typically the first month of the year finds many of us making New Year's Resolutions that involve some kind of vow to living better, healthier and physically fit. Skadi is a perfect Goddess to help in this department. In this workshop we will simply take our existing shoes or new ones, place a few drops of anointing oil and say a blessing onto them, *"that they may serve us well in our endeavors to walk a healthier path and fulfill our goals, in the name of Skadi. So Mote it Be!!!"*

WORKSHOP VI: Learning a Northern Oracular tool. In this workshop several **Rune** sets will be made available and together we can explore these beautiful ancient symbols and their meaning. By the end of the workshop each of us will chose one Rune to consult and receive answers to our deepest question.

WORKSHOP VII: We will be creating a **Collage of Inspiration** in the name of Skadi. With Wood plaques and a few glued on magnets behind it (both easily acquired at a hobby craft shop) we will create this tool of magick to remind us of our vows to fitness and good health. It can be hung on our fridge to help serve as a reminder of our promise every time we open our refrigerators. Onto these plaques we will glue a small picture from a magazine, of someone whose body we admire and believe to be healthy and inspirational. We will also clip and glue words of inspiration, rune symbols and anything else that might motivate us to keep our promise to Skadi and honor our physical body. A nice touch at the end would be to have nearby systers, within the circle, add one word of encouragement to one another's plaques.

WORKSHOP VIII: Lastly in this workshop we will discuss the **Sword** and its attributes and usage in Wicca. A blessing and charging of our Athame or swords will be performed and it will involve presenting it through all the elements starting with Air, Fire, Water, Earth...

REFLECTIONS ON SKADI
When meditating on this Goddess she appears to me as a righteous fierce spirit, very athletic, engaged in the various Winter sports, like skiing and hunting, with her bow and arrow. She appears fearlessly, delighting in the rough mountainous terrain, challenging herself both physically and mentally and all the while enjoying the companionship of her animals -the wolves. There are some similarities between Skadi and the Greek Maiden Goddess, Artemis, as both are lovers of the Wilderness, competitive sports, animals and both take great pleasure in their freedom. As wommin, she has much to teach us regarding our own autonomy and freedom. And yet her love for battle and her numerous depiction, in shield and armor attire, almost reminds me of Athena. She is tall, fair skinned and unlike other popular depictions, I do not

always see her as blonde but rather with brilliantly white hair to match the snow. Although I've also seen her with dark hair, very long, unbridled hair, sometimes braided, usually loosely kept back, which she sometimes likes to wear in a low, lose pony tail. After all, she is athletic and requires her hair away from her face, like most active people. When she runs or skis, on the mountains, her hair almost resembles that of a horse's mane. I see her, yes, as a ski snowshoe Goddess, dressed all in white, camouflaging with the sparkling white snow. She is the one who penetrates the earth with her vibrant energy and thaws the snow in time for spring and thus, I see her both in Winter and at the onset of Spring.

Almost all things seem small and trivial from a Giantess' point of view and thus Skadi appears to me with this enlightening message about perspective, how it influences reality and our own capacity to master almost all stressors that come our way. When you approach something fearful from the perspective of a giant, it all seems rather insignificant and easily overcome.

I see Skadi as fiercely bold, independent, believing herself to be quite superior and rightly so, as the daughter of the giant, Thjazi. Through-out Norse and Germanic mythology she repeatedly breaks and redefines gender stereotypes by always being depicted as beautiful, yet behaving in a rather, unconventional, "masculine manner" - not by Northern standards but by our modern day perspective. When her father is wrongly killed she does not waste any time to take proper action . Suiting herself up in her helmet, warrior attire and all battle field ecoutrements, she proceeds, fearlessly, to Asgard to demand retribution. She does this without concern for her own safety, but acts rather from a place of justice. She is moved simply by what is *"just and right,"* in this way she is reminiscent of a Goddess like Themis. Her message is, *"This is what is Right," "You owe me" "This is proper and just..."* and thus, she moves and acts from this righteous starting point.

When the God Loki , who was always getting into trouble, accidentally kills, yet another man she loved, she quickly executes proper punishment by binding a venomous snake above his face. When she finds herself married to a god (the Sea God-Njord) who she can't even live with, she attempts to resolve their difference fairly, but when that becomes impossible she again takes judicious action, to remedy the situation. After eighteen nights of trying to make their marriage work, she determines that a separation is in the best interest of all parties.

Skadi loves the mountains and wants to live on her ancestral land and clearly, she will not betray her authentic nature for anyone. This is a wonderful message for wommin who might find themselves in unhappy relationships or marriages, where they are losing their sense of self, feeling trapped, trying to compromise, making all sorts of painful unappreciated sacrifices for relationships and partners that might not be worth it in the end. Skadi tries to make it work, but when it becomes obvious that it is not in her best interest, she does not hesitate to leave. And here again we see reflections of courage for us to emulate in our own lives. *"Take action! Do not let others decide for you. Do what you know in your heart to be right...."* Life for Skadi, after this failed relationship (according to her myths) manifested several other more fulfilling unions, most notably the Gods Ulle and Odin, proved to be more compatible and better suited for her.

Strong, confident and assured of her own abilities, these are Skadi's attributes and her lessons to impart on us. She is an inspiring image of autonomy, positive sense of self-worth and an example of fearlessly taking action, when action is needed. She is an advocate for being physically fit and embracing our athletic selves. Her renown athletic and physical form, encourages wommin to eagerly get acquainted with that part of themselves and thus tap into yet another, important, aspect of the Divine. Her beauty is often associated with Winter and Snowstorms, in the awe-strikingly beautiful appearance of crystallized white snow canoodling the high mountains. However, she is a remarkable example of how beauty and strength can indeed go hand in hand, when we remember how serenely beautiful, yet relentless, winter snowstorms and those deadly snow avalanches can be.

As people begin to set new year's resolutions and some rededicate themselves to their physical fitness goals at this time of year, consider the Goddess Skadi and what she has to offer. For she is the one to call on during athletic feats, marathons, competitive sports, justice, courageous actions and, most importantly, when we ourselves are seeking to cultivate and nurture unwavering confidence in our core.

SKADI GODDESS GROVE GATHERING RITUAL

Purpose: We will honor the Norse Goddess, Skadi, who teaches us about fierce courage, determination and honoring our bodies.

Asperge/Smudge: Greeter will ask each womyn, *"How will you enter this space?" Our traditional answer will be, " In Perfect Love and Perfect Trust"*
Participant will then enter through the veil of incense, music is played in background as we gather, formulating a circle.

Welcoming and Intent of the Circle is Declared

CIRCLE IS CAST (*with a Hunter's Bow and Arrow*)
With a warrior's heart we stand today,
Erect the shield to keep us safe.
We conjure now this sacred space,
Container, preserver, invoked here today.

By will and word we open these gates
To stand outside of time and space
We call on ancient, sacred ones,
To guard our work until we're done

Cast out and keep all Evil at bay
Let Good draw near us as we pray
We call forth now to Northern lands
This circle is cast, with joining hands.

Calling Elements by incorporating the Sacred Dwarves, the ones instructed by Odin to forever hold up the sky and guard the four directions.

Hail to NORDHRI, Guardian of the North, Earth whose powers of regeneration makes us aware of our own resilient physical forms and how it's nursed in thy realm. We bid you to bring your transformative energy, come and guard our sacred space.

Hail to AUSTRI, Guardian of the East, Air whose powers of the mind, clarity and imagination. We bid you to bring your winds of vision and awakening energy, come and guard our sacred space.

Hail to SUDHRI, Guardian of the South, Fire whose powers drive us with conviction and passion. We bid you to bring your driving ambitious energy, come and guard our sacred space.

Hail to VESTRI, Guardian of the West, Water whose powers flows thru our blood, our sweat, our mouths, our yoni, our emotions, move our hearts. We bid you to bring your ebb and flow and harmonious energy, come and guard our sacred space.

CHANT: *"Earth my Body, Water my Blood,
Air my Breath and Fire my Spirit..."*

SKADI GODDESS INVOCATION

Hail beloved Giantess,
Who reminds us of our strength
Courageously fighting
for justice at all length...

I call you in my body
and honor you this day,
Receive these offerings
and teach me your ways...

Awaken the athlete
That will honor this flesh
Delight in my muscles,
My diligence and sweat.

Strong and tall
with your flowing long hair
In Utgard I see you running,
Piercing, the Wintry air

Amidst the white Wolves,
on mountaintops
With Helmet and armor
and causes you won't drop.

Demanding what is right,
beloved daughter of Thjazi,
Passionate, Free roaming
Hail to you, Skadi....

WORKING:

PART I: *A plastic, zip lock bag, filled with ice or snow, will be given to every participant. They are asked to place inside this bag, a representation of something or someone they need to eliminate from their life. It can be a bad habit, a person or a negative situation. A piece of paper naming that which needs to be banished or an actual representation of it (as in the example of a cigarette, when trying to eliminate a smoking habit.....) Afterwards, they can bury the entire content of the bag when the ice/snow has melted.*

Northern land, I bury in your terrain,
The content of this bag and these things I've named....

Chant: *"I am Magick Womyn"*

PART II: *Wommin are asked to select two small, round pieces of leather and these will be sewn together to create a Skadi Talisman pouch of strength. Wommin decorate these, adding rune symbols and they can carry these pouches around their necks or anywhere on their body. They can write their request to Skadi on a piece of paper and place it inside this pouch, along with adding special stones as well. Through-out our creation we will sing and channel our energy for strength and good health into this tool of magick. When we have completed it, each wommin will be invited to recite and enchant this spell over it:*

**"Remind me of my strength,
and all I can do,
with this magick pouch,
Skadi I invoke you....."**

Chanting Afterwards: *"We all come from the Goddess..."*
Begin Devoking, the Goddess
Devoking the Quarters.

Thanking one another for being present. As we open the circle, turn to your syster look into her eyes and say, "Ever mindful that you are Goddess, thank you for being here"

CLOSING CHANT: *"The Circle is open but unbroken....."*

SKADI NORSE MAIDEN GODDESS MEDITATION

We begin, like most pivotal journeys, emptying our minds momentarily and suspending the everyday chatter that incessantly consumes our brain. Allowing silence a sacred niche in this moment, closing our eyes to observe the darkness in that silence. Being mindful of our bodies and the breath that travels in and out, filling our lungs with new life, cleaning and giving it health with each exhalation at this very moment. Breathe in, then exhale. Taking in a deep breath to relax all of our senses. Exhale the stressors of our day. Take another deep breath and relax those sore tensed muscles, let them drop and flow away from you as you exhale.... Breathe. At this moment expect to be transported into a different time and space with your breath. Breathe.

As you exhale release your tension and feel light...lighter than you've ever felt before....breathe and allow your breath to spin you gently, like a feather. Here and there, you spin like a feather spun by a sacred breeze. Breathe.... as you spin lighter and lighter, until you land at the foot of an enormous, snow covered mountain. The tallest mountain you have ever seen. Your studious gaze notices there are four resting points upon this huge, gargantuan white mountain and when you look even closer, you notice a winding, upward road, leading higher than imaginable, leading to what appears like a crystal diamond, touching the clouds. You adjust your eyes and note it is a castle in the sky. There, is where "She" resides, high above the snow covered mountains, it is Thrymhein, her beloved home. And in the realm of Jotunheim, is where you must travel through, in order to meet her.

This journey begins at the foot of the mountain, where a seemingly tranquil pond lures you in for a closer look. Look deeply within its aquatic, blue -green, reflective waters (pause). Ebbing and flowing, study the hypnotic movement of the pond water. It is deepening your trance now. Something stirs gently, a ripple begins and from those gentle ripples an aqua marine Dragon swirls upward, and springs forth near you. Rising from the waters, in a sort of dance, she moves and spews water from her long nostril, to your surprise, she speaks....

"Those that endeavor to meet "Her," must begin their journey, where you stand right at this moment. Here at the foot of her mountain, here in the realm of the Dragon's heart. Water asks you to deeply contemplate your present situation, the emotions they conjure....How do you feel? Examining where you desperately need the gifts of a warrior now. Only in answering can you past to the next station..." (pause) There is silence for a short period, as you consider the events that have led you to this moment in time. With your answer, the Blue Water Dragon points you in the right direction for your next encounter.

Onward you go, engaging your leg muscles into the climb upward. You continue further up on your journey when all of a sudden you feel a blaze of heat. You consider for a moment that it might be your own body's furnace, keeping you warm in the wintry terrain, but soon you see the source of this magnanimous heat. A massive bonfire with no one insight to tend to it, appears before you. With reverence you approach it, as you were taught to always honor Fire. You draw near it, unsure if such wild flames should be left unmonitored and as you get closer to the flames, out jumps a living breathing Red Fire Dragon. Quite animated, it lifts its long enflamed tail and swirls in and out of the bonfire as if its trying to impress you with this tribal dance of sorts. Watching it go in and out of the rapturous bonfire flames is deepening your trance.....(pause)

The Fire Dragon stops momentarily to face you, breathes in and out hot breath that you feel on your skin now. It creates bubbles of bright colored flames from its long nostril and then it speaks.

"Many have stood where you are now, Aiming to touch the divine.
But you won't get past this fiery blaze till a Warrior's job you can define..."
You consider for a moment, what does it mean to be a Warrior? Search for your own personal images of what a warrior looks like? What does a Warrior Wommin engage in? Define a warrior.... (pause) As you submit your answer to the animated, blazing red Dragon, the flames simmer and you are directed to the next leg of your journey.

Your journey continues further upward on the omnipotent mountain. Gravity commences to pull at you and the journey begins to wear on leg muscles, you didn't even know you had. It is quite a physical work out to meet this Goddess but "She," wouldn't have it any other way. A peculiar sound stops you in your tracks. At first it is a faint "whooshing" sound, but within seconds, it triples in volume, becoming almost deafening. You search for the source of this sound, looking to the left, then looking to the right and finally you raise your head up to the sky. There above you, in the serene blue sky, is a White flying Dragon. You watch it in the sky, flying back and forth...back and forth, allowing its movement to deepen your trance. With its wings expanded, it flies gracefully, freely, unsuspecting of an admirer. But lo, it quickly spots you on the ground and immediately charges in your direction and swoops down to take you up in flight. *"Light as a feather, light as a feather, light as a feather,"* you hear it chant and you consider the question it immediately presents to you.

"Who is your warrior? Who in your past has exemplified the Warrior? Who in your past has fought for you?" (pause)

You wildly search your mind for an answer and as it comes to you, it brings back long forgotten, suppressed memories of someone very dear to you. The Air dragon knows this is a very emotional subject and with your answer, he releases you back to your journey, unto the mountain, ever closer to your destination, near your next station.

At first you are unsure where the Air Dragon has dropped you. Perhaps he made a mistake, as this does not look like the same mountain you were traveling on earlier. It looks different. There are many trees in this area of the mountain and it is unusually dark. You wonder if it is nightfall or have you entered another realm. In the dark, the trees appear to take on a life of their own, as they sway back and forth creating unusual shadows. Back and forth the trees sway... swaying back and forth, their movement is deepening your trance..... (pause)

You have been on this journey for some time now and in the dark you begin to have reservations. Should you really be taking this journey? You wonder (pause) You try to make out the road before you but it is covered in a plethora of trees and in the dark you wonder which way to go. Stop...calmly look at your surroundings with your inner third eye and listen... (long pause)

"You are quite close to Thrymhein... but do you think you have what it takes to make it all the way up there? When have you proven to be a warrior?" says a booming dark voice from the trees.... The brown Earth Dragon makes himself known, with its massive size pushing through the tangled tree branches in an effort to reach you, a

frightful sight, as he is now, face to face with you. With his solid, moist, dragon's breath upon your skin, confronting you, you almost want to run - instead, you contemplate his question and for a brief moment, survey your life thus far, to see images of all the times you were forced to take on the role of a warrior. (pause)

As you speak with your answer, the trees part to expose a clear bright road and simultaneously you watch, as the dragon sinks unto the soil of the earth. You step upon this soil and continue upward to Thrymheim. Indeed the Earth dragon was correct, you are a lot closer than you realized. Upward.... you climb the mountain. This road you are on continues upward. Much to your surprise, what appeared like a dotted crystal from down below, is now a massive castle, reachable in just a few short steps. You continue to walk forward with much vigor now and a renewed strength. With much determination to reach the regal cast iron double doors. Stand before this door, study its intricate ancient carvings of dragons, spears and heroic warriors... (pause) Then you knock. The door opens and you immediately notice a long rolled out crystallized, sheet of ice, in place of a welcome runner rug, it leads your eyes to the forefront of the dark hall, where a tall, larger than life figure stands. It is a woman with long, white silvery hair, dressed in what appear to be a ski suit, wearing snowshoes and donning her archer's bow, across her shoulders. She stands among a clan of wolves. Even in the dark you can see her astounding brilliance, strength and beauty and immediately recognize her as Skadi.

Two massive protective wolves from her clan decide to greet you personally at the doorway, but others follow, and soon, you are surrounded by the pack of white vicious looking wolves. Slowly they approach, low dark grunts heard among them, sniffing... snorts, their breathing seemed heavier now... and fear....fear is starting to take over, paralyzing you. You dare not move or even look, as they get closer to your skin, but suddenly it appeared all eyes were on you and from across the room, there "She" stood....the reason for this journey.

Find the strength and let your eyes meet their scrutiny. (pause) Time appears to stand still during this intense moment of staring, as if conversations in foreign tongues were taking place telepathically. You try to understand. Transfixed, their deep gaze penetrates yours and strangely, you no longer feel scared. (pause) Slowly, their eyes convey a familiarity, a gem, a mirror and you can indeed, all of a sudden, hear them. Hear them through your heart...(pause) You understand their language now, for it is your own. Stare deeply within the wolves eyes, to see this reflection of understanding among you, unearth this familiarity.... (pause) Within minutes you feel something take over your sight and skin........ (pause) More wolves appear, surrounding you and you realize then, that you are among your own clan now. You have become one of Skadi's sacred animals- the Wolf.

In wolf form, you are able to run to her, on the sheet of ice, with your wolf brethrens and she greets you with much enthusiasm, rubbing the coat of your scalp. Playfully she begins to tug at you and boisterously, roughhouses you, playing, rough and tumble, for a few minutes. Then she stops and gently runs her fingers through your thick, white, furry wolf mane and begins to speak.....listen. (pause)

"You've made a long journey to my Realm - from the Elemental Dragons to the shape shifting that has transformed you into your Wolf-self. (pause) What you seek is already deep within you and this journey is a testament to this truth... Take this talisman as a reminder of our union today." She places a metal medallion around your

thick, scruffy, Wolf neck. Take this moment now to admire it and speak with her further, after all, it is not every day you get to visit with a giantess. (pause) When you are ready, thank her and respectfully, bid her adieu. Looking at your wolf companions, do the same for them and begin walking across the ice crystal carpet, back towards the regal, iron door entrance. In your wolf body form, feel the weight of your four legs upon the cold, hard ground. Feel the throbbing pulse of your heart, as it strongly, pumps blood thoughout your animal form. Feel your wolf blood generating a fierce heat that is coursing through your veins now. Run....

Run like you never have before.... Run Liberated..., free. Maiden, wild and untamed. Run in your Wolf form, like Skadi has inspired you, Run liberated and free in your wolf form, joyfully gliding down the steep mountains that had once been so challenging to climb. Run now feeling every magickal step. Run down the mountain, passing through the grove of trees and the Dragon of the Earth. Bid him adieu and continue down the mountain. Hear the "whoosh" of the Air Dragon flying overhead and bid him adieu as well and continue downward. Run freely. Run with the energy of the maiden. In your wolf form, dear maiden, down the mountain you go, running with ease in your Wolf form, down pass the Fire Dragon whose sparks nearly caught on your fur. Bid her adieu, and continue down, now to the pond, where initially, the Water Dragon had inaugurated this special journey.....slow your pace and bid her adieu, as she swims half asleep now. You take a moment to catch your breath, take a sip of water from that pond. Thirsty, you realize it was a long journey, but now it appears we're reaching the end of it. As the water passes through your lips and throat, slowly you transform back into your human form once more. Your heart still beating wildly from the rigorous physical task of this journey and now running down this steep mountain, you feel taller, more confident, stronger than ever. You are delighting in your body with each heart beat and You feel ALIVE!!!!

Take one last look at Skadi's home, up high on the mountain, the vast white covered terrain and your immediate surroundings (pause). Bid adieu to the last Dragon and now, while standing tall and grounded, take a deep breath. Breathe in the fresh, crisp air around you, then let it out. Breathe and feel your breath transport you once more. Deeply Breathe in, opening up your lungs with each inhalation, now exhale. Slowly breathe in and exhale counting backwards from four to one ...4,3,2,1. Take another deep Breath and close your eyes, this time feeling the feather-like, gentle breeze passing through you. Breathe.... Inhale and exhale, feeling the gentle shift in the air. Keep breathing in and out, breathe slowly.... until you sense your return, in your body and the feel of the air on your human skin...When you are ready, slowly open your eyes and join us here, in this room....in this very moment, in this time and space.... Return... With your exhalation, return to this moment...
Welcome back.

You are encouraged to journal your thoughts or any impressions from this deep meditation. Take your time returning back . Eat something or drink water or simply chew to fully return. Request for assistance from others, if you are still having some trouble returning and grounding and make sure you do not get up until you are fully ready.

May Skadi's Gifts and Blessings continue to stay with you...

ENERGY SPELL INCORPORATING MY FAMILIAR

It was Beltane, the season of frolicking, Maiden energy and I couldn't be further from this happy, bubbly state of being. Believe me... I wanted to feel that surge of youthfulness, passion and *"umpf"* but it seemed so laborious and so foreign to me at that very moment. It appeared that in the last year or so, I had forgotten my body. Now, this was a very strange phenomenon, as I had prided myself in being a bonafide Maiden; always full of life and energy and very athletic. Yet, for some odd reason, I had fallen into a damning slump of a vicious cycle, that like an ocean wave, kept taking me further and further away from the shore of my true nature and straight into the abyss of corpulence and unhealthiness. Despite always being a Magick, spiritual womyn, I was not treating my body with much reverence and my spirit was feeling a direct disconnection, causing an even greater concern for me.

I knew I needed help that went above and beyond the mundane but I didn't know how to get access to that Divine help when I was feeling so tired, depressed and hopeless half the time.

This Beltane, music played from the speakers of my home's stereo and I sat there very sad and still, almost matronly. I watched with envy as my radiating, little children bounced around, full of vitality, dancing carefree to the blaring drum music. Their bouncing bright auras emanated all these bright swirling rainbow colors..... and then to my surprise, I caught sight of my dogs... They seemed to carry their own kind of peculiar energy. At this time in particular, my Dame familiar caught my attention, as if she whispered my name at that very moment. She has always been a source of comfort and often, very connected to me and it was at that moment I felt her and how much she totally understood me.

"I have enough energy for both of us, play with me and you'll see...." I heard her say. She was right. I share this story because, although we don't often come across Skadi's Wolves and this revered sacred animal isn't physically readily available to us these days, dogs are believed to be their direct descendants and indeed they have much to teach us, both physically and spiritually.

I watched my female dog playfully, running back and forth, with her chew toys, for a very long time, so long that I felt myself trance as the drumming music continued to play in the background. She had me spellbound as I marveled at her energy. I barely could take my eyes off of her and wanting to get a closer look at her, I soon found myself low to the ground on all fours – with the weight of my body on my arms and legs and, as it was a warm day, sweat was now pouring down my neck. Rather unexpectedly, I began to feel a strange sensation rise from within me. It was animalistic, primitive and touching a part of myself I had long suppressed. A strange feeling came over me then, as I found myself wanting to experience my beloved bitch, fully. I wanted to feel that radiating heat course through my **own** body, the way it was so obviously coursing through hers. I wanted my legs to feel her energy. I wanted to run carefree like she so effortlessly was running. I wanted to run like the maiden...run with my pack of wolves. I wanted to experience her freedom, her panting breath and that pulsating, strong thumping, heartbeat. I wanted to have paws to delight in, and run... just run... wild and carefree. I wanted to be her and soon I was.

Somehow, I wanted to contain her electric primal energy within my own body with no thoughts, just purely instinctual, like her. And I wanted to RUN!!!! For the first time in a very long time, I actually WANTED to run. Clearly I had made the journey to my long forgotten body and it was amazing to experience. I think I started to instinctively pantomime her moves; crawling on all fours, back and forth and my cheeks felt a strange sore sensation. I was actually smiling, something I hadn't done in a long time. Chucking out my brain momentarily and just feeling sensations flowing through and within my physical form. Our eyes even locked a few times in shivering moments of acknowledgment and I knew then we were experiencing a powerful exchange of energy.

She allowed me a brief, yet monumental, magickal moment, I will cherish and forever be indebted to her for it, because it inaugurate my ascent back to my body and back to good health. Thanks to my beloved dog, I re-connected to the joys of my physical, earthly form. I touched upon the primal message and the power of a Goddess like Skadi and learned the invaluable importance of honoring my body, as it directly correlates to both my physical and spiritual health- an important lesson for every Priestess to learn.)O(Hail Skadi!!!

Dream Sharing: The Giants arrive for a Nocturnal Visit

Today I woke up from many vivid dreams but the most revealing was the last one I am able to recall in greater detail here.

I was in our home as the dream began, when I received a phone call from my husband's company. They were inquiring about him and informing me that he had been tardy quite often in the past few weeks and wondered if everything was okay. It immediately set off my suspicions of infidelities and I became infuriated at the mere thought. It has always been a recurring concern of mine as a notoriously jealous womyn and in the dream, here it was again, exerting attention. I confronted the scoundrel, demanding that he tell me, and his boss, what he has been doing to cause him to miss work. As usual, he denied any wrong doing. All of a sudden, the television came on like magick and the bright blue screen exposed the truth to me in vivid, graphic images. He frantically tried to change the channel, but it came right back on to the exposing truth and that is when I knew, he was guilty, with a lot to hide.

At that moment in the dream, I experienced this all consuming surge of anger and power swell up within me and I heard myself, with much intensity, call out and invoke Hekate, Kali, Oya, Medea and all the powerful, vindictive Goddesses, to Hex him with all the powers that be, and take him down... I mean, I truly felt this surge of intense energy come pouring through my finger tips, straight at him, like a lightning bolt, and in the dream, he stumbled to the floor. He crashed to the ground and passed out right then and there. Strangely, his boss or co-workers approached the scene rapidly, to do their own examinations. His mom was there too and a private investigator. The suited man, with a pad and pen was taking notes from my answers to his inquiry, but all I could say was that I really didn't know what happened to him. Quite randomly, my husband then awoke from his coma and like an infant wrapped his arms around his mother, who then carried him off and away. In the dream it was quite pathetic to see this grown man being carried away, like a baby, by his mother but I now understand some of its message.

The scene quickly changed to some type of large medieval brick castle, with lots of connecting rooms *(Wow... I just realize how often I have dreams of multiple rooms.)* Anyway , the first room was like a type of love chamber with a large, round bed in the center, heart décor and lots of reds hues and there were two men on the bed. I marveled, in the dream, at how their members were very long and mused at how fulfilling it would be to experience. A tall woman came into the chamber, as if they had all been expecting one another. I removed myself from the room when I realized I wasn't suppose to be there and tenderly touched a little red heart décor by their window. I entered the next room and then the next and passed one room that had a red dressed, fancy doll. It had a matriarchal feel, like perhaps my mom's room or my grandmother's or maybe even my mother-in-law's room (?). I kept walking from room to room, through several corridors and found myself in a different room, with my friend J. and another friend. Together, we were sitting around with teacups or coffee, talking about our only vice; yummy sweets and sugar and we talked about the numerous times we eat it, hum... I heard myself mentioned that I was from New York City and the other woman listened attentively. *(Must make note that every single room had exposed brick walls like the ones you would find in a castle and this was clearly very important, as my eyes kept noting their texture.)* Then I left this room to continue exploring the rest of the castle. With the corner of my eyes I could see my husband was nearby but our paths did not cross. He was going somewhere else and I was heading outside.

The magickal wintry landscape outdoors called me. So strange that the ground was covered in snow and there were high, snow capped mountains and yet down below, I could see the ocean. It was a breathtaking beach and I could see my boys playing near the water. It was quite an idyllic scene to watch.

I sat on a large boulder, which really appeared like a fancy bench and before me there, stood a tall, strong, handsome man. He stood right in front of me, like a type of knight or warrior, and to my surprise he professed his undying love to me and then he proposed. He pointed to his chalet, a smaller stone brick castle nearby, up a hill, and said he needed a wife to complete his home. I listened in awe, as something seemed very peculiar about this man and this white wintry land my eyes were beholding. Something in the atmosphere had shifted and seemed very strange, ethereal and so unusual, as if I was having an out of body experience. Then, I detected, the faint sound of marching footsteps. The synchronized sound grew louder. I turned behind me shocked to discover a procession of Giants (yes, Giants!) coming towards me. They were giant warrior men, strong, with a rather formidable air to them. Each one approaching me, dropping their regalia and helmet-like hats on my lap, as they proceeded to pass me, on their way to go down to the waters. This was highly significant in the dream as their regalia weight so heavily upon my lap. A flash of insight came to me instantaneously, I was going to be their helper. Then a young, blue eyed boy, who was traveling with them, confirmed this and explained it to me in greater detail. It was then that I realized, the man who was before me, professing love and marriage, was actually a giant too. Excitedly it was then that I also realized, I was in the land of Jotunheim….in Skadi's domain and indeed this was an ethereal, breathtaking magickal terrain.

The young boy I saw was about seven years old and he appeared so happy to see me because I was, like him, a non-giant. Then from the corner of my eyes I could see my husband again, sitting on a nearby rock witnessing all of this in a very distant way, giving me space as if we were separated by glass partition and finally… surrendering his hold. The fight was over and he lost me to the Celestial Giants. Needless to say, I woke up assured there was a powerful message for me, amidst these multitude of random symbols and thus felt a need to document it in writing as best I could.

I've been working with Skadi this month and her intense pull and energy has been undeniable. Herein this dream, as strange as it my seem, I felt inaugurated into her wintry landscape and understood parts of her sacred realm and lineage in Jotunheim. Blessed be!

SKADI GODDESS INVOCATION

Hail beloved Giantess,
Who reminds us of our strength
Courageously fighting
for justice at all length...

I call you in my body
and honor you this day,
Receive these offerings
and teach me your ways...

Awaken the athlete
That will honor this flesh
Delight in my muscles,
My diligence and sweat.

Strong and tall
with your flowing long hair
In Utgard I see you running,
Piercing, the Wintry air

Amidst the white Wolves,
on mountaintops
With Helmet and armor
and causes you won't drop.

Demanding what is right,
beloved daughter of Thjazi,
Passionate, Free roaming
Hail to you, Skadi....

CIRCLE CASTING

With a warrior's heart we stand today,
Erect the shield to keep us safe.
We conjure now this sacred space,
 Container, preserver, invoked here today.

By will and word we open these gates
To stand outside of time and space
We call on ancient sacred ones,
To guard our work until we're done

Cast out and keep all Evil at bay
Let Good draw near us as we pray
We call forth now to Northern lands
This circle is cast, with joining hands.

SKADI GROVE OF THE FEMININE DIVINE CHANTS

***Mother of Darkness
Mother of Darkness
Mother of Light
Earth Beneath the Soul in flight
Songs of love and Love of life (lower)
Guide us to our heart..... *(unknown)*

SPARKS
Sparks from the Hearth
Of the Queen
Of Death and Light
Swarm through the dark,
Dance through the night
By J. Robin Gall For Starhawk's Reclaiming Tradition

SHE GATHERS HER DAUGHTERS by Ruth Rhiannon Barrett
She gathers her daughters by Moon and by Sun
She gathers her daughters it has begun
She gathers her daughters to turn the wheel
She gathers her daughters to learn and heal
She gathers her daughters by Night and by Day
She gathers her daughters to lead the way
****(Counter Melody, higher octave and melodious)
 By Moon and Sun
We have begun
To turn the wheel
to learn and Heal (continuous repetition)

EIGHT BEADS CHANTS by Carolyn Hillyer
Girlseed
Bloodflower
(dip it)Fruitmother
Spinmother,
(raise it) Midwoman
Earthcrone
Stonecrone
Bone

EARTH, MOON, MAGICK, I DRAW IT IN: by B.M.M.
In the Earth, deep within,
There is A Magick, I draw it in.
        In her Caves, in the Trees
        Hear her Heartbeat, Pulsing thru me.
When I Rise, I feel her Love
With feet Grounded, I'm soaring high above,
        In the Earth, deep within,
        There is A Magick,, I draw it in
Ancient Moon, my Soul reveres
With my Singing, I call you here.
        When this flame, ignites tonight,
        Priestess dancing, Under the moonlit night....
In the Earth, deep within,
There is A Magick
I draw it in....   There is A Magick, I draw it in }3x

Skadi Chant by B.M.M.
On High, above
In mountains,
I take pleasure alone
On my own,
Connecting with
The Soul of Nature
and the Animal's
expressive groans/moans.
I am One,
I am One with that Beast,
I am One,
I am One with the Leaf,
I am One,
I am One with the Breeze,
I am One,
I am One with the Flames of my Heart,
as it sways in the Trees......

MY BODY
My Body is a living Temple of Love
My Body is a living Temple of Love
My Body is the Body of a Goddess (3X)
My Body is the Body of a Goddess

CHAPTER FIVE
" You have to believe in yourself when no one else does, that makes you a winner"
Venus Williams- professional Athlete

"A mind focused on doubt and fear cannot focus on the journey to victory..."
Mike Jones

WELCOME NIKE

OUR ALTAR

Altar cloth : Blue, or golden altar cloth, a second altar cloth maybe in white or one with symbols of success, whatever those symbols may personally be.
Image: Statue of the Winged Goddess, although it's also appropriate to have angel statuaries as well. Canvas art or photo of the Victorious Goddess, Greece, the Parthenon, Laurel wreath or Athletic events commemorated in photos are all appropriate to display.

Always present on the altar;
A cast iron cauldron, drums, speaking stick, a silver pentacle, athame, elemental representations.....

Air: *feather bundles, angel wings, eagles or owl statuaries, bells, chimes, Incense type sticks, cones, charcoal brisket and fine powdered herbs, frankincense , myrrh and angelica.*
Fire: pillar *candles, glass enclosed candles in yellow, gold, white*
Water: *Small glass bowl with Water and or chalice with Champagne, Cranberry Juice or Red wine.*
Earth: *Green plants to decorate altar, a small dish of soil and or herbs like Laurel leaf, Vervain and Hyssop.*

Other items pertinent to this particular gathering
Laurel Wreath
Trophy or medallion
Chalice
Feather bundle
Plate offering of Olives
Our Creative work in progress
Workshop items
Tarot- the World card
Pitcher of red wine or cranberry juice
Our photos
A Red ribbon

Offering *example of Greek Culinary food, hummus, olives and tzaziki and pita, orzo etc....*
Sacred objects from members:
Notes:

Nike

Nike Altar

Nike

Nike is the immortal spirit of triumph, the Greek Goddess of victory and success. In Rome she was better known as Victoria. Often depicted standing on a globe with wings, and holding palm and Laurel wreath, she was described as quite beautiful by most of the ancient literature of her time. It appeared she was desired by everyone, for, of course, victory is that prized attribute longed for by both, men and women, mortal and immortal alike. That perpetual spirit of victory is present in all wars, competitions, award ceremonies and athletic events today, as it was in ancient times past and thus her presence can still be felt today. Perhaps this is why the American athletic shoe company which began in Oregon, in 1962, adopted its name, Nike, in honor of this great immortal Champion Goddess. Today, it is one of the most successful conglomerate corporations in the world, doing its part to campaign for this beloved Greek Goddess and maintain her name alive in our vernacular.

In Greek mythology she was the winged daughter of the dark River Styx and the Giant Titan Pallas. Her siblings, interestingly enough, were "Cratos," which means Strength, "Bia," which means Force and "Zelus," which mean Rivalry, an indication that all three attributes were ever present, when Victory was invoked.

In Rome she was worshipped quite early on and was considered the divine protector of the senate. There isn't a whole lot of detailed information on the Greek Goddess, Nike. Most of what we do know about her is extracted and derived from mere mentions, every now and then, in various ancient Greek writings. There are no long epic myths associated with her, nor any indication that she had conflict with anyone in particular. And although she was desired and welcomed by all, there is no indication of any romantic liaisons with Gods nor humans.

Although, in Greece, she had no known cult following, nor any special festivals or temples, as many of the other Greek Goddesses did, she was often associated with both Zeus and Athena. Most art and sculptures of her time depicted her as a small figure held in the hands of Athena, the Greek Goddess of War and Wisdom. There is even some literature that allege, Nike was simply another aspect of the beloved Athenian Goddess. However, more evidence reveals that indeed they were two separate entities, with many impressive similar attributes, which would explain the conflicting tales. Athena, being a Goddess of Wisdom, debates and war, would certainly want near her, the continuous blessings from the Goddess of Victory. They were considered as having a close alliance and there is even some contention in the Greek myths that directly connect Athena with the death of Nike's father, but she suffered no grave punishment due to their close relationship.

Her worship would have been compulsory on the battlefield, pageantries, athletic events and numerous other competitive situations for both mortals and immortals alike, with libations, offerings and sacrifices. The patriarchal Olympian head God, Zeus, cherished Nike immensely due to her help in attaining victory in the battle of the Titans. It is perhaps this reason why Zeus appointed Nike as his official charioteer and employed her family as attendants, allowing them, the rare privilege, to reside with him in the royal palace among the divine Gods.

Her most famous depiction is found in "Nike of Samothrace" a sculpture by Paeonius (c.424 B.C.) which was discovered on Samothrace in 1863. Presently this illustrious creation is contained at the Louvre Museum in Paris, France.

Wherever victory and success is, Nike is there too, immortal , ever present as the spirit of Victory, a pure ambitious drive, ready to award you with success. She is forever the Maiden archetype and a wonderful Goddess for modern wommin to connect with, when we are ready to tap into our fierce competitive spirit . As the Divine Charioteer, she is also an excellent Goddess to call upon for, not only Victory, but also in driving and travel spells. Invoke her when you wish to succeed in a personal endeavor or anything requiring ambition and drive. She is the energy of the marathon runner, reaching the finish line, hands outstretched towards the heaven, in pure elation and accomplishment..... This is Nike- the Goddess of Victory!

NIKE - GROVE GODDESS GATHERING

Purpose: Purpose of our Gathering is to invoke the powers of **Nike/Victoria**, To visualize success for the coming year and the fruition and manifestation of our wishes...

Check ins: We gather forming a circle and introduce ourselves to one another while incorporating our beloved talking stick, with the inherent rule that allows us to speak freely, openly, without interruptions or fear of judgment.

Chanting: *"Nike Chant," "Sweet Surrender," "May all go as I will"* (see song text sheet)

Drumming Trance: Inviting Participants to listen to a powerful drumming musical track (on CD), to help them surrender to this moment, leaving the mundane behind and ground into the present. Some might sit still and trance, while others might be moved to dance, hoping to raise energy.

Check ins II: Discussion about how we personally **define success and victory**. How will we know, we have reached the finish line? What does Nike feel like in our bodies?

LECTURE ON THE GODDESS, NIKE

and how to best utilize her Divine gifts of confidence and the guarantee of Success.

GODDESS WORKSHOP
WORKSHOP I:
Medallion Amulet Creation. In this workshop we will craft with Clay to create a Winner's Medallion pendant, imbued with Nike's energy and our own personal intention. As we are sculpting and creating this medallion, music is heard in the background and our most vivid vision of success is carried forward into our creation.

WORKSHOP II:
We will re-created the type of **crown**, Nike would bestow on us- a Laurel Wreath. Using silk floral flowers, wires, floral tape and piper cleaners we will craft a Nike crown.

WORKSHOP III:
The Tarot Card of "**The World**", best represent Nike. What does it mean to you?, What is (The World Card) saying to you personally.... The World Card, which is traditionally a card of attainment and success in the Tarot deck, will be passed around the circle. Every participant will hold it, study the card, look into its symbols to unearth its personal message being conveyed and how it relates to the Goddess, Nike.

WORKSHOP IV:
Drumming circle to raise energy- Actually creating a drumming circle with wommin, individually drumming. Collaboratively infusing our energy, movement will lead to next part.... An effective way to synchronized with our rhythm as one......it naturally leads to the energy raising of our names.

WORKSHOP V:
Toning each other's name until it becomes a **Cone of Power**.
A woman will stand in the center and receive our energy as we chant her name, first quietly then increasing in volume, raising her energy, so that she can pursue her heart's desire. We do this for our working space, why not for our own body and soul. Often wommin jump in and love being showered with the rattles and loads of vibrational positive energy, leaving them feeling tingly and euphoric.

WORKSHOP VI: The Chalice. In traditional Wicca you will often find a chalice upon the altar in the place of the West, to represent the sacred element of water. In this workshop we will discuss its usage and meaning. We will also reflect and share our own personal thoughts and experiences working with our chalice. Participants will have a chance to bless, via the four elements, and prepare their own chalice for ritual work.

WORKSHOP VII:
A Visualization or Nike Meditation will be presented. It can be offered at this time as a workshop or saved and presented during the ritual.

Nike Success Visualization - This will Not be a meditation but a Visualization:

So often we focus on what we don't have or what we need, coming from a place of lack, which can be depressing and discouraging. Perhaps one of the most powerful things we can do is visualize ourselves already in that victorious realm. We take this moment now in the present to see ourselves, already where we want to ultimately be and imagine ourselves already successful with all our needs met. Transport yourself to the end of the story. Focus, not on the process nor where you begin, but instead focus on where you intend to end up. This can sometimes be the most effective form of Magick and shifts us into a more positive state for victory . Focus on that finish line right at this moment and experiment with how much easier it becomes to manifest your wish.

It is a known secret to many athletes, like marathon runners, that focusing on the finish line can manifest its attainment quicker. Instead of coming from a place of need, instead of getting overwhelmed with the actual process, which can sometimes be hard to discern and even more discouraging to visualize, it's best to come from a place of abundance, already having achieved. We are going to shift our minds through creative visualization and see ourselves already having achieved our goal. See your spell or wish manifested. Let it trigger in you, confidence, security and greater likelihood of achievement. See your success manifested and it will trigger positive energy which will spill over to your present magickal workings. Inspiration swells and pours in when you see yourself already a winner. And you will find pleasure in the attainment of your heart's desire. This will become a tool for projection into the future. Experiment with a simple positive mantra or affirmation repeated continuously. See yourself as a success.... already having acquired your goals.

We take this moment now to engage in a few exercises that will help us in this process.

I. Write a short Bio about yourself, your journey and how you came to succeed.
Write an outline of your life. Create a simple five stage graph with the intent success date and write one accomplishment for each stage.
For example Luisa Fictious wishes;
1. six months from now, Enrolled in a good academic institution -
2. one year from now, Met the lover of my dreams
3. two years from now, Attained a great job with much potential and loads of money
4. five years from now, Courageously, opened my own business
5. seven years from now, Give Birth
6. twenty years from now, Retired in Hawaii, with lots of money, friends and lover.
   Journal the end of your intention as achieved successfully,
   share in your writing how it felt to attain your goal and win.

II. Write your Obituary. This is one sure way to shift your focus onto the end result and see what and how you wish to live in this lifetime.

III. Storytelling your success within the group is a nice way to also inspire one another.

<u>REFLECTIONS OF NIKE</u>
She is Victory. She is the immortal presence of Success and naturally desired by all. It is not surprising that the infamous beloved sports company has adapted her name and her imagery as their logo. I sometimes put on those sneakers for a morning run and I can't help but think of Nike and invoke her gifts with every step. Wherever she is –Success & Victory are present and thus as competitive wommin (whether it's in the boardroom, athletic feats or handling day to day challenges) we want her energy because we want to have the guarantee of victory. With her, we reach our goals and wear the crown of a winner!!!

NIKE GROVE GODDESS GATHERING RITUAL

Purpose: To Connect with the Goddess of Victory, Nike and project into the future, success and manifested goals.

Purifying space with feathers, the element of Air, and use of cauldron burning sage
Anointing each participant's third Eye with Sabbat Oil

Casting Circle *(with Athame)*

Invoking Quarters
each syster holds an element while priestess calls and invokes the Quarters.
Hail Eurus! Hail and Welcome Eastern Winds. Bringer of enlightenment, awakener of our dreams. Upon thy sacred Eagle you journey to us as we call upon you. We bid you, come to our aid and guard our sacred space.
Hail and Welcome **Air.**

Hail Notus! Hail and Welcome Southern Warm Winds. Bringer of pleasure and all that ignites our core, passion's elevator, drive and thy spirit of rapture. Upon the fire of our desire you journey here, to us. We bid you, come to our aid and guard our sacred space.
Hail and Welcome **Fire.**

Hail Zephyrus! Hail and Welcome Western Winds. Bringer of the waters that sing to our hearts, inspiring a river of expressive creations. Upon the moist, secret melodies of our hearts you journey here, to us. We bid you, come to our aid and guard our sacred space.
Hail and Welcome **Water.**

Hail Boreas! Hail and Welcome Northern Winds. Bringer of strength, awakening us to our solid earthly form. Teacher of prosperity and creator of all that richly grows upon this earth. Upon thy stones, our flesh and bones you journey to us, here. We bid you, come to our aid and guard our sacred space.
Hail and Welcome **Earth**.

CHANT: *"...Do you remember when God was a Woman..."*

Intent of Ritual Declared:
To Honor Nike, ourselves and celebrate the Victories we will soon experience.

INVOCATION TO NIKE...
At the altar, Priestess will read Orphic Hymn....

Invited wommin to rest for Visualization...
NIKE MEDITATION OFFERING
As they came out of the meditation trance, play a musical CD to help them transition. Paper and pen will be made available so that they may write their goals for the New Year.

Upon completion of our wish writing we come together to Sing:
"Nike's Song"
Invitation to Toast and now to pick up their Goblets. *(Tell them what we are about to do... we are already celebrating our victory!!!)*

Priestess will pour libation into each wommin's goblet as we all say the following incantation together:

**A TOAST TO YOUR VICTORY
AND WHAT SHALL IT BE?
SPEAK IT, SAY IT...
SO MOTE IT BE...**

Every lady will clasp her Goblet, raise it and say what she hopes to manifest in the year while raising her Goblet for a toast. Every womyn within the circle follows her lead when it is her turn. This needs to be very celebratory and full of joy and support for one another. Everyone must be committed to that very moment, to draw in the Magickal energy, visualizing all wishes and goals manifested already. End holding hands and containing this energy, then grounding it.

We End with **Chant**:
"We all come from the Goddess...."

Thanking and Devoking The Goddess
Nike, Beloved Goddess....
From you we have gathered
much inspiration
and confidence to see our own Victories.
We give our sincere gratitude
for your gifts, as we bid thee adieu.
Stay if you will,
Go if you must.
Hail and Farewell Nike!!!!

Devoking The Elements
Our Thanks to you **Boreas** for your Northern gifts and protection as you guarded our sacred space. We bid you adieu now in gratitude. As ye arrived in peace, depart in peace, Hail and farewell Earth.

Our Thanks to you **Zephyrus**, for your Western effervescent gifts as you guarded our sacred space. We bid you adieu now in gratitude. As ye arrived in peace, depart in peace, Hail and farewell Water.

Our Thanks to you **Notus,** for your Fiery gifts and passionate protection, as you guarded our sacred space. We bid you adieu now in gratitude. As ye arrived in peace, depart in peace, Hail and farewell Fire.

Our Thanks to you **Eurus**, for your Eastern gifts and winds of inspiration, as you guarded our sacred space. We bid you adieu in gratitude. As ye arrived in peace, depart in peace,
Hail and farewell Air.

  OPEN CIRCLE: "Circle is Open, but unbroken, may the peace of the Goddess,
be ever in our hearts......" 3X

*Encouraged the raising of Good, High level of energy for us to End the day with-
for it is just as important how we begin and end this ritual.*
Potluck/Festivities follow.....

NIKE GODDESS MEDITATION

I invite you to find a comfortable spot, sitting down or laying on the floor. Take a deep breath in and exhale releasing any pre-occupations or stress from your week. (*audibly inhale...and exhale*). Take another deep breath to further cleanse the mind of any clutter and with this next exhalation, release the remaining stressors and all mundane concerns. There is stillness and quiet anticipation. Breathe and let your body sink itself even further into your chair or the ground, if you are laying on the floor. Let it feel heavy and attached to the earth, while you bring your attention to your third eye....located in the middle of your forehead, between your eyebrows. Pierce within to see what it reveals. *(pause)* Then move on to connect with your heart chakra and again face it, see what it reveals *(pause)* Ask its willingness to take this journey with you. *(pause)* And now move to the top, the crown of your head. Study it and see if it is open to you now. If not, imagine a small door unhinging and opening right there, for, it is from this place that our journey begins.

With eyes closed, follow my voice, you will be safe as I lead you on this journey. Breathe, I will take you to a house, a beautiful home, an old home built many, many years ago and standing tall and strong today, still with integrity and all of its original beauty, pride and strength. See this home now manifest in your mind's eye and enter it. *(pause)*

You survey the home closely; the walls, the furniture and knick knacks, and you see a young girl is running around the house. Like most children you've known, this child is vibrant and full of energy. She is running through-out the house like exuberant, restless children normally do. Run behind her and try to catch up with her, follow her every movements. Notice she is going up a staircase now and up she goes... keep your sight on her. It's a bit hard to catch up to her but you do, and you watch and observe studiously. She's running up the stairs now, going up those stairs, follow her up .... She is going up until she reaches the attic.... And you follow her there. Unnoticed, you simply watch her.

Playing carefree, this young girl, to you, appears to be about nine or ten years old. You study her carefully to assess any other important details about her. She appears to be unaware of your presence. In the attic she seems preoccupied, rummaging around some old stuff, old toys, old china, old photos in broken frames, old mementoes, old books, knick knacks and old boxes, looking for something to tickle her fancy. Bored, she continues searching for something new to play with, something that will intrigued her.
What will spark her interest? *(pause)*
You see her picking up an old photo, in a broken Frame.
Who is that in the Photograph? What does she see? *(pause)*

She puts the photo back down to free her hands to pick up yet another item that catches her eyes. A shinny Brass and Gold trophy. In awe, her fingers trace and go over the outline of this very large brilliant trophy. Then she gently picks it up with both hands and feels the weight and heaviness of this grand prize. She twirls it around within her hands and holds it over her head like she imagines, champions normally do. Then she brings it down to her face for further curious inspection. With your mind's eye, step closer to see what she sees.
On the bottom, the girl notices an inscription. It is very pale and faded, but she's able to make out the words. Attentively, you notice all of this, as she mouths and whispers the words... **What does it say?**
What does she read? What do you hear her say? *(pause)*

The young girl puts down the trophy and continues to look about the room. She appears super delighted and continues looking around for more treasures while she hums a sweet tune.

You notice she stops for a minute. Before her, on a short, low coffee table are many books, but she is drawn to the largest one. A book that is impressive and enormous in size... it's larger than most she's ever seen and stands out from the rest, in its craftsmanship. Continue to watch what unfolds as the girl approaches the book with great reverence because, after all, she was taught from an early age to value the written word. Carefully she kneels down, sits and begins to turn the pages.

The first chapter tells the story surrounding the photo she had first grasped in her hands upon entering the attic. When it was taken, the names of the people present when the photo was taken and the preciousness of the occasion. It told of the time of day, its importance and why it was commemorated with this photo. The girl in the attic is intrigued and absorbed in the tale. She returns to the photo she had left in the old box. Now with an even greater smile, she looks at the photo with deeper understanding and respect.

The girl continues to read on from the book. The next chapter tells of the trophy and the day it was won. By the look on her face, she is pleased at what she reads. She seems in awe and overwhelmed with joy to learn of the special event that led to this great prize. You notice now she is beaming with happiness to learn of the value of this trophy... And you see her running ecstatically back to where she left it earlier. She runs back to find it and holds it in her hands once more. Strangely, as you witness this, you are experiencing your own heart chakra five times its size, pulsating vigorously, as you touch upon her great pride and joy in this very auspicious moment. It is as if there is a link between you and this child. It is as if she has unearth your most prized posessions. Stay with her in this scene for a moment and consider what has transpired *(pause)*

Exhale and breathe... In the air you take a whiff and smell something sweet and soon the young girl notices the scent too.

"Ambrosia... Chocolate chip cookies..." she whispers as she hears a Call.
Call her...
Call her by her name...
Nike can only come when she's invoked and called upon by name.
Call her!!!
Nike, who delights in your triumphs!!!
Nike, who's breath is our success and accomplishments.
Nike who's spirit rejoices and comes to life amidst our own Glory.
Call her now with this offering!!!
Celebrate with this immortal Goddess your success- past, present and future successes. Honor Nike with your pursuit and attainment of your goals.

Take a moment to sit with her, absorbed in her pleasure of Your work. Bask in her light of Victory and Success. Thank her for her support and her visit and then prepare yourself to say goodbye.

With your inhalation... return. Breathe and with your exhalation, you are returning... Breathe and remember this room, follow my voice as we journey back. Breathe...exhale and surrender the images, return with your breath, return to my voice, return to this room. Breathe and come back to your body. See your crown chakra open and welcoming you back. *(pause)* Visit with your heart chakra once more and thank it for its investment in this moment. With your breath return to this time and place. Now breathe into your third eye and again pierce through, to return to where you began this journey.

Breathe, feel yourself back in your body, stretch a little and pull up your body weight back to its normal position...exhale, breathe and when you are ready, open your eyes and join us here. Welcome!

ASPECTING NIKE/VICTORIA

I am **Nike**, Virgin Maiden, Goddess of Victory
Daughter of the Giant Titan Pallas, the God of Warcraft.
Born unto My mother, She of Oath & Dedication,
Goddess River Styx.
Three more siblings she birth to this realm,
Cratos (*strength*), Bia (*force*), Zelus (*Emulation*)
and we all resided in the home reserved for Gods.
I was often in charge of Zeus' chariots,
consulted and revered by all.
My worship came from many in Athens.
I am Goddess…immortal
Do you not feel me live on today?

I am the spirit of **victory**
And when I am present,
I guarantee success.
My gifts will make you see,
That Victory is yours to behold.
What starts as a simple **seed,**
can grow to great heights with me.

I show you the possibilities and
give you what you need to take **flight**
My wings are yours and you too can also fly high.

I stir ambition
I light the **Fire,**
I awaken in you tenacity and persistence
My perseverance is intense
and it is now upon you,
What will you do with my gifts?

Victory comes in many guises
It could be victory over your oppressors, a job,
a creative endeavor, a lover, health, a competition,
If it's something that you wanted and attained
it is victory and I am there!
My spirit lives in every goal achieved.
I am Victory!
I ask you to look within to find your true desire
What's worthy of such intense drive?
What Cause- merits my presence and devotion?,
I require you to investigate those stirrings,
and those gnawing **emotions.**
That raw drive…
What will ease it? What feeds it?
What will conquer it away?
I am the guarantor of Success & Victory.
Will you take flight with me today?

HOMERIC HYMN TO NIKE
Orphic Hymn 33 to Nike (translation by Taylor)
Greel Hymns C3rd B.C. to 2nd AD)

To Nike (Victory)
Fumigation from Manna.
O powerful Nike,
by men desired,
with adverse breast
to dreadful fury fired,
thee I invoke, whose might alone
can quell contending rage
and molestation fell.
"Tis thine in battle to confer the crown,
the victor's prize, the mark of sweet renown;
For thou rulest all things,
Nike divine!
And glorious strife,
and joyful shouts are thine.
Come, mighty Goddess,
and thy supplicant bless,
with sparkling eyes,
elated with success;
may deeds illustrious
thy protection claim,
and find,
led on by thee,
 immortal fame."

Public domain, source from, http;//www.theoi.com/daimon/Nike.html."

This spell is best done when the Moon is waxing and preferably on a Sunday or a Friday, during the first hour of Sunrise. Light your frankincense incense and let the smoke rise twirling and swirling around your altar items. Place a statue or photo of Victorious Nike and next to her, place your photo, along with the creative work you seek her blessings for. Attain a bright yellow pillar candle and carve it with any symbols that represent success to you, whether it is the dollar bill sign or a happy face -carve it on the wax. Then rub and charge your candle with "get it done oil", (see appendix) or Success oil. To raise energy before lighting your candle, you may drum, sing or just hum, until there is a ringing sensation in your whole body. Channel all of that powerful energy into your working candle and begin to recite the incantation three times; each time louder until the energy is sent upward, given away to the Universal auric field.

YELLOW FLAMES OF VISION
*Bring to me,
Bring to me
Vision and clarity
Allow me to follow my dreams

Yellow flames and open mind
To the path that's only mine

What shall I do?
What Shall I pursue?
What will fulfill my soul
and you?

Goddess in me,
awaken and breathe
My life's calling
help me to see

Journaling -Nike Grove Gathering-
Projecting and Manifesting Victory

It was really interesting, as usual we were not all gathered together fully until much later than planned. It appears we always start half an hour later than our start time because it takes that long for some of us to come through the door, unpack, prepare our personal altar offerings, while simultaneously carrying on conversations and catching up with our old friends. It's quite a conodrum for a facilitator, especially one that values the interaction of wommin, but it seems to be something I'll need to work to improve upon.

This particular month, the first to arrive, thankfully was the newest member to our group, and it was nice to have that chance to connect and bond before the chaos of everyone's arrival. During this time, I was able to calmly answer her questions and tell her about myself and what my background is and what Grove is all about.... I think in this quiet, intimate moment I was able to speak very openly and honestly, stressing how I had no intentions of being the dictator leader in our group, unlike other groups I witnessed, because my vision is for a Sisterhood. That has always been my vision and the inspiration for "Grove of the Feminine Divine" - sisterhood, and to this end I want to make sure I stay loyal to this initial vision. Our grove is small and maybe it will develop into a Coven one day, but if it does, it will be organically because we have a consistent group of women who want to gather regularly not because it is forced upon them....

Very soon afterwards, the next womyn arrived, excited with her new Tarot Deck and eager to share it fully with us. I took that opportunity to excuse myself, so that I could get dressed, as I was still in my mundane ordinary clothes. More wommin came and then the last Two members arrived a few minutes after, a bit late, but it was nice to finally feel like we could begin our Goddess day.

Initially, there was a lot of chit chatting as usual. We all talked about ourselves and what was going on in our respective world etc... We talked a whole lot, trying to catch up and eventually used our traditional speaking stick to keep us more organized. Chanting songs followed, but it did not start till much later. It was fun when we did get going because they actually sang all the songs very nicely, boisterously, and they appeared to enjoy themselves. Excitedly, I was able to also create some harmony with their beautiful singing voices. I used this time to also explain how we run the monthly gatherings and what to expect, so that our newest members would not be taken off guard.

The next part was actually creating a Drumming Circle to raise energy- with every individual contributing a drumming pattern. This was quite effective and I could hear when we were synchronized with our rhythm......it naturally led to the energy raising of our names. THEY REALLY LOVED THIS!!! This came about, by following my instincts on the spur of the moment and trusting my intuition, when I sensed the energy level of some wommin beginning to wane. It was very effective as I felt it indeed resulted in an elevated, astronomical energy. After drumming, we flawlessly went to the next stage of our day, the toning of each other's names until it actually becomes a powerful Cone of Power. Each wommin was invited to stand in the center and receive our brightest of energy, as we chanted her name repeatedly and raised her auric energy so that she can tap into Nike and pursue her heart's desire. This was truly cathartic and awesome to witness. And they loved jumping into the center, being showered with rattles and the vibrational powerful energy, gifted from their systers.

After these effective exercises, I felt we needed to ground a little now with a drumming CD track. Two of us could not stand still, however, we danced in delight to the frenetic drumming rhythm, we had successfully raised the right level of energy to continue our work.

Somehow, I went right into aspecting Nike after all that good mojo energy and I just started speaking and reciting prose, while gazing into their eyes. I felt a strange split pathway that allowed me to see they were really moved by Nike's appearance and presentation. On the spur of the moment, this was the best way to bring Nike's Energy into our day, rather than a formal sit down lecture. Here, I just trusted the spirit that was moving through me at that particular moment and I didn't question it while it was happening.

We transition from this place to the World Tarot Card exercise- connecting with our definition of Success and Victory. Around the circle we went, as each woman, holding the World

Card, defined out loud what it represented to her personally. This was another wonderful part of our day, as we each had something very diverse to say about Victory and the World Card. "..Clarity, clear lit path, daylight not the dark, how fertile everything becomes in its presence, the requirement of putting work and effort to achieve, Prosperity/Peace comes with it etc....etc..." It was wonderfully insightful!

Right after our Tarot exercise, I did not skip a beat and led them right into a recorded Meditation. It cannot compared to actual live meditation but it is another strong and valid way to offer a trance in a group. Sometimes offering a pre-recorded meditation allows me the chance, at that particular part of our day, to participate in the connection to the Divine. And, quite frankly, some gatherings are so intense that a chance to trance and meditate in the middle of facilitating a gathering helps recharge me. Being able to listen with them was a nice way of experiencing the meditation with them. I must admit that I immediatedly notice our energy shifted and slumped a bit after this recorded trance and I believe it was because one or two wommin were really processing difficult personal issues that were surfacing as a result from the meditation. After doing a check-in briefly and making sure everyone was okay, we proceeded to prepare for our Ritual and our toast to the Goddess of Victory.

The ritual to Nike was by all accounts fun, light and joyful, as we projected success and stood at the threshold of victory. We raised our chalices and toasted to our achievements, as it had already happened, projecting success into our future and that was quite positive and moving at the same time. I then conducted a live short visualization which had a completely different hue, much lighter, resulting in what appeared to be a more positive effect on them.

Feasting naturally, took place right after our ritual and by this time, we were all very famished. Aside from the ebb and flow of wonky energy battles with others' emotional sweeping terrains, this was a wonderfully positive gathering. All Hail to Nike, the Goddess of Success!

NIKE-GROVE OF THE FEMININE DIVINE CHANTS

***NIKE"S CHANT
I call Nike's Energy, I call Nike's Energy....
Charioteer, Our call Hear,
Victory's not Far from here
Victory's not Far from here....

    I call Nike's Energy, I call Nike's Energy....
    Charioteer, Our call Hear,
    Victory will soon be here
    Victory will soon be here...repeat   *by B.M.M.*

I AM MAGICK WOMAN (?) Shelley Graff
I am Magick /Sacred Woman, Giving Birth to myself
I am Magick /Sacred Woman
Giving Birth to myself
from deep inside the wells,
From your loving eyes and wisdom
My truth that I must tell,
I am Magick /Sacred Woman
Giving Birth to myself....

2009 DOD CLOSING CHANT by (? Ruth Barrett?)
May all go as I will
And the Road that's clear behind me, May all go as I will
And the Solid Earth beneath me, May all go as I will
And the Goddess light above me, May all go as I will
And my Sisters all around me, May all go as I will
And the Road Ahead before me, May all go as I will
And my Heart that lies within me, May all go as I will
And the Road that's clear behind me
May all go as I will
And the Solid Earth beneath me
May all go as I will
And the Goddess light above me
May all go as I will
And my Sisters all around me
May all go as I will
And the Road Ahead before me
May all go as I will
And my Heart that lies within me
May all go as I will, May all go as I will.... (continuous chant)
May all go as I will....May all go as I will....(keep repeating until hush)

***I circle around Arapaho Chant
I circle around, I circle around, The boundaries of the Earth 2X
Heyana, Heyana, Heyana Heayana
Wearing my long wing feathers as I fly
Wearing my long winged feathers as I fly. *(repeat)* *by Arapaho Ghost Dance Song*

****We Are Sisters
We are sisters on a journey, Singing in- the Sun
Singing through the Darkest night.
The healing has begun...Begun....
The healing has Begun *(repetition...3x)*
SUNG & Created(?) BY Susan Weed and Robin Rose Bennett

***Elemental Song to Devoke
introduced to me by Robin Rose Bennet
The earth, The air, the fire, the water,
Return, return, return, return,
Below above, the Center is Love,
Return , return, return, return....

February

According to the Farmer's Almanac, Snow moon and Hunger moon are just some of the many names for this month's Full moon. For our ancestors, this time of the year may have seemed dangerous, as the crops harvested, canned and pruned back in the Fall (and meant to last all winter long) might be dwindling and coming to an end. And in some parts of the world at this time of year, nothing can grow on the cold frigid land and the best you can do is hope that Spring does not delay and that your food supply will last you till then.

February's full moon is also commonly known as Quickening moon because at this time of year the core of the earth appears to be quickening and new life seems to be on the edge, underneath, patiently waiting to be born. There is a quickening towards longer hours of daylight, as the sun grows in strength. Some might begin to plant seeds indoors in preparation for Spring. Many pregnant animals now are also feeling the fluttering of their unborn within their wombs and soon, in the Spring, they too will be born. The sabbat of Imbolc, which means "in the belly," is a reference to this magickal moment in nature and the precious cycle of our Mother Earth. Many Pagans, at the start of the month, celebrate this ancient Celtic sabbat that honors the new precious life, and the seedlings, nursing in the womb and belly of the Earth, awaiting to be born in the Spring. On a spiritual level, both figuratively and literally, this is a time of incubation and gestation, as we prepare for what will transpire in the coming Spring.

February is known as the shortest month of our calendar year. It probably received its name from the ancient purification festival, "*Februa*," derived from the Latin word, "*Februare*", which means "to purify." Indeed February can be seen as a perfect time to purify our land, our homes, our families and ourselves, in preparation for the coming of Spring. Perhaps it is this reason why the Full Moon of this month was also sometimes refered to as the Chaste Moon.

Numerous Pagans, at this time of year, go through Craft and Coven initiations and elect to dedicate or rededicate themselves to their spiritual practice. As this time of year resembles our Pagan ancestor's new year, there are some that refer to it as the true Wiccan New year. It is also considered the start of the season of the Maiden and the astrological sign for this month is water bearer, Aquarius, ruled by Uranus (Jan 21-Feb 20).

Throughout all of nature we are now looking for early signs of Spring's impeding arrival- birds chirping, thawed soil, the first flower buds. Today, the sight of a groundhog inaugurates much hope and excitement in the U.S.A. as we rely on this tradition to foretell if Spring will come early. In ancient time, however, Celtic myths reveal that initially our ancestors searched for a slithering snake (who represented the Goddess Brigit) that would come out of the mountain and slithered down to announce Springs arrival. February also has many of us celebrating the great, fire festival of the Chinese New Years, with fireworks and festive processions. By mid- month we are honoring old Presidents in the U.S.A., but also celebrating our own romantic relationships with Valentine's Day. It seems so appropriate that on the coldest month of the year, we have what is, traditionally, known as a warm-hearted, romantic holiday, called Valentine's day -named after the legendary Celtic patron, St. Valentine.

Beneath the seemingly cold, barren, hard Earth there are great stirrings, that we will only be privy to see when the weather begins to get warmer. It is thus a time of magickal transformations, as the Earth begins to thaw and slowly transform itself into the lush, fertile, oasis for Spring. We call upon two Goddesses of major transformation this month, the Yoruban Goddess Oya and the Celtic Goddess Brigit. Within these fiery deities, we are encouraged, as they exemplify beautifully how inner transformations can produce the most fertile, productive, magickal realms of healing for our inner and outer selves.

CHAPTER SIX

"Whatever the theories may be of woman's dependence on a man, in the Supreme moments of her Life, He cannot bear her Burdens..." Elizabeth Cady

"It is the creative potential itself in human beings that is the image of God..." Mary Daly

WELCOME BRIGIT

OUR ALTAR

Altar cloth: Large White altar cloth, red silk scarf and some green silk scarf.
Image: Statue of the Celtic Raven haired Goddess or Saint Brigit.
Canvas art or photo of the Goddess, Ireland, Snowy Landscape, Water Wells, or photo of Flames, hearth, cauldron, Brigit's Cross.

Always present on the altar;
A cast iron cauldron, drums, speaking stick, a silver pentacle, athame, elemental representations......

Air: Bird statuary, smudge wands, Incense type sticks, cones, charcoal brisket and fine powdered herbs of Clove, Cinnamon and Sandalwood.
Fire: candle, glass enclosed candles in white, you can green as it is a Celtic color, many Red candles as can be, to light an entire room, since she is a Fire goddess and one single large candle in the center.
Water: Milk, Chalice or glass bowl with herbed Water, ice, well spring water.
Earth: Bread, Bare branches, seedlings newly sprouted, a small dish of soil and or herbs and best to decorate with floral arrangements of bare branches in red colored vases.

Other items pertinent to this particular gathering
Anvil,
Representative of a water well
A head circlet
Small cast iron cauldron or other metal piece
Glass bowl of ice/snow
Offering of Homemade Loaf of Bread
Bowl of herbed consecrated water
Or a representation of a well
Gauzy Red fabric or sarong to represent Fire
Musical instruments like drums and tambourines
Workshop items
Tarot
Pitcher of milk
A _creative project;_ Book, song, glasswork, metal art, canvas art, crochet blanket etc

Offering example food; milk, cake and a bread loaf
Sacred objects from members:
Notes:

Brigit

Brigit Altar

Handmade Sculpture of Brigit

BRIGIT (Pronounced Brid)

The Celtic Goddess of the Forge, The Fiery Goddess of Poetry and Inspiration. She is Goddess of the healing well waters and of the hearth. She is a Goddess of transformations, smithcraft, midwifery and the bard. This beloved agricultural Goddess was known by many names like; Brigit, Brigantia, Brighid, Brigid, Briget, Brid, Bride. Her name means *"the Exalted One"* and Breo-Aigit (another one of her many names) means *"Fiery Arrow."*

One story tells us that Brigit was the wife of the ruler of the Children of Danu, Bres. With him she conceived one son who was tragically killed in battle. She mourned for her beloved son on the battlefield and introduced the Celtic practice of Keening. Caoine or keening, as it is better known, was the act of sorrowful, very audible, weeping and wailing and Brigit is credited for inventing this practice when she herself lost her beloved son.

There is another known tale of Brigit being the wife of Tuirean and with him birthing three boys; Ircharba, Brian, Luchar. These three sons were said to have killed the God Cian, Lugh's father.

There are many myths about Brigit and her life. Some of these tales conflict with one another. For example, in a 10th century text she is described as the daughter of the Daghda, who was the God of the Tuatha de Dannan. In her role for the Catholic Church, as Saint Brighid, she was known to have been the daughter of a Druid, pagan priest, by the name of Dubthach. Some believe she was actually baptized by St. Patrick himself and some early Christian poetry of the time, claimed that she was the beloved, foster mother of Christ himself. According to one legend, as a young maiden, she feared her father would push her into marriage. To make herself less desirable to romantic suitors, she disfigured herself by making her eyes pop out. Supporting this story is the numerous myths regarding the eyes and Brigit's sacred well waters bringing miraculous healing to people with opthalmological disorders.

This Pagan Celtic Goddess was so beloved by her people that there was great resistance when the Catholic church tried to assert its power to eradicate Paganism across the land. Her shrines and temples were converted to Abbeys and monasteries and she was thus converted to the Christianized, St. Brighid. Her Gifts of transformation were exemplified best in this very act, as her survival all these years has come about because of that transformation. From Pagan deity, she allowed herself to be transformed into the Christianized saint and thus her devotees grew and remained throughout the decades.

At Kildare, her sacred shrine was kept and sustained allegedly, by nineteen vestal virgins tending to her sacred flame in the guise of nuns. Nineteen has thus become known as a special number associated with this Goddess. These sacred Brighid flames had been tended to for over six hundred years, but the Archbishop of Dublin, Henri de Loundes, put out Brigit's divine flames when he feared and suspected these as Pagan rites. Thankfully, in 1993 her sacred Flames were re-lit again by Sister Mary Minchin. Today her undying flames are maintained by the Brigandines, an order of Sisters of Bridget.

Brigit was known to have provided many gifts to her people. She was attributed to inventing whistling as a way to call her friends, after the death of her son. She was credited for inventing Ogham, an ancient form of writing.

Beloved as a Healer, she healed with the waters from her numerous sacred wells. At Kildare there were more than 30 known wells dedicated to her. The largest well is still in use today and famous for bringing all sorts of healing, particularly healing of eye diseases. In her myths there were many known stories of miraculous cures for all sorts of ailments at her numerous sacred wells. It was a common practice to highly decorate these special wells with ribbons and flowers and leave various gift offerings to the Goddess there; like cakes, milk and honey.

Brigit was worshipped as a triple Goddess of healing, inspiration and the forge. Her symbol was the fire, like the sacred fires of creativity and the forge, but her symbol was also of the waters, with her healing sacred wells. Interesting to note how she can rule over two such opposing elements but certainly, a lesson about balance is to be learned here. In this example, she is reminiscent of the Hindu Goddess Saraswati, who also rules over two opposing sacred elements- fire and water.

Brigit was the muse, inspiring the bard, the poet, the storyteller and the songsters. She was Goddess of the blacksmith, the glasswork creator, the artist, the sculptors, the weaver, the jewelry maker, needle worker and knitter. Brigit is a Goddess for those who use their hands to forge and create, for inherent in these skills, is the sacred act of transformation, which she rules.

This Celtic Goddess, whose sacred trees were the Rowan, Apple, Birch and Willow trees, was closely associated with the sabbat of Imbolc. Oimelc or Imbolc, was also known in its Christianized name as Candlemass. Imbolc, means, *"in the Belly"*, a reference to the Earth's potential Spring stirrings in the womb. According to the Carmina Gadelica, the Celtic Goddess, as a snake, would emerge from her wintry hibernation. She would appear slithering from the mountains or a cave, where she had been all winter long. The tale was similar to our modern custom of the male Groundhog announcing the season's status. The snake was seen as a prediction of Spring's arrival, to inform us whether the Goddess will allow Spring to arrive early or let Winter linger on. During this Sabbat, cakes were left out for the Goddess. Loaves of bread and pitchers of milk were often left at the entrances of homes, as offerings, or they were shared with neighbors to attract Brigit's goodwill and better crops for the coming season. The cross plaiting with straws from the harvest was believed to protect the home from fires and bring good luck through-out the year and they were often hung around the home and farms.

Brigit is a Goddess of great transformation, for she takes our pain and transforms them into healing. She takes ideas and transforms them into creative works of arts, like songs, art works, sculptures, poetry, stories. She transforms us at the forge and with her flames forges our soul -as metal works are transformed into smith craft, so is our soul able to metamorphosize and undergo magical transformations with her imput, guidance and blessings.

BRIGIT GROVE GODDESS GATHERING

Purpose: to celebrate the turning of the sacred wheel, as we commemorate the sabbat of Imbolc and honor the healing, Forge Goddess of Creativity-Brigit

Check ins: As we always endeavor to do, at the beginning of our Gatherings, we stand in a circle and introduce ourselves. In this introduction we will sing our name aloud and hear it immediately repeated and sung by our fellow systers.

Check Ins II: What have we been up to lately since our last gathering? And how did we experience the last Full Moon...? and our Astral spell weaving? Perhaps sharing our Lunar art collages as well.

Chanting Workshop: *"Spirits of Fire..." "Hymn to Brigit"* (see song text sheet for suggestions)

Drumming: Body works-
With music CD Drumming track, we will engage in a drumming circle that will incorporate our bodies to shake and shift energy throughout our chakras. Begin by shaking your hands before you, like you are dusting off something and shake your hands this way, passing through all of your seven centers in front of your body. Raising energy, sway and transfer that rhythmic energy into your hips, pelvic and up through your body. Let this raised energy continue to swirl, awakening your chakras and then, send out the excess to the universe and to those who may need it most. We have engaged our sacred bodies. It is done!

Connecting with the Goddess: An image of Brigit is passed around the room so that every womyn has a moment to connect with this beloved Celtic Goddess. How does she appear to you? Which one of her numerous attributes stands out, beckoning you, at this point in your life? One by one, womyn are invited to study her image and speak aloud and answer from the heart... How does she appear to us personally?

GODDESS LESSON
Learning of the Celtic Goddess Brigit, her attributes and relevance for womyn today.

GODDESS WORKSHOPS:
WORKSHOP I:
In honor of Brigit we will be crafting a traditional Brigit Cross to Bless and bring protection to our home. Using fuzzy sticks aka pipe cleaners we will meditatively create a cross and imbue it with our intention while music plays in the background *(Celtic music playing in the background)*

WORKSHOP II: MEDITATION
Invite the women to find a comfortable spot to rest and prepare for our journey and trance meditation. The **Meditation** will bring us into the Belly of the Earth as Imbolc approaches.... Use CD trance drum as background if necessary.

WORKSHOP III:
Learning a few basic crocheting/knitting stitches and imbuing our handicraft with our energy. Brigit was known as a patron Goddess to those who handcrafted and needle work was one of her gifts as well. In this workshop we will crochet or knit a basic chain to be used as the foundation of a future larger work or to save for a knot spell.

WORKSHOP IV:
Knot Spell Working. Continuing with the theme of handicraft and needlework. Together we will do a traditional knot spell. Choose a color that closely relates to your intended wish for example; Green yarn for money or fertility spells, yellow for studies or mind related spells, Red for an energy or sexual natured spell and Pink for love and friendship desires etc...The accompanied invocation for your knot spell can be found at the end of this chapter.

WORKSHOP V:
Creating a Metal or Glass offering to the Goddess (for example a metal altar tray or a Glass beaded bracelet). Brigit was known as the Goddess of the Forge and therefore beloved by Blacksmiths. In this workshop, supplies of glass and metal will be offered to serve as inspiration, so that participants may have a chance to experiment and connect with yet another aspect of the Goddess. Another option is creating a prayer necklace dedicated to Brigit, incorporating both metal and glass beads.

WORKSHOP VI:
Bardic exploration. We'll take a break from handicraft in this workshop, to tinkle and experiment with the art of the bard. Every womyn is encouraged to write a four line poem or song in honor of Brigit, the Goddess of the Bards.

WORKSHOP VII:
Crafting Homemade Candles, or carving and charging our store bought candles and imbuing them with this Fire Deity's energy and our intentions. Wax paraffin, metal candle molds, crayons to color the wax and wicks, will be needed and almost all supplies can be readily found at your local craftstore, to create homemade candles. This project might be best suited for full weekend Goddess gathering retreats, since it requires more time.

WORKSHOP VIII: Bread Baking as a community.
As is the tradition in some parts of Ireland at this time of year, we will bake together a loaf of bread (recipe found in this chapter). Participants were invited to bring ingredients from their home and together we will knead the dough and imbue in with the most positive energy to Bless us during the season of Imbolc.

REFLECTIONS ON BRIGIT
This ancient beloved, Triple formed goddess, presents to us metamorphosis and the gifts, inherently found, in our deliberate transformations. She comes into our lives to help us heal by taking our pain, acknowledging it and torching them, to manifest something even greater. In her sacred wells, we cleanse our hearts and in her forges, we are transformed, to reflect her powers of transformation. As a triple aspected Goddess she has much to offer us as we journey through the various sacred stages of womanhood. She also represents the value of those initial artistic inspiration found in our belly, those that may have come as a cathartic way to mutate pain into artistic expression. She is that fire of initial inspiration that beckons you to create, pour it out and express what is deep within your soul. With her, we are able to take our visions and forge them into transformative works that ultimately unearth our own inner healing.

BRIGIT GROVE GODDESS GATHERING RITUAL

PURPOSE: To experience Brigit's healing, inspiration and allow her fires in the forge to begin your Personal Transformation.

Anointing/purification by Brid's Healing wells. Consecrated Herbed waters offered and oil for third Eye, blessing.

Casting Circle with the ting of an Anvil as you go around the circle striking it gently as you cast the sacred circle.

Quarters
* Guardians of the Watchtowers of the **East**, Ye Powers of **Air**,
Place of breath and healing sighs, new beginnings and conceptual breezes,
We call on you to bring us your gifts
Guard and Hold our sacred space, Hail and Welcome
(attendants repeat) Hail and Welcome!!!

*Hail Guardians of the Watchtowers of the **South**, Ye Powers of **Fire**,
Place of the Hearth and burning forge, Fires of creativity, Fires found in the pit of our belly and in our soul,   We call on you to lend us your gifts
Guard and Hold our sacred circle, Hail and Welcome
(attendants repeat) Hail and Welcome!!!

*Hail Guardians of the Watchtowers of the **West**, Ye powers of **Water**,
Place of Brid's healing wells, cleansing waters that soothe and wash the slate clean,
We call on you to bring us your gifts
Guard and Hold our sacred space, Hail and Welcome
(attendants repeat) Hail and Welcome!!!

*Hail Guardians of the Watchtowers of the **North**, Ye powers of **Earth**,
Place of sprouting growth and transformation, wintry land, nurturer of our seeds,
We call on you to bring us your gifts
Guard and behold our sacred circle, Hail and Welcome
(attendants repeat) Hail and Welcome.

Invoke (see suggested Brigit's invocation)
Chanting *"We can Rise with The Fire of Freedom"*
Goddess Brid Appears:
speaks of her Gifts and instructs them to come to her sacred wells.
(See below for Goddess aspecting suggestion)

WATER ALTAR*(quiet/introspection at the altar where water bowl is available)* At the water well that heals our infirmaries. Heal yourself. Water will ask- **What do you need to be healed of? Do you know? Can you name it?** You can speak what needs to be healed aloud or simply hold the image in your mind.
After being healed by water attendants return to the circle and now visit the place of Brid's Inspiration.

INSPIRATION CIRCLE *(place of artistic celebration)* They enter and create one big circle. A Bardic circle begins with songs, someone will sing, drum, others will join in and offer poetry, jokes, dance, knit, recite verses, show off handiworks, tell tales and simply share their artistic gifts and inspiration within the circle.

When all have shared joyfully and they are ready -
Brigit will ask them to follow her to the Forge…

FIRE ALTAR: (At the Altar amidst many candles) Now that healing & inspiration has been experienced, **what will be transformed as at the Forge? What will Fire Forge you to be? What will you become?**

Attendants are invited to scry and study the fire. *** Gaze, Stare, commune with the Fire either a bonfire or a collection of flames in the center of the room. Moment of silence as all participants scry silently.

Brigit (*will tell them of her abilities to transform with her Fires*)
When they are ready, attendants will jump over the actual flame. Alternatively, hang a reddish Gauze fabric from somewhere as a symbol of fire that attendants will walk through to be transformed like at an actual Forge. We are recreating here the feeling of entering fire, entering a forge to be transformed. Participants are encouraged to state aloud who or what they'll transform at the forge, as they jump the candle flames and go through the reddish veil. Walk through this reddish Gauze fabric and become transformed by the representation of fire at the Forge then begin to sing….
Chanting: *"Brigit's Songs"*
Chanting *"We all come from the Goddess"*
Holding hands to ground, Sharing any final thoughts before devoking……

Thanking & devoking the Goddess
Healer, Inspirer Great Goddess Brigit.
We thank you for your presence here today.
Though your flames of inspiration permeate our bellies
and in our hearts you will forever remain,
for now we must bid you adieu from this space.
Receive our Thanks as we say,
Hail and Farewell Brigit!

Devoking Quarters
Earth the guardian, protecting our space,
With gratitude, we bid you adieu,
Hail and Farewell **Earth!**
    Waters of her well, your healing ebb and flow
    was constant in our circle,
    as you witness and protected our rites.
    With gratitude, we bid you adieu,
    Hail and Farewell **Water!**
Fire, your flames of protection
was felt through-out our ritual,
we Thank you -simmering cauldron of the South.
With gratitude, we bid you adieu,
Hail and Farewell **Fire!**
    Air, your gentle breezes ever present in our rites
    assuring us divine protection, we thank you.
    With gratitude we bid you adieu,
    Hail and Farewell **Air!**
******Open Circle,** with our Merry Meet Song****
Potluck Meal follows

IMBOLC BRIGIT -GROVE GATHERING RITUAL-II

Purpose: to celebrate the turning of the sacred wheel, as we commemorate the sabbat of Imbolc and honor the healing, Forge Goddess of creativity-Brigit

Asperge & Oil anointing and sharing

WELCOMING:
It is better for you to rush upon my blade than to enter with fear in your heart....
PARTICIPANTS' REPLY: *"I enter the circle in Perfect Love and Perfect Trust...."*

Circle Casting
Goddess before me, Goddess behind me,
Goddess above me, Goddess below me,
Goddess to the Left, Goddess to the right...
Together this circle is cast by our will and might.
The Circle is cast, we are between the worlds,
We stand on Hallowed ground. Let our work be blessed!!!

*Declaring the meaning of this Sabbat and <u>announcing our intent</u> in this ritual-this can be done with prose

****

<u>Elemental</u> calling as per volunteered by Participants: **Air, Fire, Water, Earth**

INVOCATION
We are your Priestess
and we endeavor to connect with you herein this moment.
We come together as sisters to honor you Beloved Goddess,
and commemorate the turning of the sacred wheel.
In this magick circle,
We welcome and honor you
and call back your ever -returning light....
BLESSED BE!!!!

Making an **Offering of Milk and Oats upon the altar for her**
MUSIC/CHANTING... *"Hymn to Brigit"*

*****INVOCATION TO BRIGIT** ****
"Hail Goddess of the Forge, Ancient Goddess in triplicate form,
Inspiring Goddess- who blesses the Bard,
Bestower of Creativity, Come near us, not far.

We call you into this sacred space,
bring your healing gifts and let us see thy face,
Around this circle, as we turn to one another,
Reflected in our systers' eyes, we see you Ancient Mother.

Goddess of transformation, Who withstood the test of time,
From pagan Goddess to the Saint,
you were Christianized.
We call you Brid, Brigit, Brigantia, the Bride
Goddess of the healing well waters,
bring blessings to our sight.

You who leads us into the depths of our soul,
bringing us to our womb and belly for here...we know...
Deep connection, quiet and still,

deep in the belly we are working our will.

In preparations for all that will bloom,
Wishes, like roses, sprouting in multitude.

May your fires inspire and gently awaken us from slumber,
May your fires Heal what needs nurturance, support and guidance
May your fires burn and transform what needs restoration and revitalization.
Fiery One, All Hails to you! Welcome Brigantia!

AFTERWARDS MUSIC: *MA -Sinead O' Connor or Enya Musical CD piece,
as we prepare to gather our supplies and consider the season and what we are about to undertake....*

As this is the season of the Maiden, let us **invoke the Maiden archetype**, here now communally. As we go around the room, clockwise, announcing aloud, our own personal view of the Maiden and her various attributes. We share aloud her numerous qualities all the while rubbing our hands together, raising heated energy and drawing her within us .... This energy once raised will be imbued into our heart chakras, then into our spell working candles.
We begin; *"youthful, energy, exuberant, buoyant, giggling, joyful, rainbow, autonomous, healthy, carefree, bouncy, virginal, pink, brave, arrow, green, fast, shiny etc..."* when the maiden energy has reached its zenith we begin our spell....

SPELLWORKING:
1. I invite you to take up your black or **darkened candle**.
This is to honor the season passing, the Crone, the Winter.
Upon this candle imbue the memory of an experience or moment you are Grateful for these last couple of months, during the Winter season.... For without Winter we cannot appreciate Spring and the brightest lights emerge from darkness, so let us honor the Dark first and foremost.
I HAVE GRATITUDE:_____
2. Now take up your melting ICE CUBES
Consider the season of Winter, with its cold winds and snowfalls. which is now passing. Look deeply at your own life and consider what is ready to thaw and melt away. Let the flame from the candle help melt the ice cube. Hold the vision of what you want to purify. Within this ice cube, imbue this vision, bid it adieu and release it....
I SURRENDER: _____
3. Now take up your white, red or green working candle and try to reflect on what's before you. Remember the lay of the land in the spring time. Remember the bright green grass, flowers blossoming and lush full trees swaying in the warm breeze. At this time of the year, what do you birth? What do you contribute to this idyllic spring scene? Project unto this future and reflect on what you see yourself creatively birthing by next sabbat.
Hold this vision in your mind, imbue it upon your candle and ignite this spark of flame.
I MANIFEST: _____

CHANT/Song: *"Mother I feel you under my Feet....."*
CHANTING as Cone of Power: *"It is done..."*

***

Devoking Elements as per participants...

Devoking Goddess, "Thank you Great Goddess for joining us today. Be with us as we go about our days during the cycle of growth....and transformation"

Giving thanks and Opening up the Circle with our traditional Chant...

*******Pot luck follows...*

*INVOCATION TO BRIGIT *
"Hail Goddess of the Forge,
Ancient Goddess in triplicate form,
Inspiring Goddess- who blesses the Bard,
Bestower of Creativity, Come near us, not far.

We call you into this sacred space,
bring your healing gifts and let us see thy face,
Around this circle, as we turn to one another,
Reflected in our systers' eyes, we see you Ancient Mother.

Goddess of transformation, Who withstood the test of time,
From Pagan Goddess to the Saint, you were Christianized.
We call you Brid, Brigit, Brigantia, the Bride
Goddess of the healing wells waters,
bring blessings to our sight.

You who leads us into the depths of our soul,
bringing us to our womb and belly for here...we know...
Deep connection, quiet and still,
deep in the belly we are working our will.

In preparations for all that will bloom,
Wishes, like roses, sprouting in multitude.

May your fires inspire and
gently awaken us from slumber,
May your fires Heal what needs nurturance,
support and guidance
May your fires burn and transform
what needs restoration and revitalization.
Fiery One, All Hails to you!
Hail and Welcome Brigantia!

TWO BAKING RECIPES FOR
BRIGIT'S GROVE GODDESS GATHERING WORKSHOP

From the Irish Soda Bread Society
IRISH BROWN BREAD
4 cups Stone Ground Whole wheat flour
2 cups White flour
1 ½ tsp Baking Soda
1 ½ tsp Salt
2 cups Buttermilk (sour milk)

Mix together the flour, baking soda, stone ground wheat, the salt.
Make the traditional well in the center of this
Pour gently the liquid/buttermilk and slowly
Knead the dough into a ball, adding more or less liquid, depending on the quality of the dough.
Knead it then Flatten it into a circle
Make a cross with knife in the center, before baking.

Bake at 425 degrees for 25 minutes
Then reduce heat for 350 degrees, baking further for 15 minutes
Take out and if the crust is too hard,
cover with a damp cloth to regain its moisture
Do not cut the bread until after it has had a chance
to cool off for six hours
   Source: "The Art of Irish Cooking" (published 1965) by Monica Sheridan

IRISH WHITE SODA BREAD
4 cups (16 oz) of all purpose flour
1 teaspoon of Baking Soda
1 teaspoon of salt
14 oz of Buttermilk
Preheat oven to 425F degree
Lightly grease and flour cake pan

Combine all dry ingredient,
Gently add buttermilk to form a dough,
Gently knead the dough on a floured surface,
Shape into a flat circle and place in a round cake pan
Cut a cross upon the top before baking,
Cover the pan with another pan in the oven
And bake for thirty minutes
Then after, remove cover and bake for additional 15 minutes

After you take the bread out of the oven,
cover it with a damp cloth to keep the bread moist.
   Source: http://www.sodabread.info traditionalirishsodabread.

IN THE BELLY-AN IMBOLC MEDITATION

Frost.... cold on the ground, frozen land under your feet and you feel the crisp piercing, cold breeze upon your skin. From where you are, you study the long bare branches from a nearby tree and survey the vast frozen landscape before you. It seems like forever since you last saw a fertile green tree. Holding this bare cold branch in your hand, you recollect the last time you saw this tree full, with bright green leaves and an array of plump berries ornamenting it's crown. It brings lively, bright images of last Summer..... and last Spring... and conjures up a vast collection of happy memorable vignettes from your past. You come back to the tree, reflecting on how full they were then, in contrast to their barren, nakedness now and how cold and stark they appear...

The more you remember about last summer and last spring, the lighter you feel and the softer the ground beneath you appears to become....and suddenly you feel its subtle shift....warming, dissolving, its metamorphosis, awakening from long slumber... Beneath you, the Earth yawns and she softens to your weight. You slightly slump and then gently sink; first its imperceptible, then it becomes more obvious, you are indeed sinking. The weight of your body upon the soles of your feet now, as you sink deeper and deeper into the earth.... Comfortably let yourself go deeper and deeper, as your legs relax into the ground that seemed impenetrable by frost, a few seconds before. Like a magnetic pull from the underside of this soil, it pulls you deeper, ever deeper still, until you are no longer above the ground, but rather underneath, submerged. Your entire body now, nestled in her womb, surrounded by the deep dark rich soil of the Earth. It's profoundly dark hues of brown and black, moist, warm, fertile soil. The air has changed and even your nose detects a different scent. Her womb cradles you now, holding you in a protective, warm embrace and here, deep in her cavern, you feel more charged and alive than ever before.

Adjusting to this new environment, you slow down your breathing and slow down the constant chatter of your mind to detect a golden silence, soon interrupted by a sound.... (pause) You start to hear a thump... A consistent faint thump....Her heartbeat or your own? or both- indistinguishable now. The sound seems to be coming from a glowing light further inside on your right. Surrounding this light, you discover the source of the thumping, it is water leaking. Trickling water, falling from above. Take this healing water, cup it inside your hand if you can. It is embryonic, uterine water from Her womb and it has the great power to heal. Place this water now, wherever you need healing, most, on your body..... (Pause)

The glowing light becomes a strong, bright flame now, after having blessed yourself with her waters. It is quite beautiful, with its orange, red and yellow hues. As you trance, deeply studying the quivering flames, you detect an inaudible murmur. The faint tone of someone's voice can be heard and it appears to be coming from this glowing light. Scry into the flames and look deeply at the shapes and images appearing before you. Listen carefully to discern what language is being spoken - for it does not initially sound like a language you are versed in. Listen now, with your whole heart and body, to translate and interpret the flame's message to you. (pause)

"Mine are the flames that bring healing, creativity and great transformation. How will you best utilize my sacred fires? (pause) What do you place in my forge of transformation? And when the snow has melted and the Earth is reborn anew, what will my fires help you manifest?" (pause)

Consider carefully your response and take this time now to share with her, your goals and heart's desire.... (pause)

From the flames, out appears the form of a woman with scarlet, long red hair. She has lovingly heard your every word and now protrusively steps out of the flame. She places her warm hand upon yours and takes you on a journey through a labyrinth. The labyrinth appears to be ascending as you walk further upwards, up it takes you, with her leading the way. Slowly you walk through the deep dark soil, crystals, minerals and waterfalls. Like a spiral upward you continue now on this journey, and the familiar uterine warmth, felt down below, now begins to feel dry and cool. (pause) Upward you continue to walk this spiral, upward with her guidance.... (pause) The air is feeling very cold now and She stops momentarily to turn to you. Deeply gazing into your eyes she has one last message for you. Listen carefully (pause), then thank her and respectfully bid her adieu.

She now opens a passage way door and invites you to walk through. You hear her say; *"For now this is the end of our journey and we must part, but you may call on me when you thirst for my healing waters or when Fire medicine is needed to create, heal and transform. Come during these sacred transitional moments in your life, when you find yourself at a threshold before embarking on change. Come during those pivotal seasonal moments, as the wheel of the year turns once more. Come when you crave and seek to rest in the womb and belly of your Ancient mother. Until we merry meet again, I bid you farewell, with peace, wellbeing, fires of creativity and love. Blessed Be...."* (pause)

Seven steps lead you upward back to where we started. Follow the sound of my voice as we return to our body and this room and this time and place.... We begin and you are called now to return. **Seven**.... Inhale and exhale, **Six**... follow my voice and return to this space, **Five**... breathe in deeply and exhale... **Four**... return here to the now. **Three**, take a deep breath in, hold and now let it all out. **Two**, return to this room and to the sound of my voice, continue breathing... **One**..... When you are ready, open your eyes and please, join us in this room....

JOURNALING -IMBOLC GROVE GODDESS GATHERING

Music played in the back ground as wommin came in through the front door of our home. From these very first tender moments, the house becomes a wommin's gathering temple. They strolled one by one and settled themselves into the space, unpacking and collecting their things and warmly greeting each other, as we always do upon seeing one another. There is always a lot of buzzing and bouncing colorful auras expressed at this time. To begin to draw them into this sacred moment, I play the chant sung by Elaine Silver, "By the Earth that is her body, by the air that is her breath..." and this beautiful chant, heard on the loud speaker, instantly drew all the wommin into the center of our space to begin our Grove day.

Our First Check ins *started with simple introductions and sharing what we've been up to since our last gathering?*

The second Check in, *we talked and briefly touched upon the last Full Moon and how we experienced this recent esbats. I talked about "Lunar Collages," mandalas and their effectiveness in attuning us to the energy of the moon and the potential for great magick in their usage. I shared my own recent Lunar Collages and encouraged them to get into the practice of doing these, as I have found them quite cathartic and a wonderful way to connect with my subconscious.*

We then started our singing and chanting Workshop. *First we started with a most beautiful teaching recording of Brigit's song by Isaac Bonewits. Using a tape recording to teach it first, we learned it quickly and sang it several times together. It was very moving and the wommin were excited to learn of a new chant to Brigit, now available to them. Then one exuberant sister suggested a wonderful chant which we sang incorporating body movement. It helped, fantastically, shift our energy and it inspire me to add more. Next I suggested a "MA" cone of power chanting, right after.*

Cone of power thru the Chakras!

Somehow we found ourselves afterwards, **talking about my beloved elder**, *Z. Budapest, the numerous foremothers of the Dianic Feminist witchcraft movement. We talked about their radical struggles in the 70's and the complacency of today's feminist or rather the realization that women's issues today are more subtle and the terrain of our war and struggles are different than those in the 70's. I reflected on that recent broadcast interview I heard, with Margo Adler, author of "Drawing Down the Moon" and the impact her words had on me. She wondered, where were the Radical wommin, radical Pagans, the innovators, the warriors, the ones who will break new grounds as her fierce generation did back in the late 60's and 70's? Her message certainly woke me up and made me contemplate on my own need to break the mold and unearth my inner warrior.*

At this point, wommin wanted **Drumming** *and some even wanted to dance and I'm not sure what we did, was what they had in mind, but it was amazing! I played a Soweto Drumming track and it manifested a powerful moment in our gathering. I got them to move- even though initially it wasn't planned. Somehow I got them to shake their hands to release and awaken their own energy and then transfer that shaking movement, energy, up through their body, through their hips, pelvic then through their own chakras. As there was plenty of energy conjured up, I asked them to share it with those, in the universe, in need of our energy, send it out as there is plenty, and then, I asked them to go even deeper, deep into the earth, share the energy with the earth and with our sacred ancestry in the spirit realm, then full circle back to us. It was intensely beautiful and I felt my whole body metamorphosing from a dull grey to the brilliance, of the Green maiden energy. The intense Soweto Drumming heard loudly on the stereo awakened all of our senses and the energy that we raised was undeniable. Intuition begged me to put this great energy to immediate use into our first spell crafting. So even though the order of the day went against what I had originally planned, I followed my intuition and brought out our crafting tools right then and there, so that we could immediately* **create Brigit's cross** *and imbue it with protective energy for our personal homes. Normally, the Goddess lecture of the day would've led right into this craft, but seeing as how we raised an exorbitant amount of energy, at that very moment with our drumming, it seemed best to pour it now into our Spellcasting. Our tools were taken out of the cauldron and we began to craft Brigit's cross with fuzzy pipe cleaners. It turned out wonderfully and many wommin were so impressed and appreciative of the opportunity to have an alternative way to create a Brigit's* cross without the traditional straw reeds. I am also really glad I am starting to learn to surrender to spirit's counsel more often in times like these, as it never leads me astray.

Plaiting Brigit's Cross

After our crafting I suggested we do our meditation, this time it would be an **underworld Meditation**. I tend to always have several meditations (pre-recorded and scripted) ready to offer the wommin at Grove and today I elected a meditation that took them to the underworld. Although, on the surface this meditation would seem more appropriate during Samhain, I really felt the need for us to connect to the underworld at this pivotal time of the year. I thought the meditation poured out of me effortlessly, the words came out clearly and I believe it was very effective. The theme of the underworld, while typically presented during Samhain or when speaking of Hekate and Persephone, worked well as we prepare to bid Winter adieu and welcome the coming of spring. I felt strongly about its appropriate nature at this time of year as we sit deep in the womb of the Goddess, under the earth, in her belly at Imbolc. The women seem to really resonate with it as well.

After wards I passed around an **image of Brigit** from the Goddess Oracle Tarot and each of us connected with this image, as I began **our lecture** portion of our day. I must admit that it was quite challenging for me to present all of Brigit's numerous folklore tales and documented mythologies. Ancient Goddesses, who have also been Christianized are very saturated with immeasurable conflicting stories and lots of tidbits and half tales as well. So, attempting to present each and every one of them made my head spin, literally, but I think I presented the gist of some important facts and I know, I offered them a lot of information to utilize for their own future personal devotional rituals to her.

<u>Ritual followed</u>

We walked procession like around to the other side of the room to make our threshold entrance, as Enya's beautiful voice played in the background. Once inside the circle formation, I lit all the votives candles around the altar and it immediately set the tone for our ritual. It created a most vivid, beautiful image that literally moved me to tears right from the start. An anointing oil was passed from womyn to womyn, as we blessed, then hugged our neighboring syster and this was quite moving to experience. Dear friends, who were so bouncy and chatty all day long, to see them now slow their pace and take the time to hug and genuinely welcome their syster into this sacred moment in time. It was precious to the say the least, and here in this tender moment we begin to cast our circle. This is an aspect of wommin gathering that you will not see often enough in large mixed open rituals. It's always beautiful to see this welcoming because among our very busy day and numerous activities, we intentionally set apart this sacred time to commune and connect with one another and the Feminine Divine.

A more formal Circle Casting followed, as I walked around the group with athame in hand, calling on all the protection from all the directions to keep us safe and bless our work. The intent of the season was read before them and then the Elements were called by Priestess volunteers within the group. They invoked the elements beautifully and some of them did it for the first time and it was wonderful. Corresponding candles were lit after and then I shared an invocation before making an offering of Milk to Brigit. This bowl of milk was passed around the circle for each woman to partake of the blessing. I then held up a sculptured image of the Goddess Brigit as I invoked her. At this pivotal point, I was hoping we could sing Brigit's new song but fearing we wouldn't remember the melody, I quickly opted instead for Celtic Music via our stereo. It was effective, as we gathered our crafting candles and began to prepare our minds for the spell. Sinead O'Connor's beautiful voice lulled us and put us in a magickal trance and when her song ended we were ready.

I looked around at everyone's face and realized that we were all so calmed and relaxed after listening to the songstress that we really needed to wake up. I looked at our candles and realized that before we could execute this spell working, and for that matter, ANY working, we would need to raise plenty of energy to give it "oomph". We had already done plenty of that through-out the day with drumming but now at this pivotal moments we needed to bring it through again. So I verbalized my thoughts on this and invited them to rubbed their hands together. Rubbing your hands together is the quickest, most effective way to raise energy, in my opinion, and as we started to do this, I remembered that this is the season of the Maiden. At the beginning of the day I had initially wanted to talk about what this looked like to us, individually but was side tracked and here I found the perfect time to retrieve the exercise. As we rubbed our *hands together to raise energy, I had everyone one by one in circle formation, state how the Maiden personally appears. What does she look like to you? Around and around we went naming her various attributes; giggling, touching her, invoking her with our words, feeling her energy surging and swirling all around us and from within. It was amazing to see myself and these women, instantaneously, manifesting the maiden within themselves. Suddenly, women that had previously looked heavy, burdened and aged, now they appeared brighter, lighter, giddier, sprightly and just plain happier... Yes, The Goddess is alive and magick is afoot in moments like these.*

When the energy was raised fully I told them to place that newly raised Maiden energy and now put it over their heart chakra and then anywhere else they personally feel they need it. Lastly, they were to put their hands over their working candles and pour out the rest of that maiden energy into their candles. In this moment of intense electric quietude we began our spell working.

Black candle lit to give thanks to the crone and the Winter now passing. With gratitude give thanks for a lesson learned or something that happened in the past winter season. Next we took the ice, everyone had to make sure they had a container for their melting ice. This ice represents that which we are ready to thaw and surrender in our lives. As the ice melted we envisioned what we surrender at this time of year before moving into spring. That was a very powerful act, to see and feel the ice melt away and hold this representation of what we personally surrender. It was moving and our hushed silence reflected the intensity of our work. Then I invited them to breathe and now move onto the spring. Project into the future and think about spring and the Maiden and upon our white candles think about what we hope to manifest when the first blossoms sprouts through the earth. I don't know why, but I found myself singing "Mother I feel you under my feet, Mother I feel your heart beat....." and I passed instruments around too and all together they joined me in this chant. We sang it over and over again feeling that energy rising. Again, there were so many other songs I could've suggested, but somehow staring at my candles, thinking of the Imbolc womb and what would sprout out of the earth in spring and then reflecting on my own spell, well... spirit just moved me to sing this particular mother song,instead of the expected maiden chant. Beautifully, they all joined in the singing without a glitch and we rattled and drummed and placed all of that passion and energy into our spell working via this powerful song. To end, I showed them how to cap a spell with the chanting taught to me by Z. Budapest, "It is done"... As it accelerated, our voices grew with intensity and the words became its own powerful Cone of Power. Spectacular!!!!

We did a final check in to see if everyone was okay before beginning our devocation. I devoked Brigit, the ladies still sitting on the ground devoked the elements beautifully. Then, it was declared that we would end our ritual the way we started our day and played Elaine Silver's song..."By the earth...that is her body..." some of us chanted with the track and some just swayed to it, while holding one another's hands and it was intense and a beautiful way to end but we didn't. We cleared the area, gathering our things placing candles on the altar etc... then with music in the background, in a procession style we went to the bathroom to dispose our ice water (that which we surrender) into the toilet. That was a cute witchy, sisterly moment, as those water droppings made an awkward sound. When we returned to our circle for the last time, we held hands and one of the ladies helped start us off into our, circle opening song, "The Circle is open but unbroken..." to fully conclude our day and open our space. So we kind of did a double opening of sacred space but considering our multidimensional working, it was most appropriate.

A yummy rich Potluck followed afterwards and we talked and ate and communed. It was so wonderful. I got very sentimental when I looked across the table and noted that some of these wommin have been with me since the very first Grove gathering and here we all are, sitting among new Grove systers as one big family. It was truly a moving day.

Acquire a piece of yarn, about the length of your arm and choose a color that corresponds best with your wish. Take your cord and bless it by all the elements before beginning your invocation. Let the smoke of your burning incense pass thru it, carefully pass it above the flame of your candle and sprinkle it with a touch of water or scented oil. Lastly, roll it into a ball and hold it tightly in your hands, warming it with your earthly essence. Invoke the Goddess to bless this tool of magick. Concentrate on your wish all along and visualize what you hope to manifest with this spell. When you see your spell actualized in your mind begin. Tie a knot on your cord for each line you recite aloud.

SUGGESTED KNOT SPELL INVOCATION

By the Knot of One,
this spell has begun

By the Knot of Two,
it will come true

By the Knot of Three,
I draw it to me

By the Knot of Four,
it opens all doors

By the Knot of Five,
it's radiating alive

By the Knot of Six,
this spell is fixed

By the Knot of Seven,
it connects with the heavens.

By the Knot of Eight,
its power is great

By the Knot of Nine,
It IS DONE and now mine...

An it harm none,
these things or better,
So mote it be....

Knot spells have been around for centuries. This one in particular is my own creation but I must give credit for the inspiration and influence of Doreen Valiente in her book pg188, "Witchcraft for Tomorrow" -Phoenix publishing, Washington, 1978, 1987

A Spell at this time of year to rededicate self to the Goddess. Prefer to do this on the Full Moon, sometimes sky clad, while drawing down her energy in the evening. Charge your white, silver or any preferred goddess candle you've dedicated for this spell with Priestess oil (See appendix). Include a bowl of water with fresh mugwort and an incense on your charcoal brisk with burning vervain, hyssop and mugwort. Upon your altar place your special tools of the craft, like your Circlet, Athame, chalice and bowl. Bless these tools using the four elements; earth from your herbs, water from your chalice of Spring water or red wine, fire from your candles, air from your burning incense.

REDEDICATIONS

*Never deserting
Watch how I bloom
After much time off
I return to you
> Goddess within
> Take your place on this stage
> Herein this ritual
> You are honored today

Let thy elements inspire
What was dormant inside
Earth, Air, Water
Fire and the Divine
> Priestess I am
> Always for you
> Crafter, weaver
> Bless what I do

Witch, Enchantress
Priestess are my name
Herein I dedicate myself
To your domain
> Crafter of Magick
> Weaver of Spells
> Student of the Goddess
> Daughter of the Moon-well

I re-enter our temple
Where love is ever abound
And open myself
To my Priestess Goddess Crown.
> I'll accept my journey
> As long as it's clear
> My calling to be
> witch and foreseer

I'll embrace my path
And the positive course
life emanates within me
Like a charging life force
> Ancient bright moon, bless my path
> And keep me mindful of the spiral dance
> Strengthen my gifts as you feed my mind
> With knowledge of magick and the sacred divine

Herein I connect
to She who is Breath
All powerful,
Ancient Wise
Full of strength
> Goddess within, take your place on this stage
> Herein this ritual, you are honored today.

BRIGIT GODDESS GATHERING SONG TEXT SHEET

ELEMENTAL CHANT
Earth my Body, Water my Blood
Air my Breath and Fire my spirit
By unknown

WAY TO THE WELL
We will never,
never lose our way to the well
of her memory
and the powers
of her living flame
it will rise,
it will rise again.....*By South African melody/words by Starhawk*

HYMN TO BRIGIT BY ISAAC BONEWITS
Oh Brigit our heart
Our brightest Queen
Cast your blessings unto us.
    We are your children
    and you are our Mother,
    so hearken unto us...
You are the Cauldron,
Now in our Grove,
Wise Woman inspire us
    Oh Fire of love
    Oh Fire of life,
    Please Brigit,
    Come to us...

SONG TO BRIGHID BY LISA THIEL
    Blessed Woman come to me
    Woman of the Fires,
    Woman of Poetry
    Blessed Woman come to me
    Woman of Healing,
    Woman of Skillful Means
Blessed woman of the land
Guide my heart and guide my hand
Blessed Woman of the streams
Guide my soul and guide my dreams
Blessed Woman come to me
Woman of the fires
Woman of Poetry,
    Blessed Woman come to me
    Woman of Healing
    Woman of Skillful Means.
    Blessed Woman of the hills
    Heal all wounds and heal all ills
    Blessed Woman of the flame
    Awaken me to renew again.

SPIRITS OF FIRE
Spirits of Fire come to us , We will kindle the Fire,
Spirits of Fire come to us , We will kindle the Fire,
We will kindle the Fire,
Dance the magic circle round,
We will kindle the fire dance the circle around (repeat)

LET ME FIND MY WAY TO THE WELL
Let me find my way to the well, (2X)
Let me quench my thirst
with the waters of the earth,
Let me find my way to the well
    Let me find my way to the fire
    Let me find my way to the fire
    In Brigit's sacred Fire,
    Let me find my heart's desire
    Let me find my way to the Fire.....*By Song and Text Diane Baker*

Mother of Darkness.
Mother of Darkness, Mother of Light
Earth Beneath the Soul in flight
Songs of love and Love of life, Guide us to our heart.....

CHAPTER SEVEN

"Everyone thinks of changing the world, but no one thinks of changing himself..." Leo Tolstoy

"Courage doesn't always Roar. Sometimes courage is the quiet voice at the end of the day, saying, "I will try again tomorrow..."
Mary Anne Radmacher

WELCOME OYA YANSA

OUR ALTAR

Altar cloth: Deep reds & burgundy altar cloth. African designed Textiles.
Image: Statue of the Yoruban, African Goddess or Saint Barbara.
Canvas art or photo of the Elemental Orisha, sacred sigils, Photographs of Thunder and lightning documented photographs. You can even have a doll or image of a fierce warrior woman, like Xena.

Always present on the altar;
A copper cauldron, drums, speaking stick, a silver pentacle, athame, elemental representations.....

Air: Smudge wands, feather bundles or bell, Incense type sticks, cones, charcoal brisket and fine powdered herbs of Angelica, Mandrake, Benzoin, Frankincense, Myrrh.
Fire: candle, a glass enclosed candles in colors of plum or burgundy, as many as can be to light the entire room since she is a Fire/Lightning Goddess.
Water: Chalice or small glass bowl with Water or red wine
Earth: Green lush Plants, a small dish of soil and or herbs. Do not have salt on your altar. Symbols of her sacred animals like the Buffalo, which she was believed to be or horses, ox and roosters.

Other items pertinent to this particular gathering
Machete or sword
Aboriginal African Face Mask
Small toy Horses or ox
Copper Pennies
Chalice of Red wine
Red and black beaded necklace
Feather bundle
Small copper cauldron or other Copper metal piece
Skull or cemetery stone hedge
Shea Butter offering dish
Copper or gold embroidery thread
Workshop items
Tarot, "The Tower Card"
A Cutting implement

Offering example food; chocolates, purple grapes, eggplants, nuts, black beans, spicy foods, Rice, Red Wine.
Sacred objects from members:
Notes:

OYA

OYA ALTARS

OYA-YANSAN, IANSA,

Her name means, "Mother of Nine" and in the Yoruban language it means: "She Tore". In Brazil they salute this Goddess with "EPI, EPA HEYI", while her Afro-Cuban salute is: "HEKUA HEY YANSA", thus, we begin our journey to Oya with this salute.
EPI, *EPA HEYI Oya-Yansa!!!!* HEKUA HEY YANSA"

Respectively known as Oya-Yansa, Iansan, Iansa and Yansa, Oya is an Elemental African Goddess, attributed with the gift of bringing sudden drastic change. She is called upon for dramatic transformations and is considered among one of the most powerful Orishas (meaning African Deities) in the Yoruban pantheon.

Oya-Yansa is a Goddess associated with the Niger River, where it is believed she originates from, but one of the most amazing fact about this Goddess is how she permeates numerous cultures and traditions. From African and Yoruban practices, to Brazilian and Candomble, her worship stretches into the Americas and Cuba, touching upon Catholicism, Voodoo and the practice of Santeria. In the Catholic religion, she is associated with Joan of Arc and Lady Candelaria. In Santeria, she is sometimes known as Santa Barbara. In New Orleans, some see her manifested as Maman Brigitte. It becomes quite evident that she is revered and embraced by numerous cultures and various religions and this substantiate her supremacy among the African pantheon.

Often portrayed holding her sword, (her Machete) for she cuts through illusions, she is notoriously known for her abilities to cut through deceit, dishonesty and injustices. She is a force of change and anywhere she is invoked, Oya clears the way for new growth. Like cutting out that which is no longer needed, she amputates that which serves no purpose and extracts the tumor growth to make wave for healing. These are just some of Oya's powerful gifts.

Oya is known to have many attributes, but is best known as an Elemental Goddess because of her connections to strong winds, earthquakes, roaring fires, omnipotent rainstorms, thunder-filled lightning and the drastic changes that natural disasters impart. As a matter of fact, all the elements (Air, Fire, Water and Earth) seem to be embodied by this all powerful African Goddess. In the howl of a strong wind, you can hear her name... Oya... She stirs and brings the winds of external and internal changes. It is perhaps why she is so easily embodied in the Tarot, Tower card, for she brings about structural changes. Tornadoes, cyclones, earthquakes, hurricane, lightning, rainstorms, thunder, fires etc... all of these Earth/natural disasters fall under her domain and naturally make her one of the most powerful Goddesses and a force to be reckon with.

This highly revered Orisha was known to have two husbands. Her first husband, Oggun, also known as Oba and Ochun, was later replaced by the warrior God, Chango, who was more suited to her fiery personality. It is often stated in the Orisha lores that she joined him in battles and together they fiercely fought side by side. While Chango is considered the lightning in the midst of heavy rainstorm, it is Oya who is the torrential rain that brings flooding and the thunder and deathly electric bolts that catapults and destroys anything in her sight.

Oya is known to be very protective of her initiates and is a beloved, patron Goddess for wommin and in particular those in leadership roles. Known as a goddess of movement, her initiates would often dance, swirling in their long wide sweeping skirts, as they do a dance, that can either invite the dead to join in or, with the simple sweep of their hands, keep them at bay. As can be expected from a Fire Goddess, she is known to be very passionate and independent and like most fire Goddesses, angers easily with a fierce temper much like the Volcanic Hawaiian Goddess, Pele. It is therefore of no surprise that she has garnered the reputation for being a warrior Goddess. Yoruban folklore claim she is a Warrior Goddess, who can sometimes even grow a beard, alluding to her great powers and strong, masculine energy. It is said *"...She puts on the pants to go into battle..."* Again, in this very patriarchal statement, there is a reference to Oya's great powers matching that of a mans' and therefore equal in strength.

Oya is also known as Lady of the Cemeteries and in New Orleans, she might take on the name of Maman Brigitte, as both Goddesses are considered guardians of the dead, cemeteries, skeletons and skulls. They were to guide the souls of the dead and brings them to the underworld. Like the ancient Goddess Hekate, this aspect of Oya-Yansa is known as a Goddess of Sorcery, Magick, intuition and the psychic arts. Thus she is a patron Goddess of Witches and beholder of ancient occult knowledge and the Magickal arts. Some of her other numerous titles are Lady of the Masks, as they were sacred to her and Lady of the Market, for she will always find you a good deal when shopping. Her energy is often described as swirling prevalently in the market place, in the midst of haggling and in the, fast- paced act of sale pitches. In the act of procuring the best deal for your money, Oya is ever present. She is also titled as, Lady of the mind, because of her great intellect and shrewd business sense. It is said she can impart genius and great memory or toil with you with the curse of insanity.

According to Yoruban cosmology, she is considered to be one of Yemaja's daughters, although it is best to never invoked them together in rituals, as they have quite a volatile history and some animosity towards each other. Some of this has to do with her philandering husband, Chango, but there are numerous other tales. According to Yoruban Lore, long ago Oya, first ruled over the Ocean and thru trickery, the Mother of all the Gods and the sea, Yemaja, managed to trick Oya into relinquishing her Ocean Realm, in exchange for the Cemetery, she now rules over. Thus this aspect of her as ruler of the cemetery is probably not one fully embraced by Oya, but there are varying opinions on this.

Oya is indeed a powerful Goddess and there are many ways to begin working with her energy. Perhaps begin by calling her, on her special day -Wednesdays and incorporate her favorite number -nine. To honor this Goddess, offer her special ritual masks, sharp machetes and swords, and anything made of copper, like pennies and copper cooking pots. Her favorite colors of maroon, purples and reds can also adorn an altar or shrine for her and she will always appreciate jamming, drumming session with lots of frenetic, ecstatic dancing. Beware though, Oya detest smoke, palm kernel oil, ram and pork, but eggplants, grape, wine, gin, rum, kola nuts, roosters, hen, porridge, fruits, fish, anything spicy are all sacred to her and a most appropriate offerings for this powerful Yoruban Goddess.

OYA-YANSA- IANSA- GODDESS LECTURE NOTES

- Yoruba African Goddess. Oya means "She tore" in the Yoruba language.
- Goddess of the Niger River
- Worshipped in Africa, Brazil, Cuba, Haiti, New Orleans etc…
- Her name also means "Mother of Nine"….(she had Egungun and four sets of twins…)
- She is Winds of Change, Structural change, Known as a Weather Goddess
- She destroys Outworn structures, sweeps away debris making room for new growth.
- Goddess of Transformation
- Unpredictable,
- She can be as a gently breeze upon your skin or as destructive as the winds of a hurricane
- Lightning, Torrential rain storms with her tears
- Cyclones, Tornadoes, hurricanes, earthquakes her domain,
- Strong Storms , Fast paced movement,
- Fast paced energy of the marketplace,
- Patron of Woman leadership
- Wild Woman, Amazon,
- Protector of Women
- She is the power of Feminine leadership
- Mistress of Masquerades
- Fiercely independent
- Shrewd Business Woman
- Queen of the Marketplace
- Goddess who Can impart Great intellect /genius or Insanity
- Library/ Den in your house should be dedicated to her
- Speech is her domain
- Her Symbol is the Machete or Sword and she Cuts thru illusions, to get the truth
- She is Justice Seeker
- Fierce Warrior Goddess, fights with Chango her 2nd Husband, 1st husband was Ogun.
- She is Known as the one who grows a beard and puts the pants on to go to war.
- As a Goddess of Movement, Loves to Dance and those who she possess do a special dance.
- Like Celtic Goddess Brigit with her association with Fire and water thru her Niger River and thunder and lightning rain.
- Like Athena, She is armed and helmeted to fight injustices and is associated with Wars, Air, intellect, swords.
- Like Hecate affinity to the dead and Sorcery and the magical arts
- Like Maat with her dedication to injustices, exposing deceits and dishonesty
- Like Voodoo Loa, Maman Brigitte, Guardian and Keeper of the Cemetery and the newly dead.
- She is Lady of the Cemetery… She lead the spirit of the dead. She can call forth the spirit of the Dead or hold it back.
- Grim Reaper association.
- She was known as the Buffalo before she came to have human form.
- Associated with the Dark Moon and the planet Uranus

- Her day is Wednesday
- Her number is Nine
- Copper is her metal
- Burgundy, Reds, Browns, purples, Burnt orange are her colors
- Eggplants, Plums, chocolates, red wine, roosters, hens, goats, bean fritters, fish, kola nuts,
- Shea CocoButter, Buffalo Horns, fruits or anything spicy are appropriate offerings,
- Taboos: Smoke, palm kernel oil, ram and Pork.
- Saints associated with her are; Santa Barbara, Catherine, Theresa Dymphna, Joan of Arc, our Lady of Candelaria (whose feast day is like Brigit's -Feb2nd)
- Oya is therefore honored on Feb 2nd but also on her Feast day-December 4th.

- ***She is said to be the daughter of Yemaja- Yemaja being the mother of all --But you cannot invoke both goddesses together because of a love rivalry. Chango her husband, was like Zeus with infidelity issues and at some point he was a lover of Yemaya and her Sister Oshun, according to some of the oral Yoruban myths.

HEKUA OYA
EPI HEY YANSA

Oya Grove Goddess Gathering

Purpose: To honor OYA, the Yoruba Goddess of Drastic Change.

Check Ins: We gather around within a circle and introduce ourselves, while also voicing what we happily relinquish at this time of the year.

Chanting: *"Hekua Hey Yansa Chant", "She Gathers her Daughters," "I am Magick Woman,"* (see song sheet)

Drumming: A drumming musical CD track will be played, to give participants a chance to connect and ground to this very moment. They are invited to find a comfortable seat or stand and add movement, however they are most inspired by the drumming.

Agreement: We go around the circle reading a few lines each, of our Group Agreements and add any new ones that seem necessary. Agreements are signed and submitted in confidence.

Check Ins: Reflect on The Tower, tarot card and individually unearth its personal message to us. What does the Tower Card mean and how does it relate to Oya?

LECTURE ON THE GODDESS:
Discussing the Yoruban Orisha, Oya. Gathering information about her history, her numerous folklores, when to invoke her best, her relevance to wommin and some information on her traditional worship.

GODDESS WORKSHOPS
WORKSHOP I: A discussion on the Indigenous use of Sacred Masks in Rituals and its potency and effectiveness in sacred space. We endeavor to create our own African masks. Using plaster of Paris strips and either a face mold or a mirror and our own faces, we will create an aboriginal mask. Later on, if time permits during our day, we will paint, decoupage, varnish and decorate them with special sigils.

WORKSHOP II
Another workshop utilizing mask, we will decorate, store bought simple eye masks with words/emotions that we wish to abolish at this time. These masks will later be incorporated into our special Oya ritual.

WORKSHOP III: The use of percussive instruments, like maracas, is very prevalent with indigenous cultures. In this workshop we will create our own personal percussion instrument like a shaker or a maraca, using gourds, dry beans, rice and pellets. We will also take the opportunity to decorate them to our personal taste, charge and bless them.

WORKSHOP IV: Creating mini Ancestral Shrines for our deceased loved ones. Briefly speaking on Oya's other aspect as, "Goddess of Cemeteries." We will take this time to honor our ancestors with a small shrine with a recycled, decorated box.

WORKSHOP V: A Meditation Offering is presented or we gather around for storytelling time as one of Oya's lore is read aloud.

WORKSHOP VI: Discussion on the many potent usage of Athame, swords and daggers in Ritual Spell workings. If possible we can rededicate, charge and bless our tools.

WORKSHOP VII: With music playing in the background, we will have a chance to contemplate on what needs to be severed in our lives. Take a good hard look at the cancer that is festering, what is causing disease in your realm?, What has the potential to completely destroy, if we don't do something about it at this instance. Write it down on a sheet pf parchment paper. Write down what needs to be eradicated from your life? Then together around the smoldering cauldron we will state aloud and surrender our written words and ask Oya to burn these things away. An it harm none and for the greater good of all, so mote it be! We release what needs to be.

WORKSHOP VIII: An image of Oya is passed around the room, as each participant states one word that immediately comes to mind upon seeing her image, what does she conjures in us?

WORKSHOP IX: Percussion instrument will be made available so that together we will create an actual **Drumming Circle**. One syster begins rattling her maracas, then another will add the sound of the tambourines and then others will join the cacophony with various drum beats, until we slowly begin to synchronize our rhythmic pattern and the energy is raised to ideal levels. This is a fun workshop that experiments with energy raising skills.

Preparing for our upcoming Ritual to Oya.

REFLECTIONS ON OYA-IANSA

Do not fear this powerful Orisha, wommin, for she is the spirit of severing the old and outworn, the spirit of Drastic change. She gifts us the power to take down old beliefs and outworn structures that no longer serve us well and quite possibly, might do us more harm than good to hold on to. She comes into your life, armoring you with courage to honestly assess your situation and essentially clean house. She is the warrior Goddess who mercilessly, and without hesitation, amputates with one slash of her "machete," cutting out that which does not serve well anymore. Whatever is sickly, diseased, causing pain or useless, gets severed and wiped away. As wommin we need not fear this process but rather run to embrace its liberating sovereignty. Oya's gift to us can be seen as cathartic and almost downright crucial…. for even the most beautifully, fertile growing plant will, at some point, need to be cut and pruned, in order to maintain its health and guarantee even greater potential for growth. And so it is for us as wommin. Oya's message to us is indeed very powerful. Unapologetically, She says good riddance, and helps wommin clear the house and starts anew with courage and the heart of a warrior.

OYA GROVE GODDESS GATHERING RITUAL

Purpose: To honor the Yoruban Goddess of Drastic Change and willingly cut off and amputate that which no longer serves us well.

Asperge and Purification. The Cast iron cauldron will have herbs of Angelica, Frankincense and Myrrh burning as purifying incense. The swirling smoke will gently cascade around the room and its inhabitants.

Anointing: Each participant will receive **anointing oil** upon their third eye with a traditional wiccan question.

"...How do you enter this sacred space?" asks the gatekeeper.

Participant contemplates and when ready, answers; *"In perfect love and perfect trust."*

Circle Casting

With Sword I conjure this magick sphere,
outside of space, outside of fear
For love is all that shields us here
Bright lights to quell the baneful and weird.

Upon this Sphere, this Circle is cast,
Keep evil at bay, let kind spirits pass.
No more a room, but your Holy Space
To worship and invoke, your essence and grace

Container, Preserver,
all within thee
this circle is cast,
SO MOTE IT BE!

Quarters Called communally,
as each womyn will face the corresponding direction and all will call and invite the elements, making the respective **"sounds"** we personally associate with that element. For example; when calling Water, we face the West and perhaps a stream of giggles or audible sobbing is heard from participants.

Welcome Water.

For the Eastern invocation, it might stir in the sounds of Winds, fans, helicopters or chirping birds.

Welcome Air.

Facing the South, we call in Fire, with shrieking sparks, higher pitched shrieks, the sounds of crakling fire, or firecrackers, sharp darting sounds and or movements.

Welcome Fire.

As we face the North, the element of Earth, there might be loud pounding on the ground, thumping or low moaning sounds of a birthing mother, or growling, deep moans of animals, or sounds we believe are deep inside the Earth

Welcome Earth.

Chanting: *"Let it in, let it flow"*

Legba Rum Offering:

We call on Legba to open the way so that the Orisha may bless us with her presence during our working.

Blessed Legba,
We are at your sacred doors,
Let us in!
Open the passageway, most holy one,
so that we may greet her,
our beloved Orisha, Oya.
Open the Way so that we may visit
even if only for this short moment.
We bring you offerings of Rum
to connect us as alliances,
that we are working together, in harmony,
while in this spirit realm.
In gratitude for the open gates, Blessed Be and Thank you!

Oya's chant: *"Hekua Hey Yansa"*
INVOCATION TO OYA-COMMUNAL CALL
(see invocation sheet)

Intent of Ritual Spoken: *Oya is the mistress of masks, at this point in our ritual She invites the wommin to take up their masks and machete/athame/sword. She asks you to put on your masks, which will have handwritten attributes that you'll surrender and relinquish at this time. Participants are invite to grab their masks and their swords and one by one, stand in the sacred center, surrounded by the remaining sisters.*

Ritual, Music...and Pantomime Working

<u>Masks will say what we willingly surrender like:</u> Shame, Pain, Loneliness, Guilt, The Past, Weakness, Ugliness etc...,
Wearing our masks, Contemplate on the change you want to create, what needs to be cut off, what will Oya help you cut off with your Machete?... Have this thought clear in your mind for at any point you will need to take up Oya's sword to defend yourself.
Each womyn Standing in the center with sword, will take the Stance of a Warrior Goddess, ready to defend herself...
The other wommin will swarm, humming, wearing their masks, representing ALL that will need to be cut off. Making the movement/pantomime, center womyn will cut them off, proceed to defend self until they've moved away.
End by lighting your candle at the altar,
That flame will represent your achieved goal, after the Mask-battle is fought.

When all wommin are finished with this exercise, **Chant as we sway:**
"She changes everything she touches and, everything she touches change..."

GROUNDING:
Sit in the circle now, ground and talk about the exercise- make sure all are well, communicating and grounded, after such an intense ritual. *(Pass along chocolate, grapes or something sweet to help with grounding...)* Prepare to Devoke...

Hold each other's hands as we **sing**.... *"We all Come from the Goddess..."*
Begin Devoking and thanking the energy of the Goddess. See **Oya devocation** page...
Then **Devoke Legba**

Legba, Gate Keeper.
We thank you for allowing this sacred communion,
to take place today.
You heard our call and opened the doors
With gratitude, we call you once more.
Let all return to their rightful place
We bid thee adieu from this ritual space.
Thank you , Hail and farewell Legba!
*****

Thanking and Devoking the Elements
Earth , Fire, Water and Air,
we thank you for your presence in this ritual affair,
as ye was called and arrived in peace, depart in peace .
With gratitude we bid thee adieu,
Hail and Farewell, Earth , Fire, Water and Air........
****

Opening the Circle,
with the sacred song while walking counterclockwise....
"By the Earth that is her Body, by the air that is her breath..."
**Potluck begins*
*

SHARED INVOCATION FOR OYA INTO OUR CIRCLE

Each participant in the circle reads an attribute to help invoke Oya communally.

1. BELOVED OYA
Twirls and Swirls... I hear your name in the howls of the Winds.

2. GODDESS OF THE STORMS
In the gentle breeze or the Harsh relentless winds I feel your essence.

3. MOTHER OF NINE:
We are your daughters, Come to us, Teaching us your ways of Sorcery and Magick.

4. WARRIOR GODDESS
Shield us- Protect us -Strengthen us in battle, when we need to call forth on the Warrior Goddess within.

5. QUEEN OF THE SWORD
Let your Sword cut through illusions and deceit to help us see clearly the truth in all situations.

6. MISTRESS OF THE CEMETERY
Keeper of our ancestor's spirits....With our last breath on this Earth, may you guide us as you did upon our first breath as Newborns.

7. QUEEN OF THE MARKETPLACE
You who always finds us great deals. May your gifts of Great intelligence and shrewd business sense be with us now and always.

8. LADY OF THE WINDS
Let your Winds destroy, and sweep away THAT which does Not Serve us any longer.

9. GODDESS OF TRANSFORMATION
Ease us into Positive Change and like the Alchemist, may we be transformed into our most positive Authentic selves....

We honor and Welcome you now OYA-
Hail and Welcome!!!!!

DEVOKING OYA

Warrior Goddess,
Strong and true
Revealing your strength
and your love too.

You came to us Goddess
when you were called,
Oya's energy
felt by all.

We thank you for your lessons
of Courage and Truth,
the Swords you placed in our hands
When we sought to know you.

The energy that transforms us
after all is cut away,
The Knowledge and Comfort
that the Goddess doesn't Stray.

Within us we'll cherish
that portion of you,
Receive our Thanks Oya
as we bid thee Adieu............

Hail and farewell Oya Yansa...

All say.... Hail and farewell Oya Yansa...

Executed and created during the Waxing Moon,
at its most potent as tomorrow is the FULL MOON.
I sang her name continuously and felt my voice with much power, beauty and strength....

A PERSONAL PRAYER AND RITUAL TO OYA YANSA

Long have I loved you
Long have I sensed you near me,
Long have I felt you- sometimes within me, sometimes like a shadow near me.
You and I, we've journey together for quite some time now.
Long have I known you -yet never by name
How you patiently waited for this day when I would learn of your name and call you properly... Hekua Hey Yansan....Oya-Yansa-Iansa....
And take on your name as mine own.
I look to you and see that missing piece of my ancestry and lineage. You open the door to my family...you are my family.
I humbly call on you.....

We have many things in common beloved Yoruba Goddess...our love of Roosters, eggplants, black beans and white Rice, red wine and dark chocolates....
I begin this ritual, as one of many, to simply give honor to you, beloved Orisha.
Receive my offerings the first of many...

Herein I offer some items that we both seem to enjoy, dark chocolate, the silky lotion of Shea Butter, nine copper pennies, a necklace of red and black beads which I made a long time ago and now I realized it was made for you, delicious Black Cherry dark burgundy and Blood Red candles blessed with Hyssop and Courage oil, tiny toy horses and machete to represent your beloved symbols....

While others may fear you and run from you...I see ALL of you, your beauty, power and strength and in that strength I see Great beauty.... It holds me in a trance of deep infatuation. Oh my love for you goes beyond this time and place -for we have known each other long before my birth...we have met in previous lives and you have been loved by me through the ages.

Beloved Oya-Yansa-Mother of Nine take me on now as yours. Your strength and protective powers of a Mother are unmatched. You and I know that all too well.
I beseech you to take me on now as your daughter that I may receive your teachings with patience, love and firmness. That you may guide me gently and come to me as Mothers always do with compassion, gentleness and patience

OFFERING:

I humbly make my offerings to you and light this flame. With this light I welcome your energy. I call on you to bring me your Courage & Strength.

To help me in the role as Priestess in this group "Grove of the Feminine Divine", Strengthen and protect me as a Spiritual Leader for women.

Let your winds sweep in the right people into my life and the right opportunities so that I may prosper in your name.

Warrior Goddess, with the physique of an Amazon, I seek to embody your sculpted physique, strength and good physical & mental health.

Lady of the Sword I seek your Powers of intellect to awaken my mind during my research, writings and studies, bestow me with the gift of great memory & intellect. Bless me with success in my writing & publishing pursuit.

Bless me with Clarity of mind, thinking clearly. Help me to cut through illusions, delusions and deceit. Help me cut the bull, be able to see the truth. Seeing right through deceit to discern with clarity your path. Oh Lover of justice be by my side, Oya.

You know the trials and tribulations of the wife. The one rightly suspicious of her mate, the married wife and her challenges. Queen Oya -Yansa help and strengthen me in my role as Wife.

Known as a Shrewd business woman I call on you to imbue me with money and abundance, that I may finally attain independence and financially be able to stand on my own two feet!

Gingerly tear what does not serve me well, so that I may rebuilt even stronger Structures that are more successful, positive and more effective for me.

Teach me your ways of Sorcery and Magick, the secrets of the psychic arts, Enchantments and spell workings, teach me my lineage, voodoo, stregheria , witchcraft, invocations and magick...

Lady of the Cemeteries, Guardian of the dead, Teach me the dance that pushes and keeps the dead spirits away and is able to invite them or keep them at bay as I will it. Let us dance by the graveyard under moonlit nights.

With your winds, sweep in the right opportunities
Wake me,
Shake me,
and Wake me up to see those opportunities

Let me NOT stay stagnant, Shake me and awaken me to opportunities that you offer and continually stir me in the right directions, Beloved Oya. Help me to see and seize opportunities, as they come before me.

Mother of Nine, you know the love and protective powers of the Mother. Kindly take me into your bosom as your own. Take me in as your daughter and gingerly teach me your ways all the while protecting me fiercely from harm.

Gentle... Gentle with me Beloved Oya...let your winds of Courage and Positive Change Come with ease..... Hekua Hey Yansan.....
So mote it be....

***Light Nine votive or pillar candles
surrounding her image on the altar
along with her traditional offerings....***

OYA and Tower card, Goddess Gathering - Grove of the Feminine Divine

This month, She comes in the form of the Tower card from the Tarot. She presents herself as the Goddess of Transformation and swirling, drastic Change. As the one who pulverizes, knocks down, tears down, strips you bare, amputates, so that new growth can manifest in its place and ultimately catapults within us - transformations. As the wheel turns once more and we transition into a new season, we face yet again, the unknown, the unforeseen... but also, the great hope and anticipation that Spring always brings. I am writing this as our nation witness a historical monumental newly elected President, the first African American President and one who is a stauch advocate for Change, it becomes quite obvious that we, collectively, are indeed facing a major Universal turning point here.

It also becomes quite apparent that change **NEVER** comes with ease. No matter how much we may say we want it and no matter how ready we think we are willing to embrace it.... change never comes without great upheaval of some sort. Think how often we are paralyzed in mid pursuit of our dreams, as we contemplate the change requirements and consequences of our fulfilled dreams. To move to a new house, requires you to sort thru, pack up the old and temporarily live with messy moving boxes. It also requires embracing the stress of catapulting already set routines and a temporary welcome to disarray and chaos. To find new employment requires a surrendering of the old and familiar, previous routines, of an old job. To find new love might require you to completely revamp, strip down the old you or strip away the old expectations and false ideals that do not serve you best in this pursuit.

Think of how often we wish to manifest something Great but fail because of our **Unwillingness** to voluntarily Change. Think of examples like: wanting to be twenty pounds lighter, but unwilling to modify eating and exercise habits or wanting to quit smoking, drinking, other substances, but unwilling to go thru the inevitable painful withdrawals. Think of those times when we wanted a new circle of friends or lover, but were too scared or unwilling to leave the house or change our comfortable routines. Think of those times when we can no longer deny our true life passion and yet, to change careers and surrender what you've become accustomed to, becomes almost unfathomable. Those life passions, then, just get regulated to being lived only in the mind, due to the unwillingness to place effort and the discomfort of new training and new education....yes, the list goes on and on, of the many ways we turn away from the cathartic powers of change. No matter how much we may want something new and no matter how many spells we do, what we want most, cannot manifest itself until we are willing to surrender to the Change it requires of us individually.

Last Month, we called on Nike to guarantee our Success. We voiced our goals and aspirations for the New Year. We looked at the World Tarot Card which always denotes completion, success and accomplishment of our Goals when it appears in a tarot spread. This month we bring our attention to The **Tower Card** and honor **Oya-Iansa**, the Yoruban Goddess of Change and Transformation. A Goddess mostly associated with Storms, Fires, hurricanes and brutal winds that sweep away anything in its path. ...Oh, but how she is so much more.....

We will learn of her Powers and how we need not be intimidated, nor fear them, but rather embrace all that she has to offer and tap into this great power available to us. I hope many of you will join me.

I quietly sit here and muse, wondering what Changes are being asked of me at this moment?

Where have I become too complacent and imprisoned by my own comfortable sets of routines? _____

How has fear of the unknown, stifled change and any chance of my personal growth?
_____

Where and how will the Tower card of the Tarot, manifest itself in my life?
_____

What will OYA destroy but transform and rebuild in our lives now, as we approach Spring? _____

    You see, I am all too well aware that for the Fool's Journey, the Tower is encountered early on, it precedes the much beloved World card. And as we all know, the World Card and Success, comes at the end of said long journey, for the Fool.
What Changes must we face and welcome now, on our own personal journey towards the World Card and in preparation for the Success Nike Guarantees?
_____

    Last month when we invoked Nike -The Goddess of Victory- We held our Future Success in our minds, our hearts, and in our hands as the World Card. This month We will invoke Oya-Yansa, the Goddess of Change and Transformation and see some of her attributes exemplified in the **Tower card** from the Tarot. Drastic change in our values and beliefs are represented in this card. Something is being destroyed and shaken down. Change is evitable and our inner landscape will never be the same, when this card appears in a spread and thus it is the same with Oya's formidable entrance.

    Change doesn't always arrive quietly, nor neatly, nor the way we might fantasize or envision it. Oya's presence can be felt when we look at how, sometimes, the most monumental cathartic changes come drastically and unexpectedly. It often has a way of disrupting our comfort zone, challenging that which we revere and have become accustomed to (like all those cherished little habits- good or bad- we hold on to). Warrior Goddess Oya does not come pristinely, nor painlessly but.. neither does Transformations of any sort.

    I invite you to contemplate on Change and Transformations. Gaze into your own Tarot, <u>Tower Cards,</u> and think about what changes have you been avoiding and how might you be willing to surrender to them now.....
Blessings on the Fool's journey....)O(

A Summer Amidst Change

I remember the Summer of 2007. Up until then, it was a grueling year of struggling to manifest great changes in my life, breaking molds and taking leaps of faith. And then, finally attaining success, needing to adjust to it and welcome the trillions of blessings that were coming my way rapidly.

Our house had been placed on the market at the very beginning of the housing slump (little did we know it would get far worse) and the house was not selling as fast as we had hoped- creating, not only stress, but self doubt about our big plans. My husband and I had enough of the East Coast stress; the hustle and bustle, financial strains and cold climates in the Winters. After giving birth to my third and last child, I personally was hoping to raise my boys in a more idyllic setting. San Antonio, Texas, seemed to fit the bill just right. We learned a great deal about San Antonio through HGTV shows, that featured it's larger homes and beautiful properties. We also were educated by the Montelongo's show called "Flip this House", which we watched religiously every weekend. Suddenly, a seemingly big dream became a possibility. The universe seemed very supportive of it too and we pushed forward to make it a concrete reality. There were numerous obstacles and stressors, some anticipated and some unexpected, but by the time August came around, it all seemed like a distant memory. We were unpacking, settling into our new home and acclimating our New York selves, and the little ones, into Texas Living.... And as the old saying goes, *"the dust was finally settling down..."* and all was good.

Back in Long Island, New York, I was a bona fide hermit...A non-driving housewife, a stay at home mom, birthing three boys (two were like twins-17 months apart) and a newborn in 2006. Money being very scarce, with only the husband's source of income, I had no vehicle, nor access to a fully functional computer, nor internet and looking back now, I don't know how I survived!!! Those days really felt like the dark ages, as I stayed in my dungeon, catered only to my small children and husband, crafted and crochet to keep myself sane sometimes and spent my days without any outside adult interactions- which is quite easy to do when you have no extended family, like me. Slowly I had resigned myself to being a solitary and surrendered to the isolation.

Imagine how my world was instantaneously opened, when I plugged in our first computer here in Texas and hooked onto the internet...BANG!!! All of a sudden I was connecting with others who had similar interest and who shared my belief system. I was learning about all kinds of womyn spirituality groups, which I had been heavily involved with before marriage, back in New York City, but upon marrying, I found myself willingly relinquishing these connections. It seemed like I tried to replaced human connection with my continuous love of books on the subject during my Hermit years. I was only now catching up with my life, after eight years of Hermit living.

One night, I discovered "Youtube" and came across Z. Budapest and her Goddess Gathering series, taped in Austin, Texas. She had always been one of my favorite authors on Woman's Spirituality. I had all of her books and often referred to them throughout the years; both when I was a young witch maiden and during my solitary days as a married Hermit. It was amazing to watch someone I had admired and loved all these years, now in the privacy of my own home on my computer screen, late at night when I should've been sleeping. Oh the joys of discovering "YouTube....!"

After the initial thrill came the pangs, however.... I felt a strange, unexpected pang in my insides, a feeling like I had been missing out on something crucial and vital to my very own wellbeing all this time. It was then that I noticed the hunger rising within me, and a deep part of my neglected soul, craving to be whole, made itself known. I craved to actually be there in that circle of wommin, in Z's presence, worshipping the

Goddess. *"One day..."* I said to myself, as I always do and I continued looking around the internet, exploring the overwhelming landscape of this brand new intergalactic, techno world.

I decided to look up another one of my beloved Womyn Spirituality Author's, Shekhinah Mountainwater. It was always my intention to one day, contact her, meet her and maybe scrounge enough money to take a workshop with her or something. Imagine my devastating surprise to learn right then and there that she had been struggling with Cancer and loss her battle to the disease on August 12th 2007. I sat there, jaw wide open, dumbfounded, staring at the computer monitor in complete disbelief and then, within seconds, a stream of tears and painful sobs followed. I still get choked up at this devastating realization of her untimely death. I didn't sleep that night and I mourned her death as if she was my very own relative because indeed she (like a handful of Wiccan and Goddess Spirituality Authors) had become my family, especially during those lonely years as a stay at home mom. I cried and still do at the thought I will never get to meet her, work with her, thank her, the way I had always dreamed I would.

When I learned of the Z. Budapest 2008 Goddess Gathering, something clicked inside of me -well, more like ROARED.... There was no way I was going to let this opportunity pass me by, especially since it was being advertised as Z's last festival and there was no way I was going to experience a repeat of the painful remorse I felt after hearing of Shekhinah's death. I saved my pennies literally. Slowly, I convinced my husband and family that this was a matter of life and death and I needed to do this for my own wellbeing and indeed it was. I needed to step outside of the self -imposed hole I had been hiding in all these years. I needed to connect again with the me who was, before marriage and children started to chisel and define me. I needed to get back to me, the core of me, which had been supported all along through the writings of Z. Budapest and Shekhinah Mountainwater. I needed to come up...come up for air and breathe life into myself....and celebrate that tiny spark of life and maiden energy, that had emaciatedly remained and was only now beginning to take form, once more.

It has only been a month since the Gathering has come and gone and indeed it was a transformational event for me. It was amazing and the highlight of my year. I can breathe a sigh of relief now knowing that I have met, worked with and was initiated by my Beloved foremother, Dianic author of Woman's Spirituality- Z. Budapest.

It was a remarkable experience to be swept up in the wave of the Goddess movement but even more monumental is the realization that I am now an intrical part of "Herstory." And to think it all started with that one pebble upon the water, the welcoming of change and the continuous surrendering to its power. One day... one day, a woman somewhere in the world will find herself much like I did, alone late at night with pangs for something ancient and familiar. She will be exploring the internet, maybe come across a new "You tube" video of Z. Budapest and this time, the 2008 Goddess Gathering, and she will feel the urgency I felt that night and the gnawing call from the Divine Feminine. Somehow it warms my heart and gives me great pleasure to know that I was a part of that energy and now, it may bring healing and transformation to someone out there, as it so strongly did for me.

My move to the South West has been life altering, at times challenging, forcing me to just flow and perfect my dance with *"She who brings Drastic change."* It brought about a ripple of magnanimous new changes in my world and after a long winding road, I find myself part of the human race again, alive, reborn, transformed, reclaiming my inner spark for change, among Goddess Systers and the Great Feminine Divine.
Blessed Be....

Journaling Grove Gathering; Lady of Transformations, Courageously Invoking the powers of Oya

This for me was one of my favorite, most powerful, Grove gatherings. Perhaps because I've been so intimately connected to Oya in ways that surpass human understanding. I mean, I feel this Orisha, not just in the present tense, but in a timelessness that links us to so many reincarnations ago. I feel a deep ancestral nexus that make us part of the same sacred pantheon and that might seem weird for some to understand, but Oya feels like my "momma." It is that rare, soul familiarity that makes my approach to her so comfortable and thus a presentation of her, to Grove, enjoyable.

Our day with Oya, according to my observations, manifested in some long lasting, jolting effects and stirred every womyn present and that is to be expected, when you do powerful ritual work with a Goddess of her caliber. Ironically not every woman shared in my sentiments for Oya, you know, she's garnered quite a misunderstood reputation for being a feared, brutal relentless force that can swallow one whole and bring terrible destruction in an effort to birth transformation. To my surprise, not everyone is on the path of spiritual enlightenement and not everyone is seeking "kick ass" transformation in their lives. As a matter of fact, it saddens me to realize that some people prefer the state of ignorance, denial, suppression and false sense of safety- opting never to even attemp at opening closed doors in their psyche. So, for those who champion the mantra that, " ignorance is bliss" or who prefer to stay put and live in stagnant waters, Oya can be downright frightful. What she brings to the surface on the psychic level, can scare some people, if they are not ready for change. It can take some womyn off guard and it can bring up issues that they would rather not face and conveniently suppress.

Despite theses revelations, I cannot ignore Oya's cathartic, transformative powers for us as wommin, moreover I cannot discount her enormous contribution as another significant face of the Feminine Divine. There is great value in working with such a powerful deity and as wommin, it behooves us to put aside our fears and open ourselves up to her energy.

I loved working with Oya during this Grove gathering, and relished every morsel of insight she blessed me with. Some womyn, right from the very start of our Grove day expressed great trepidation and reluctance and clearly did not share in my enthusiasm for Oya. I don't know if there was a racial or cultural barrier influencing their opinion. I think, for whatever reason, there was a lot of fear of Oya and her legendary powers of destruction and transformation. I realized then, that while I was wholeheartedly able to embrace Oya and all that she entails (both negatively and positively), this was not a Goddess, women (or at least the women who were in attendance that day) could identify with or sadly, even want to encounter. She begs you to tap into your own powers and reclaim them for yourself. Wielding a machete, going into battle, growing a beard, knocking down eddifices, amputating the cancer and sweeping away cherished value systems, I suppose it can be intimidating for some wommin, especially if they were hoping for someone else to do all that work for them.

For me, I relished everything about Oya, feeling an ancestral connection to her. I felt her presence guiding me through-out the day and it effortlessly matched up to my initial planned outline and visions for our gathering. I felt totally confident and on top of my Priestessing. As a Goddess who blesses the work of a leader, I felt her unwavering guidance. Perhaps my great love and reverence for this Goddess made it super easy for me to conduct, what I believed to be, a successful gathering, honoring her. However, with some fearful womyn in my midst, showing resistance to celebrate this supreme Orisha, I had my work cut out for me as a priestess.

Afterwards, I think Oya made herself known to some of those womyn that had refused to show proper respect and reverence to her. While I felt absolutely spiritually charged after our day, there were one or two wommin who later experienced headaches, insomnia and their once suppressed past negativity, resurfacing, forcing them to handle and finally confront some of their personal issues. Confrontation, I have sadly learned is not a strong point for a lot of wommin, especially when we are so often conditioned and socialize to "play nice", "don't make trouble" and "smile." As I witness some of these womyn struggling with shadow work, this dark deity of Drastic Change and Transformation, I couldn't help but also see the mind blowing, transformative ways Oya is capable of working in a womyn's life....

Oya's ability to empower us as Wommin is one of her greatest gifts. I am forever grateful for the challenge she brought me. As a Priestess, I touched upon, yet another powerful, beautiful face of the Divine with Oya, and I felt honored to have been given the chance to work with her and introduce her to the Grove of the Feminine Divine.

This spell calls upon some of the strongest, protective Goddesses to come to our aid and Oya is among them. Hekate, Medea, Durga and Kali are also invoked. If you have photos or images of these Goddesses, placed them around you or around your working candle. You may use a black candle, charged in "Shield me Oil"(see appendix). As incense, you can use a Sage and Copal Smudge wand or a charcoal brisket, to burn herbs of elm, mandrake, patchouli, pine, rosemary and sage. This spell can be done at any moon phase but the dark of the Moon is most effective.

PROTECTION SPELL
*Shield, protect me round and round
Hekate's arms shield me now,
Kali, my defender,
Help me with this war,
like Durga, please save me Kali ,
I am yours.

Oya remind me, I am not alone
Let my ancestors come,
to secure me in my home
Enchantress Medea,
Beautiful and skilled,
I conjure the right love,
with my words and my will

Surround with powers,
this magickal spell
From this day forth,
all will go well....

By all the powers of Universal light,
Infuse this spell with magick and might,
I draw upon my Goddess power,
this spell manifest on this sacred hour...
It is done......!

OYA GROVE GODDESS GATHERING CHANTS

I circle around, I circle around
the boundaries of the Earth
I circle around, I circle around
the boundaries of the Earth
Heyana, Heyana, Heyana, Heyana,
Wearing my Long Wing feathers as I Fly
Wearing my Long Wing feathers as I Fly
By Arapaho Ghost Dance Song

A fu lele A de-o, A fu lele
A fu lele A de-o, A fu lele
Oya Cara Bel Oko, A fu lele
Oya Bamba la yi le, A fu lele
Storm Wind is arriving, Storm Wind is arriving,
Oya likes a Good Hard lover, Strong Wind
Oya dances a wicked Bamba, Strong Wind, (Gleason Bk)

In the Darkness of the Night
Plaaaaant a Seed
Magick made by candlelight
Stirring Silently
Growing, Growing By my might
Words I speak and Charge tonight
____Cast a Circle, Raise the Vibe
With my Energy
Magick made by Candlelight
Sing so mote it be....Sing So Mote it Be!!! *By B.M.M.*

Hekua Hey Yansa *by;B.M.M.*
Oya, Oya
On Storms she comes
Oya, Oya
Her Winds Transform
Oya, Oya
We call on you
Oya, Oya
Dance to this Tune(*repeat*)

We are Sisters on a Journey
Singing in the Sun,
Singing thru the Darkest Night
The Healing has begun,
Begun.
The Healing has Begun... *by Susan Weed*

EIGHT BEADS CHANTS by Carolyn Hillyer
Girlseed
Bloodflower
(dip it)Fruitmother
Spinmother,
(raise it) Midwoman
Earthcrone
Stonecrone
Bone .....

By the Earth that is her Body
By the Air that is her Breath
By the Fire that is her bright Spirit
By the Living waters of her womb
May the Peace of the Goddess
Be forever in our Hearts
The circle is open but unbroken
Merry Meet and merry Part
The circle is open but unbroken
Merry Meet and merry Part (continue from the beginning)

She Changes Everything She touches and everything She touches Changes(*repeat*) *by Starhawk*

EARTH, MOON, MAGICK by B.M.M.
In the Earth, deep within,
There is A Magick,
I draw it in.
    In her Caves, in the Trees
    Hear her Heartbeat,
    Pulsing thru me.
When I Rise, I feel her Love
With feet Grounded
I'm soaring high above,
    In the Earth, deep within,
    There is A Magick,
    I draw it in
Ancient Moon, my Soul reveres
With my Singing,
I call you here.
    When this flame, ignites tonight,
    Priestess dancing,
    Under the moonlit night....
In the Earth, deep within,
There is A Magick
I draw it in....
    There is A Magick, I draw it in }3x

March

March is the third month in the Gregorian calendar. Interestingly enough, it originally was the first month of the Roman year, known as Martius. In Rome this was not only the beginning of Spring but also the start of the military campaign season and it is therefore not surprising, the month was named after Mars, the Roman God of War, to honor this civic time. Many ancient cultures viewed the first month of Spring as the start of the year and according to scholars, it wasn't until about 450BC, when perhaps King Numa Pompillius made the change, making January the first month of the year. *(wikipedia)*

The full moon, this month, was known as Crust Moon, a reference to the crunchy crust layer of thin ice, that formed over the earth throughout the evening hours and thawed by the midday sun. It was also known as Sap Moon and Crow Moon due to the arrival of cackling crows. And because there were many rainstorms that developed at this time of year, it also garnered the name Storm Moon. According to the Farmer's Almanac, March's Full Moon was also named Worm Moon, by the Native Americans, because at this time of year, as the earth began to thaw from the long cold winter, the earth worms would rise up to the surface of the earth and announce the arrival of spring.

All around us are the very first visible signs that we have entered a new season. And in no time, Spring will make the harshness of Winter a distant memory. In some parts of the world, the snow may not have thawed on the ground and there may even be fresh snow still falling. Some days give hope for early Springs arrival, while other days, stubbornly cling to Winter. Unpredictability clearly reigns this month and although winter can still be felt, we've survived the worse of it. If we look closely we'll see, that although Winter might linger faintly, its bitterness, begins to wane.

March's astrological sign is the fish, Pisces, and it is ruled by dreamy, elusive fantasy driven, Neptune (Feb 21-march 20).

There are some important holidays for us, as wommin, to make note of. The entire month of March is considered Woman's History Month and March 8th is officially International Woman's Day. March 17th is dedicated to St. Patrick's day and Mardi Gras is also grandly celebrated during this month. Night and Day are in perfect balance on the Vernal Equinox on (March 20-21st) as most Pagans celebrate the sabbat of Ostara. To experience this phenomenon try to stand an egg (her sacred symbol) at the exact hour of the Equinox and feel the Earth's magnetic pull and current on this special day. It's quite magickal to experience this, especially when incorporated within a sabbat ritual. The season of the Maiden is fully present in March and her inquisitive, sprouting energy can be represented in the numerous symbols of Spring, including seeds.

One of my favorite names for this month's Full moon is, Seed Moon. For me this is an equally appropriate name among the many already mentioned. Traditionally, this is the time for planting seeds, whether figuratively or literally. It is an ideal time to hope and dream, plan and plant our wishes, as nature itself is supporting our very own endeavors. As we bear witness to the amazing powers of Mother nature and delight in the robin's arrival, let us plant those seedlings in the soil and be confident that they will sprout soon and manifest into a multitude of beauty, before too long. This is the season of great optimism and potential.

Witnessing nature's magical transformation, inspires us to look into our own personal transformations and the work that began at Imbolc continues to transform us now. We call upon the Greek Maiden Huntress-Artemis and the Fiery, willful Hawaiian Goddess-Pele, to move us with Courage into this new phase in our lives, as the wheel of the sacred year turns once more.

CHAPTER EIGHT

"By Believing passionately in something that does not exist, We create it. The non-existent is whatever we have not sufficiently Desired..." Franz Kafka

"The Tongue kills without drawing Blood...." Buddha

WELCOME PELE

OUR ALTAR

Altar cloth: Deep Reds & Orange altar cloth and maybe a second brown altar cloth underneath.
Image: Statue of the Hula dancers, Tahitian tiki, Hawaiian Polynesian Goddess, a volcano sculpted image. Canvas art or photo of the Goddess or images of Hawaiian lush landscape, Hulas and erupting volcanoes. Glassworks and images of Black lava Rocks.

Always present on the altar;
A cast iron cauldron, drums, speaking stick, a silver pentacle, athame, elemental representations.....

Air: feather bundles, bird statuaries, smudge wands, Incense type sticks, cones, charcoal brisket and fine powdered herbs; Cinnamon, clove and orange peel..
Fire: lots of candles, glass enclosed candles or pillars in red, Suggesting Red or black pyramid candles, which can be found in occult shops orange and black or image candles of volcanoes, yoni with its cavernous images also work well
Water: small glass vessel or bowl with water, wine and preferably rum.
Earth: a small dish of soil and or herbs, coffee grains.

Other items pertinent to this particular gathering
Special photography book on the beauty of Volcanoes
An actual volcano statue or toy
A lei, tropical flowers
soil
Plate of black volcanic rocks
Pack of Red balloons
Small cast iron pot or cauldron
Plate Offerings
Gauzy Red fabric to represent fire
Anything that represents the element of Fire
Workshop items;
red balloons, markers, pen and paper, red and black rocks
Tarot or other Goddess oracular items with her image

Offering, example of food; rum, coffee, pork, chicken, honey, sweet breadrolls, hair clippings
Sacred objects from members:
Notes:

Pele

Pele Altar

Candle Crafting

PELE

The Polynesian Volcanic Goddess, Pele, is a Fire Goddess known for her passionate, unpredictable, lava spewing insatiable ways. To the people of Hawaii, she is beloved "Tutu Pele" (grandmother Pele), a demonstrative name revealing much respect and adoration. She is also known as Pele-honua-mea (Pele of the sacred land) and also as, Pele-ai-honua (Pele the devourer of land). This Hawaiian Goddess of beauty, anger and sexual liberation among her many other titles was also known as Ka-ula-o-ke-ahi, a reference to the redness of her fires.

According to Polynesian cosmology, in the beginning was pure darkness. There was formlessness, the infinite, similar to the cosmology of numerous cultures and in this darkness we find the Earth's womb, the feminine, the Goddess- Papa. Then light was born and this light was the masculine, known as the Sky God –Wakea. When this union between light and darkness joined, the Universe was thus formed and first born. From this union of opposites, mother darkness and father light, emerged all the Gods and all of creation. The creator God, Kane came to be and numerous other important deities followed like Lono, the agricultural God and Kanaloa and Ku, to name a few. Pele is the daughter of the Earth Goddess, Haumea and holds the spirit of the Female Goddess, Hina; as all female deities were considered her direct descendants. In some legends her father was Kuwahailo, a sky God and brother to Hina.

There are many legends about Pele and her vast extended family. We know for example that she had numerous brothers and sisters, as can be expected from her fertile Mother, the Goddess of the Earth. Most notably, her sisters were the patron Goddesses of Hula dancing; Laka and Hiiaka. Laka was a fertility goddess but she was also known as Kapo, in another incarnation, the shape shifter Goddess of dark powers and sorcery. Pele's youngest sister, Hiiaka, was especially dear to her. Hiiaka was born in the shape of an egg and Pele assumed big sister duties by being in charge of caring for that beloved egg. In Hawaiian folklore, we learn of how Hiiaka was held by her sister, as an egg, close to her armpit during the journey to the island of Hawaii, until the egg one day changed into a beautiful little girl. Some of her other important siblings were; Komohoalii, a Shark God. He was her eldest brother and guarded the fiery Goddess often. In some legends he was the Sea God who provided the canoe for her journey to Hawaii. Kane-hekili was also her brother, the God of Thunder and Kauila-nui was yet another brother, the God of lightning. Namaka was her rivaling sister, the Goddess of the Sea, and they had numerous intense battles according to Polynesian folklore. The most famous of these had to do with Pele seducing her husband and Namaka chasing her sister, away from the rest of the family.

In ancient times, Pele was considered part of the Aumakua, family of lesser Gods, and thus her worship did not require the elaborate, formal structured rituals of the major Hawaiian Gods. Perhaps this is one reason why her myths and her worship has survived all this time among the Hawaiian people. Her worship and the practice of her rituals were very informal and individualize, allowing the average laymen the ability to connect with this Divine deity and call on her, in their own personal way. Pele remains one of four most powerful Hawaiian Goddesses still revered and worshipped by natives and non-natives alike on the island. A visit to modern day Hawaii will confirm her as one of the most well known, venerated deities still commanding our attention today.

Often, Pele was described as beautiful, but easily angered, very volatile, impulsive and jealous. Depicted with long brown hair and sometimes just as an erupting volcano, her priestesses were not allowed to cut their hair, unless it was done so as an offering. Frequently, her priestesses, and those seeking to connect with the Goddess, would cut their long locks as an offering and place it at the edge of the volcanic craters, where many forms of rituals and gifts were offered to her. Gin bottles would be left at

Halema'uma'u crater within Kilauea caldera, as well as baked pork, coffee, flowers, fruits and vegetables.

Pele's known home was in Mount Kilauea, Hawaii, but all volcanoes were sacred to her and thus viewed as her ruling domain. Not surprisingly, lava rocks were sacred to her, as well as natural glass. Her colors were the colors of fire; red, orange, yellow and black. The red Lehua flower, from the Ohi'a tree was also sacred to her. During childbirth it was a common practice to call on the midwife aspect of Pele. Polynesian women would invoke her strength and the esteemed Lehua flower was used to entreat her help and ease the pain in childbirth.

Legend tells of how often she would disguised herself as an old lady to test the loyalty of her people. As a crone, she would ask for a plate of food and bless those that complied. Conversely, she would curse with fire, those that were less than generous, as is evident in many of her known tales. Similar to the Greek Goddess Hekate, Pele was seen as a Triple goddess because sometimes she would appear as an old Crone woman, or sometimes as a child. And still at other times, she would appear as a beautiful, insatiable, passionate young maiden. There are myths that tell of Pele truly being an old Hag that reveals her true self, only in dreams.

The Goddess Pele garnered herself a reputation for being, strong tempered, passionate, lustful, wanton and free. As the Goddess of liberation she was a pleasure seeker, a sexual Goddess and what we might term as a minx. Living solely in the moment without thought to consequences, she pursued her passions. Whatever and whomever she wanted, she targeted, pursued and often achieved at attaining. She was a beautiful enchantress, few could resist her and, needless to say, she had many lovers. However, her volatile persona caused much problems within her family and all around the island of Hawaii. Her myths reveal she had many problems with her siblings and was known to have slept with her sisters' husbands. Pele had a rival in the Goddess of the snow-capped mountains-Poloahu. This rivalry is not surprising, due to the fact that Fire never gets along with ice or water.

Pele was known to have had a tumultuous relationship with the Demi Pig- God of agriculture, Kamapua'a. Together they were believed to have had one child who later becomes the ancestor of Polynesian chieftains, intimately connecting the people to their Gods. Kamapua'a appeared to the Fiery Goddess as a handsome chief, who could shapeshift into numerous images from a huge, eight eye boar to plants and fishes. He was known to have had quite the sexual appetite which meant he pursued numerous dalliance. The first sight of Pele excited him greatly and although she had no interest in him, he pursued her relentlessly, causing the Hawaiian landscape some distress. When she finally surrendered to their union it was riddled with many battles for they were polar opposites. Even their home land had to be divided, as Pele required drier land for her lava to flow and Kamapua'a required verdant, moist and fertile land and thus the two could not live together. Yet interesting to note that although, Pele makes the land from her spewing Lava seemingly separated from her mate, evidence of his bountiful gifts are seen when seeds somehow take root upon the lava, eventually becoming fertile soil. According to author, Herb Kawainui Kane, in his book, *"Pele, Goddess of Hawaii's Volcanoes"* (pg 31), "...Pele may build the island with her lava, but it is the incessant attentions of Kamapua'a that makes it fertile."

There are numerous tales of Pele and her volatility causing much conflict and drama on the island of Hawaii. One tale in particular reveal much about this Goddess.

Pele was madly in love with her new lover, a mortal hula dancer named Lohiau, whom she had a passionate love affair with, when she visited the Earth. They were separated after she had decided to return to her realm in her moment of restlessness. But soon after leaving the earth, she began to long for him. She asked her little sister,

Hiiaka, to retrieved him and bring him back to her. Her sister agreed, but only if Pele would tend to her beloved garden during the time she was away. Pele agreed. Hiiaka ran into some trouble however, in this endeavor, and could not bring Pele's lover back to her quickly enough. Lohiau had died from a broken heart during the journey and Hiiaka had to revive him.

Their journey back to Pele was full of challenges. Much time lapsed and Pele, being a jealous Goddess, assumed her sister had betrayed her by taking her lover for her own self. Pele angry, and in a fit of uncontrollable jealousy, destroyed her sister's garden in retaliation. When Hiiaka finally returned and saw what her sister had done to her garden, she in turn retaliated by giving in to her own suppressed desires for the mortal, Lohiau. Throughout their journey, the two had fallen in love with one another, but resisted temptation. Lohiau had confessed, at this time, to loving Hiiaka more but the fear of Pele's retribution helped him resist his desirous impulses. The couple did not give in to their passions due to their vow to Pele but upon discovering Pele's betrayal, Hiiaka took Pele's lover to the sacred crater of the Volcano, where the Goddess could bear witness to what would unfold. Hiiaka took Lohiau and there proceeded to make love to him. As you can surmised, this act angered Pele, the great Goddess of violence . She wasted no time in killing the mortal, sending him quickly to the land of the dead and making Hiiaka terribly distraught and heartbroken. The end of this tale reveals Pele's fickleness with lovers, as she later resurrects Lohiau from the land of the dead. She willingly gives him up to her sister in exchange for a new love found in the Hula dancer's best friend. Clearly, honesty was crucial to Pele and she did not hesitate to punish those that failed her. She was known to hurl Lava at her lovers when they would not meet her expectations.

Despite the introduction of Christianity by the missionaries in the 1700- 1800's Pele is one of the most well-known, venerated Polynesian deities today. As a Volcanic Goddess, Pele symbolized the internal fires found in the core of the Earth but also within womyn. She is the unbridled power of anger that move us and becomes a catalyst for great change.

This Polynesian Goddess is a symbol of passion and perseverance and raw power. Pele is about asserting will and the expression of anger. She teaches us to honor our feelings and allow them to move us into courage and action. Pele teaches us to honor and embrace our deep rooted passions and allow them to surface, so that we can effectively pursue and attain our heart's desire. She teaches us how anger can be a catalyst for great change in our lives. She knows what she wants, is self -assured and may sometimes appear brat-like in her relentless pursuit of her desire, yet, this is a Goddess who will not allow you to become a victim or self -martyrdom, she has no patience for the weak. Like her, she expects you to be strong and passionate... And in Pele, we find the qualities of strong will, action, strength and women's empowerment.

PELE GROVE GODDESS GATHERING

Purpose: To honor the Hawaiian, Volcanic Goddess, Pele and tap into her cathartic powers of anger and a call to action. To meet and honor our inner Bitch.

Check Ins: We gather together, forming a circle and take the time to introduce ourselves within this space, while also reflecting on a color that best describes our character.

Chant Workshop
"Pele's Chant," "Spirits of Fire..." and "I align my desires with the Spirit Divine," (see song text sheet)

Drumming Circle, and play CD: Best to unearth and play authentic Hawaiian Drumming Music or Hula inspired music to set the tone for our day with Pele. Listening to this music allows participants a chance to begin to travel to her land, connect with Pele and ground into this moment. Bora Bora Tahitian drumming music is offered.

Check Ins II: Sharing her image from the tarot card or from one of the numerous artistic images available. The image of Pele will be passed around the circle and every womyn will have a chance to study, reflect and consider how this Goddess is manifesting in her own personal life..... Communally Invoking Pele thru artistic images.

Lesson on the Goddess Pele
her myths, etymology and the spiritual practices of the Hawaiian people.

GODDESS WORKSHOP
WORKSHOP I: Energy Work. Each Wombmyn will stand in the center of the circle and expresses the anger or other emotions she is feeling with her body and no words, silence . She will pantomime her emotions and where she hurts, via her body alone and Grove systers surrounding, will interpret and witness her voiceless, passionate expression.

WORKSHOP II: A Special discussion on the word **"Bitch"**. Personal reflection and Discussion on what does it mean, in today's world, to be a "bitch"? How do we feel today about this label?

WORKSHOP III: Crafting a Volcanic mini altar creations with paper mache or clay and Black stone/lava rock artistic creation. A perfect, light crafting outlet, after working intensely with our "Anger."

WORKSHOP IV: Chakra Exercise; working with our **Red root chakras** and our powers of "will and intent". Sitting with anger....learning to work with such a powerful emotion.

WORKSHOP V: Lighting our individual candles and having a quiet moment at Pele's altar to contemplate on our initial feelings on this Goddess, aggression and what she personally means to us as wommin. One by one, wommin can present their personal, **Red candle to the altar**, visit with the images of Pele and light their candle with their own special intention.

WORKSHOP VI: Hawaiian movement Dance- **Lual** style- engaging our body in the slow and methodical movement of a very ancient form of storytelling. Connecting to a cultural tradition closely linked to Pele and her sisters. We will have a mini lesson,engage our body to Hula dance.

WORKSHOP VII: Blowing up red balloons with our intention. As you blow up the balloons place the goals you have set for yourself within your hot breath and now into the balloons. These balloons will be scattered around our sacred space and become a part of our upcoming ritual to Pele. A discussion and the logistics on the upcoming ritual to Pele, the balloons and the goal of our day will ensue afterwards.

WORKSHOP VIII: Sharing various photos from a beautiful **Volcano Art books** or viewing an actual National Geographic Documentary film about Volcanoes in Hawaii. Connecting with the thoughts and images that transpires from viewing her powerful images.

WORKSHOP IX: Aspecting Volcano energy. Cone of Power working- recreating the sounds of an erupting volcano. Starting with a low, buzzing, grumble and slowly rumbling, organically letting it grow and rise, the sound bubbling over and shooting out explosively. Obviously, this kind of work needs to be done in an area that will not disrupt others...perhaps a sound proof room or out, amidst nature. It is quite an effective exercise in unearthing our primal self and releasing a lot of pent up emotions.

WORKSHOP X: Wand Blessing-Participants are encouraged to go outdoors, briefly, to search for a tree branch that speaks to them personally. In our own backyard you can almost always find various sorts of branches from the local Oak and Ash tree on the land. If it proves too difficult to have the group go outdoors you can always scatter, around the temple, an array of pre-selected branches, from various trees, and encourage participants to intuit which one is best for them personally.

The next step is to gather your supplies; colored tissue papers, Elmers glue and long strips of ribbons in various colors. After lightly sanding and cleaning your branch you are encourage to spend a brief moment connecting to this new tool of magick. Contemplate on how you wish to incorporate this wand into your spiritual practice and listen carefully for what attributes the wand itself wants to impart on you. This is an important part in linking and merging your energies and should not be underestimated. Continue to focus your energy in this way as you prepare the wand. Saturate the branch and the strips of paper and ribbons in the glue and begin to layer the various components over the branch. Place it over a chalice, or any other helpful item, to dry safely. When it is fully dry, prepare to charge and bless this wand by presenting it, formally or informally, to all the elements. This can be done communally among your sisters or you can take the wand home and elect to do this as a solitary, at your desired lunar stage (preferably Full moon, though some might opt to do this at the New moon).

If done Communally, participants can approach the altar and use the Incense for an air Blessing, Fire flames of the altar candles for Fire Blessing. Then follow with a water blessing by dabbing oil or scented rose water and utilize herbs or salt as an Earth blessing. A drop of your blood, saliva or other bodily fluid links it even more to you personally and enhances its power. Finally, enchant a prose like the suggested one below;

WAND BLESSING
From branch to wand to unearth your spark,
By will and word I feed you the mark.
By all the elements sacred to us,
I Charge this wand in the name of Goddess.
I Mark it now with a Witches touch,
By Air, Fire, Water and Earth's crust.
Be ye charged and bless,
for my intended purpose,
As a powerful tool of magick,
I herein nurse it!

REFLECTIONS ON PELE

She is ferocity, uncensored passion and eruption of emotions. She teaches us to value our feelings, those dark overpowering emotions, that would on the surface, seem to overtake us, or shift us into a much feared, dangerous terrain. She encourages us to go there. Pele's gift to us is the roar of her volcanoes, echoing the potential of our own voice. She is the overflowing erupting hot lava that is so reminiscent of our own womanhood and our own erotic spewafication. She is our liberating climax. Do not fear your wild, passionate nature. She is her own womyn and reminds us that we are too. She enters your life so that you may acknowledge and value your roars, your emotions, especially anger, which is so often suppressed by wommin, yet so often necessary to catapult enormous, monumental change .... There is power in our anger and Pele teaches us to unearth and connect with that power.

PELE GROVE GODDESS GATHERING RITUAL

Purpose: To honor the Hawaiian Goddess Pele and tap into her cathartic powers of Anger and a call to action. To meet and honor our inner Bitch.

Purification & Anointing with the rising smoke of incense or a sage smudge and ashes on the forehead and a cultural, audible lamentation sound is heard (this can be a recording).

***As they enter sanctuary, Place in their hands the offering *(if they don't have one already give them coffee or a flower)* they will use & offer it to the Goddess at the altar.

We gather around in a circle...

Speaker states intent of ritual

Cast circle with actual lava rocks or black /red rocks to simulate lava rocks and prose.

Quarters called

We call on **Fire** with our flesh. Rub your hands together fast and furious, feel that heat you have generated. Now place this heat upon your chest. Feel the heat upon your heart.
We have invoked the powers of Fire.
Fire is here now.
Aloha Ahi Wai'ona, Komo mai Aumakua (Greetings Fire Spirits, Welcome Ancestors)
All say: **Welcome Fire**

We call on **Water** with the moisture found on our lips, lick your lips, wet them with your saliva. Feel how this element is living within you.
We have invoked the powers of Water.
Water is here,
*Aloha Wailele Wai'ona, Komo mai Aumakua (*Greetings waterfall Spirits, Welcome Ancestors)
All say: **Welcome Water**

We call on **Earth** with the solidity of our own bodies, give your neighboring Sister an embrace.
All embrace each other.
We have invoked the powers of Earth
Earth is here
Aloha Ao honua'aina Wai'ona, Komo mai Aumakua (Greetings Earth Spirits, Welcome Ancestors)
All say: **Welcome Earth**

We call **Air** with our breath, panting and sighs.
Altogether, all the attendants breathe audibly.
We have invoked the powers of Air
Air is here now.
Aloha Lewa Wai'ona, Komo mai Aumakua (Greetings Air Spirits, Welcome Ancestors)
All say: **Welcome Air**

INVOCATION GODDESS WITH PROSE

SING PELE'S CHANT

He Pele mai Kahiki (Pele Comes from a distant place)
He Ola mau (and is eternal and everlasting)
Ka ikena O ke akua (the Gods have a higher vision)
E Homai, E Homai (we ask that it be transferred to us)

Reflection, Priestess Speaks...

There are times in one's life when we need to get angry before we are moved to great heights of success. There are times when our mere silence cannot move the mountains that the passionate roar of a volcano can. When we desire something or someone and fear keeps us from moving forward, we need to tap into the passionate Fires of Pele in those instances, for she fearlessly pursues what her heart desires. She answers to no one and attains her target every time

-without fail. Pele is particularly sympathetic to women's struggles in our patriarchal society. She makes herself available to you now, if you allow it to be, so what do you need her fires for? What do you intend to manifest in your life? (pause)

I think as womyn we are so often raised and taught to be passive and simply receptive in all areas of our lives; from sex, to relationships to finances and our careers and workplace. We are not so often encouraged to speak up and voice our thoughts or be aggressive and openly passionate. It appears so often, that we are discouraged from showing any type of competitive edge, drive or aggression or call to action, for fear it might make us appear uncooperative, unladylike, troublesome or just play "mental." Any display of such intense emotions often gets us classified as the "Bitch" or a "winch," or "crazy," "chemically imbalanced" or the "dyke- in need of the remedy of a man." Whatever the label- aggression in women is deemed as unattractive, whorish, lesbionic or and problematic, not just by men, but sadly by other women as well. Yet as the actress /producer Tina Faye puts it, *"...bitches get things done...."* and sometimes in life you have to tap into that inner bitch and unleash her onto the world, in order to move from point A (paralysis) to point B (Action and Empowerment). Sometimes you have to get ANGRY...and you have to let yourself get mad and feel that Volcanic eruption in order for the lava to spew and those oceans to part... and those villages and people to MOVE!!!!!

Pele invites you to unearth that hidden aspect within every Goddess womyn. Pele invites you to meet, face to face, with **"The Bitch"**, the one who won't put up with crap. She is the one who is clear on her agenda and knows exactly what she wants and with full drive, piercing ambition and passionate pursuit, attains her goals. Oh Yes...we NEED to feel Pele's Fire. We need to tap into our own inner fierce Pele. For without her, we let life pass us by. For without her, we remain stagnant, paralyzed, fearful and much too passive for this lifetime.

Pele is Drive! Pele is that boiling point!

Pele is that day when you wake up in the morning and you finally say, "I HAVE HAD ENOUGH!!!!!" I am leaving this toxic relationship or I am losing this weight now or I am getting that promotion or I will make him/her my lover, today or I quit smoking now or I am going to get out of this neighborhood, etc, etc...

Pele is active. She does not accept weakness and we meet her, within our own selves, when we too, finally, refuse to tolerate weakness.

We are going to start here in this sacred space...by getting angry...and if we are afraid of getting angry and afraid of feeling the depths of such intense strong emotions know that you are with your systers in sacred space and you will be safe here. We are going to start by freely opening our throat chakra and screaming....SCREAMING off the top of your lungs. Scream as loud as you can, let it out. Scream because you have had enough! Today is the day you have reached your boiling point and in your screams, you will release your fear and above all, **all** those things that have comfortably silenced you....release.

Your collective screams becomes Pele's Volcanic eruption

There will be silence afterwards and we will honor that silence as Mother nature always leaves us in awe.

When you are ready, state aloud what you "**will**" with Pele's fires....

One by one they will speak.

"I will_____"

Then right after statement of intent, Find one of the floating red balloons among our space. Flighty, red, Air Balloon, tricky to grasp but you will -for it represents your goal pursued. When you have attained it and grasped this balloon in your hand, **POP the Balloon** as you say, " **IT IS DONE!!!!!**"

Every woman follows the same action and is cheered by her sisters within the circle. When all have experienced this we begin....

PELE CHANT

With movement around the room **GODDESS CHANT SUNG*****

Holding hands we begin Thanking and devoking the Goddess Pele,
**Devoking the Elements...with Elemental Song
**Opening the Circle....

**Potluck feasting flows

PELE INVOCATION
Fires of Pele
invoked here today
In me lives the passions
and her lusty ways

Captivating Beauty,
Ensnares who she wills
Draws her many lovers
to mount her luscious hills.

There near volcanoes
on the edge of explosions
Feel the depths of her powers
And swells of emotions

To will and to know
Defiant and clear
Your targets and goals
Can't escape you
My dear.

Hail to you,
that lives and breathes
that passion, that focus
that fire in me.

Gather several Red candles and include a black one and yellow as well. Carve, charge and anoint these candles with "Get it done oil"(see appendix). Upon your altar place a statue of the Goddess Pele and a photo or image of an actual Volcano. Place near her image, a symbol of what you seek her assistance with. Create an offering plate with; flowers, coffee grains, honey, rum/gin, chocolate sweets, a snippet of your hair, glass/gemstones and any Hawaiian items. Burn pleasing, smelling incense and let the smoke swirl and twirl around you and your altar items. You are going to need to raise a lot of energy for this spell and drumming, as well as heavy dancing, is highly suggested to fuel this work. Call her loudly and strongly and feel her energy, passionately, move in your entire body as you perform this spell and light your candles. Waxing Moon on a Tuesday (ruled by Aggressive Mars) will best serve this powerful spell work.

PELE INSPIRED-SPEAKING OUT
Pele I call you
From the depths of your Terrain
Pele Here before you
I invoke your Lava rain.

Getting Angry enough
To do something real,
Pele move me to action
So that I may heal,

Courage surging within me,
And down to my Roots,
Roots of Black, Yellow, Red,
Roots volcanic, flaming soot.

Pele Willful and Focus,
Undeniably Free,
Roaring Fires, Inflame me,
so that I may speak.

Tapping into our Voice
As it touches my heart
Letting pleasure dissolve,
What once tore me apart.

Pele now hear me,
From the depths of my Terrain,
Cathartic transformation,
Unearthed in your Lava rain.

PELE DREAM

I was sitting at a long conference table among various other Goddess systers, there was some type of meeting among us. I recall the long table was near a double glass doors, leading to the outdoor courtyard. We were in the middle of planning some very important spiritual event (like the next Goddess Gathering) and I was there with clipboard and pen, taking notes. A boyish looking womyn or possibly an actual boy, sat to my left and I chose to sit right across from renown Priestess M. We all talked passionately, laughed, brainstormed and discussed things among ourselves. Then the meeting was quickly adjourned and the wommin started to pack up and leave.

I started gathering my belongings carefully, placing things in my bag, when I heard my own inner voice say aloud, *"....but you didn't ask her about.... and this is your chance, you can't possibly leave yet...."* I looked over at Priestess M. just sitting there alone now and I realized my inner voice made a convincing point. I needed to know and I couldn't leave until I spoke to her. So shyly, but hopeful, I approached her with reverence and asked.... *" Excuse me, can I ask you a question, Priestess M?* In my most serious tone of voice I asked, *"Do you always pre-prepare a ritual for every Goddess Festival? How do you invoke her?"* She looked up at me and answered with something about trusting your inner guide, listening to your heart...and all of a sudden it appeared she was speaking to me in some archaic language and in this breathtakingly beautiful prose. It was so eloquent, but too cryptic for my own ears and I felt spellbound by her words, though I could barely understand what she was saying to me. I knew, however, that she was imparting spiritual occult knowledge to me at that very moment and her words were meant for my soul, not my ears.

When she finished speaking, I humbly thanked her, grabbed my bag and proceeded to walk over to the nearby counter and glass showcase. It looked like the type of counter you find at a pastry shop, but instead, there were no pastries behind the glass, no... there were important occult books, very prized, antiquated books.

There over the counter, I was thrilled to have the opportunity to hold in my hands a very old Hawaiian book of Deities. Pele, Hina, Huna and many Polynesian Gods were among the names highlighted in this very large, impressive, hardcover book. But almost as if the Goddess yanked my head to the left, my heart stopped, as I quickly noticed another book within the glass showcase...one that literally made my palms sweat and my heart race, a mile a minute, at the mere thought of actually holding it. She was calling me and I was strangely drawn to her book. Clearly She was making herself known to me and insisting, *"this is the book you need to own and study now."* Within the showcase, as clear as can be, I read the title of this ancient book, *"Pele"*. While the first book mentioned numerous Polynesian Deities and Pele was among them, this book before me, was dedicate entirely to the Volcanic Goddess and I felt this strange urgency to hold it in my hands. I needed to hold it and read it with my own eyes. From behind the glass showcase, I ogled at it and noticed it was very old, yellowing, with a torn front flap and what appeared to be an encircled price mark, P16.

Seeing how I was hanging around for a long time, the store clerk approached me, and asked if she could help me. I expressed my curiosity and desire to see the "Pele" book and in a witchy manner, she quickly said to me, *"Nooooo, you want **THIS** book instead..."* and right before me, she laid down this heavy, archaic, enormous book with a strong leather, black cover. It was clearly an ancient Grimoire, a Book of Shadow with a multitude of handwritten spells for all occasions. My hands gently touched the yellowing paper, I perused through the book in complete amazement, noticing a trillion spells for everything imaginable. I mean, you name it and a spell for it was found in this book and it made my head spin. The more I looked through it, the more I realized it was not the right book for me. I said to the waiting store clerk, *"...No, I am doing scholastic... um..*

*academic research on the Goddess. I need **that** book in the showcase, not this Book of Shadows. I am doing research, serious Goddess studies. I need Pele's book."* The store clerk, who was dressed like a New York City East Villager, all in black, turned and retrieved the book. When she handed it to me I felt an electric surge course through me and the giddiness of a three year old child and I knew I had made the right decision. It felt as if in that very moment, when the book touched my hand, I was inducted into her Sacred Temple.

With my prized book in hand, I now returned to the long table where the conference had taken place earlier on. Clearly I had forgotten some of my belongings and was now gathering sheets of paper and all of my other things. I only spied that one tomboyish girl/boy again. She teasingly patted me on the back with a smirk, as she proceeded to get her things and leave. The other wommin were now in another area to my right. They were on the Cafeteria line, getting ready to have lunch. I followed suit and proceeded to join them, as it was getting late. On line we were all getting our trays and utensils, the way school kids do for lunch at the cafeteria and then I heard one wommin remind me to pick up a plate for myself. Strange, but I woke up soon after that and although I have glimpses of other dreams that night, this was the only one documented in my journal due to its vivid, unquestionable significance and association with the Goddess Pele. Hail to you Volcanic Beauty!!!

Pele Grove Goddess Gathering Chants Text sheet

Pele's Song:
Pele...Pele...
Passion Fire stirs in me
Pele...Pele....
I attract what my heart seeks
Pele...Pele...
Fire stirs and stirs in me
Pele, Pele
What I will shall come to be... (repeat) *by B.M.M.*

Spirits of Fire
Spirits of Fire come to us
we will kindle the Fire,
Spirits of Fire come to us
we will kindle the Fire,
We will kindle the Fire
dance the magic circle round
We will kindle the fire dance the circle around

We Can Rise With the Fire
We can rise with the fire of freedom
Truth is the fire that burns our chains
And we can stop the fire of destruction
Healing is the fire running through our veins By: Starhawk

Mother of Darkness
Mother of Darkness,
Mother of Light ,
Earth beneath the Soul in Flight
Songs of Love
and Love of Light,
Guide us to our heart...

Mother I feel you under my feet
*Mother I feel you under my feet, Mother I feel your Heart Beat 2X
Heya Heya Heya, Heya Heya Ho 2X
Mother I hear you in the Rivers Sound, Eternal Waters going on and on 2X
Heya heya heya heya heya ho 2X
Mother I see you in when the Eagles fly, Flight of the Spirit gonna take our time 2X
Heya Heya Heya, Heya Heya Ho By: Unknown source

Elemental Chant
*The Earth, The Air
The Fire, The Water
Return, Return, Return
Below, Above
the Center is Love
Return, Return, Return By: Robin Rose Bennet -addy, Origins unknown

SING PELE'S CHANT
He Pele mai Kahiki (Pele Comes from a distant place)
He Ola mau (and is eternal and everlasting)
Ka ikena O ke akua (the Gods have a higher vision)
E Homai, E Homai (we ask that it be transferred to us)

*Isis, Astarte, Diana, Hecate, Demeter, Kali, Inanna....
By: Deena Metzger & Caitlin Mullin

*The Earth is a Woman and she shall rise..... By: Z. Budapest

CHAPTER NINE

"Promise me, you"ll always remember you're braver than you believe and stronger than you seem and smarter than you think..." Christopher Robbin to Winnie the Pooh

"You've got to rattle your cage door. You've got to let them know that you are in there and that you want out. Make Noise! Cause trouble! You may not win right away, but you'll sure have a lot more fun..." Florynce Kennedy

WELCOME ARTEMIS

OUR ALTAR

Altar cloth: *Green and maybe a second brown altar cloth underneath.*
Image: *Statue of the Huntress, Greek Goddess Artemis or the Roman Diana, or statue of the multi breasted-Artemis of Ephesus*
Canvas art or photo of the Amazonian maiden Goddess or and photos of Greece and a Forest. Animal images are also appropriate to have on the altar like, stags, bears, hounds, rabbits, horses etc..

Always present on the altar;
A cast iron cauldron, drums, speaking stick, a silver pentacle, athame, elemental representations.....

Air: *Arrows and Bow, Smudge wands, Incense type sticks, cones, charcoal brisket and fine powdered herbs Mugwort and Cypress, Hawthorn, Vervain*
Fire: *candle, glass enclosed candles or pillars in Green or Silver and or a lunar shaped candle.*
Water: *Chalice or small glass bowl with Water*
Earth: *Plants-lots of Greenery and fresh flowers, branches, a small dish of soil and or herbs like cypress. Large Branches, Deer Horn, wolf fur, rabbits foot or other animal symbolisms.*

Other items pertinent to this particular gathering
An actual Bow and Arrow Archery set
Plants and lots of Greenery
Symbol of the Horn Crescent Moon
Plate of soil
Head wreath or Circlet
Figurine of animals like deer, bears, rabbits and dogs
Writing pens and paper, safety pins,
Green gauzy fabric to represent the fertile earth
Small cast iron pot or cauldron
A bell
Plate Offerings with olives, grapes, fruits that grow on vines
Workshop items
Tarot or other oracular item

Offering *example food; olives, orzo, hummus, appetizers, avoid meat or animals as food offerings.*
Sacred objects from members:
Notes:

Artemis

The Huntress

Altar

Artemis Altar

Aspecting Artemis, The Huntress

ARTEMIS

Virgin, maiden, whole unto herself, Artemis is the Greek Goddess of the Crescent New Moon. She is the Huntress, known in Rome as Diana-Artemis. She was Goddess of the wilderness, Goddess of Archery and the Hunt. Artemis was considered a leader to the Amazons and a patron Goddess to all wild animals, women and children. She is the immortal spirit of the wild, free maiden and her name is derived from the Greek word, *"Artemes",* which means, healthy and energetic and a reference to strength and vitality - all attributes she exemplifies.

As Lady of Ephesus, she was depicted with a multitude of breast and worshipped more as an ancient, pre-Olympian, Mother Goddess. In Rome she was known as Diana-Artemis, mother of Aradia, and thus Goddess of the Witches, according to Charles Godfrey Leland.

The Greek Huntress was associated with the crescent new moon and was often depicted wearing a short tunic and a circlet of the crescent moon upon her brow. Artemis was sometimes viewed as the maiden aspect of Hekate. There are numerous variations of this trinity, but a common one makes Hekate, the crone, symbolized by the darkmoon, Selene (a Titaness moon Goddess) as the mother, symbolized by the Full moon, while Diana-Artemis, as the maiden, was symbolized by the crescent.

As a lunar Goddess she shares some characteristics with Hekate and their connection is undeniable. Some text reveals that Hekate was actually a cousin of Artemis because her mother's sister, Asteria, was mother to Hekate. Their great grandmother was the primordial Goddess, Gaia, and their grandmother was the ancient Moon Goddess, the Titaness, Phoebe. Phoebe, interestingly enough, translates as *"light-bearer"* and this is an attribute that all her familial descendants possess.

Artemis was the daughter of Zeus and the Goddess Leto and she was a twin to Apollo-The sun God. Though she herself, as a Virgin deity, never gave birth, she was considered the Goddess of Childbirth, and often called upon by women in the midst of labor. She was immortalized in the writings of her time as the young one who was immediately employed to be her mother's midwife, as the birth of her twin brother proved to be difficult.

According to the well-known myths, documented in the Callimachus, and the Homeric hymn, Artemis was born on the Greek Island of Delos, also known as Ortygia, Isle of Quails. Perhaps this is one reason why she is also known by the name of Cynthia, a reference to her birthplace on Mount Cynthus, in Delos. According to one account, her mother searched tirelessly to find a safe place to birth her children, away from Hera's jealous wrath. Zeus's wife, Hera, had decreed that Leto would not be allowed to give birth anywhere on the earth, but with some divine intervention, the Greek island of Delos emerged from deep within the sea, as an enchanted island immuned to Hera's curse. Although there are some variations to this story, Artemis was first born and witnessing her mother's distress and struggles to birth her twin brother, she wasted no time in immediately helping her beloved mother and easing her labor pains. This is one reason why she is so often associated with women and childbirth and the practice of midwifery. In this capacity she is known as, *Kourotrophos*, the nurse for the young and as *Locheia,* the Goddess of childbirth.

Throughout mythology, this maiden Goddess was often seen coming to her mother's aid and protecting various women in distress. She became known as the protector of the hopeless, the vulnerable and the defenseless, such were at the time; children, women, young girls, animals beast, babes. In the tale of Niobids, the Queen of Thebes made the grave mistake of boasting about her fourteen children and comparing her rather fertile birthing abilities, as more superior than that of the Goddess Leto, who had only given birth to one male and one female. For Artemis and Apollo, who loved their mother dearly, this was gravely offensive. They wasted no time in defending their mother's honor and succeeded at killing the Queen's children by shooting at them with poisoned arrows. The father, Amphion, completely distraught, killed himself upon witnessing the tragic death of his sons. The Queen, Niobe, and her remaining children were quickly turned to stone by Artemis as they mourned the tragic, demise of their family. It becomes clear in this tale and many other Greek lore, that Artemis, while very protective of the vulnerable and defenseless, could also be just as fierce, unapologetic in her defense and quick to retaliate if offended. A Goddess of swift action, there were many men, as well as women, in Greek mythology, that fell victim to her volatile wrath when they dared to fail her expectations.

    The Cypress and Laurel wreath were sacred to her, as were the mountains, wilderness and the raw powers found in nature. Here is a Goddess who perfectly exemplified this wild, untamable, raw power. All wild beast, in her beloved forest, fell under her love and care. Artemis was sometimes known as the stag lover and some of her totem animals were the deer, bears, horses, hare, and like Hecate- the hounds. She was often associated with bears, perhaps because she too, exemplified the same fiercely, protective nature towards the young, as bears do with their cubs. In many artistic depictions of the Moon Goddess we see her holding her bow and arrows, surrounded by stags, hare, wild beast and dogs. She was indeed the huntress, but engaged in this sport with great reverence. The act of killing an animal, for mere pleasure, was sacrilegious to this Goddess and resulted in her unforgiving retaliation.

    All forest animals were under her protective domain, as were young girls. Young maidens were expected to dedicate themselves to her and traditionally spent a year in her service prior to marriage. Some of the text of the time reveal interesting rituals young girls performed in her honor, like wearing yellow tunics and mimicking animals in a special bear dance. Numerous priestesses took vows of chastity and exemplified the virtues and attributes of Artemis in their service to her. She was depicted as pure and chaste and demanded her priestesses to also live their lives in the same manner, devoted to her. Her numerous temples were found in Sparta and the town of Brauron and the largest, in Delos, her birth place. At Ephesus in Ionia (Turkey) her temple became one of the Seven Wonders of the World. Erected in 550bc, but was burned down by Herastratus, by 356bc.

    Artemis was the Goddess of the Hunt. Her Archery skills were unmatched and her aim and focus unsurpassed. She did not back down to any man and proudly displayed her archery skills at every opportunity. It was also apparent, she preferred the company of women, over men. Greek lore reveal that she probably was once in love, with a mortal hunter named Orion, but she vowed never to love again when that love ended tragically and of course, there are various accounts of this tale. Her brother, who was also a fine, competitive archer, engaged her in a little competition one day, which subsequently resulted in her arrow killing the love of her life. According to one myth, Apollo loved his sister greatly and perhaps was jealous of the relationship she was forming with Orion, but some speculate, that he also wanted to protect his sister's chastity. One day he challenged his competitive sister to see if she could hit a shiny target, far away, near a lake. Artemis, lover of challenges and never one to miss her target, aimed... and unbeknownst to her..... shot the arrow, killing Orion.

    Although she interacted very little with men, she had an extremely close relationship with her brother, but it becomes apparent through some of the Greek literature of the time, that she also had a special relationship with her father, Zeus. Artemis was always confident, focus, strong willed and very decisive. She displayed these strong attributes at a very young age too. According to the popular Greek writings of the time, by her third birthday she already knew precisely what she wanted as a gift and made her request known to her beloved father, while sitting upon his lap. Without hesitation, Zeus complied to his bold, confident birthday girl and provided her with the desired bow & arrows, sixty nymphs, as well as stags and hounds, just as she requested at age three. She wanted to be chaste and free of the confinements of marriage and she wanted a silver bow and arrow, like her twin brother. According to the legend, at this tender age, she let it be known that she wanted to reside among the wild, in the mountains and Zeus was only too pleased to comply. The Hellenic Goddess, didn't want to wear the traditional attire that women of her time wore. She wanted a short tunic as her hunting attire, which gave her freedom to run. She wanted to bring light into the world, in the same way her twin brother did, as God of the Sun, and she was not at all interested in the distractions of love and thus she was given immunity from Aphrodite's charms.

In Artemis we see the roots of feminism, leadership, sisterhood and the spirit of independence. She embraced being a leader to her clan of nymphs and amazons, yet the young Artemis passionately valued her freedom and those moments of solitude. She fiercely defended her privacy and there are numerous tales of her retaliations on those who dared violate her privacy, especially if they were men.

Artemis was known as a maiden, virgin Goddess because she belonged to no one. Virgin was a title in ancient time, referring to societal position -not necessarily sexual and more than anything it pointed to her autonomy. The Hellenic Goddess was never married and had no known children and thus she was considered whole unto herself, belonging to no one. In mythology we see how she was fierce and impulsive, if pushed to anger and often men, and some women, fell victim to her wrath if they failed to meet her expectations. Still, this immortal Greek Maiden Goddess is a champion of wommin and exemplifies for us; autonomy, strength and the power inherent in our focus and passionate will. She demanded to live her life on her own terms, unconventionally, not conforming to the traditional roles of women of her time and She can be quite a force of empowerment for today's struggling women and feminist alike.

LESSON ON ARTEMIS

- **Known as:** The Greek Virgin Maiden Goddess Artemis
- Goddess of the Hunt, Goddess of Archery, Goddess of the New Moon, Goddess of the Amazons.
- Patron Goddess to Women, Children, Animals.
- Her name also translates as "protector/safety"
- Virgin meaning: whole unto herself and no one else. It was a word referring to a societal position -not sexuality. She was never married, no known children.
- She was also known in Rome as Diana, Diana Artemis, multi- breasted Lady of Ephesus.
- **Birthplace:** Born on the Greek Island of Delos, she was daughter of Zeus & Goddess Leto (Goddess of Child birthing). She was twin to Apollo-The Sun God. Thus she shares a lot of characteristics with her brother, such as being a light bearer. When she was born, as mythology reveals, she was immediately employed as midwife to assist her mother, who was having a difficult time birthing her twin brother. This is one reason why she is often associated with women and childbirth and is the Patroness of midwifery though she, herself, never had any known children.
- **Her Symbols:** Associated with the Crescent new moon and is often seen as the maiden aspect of Hekate and thus part of that trinity(maiden, mother, crone). Selene, Hekate, Diana-Artemis many variations on this trinity like Demeter, Kore & Hekate etc.. She is Light bearer sharing similar characteristics to Hekate.
    - She became known as the protector of the hopeless and defenseless, which at the time were; children, women, young girls, animals beast, babes etc. Young girls would often dedicate themselves to Artemis and she had numerous priestesses and temples.
    - Her totems were the Stag, Rabbits, Bears, and like Hekate, Dogs, all wild beast and offspring were sacred in her beloved forest. The mountains wilderness were sacred to her. Perhaps because she was the known defender & protector of women and the defenseless, she became the Goddess of the Witches as her Roman counterpart, Diana.
- **Her Mythology/stories:** When her mother was ready to give birth she ran into trouble trying to find a safe place to deliver her twins due to Hera's wrath- no one dared assist the pregnant Leto. A magical island (the Greek island of Delos) was made available and there she was able to give birth to Artemis.
    - Through out mythology she was often seen coming to her mother's aid and defending and protecting her, along with other women.
    - Artemis was confident, even at the early age of three, she knew she wanted; her bow & arrow, sixty nymphs, hunting dogs. She wanted to reside among the wild in the mountains. She knew she didn't want to wear traditional dress and wanted her hunting costume as her attire, she wanted to bring light into the world. She did not want the distractions of love and thus she wanted immunity from Aphrodite's charms.
- **Her Gifts:** She was seen as pure and chaste and she expected her priestesses to live in the same way. Artemis valued her freedom and could be quite fierce if angered. She loved her time in solitude but also being a leader, to nymphs and to her clan of Amazons. She was very competitive and no one could match her aim & focus as an Archer and she backed down to no man. The beautiful Callisto was her known, beloved companion. Artemis was self-confident, strong, decisive and loved the company of women.

ARTEMIS GROVE GODDESS GATHERING

Purpose: To strengthen some of Artemis attributes in ourselves, namely; 1.Sisterhood, 2.Empowerment and 3.Success aiming at our new target.

Chanting and Music making
"Artemis Song", "Lady of the Moon",
"She gathers her Daughters", "Equinox Chant" *(see song text sheet)*

Check Ins: We gather around in a circle formation to introduce ourselves and share aloud our personal views on "*Sisterhood.*" *What does Sisterhood mean to you?*

Drumming Circle: A drumming indigenous musical track (CD) will be played to raise vibrational energy of the room and celebrate this moment. We will re-enact the Sacred Bear dance, documented in the myths of Artemis, by pounding on the earth with the soles of our feet like bears.

Sharing her Image from a tarot card Deck, like the Universal Goddess Tarot or, one of my favorite, The Goddess Oracle by Amy Sophia Marashinsky or from any one of the numerous other artistic rendering of the Goddess available, we endeavor now to connect with her energy. The image of Artemis will be passed around the circle and every womyn will have a chance to study, reflect and consider how this Goddess is manifesting in her own personal life. Communally Invoking aloud, the maiden Goddesss, Artemis, through her visual image.

LECTURE ON THE GREEK GODDESS ARTEMIS
Learning about her etymology, her various myths and her relevance for today's modern womyn. Connecting with her energy through her infamous attributes.

GODDESS WORKSHOPS
WORKSHOP I:
Invoking Empowerment: In this workshop we will have the opportunities to define and discuss what is empowerment in today's day and age. Wommin will have a chance to invoke Empowerment by personally defining it openly within our sacred circle.

WORKSHOP II:
Forest Totem Animal Work . Our Totem and how these beloved creatures can assist us in our own spiritual journey. Animals were very sacred to this Maiden Goddess and become a natural subject when connecting with Artemis. We will look into our personal totem animal and the message they have for us, through a drumming meditation. We will also incorporate the use of Oracle cards by Steven D. Farmer, *"Messages from your Animal Spirit Guides"* and unearth our own personal totem via its suggestion.

WORKSHOP III:
Ritual Head **Maiden Circlets**; Attendants will gather around to collect silk floral flower pieces and tie them up to create for themselves Spring, Floral, Head Circlets. There will also be a discussion on the Head Chakra and the Customary adornment of the head through out the ages.

WORKSHOP IV:
Empowerment meditation. Inviting Artemis and her Nymphs via a special

meditation and a discussion will ensue afterwards to share our experience during trance work and the meditation.

WORKSHOP V:
Archery. Since this is Artemis' domain this can really help attendants tap into her energy and her attributes. The very act of holding a Bow and arrow correctly, quickly attunes you to this beloved, maiden Huntress. In this very act we hone into her "Sacred Will" and the gifts of "Focus and Aim". It can be very Empowering, as some wommin may never have practiced archery before. Holding Archery equipment, thinking upon the goals you wish to attain and grounding into the Archer's stillness & courageous techniques needed to ground, Aim and Focus to attain desired target. These skills are applicable in our magickal workings.

WORKSHOP VI:
A discussion on **Astrology** and looking into the attributes of Earth Signs and what they can reveal to us. Artemis is almost compulsory related to the crescent moon, but there is a strong aspect of her related to the earth, as she is the wild, untamable maiden force that dwells in the mountain tops and in the raw uncultivated forest. In this workshop we will look at the three astrological earth signs;
Taurus (fixed),
Virgo (mutable),
Capricorn (cardinal),
Looking into the attributes and influence of these earth signs to see what they bring into our astrological charts. Some qualities are being grounded, slower paced, concern with those things that are tangible, concrete and measurable.These earth signs have an ability to manifest things on the earthly plane, turn dreams into reality, be productive and abundantly creative, but they can also be stubborn, workaholics, tenacious and unimaginative. Together we will delve deeper into how we can best utilze this knowledge.

REFLECTIONS ON ARTEMIS
    Artemis comes into our lives and teaches us a lesson on the value of sisterhood and embracing the power found within our gender's community. For when we gather together in the fields, amidst nature, under her crescent moon, at gathering where there are wommin, there is much that we CAN accomplish together. Yet, she also champions the necessity for solitude, balance and relishing our privacy and seclusion, every now and then. The ocassional solo retreat, among the wilderness and even mountain tops, is almost quintessentially mandatory for our gender. It feeds the soul and it is an invaluable gifts to ourselves as wommin.
    Endearing animals to us, she introduces us to our primal connection to the animals in the wild. They have much to teach us, if we give them proper respect and reverence. They can greatly enhance our spiritual work. Artemis awakens the autonomous, free roaming, wild One and she introduces mother bear, protector of the young. She awaken our inner strength and teaches us the power of our Focus and Will, to attain our target. When she enters your life you know what you want and how to wield it to fruition. She shares her gifts, as the Divine Archer and teaches us to the art of competition, targeting, focusing and attaining our goals with clear sight and ambition. Whether alone or in community, among a Systerhood, she connects us to the beloved creatures of the land,the magick of nature, the power of the moon and helps us value our sisters, our own autonomy and the gifts of the Archer -confidently, attaining our target every time. Hail to the wild MaidenGoddess, Artemis!

*"Women need real moments of solitude and self reflection to balance with
how much of ourselves we give away..." Barbara De Angelis*

ARTEMIS GROVE GODDESS GATHERING RITUAL

Purpose: To strengthen some of Artemis attributes in ourselves; namely her gifts of Empowerment, Sisterhood, Strong aim & focus on a goal until manifested...
     Also, as Sisters we are going to be planting each other's Equinox Seeds/Wishes to strengthen community and make us aware of our interconnectiveness. Celebrate Spring!

ALTAR SET UP:
     Bell is rung and heard to denote we are ready to begin, Procession is formed, walking towards the entrance
PURIFICATION: with Artemis Oil -Entry into sacred space.
Musical selection is played and heard as they enter. It sets the tone for our ritual. The Women enter into the room already lit with candles, and an altar in the center.
Season Intent Announcer : Defining for us this Ritual and its purpose.

     CIRCLE CASTING using Bow and Arrow or Wood Branch Wand, and recite an appropriate Prose. (see appendix for sugggestions)

ELEMENTAL CALLS

Hail Realm of the East! Flight of the arrow from the Huntress' arms, Gifts of the strong, focused mind, we call on you Air, to bring your energy to our circle, as you witness and guard our sacred rites.
Hail and Welcome Air.

Hail Realm of Fire! Pulsating Heart, Heat of our blood, Bubbling and rising in the Cauldron of our wombs, we call on you Fire, to bring your energy to our circle, as you witness and guard our sacred rites.
Hail and Welcome Fire.

Hail Realm of the West! Our Tears, our joys, our well earned sweat, Compassionate realm that unifies us as wommin, we call on you Water, to bring your energy to our circle, as you witness and guard our sacred rites.
Hail and Welcome Water.

Hail Realm of the Earth! Where we play, where we love, where we diligently work... Holder of our earthly body and our manifested visions, we call on you Earth, to bring your energy to our circle, as you witness and guard our sacred rites.
Hail and Welcome Earth.

     Invoking Artemis *(prose suggestion in this chapter)*
     Invoking Artemis with **song**: *"Honor maiden Huntress..."*
          Chant: Artemis Song
Priestess aspecting Artemis appears and speaks... (see suggestion), Dressed in her tunic, Ready to move and dance like the Maiden she is. Holding her bow and arrow and medium Cauldron to hold journaling sheets...enter...

Aspecting, Artemis speaks of her gifts,
Next she instructs them to pin her Sister next to her....
In a circle each woman will Pin a safety pin unto her neighboring sister's breast/chest saying *"...Be empowered my sister you are of the Goddess..."*
     Meditation Offering...
After meditation the Goddess will **pass out sheets of paper & pens** so that the women can journal unto their paper what IT IS they require of Artemis. **What do you hope to manifest in this season of growth?**   *There is simple quietude now but this journaling should NOT take long...Anonymous neat journaling as someone else will be reading your wish.

Afterwards, the Priestess goes around **collecting these papers again** back into her basket or cauldron. She will now place her hand in the batch, mix it, imbue energy, enchant and begin a Frenetic maiden Bear Dance with the cauldron of wishes. She dances and shows it off for all to see and encourages all to join in the center.

Wommin Sing for her, drumming, chanting to raise the energy
1. "Lady of the Moon be with us come to us..."
2. "I feel her power running thru me Artemis Blessings..."
*3. "Onward we go round the Spiral song"

When the energy has been raised. Stop-
A very long **Green Gauze scarf** will be passed around, placed in the hands of every woman there in the circle.

Artemis will speak, instruct, and invite each womyn to select a seed (a slip of paper) from her basket, containing a sister's seasonal wish

*Sisterhood: We are planting each other's seeds, NOT just our own,
to strengthen our community and to make us aware
of our inter-connectiveness as sisters....
Each sister in the circle will take one of the
notes in the batch and read it aloud;
womyn read the wish aloud saying; "For my Sister I will Plant her seed of____(read the anonymous wish)_____"

After reading the note, take safety pin and pin the wish unto the green gauze fabric(*we are planting with this act.*)When all have done this and the scarf is covered in pinned paper wishes begin **Singing in the circle** while holding this scarf.

Music: Equinox Chant

If we are able to, we can continue this singing, moving outdoors while holding up and exalting the Green gauze, then returning back to our circle space.
Chanting: **"She changes everything she touches and everything she ...."**
As we Return come back to center of the sanctuary
*Artemis invites you to *"PLANT YOUR SEEDS NOW"*. Each woman comes to the center and **drops her part** of the green gauze until there is a big pile of green grass looking gauze in the center. (this symbolizes the green Spring earth/grass and our wishes with the potential to rise and manifest...)

Season intent Announcer Summarizes:
*"We have touched upon the Spirit of the Maiden Huntress and in this sabbat, planted our sacred seeds and commemorated the sabbat of Spring. May the Magick we made today, continue to blossom and reverberate into the astral plane!
So mote it be...."*

Devoking & Thanking Goddess
Dearest Maiden of the Moon
Beloved Huntress, receive our thank you,
Your gifts we hold dear in our hearts
though at this moment we must depart.
Syster Goddess, we are grateful for you,
receive our gratitude, as we bid thee adieu.
Hail and farewell Artemis!

Devoking all Quarters
Earth, the protector and supporter in our Rites,
we felt you as you guarded our sacred space.
With heartfelt thanks we bid thee Adieu.
Hail and Farewell Earth.

Water, your flowing streams became our Divine guard,
With heartfelt Gratitude we bid thee Adieu.
Hail and Farewell Water.

Fire, your passionate flames encircled us warmly in safety.
With heartfelt Gratitude we bid thee Adieu.
Hail and Farewell Fire.

Air, we felt your stirring winds guarding our sacred circle.
With heartfelt thanks we bid thee Adieu.
Hail and Farewell Air.

<u>**Equinox Gifts**</u> of colored eggs will be passed around the circle now, you may also offer eggshaped chocolates to help with grounding as we do a final check in before devoking.

Opening circle,
with our traditional song, *"The Circle is open, but unbroken...may the peace of the Goddess be ever in our hearts, merry meet and merry part and merry meet again..."*

Cakes and Ales to complete the celebration of Spring!

Artemis Meditation for Sisterhood Empowerment

...Rest soundly, rest deeply, follow my voice as it lulls you into this moment and gently leads you through the astral plane to this new realm. Breathe! All journeys begin with our breath. As I count backwards, from five to one, breathe as we go deeper into this hibernation. Breathe, five, and allow my voice as it leads you to go deeper into this realm... four (breathe and exhale) three, (deeper still, breathe), two. When you awake it will be Spring...One.

Breathe into this moment and with your mind's eye, awaken from this deep... deep slumber in the cool damp, dawn of Spring. It does not feel like Spring yet, but you sense something different in the air. As you awake, look around you and then let your gaze fall to the ground. Look down at your feet... notice where you stand now....(pause)

A grey, furry, Hare is spotted by your toes. How strange you think, but quite impulsively feel a need to reach down for it, as you can't help but want to caress it. As you reach for it, the Hare scurries off. **"Come back,"** you hear yourself cry aloud and barefoot you instinctively, run out to chase after it. (Pause)

Keep your eye on this hare and follow it as it is very quick. It seems to be heading towards the expansive, dark forest, but that doesn't worry you and you continue running after it. (pause)Feel the strength and the vitality coursing through you, birthing from within. Run now..run feeling your heart beat beginning to accelerate with each step.... Get comfortable in this new body, in this realm, as you feel your body take on speed and run. Feel the renewed strength, coursing through your legs as you chase after this furry little earth creature. Unearth your maiden self and run, you are almost catching up with it... (pause)

The ground feels crunchy, so hard and cold upon your bare feet now. Did you even notice you were barefoot the whole time you were running? After a while the soles of your feet become so numb from the cold that you can't even feel them. Deeper into the forest you go, still deeper down a winding road, running without hesitation, deeper into the forest where the Hare leads you...until all you see are tall trees and the brown soil under your feet. Suddenly you notice it feels so much warmer. You notice now the ground feels delightfully softer, mushier and warmer now. Its color and scent has even changed before your eyes. It is looser and moist, where you stand now. You stop and take in a deep breath (breathe) and exhale to slow down your heartbeat. Look around this new magickal realm. Have you ever traveled so deeply into the forest? You don't see the Hare anywhere now and you don't know how to get back either.... Breathe calmly. Take a minute to survey your surrounding and with your mind's eye, see through the darkness. (pause)

Suddenly, to your left, you hear a rustling... *"that must be it,"* you think, as you prepare to go, but another sound permeates the air... From the right it sounds like whispers... Curiosity beckons you to follow it. Who? or what? could that be?

You walk deeper and deeper still into the forest. The whispers become louder and louder. As you get closer they become a loud Chatter of voices. The chatter of women, happily conversing, giggling and boisterously engaged in conversations.... They look so majestic from a far. They seem like giants.

You cautiously get closer and See. .. some faces look familiar, some do not. Study them closely with your mind's eye, who do you see? (pause) One of them spots you and before you could hide, they **all** turn around and notice you, and the chatter now gets even louder as it turn towards you...

"...We've been waiting for you..., We've been waiting for you... , so glad you're here..., we've been waiting for you... the voices swelled from the group.
They called on you as if, to this clan of women, you were a looong lost relative. You begin to attempt to reply,"*...I was just chasing...*" *"Yes we know... Are you ready?"* They interrupt. *Ready for what?*, you wonder... Overwhelmed, You want to Run again... run as far as you can in the other direction..but...then... you see **"Her"**... In full view with her bow and arrows and her Stags by her feet and that beloved Crescent Moon upon her brow. Captivated by her unusual brilliance and strength, you can't move. You can't leave now...

The clan of wommin gather around you, surrounding you....embracing you... the way the green trees in the forest had earlier. Can you feel their breath and the heat emanating from their bodies surrounding yours now? They are so young and energetic, though they were all representing different ages.

"Are you ready to receive my gifts?" *You heard Artemis inquire.*
"Each priestess here will present it to you. You have the option of accepting or not." You step forward and Accept...
One by one they begin with an energetic exuberant Wave You have never felt before....
The flurry of young Maidens and Amazons begin to speak;

I give you Courage
I give you Protection
I give you Physical strength

I give you Confidence & Competence
I give you Hope
I give you the Aim & Focus of an Archer

I give you Sisterhood & Equality
I give you Discipline
I give you Knowledge of your Choices

I give you Mental Strength
I give you Light
I give you Success in your Goals

I give you Freedom
I give you Delight in your own Body
I give you Womyn Power

I give you Decisiveness
I give you Clarity
I give you Rule over your own body

I give you Endurance
I give you Victory
I give to you **Self Love...**

With each gift presented to you, you feel their spirit penetrate and meld with your own. In the end, you feel saturated beholding **All** of their gifts and yet, you have never felt such Liberation and this tall sense of Empowerment from within.

Artemis was the last one to present you with a gift...
Artemis places her laurel wreath upon your head, as the last gift.
Can you feel the weight of her laurel wreath upon you? (pause)
Can you feel her gifts on you... IN you? (pause)
She shut her eyes, nothing needs to be said and then she too melds, into you.

For a moment you stand still, alone, holding all of them as your gifts. Knowing NOW that Spring has finally come. That renewed spirit of the season stirs in your heart now as it pulsates. Artemis, Maiden Goddess, stirs in your heart now... Breathe... Breathe.... Breathe with your renewed maiden heart, Breathe in with your renewed lungs, breathe with your renewed spirit and body. Just Breathe... (pause)
With your mind's eye, take this moment to survey this realm and commit to memory any memorable images before you. Breathe (pause)
   Begin to walk back... perhaps you now realize you are unsure of how to get back home...Suddenly, the Hare appears once more and this time it is not running, but walking slowly, inviting you to follow. Follow its slow movement, as it leads you through the forest once more, carefully retracing your steps back home. Breathe with every step you take to return back home.
**With your mind's eye, when you see your home again and you are safely in your familiar environment , you may open your eyes then and join us in this time and this space. Follow my voice and join us here. With your exhalation return to this room, return to this moment here now. Return....Welcome back ....

ASPECTING ARTEMIS SPEAKS

My beloved sisters... You are of my utmost concern. I live and breathe for you.
*To protect you,
*To Encourage you,
*To remind you of your Strength.
*To bring your consciousness back to the beginning,
Back to a time when the Divine Feminine was honored.
Do you Remember ?-----

    I serve to remind you from whence your strength comes from, To remind you of your origins. ...OH... Do not let society erase our history. How often society will make you feel insignificant, unsupported and irrelevant.
Form from Rib???? How they'll make you feel secondary and leave you doubtful.
But I am here to tell you It is NOT how it was, nor how it is.
*It might've become **their** Reality... But it is **not** yours.*

    Let me remind you of
*Who you are,
*Where you came from and
*What you have inside of you.
Let me remind you-of **ALL** the wommin that have come before you;
Strong, Significant Impactful
    And how **All** of their strength lies within you.... Including mine own.
*Mine is the gift of **Courage** to accept yourself as you are and not conform
*Mine is the gift of **Confidence** for you are of the superior species not inferior
*Mine is the Gift of **Straight forwardness** for each of us has the right to be heard
*Mine is the Gift **of Sisterhood** for we are NOT enemies but of the same Blood line,
*Mine is the Gift of **Mind over heart** for we are not to be
    enslaved, consumed by our powerful emotions.
*Mine is the Gift of **Physical Vitality** for our bodies are our Sacred Temples

I am **NOT** some image in your history books. I am NOT some image in the sky or in mythology. I am here NOW living and breathing in the hearts of womyn who choose to see me and Acknowledge me.
*I am in the Women Politician
*I am in the Teacher who teaches young girls to become women.
*I am in the Child Advocate (Advocating for Children's rights)
*I am in the Defender of Abused Women
*I am in the Midwives helping in childbirth
*I am in the Competitive Athletes
*I am in the Animal Rescuer and the Ecologist
*I am in the Feminist
*I am in the lover of women and in the women experimenting with her sexuality
*I am in the Solo Traveler who loves being among the wilderness.
*I am in that Friend that never lets you down and at your weakest hour gives you words of encouragement.
*I am in the woman who DEFIES convention and lives her life according to her own rules.
*I am in EVERY Priestess and deep down inside I am in Every one of you.
See me ...Recognize me....Acknowledge me
**My gifts will meet all of your needs!

ASPECTING ARTEMIS

Behold I am Queen of The Hunt
Leader of the Amazons,
Virgin Goddess,
whole unto myself.

Patroness of Midwives,
Protector of Children,
Women and all beast,
Goddess of the Crescent New Moon.
I am Artemis...

From the time I was a child, I defied convention
and vowed to live my life
according to my own rules.
When women were in need
or found themselves in great danger
I was their Defender and Protector.
I still am.

Call on me, as others have for centuries,
when you're birthing new life,
for I have much experience as a midwife.

I am lover of the Trees,
the Forest and the Mountains...
I am lover of the hare,
the stag, dogs and all beast,

I am Queen Archer
And no one can match,
my keen Aim and Focus
Feel my Strength surging thru you
it is called **WOMYN POWER.**

Look around,
See the Beautiful faces next to you,
unified in my worship,
It is called **SISTERHOOD**

My gift to you,
is confidence
and that keen Aim & Focus of an Archer.

What will you <u>chose</u> to use my gifts for?
What will you **Aim** and **Attain** this season?

Let's invoke Power/Empowerment....

If I were to invoke Empowerment like We invoke the elements (Earth, Fire, Water, Air), here's what I would say:

I invoke you Power
I invoke the color red, burgundy, deep Blood red
I invoke the powers found in A woman in the midst of giving birth with her pants and grunts, pushing new life out of her.

I invoke the powers found in A runner, running full force past the finish line.
I invoke Madonna during her "Truth or Dare" stage.
I invoke the power found in My mother, *may she rest in peace.*
I invoke the power to stand Tall, with an upright posture
I invoke the powers found in The crash of waves
I invoke the powers found in my own voice when at times I needed to be heard
I invoke the powers needed to face a test and challenges
I invoke the power found in The bonds of women
I invoke the roar of a Large Mama Bear
I invoke the _____

ARCHERY WORKSHOP INCANTATION FOR FOCUS & AIM

Artemis' Gift
Of Focus and Aim
Gather now in me
As we play this Game

Bow and Arrow
Charged thru my hand,
This wish I make true
By will and command.

As I pull this Magick bow
Let my spell wish take hold
Strength I call from Artemis
Maiden Goddess now bless us.

Exemplifying Artemis

I have Courage,
I am not afraid,
See how I roam the forest
Night and day.

Communing with Beast.
Donning the scent of Cedar,
I am Confident as
the Amazon's beloved Leader.

In the mountains alone,
or with my clan of sisters
My soul now has melded
To commune with her.

I am beautiful and chaste,
Nature's beauty upon my face.
The moon on my brow
Wolf and Stag answer my howl.

I am heard and respected .
I am eloquent when I speak,
I run with delight
across the mountain peaks.

With my Bow and Arrow
Focused as I am,
Grounded and fearless,
Steady are my hands.

My voice is desired
and it is heard aloud,
clear and deliberate
as I am confident and proud.

See my posture,
See how I walk
See how I carry myself
when I talk.

I have the gift to inspire,
all the wommin that come to me
travel my sisters,
find strength in our blesed journey,

As Maiden I do stand,
Excelling in all I do,
Hear me because I am Artemis,
Immortal Goddess of the Moon.

A CALL TO ARTEMIS IN JOURNEYS, IN DREAMS

I woke up this morning praising the Goddess for I knew she had blessed me with her presence in my dreams. I woke up feeling loved and an electricity I hadn't felt in a long time. Between wake and dream realms, I heard myself saying *"....I exalt you Diana Artemis, I revere you most holy one, I am blessed, Thank you for your love..."*

In this dream I was in some sort of, shopping mall, on the bottom, main floor, where some kiosks were set up and I remember walking along a pathway. There were numerous stores, the way most malls are set up, all around the perimeters of the second level above me. There was a notably festive, jovial feeling in the air- people scattered around; walking, eating, shopping and just carrying on normally. Intrigued, I looked all around, my eyes trying to savor and record every image that passed my way.

I started walking, but suddenly I was trying to quicken my pace. I desperately needed to run to get somewhere. I felt an unusual urgency and I needed to go faster, but I felt heavy. I could feel the weight of my own legs, like anchors in molasses, not cooperating and holding me back. My body was not in harmony with my strong will and spirit and I heard myself call out to "Her" in supplication. *"....Artemis... Artemis, I call on you Diana Artemis, give me wings....Goddess lend me your fires to quicken my pace, lend me your legs and feet to carry me far. Beloved Artemis, lend me your wings and imbue me with the light and quick pace of the Huntress...."* As I was praying to her, all of a sudden, all those people in the mall, all those strangers, scattered around the whole mall began to sing in a heartwarming, celestial choir-like, manner. Slowly they drew nearer, slowly they gathered like bees, surrounding me with their voices, while singing the beautiful "Triple Goddess Chant". I heard them sing:

Honor Maiden Huntress, Artemis, Artemis,
New Moon Come to us...
Silver Shinning Wheel of
Radiance, Radiance,
Mother Come to us...
Honor Queen of Wisdom,
Hecate , Hecate,
Wise one Come to us....

I heard the lyrics clearly at this moment in the dream and my heart swelled and was overtaken, bursting with such an overwhelming feeling of love, hope and joy, by what I was actually experiencing. And the faint distant singing became stronger and more beautiful, fueling me with strength, giving my legs the power of flight. There were children and adults and people of various ethnicities singing this beautiful Goddess chant. Around my feet, I could see three little black dogs running by me, which for me, have always been a sacred symbol of Hekate's presence. When I saw them in the dream, I knew that I was being visited, not only by Artemis -the Maiden, Crescent moon, but also by the beloved Crone -the Dark of the Moon and the triple aspect of the Goddess was unmistakably present. I felt such an immanent, deep love. I felt light enough to fly with my feet, like the Huntress and I started to feel like I could. The people in this mall moved closer to me, gently pushing me forward, while they continued singing. And with their energy, gently pushing me, begging me to start running. They followed me and it was almost as if they were forcing me to go, only one way now - onward and forward, with full speed and grace.

In the dream, I continued to run partaking in a kind of journey, or a quest and it led me to some sort of college dorm room with various over-cluttered rooms and a long corridor that seemed to connect each dormitory room to the next. What stood out about these rooms was the clutter, the myriads of special mementoes and unique bohemian décor. There were Arabian sheer veils, Moroccan sarongs in fuchsias, reds and oranges and coppers. There were beautiful, colorful rich tapestries hanging from one room to the next and I was going through each room, the way a backpacker travels around Europe, collecting faces, idle chit chats, intimate conversations, tempestuous experiences and memories with everything and everyone I encountered.

I reached, what seemed like, the end of this journey, a small bohemian café. With intimate small bistro tables and a few people inside sipping their tiny demi-tasse, delicately drinking their tiny espressos. I watched two ladies sitting rather closely-talking....whispering. They were obviously good friends. I approached them and handed them my business card. They took my card, then studied my face ever so deeply and then looked down at my card. One of the woman commented to her friend and then turned to me, saying how beautiful she thought I was... Her comment had so much scrutiny and depth and a sincerity that it moved me to tears. She said to me, I was more beautiful than anything she had ever seen and she made a comment about my "gift." At this point, I can't remember exactly what she was referring to, but I was moved by her kind words, which had been spoken to me like an older, wiser syster, like an all-knowing Gypsy or psychic who was looking into my soul, doing an impromptu mystical tarot or psychic reading just for me.

My pace, which all along had been frenetically fast and fiery, after the magickal event at the mall, had now slowed down quite substantially. In this Parisian like café, I found myself calm and cool, as if this was the destination I needed to hurry to. Perhaps in this café I had finally reached a goal, an awareness or some level of self-worth and value. I began to walk away after meeting these ladies and I headed towards the door. There to my right , near the exit, was another small bistro table with a gentleman (although now, I think it might have been another woman)- not sure of gender. Before heading out, I confidently walked to this person and placed my business card again on the table, offering it for the person to read. Together we engaged in a discussion about pursuing our goals and I was strangely, greatly encouraged. At this point, the dream gets a little foggy, as I was preparing to wake up...and indeed I woke up praising Artemis and singing her Goddess chant.

I think it can be extremely hard and quite challenging to remember our dreams and then be able to describe them in <u>words,</u> as I just tried to do in sharing this powerful Artemis dream, and so often find myself attempting to do elsewhere. Whether it's in writing or in actual conversations, dreams are loaded and chockfull of various bright, and, not so bright, images and at times, so multi-dimensional with their rich symbolisms, making them extra difficult to translate, but well worth the effort. Some dreams are ripe, with a myriads of personal details, easily interpreted and these, coupled with intense feelings, can truly complete the whole spiritual message of a dream. It is not always easy to translate these series of compelling symbolisms well in writing. Still it doesn't stop me from continually trying to do so and sharing those dreams I feel are pivotal in my spiritual life with others. This happens to be one of those powerful dreams; as I truly felt Artemis coming to my aid when called, but more importantly, I saw the connection between my life's journey and her divine manifestation in my life. I felt her presence, supporting and guiding me through other wommin and I directly experienced Artemis' definition of sisterhood and our connection to one another as we all embark in our respective journey. This is how I approach this month's Goddess gathering, as Artemis comes to me as big Sister, reminding all womyn of our common bond. Blessed Be....

A spell to welcome and invoke the Huntress Goddess, Artemis. Have a statue of this beloved Goddess or a photo image of her. You can also have a sacred symbol of hers, like hounds, stags or bow and arrows. You can also present and bless your crescent moon circlet. Charge a silver, white or green candle with "Maiden oil" (see appendix) and carve it with the image of the crescent moon. Fill your chalice with rain water and as an incense; use Mugwort, also known as Artemisia and a bay leaf. Since Artemis is the Maiden Goddess of the Crescent New moon, do this spell outdoors, right after the New Moon- upon seeing the first sliver of the moon, a reflection of her sacred bow.....

ARTEMIS
*Virgin Goddess of the Moon
Born of Leto and of Zeus
Friend of Hounds, of bears and trees
Huntress, Queen of Archery.

Virgin, Mother, Crone
Triple Goddess make
You and Selene
Joined by Hekate..

Midwife to your Mother
For nine days and nine nights
To deliver your brother
The God of Sunlight.

Now you are called
By women in need,
To help with delivering
Our healthy babies

Defender of Women
Protector of the young
Twin sister to Apollo
The God of the Sun

Virgin, Mother, Crone
Creating a divine trine
Triple Goddess formed
Revered since old times

Hail to thee Artemis
Goddess of the Moon
Receive my reverence
And my gratitude.

Hail and Welcome Artemis!

To invoke Artemis, in a sacred Circle, on the first night of the Crescent New Moon. Use a Silver, white or even a blue candle, carved with an image of the crescent moon. Charge your candle with Cypress oil, or Maiden oil (see Appendix). Use an incense of earthy scented patchouli or mugwort herb upon your charcoal brisket. Decorate your altar with images of the Maiden Greek Goddess; statue of the Goddess, or hounds, stags, hares, bow and arrow, tree branches and moon circlets are all appropriate for her.

ARTEMIS
*We call upon Artemis
Beloved Goddess of the moon
Amidst this sacred circle we invoke you

Enchantress, Protector
Queen of Mountains up high.
We celebrate you on this lunar night

Illuminate our spirits
Illuminate our minds
Our journey begins
With words of rhyme

Artemis Luna
We hail to thee
Show us now our own divinity

Here do we stand
To receive your insight
Make us the reflection
Of your divine light

Charge us as the Witches
That we are
Fill us with the magic
of the moon and the stars

Powerful and wise,
as ancestors of ol'
This spell is now cast,
Let magick take hold

For this spell I use a red candle, as red is a color associated with energy, life force and vitality, but you may use any color that speaks to you personally. Decorate altar with images of strong wommin, Amazonian wommin that speak to you personally about strength. See yourself already embodying the essence of the Amazons and having their full support in your endeavor. Charge your candle with "Maiden Oil" (see appendix). Place your running shoes, or any workout attire, on the altar to be charged and blessed. Include a small crystal to imbue with this renewed Moon Goddess energy, for future use in times of weakness. To drink, prepare a glass of clean, clear water with this charged crystal. Ingest a new you -healthier and stronger. Do this spell when the moon is waxing, preferable when the moon is in Sagittarius or Aries, which are fiery energized astrological signs.

TO INVOKE HER POWERS OF VITALITY

Beloved Huntress,
Dearest Amazon systers
.....Artemis come and bless me
Help me to unearth the energy,
vitality strength of the Amazon
and great health.
From the depths of my soul,
Let me draw upon you,
your essential omnipotent energy of life,
Your vitality,
Coursing thru my blood.
From the toes of my feet,
to my blessed crown chakra
Let me feel you, Pulsating through me
Fueling me with divine energy,
embedding in me,
thy fiery immortal spark and zest for life....
I run with thy feet and
breathe with thy lungs
and sing of thy beauty,
I Dance with thy surge of creative expression
in your sacred circle,
I sing of you, with you,
exemplifying your strength
and magick.....

SISTERHOOD

Maiden Huntress, Swirling in Green
I draw you from the depths of my dreams
Stepping forward you take my hand,
Together we are the Spiral Dance,

I turn, you turn and sway with me,
Friendship, sisterhood now forming,
And In this spell, Camaraderie and trust,
I invoke your gifts, Maiden Huntress.

Herein I call the Most sincere
And in their light, loneliness disappears,
Beloved Goddess reveal yourself to me,
Thru encounters with those that are friendly.

Around me stand Callisto, and my Amazon friends,
I am comforted knowing, it is me they defend.
From my left, to my right,
From before me and behind
The circle is cast and all are allies.

I am never alone, when you are near ,
You bring the clan of those who are dear.
Howling Goddess of the Moon
Tonight we invoke our Sisterhood.
Donning Bow and Arrows Bright,
True friends I draw in with this candle's light...

ARTEMIS GROVE GODDESS GATHERING CHANTS

SONGS FOR ARTEMIS
I feel her Powers,
running through me,
Artemis Blessing
I am you, you are me.
Queen of the Moonlight
Maiden and Free,
Lover of Women
Empower me,
Empower me,
Empower me....*By: B.M.M.*

LADY OF THE MOON-ARTEMIS
Lady of the Moon,
Be with us... Come to us....
Lady of the Moon,
Lady of the Moon.
Lady of the Hunt,
    Artemis, Artemis
Be with us.... Now be with us.... *By B.M.M.*

NEW MOON COME TO US
*Honor Maiden Huntress
Artemis
Artemis
New Moon Come to us
Silver Shinning Wheel of
Radiance
Radiance
Mother come to us
Honor Queen of Wisdom
Hecate
Hecate
wise One come to us........*By: Peter Soderberg*

Chanting: ARTEMIS....ARTEMIS..... ARTEMIS....
***She changes everything She touches and everything She touches changes**
By: Starhawk

EQUINOX CHANT
Onward we go round the Spiral
Touching darkness, touching light
Twice each year we rest in balance
Make choices on this night
Make choices on this night *By: Marie Summerwood*

SHE GATHERS HER DAUGHTERS
She gathers her daughters by Moon and by Sun
She gathers her daughters it has begun

She gathers her daughters to turn the wheel
She gathers her daughters to learn and heal

She gathers her daughters by Night and by Day
She gathers her daughters to lead the way

(Counter Melody, higher octave and melodious)
 By Moon and Sun
We have begun
To turn the wheel
to learn and Heal (continuous repetition) *by Ruth Rhiannon Barrett*

ARTEMIS GROVE GODDESS GATHERING CHANTS -II

MAIDEN DANCING by B.M.M.
Spiraling Dancing, Up and Down
Reaching the Center with Floral Crown
Laughing Maiden, Giggles are free
I've awaken the Maiden in me.
>See me Jump, Jump, Jump,
>Cross the meadow Field
>See me Fearless and Beautiful
>and dancing the Wheel.

STANDING LIKE A TREE
Standing like a tree with my roots thrust down
My branches wide and open,
Come blow the Wind,
Come blow the Rain,
Come blow the Love,
To a heart that is open. *By Starhawk*

>**MAIDEN MOTHER CRONE**
>Smiling Virgin, Shinning Crescent
>Waxing fullness
>Luminescent
>Sickle of Silver,
>Weaver of Bones
>Maiden, Mother and Crone . *By Abby Spinner*

SHE WALKS WITH SNAKES
She walks with snakes, she stands on the moon
She walks with snakes, she stands on the moon
She walks with snakes, she stands on the moon
Mary, Mary, Mary, Mary stands on the moon
(repeat)
Touch me with your hands of light
Crown of stars to bless the night
Mother Mary give me sight
That I may see
She walks with snakes she stands on the moon
She walks with snakes she stands on the moon
She walks with snakes she stands on the moon
Mary, Mary, Mary, Mary
Mary, Mary, Mary, Mary
Mary, Mary, Mary, Mary
Mary, Mary, Mary, Mary
Stands on the Moon   *By Marie Summerwood*

SWEET SURRENDER
We are Opening up in Sweet Surrender
to the Luminous Love light of the one
We are Opening up in Sweet Surrender
to the Luminous Love light of the one
We are Opening.....We are Opening (2X) *by Gladys Gray*

>**ELEMENTAL GODDESS CHANT**
>Earth, Air Fire Water, I am the Witches daughter
>Oya is me and I am she.
>Earth Air Fire Water, I am the witches daughter
>Brigit is me and I am she,
>Earth, Air Fire Water, I am the Witches daughter
>Hathor is me and I am she,
>Earth, Air Fire Water, I am the Witches daughter
>Gaia is me and I am she. By Unknown

April

The Astrological sign of the month is Aries, the ram, and it is ruled by Mars, (March 21-April 20). April is the fourth month of the Gregorian calendar, though originally it was known as the second month in the Roman year. It is believed that when King Numa Pompillius changed January, electing it to be the first month of the year, April thus became the fourth month. Because the Romans named their months to honor their deities it would seem likely that this month was named after the Roman Goddess of Love, Aprilis. She shares many similarities to Aphrodite, the Greek Goddess of Love, who was also known to the Romans as Venus. April, also comes from the Latin word, *"Aprilis"*, meaning "to open" and we can only assume this is a reference to the number of trees and flowers opening up and blossoming during this season. This is truly a magickal time of the year to relish the many wonders of nature, the multitude of colors beginning to sprout amidst our landscape and enjoy the milder temperatures outdoors. With gentle breezes felt throughout the month of April, it is not surprising the month's full moon is also called, Wind Moon.

If we look even further at the word April, it is derived from the Latin word *"aper"* also meaning *"boar."* The boar was considered one of Aphrodite's sacred animals, another indication of how connected this month is to the Goddesses of love; Aphrodite and Aprilis. The hare was considered another sacred animal to the Goddesses of Love and thus, it is only fitting that the Full moon of this month is sometimes known as the Hare moon. According to the Farmer's Almanac, April's full moon was also referenced as Fish Moon and Egg Moon, which can be viewed as alluding to Aphrodite's beloved food offerings and the predominance of eggs as a sacred symbol of rebirth, Spring and the Goddess.

Other names for the April Full moon are Pink Moon and Sprouting Moon, due to the numerous beautiful flowers sproutings at this time of the year. The Earth indeed, appears ripe, verdant and at the height of its powers of fertility. All around us are signs that Spring is finally here and we are showered with ancient symbols of the Goddess; the hare, eggs, chirping birds, the bright sun, blooming flowers, crafted baskets filled with goodies, colorful ribbons and bonnets, gardens with green lush landscapes. And it appears that the offspring of both humans and animals begin to make themselves better known as they come out to play more often in the warming climate.

Those seeds we planted in the previous months, now begin to sprout into small blossomings and, excitedly, we begin to see signs of hope, fruition and beauty everywhere. Even in the Christian holiday of Easter, there is hope and renewal and the theme of resurrection. The value and the beauty of the Earth is also commemorated on National Earth day, also known as Arbor day, on April 22nd. This holiday that started in Nebraska in 1872 by a newspaper publisher named, Julius Sterling Morton, aimed to plant more trees and honor the earth. The first of the month is reserved for all kinds of mischievous pranks and youthful joviality, with the advent of April Fool's Day. The Maiden energy is truly exemplified right from the start of the month and reaches its zenith upon the following months.

This month, we take the time to recognize the beauty that is manifesting itself all around us, in nature and within us. What better Goddess to work with, at this time, than the one this month was named after. We call on the Greek Goddess of Love, Aphrodite, and touch upon her gifts of love and attraction, through a traditional self-blessing. We will also be working intimately with the energy of the Mayan Moon Goddess, Ix Chel. She has much to teach us, as wommin, about our amazing connection to the moon. Both deities rule over the realm of Water and together we will connect with the beautiful gifts of our gender and the various cathartic powers of the sacred element of water.
All Hails!

CHAPTER TEN

"I am Beautiful as I am, I am the shape that was gifted. My breasts are no longer perky and upright like when I was teenager. My hips are wider than that of a fashion models, for this I am glad for these are the signs of a life, lived...." Cindy Olwen

"Sex is energy exchange, communion, relief, release, a dance, sometimes healing, sometimes fun, mostly a ritual to her...." B.Melusine

WELCOMING APHRODITE

OUR ALTAR

Altar cloth: Pink and maybe a second white or gold altar cloth underneath.
Image: Venus de Milo Statue of the Greek Goddess, or any other esthetically pleasing looking female statuary, nudes are also perfect for this altar.
Canvas art or photo of the Sea foam Goddess or and photos of Cyprus, its flag, Greece and the Ocean or mermaids and or lovers in heated passionate embrace. You may also include photos of yourself, mirrors and images of your beloved or things that evoke warm feelings of love and joy.

Always present on the altar;
A cast iron cauldron, drums, speaking stick, a silver pentacle, athame, elemental representations.....

Air: Bird statuaries, especially lovebirds or doves, peacock feathers, sweet smelling incense (sticks, cones), charcoal brisket and fine powdered herbs, gentle wind chimes.
Fire: candles, glass enclosed candles or pillars in pinks and whites and or a women shaped, also seashell image candles. You may also use yoni shaped, heart, rose-like shaped candles, which are popular during February's Valentine day holiday.
Water: Chalice or small glass bowl with Water or pink Champagne
Earth: Most appropriate is to decorate your altar with as many beautiful roses as possible. Lots of fertile green lush plants, a small dish of saltl and or herbs like Jasmine, Yarrow, Damiana, Basil.

Other items pertinent to this particular gathering
An abundance of Seashells and large scalloped ones,
Sand and pearls,
You can gather mini chocolate eggs from Easter sales or actual hard boil eggs
Statuaries of birds and feathers
Figurines of dolphins and fishes
Statuaries of Bunnies to represent fertility and friskiness
Red Roses -lots of greenery
Bowls of perfumed water
Lipstick tubes
Rose quartz, Amazonite, Howlite, Green Aventurine gemstone
Plate offerings with Apples
Writing pens and paper, safety pins,
Light blue gauzy fabric to represent water
Workshop items
Tarot or other Oracular items

Offering example food; apples, peaches, doves heart, oysters, clams
Sacred objects from members:
Notes:

Aphrodite Altar

Aphrodite Altar

APHRODITE

Greek Goddess of Love and Beauty, her Roman counterpart was Venus. Aphrodite is one of the oldest and most recognized, powerful deities of our time. Her origins can be traced to the East of Cyprus and Cytheria. She is known as the Goddess of Beauty and Gracefulness. She is cherished as Goddess of Attraction and the iconic, beloved Goddess of love, but more specifically, she is about that instant attraction and she can bring pleasure as well as pangs of love. Aphrodite doesn't concern herself with consequences for she is the one that arouses desire and great passion, regardless of the situation. She is about physical coupling, infatuations and sexual longings. She is not about the institution or sanctity of marriage but rather that of sexual attraction, first experienced and necessary to maintain within a marriage.

She was sometimes known as the Goddess of the Prostitutes, for here again, in this profession, her powers of seduction and attraction was greatly needed and called upon. Hetairai, as they were called, were not only beautiful, but were highly skilled in music, dancing, art, eloquent speech and the art of seduction -all Aphrodite's domain.

Sea foam born, according to one Greek myth, she was born of the severed genitalia of her father, Uranus and this myth clearly supports her role as a Goddess of sexual pleasure - strongly emphasizing her own sexuality. Sometimes her sea foam birth reveals her coming out of a scallop seashell. This again is hinting at her role as a Goddess of Sexuality, as the sea shell highly resembles the form of a female's genitalia. The word scallop in Greek is, "Kteis." In Greek literature this word is also used to describe a woman's yoni.

Golden Aphrodite was often depicted and described as nude or half naked, dressing, undressing, or being adorned. This called attention to her incredible physical beauty as a sexual Goddess. Often she was depicted with the Three graces: Algaia (*the bright one*), Euphrasy (*the glad one*) and Thaleia (*the abundant one*). They are reflections of Aphrodite herself and they assist her in ornamenting her curvaceous body. The Graces are often employed to help with anointing the Goddess with divine oils, bathing, dressing and adorning her according to the writings of her time. They were always seen happily dancing, acting maiden-like and again emphasizing the flowing elements of the Goddess of Love.

The laughing One, giggling with a smile that would reduce men to babbles, her skills and art in seduction were unmatched by any other being. Aphrodite was the definition of feminine warmth, sweetness and lightheartedness, rarely ever depicted as scornful, sobbing or angry but rather always light and inviting. She was portrayed as the Golden one, whose fragrance lingered long after her absence. Her presence aroused great passion and often as a result, some tricky situations. Some of her many symbols are; honey, semen, gold, sweetness and flowers; like Roses. Sweet smelling fruits like the apple and passion red pomegranate are also her symbols.

There are two different tales about her birth according to Hesiod and Homer. Homer states that Aphrodite was born out of the union between Zeus and a Sea nymph. The most commonly accepted tale of her manifestation comes from Hesiod's literature. According to Hesiod, Gaia's consort, Uranus, was causing upheaval by not allowing Gaia to give birth to their children. Cronos, one of their sons, sought to come to his mother's aid and took a sickle and cut off his Father's genitalia. The severed Penis was thrown into the Sea, where its semen mixed with the ocean creating foam. Aphrodite emerged from this foam as a fully grown Goddess in all of her curvaceous splendor. In the early Renaissance, the Florentine Artist, Sandro Botticelli (1444-1510), created a masterpiece artwork around 1485, called *"The Birth of Venus"*, that will forever encapsulate this moment in Greek Mythology, when newly born Aphrodite came ashore the Island of Cyprus.

She was the only Goddess allowed to choose her own consorts, unlike some of the other Greek Goddesses that were either raped, seduced, abducted or tricked. In mythology there are countless of stories of her amorous conquest and entertaining tales, involving her many dalliances.

She married Hera's son, Hephaestus, the Smith God, deity of craftsmen and the fire of the Forge. They had no children together. She also consorted with, Ares, God of War. This was a known, long term, love affair that resulted in three children. Together they had a daughter Harmonia (*Harmony),* and two sons, Deimos (*Terror)* and Phobos (*Fear).* The boys, according to the writings of the time, were often depicted joining their father in the bloody battlefields. Aphrodite also found a consort in, Hermes, Messenger God, God of science, magick, and trickery. With Hermes, She bore him Hermaphroditus, the Bi-sexual God, who had both sexual characteristics of his parents. Eros, who also had a very mystical birth and who has a number of conflicting tales describing his manifestation, was in later mythology considered Aphrodite's fatherless son. He was also known as "Amor," in Rome and today is depicted as the beloved, celebrated Cupid, exalted during our U.S.A. Valentine day celebrations.

Aphrodite also found lovers in mortal men. She was aroused with great desire upon seeing, Anchises, the Mountain sid cattle grazer. With him she conceived a child that later would become the founder of Rome, Aeneas. Aphrodite was also completely smitten with Adonis, a youthful handsome hunter, who was later torn to pieces by a wild Boar. According to Greek myths, he was sent to the land of the Dead, but was permitted to return to his beloved Goddess part of the year, as a symbol of returning fertility. The Cult of Adonis performed this sacred rite -commemorating the annual return to Aphrodite in the same way Demeter and Persephone did in the Eleusinian Mysteries.

In the story of Pygmalion, the King of Cyprus creates his ideal woman by carving a large ivory sculpture. Little by little he becomes completely enrapture with his creation and falls in love with this image. During a festival honoring this great Deity he beckons Aphrodite to help him find this ideal woman in the flesh. Aphrodite in turn allows the sculpture to come to life. With one kiss from the king, his work of art comes to life, and the king finds love and marries his ideal woman.

There are also numerous tales involving women being touched and effected by Aphrodite. Throughout the story of Hera and Zeus, we learn of Aphrodite's powerful girdle and its ability to make its wearer irresistible, when Hera lays hands on it. Myrrha was made to fall madly in love with her own father and have relations with him because she neglected her Aphrosinian worship, still another probable cause was because her own mother had boasted that Myrrha was more beautiful than Aphrodite.

In yet another tale, Aphrodite caused Phaedra to have great desire for her own step-son. Uncontrollably, she finds herself in love with her step-son, Hippolytus, because Aphrodite was displeased with the son's disregard for the Goddess of Love. Hippolytus had taken vows of celibacy and devotion to the Virgin Moon Goddess, Artemis. To punish him, Aphrodite created a horrible situation in which Phaedra committed suicide and left a note falsely accusing her step-son of rape. As a result, Poseidon was summoned to kill Hippolytus.

Another interesting tale was that of Psyche. Psyche was considered so beautiful, that she was often revered as a Goddess herself and she had garnered the reputation of often being compared to the Goddess of love. Obviously, this did not sit well with the supreme Goddess of Attraction. Aphrodite created a number of challenges and road block that Psyche, eventually, was able to successfully master and as a result, she received Aphrodite's blessings in her union with her son, Eros.

Aphrodite had many important symbols like the apple and the pomegranate fruit. These fruits are commonly associated with fertility and sexuality. Sweet scents and flowers, in particular; roses and the lily, are also her sacred symbols, again suggesting sexuality and generative sexual organs. She is often depicted with dolphins - a reference to her birth at Sea and perhaps because dolphins were considered sociable, frisky and very friendly, particularly to sea travelers. Doves are associated with her because they coo and are publicly affectionate. Sparrows were said to be her charioteers and they too were her beloved symbol for their wantonness. Their eggs were often eaten as an aphrodisiac in her honor.

Anything gold and shimmering was attributed to her divine essence. Throughout the literature of her time the Goddess of love is often described with these complimentary, golden, demonstrative words. Gold is a metal that is brilliant and does not tarnish and is appropriate for this Cypriot Goddess who seem to exemplify those same qualities.

This immortal brilliant goddess is ever present in romantic and sexual unions but her engrossing spirit is easily detectable in so many other areas in our lives. In our very own creativity we can also encounter Aphrodite's gifts. For as artist, sometimes we find ourselves creating things of beauty and sensuality. When the artist is at work, there is a feeling of enrapture, drive, obsession and the type of attention and focus that most lovers experience for one another at the beginning of a romantic relationship. This is an Aphrosinian experience. In creativity there is great love, cultivations, attraction and engrossment throughout the creative process. A heighten sense of aesthetics is experienced as well as during the creative process and here too, this is Aphrodite's divine essence and gift to us.

Hail to you, captivating Aphrodite!

APHRODITE GROVE GODDESS GATHERING

PURPOSE: To invoke Aphrodite, the Goddess of Love and unearth our own beauty and powers of attraction.

CHECK INS: Within the circle, we gather among our Grove systers and introduce ourselves, with our name and a declaration of two things we adore, love and feel passionate about. It could be a person or an inanimate object or a special place or even an emotion/sensation.

CHANT WORKSHOP: *"Born of Water," "The Ocean is the Beginning of the world," "My Body is a living Temple," "The River is Flowing"* (see Song Text sheet provided)

DRUMMING CIRCLE: Participants are encouraged to select a percussive instrument from the center basket of musical offerings and, one by one, we begin awakening the Kundalini energy with our sounds of rattles, tambourines, chimes, bells and drumming. We add snake, body movement, as our Cone of power progresses and begins to synchronize.... then ground this ubiquitous energy.

CHECK INS: The images of the Goddess Aphrodite are plentiful. At this point, each womyn within the circle will have a chance to connect with Aphrodite via a statue of the Goddess of Love; with her flowing golden hair, her full pendulous bosoms and her enchanting curvaceous hips. What Aphrosinian attributes speaks to you personally as you behold her image.
LESSON ON THE GODDESS APHRODITE
A discussion on her various myths, and images, sharing how she appears to us personally and her relevance for today's modern womyn

GODDESS WORKSHOPS
WORKSHOP I: Gentle Kundalini Yoga. In this workshop we will learn and practice a series of Yoga moves that awaken our Kundalini, the serpent at the base of our spine, that travels, dispersing energy through our Chakras.

WORKSHOP II: Have you ever personally felt the surge of this Goddess calling? A lively discussion is assured. As wommin we have numerous tales to share on moments of attraction, the powers of passion, fulfilling relationships and memorable sexual escapades. Around the circle, with speaking stick, we will each have an opportunity to reflect on a time, when undeniably, the presence of Goddess of Love was felt.

WORKSHOP III: Creation of a personal **Love oil**, by combining 3-4 essential oils and charging it with our intent. You may use suggestions found in the appendix of this book, but it is also fun to experiment and combine a few oils to make our own unique, personal fragrance.

WORKSHOP IV: Ingredients of a Love Spell. Ever wonder how to cast a successful Love spell? In this workshop we will discuss the components of a love spell and traditional ingredients utilize. Presenting various resources and grimoires, we will pen our own magickal spell for love and prepare our own candles for the spell.

WORKSHOP V: Defining for ourselves **what is beauty** and what personally attracts us? Reflecting on what we believe, inside of us, would attract others? Participants were asked ahead of time to bring to the gathering, a magazine clipping or a photo of something they are attracted to and verbally sharing their thoughts on the subject. A lively discussion should ensue as everyone has various definitions of beauty.

WORKSHOP VI: A lesson and discussion on Casting **"Glamour."**

WORKSHOP VII: Creating and imbuing scented bath soaps and salts. Dedicating our yummy bath creations to the Goddess of Love. Adding Epsom salt, a few drops of ylang ylang oil, dried roses, yarrow, lavender, hyssop herbs into a special infusion.

WORKSHOP VIII: A fun discussion on body modification and tattoos. We will share our thoughts on the subject and even share our own actual body art (tattoo) with one another- opening up a lively, inspiring discussion on our reasoning. Temporary tattoos will also be available to consciously experiment with this magickal practice of body adornment.

REFLECTIONS ON APHRODITE

Love at first sight, being enraptured, smitten, overtaken by strong sexual attraction, Love sickness, enchantment, obsession, desire....these Aphrosinian attributes exist today as they did in ancient Greece. Surely we can see the value of this world renown, iconic, ancient Goddess even in our most modern lives. She brings us the powers of love, attraction, sexuality, beauty, the arts, music - elements that transcends time and will always be sought and valued by Gods and humans alike. For Wommin, more importantly, she is an advocate for self-love and self worth and teaches us to recognize our own internal and physical beauty. We are indeed worthy of Love no matter where, or what stage, we are in our world.

When I look around and see a myriad of examples of this Goddess, reflected in the various looking couples, I am convinced of her breathing, living existence ever more prevalent today than ever before. There is not one size, nor one look, nor one race, nor one gender, nor one type of person, that is solely visited by the Goddess of love, for She does not discriminates and her presence can be experienced by ALL; heterosexual or gay, white or black, petite or large, scientific Einsteins or the uneducated, rich or poor... All living beings are vulnerable to her great powers. Even the plant and animal kingdom cannot escape her influence, for they too exemplify the urgency to mate, love and express tenderness.

Powers of attraction, beauty and sexuality are awaken with her Divine presence in our lives. This magnetic power of attraction is a formidable engulfing force, reminiscent of the very wild, sea foaming, playful oceans she was born in. It can sweep you up, taking you further deep into the unknown parts of you, the suppressed realms within your own self that perhaps you neglected to acknowledge. Her Aphrosinian waters can take you away, far away from the comforting shores that made you feel so stable and grounded and sweep you into a primordial vortex of love's ancient history, making you now an integral part of its moist sustenance.

Her powers of infiltrating our heart and our senses, and passionately moving us into this euphoric state of ecstasy, is ever prevalent today as it was eons ago. She teaches us, that reflected in every single human being, there exist the same juiciness and raw passion that has touched humanity since its inception. More importantly, she teaches that there is much love and beauty to be unearth in our lifetime and it always begins first and foremost with the acknowledgement of our own beauty and self- love.

APHRODITE GROVE GODDESS GATHERING RITUAL

PURPOSE: To invoke the Goddess Aphrodite and unearth our own beauty and powers of attraction.

Purification: a gentle rose incense will be lit and its smoke will fumigate and permeate our ritual space to begin.

Anointing: A priestess will stand at the entrance of our temple, holding in her hands a small bowl of rose water, or scented blessing oil. She will offer it to each womyn that approaches her and anoint their heart chakra,
as she asks; *"How do you enter this sacred space?"*
Participant answers when ready, *"...in perfect love and perfect trust"*

Circle Casting,
with Red rose petals scattered around the circle, collective gentle humming by the wommin and eloquent prose spoken, the circle is cast.

Quarters called
* Guardians of the Watchtowers of the **East**, Ye Powers of **Air**,
Place of Conception, beginnings, Breezes that caress, invite and seduce our flesh.
We call on you to bring us your gifts
Guard and Hold our sacred space, Hail and welcome
(*attendants repeat*) Hail and Welcome!!!

*Hail Guardians of the Watchtowers of the **South**, Ye Powers of **Fire**,
Place of great passion and burning desire, cavernous flames of attraction and love
We call on you to lend us your gifts
Guard and Hold our sacred circle, Hail and Welcome
(*attendants repeat*) Hail and Welcome!!!

*Hail Guardians of the Watchtowers of the **West**, Ye powers of **Water**,
Place of Aphrodite's birth, sea foam juices that stir and awaken ecstasy in our womanhood,
We call on you to bring us your gifts
Guard and Hold our sacred space, Hail and welcome
(*attendants repeat*) Hail and Welcome!!!

*Hail Guardians of the Watchtowers of the **North**, Ye powers of **Earth**,
Place of our physical unions and scintillating bodies, Flesh upon the ripening Earth
We call on you to bring us your gifts
Guard and Hold our sacred circle, Hail and welcome
(*attendants repeat*) Hail and Welcome.

Invoke her
(*see suggested Aphrodite invocations*)

ASPECTED APHRODITE (*Goddess Aphrodite appears, Aspected and speaks...*)
**Behold I am Aphrodite, Goddess of love,
Goddess of Attraction,
Rider of the Dolphins and Doves
Golden, Sea Foam, Pleasure seeker,
Acknowledge my immortal self,
breathing in you,
throbbing in you,
waiting to be unleashed.
I am lover of all that is beautiful and that includes you.*

Have you looked within my mirrors? Do you see what I see?

Immortal and forever at your service
to stir the waters that live within you
To stir the juices that want to flow out
from under you,
To bring you to the doors of ecstasy.
To bring you to Self- love
To bring you to your own beauty.

Look to me, within yourself
Behold for you are me
Expression of seduction and love.
You are divinity.

*Participants should have the new shirt/top to change into for the self blessing.
Priestess as Aphrodite asks each woman in the circle to help remove her sister's top and thus remove her old ways. *(Semi sky clad work ex: come with your old blouse, undress, abandon it, after the self-Blessing attendants will re-dress in their new tops within the sacred circle to express a new more beautiful you being born.)*
When the attendants are ready, one by one they will come and retrieve from the Goddess the consecrated **holy Rose water** which will be used for her own self blessing. As Aphrodite was born of the Sea and the rose was sacred to her, rosewater is appropriate for this ritual. When each woman has attained her rosewater the Goddess will begin.

Aphrodite Speaks:
"Tonight I will serve to remind you of your own powers of attraction with an ancient self-blessing rite. Follow my lead and Bless yourself..."

SELF-BLESSING RITE

Blessings upon Thy Feet
That you may walk in her Light, confidently on your personal, sacred journey, may your feet lead you to the right path, where you're called to be.

Blessings upon Thy Knees
That you may kneel at the altar of the Goddess, not groveling, but in reverence for yourself and the Divine that is encased within.

Blessings upon Thy Yoni
That you may receive and bestow great delight and pleasure and behold life, security and vitality.

Blessings upon Thy Womb
That you may know and recognize your own gifts of regeneration, nursing within you. And if you chose to do so, bring forth creativity and new life.

Blessings upon Thy Heart
That you may know love, and in its presence, recognize its awestricken power. That this sacred seat may be a receptor for genuine, divine love and be a conduit for affection to flow freely, effortlessly into your life.

Blessings upon Thy Throat
That your unique songs may have ears and heart to fulfill, May your speeches have eloquence and clarity and may your voice be honored, respected and heard always.

Blessings upon Thy Lips
That your lips may touch only that which is good for you and when invoked, utter the words of power. That your sensually gifted lips may be the sacred threshold for greater pleasures to follow, if you choose.

Blessings upon Thy Nose
That you may smell many pleasant scents in your lifetime and have ease of breath connecting you to heathy awakened lungs.

Blessings upon Thy flesh
That your skin may reflect the spiritual sunshine created in your soul- supple and smooth, representing you, always divinely beautiful.

Blessings upon Thy Eyes
That your eyes may never fail you, always bringing you sight, direction and clarity. May you see all things needful, monumental and beautiful.

Blessings upon Thy 3rd Eye
That it may be blessed with health, strength and clarity, seeing both the unseen and seen and alerting you on all spiritual matters.

Blessings upon Thy hair
That your hair, short or long, sparkle with health and a beautiful reflection of the unique Goddess you are.

Blessings upon Thy Crown
That your crown may be a receptor of Divine light, functioning to its fullest potential awakened to communicate and unearth the wisdom within and without.

Blessings upon Thy Soul
That it may receive the ultimate blessings from the Goddess and lead you continuously to a happier, more fulfilling life journey.

*******Inspiration and credit given to Z. Budapest and her book, "Holy Book of Women's Mysteries"*

Singing Goddess Chant:
"My Body is a Living Temple of Love"
"The Ocean is the Beginning of the World"
****

Aphrodite speaks as she prepares to leave:
....Remember this night and our sacred rite.....

<u>Ending Ritual:</u> The Lipstick Spell, in which new chapstick, gloss or lipstick, will be enchanted with good positive, beautiful energy and it will be newly opened, placed on our sister's lips then gifted as a ritual gift for the evening. The woman standing next to you will be *"lipified."* As we, one by one, turn to our sister standing next to us and lovingly, line the lips of our Grove Syster, while carefully saying...

"Be ever mindful that You are a Beautiful reflection of the Goddess, so mote it be!"
****

Holding hands, Humming to Ground and begin
Devoking....
Thanking and Releasing the Goddess
in whatever way you feel inspired to do so.

Devoking Quarters by Singing Our **Closing Chant:**
"By the Earth that is her Body, by the Air that is her breath......"
"The Circle is Open,*but unbroken, may the peace of the Goddess be ever in our hearts.."*

Potluck festivities begin

April- Grove Goddess Beltane Gathering II

Purpose: To honor the season of Love, fertility and frolicking and call forth the Love Goddess within our selves.

MOOD SET: *Begin with Rattling and Percussive drumming immediately to set the tone for our day and elevate vibrations to a good start right from the beginning.* ***Greek Music or Shamanic Drumming CD***

Check Ins: Since last Gathering, What has transpired, what Magick had manifested?

****Chanting Songs see text Sheet***
1. I honor what is sacred, 2. I am Magick Woman Giving Birth to myself, 3. My Body is a living temple of Love (as we move) 4._____(suggestions)

Check ins: How was last Full/ New Moon experienced? Lunar Collages, show and tell.

Sharing her Image: an image of the Goddess will be passed around the circle to allow every Wombmyn the chance to personally connect with her and verbally state aloud what attributes speak to you personally. This is how we begin to invoke her into our circle.

Meditation
CD Meditation played or read, to help participants connect to The Lover archetype

CREATING A PERSONAL INVOCATION: Sharing our personal <u>Love Goddess</u>- What attributes does she most exemplify to you personally. Take a moment to connect with her. With Music playing in background, Let us create a special invocation to her, which we will read within ritual.

" Oh Beautiful Aphrodite,
In you I see_____(list attributes)_____
And I honor you for your gifts of_____
At this pivotal time, on the Sabbat of Beltane,
You come into my life to awaken in me_____
With this flame, I unearth you now within me -*(during ritual, light the flame)*

Lecture and Check ins: Components of a Love Spell, Conversations about Love, beauty and sexual attraction and all things of that nature. Brainstorming, what we have learned, our best love lessons in this realm...
When have you ever felt obsessive over someone or something? What and when?
_____
Have you ever been a target of someone's obsession?_____
Have you ever had or wanted a purely sexual relationship?_____
What or whom do you feel passionate about?_____
What attributes first attract you in a stranger?_____
What have you learned thus far about Sex?_____
What do u consider to be the sexiest part of you, what is the least?
_____
If you had one love wish what would it be?_____
CHECK INS:
What have you learned about love thus far? Around the room we go, Sharing our lessons and personal view on Love...

CRAFTING WORKSHOPS
Scented Love Goddess Oil Creation
Carving and Charging Candles
Sharing our stories of Love and Enchantments
Pendant creation
Creation of a Rose, Ylang-yang, Scented Body Lotion and Body Massage...

BELTANE-GROVE GATHERING- GODDESS RITUAL II

<u>Purpose:</u> To honor the season of Love, fertility and frolicking, call forth the Love Goddess within our selves.

<u>Asperge</u>, We welcome each sister into the circle with a scented hand crème placed on your sister's hands, neck or heart chakra

<u>Circle cast:</u> Some percussive sounds in background, as we walk around the perimeters of the circle scattering Rose petals and with prose casting our sacred space.
We cast this circle, May love abound,
From our feet below to the top of our crown,
We cast this circle, make sacred space
Create this shield to keep all
herein safe.!!!

<u>Elemental called:</u> *very reflective with initial primal sounds of those elements, connecting with their attributes, elemental candles lit along with every incantation. (See accompanied prose in this chapter....)*

Elemental Call
**Hail to the Element of the East, Ancient Spirit of <u>Air</u>
Warming inviting Summer Breeze that tickles and caresses our skin.
We call your gifts of Awakening......
Come Join us in our sacred Circle today, Hail and Welcome Air!

**Hail to the Element of the South, Ancient Spirit of <u>Fire</u>
Passions, quietly murmuring and brewing, rising with the flames of our Loins.
We call your gifts of Drive and Desire.....
Come Join us in our sacred Circle today, Hail and Welcome Fire!

**Hail to the Element of the West, Ancient Spirit of <u>Water</u>
Place of all Births and creations.. of wombs and nurturance, of sighs and delights, of all that seeps and leaks from our "Wombmynhood."
We call your gifts of Surrendering and Thirst Quenching...
Come Join us in our sacred Circle today, Hail and Welcome Water!

**Hail to the Element of the North, Ancient Spirit of <u>Earth</u>
Place of transformation, of fertile seeds taking root, coming to fruition, of trees, and hills, of land and pulsating beings, of all that grows and manifest by "Her" will and word...
We call your gifts of Fertility and Fruition.
Come Join us in our sacred Circle today, Hail and Welcome Earth!
****
Hail to the Element of the Center,
A moment of silence to honor and call forth Center, our Spirit.
Come Join us in our sacred Circle today, Hail and Welcome Core Spirit!

CHANTING: *"I honor what is sacred and what's sacred honors me...."*

INVOCATION: A call to each Goddess- *every participant will call upon her Deity reading what she wrote or while gazing and reflecting on an image of the Goddess....then lighting her personal candle to invite her energy in the circle.

INVOCATION
Cypriot Born, Cytheria, Golden Aphrodite,
I call you from the depths of my Soul,
Come Hither,
Transcend all time and space,
To join me here as I search your face.

I call to invoke the Coquettish,
Let thy Fertile, deep waters

Unearth the Pearls of Love's Ancient Wisdom,
That will lead me to your Divine realm of ecstasy....

Let parched crevices be quenched
By your irrefutable moisture,
Sweltering, heaving...
Let your waters bring back the suppleness of my Skin,

May your Cypriot, champagne like essence, spread effervescently,
seeping across forgotten parched fields.
Let me unearth this Magick that is you, within me,
For I have known you before....

In the distance of youth,
Where drive and passion partnered with great pleasure and pain
Yet in my haste and immaturity,
I could not navigate the powers of your engulfing waters
And slowly I pulled away, pulled away...

I call you now, Return to me.
Let dry forgotten realms, awaken to your arrival,
By the presence of your divine accoutrements,
Golden Liquor, sea-foam oceans, seashells and pearls and
Pink Hues of engorged clitoris and the wands of erupting drive.

Come Golden One Share your light with me,
That all I see, touch, create and love
reflect back your effervescent juiciness,
Magnetisms', beauty and desire...
All Hail to thee, Aphrodite!!!

MEDITATION: a short meditation is read to connect with the gifts of pleasure, beauty, love and Aphrodite....or a simple musical selection will be offered to allow a moment of meditative trance.

OFFERING of Honey in the center of our circle
and each woman is encouraged to taste of her sweet nectar offering and connect with Goddess in this way...

SPELL WORKING: *Maypole Ribbon adornment*

We gather our own personal colored ribbon and begin by tying an initial knot on the top of the wand. Then speaking our wish for the season as we wrap the ribbon around the Maypole. Our spell is affirmed by our systers with a loud, "So Mote it be"

*CHARGING OUR MAYPOLE: raising energy with movement and rattle/Shamanism CD can be played here. Using our scarves we will dance around our cauldron and the sacred Maypole.
With lively Music still playing in the background we will now honor a long standing Pagan tradition, that of jumping the bonfire with Maypole in hand. The large Cast iron Cauldron is put in the middle of the circle and we gathered all of our lit candles in the center-this acted as our Beltane Bonfire. Raising a lot of energy for the sabbat this is done three times, each time we jump higher...As is an old pagan folklore which states the higher you jump the more likely spell comes to fruition....

Jumping our Flames the BelFires******IT IS DONE!!!!!
Each one of us goes to the center to share in the **Devoking** of our personal Love Goddess...

Devoke and **Thanking** Elements
Song to Devoke Open Circle....
"The Circle is open but never broken, may the peace and Love of the Goddess be forever in our hearts. Merry meet and Merry part and merry meet again..."

*****Potluck begins around the circle as we feed each other the first Morsel**

APHRODITE GODDESS GATHERING RITUAL PROSE

CASTING CIRCLE
We cast this circle, May love abound,
From our feet below to the top of our crown,
We cast this circle, make sacred space
Create this shield to keep all
herein safe.!!!

Elemental Call
**Hail to the Element of the East, Ancient Spirit of <u>Air</u>
Warming inviting Summer Breeze that tickles and caresses our skin.
We call your gifts of Awakening......
Come Join us in our sacred Circle today, Hail and Welcome Air!

**Hail to the Element of the South, Ancient Spirit of <u>Fire</u>
Passions, quietly murmuring and brewing rising with the flames of our Loins.
We call your gifts of Drive and Desire.....
Come Join us in our sacred Circle today, Hail and Welcome Fire!

**Hail to the Element of the West, Ancient Spirit of <u>Water</u>
Place of all Births and creations.. of wombs and nurturance, of sighs and delights, of all that seeps and leaks from our Wombmynhood.
We call your gifts of Surrendering and Thirst Quenching...
Come Join us in our sacred Circle today, Hail and Welcome Water!

**Hail to the Element of the North, Ancient Spirit of <u>Earth</u>
Place of transformation, of fertile seeds taking root, coming to fruition, of trees, and hills, of land and pulsating beings, of all that grows and manifest by "Her" will and word...
We call your gifts of Fertility and Fruition.
Come Join us in our sacred Circle today, Hail and Welcome Earth!

**Hail to the Element of the <u>Center</u>,
A moment of silence to honor and call forth Center, our Spirit.
Come Join us in our sacred Circle today,
Hail and Welcome Core Spirit!

INVOCATION
Cypriot Born, Cytheria, Golden Aphrodite,
I call you from the depths of my Soul,
Come Hither,
Transcend all time and space,
To join me here as I search your face.

I call to invoke the Coquettish,
Let thy Fertile, deep waters
Unearth the Pearls of Love's Ancient Wisdom,
That will lead me to your Divine realm of ecstasy....
Let parched crevices be quenched
By your irrefutable moisture,
Sweltering, heaving...
Let your waters bring back the suppleness of my Skin,

May your Cypriot, champagne like essence, spread effervescently,
seeping across forgotten parched fields.
Let me unearth this Magick that is you, within me,
For I have known you before....

In the distance of youth,
Where drive and passion partnered with great pleasure and pain
Yet in my haste and immaturity,
I could not navigate the powers of your engulfing waters
And slowly I pulled away....and pulled away...

I call you now, Return to me.
Let dry forgotten realms, awaken to your arrival,
By the presence of your divine accoutrements,
Golden Liquor, sea-foam oceans, seashells and pearls and
Pink Hues of engorged clitoris and the wands of erupting drive.

Come Golden One Share your light with me,
That all I see, touch, create and love
reflect back your effervescent juiciness,
Magnetisms, beauty and desire...
All Hail to thee, Aphrodite!!!

Have champagne served in your Special chalice and a bottle of your chosen perfume. Lay out lacy lingerie and any other personal symbol of romance, like pearls and gold jewelry. Begin this spell after taking a cleansing bath and massaging scented moisturizer on your flesh. Do Find a statue, photos, art, images of the Goddess of love to prominently display on your love invoking shrine. Place a photo of yourself near it and Surround it with rose petals. Carve symbols of love, such as hearts, xoxo, Venus sign etc.., on your Red or Pink candle. Charge your candle with Rose oil or Love oil (see appendix). On your altar, offer fresh flowers like Roses. Also surround your candles with sea shells, sand and ocean water. Include in your offering, gemstones like Rose quartz placed on a bowl filled with Aphrosinian herbs of Jasmine, vervain, cinnamon, Damiana; all of which you may also burn on your charcoal brisket. You can also burn Rose, vanilla or jasmine incense sticks. Do this spell on a Friday when the moon is waxing and preferably when the moon is in Libra or Taurus both ruled by the planet of Love.

CALL TO APHRODITE
*Queen Aphrodite
Goddess of love
Unfold and blossom
like a rose bud

Seductress,
Enchantress
Laughing Queen
Tonight in my ritual I'll honor thee

Come to my circle, Receive my thanks
For love and Passion are in my life
For spells and Magick have come true
Accept this ritual as Gratitude

I honour thee,
I honour myself
In Giggles and lovemaking
with beauty and health

Expressive eyes, Delicious lips
Sweet moist womanhood and swinging hips
These are my treasures to use as I please
Proof that the Goddess lives within me

Goddess of love
HAIL to thee
Tonight and always
So mote it be!!!

After a long, sensual cleansing bath, prepare your altar, dedicated to The Goddess. Find a statue of Aphrodite or photos, art, other images of the Goddess of love to prominently display on your love invoking shrine. Acquire a red Yoni shaped candle and also use a gold, red or dark pink candle. Charge your candle with Rose oil, Love oil, Enchantress oil (see appendix). On your altar, offer sea shells, fresh flowers like Red and Pink Roses, place gemstones that correspond to your second and root chakra, like Fire Agate, Red Jasper, Rubies and Garnets. Burn Rose, vanilla, jasmine incense sticks or Aphrosinian herbs, like Vervain, Damiana, Yarrow, Jasmine, Cinnamon. Offer her fruits; the Apple, and don't be afraid to fill the space with the sounds of seductress, moving music. Let your heart, body and soul, sway to the music, the sight and delicious scents of love you've crafted. Enjoy this moment with the intention to project it also into the future. Do this spell any evening when the moon is waxing but preferably on a Friday, when the moon is growing or even on the very night of the full moon and preferably if the moon is in Venus ruled Libra or Taurus, also Moon in passionate Scorpio works well.

AWAKENING ECSTASY
* I awaken myself
to the sexual seas
as I invoke here now
Queen Aphrodite.

Stir and awaken my root chakra
Red is its color, hot temperature
Awaken, Awaken, Dormant no more
Awaken to ecstasy & pleasures galore

Waxing moon fuel this spell
And by my words
Let it work well

Aphrodite, Aphrodite
Alluring as you
Help me enjoy the swells as you do

Hum ...Hum...
With my consort, my love
Climaxing swells
soaring higher above.

GLAMOUR CASTING
* Cast a Glamour round and round
From my Red root to my crown
Passing energies through our souls
Let this magick now take hold.

Visions hazed by Cupid's Dust
Stirring up delicious Lust
Logic out and passion in
Give this spell its magic spin!

On your altar offer everything that you associate with Aphrodite and the Goddess Of Love. Include Sea Shells, pearls, gold jewelry, apples and champagne flutes. Have a statue of the Goddess, a toy rubber dolphin, images of doves, or art/photo images of her. Offer a vase of fresh flowers, like Roses and photos of yourself or intended love. Include gemstones like Rose quartz, green amozonite, pink rhodonite, garnets and a bowl of clean ocean water as well. Gather herbs of Jasmine, Vervain, Cinnamon, Damiana; all of which you may also burn on your charcoal brisket. Carve symbols of love, such as hearts, xoxo, venus sign etc.., on your green, pink, or red candles. You may even use those special image candles of a womyn/men. Charge your pillar candles with Rose oil or Love oil, Enchantress oil. (see appendix) . Do this spell on a Sunday or Friday when the moon is waxing and if the moon is in Libra or Taurus, all the better. Perform this spell sky clad or in your sexiest robe and have fun, as this Goddess enjoys pleasure and laughter as her shrine offerings.

INVOCATION TO VENUS
*With Waxing moon
and the rising Sun
I conjure thee,
Oh Goddess of love

On Venus day
and Venus hour
Bestow upon me
Your feminine powers

Awaken in me
The Goddess that lives
And give this spell
It's magick spin

I weave this spell
To draw to me
My perfect mate
My lover to be

Protect our love
And let it grow
Merge my spirit
with his soul

Goddess of Love
I thank you in advance
Let true love and union
Rise from romance

It is best to do this spell when the moon is waxing, on a Friday , which is a day sacred to the norse Goddess Freya and Venus and all the Goddesses of Love. Find photos, art, images of Aphrodite, to prominently display on your love invoking shrine. Carve symbols of love, such as hearts, xoxo, venus sign etc.., on your pink candle. Charge your candle with Rose oil, Love oil, ylang-ylang, gardenia oil (see appendix). Place near your candle; seashells, pearls and gold jewelry and any sweet foamy edible, items like whip cream or ice cream. On your altar offer fresh Red Roses and include gemstones like Rose quartz. Create an herbal placket made of pink felt and filled with herbs of Jasmine, Vervain, Cinnamon, Damiana; all of which you may also burn on your charcoal brisket as an incense. Include photos of either yourself or romantic looking couples, that exudes the energy you are endeavoring to manifest in your life.

EXALTING VENUS
*In celebration of Venus
The Goddess of beauty and love
I make this holy offering
With spiritual guidance from above

I call upon the elements
Water, Earth, Fire and Air
To help me celebrate
this ritual affair

Red roses I offer
And Jasmine incense
I burn these pink candles
with loving intent

With Blessings of Venus
And the powers of these words
I enchant this pink placket
with these sacred herbs

Bless me with your presence
Fill me with your soul
Share with me your beauty
Glamour now take hold

I invoke thee, Goddess
to bless me tonight
with love and great beauty
Come guidance and insight.

So mote it be!

Encounters with Aphrodite- My dream, during the Season of Rebirth and Spring

It seemed like a Doctor's office as it was a large white, very sterile room. My vision was being checked by this (nondescript) doctor who somehow became my love in this dream or the catalyst for love to travel through. He checked my vision in this strange white, bright room, while I sat on the metal table. He said, "you are fine and your vision is great...." Then somehow his luscious lips ended up on top of mine, pressing sensually, like an angelic pillow upon my lips. I remember feeling swept away by this most celestially, beautiful, earth shaking kiss. It was moist and deeply knee buckling. I have never been kissed like that and I could still feel the warmth of his lips upon mine own, even hours after waking up.

As beautiful and monumental as this dream may have appeared up till that point, it became even more profound. The scenery changed. It was still a bright, white celestial room, but now I found myself sitting at some sort of hospital waiting room with my son- the oldest one. Well, a woman appeared right before us. She really appeared before me. My son seem to have been there simply as a symbol of sorts, for there was little interaction with him in the dream at this point.

I think, in the dream I was confused about this woman who was now before me and I searched my own psyche, trying to link the two, confused about her actual connection to the doctor. It seemed like the doctor who had earlier checked my vision and kissed me passionately, had become a woman- or so I thought. I continued to study this woman who was completely naked and appeared to be modeling for me. In her voluptuous naked form, she appeared to be posing, being very coy and appeared to absolutely love all the attention I was now giving her. She wanted me to look at her, adore her, embrace her with my eyes and I, in a sense, felt captivated and enchanted by her. Who was this beautiful woman? It was a perplexing mystery.

I studied the color of her peach flesh, her free flowing hair, I traced the curves of her breast and noticed the pinkness of her erect nipples. I studied her curvaceous milky thighs and how they swayed back and forth, as if she was modeling in some "Mademoiselle magazine" fashion shoot, back and forth as she demonstrated her various model poses, demanding all eyes on her. She was beautiful, with a brilliant celestial glow about her and she relished her own Divine beauty. She was voluptuous and exuded sex. I did not know who she was and in my head, I tried to figure it out during the dream. She stayed stationed, like an alabaster art sculpture, only turning slightly in place, every now and then, to give me a better look. The room was all white and, she seemed confined to a small area like within a glass showcase, she welcomed my studious gaze and almost demanded my admiration. And I kept my eyes on her, almost obligated to watch, transfixed. Would she be my new lover? I thought in the dream.....even though I am Not a lesbian, I actually wondered why she was before me and what was the implication of her vividly bright presence in my dream. And then I wondered why would my eldest son be there, sitting next to me, he, so unmoved by all of this....it was quite perplexing.

It wasn't until I woke up and started to write and record this dream that it finally dawned on me. I finally saw the monumental meaning of this dream. All of the details of this amazing dream came to me and alarmingly unfolded. With a squeal of joy, I came to realize that I was visited by the brilliant Goddess of Love, sex, beauty and attraction. Queen Aphrodite. She finally, after all these years, came to me.

The vision checked, male doctor affirming my vision is just fine and kissing me. A symbol that affirms my perspective and my sight is right on target. I am not blind, what I see is indeed valid and what I sense is real. The kiss affirming that, yes, this is what you want and you are right to want this because it is indeed beautiful & magickal...

What of my son -the oldest- sitting next to me through out this Aphrosinian experience...? With his birth, he made me into a Mother, so his presence in the dream was a symbol, it pointed to my role as mother. Balancing who I am now, a mother, with that elusive beautiful, Aphrosinian, sexual woman who stood before me- an aspect of me that I can never seem to touch within myself, for she always seems to be out there, so elusive, so glass enclosed shielded from me, outside in others, but never me. Aphrodite, always the distant one in my life and there she appeared as if to say; *"Here I am ...stop, claiming that I don't come to you, for I have been here all along. I just require you to look at me, LOOK AT ME!!!!"* That is exactly what she was saying to me in this dream. She was demanding that I look at her and thus look at myself - embrace the sexual, beautiful Aphrodite within my own self!!!

Aphrodite has always seemed rather elusive to me, but it appeared that in marriage and motherhood she almost completely disappeared. I often wondered if she was mad at me or had some issue with me personally, for I felt that my prayers, special rituals and love spell to her never amounted to any changes in my situation. It seemed like my supplications to her were on deaf ears, for she was not going to give me the time of day. Period! After a while, a witch can start to feel despondent and hopeless and I honestly started to question if we ever had a cool relationship. I mean, in my youth we seem to be alright... so I thought. I knew the pangs of lust and the occasional passionate love affairs. I had intense relationships and experienced those emotional, tumultuous young love and heated passions. They didn't always end the way I had hoped but Aphrodite's powers were unquestionably present. And yet, if deceit falls under her domain? then she and I have much reasons to be miffed with one another, for I have had my share of that too.

Quite honestly, I wondered if Aphrodite was just **not** a patron Goddess for the woman who, like me, found herself in a marriage with children. I was always a devotee of Athena and Artemis, the supreme Virgin Goddesses. Even Hestia had a hold on me that continues today, but I wondered if that devotion to strong, virginal Goddesses, was wrecking my chances of getting good with the Goddess of Love. Did she consider me in the same vein as Athena and Artemis? Since I hung out with them a lot, was I being scoffed at by Aphrodite? Given the cold shoulder, the way those high school cheerleaders do to nerdy geeks? As time went on in my marriage, I started to believe that maybe I just wasn't meant to know Aphrodite anymore. Maybe I should just be happy with Athena guarding my sanctity of marriage and gifting me with the numerous gifts of domesticity. Maybe I should be ever grateful that Artemis took me under her loving, protective, sisterly wings and even helped me birth life into this world, three different times. How lucky am I and I say this with great sincerity. For indeed, for me, the Goddess is alive and magick is a foot in my life but what about Passion and Love and Beauty? What about that gift to turn heads and make men drool over you sexually? Hum..

Does Aphrodite not visit older mothers and wives? That has been my question for a number of years and now with this dream, She has finally answered me. A roaring; *"Of Course..., but it is not I who comes to you, it is You who must make the journey to me. For I am here, where I have always been. Can't you see? It is you who have scoffed at me and abandon me, thinking of me as just a luxury you can live without. Maybe some can, but I don't consider that really living authentically. Look at me!!!.... I ask you to look at me, deeply look at my beauty, for it is a reflection of you. I ask you to search for me within your heart and soul, search for me in your own beautiful reflection, search for me in your smile and seductive gaze, for I haven't left you. I am here waiting to be seen, acknowledge and admired. I am here waiting to be loved, touched and adorned. I am here waiting to be perfumed, tickled and scantily dressed. I am here waiting to be admired and adored by you. Make that journey to me and it will lead you straight to that treasure within your own passionate heart."*
Blessed Be)O(

GROVE OF THE FEMININE DIVINE GODDESS CHANTS

MY BODY
My Body is a living Temple of Love
My Body is a living Temple of Love
My Body is the Body of a Goddess (3X)
(lower)My Body is the Body of a Goddess

THE RIVER IS FLOWING
The river is flowing,
Flowing and Growing,
The River is flowing,
down to the sea,
Mother carry me
a child I will always be,
Mother carry me down to the Sea. *by: Diana Hildebrand-Hull*

THE OCEAN
The Ocean is the beginning of the world
The Ocean is the beginning of the world
All life comes from the sea
All life comes from the sea.
By Delaney Johnson, Starhawk and Reclaiming collective

SISTER RIVER
From Victorian Christian's creation, Elijah The band of Light
Sister, River, Giver...Returning Whole,
Sister, River, Giver...Returning Whole
    Open up, To receive
    We are what we Believe. *(REPEAT)*
    Sister, River, Giver...Returning Whole,
    Sister, River, Giver...Returning Whole
Growing Roots like the Trees,
We are planting seeds. *(REPEAT)*
Sister, River, Giver...Returning Whole,
Sister, River, Giver...Returning Whole,
    Stored in Deep, Stories Sleep,
    Within Us, These Tales we Keep. *(REPEAT)*
    Sister, River, Giver...Returning Whole,
    Sister, River, Giver...Returning Whole,

DON'T YOU KNOW *by Elaine Silver*
Don't you know, Your body is a Temple
And Don't you know, Your Spirit is a Shrine
The other side of Fear, Is a never ending Love
Don't you know,
You and I Are both Divine
    You won't know, What it means to really grow
    If you don't open up, To whose inside
    The other side of Fear, Is a never ending Love
    Don't you know,
    You and I Are both Divine
And I lift up my glass, And drink a toast
to all the women in me, I hold them so close
The other side of fear, Is a never ending love
Don't you know,
You and I Are both Divine.
    I am part Princess, part Witch,
    Part Goddess, part Bitch, part Spirit,
    And I am Divine.
    Don't you know,
    You and I Are both Divine.

BORN OF WATERS
Born of Waters,
Cleansing Powerful.
Healing, Changing,
We are... *by Starhawk*

GODDESS NAMES
Do you remember,
When God was a woman,
She had many, many names,
They called her Isis, Astarte, Diana, Hecate,
Demeter, Kali, Inanna...

WE ALL COME FROM THE GODDESS
We all come from the Goddess
And to her we shall return,
Like a Drop of Rain,
Flowing to the Ocean *By Z. Budapest*

CHAPTER ELEVEN

"If One dream should fall and break into a thousand pieces, never be afraid to pick up one of those pieces up and begin again..." Flavia Weedn, Flavia and the Dream Maker

"Everything you can imagine is real..." Pablo Picasso

WELCOMING IX CHEL

OUR ALTAR

Altar cloth: White or Silver and maybe a second Blue altar cloth underneath.
Image: Statue of this Lunar Mayan Goddess or images of the moon.
Canvas art or photo of the Goddess and or photos of Cozumel, the ocean or the Moon and a rainbow. Also images of flowing water are appropriate.

Always present on the altar;
A cast iron cauldron, drums, speaking stick, a silver pentacle, athame, elemental representations.....

Air: Eagles or vulture statuaries, feathers, Smudge wands, Incense type sticks, cones, charcoal brisket and fine powdered herbs, Mugwort, Sandalwood, Damiana.
Fire: candles, glass enclosed candles or pillars in whites, or silver and or a women shaped, or lunar shaped candles.
Water: Chalice or small glass bowl with Fresh Spring Water or newly attained Rain water
Earth: Lush Green plants, fresh cut flowers, a small dish of soil and or herbs, rubber toy snakes.

Other items pertinent to this particular gathering
Dragon Flies, lots, either in an art piece or toy figurines
An abundance of Snakes they can be toy rubber snakes
Jaguar statue
Rainbows, either in art or figurines
Lunar pendants
Bunnies to represent the moon's totem symbol of fertility
Flowers and Red Roses, lots of greenery
Bowl of consecrated Water
Rocks and Gemstone
Plate offering with eggs
Chalice of Lunar water
Healing Poppets or Plackets
Writing pens and paper, safety pins,
Light blue gauzy fabric to represent water
Workshop items
Tarot; "Temperance" and or other oracular items.

Offering turkey broth, avocado, grains, rice, bean, guava, tortilla, crabs, coffee,
Sacred objects from members:
Notes:

Ix Chel

Crone Ix Chel

Ix Chel Altar

IX CHEL

She is the ancient Mayan Goddess of the Moon. Also known as "Lady Rainbow" due to her association with moisture and rain. She rules over the various phases of the moon and thus a woman life. Ix Chel is a Goddess that rules; fertility, creativity, sexuality, intuition, childbirth. Known also as patron Goddess of expectant mothers, healing and medicinal arts. She was the Goddess of artisans and weavers. Textiles, decorative cloths and weaving were sacred women's handicraft, considered very important in many cultures, including Central and South America. Ix Chel was called upon to bless young girls with this vital, prosperous skill.

As Goddess of the Moon, which rules over the ebb and flow of the ocean waters, it is not surprising, all waters are her domain. She ruled over intuition which also falls under the Moon's realm. This Lunar Deity was in charge of regulating the waters that can bestows fertility onto the land or great destruction, with her uncontrollable floods. In this respect, she is seen as a Goddess of abundance and fruitfulness, in the same way that Demeter and Gaia (Earth Goddesses) are seen as bringer of abundance and fruitfulness to their native land.

According to some mythologies it is believed that the well documented (Haiyococab) flooding of the Earth, many years ago, was attributed to Ix Chel who unleashed her sacred waters from a giant earthen vessel. According to this part of Mayan cosmology, she poured out her waters upon the earth to cleanse it and revitalize new growth. In this depiction we see her great powers as a water deity providing nurturance and quenching the earth's thirst but here, we also see her potentially destructive nature if she inundates us, pouring forth an inordinate amount of water with the potential to destroy.

As a water deity she was also regarded as a Goddess of medicine and healing. It was believed she would approach and tend to the sick. If proper supplications and offerings are made, some claim to see her shadow, as a crone, by the foot of the bedridden and it was believed she could heal, as well as make the transition smoother for those who would need to cross over into the realm of the dead. The rising smoke from a smudge of Copal and tobacco would draw her near, as well as other offerings like; guava tips, sap of a rubber tree, turkey broth, haaz papaya and pulverized crab powder. Here was a Goddess who unquestionably ruled over the realms of life and death for Mayan people.

Ix Chel also has been seen as Goddess of creativity and commerce in her ability to inspire and teach wommin to provide for themselves by way of their handicrafts and creative arts. A Goddess of wommin who need autonomy and financially independent, She thus became a patron Goddess of weaving and textile because these were the skills and trade accessible for wommin to excel in. One myth tells of her intense concentration upon a spider weaving her web and from this act, she was able to pass on this critical knowledge and imperative skill (which would prove to be profitable) to wommin on earth. Textile knowledge, like how to work with looms, spinning cotton, and how to dye cotton in various colors, were examples of her Divine gifts to wommin. Most importantly she championed wommin's use of their sacred hands in various hand-crafts, artistry and numerous creative and profitable outlets.

She was sometimes depicted holding a sacred urn (vase) upside down, which was a symbol of her watery wombs being released upon the earth. Water lilies were also sacred to her. This Mayan Goddess of the Moon was most beloved by wommin because of her well documented ability to impart fertility and ease in child birthing. It was a custom, in ancient times, for all pregnant wommin or those wanting to conceive, to make the journey to her famous Shrines in Cozumel or "Isla de Mujeres", for it was believed that in these sacred waters, fertility and her blessings were guaranteed. As a Moon

Goddess, she unquestionably rules over all the waters; including the waters of our womanhood, blood, our urine, our moisture, sexuality, amniotic fluids and childbirth. Her Shrines can still be found today on the island of Cozumel, near the Yucatan Peninsula... just to the northeastern coast of the Peninsula. A quick Google search on the internet will provide a list of numerous tour companies eager to share Ix Chel's Temples, waters, caves and ruins, still accessible today.

As an ancient Deity, Ix Chel was known as a triple Goddess that could take the form of a beautiful young maiden, brushing her hair upon the moon, or as a nurturing mother helping her people and or a crone, a hag with a skirt of bones. Other popular images show her with a crown of snakes upon her head, pouring water from earthen vessels. Still other depictions show her as a voluptuous, naked, sensual enchantress alongside her totem animals; the hare, the snake or the jaguar. Sometimes she is depicted with eagle feathers and was known also as "Eagle Woman" because the eagle was known as a messenger of the Moon. For the people of Guatemala, Campeche and the Yucatan region she was considered the First woman of the world, and thus a mother deity who gave birth to all succeeding wommin and Goddesses.

THE STORY OF IX CHEL and THE SUN

According to Mayan cosmology, the earth began with two very bright, luminous beings in the sky; the Sun and the Moon. The Moon, Ix Chel, was known to be the most beautiful enchantress, but she had a notoriously jealous grandfather who guarded her carefully and as her numerous tales reveal, her life was plagued by this theme of jealous, oppressive beings trying to control her. The Sun God, was in love with Ix Chel and infatuatedly watched her daily, although in some tales it is Ix Chel who is greatly enamored by the Sun God, Kinich Ahau. While she was actively pursued by numerous deities, she only had eyes for the great Sun God and she tries to attract his attention, despite her vicious, jealous grandfather's threats.

One Mayan Tale, reveals that Kinich Ahau, the Sun, endeavoring to endear Ix Chel and get closer to her, disguised himself as a Hummingbird. In his Hummingbird form he flew to her home and as a bird he was quite welcomed by the Goddess. She offered him honey from the tobacco flower and as they were sharing a quiet moment, the hummingbird fell down, wounded by a fierce clay pellet that had been shot and aimed at him by her jealous grandfather. With great empathy she quickly safeguarded the helpless bird and nursed him to health in the privacy of her room and, according to folklore, this very act awakened and stirred in her, deep, unknown affections for him. When he recovered and flew robust and full of life again, he revealed his true identity and convinced her to leave her home and her monstrously, oppressive grandfather and so... they fled together.

When Ix Chel's grandfather caught sight of the two luminous divine lights escaping, he became greatly infuriated and in his raged he called upon the assistance of Chac, the one who controlled lightning and the storms. According to this tale Chac hurled lightning bolts to both the Sun and the Moon deity as instructed by her grandfather. Although they appeared to be able to retreat momentarily into the water, Ix Chel as a crab and the Sun as a turtle, the Moon Goddess was not able to escape and she was eventually killed by the lightning bolt. In another tale, it is Ix Chel's grandfather himself that aims and shoots the lightning directly at Ix Chel, killing her instantaneously.

The next part of this ancient tale is retold differently by various accounts, but they all reveal a great deal about Ix Chel's sacred symbols and her connection to dragon flies, the number thirteen, death and resurrection and snakes. Some tales tell that while she lay lifeless, thirteen dragonflies sung to her and brought her back to life. Another story tells of how her lifeless body was nursed for thirteen days by a multitude of celestial dragonflies, that sang to revive her. And in this particular story we learn of how the dragonflies created thirteen hollow logs and on the thirteenth night, twelve logs broke open to reveal twelve divine snakes -while the thirteenth log, broke open to reveal the Goddess Ix Chel, alive, resurrected and brilliant once more. The Sun God, who had been mourning her death up to that moment, rejoiced to see her come back to life, bright and whole. He immediately proposed marriage to his beloved and she agreed. Together they set up their home in the heavens, side by side, they were also believed to have given birth to the four Jaguars Gods, who became the guardians of the four corners of the world. But alas, married life soon proved to be very difficult and more challenging than anticipated for the Moon Goddess.

The Sun's brother, the morning Star, Chac Noh Eck, was known to visit their marital abode much too often and apparently he appeared to be quite fond of the Moon too, lingering closer to her than to the Sun himself. This made the already hot tempered, volatile Sun, extremely jealous. He accused the brilliant Ix Chel of unthinkable infidelities with his brother, Chac Noh Eck, lashing out cruel words and false accusations. Refusing to hear her defense, the Sun God, expelled her from the heavens.

Ix Chel, banished from the heaven, landed near a volcano, not far from Lake of Atilan and there she contemplated this horrible turn of events. She was angered at the unjust accusations made by her husband and was of course saddened by his abuse. A vulture appeared nearby and having sympathy, offered her a ride to his home, way up high in the mountains. Here she met the King of Vultures and together they took residence in the mountains, where they also became lovers.

When the remorseful Sun God learned of this amicable union, it did not sit well with him and he soon grabbled to devise a scheme to entreat his wife once more to forgive his brute ways and return to the heavens. One story tells that he hid himself in the hide of a dead deer and waited for the predictable vultures to approach the carcass. Unsuspectingly, he jumped on the vultures back and was flown to Ix Chel's new abode. When he arrived, he managed to corner Ix Chel and pleaded with her to give him another chance and to recall all the wonderful moments they had shared as young lovers. Tugging at her heartstring, she allowed his words to move her and… sadly prepared to leave the home she and her Vulture lover had so successfully created. She returned to her throne in the heavens, but the story does not end here.

No sooner had she returned to the heavens, when the jealousy and volatile accusations of her husband started up again. According to some tales there was incessant verbal abuse but also physical abuse, as the Sun God tried to destroy her beauty and disfigure her with scars, to lessen her enchanting nature. They say this is why the moon has visible carved craters on its surface.

One night, the Moon Goddess had endured enough and with all of her willpower and strength she left into the night, some say as a jaguar, vowing to stay away from the Sun for eternity. She is known to hide in the day when he is awake and wanders through the dark of the night and although her beauty made many lovers propose marriage to her, she opted to embrace her freedom, belonging to no one, but herself. Ix Chel was known to truly relish her freedom after this ordeal with the Sun God and vowed never to become owned by anyone else. It was believed that she retreated to her Island in Cozumel, where she could enjoy her freedom and delight in assisting women in child labor and all aspects of feminine activities.

In this myth we see her as a champion for the oppressed and a Goddess of bold action, who teaches us as women not to become victims of abuse. She teaches us to assert ourselves and not allow ourselves to be victimized; emotionally, nor physically, because anything that negatively effects our soul and wellbeing…must be eradicated in order for our inner light to shine. Much like many Moon Goddesses from various cultures and through-out the ages, she exemplifies the independent spirit of a woman with no ties to any man. Some believe she was touched by the cries of myriads of struggling wommin everywhere on earth, but especially those making offerings, prayers and supplications at her shrines on the island of Cozumel. She proudly devotes herself to wommin, their struggles, answering those prayers and being an advocate for women's freedom, strength and creativity.

IX CHEL GROVE GODDESS GATHERING

Purpose: to honor the Mayan Moon Goddess Ix Chel and welcome her healing waters into our realm, while also commemorating the season.

Check ins with Speaking stick, sharing what has transpired since our last gathering

Chanting: ****(see song sheet)**** *"The River is flowing," "The Ocean is the beginning of the Earth," "Born of water."*

Agreements: Participants will read one to two bylaws from our Groups' Agreement and add, as they see fit, any new request or concerns to the existing list. After a brief discussion, they are encouraged to submit their sign agreements.

Check ins: sharing an image of Ix Chel (I like to use the card from The Goddess Oracle by Marashinksy). As the oracle card is passed around the circle, wommin will be asked to speak aloud any personal thoughts or images that come about as a result from this image. What does her image personally conjure up for you?

Drumming: hearing a Shamanic CD Drumming Track, allowing the space for a moment of trance and connecting with the sacred heartbeat. We may also choose to create an actual drumming circle. Percussive instruments always provided.

Lecture on Mayan Goddess, Ix Chel and her various folklore

GODDESS WORKSHOP

WORKSHOP I: Ix Chel is a Mayan Lunar Deity, She comes as a water Goddess. Think upon water and its grand significance in our lives. The West is the realm of water, our heart chakras, realm of expressions, intuition and the Moon.

Water through our Seven Chakras. Connecting with each chakra as we honor the various kinds of water.

Water in our Blood -**1st ROOT CHAKRA** - helps us rejuvenate/rebirth ourselves monthly

Water in our Sweat- which purges out our toxins

Water in our Pleasure- **2nd SACRAL CHAKRA**- evidence of our ecstasy

Water in our Digestive system -**3rd CHAKRA** -that functions to keep us healthy

Water in our urine

Water in our Emotions -**4th HEART CHAKRA**- that when unblocked, can allow ebb and flow mirroring her sacred oceans

Water in our Tears and mourning, evidence of our human compassion connected to divine compassion

Water in our Creative Expressions - **5th THROAT CHAKRA** - ever moving, beautifully expressive of inner spirit, vehicle for divine expression.

Water in our Intuition - **6th THIRD EYE CHAKRA** - meeting place for us and the divine

Water in our Connection to Source - **7th CROWN CHAKRA** –connected to Source, conjoined and we commingle on this great planet.

WORKSHOP II: Conjuring Water... discussing our relationship to this realm and briefly talking about astrological water signs like; Pisces, Scorpio, Cancer and exploring where they fall in our own personal astrological charts and consider what qualities they offer to our astro charts.

WORKSHOP III: Snake Meditation. Script read included in this chapter and we can then share within circle. Trance drumming in the background as meditation is heard or even done within our ritual.

WORKSHOP IV: Water Magick. A discussion on the various ways Water can be utilized in our Magick. See article in this chapter for a starting point to this discussion.

WORKSHOP V: Gratitude. Typically during the first harvest, August 1st, we give gratitude and count our blessings, but we can do this at **any** time of the year, to check on our progress and the vows we have made to ourselves. A prepared handstamped parchment paper will be passed around the room and music will be played in the background to set the tone of gratitude. Take this time to quietly contemplate and jot down for yourself, a few things that have come to pass or that still needs to come to pass and what you can be most grateful about at this time of the year.

WORKSHOP VI: Ix Chel was known as patron Goddess to all **handmade Crafters**. In this workshop we will endeavor to utilize our hands to honor her, with a handmade creation. Weaving, crocheting or decorating mini altar cloths and imbuing them with her energy.

WORKSHOP VII: Dragon fly creations. As the myth reveals, Dragonflies revived the Goddess, Ix Chel, bringing her back to life after she had been killed by her grandfather. It is only appropriate to incorporate their wings, in our efforts to connect with Ix Chel. With wire hangers, gauzy fabric, sparkles, furry boas, and fabric glue, we create Mardi Gras Gauzy Wings for ourselves, to be worn at future rituals to Ix Chel. We will also simultaneously, tell our own tales of Dragon fly Myths and any personal experiences we've had with them.

WORKSHOP VIII: Looking into the eyes of the Jaguar. Ix Chel was also closely associated with the Jaguar. In this workshop, we will connect and invoke this powerful totem animal, to unearth what it can reveal to us about the Goddess, Ix Chel and our own spiritual journey. Connecting to her Totem animals; the jaguar, snake, dragonfly, eagle.

WORKSHOP IX: Painting our own rainbow art on canvas. The Rainbow was obviously sacred to Ix Chel. In this workshop, art supplies will be made available to participants, to tap into the inner child, paint and re-create our own unique, spirit inspired, artistic version of a Rainbow. We are endeavoring to awaken our inner child.

WORKSHOP X: Elements of Drawing down the Moon.
I wondered how many of you will celebrate the Full moon? Do you celebrate full moons or New moons and what is your preferred method? Has anyone ever drawn down the moon? Open up a discussion on the various methods for drawing down the moon and the purpose. Typically, we do this to connect with Lunar Goddesses, rededicate ourselves to the craft and tap into her divine gifts. Take a moment to compose a short prose for this.

REFLECTIONS ON IX CHEL

The Water's ebb and flow, regulated by the powers of the moon, connects us intimately to her. She brings us the powerful symbols of the moon, the snake, the hare, the jaguar, night and the restorative powers of water. Water, in its many forms is healing, sexual, creative, fertile and the very nature of wommin.

Since the earliest of times, Ix Chel was invoked by Mayan wommin for her legendary powers of fertility and protection. Wommin would make long journeys to reach the shore of her beloved island of Cozumel, to receive her blessings of fertility and ease with childbirth, through her waters. Yet, it appears she is a Goddess available to wommin at all stages of their respective lives and today, her worship is still prevalent for those who seek to connect with her ancient feminine powers. There are still numerous temples in her honor on Isla Mujeres and in Cozumel and modern day wommin who make the pilgrimage today attest to the cathartic experience of bathing in her waters.

Yet, Ix Chel is a Goddess intrinsically connected to wommin's plight and journey. From the young maiden, seeking her first true love, to the womyn fighting for her autonomy and financial success... to the new mother seeking help with fertility and childbirth, to the crone with health issues, needing help transitioning....Ix Chel hears all the prayers of wommin. And because she herself knows all too well the uniquely challenging journey of our gender, she is only all too eager to be of help. She knows death and rebirth and the cycles in a womyn's life. Her myths reveal her familiarity with abuse, survival and patriarchal control and oppression and thus, this is a Goddess who can intimately understand our very own journey. A journey that for wommin, no matter what age, year, culture or country, still presents the same struggles and obstacles. Perhaps this is why she is still sought after and continues to be venerated today. For us modern wommin, she infinitely connect us to our healing powers, our strengths, our bodies and our own sacred, internal ebb and flow. And through her we begin to value the powerful element of water and its capacity to mirror healing for us.

IX CHEL GROVE GODDESS GATHERING RITUAL

ALTAR PREPARATION: Working spell candle, Smudge/incense/oil, Blue votives for all participant, Elemental Candles for each Quarter: White candle for AIR, Red Candle for FIRE, Blue candle for WATER, Brown or Green candle for EARTH. Blue altar cloth, Earthenware, rabbit, snake, jaguar, moon, sun, White Goddess image, Fruit Food Offering platter like things that have grown on a vine; grapes, cherries, oranges.

Asperge: Smudge the ritual space and participants... scented Oil, offered to every womyn sitting in the circle.

Purpose and Intention spoken:
We will offer gratitude and pay it forward with a Global wish, a special spell for the Universe.

CIRCLE **CASTING:** From hand to hand this circle is cast... Or Prose...
QUARTERS INVOKED
Winds to Sweep and stir renewed, Eastern Realm, we call on you!
Hail and Welcome Air!!!
Light White/Yellow Candle

Flames to move us to our Cause, passion guides when we are lost!
Hail and Welcome Fire!
Light Red /Orange Candle

Water flows, express our Hearts, unify our broken parts!
Hail and welcome Water!
Light Blue Candle

Fertile Earth, that births and forms, In your realm, we are Transformed!
Hail and Welcome Earth!
Light Brown/Green Candle

INVOKING IX CHEL
Snake Womyn,
Moon Womyn,
Mother of Jaguars
and All.
Rainbow Rider,
Come Inspirer us,
Let your Healing Waters Fall....

Come into this sacred space,
we've erected to honor you, oh ancient one.
We call you Ix Chel, Sweet Mayan Moon Goddess,
revered by all wommin,
because it is you,
who guides and protects us,
in all stages of our sacred lives.
As girls, as maidens, as sexual young womyn,
as wives and pregnant mothers,
as creatrix and as crones,
You are our source of strength, support and inspiration.
We call on you and bid you to visit with us....
Hail and welcome Ix Chel!!!

CHANT: Eight Bead Song
**MEDITATION (Audio CD or read)

**as they are coming out of Trance offer a reading....Aspected Invocation of belly/womb seed spell from the book, *"Ix Chel Wisdom" by Shonagh Home.*

SPELL WORKING

<u>1.Water Blood Jar offering.</u>
Participant's items-Collection of an Intentional Jar of Water from our own personal source.... Each womyn will be asked to prick her finger with a sterilized needle and place a drop of blood in her own jar. This will serve as an offering to the Goddess as a symbol of the traditional sacrifice of the time and in gratitude for our initial harvest. It will be poured directly unto the earth as a customary offering.

<u>2.Lighting blue votive.</u>
So often, when we do a spell we are asking for something personal for our selves, but the powerful energy found on the day/night of a New and or Full Moon are more conducive to grandeur spell workings that are more global and altruistic in nature.   On the day of the full moon, I propose that we do a **Philanthropic spell** and pay it forward. We should each consider a Global situation that may utilize our best of intentions and light our votives for Global healing. Examples of this may be... *"Protection for all children, Clean waters and help for Marine life, Shield of protection and a way to safety for all abused wommin, Relief for places like Haiti, Mexico and Africa effected by recent earthquakes, A cure for Cancer and Aids, Good healthcare for all of humanity, Prosperity and jobs, A resolution to our struggling economy....etc...etc..."*
***As we light our candles we say aloud, around the Circle, what global seeds and Universal visions we hope for in the world.... So Mote it Be!**

CHANT: *"We are Systers on a journey" or "We all come from the Goddess"*
Check ins: If necessary....

Thanking and Devoking Goddess Ix Chel

Dearest Mayan Mother, Ix Chel.
In your presence we were blessed
to experience your numerous divine gifts.
Surely, as wommin you will forever
have a place in our heart and soul
and our journey to you has only just begun.
Stay if you will, Go if you must.
Hail and Farewell Ix Chel.

Devoking and thanking the Elements

Earth, the nurturer, the solid protector, providing us a sacred space.
We thank you and bid thee adieu with sincere Gratitude,
Hail and Farewell Earth.
Water, the realm of Ix Chel's Lunar embrace,
we thank you for witnessing and guarding our space.
Received our Thanks as we bid thee adieu.
Hail and Farewell Water.
Fire, the protective flames that encircled our rites.
We thank you for your presence here today.
Receive our gratitude as we bid thee adieu.
Hail and Farewell Fire.
Air, the initiator that came when called,
to guard and hold our sacred space.
Received our thank you as we bid thee adieu.
Hail and Farewell Air.
****

Opening up the Circle
"The Circle is open, but unbroken, may the peace of the Goddess be ever in our hearts..."
Cakes and Ales to follow with our traditional potluck.

IX CHEL GROVE GODDESS GATHERING RITUAL II

Purpose: To honor the Mayan Moon Goddess, Ix Chel and let her flowing waters bring us courage and healing as women.

Anoint and purify with smudge
Entry, as music is being played
Intent of season is spoken
CIRCLE CASTING
simply with hands say; "From hand to hand this circle is cast."

CALLING QUARTERS

Guardian of the West, Powers of **Water**,
Moon Lover, ebbing and flowing with the Ocean tides, teach us your gifts of flowing freely with your waters. We call on you now to guard and hold our sacred space now... Hail and welcome, Water.

Guardian of the North, Powers of **Earth**,
Receptor, container reflector of the Goddesses gift. Let thy fertile fields ensue.... and powers of fertility and creation be here now. We call on you to guard and hold our sacred space. Hail and welcome, Earth.

Guardian of the East, Powers of **Air**,
Gentle breezes that moves and inspires, bringer of news, Transporter of Divine gifts. We call on you to awaken our senses so that we may feel and hear the language of your winds. Guard and Hold our sacred space . Hail and welcome, Air.

Guardian of the South, Powers of **Fire**,
Passions and Pursuits, generator of Heat, Cauldron are smoldering as magick takes hold. Lend us your gifts of inner flames and light. We call on you to guard and hold our sacred space now. Hail and welcome, Fire.

CHANTING: *"Wings chant"*

INVOKE:
Each participant will approach the altar and draw a Dragon fly upon the artist canvas resting there. They are asked to invoke Ix Chel in their own personal way as they draw and say her name aloud as they finish until everyone is chanting her name together.

A Goblet with Full moon imbued and enchanted **Water** will be passed around the circle so that each participant may drink in her **Strength and Courage.**
　　*As you drink say aloud: *"With this sip she shares with me, the Moon's gift of creativity/healing/courage etc...*_____(*every womyn states what she wishes to say...*)
.
Water Workings (on a slip of paper participants will write what they hope to dissolve and heal.)
A bowl of consecrated herbed water will be passed around the circle, in it participants will dissolve a slip of paper (one they already worked on during workshop) which will have what they surrender to Ix Chel to heal. Together this bowl of water will be poured out onto the far corners of the property or a stream of running water.

CHANTING: *"We all come from the Goddess"* or and *"Moon Chant"*
Holding hands, we prepare to give our thanks and devoke.
Devoking the Goddess Ix Chel with thanks
Devoking the elements by song with gratitude
Opening our circle with Merry meet song......

Cakes and Ales and Potluck feasting....

INVOKING IX CHEL

Snake Woman,
Moon Woman,
Mother of Jaguars
and All.
Rainbow Rider,
Come Inspirer us,
Let your Healing Waters Fall....

TO IX CHEL

Divine Ix Chel,
Let your Waters pour down on us now,
In your sacred waters
Let our healing be found.

Come thy serpent wearer,
Mayan Moon, Ix Chel,
Release thy watery womb,
And fill all empty Wells.

By your ebb and flow,
Quench all our thirsty needs,
Ye Woman defender,
Help us rise from our knees.

Release thy waters,
From your Divine hands.
From your Lunar heavens,
Unto our dry hungry land,

Come thy serpent,
Connect us to you
We ebb and flow,
With the rise of your Moon

Ix Chel release,
Thy Bountiful flow
And awaken us now,
to all that we know....

Hail and Welcome Ix Chel!

Ix Chel, Let your Waters Pour Down on us now,
to quench all thirst and bring us healing,
Ix Chel,
come thy serpent and release thy watery womb
from the heavens unto dry hungry land..
Ix Chel,
Release thy Bountiful waters,
release them unto us.
We are many on this Earth,
Cherishing and awaiting your sacred waters.
Pour forth your love, Dearest One...
Pour forth your waters,
as you do your precious Moonlight.

****AFTERWARDS:*** *These are not quite Aphrodite's waters. These are Ix Chel's healing waters that yes, can bring you healing of a sexual nature but these waters bring "long overdue" relief and healings in various aspects in our lives; from creativity, rising above abuse, to fertility, birthing and excellence in craftsmanship, to sexual awakening and nourishing those dry, neglected parts of ourselves, to moving us, inspiring us to flow and awaken those stagnant parts of ourselves and helping others...*
Where will Ix Chel's sacred waters travel to?
Where will her healing waters flow to? Where is your land driest?
In what parts of your world will her healing waters pool and gather in?

DEVOKING POEM TO IX CHEL
Waters flowed from you and me,
Joined from present, past, infinity,
Ix Chel's waters invoked to Heal
Layers of our Heart Chakras
exposed and peeled.

Mayan Goddess,
quench our thirst,
do not submerge us
when we hurt.
But give us the waters
that nourish our souls,
Strengthen our connection
to Ancestors of old.

Give us the courage
to embrace who we are,
Lend us the revealing light
of your moon and the stars.

Draw us to drink
of the resources in you.
So that we too may shine,
like you do in the Moon.

And with sincere gratitude,
We gather at this time
We bid thee Adieu...
Farewell Ix Chel, until next time....

Hail and Farewell Goddess Ix Chel!!!

SNAKE AND WATER MEDITATION ON IX CHEL

I invite you to find a comfortable spot. You can be seated or laying on a mat. However you feel you are most comfortable, I invite you to settle in and breathe. Breathe and slow it all down. Exhale....and Inhale... Surrender now to your mind's eye and let it take you where it needs to be. *(pause)*

Darkness Falls upon the sky. The Curtains part with "Her" glow.
She makes her entrance when **he** departs the night sky.... *(pause)*
Come.... Come enter into this sacred space.

Follow my voice as it carefully leads you down a path, follow my voice as it takes you down....., down to your toes, follow my voice as it takes you down to the dry soil;
to the Earth that holds your precious feet. *(pause)*

Crouch down now, Crouch down low unto the ground. Feel the Earth beneath you, with your hands, feel it's coarseness and listen to how parched it is.
Note, how does your hands feel upon this dry land? (pause)

It has not rained in this place for far too long...and the sacred beings from the underworld realm, deep down below, are starting to get restless and rise up to the surface, seeking relief. Slithering before you, dark branches seem to move, but behold- sacred beings are making their appearance. They felt your arrival upon their heads and sensed your needs matched their very own. **What needs brings you here today? (pause)**

You watch them slither and hiss, back and forth,sssssss, slowly caressing the dark earth beneath them as they move about. Ssssssss. In your deep observation of these beings you too begin to sway back and forth, Ssssss. Back and forth...Sssssss, comfortably slithering, gently adopting their seductive, languid rhythm, until like them (Sssssss) you too, become a slithering "sacred being." **How does the earth feel to you now, as one of "Her" snakes? (pause)**

Like water, you flow with them and join them in their travel. You know where you must go now. The dry Earth, underneath you, has told you. Follow...
Follow your new clan of sisters as you slither upwards now. Sssssss. Follow them, knowing you will soon reach your destination and that thirst will be quenched. *(pause)*

Follow them upwards, up a curved cratered road, as they continue to slither and hiss going up, up onto the crescent Moon now. Sssssss. *(pause)*
Under your cold, scaly skin, feel her sacred, beloved body underneath your very own, as you slither and hiss in delight and continue to travel upward around her thighs, her curves, her moist womb with the waters you've sought and craved. *(pause)*
They gather upward now and you follow to join them. Together you unite to form her sacred crown upon her head and *Ix Chel,* in delight, pours forth her waters.... *(pause)*

Healing waters... gushing and pouring out unto the thirsty landscape below. Swelling and gushing onward, filling what was empty. The Healing water you needed is here, feel it sprinkling, being soaked upon your once leathery skin, delight in this water. Healing waters poured unto your surrounding sisters. *Ix Chel's* healing waters showering you with support. You see the Goddess smiling at you, she takes pleasure in knowing her waters are being put to good use. Take this moment now to tell her how you intend to use her moist gift from this point on. *(pause)*

As you speak to her, your body begins to feel familiar, no longer a snake but rather a reflection of her light, her Moonlight. And then, just as quickly, she becomes your mirror in which you see yourself fully as you always have been- beautiful and strong. Embrace yourself and for now, Bid adieu to Ix Chel. Know that she is never far and when you seek her, she will come.. for she loves her daughters. *(pause)*

Breathe again, with my voice, you are returning.... Return back into your delightful earthly body. Returning, as I count from 5 to 1.... *(pause).* Return back to this room and this time and place, 5. Return to feel your own body 4, well quenched and healed. 3, Return to feel your weight upon the floor of this room, 2. Return ....and 1. When you are ready, slowly open your eyes, stretch a bit and join us here. Welcome!

THE SACRED ELEMENT OF WATER

There are various ways the sacred element of Water can be incorporated in our most powerful magick workings. Below I have notated just a few to give us a starting point for our own personal experimentations with water magick.

1. The simplest form of water magick is in a mere shower after a particularly, long harsh, stressful day. Soap and water scrubbed on our skin helps to wash away physical debris but also to wash away debris that might be clogging our emotional or astral bodies and our chakras as well. As you shower, utilize the water to send intentional healing energy to wherever you feel it is most needed.

2. Ritual Baths with scented oils, enchanted herbs and sea salt have been utilized for ages by various cultures and spiritual practices. It is always best to do right before a ritual or a spell. Often it is suggested to allow yourself to air dry so as not to wipe away the scented healing essence you acquired.

3. A special bath dedicated to the Goddess of Love is perfect for a personal Self Blessing ritual to honor yourself and induce a reverence and respect for your own beauty. It can be simple or as elaborate as you'd like, with a full circle casting. Rose water and rose scented oil are perfect for this potentially powerful ritual of Self-love.

4. Another way of incorporating water into our magick is with the very simple act of drinking a glass of clean, fresh water. Studies have shown that we don't include enough water in our diets and this lack of water, in our day to day lives, can have vastly negative effects to our intestine and digestive systems, not to mention our skin, energy levels and our overall well-being. To drink a glass of cool healing water, consciously ingested with positive intent, can have profound effects on our health, fitness goals and inaugurate an awareness on better beverage choices for ourselves.

5. Through-out the ages recipes for magickal Elixirs have been described in many Occult Grimoires. A simple way of creating an Elixir is with a special gemstone (like moonstone or amazonite gem) placed in a glass of water overnight and preferably under the Full moon, to absorb its energy. Then within your own personal ritual you can drink this elixir with the intention of internalizing the positive qualities of the stones and the full moon. Before choosing a gemstone for your elixir be sure to research its qualities and stay away from potentially poisonous ones.

6. Rain water, especially from a fierce thunder storm, can be utilized to bring about drastic change and wash away that which needs to be eradicated and banished from one's life, for positive transformation. We can call on the rain to moisten those particular parched areas in our lives that need revitalization via healing rain water.

7. A quiet, meditative moment drinking tea composed of hot water, honey and intentionally gathered herbs, can do wonders for calming the mind, but also as a powerful healing agent when facing physical and emotional challenges. We tend to do this instinctively when we feel the onset of a cold or when we are having a particularly harried day and we reach for the chamomile tea. Water in the form of warm tea can be quite magickal and inaugurate healing.

8. Drowning a problem and eradicating it in a pool of moving water, an ocean, a toilet, even a bowl of consecrated water dedicated for this cleansing, banishing purpose, is quite effective. This is not to be done halfheartedly, be sure you have considered seriously the consequences for banishing someone or something from your life.

9. Water by the side of your bed before going to sleep has been known to help quell nightmares and keep negative spirits at bay in various aboriginal, cultural traditions.

SOME WATER GODDESSES TO CONSIDER: *Ix Chel, Aphrodite, Venus, Oshun, Yemaja, Hathor, Saraswati, Erzulie-Freda, Scylla, Sirenne, Naiads, Tiamat, Lady of the Lake, Danu, Hiaaka, Hina Ke Kai, etc...*

RELINQUISHING & GROUNDING
Alone, so many find themselves,
In this vast world,
Alone, just as well.
In partnership or solitude…
Among the living, who claim to love you,

Yet by their actions, their words empty,
As if to fool, confuse with contradictories.

Alone, yet still,
even in your hands,
For love avails itself
to read and understand.

The void I tried to fill with you,
Like water,
Can't grasp it,
Slipping right through…

The cracks of this façade you've made.
The one I can no longer play.
It's marred beyond this moment in time,
Deceit's ill-effect to take what was mine,

Illusions of love and forever after,
Relinquishing, now hope for a savior's rapture.
Relinquishing You and the pain of deceit,
Returning to solitude
Until I find what's right for me,

Peace, stillness,
The waves to settle down,
Hushing Thunder, in Mother Earth I ground,
I ground….
I ground……

RELEASING- A SPIRIT TRANSMISSION
"The essence of the way is detachment..." Bodhidharma

Weeks before Approaching the globally, much anticipated Virgo Full Moon of the Spring Equinox, I was receiving lots of "transmissions" from the Divine. In one strange moment I found myself reflecting upon the word "***Release***" and soon thereafter held a pen in my hand, while I jotted down the wave of messages regarding this word.

"Release is the absence of holding on. Creation is releasing...
Creating is Not holding on, it is based on the act of releasing,
Every single time we create, we are performing an act of
releasing unto the Universe...
Therefore inherent in the act of releasing
is simultaneously the act of creating" (my journal notes...)

"A mother gives birth not by holding onto her child but by letting go,
opening her womb and releasing the child unto the Universe...
The performing and visual artist, the writer, the craftsman
all create, not by holding on to his/her craft, but by releasing it unto the world.
Our very breath on this planet is an act of releasing.
Observe a Dancer, as they move and breathe out with every step,
gracefully giving life to visions and choreography. It is via the exhalation (the release) that songs are sung,
dancers move, musicians and artist express, even the practice of Yoga and our spirituality
is called in this manner. And we come into this world in this way,
by our very breath-
We release and thus create." (my journal notes...)

A song's beauty is in its release unto the listener, by its very exhalation, not by holding on to it ....Observe a singer who's very craft is harmoniously connected with the ability to take in breath, manipulate and release it, like a craftsmen, delicately upon a composer's melody. The Magician, Priestess and Witch (I realize now more than ever) also touches upon this supposition. For indeed spells, our most cherished wishes, cannot come to be and manifest whilst we hold onto them, daily wishing for their fruition. It is only when we release our wish unto the Universe via a spell and then walk away, in perfect trust and love that all will manifest for the greater good, that a spell then, has the fortunate chance of manifesting.

It is only by releasing, that we move into our most creative transformational powers. From containment in the heart, mind and soul, to the sacred act of letting go, we aid our own personal growth, but also greatly effect humanities'. Our own journey suffers most when we resist and do the contrary. By clenching and holding unto the past, whether it's resentment, failures, anger and hurt or, on the other side of the coin, holding on to our gifts, our thoughts, opinions and all that is locked in our precious heart - we rob the breath of new life force. We block the potential for something monumental, cathartic and greatly necessary for humanity -we rob the Divine's vehicle of transmission.

As someone who in the past suffered from various digestive problems including IBS, I can attest to this truth and the negative effects of holding on to things that really needed to be expressed outwardly. I must note that the waste of our urine and excrement causes us great physical pain and discomfort, symptomatically as a result of blockage in our solar-third chakra. This chakra, located in the upper region of our abdomen, rules the expression of our emotions and links very closely to our digestive system. When we are unable to release stress or have other unexpressed emotions, our body's reaction is to shut down and physically reflect what the spirit is undergoing. Silencing the soul is one of the most detrimental things you can do to your encasement, and temporary physical form, it is trauma to your insides. As emotions are held in captivity, so do we begin to hold within our body, toxins and things that really ought to be released for our own holistic wellbeing. This is just one example of how negative emotions, toxins like hate, fear, unexpressed stress, anger, resentments and regrets, all have the potential to harm us in one shape or form, when not expressed and released. In surrendering, we release and in that very act of releasing, we give birth to something new and potentially better.

It is via this release and exhalation- that we are able to transition and move from one stage in our development to the next. The soul too, upon death must release the physical body and thus, only through this act can then transcend and transform into the next incarnation... I suspect this was one of the great mysteries of the cycle of life and death, revealed in the renown Great Eleusinian Mystery Rites of Ancient Greece. I continue to muse and also speculate on Sex, as it also reflects another great example of the cycle of life and death and the cathartic powers of releasing. The very magickal act of an Orgasm is in fact a form of releasing, - the release of the body into ecstasy. The release of Fear, births the Warrior. Releasing of pre-conceived ideas frees us to grow and manifest in ways we never could've imagined and with the release of ignorance, we end racism.

At this moment, I surveyed my entire life and marveled at all the numerous time I gave birth to astounding creations and then... in that same instance, sadness came over me, as I realized how many more times, I simply manifested a multitude of deaths, paralysis, stagnations due to my inability to just release.

In light of the recent natural disasters; the destructive earth Quake and horrible Tsunami in Japan, and the numerous devastations facing all of us, with the escalating global crisis, it becomes clear that the only way we can survive is by releasing and letting go of attachments. Buddhist believe that the source of great pain for humanity is found in attachment and thus I can't help but connect the two words and the helpful insight we can garnered by simply reflecting on their meaning.

At this time of year I should be happily looking at seeds, blossoming flowers, transformations and rebirth and yet, I find myself looking at the challenging act of releasing as another fundamental route to rebirth and Spring's renewal. So much sadness and confusion is facing us globally at this time but, I think, It's only exasperated when we claw and hopelessly clench with our very last breath, to all that we've known and become accustomed to, for fear of what is evolving and attempting to be born.

May we all find the strength, in times of great turmoil, to simply breathe, exhale and release, knowing full well that within us is the power to create, transform, rebuild and birth new life once more. Namaste...

What am I holding on to (4 of Pentacle)?

_____

How is holding on, hurting me?

_____

What must I release?

_____

What do I wish to Birth in the near future?

_____

Journaling about Ix Chel Gathering

Unlike the previous past months (when I was struggling with some insecurities and personal home challenges) I was very much looking forward to this month's grove gathering. I had lots of activities planned for us and I had invested a great deal of time and energy in preparation for this month's Goddess. Ix Chel unquestionably, inspired and captivated me and I was only too happy to share in my enthusiasm with my systers. She had been gracing our hearth mantel for months now, as I had painted an image of her, that came to me last year, and all too often, wommin would inquire about her, every single time they entered my home. I truly felt a sense of sacred honor to finally be able to bring her to my Grove systers.

The timing seemed just right, as last month we invoked a Fire Goddess and devoted ourselves to Fire, while just touching upon the realm of Water and we were now at the heart of Summer, in July. The heat of summer however, has many of us extremely busy, noncommittal and far away.... and so, I was initially disappointed when those I expected to come, did not. Still, if there is one lesson that I have learned as a priestess is that, honoring the Goddess requires no exact number of participants and it is a sad disservice to those, dedicated systers, who are present, to give them any less of me because the turn out wasn't what I had hoped. So I persevered and in the end, reaped great benefits for it too.

We started by first singing some Goddess chants and then doing a check in to catch up on all that we were dealing with since the last gathering. One of the womyn was noticeably very despondent due to her inability to find work in this recession and I was well aware of the effect, her lack of energy would have on the entire group's dynamic, but I kept sending her love to balance out the energy and I think it really worked throughout our day. In years passed, something like that would have thrown me off course and altered the hue of our entire day, happily it did not.

Following my notes, I briefly talked about Water in relation to all the seven Chakras and then gave a very important lesson on the various sacred ways the element of Water is utilized in our magick work, craft, and the occult. I happily shared my knowledge of Ix Chel and the numerous depictions and mythos about this beloved Mayan Goddess and I think many wommin were able to really connect with her numerous attributes.

Without missing a beat, I quickly reminded them about the upcoming sabbat of Lammas, its significance and our own annual tradition of surveying the year with gratitude. I played beautiful, serene music and invited them to write, on hand-stamped parchment paper, all the things that have manifested for them this year and their gratitude for it. On the reverse side of the paper, they were invited to write what they hope to manifest in the coming months before the end of the Wiccan year. This would be a private note, for their own personal altar and thus we did not need to share it.

The next phase of our day was the Ritual part.

We started our Ritual in a much more intimate fashion, since it was a small group, I felt it seemed most appropriate and I've come to really appreciate how physical proximity instinctively results in intimacy. We knelt close together and blessed each other with oil on our third eye and thus began our work and the circle casting.

I called all the Elements myself with prose, incorporating special elemental candles (Yellow for Air, Red for Fire, Water in Blue and an Olive Green candle to represent Earth). These candles were placed and lit in the center of our circle as the sacred quarters were called. I also invoked Ix Chel with a prepared poem and smoothly we transition into a pre-recorded meditation on the "Medial womyn" and the realm of the West. This meditation was important for me to also experience within this circle. I was most impressed with how smoothly the transition was and how close it was, to what I had initially envisioned for us weeks beforehand. Immediatedly after the Meditation, I read a passage from "Ix Chel Wisdom" by Shonagh Home, in which our belly is honored as the sacred source from which all magick can manifest from and we placed our hands upon our womb, blessing this sacred spot.

The next phase of our ritual was the Spell and like last month, this would be a two part working. The first and most challenging part, was a water jar offering with our blood. Participants came into the circle with their own personal urn/jar of water and we pricked our fingers (a bit challenging, for some more than others) with sterile needles to add a bit of our *blood into our personal Goddess offering. This was an offering of thanksgiving to the Goddess, Ix Chel. Each womyn poured a bit from her water jar into a larger communal glass jar and in this manner, together we created a communal Grove offering, in addition to our personal offering, to pour unto the earth. This went quite beautifully, as I think we all understood the concept behind the act.*

The second part of our ritual was totally altruistic and I felt very strongly that, indeed, it needed to be or maybe that was Ix Chel asserting her way. We don't often send enough good energy out there, to others who might need it more than us but are unable to reach for help. And this was a chance, as witches, to consider the ramification of our work for the greater good.

With music playing in the background, we considered a cause or a person that needed healing. I passed around blue, peacefully charged, votive candles, to each womyn and in genuine Ix Chel's honor, with much reverence for the sacred work we were doing, we went around the circle saying aloud who/what this light would burn for. This was a very touching, intensely serene moment to witness and to personally experience. When all was done, I surveyed the collection of lit blue votives, shining their light for others and felt misty at the thought that our work indeed effect healing unto the world. We did a check in, before embarking on devoking, and some expressed chills and a surge of energy running up and down their spine and I understood, for I had the same surging within me too.

Devoking presented a final challenge, but only to the one who had been a bit down on herself the entire time and I wondered if that was spirit demanding some sort of proper reverence. I want to add that, after our working, I felt a surge of confidence, love and support from Ix Chel and it really tore away any fears or insecurities I might've had about really..... anything, even something as nerve wrecking as devoking. I found myself strangely searching, yes searching, for my inner guide and that voice of intuition came in louder than ever and it propelled me to devoke from that place, deep inside my heart, trusting it and letting it flow among my Grove systers. I held each elemental candle and upon devoking with my heartfelt words, I used my hands over it to blow away the lit flame. Apparently when I came to the element of Air, the hot candle wax, shockingly, blew over, spilling unto the nearby, already troubled syster. It was initially shocking, mortifying and then... all out hilarious. No one was too scalded because it was a low level burning candle and after the initial shock, we all had a good chuckle at how elements have a way of making themselves known. For me, it was just a reminder that ritual work is serious business, not to be entered lightly. I always hold it with the highest regard and never once forget the deities, forces and spirits ever present when that circle is cast and so it behooves me to be very present and alert in ritual because anything can indeed happen and there are messages in these situation. We must be fully present in rituals.

Our circle was quickly opened after the candles had all been snuffed and we proceeded to enjoy our potluck feasting. There was exotic chocolate and homemade vegetarian pizza to be enjoyed, made by one of our most talented, crafty, kitchen-witch, beloved Grove syster and so we wasted no time to commence the feasting and thus ended our sweet day of sisterhood with Ix Chel.

IX CHEL GROVE GODDESS GATHERING CHANTS

EIGHT BEADS CHANTS by Carolyn Hillyer
Girlseed
Bloodflower
(dip it)Fruitmother
Spinmother,
(raise it) Midwoman
Earthcrone
Stonecrone
Bone

***Mother of Darkness
Mother of Darkness
Mother of Light
Earth Beneath the Soul in flight
Songs of love and Love of life
Guide us to our heart.....

THE RIVER IS FLOWING
The river is flowing, flowing and growing,
The river She is flowing, Down to the Sea.
Mother carry me; your child I will always be.
Mother carry me down to the Sea.
The Moon she is changing, waxing and waning,
The Moon She is changing, high, above me,
Sister, challenge me, your child I'll forever be,
Sister, wait for me, till I am free. *By Diana Hildebrand-Hull*

SYSTER RIVER, GIVER
From Victorian Christian's creation , Elijah The band of Light
Syster, River, Giver...Returning Whole,
Syster, River, Giver...Returning Whole
    Open up, To receive
    We are what we Believe. *(REPEAT)*
    Syster, River, Giver...Returning Whole (2X),
Growing Roots like the Trees,
Wee are planting seeds. *(REPEAT)*
Syster, River, Giver...Returning Whole (2X),
    Stored in Deep, Stories Sleep,
    Within Us, These Tales we Keep. *(REPEAT)*
    Syster, River, Giver...Returning Whole,
    Syster, River, Giver...Returning Whole,

MY BODY
My Body is a living Temple of Love
My Body is a living Temple of Love
My Body is the Body of a Goddess (3X)
(lower)My Body is the Body of a Goddess

THE OCEAN
The Ocean is the beginning of the world
The Ocean is the beginning of the world
All life comes from the sea
All life comes from the sea.
By Delaney Johnson, Starhawk and Reclaiming collective

SWEET SURRENDER
We are opening up,
in sweet surrender,
to the luminance
Love light of the one, (Repeat)
    We are opening ....We are Opening (z2X) *by Gladys Gray*

MAIDEN MOTHER AND CRONE
Smiling Virgin, shinning crescent,
Waxing fullness,
Luminescent
Sickle of Silver, reaper of Bones
Maiden Mother and Crone, Maiden Mother and Crone by Abbi Spinner

BORN OF WATERS
Born of Waters,
Cleansing Powerful.
Healing , Changing,
We are...   *by Starhawk*

WE ALL COME FROM THE GODDESS
We all come from the Goddess
And to her we shall return,
Like a Drop of Rain,
Flowing to the Ocean *By Z. Budapest*

May

The Astrological sign for the month of May is the earthy sign of Taurus, the Bull. Taurus is ruled by the planet Venus (April 21-May 20). Traditionally known as the planet of love, it is not surprising that the arrival of May brings the theme of love, joy, earthy pleasure and frolicking maiden energy, oozing out of the Universal auric field.

The Full moon for this month was sometimes called the Flower Moon or Fertile Moon, as these, evidently, are the predominant themes of the month. According to the Farmer's Almanac, sometimes May's Full moon is also known as the Milk moon and Corn moon as well.

May is the Fifth month in the Gregorian calendar. This month is probably named after the ancient Roman Goddess, Maia, who apparently is slightly different from the Greek Goddess with the same name. The name Maia means "mother" in Greek and as a Greek Goddess she indeed exemplified maternal attributes, as the reputed Mother of the God, Hermes. Perhaps this is why, on the second Sunday of May, we commemorate our beloved mothers with the U.S.A. holiday of Mother's Day. Even the Catholic Church honors the Feminine with Our Lady of Fatima's feast day on May 13th and, interesting to note, all of May is devoted to the blessed Virgin Mary.

However, The Roman Goddess Maia (also known as Majesta) whom this month is named after, is Goddess of Growth and Abundance and she exemplifies more of the maiden, frolicking energy, most reflective of the month. Most of the festivals during this month allude to fertility and orgiastic rites like the Floralia, held at the end of April leading right into the first week of May. It garnered the reputation for being a grand orgiastic festival to honor the Roman Goddess of Growth and Springtime, Flora.

Bona Dea (meaning Good-Goddess) was also an ancient fertility festival held in May that honored the ancient Roman goddess by the same name. The Rosalia festival, held around May 23rd, also venerated the magick of flowers and the Goddess of Fertility.

For many Pagans in the U.S.A. and abroad, this is the month to celebrate one of the four major sabbats of the witches year, Beltane. Beltane is a Celtic holy-day that honors the energy of the ancient Celtic Fire Gods, Belenus and Bel and there are numerous traditions linked to its observance. Traditionally, as part of the Beltane activities, Goddess and God or an appointed May Queen and May King, mated and became one in perfect balance. Their mating upon the earth's soil, assured the earth's abundance, healthy proliferation and fertility upon the land. This was also the time of engagements for young couples hoping to marry the following month, as it was considered lucky to marry in June, because it was believed the Roman Goddess of love and matrimony, Juno, would bestow her blessings on the union.

In May, it appears as if the Spring maiden has fully blossomed and reached the ultimate level of maturity. Some traditions view her menarche at this time of the year and celebrated her fertile, bright red blood of life. Precious seeds from the Equinox, back in March, have sprouted, lush, flowering, green and full. Her powers of creation and attraction are undeniable now, as bees and critters, of all kind, come out of hiding, drawn to her colors and scents. Now Spring is fully here and brings with it, all of her joys, light-heartedness, gentle breezes, and warmer climate. Colorful ribbons, floral wreaths, a jovial frivolity, sensuality, and a youthful spirit lingers in the air now.

We honor the maiden's arrival and this earthy, pleasure filled season, by pounding and awakening the fertile moist earth with our joyful steps, twirling and dancing around the sacred Maypole (which can be made of Ash or Birch tree but also of Cypress or Elm wood). As Pagans we celebrate Beltane, the way we believe she has been celebrated for numerous years by our ancestors. The Earth is awakened and alive and so are our physical bodies. Frolicking and lovemaking are a common theme this month. Everywhere and everyone is feeling friskier than ever, amidst the growing heat and power of the Sun.

In the spirit of the season, we call upon the Egyptian Goddess of pleasure -Hathor, to assist us in awakening joy, sensuality, pleasure and our heart's delight. This month, in the spirit of merriment, we will also honor Baubo, who reveals to us the greatest gift we behold as wommin- the gift of our Yoni, our womb/belly and the cathartic power of laughter.

CHAPTER TWELVE

"Witchcraft is all about living to the heights and depths of life as a way of worship..." Ly De Angeles, *"Witchcraft: theory and Practice"*

"Those who think Sex is Overrated, just ain't doing it right...." Hip Hop Rapper, Ludacris

WELCOME HATHOR

OUR ALTAR

Altar cloth: Pinks, reds or purple altar cloths and maybe a second blue altar cloth underneath to represent the Nile.
Image: Statue of this Horned Egyptian Goddess, Cows.
Canvas art or photo of the Goddess and or photos of her temples, Egypt, Bovines, lioness, water, moon and stars are all appropriate to display on your altar.

Always present on the altar;
A cast iron cauldron, drums, speaking stick, a silver pentacle, athame, elemental representations.....

Air: Sistrum, peacock feathers, smudge wands, Incense type sticks, cones, charcoal brisket and fine powdered herbs like, jasmine, mugwort, hyssop, sandalwood.
Fire: candles, glass enclosed candles or pillars in red, pink or purples and or a women shaped candle, or woman's Yoni/genitalia shaped candle.
Water: Chalice or small glass bowl with Water or better still red beer or red wine
Earth: Colorful fresh cut flowers, green plants, a small dish of soil and or herbs and branches like Sycamore, Ash, Oak tree branches.

Other items pertinent to this particular gathering
Hand held elaborate mirror
Gemstones in particular; Turquoise and Malachite
Rings, Necklaces and pendants
Beads for the Menat, a multi-strand altar necklace
Plate offerings of decadent rich chocolates, gooey sweets
Fragrant lotions and scented oil
Roses and lots of plants and greener
Statue or figurines of Cows,
Lunar Head circlet
Sistrum, rattles or other musical instruments
Books of poetry and erotica
Lipstick, eyeliners and other cosmetics
Bowls of consecrated, scented Water
Plate offering with eggs
Writing pens and paper, safety pins,
Light blue gauzy fabric to represent water
Workshop items; cosmetics, scented oils, sweets, art
Tarot or other oracular tools

Offering example food; decadent sweets, chocolate, strawberries, cherries, whip cream, peaches etc...
Sacred objects from members:
Notes:

Hathor

Hathor Altars

Bovinian Hathor

HATHOR:

Hathor is a Pre-dynastic Goddess, worshipped for over 3,000 years. She is the Egyptian Goddess of Joy, Pleasure, Beauty and Love. Yet Hathor is known by a multitude of other names and titles. As is typical of most ancient deities, Hathor appears to be an important Goddess of many names, duties and significant attributes. The name Hathor means, "House of Horus," perhaps a reference to her role as mother of Horus. Hwt-Hrw, Het-Hor, Het-Hert, Athor-Athyr are just some of the names ascribes to her in the writings of her time period.

She was most commonly known and depicted as the *"Celestial Bovine"*, nurturing all of humanity. Images of her appeared as a beautiful winged Cow with stars over her head and sometimes as a cow on a boat over water, alluding to her connection with the Nile river. This image later developed into a lady with the head of a cow, wearing the illustrious head dress of a pair of horns and a moon or solar disk in the center. Eventually she was depicted with a human head and the ears or horns of a cow, while wearing the Goddess head-dress. As a cow, she represents all of the generous attributes typical of a bovine and was believed to have given birth to the universe, according to one Egyptian cosmology.

Interesting to note, Hathor seems to embody all the elements; earth, fire, air and water. Often depicted as a Sky Goddess, existing before time and called Mistress of the Heavens, she was also the Goddess of Moisture, associated with the inundation of the Nile River. She was seen as a Solar Goddess in her connection to her consort Ra- the Sun God and also in her aspect as the Fiery Lioness, Sekhmet. She is the Goddess of the Moon and the Goddess of the underworld, protecting dead souls and guiding them to the Judgment Hall. Known as Mistress of the Necropolis, she tenderly cared for the dead souls and offered them water, with the branch of her sacred Sycamore tree, as they journey to the underworld. She was considered the Goddess of Agriculture and, to ancient Egyptians, she was called upon to assure the fertility of the land. Unquestionably, Hathor was a beloved, multifaceted, ancient Deity, greatly revered by both men and wommin.

Her main Cult was in Dendera, but she had many devotees and followers through-out the world. From Africa (places like modern day Ethiopia, Somalia and Libya) to Semitic West Asia. She was a patron Goddess for wommin and all feminine aspects of life, but she was also adored and worshipped by many men as well.

Hathor was the protectress of pregnant women and all women at different stages of their lives. From birth to death, she was believed to oversee and be invested in the many stages of a womyn's life. A Goddess of perfumery, cosmetics and jewelry, she was known as Lady of the Malachite and Lady of the Turquoise. Malachite was mined in her Providence of Sinai and thus easily attainable in this region and some of these precious stones had many sacred usage, some were even grinded and used as cosmetics. As a Goddess of cosmetics and beautification, Hathor often adorned her eyes but so did both, priestesses and male priest in Egyptian temples.

The Menat, a multi strand necklace, was her beloved symbol. This was a necklace that was not used for mere adornment but rather was used during special rituals. As a Goddess of Music, the Sistrum was also another sacred symbol of Hathor that was used mainly to bless, ceremonially cleanse and purify a place of worship.

Hathor was believed to be the daughter of Nut, Sky Goddess and Mother of all Gods, and Ra, The Sun God. She was also the wife of the Sun God and given the esteemed titled of the "Eye of Ra." This daughter- wife relationship (similar to the Hindu Goddess Saraswati and the God, Brahma) appears to be a common ocurrence among ancient deities of the time.

According to a famous legend, Ra feared his kingdom was coming to an end. He was angered at the Egyptian people and their apparent lack of respect and commitment to him, as their God. He sent his beloved Hathor as the bloodthirsty Sekhmet, to go out to kill off those who appeared to be going against the old ruler. Rather unexpectedly, however, Sekhmet became uncontrollably blood thirsty and was determine to massacre everyone in sight, good or bad, regardless of their political allegiance.

As Sekhmet, she was an irrepressible force, determined to draw blood, feast and dance on the multitude of corpses. I can't help but see the image of the Hindu Goddess, Kali Ma in this depiction of Sekhmet, but I digress. Ra feared the worse and recognized his impulsive grave error. In a desperate attempt to end Sekhmet's killing spree, he poured red colored beer and tricked the Goddess into drinking it, believing it to be blood.

According to one myth, Sekhmet became so intoxicated after ravenously ingesting all of that beer that she completely passed out and the next day woke up in total contrast, as the sweet, benevolent Hathor once more. In this myth, we see our Egyptian Goddess as the savior of Egyptian people and we also see her association with intoxication. Interesting to note how Sekhmet becomes representative of this fierce dark aspect so often seen in most revered mother archetype, like Hathor. It reflects the double aspect most often exemplified by matriarchal deities. They are sweet, generous and nurturing, yet capable of fierce protection, and severe destruction swiftly, if the situation calls for that energy.

When later, the cult of Isis and Osiris came to Egypt, it changed Hathor's popularity and worship. Many of her aspects and functions were taken over and absorbed by the new Egyptian Goddess, Isis, whose worship spread to Rome, Africa, Asia and through-out Europe. Though on the surface they might appear the same, these are two quite distinctly different deities. In the myths of Isis, we learn of her pain, tragedy and grief but with Hathor, such emotions almost seem foreign to her character. In her myths, Hathor is the embodiment of success, happiness, joy, pleasantries and beauty –in complete contrast to her dark aspect as Sekhmet. Hathor is benevolence, pleasure and the pinnacle of Solar brightness-rarely do we hear of any hints of ugliness, nor tragedies in her tales and she has remained a beloved Egyptian Goddess, who bestows joy and pleasure to her worshippers and she continues to be a Feminine deity many wommin can easily connect with in this modern era just as in previous years past.

Hail and Welcome Bovinian Goddess Hathor!!!!!

HATHOR GROVE GODDESS GATHERING

Purpose: Inviting Love, Beauty and Pleasure in our lives through Hathor. Celebrating Beltane... a day of sensuality. Encourage participants to dress comfortably in silkens, P.J. or lingerie...

Check Ins: Introducing ourselves to the group and sharing what we've been up to since our last gathering and how we experienced the last esbat.

CHANTING WORKSHOP
"Hathor Song", "My Body is a living Temple of Love..", "Mother I feel you under my feet...", Let it in, Let it Flow... "The River is flowing" (see also song sheet)
GENTLE MUSIC CD HEARD THRU-OUT
AGREEMENTS: Our Agreement Sheet is passed around and we each read a bylaw and discuss it, adding to it as necessary. It is signed, dated and submitted.

Check ins: With speaking sticks, participants will have a chance to go around the room, check in, answering a fun question that will commence our journey to Hathor, for ex; complete sentence, ***"Pleasure is...._____ or If I was a gemstone or a drink or a color, I would be called...................." etc...*** *or come up with another social ice breaker to start...*

DRUMMING Throughout the day, gentle Egyptian instrumental music will be heard, but at this time a powerful drumming or bellydancing music track will be played to allow wommin a chance to connect, feel their earthly form, and ground in this moment.

Creation of Cone of Power
Holding hands within a circle, starting with a low buzzing hum, resonating deep down within our Root chakra, we continue humming, now open it up to "Ma", raise this energy up through the seven chakras before you. Simultaneously raising our intonation stronger, louder, vibrating a heart open "Ma", blending our intonation until it is One strong voice, vibratingly strongly over our seventh chakra-the crown. Then slowly releasing the energy into our sacred space. It is done and this is how the Cone of Power is erected.

MEDITATION
Offer a CD recorded meditation or one of the numerous found in this book, a discussion follows afterwards to assure everyone is back and well grounded.
LEARNING ABOUT THE GODDESS HATHOR
learning of Hathor's etymology, her myths and her attributes
GODDESS WORKSHOPS
WORKSHOP I: With music gently playing in the background, participants are given a questionnaire sheet to help them begin journeying to Hathor's Realm. Together we will share some of our responses to help get to know one another better.

WORKSHOP II: Meditation and contemplations on the Cow as a Sacred Totem and how we may incorporate this sacred animal in our magick.

WORKSHOP III: There are numerous images of Hathor and on our altar we will have our sculpture and Goddess Oracle and tarot (which all have images of Hathor). These images will be shared around the circle so that every womyn has a chance to connect with her, speaking aloud what they see in her image. In this way we begin to invoke her in our day.

WORKSHOP IV: Beer Making. Since Hathor is so often associated with intoxication and beer drinking, a beer making workshop would seem perfectly suitable to connect with this aspect of our beloved Mistress of the Necropolis. Personally I'm not an expert on the subject but its nothing that a little research can't benefit from. You can also hire someone to come in for the day and teach a beer making workshop to the Goddess Circle.

WORKSHOP V: A Menat workshop. Sacred Altar Necklace Creations. In ancient times, priestesses not only adorned their bodies, but also their sacred temples and altars. Malachite and Turquoise were Hathor's sacred stones. In this workshop we will create an altar necklace with special, large, craft beads, that we'll imbued with Hathor's energy.

WORKSHOP VI: Music and Body work, Creating energy with the power of Dance and movement (**Belly Dancing**). For this part of our day, we will engage our bodies to help connect with Hathor's essence, using a few basic, belly dancing moves.

WORKSHOP VII: Creation of Scented oils, as this is Hathor's domain. You are welcomed to use the suggested scented oils found in the appendix of this book. It is also fun to experiment with a few essential oils to recreate your very own personal Hathor oil. This oil can be used to charge candles, ritual tools or your body, prior to spell workings and all in the name of the Goddess.

WORKSHOP VIII: Cosmetic blessings. Since Hathor was known to be the patron Goddess of cosmetics, beauty and facial adornments, we will take our most prized, brand new cosmetic (example; eye-shadow or mascara or lipstick etc...) and bless them in the name of Hathor, with our best intention via the elements. If wommin are up to it, they may pair up and give each other some form of adornment or cosmetic make over. This can be viewed as an adult facepainting workshop and it touches upon one of her important attributes as a Goddess of cosmetics.

WORKSHOP IX: Feeling her energy thru the Four Elements, this will be done as a group or pairing off participants:
Air: eyes closed ---tickling each other sensually with feathers or with our breath upon the ears/flesh....
Fire: Lighting our candles and passing it around our flesh as close as possible... maybe lighting our systers candle and then placing your systers hand right above the heat of that flame.
Water: Feeding each other juicy fruits like Strawberries, peaches, chocolate syrup, etc.. it all has to be drippy and of a sensual nature for our systers touch upon Hathor
Earth: Massages, back rubs while sitting/standing, then turning afterwards to reciprocate.... The use of scented massage oils can be incorporated, if there are no objections or allergies.

WORKSHOP X: Creating an Erotica Poetry Café reading. Words and images will be shared and intimate stories told about our wildest sexual encounters, or tales of our first love making experience... Wommin sharing confidently their best secrets for ultimate pleasure or perhaps sharing issues they wish to remedy with the advise from their other sisters. To end, a final check in for participants to complete the following sentence, "**It turns me on when......................**"

WORKSHOP XI: Depending on the members of your circle for this gathering and their level of trust and comfort you can offer a **"Passion Party"** which incorpotrates a Trusted Sextoy salesperson to come by and discuss their use and benefits and basically sell you bedroom accoutrements in the privacy of your own home. This is a wonderful opportunity, especially for shy wommin who might never have been to an adult shop or who would never have considered the addition of such a thing in their lives, to explore another side of our Hathorian Goddess. With a fun group of wommin this can be quite a blast and very informative.

REFLECTIONS ON HATHOR

Hathor teaches us that life is to be enjoyed. As wommin, though we have a myriad of roles and responsibilities, at times pulling us in contrasting directions, we still have much to take pleasure in. We are multi-orgasmic sacred beings and our very nature can be soft, sensual and beautiful. We should embrace the sensual gifts found all around us more often than we do. Music making, adorning ourselves with cosmetics and alluring clothing fall under Hathor's domain. Precious Gemstones, silken fabrics, delicious scents and tasty, delectable things that make our tongues dance also fall under her jurisdiction. Experiment with awe inspiring music and let your body mimic that of a snake. ...These are just some of Hathor's lessons and gifts to us; to dance with enjoyment in this lifetime and embrace our sexual, pleasure seeking nature -allow joy a chance to penetrate your realm.

HATHOR GROVE GODDESS GATHERING RITUAL

Purpose: Inviting Love, Beauty and Pleasure in our lives thru Hathor. Celebrating Beltane... a day of sensuality. Encouraged to dress comfortably.

Asperge: Purification by Lavender Rose Water,
Each Womyn offers her Syster a Glass of Cold Water saying may the Goddess quench your thirst. Offer a glass of Spring Lunar water (This is water that has been left under the sacred light of the Full Moon to retain its energy).

Casting Circle:
With flowers and Rose petals cast around the space, the Priestess Recites.....
CIRCLE CAST
Sacred Space I conjure thee
Safely Hold our energy
Guard and Shield us as we Work
Finding Spirit in our search.
We stand between the Light and Dark
And With these flowers
our Circle is now marked.....
***The Circle is cast we stand in sacred space...

QUARTERS CALLED:
Chant- *"Earth my Body, Water my Blood, Air my Breath and Fire my Spirit...."*
EAST
Close your Eyes to begin this elemental Journey...
AIR is Honored with your Breath and Mine....Breathe.
SOUTH
Feel The Heat of this Flame,
it is the same Flame of Goddess that lives within you, Hold candle flame.
WEST
With this offering,
I feed you and awaken the powers of Water which flow in our womanhood...,
offer juicy strawberries, watery melons or syrupy chocolate cordials
NORTH
We are Body and Soul and with this act we remember
and acknowledge the Value of our Earthly body on this plane... Rub your hands together and hug the person next to you.

HATHOR INVOCATION
With Candle lit in her honor

Short Meditation Offering, to help us connect to this moment.

SPELLWORKING: Each participant will elect a colorful ribbon to use for the spell. An **Egyptian Musical CD** track will play, giving wommin a chance to **raise Energy**, while dancing, connecting and imbuing energy into their selected Beltane Ribbons. Once energy has raised, each participant will take their ribbon and **wrap it around the Maypole** while stating aloud their wish for the season. When all have finished and the Maypole is beautifully wrapped in ribbons, we will next jump the **large Cauldron in the center of the room, with the Beltane candle fires**. With excitement and vigor stating aloud our wish as manifested we jump the cauldron with positive affirmations,

For example; *"I am working at the job of my dreams"*, *"I am in a loving relationship"*, *"I have all my bills paid"* etc etc...

WORKING II:
Egyptians were known for their usage of charcoal dark liners around their eyes to enhance this most important feature on the face. At this moment in our ritual womyn are encourage to pair off and line each others eyes with a cosmetic pencil liner, saying;

"Behold my Syster, I adorn you now as the Goddess that you are.
May it remind you of Hathor and this day...".
CHANT: Hathor song

Thanking and **Devoking Hathor** in whichever way feels best to release her...(see text)

Devoke Elements

NORTH
We are Body and Soul May we always remember.
In this sweet embrace that started this day,
I give my gratitude for your presence here today.
Our earthly forms acknowledge and honored,
We thank you Earth and bid thee adieu... Hail and Farewell Earth!

WEST
Fed with thy sweetness, we touched your watery gifts.
Your presence all around us like a gentle shower mist.
We thank you Water and bid thee adieu...
Hail and Farewell Water!

SOUTH
Heat of our inner Flames felt in this sphere,
Thank you Fire for drawing near.
We thank you Fire and bid thee adieu...
Hail and Farewell Fire!

EAST
Healing exhalations, rejuvenating breath,
We felt your divine powers circling our sacred nest.
Thank you Air for your presence here today,
We bid thee adieu until we meet again.
We thank you Air and bid thee adieu...
Hail and Farewell Air!

CHANT: *"The earth, the air, the fire, the water, return, return, return, return, Below above, the center is love, return, return, return, return,"* by Robin Rose Bennet

Final thoughts

Open the Circle with our traditional chant...
"The Circle is open but unbroken, may the Love of the Goddess be ever in our heart..."

POTLUCK: *Yummy foods of pleasure to be enjoyed...*

HATHOR GROVE GATHERING

Questions to Journey to Hathor

In moments of stress or severe depression knowing the answers to these questions can be of great help by taking you out of that overwhelming rut and putting you back in touch with the Divine....

Applying this intimate knowledge about yourself can also quickly put you in touch with some of Hathor's most cherished attributes like; Joy, pleasure, beauty (your own beauty and self-worth). and move you beyond episodes of despair. See how quickly you are able to answer these (all 5 senses included), then if you will, please let us share in our responses and begin our Grove Journey to Hathor.......

1. What 3-5X things that bring you joy and pleasure. What puts an immediate smile on your face?
   1. _____
   2. _____
   3. _____
   4. _____
   5. _____

2. What Part(s) of your body do you consider Erotic/Sensual?
   a. _____
   b. _____

3. Which animal do you associate yourself with? _____ and what comes to mind when you think of a Cow/Bovine? _____

4. Do you wear cosmetics? _____
If you do, what part of your face/body do you highlight or adorn most?
_____

5. Do you wear Perfumes? _____
Name a smell or scent (any) that immediately transports you to Ecstasy/a better place...
_____

6. Where and how should someone touch you to help you achieve relaxation?
_____

7. Rate these according to your level of preference:
___popcorn
___ice cream
___broccoli
___wine/other spirits
___whip cream
___lasagna
___water
___chocolate
___chewing gum
___coffee
___fruits
___French fries/potatoes

8. What/Who is your favorite performing artist, band group, music?:
_____

INVOKING HATHOR
Bovinian Goddess
From immortal realms,
From Egyptian land,
May your presence here be felt.
    May your musk essence linger,
    To awaken the Snake,
    To arouse the hungry swaying,
    Of hips formed to gyrate.
To dance in seduction,
By your Sycamore tree,
Invoke you in swirls,
Of joy and ecstasy.
    Hathor, sweet Lady,
    Beloved Eye of Ra,
    Tonight I'll invoke you
    In my climactic "Ahs"...
Mistress of Malachite
Of Egyptian Scenes,
I paint you and draw you
With my melodies.
    Dendera worshipped
    I leave offerings of beer,
    Whilst sweet incense swirls
    To draw you ever near.
Come Mistress of Heaven,
See how much you're adored,
Lady of Jubilation,
Let me receive you through these doors.
Hail and Welcome Hathor!!!

DEVOKING HATHOR
Lady of Jubilee, of Merriment and Love,
Bovinian, Egyptian Goddess, Hathor,
The **Sounds** of your rhythmic Pulse,
still vibrates in the Air.
The **Taste** of you,
still fresh on my lips,
Your Beauty,
always **reflected** among my Systers,
And Thy Sweet **Scent**,
still lingering evermore in this place.

A new month has begun and we endeavor
to move forward on our Goddess Journey.
As is our tradition,
We give our most sincere thanks and Bid thee Adieu...
Dearest Hathor,
Go if you must, Stay if you will...
and May you always be near enough
to embrace and **touch**,
in those moments I neglect
or forget my own self- worth
and inner Beauty...
Hail and Farewell Hathor...
All say: Hail and Farewell Hathor...

EROTICAS TO HONOR THE SEXUAL ONE

****More - More- more
Woah...
More - more- more
Woah...
Hathor, Aphrodite, Ix Chel,
Water Goddesses, Sexual Ones,
flowing within me, around me
I am the altar that exalts you
I am the screams voicing your passions
I am both the
container and releaser,
of all your great powers of ecstasy
Within the eruptions and fountains
Express your divine gifts,
May I continue to be visited by you and
be blessed.....

**Participants are encouraged
to compose their own eroticas in the name of Hathor
and share among the Circle....**

_____

_____

_____

_____

_____

Perform this spell on Beltane or a Spring day and when the moon is waxing or near Full. It may be done in the evening, but best if done, the first hour of sunrise on a Friday - which was the day, named and devoted to the Goddess of Love. Upon your altar, place images that conjure up your personal ideals of love; heart shaped items in reds and pinks, red roses, photos or magazine clippings of couples or ideal looking mates. Include also a statue of the Goddess and photos of yourself near her image. Let the smoke from your sweet smelling incense swirl around you and your altar. Watch the smoke rise and let it put you in a hypnotic, magickal trance of love and pleasure. Play moving music, drum or sing to her, as she appreciates these types of musical offerings. Acquire a green candle and a pink one as well, both carved with symbols of love on the wax; like heart shapes, swirls, Venus symbol, xoxo... Anoint your candles and your body with rose oil, love oil or draw to me oil, (see appendix). Place tasty offerings of Champagne or red wine, sweet dark chocolates and sticky, syrupy, ambrosianic edible items on your altar. Let her worship begin in you and upon this altar and visualize the results of your manifested love spell.

BELTANE
* May day, May Day
Bring Love and good cheers
I celebrate the luck and joys of this year

On Venus day and Venus hour
I invoke you Goddess to grant me your powers
To manifest beauty and love in my life
A soul mate, a partner, who is rightfully mine

Loving to me, respectful
Faithful to me and good
Passionate and giving
All is understood...

Handsome sweet soul-mate
Who will only love me
Have I met you yet,
in last night's dream?

We've yet to meet, but
Let us meet now
I am ready to behold
the Empress and her crown

On this blessed Sabbat
I call unto thee
This spell is now cast
So mote it be!

Calling Forth for Joyful Pleasures-Dancing with Hathor.

This was by far a surprisingly, very fun gathering. Although I had great visions and ambitions for our day, I didn't know what to expect due to the intimate nature of the theme and knowing how so many womyn still struggle with their own beauty and sexuality. I was wretched and tormented with initial fears that no one would even show up.... but when I looked into the eyes of the few womyn that indeed were there- I was inspired and encouraged to put aside any feelings of failure, or let down, and make Hathor proud of me as her Priestess, by bringing her energy into our day, no matter how big or how small the attendance. By the end of our day, one of the participants said it best, when she timidly admitted that she was glad for those who were present and those who were not, because the energy of the day was exactly as it needed to be....and who knows how vastly different it might've been, had the wrong members been present for such an intimate Grove gathering....

Indeed it was a wonderfully intimate day because we shared as womyn very personal stories and we supported each other's sensualities and beauties. We celebrated our five senses, chanted, drummed, read erotic poetries and shared love songs. We learned to Belly dance and in sacred ritual space, we jumped the frolicking Beltane fires, by way of my huge cast iron cauldron... Our day was wonderfully exuberant, full of high energy, sexiness and one of my favorite gatherings because as a Priestess, I stepped up to the challenge of trusting my intuition amidst a frail, doubting moment of failure and insecurities. I embraced my gut vision and passion for this Goddess Grove day. I sidestepped ego so that I could present a Goddess that I knew needed to be acknowledged, invoked and celebrated by us, as womyn, and it was a powerful, most memorable day for everyone involved, because of it. I even heard that some had returned home, to their mates, still feeling Hathor's gifts and arousals. I was tickled to learn that I wasn't the only one stirred positively by Hathor and our beautiful Goddess gathering....

Journaling Hathor Gathering
with Grove of the Feminine Divine

The wommin have just left and I'm now tidying up the place. I can't rave enough about our Grove Gathering and what began as something I thought I would be forced to cancel, ended up being such an awesome, amazing, gratifying event!!!! OH MY Goddess!!!! With only a few wommin, it was remarkable!!!! I should've known it was going to be this way, when at around 11:45am, I looked out the window and saw Three black, large Grackles, reminiscent of Macbeth. Their beaks strangely wide open and they were gathered in front of the Dog's kennel, near my home. I studied them for a while, perplexed at their appearance and why they had their beaks so wide open and now I see how they foretold the success of this day.

Okay, I am still buzzing in delirium and I'm just so happy about our day!!!! This is the highly charged energy I'm left with when experiencing a Goddess like Hathor deep in my bones. One womyn said it best in the end, when she said, ".... I love all my systers, but I am kind of glad it was just us, ...don't know if we would have had the same, amazing, intimate great energy, had others been here... " I knew exactly what she was saying. Without being disrespectful, I couldn't agree more. It became clear to me then, that not all wommin want to tap into this part of the Goddess and they willingly deny this part of themselves, opting to deny their physical, earthly forms, for various reasons. Hathor demands that you shake it up and embrace joy and pleasure and sadly some wommin struggle with allowing themselves permission to enter this realm. As a result, sometimes, womyn can become energy zappers and downers when they fail to truly be participatory, and fully present, in a group ritual. So, I really understood that Syster's statement. Indeed, their added presence might have changed our amazing experience today for when you have eager healthy participants your gatherings and rituals are greatly influenced. Jokingly, we were all in agreement about repeating Hathor every six months... They joked, but felt strongly about Hathor being a Goddess for every sister to experience and how it was too bad some wommin couldn't be there. They surely missed out on an a valuable experience.

Everything was seamless and it's funny because when I started, (seeing how it was just a small group) I thought, seams would come undone, actually. I was scared of how I could achieve structure and yet still appear casual, plesant and relax, but still accomplished everything planned for Hathor. GODDESS, thank you, because indeed it worked itself out beautifully...better than I anticipated. I guess I am growing too as a priestess and I send my wholehearted thank you, to beloved Hathor for making herself known to us.

We started completely different from the norm, but I listened to my intuition and trusted that it knew best. Drumming music was heard throughout and I bet no one wanted it to stop, so it didn't. We did our checks ins with it and it went great. Then one syster suggested we each voice our personal view on

Hathor and I thought it was an awesome idea since she is an ancient Goddess with so many numerous aspects and attributes. We each shared how Hathor came to us personally and how she was pulling us individually. I must say it was interesting to see and hear Hathor through everyone's eyes.

This led to the Lecture on Hathor, her myths, who she is, what she brings to us and her similarities to other important Goddesses in various pantheons... It was nice, not my usual way to begin our Grove day, but it worked and it was seamless. Then just as effortless, one syster mentioned a song she had written for her love and I thought that was her offering to Hathor (it wasn't), but I asked her to sing it to us anyway, as an offering and it became the start of some beautiful sweet offerings to Goddess. Next was my Erotic Poem, honoring my vagina. They loved it and saw the classiness of it as well. Afterwards, was the awesome Belly dancing workshop led by another Grove syster. Wow!!!! is the best way I can describe it!!! She took us through an amazing exploration of Belly Dancing and I was never so amazed at how effective belly dancing is for a good total work-out. I am totally hooked on this beautiful, expressive art form, thanks to her workshop. She really taught us the right technique and the historical significance as well. Afterwards, we spent time just dancing and moving lusciously, manifesting amazing heat and juicy Hathor sensuality.

Quite Harmoniously again, this led us to the next phase of our day- the Elemental meditation working. **Air** *with our breath, to calm down, slow it down after that heavy dancing experience. Then afterwards, the feathers of air, that wonderful breeze it created, as it touched our skin. It was beautiful!!!! Then* **Fire.** *I had them touch their heart and feel the heat within and then passed around our altar candle so that they may feel the flame and recognize Hathor and themselves in that flame... It was magickal!!! Then* **Water**...*Oh we had so much fun, feeding each other luscious dripping sweet melted Cordial Chocolate covered Cherries.... Oh My... talk about getting in touch with Hathor. It was the most sensuous experience ever and indeed intimate, yet this was the ideal way to experience Hathor. They understood what that was all about...* **Earth** *was next, I think they really enjoyed the suggestion of light body massages.... I explained the reasoning, how massaging was taught to me and we just massaged each other while sitting down, train style, and it was comfortable, groovy and cathartic.*

Only after this wondrous experience were we able to finally get to the Chant workshop. My Chanting workshops are usually the way I begin our Grove day, but it didn't happen that way and I am so glad. Again seamlessly, it worked, fitting perfectly right after the body massage and elemental working. Here we had now tasted Hathor in relation to all the elements. Now we were celebrating with our voices... singing freely, which is exactly how Hathor prefers to be honored. We started with "My body is a living temple of Love..." perfect after working with our bodies! Drumming seamlessly followed that song and again, I had to trust my intuition here which was guiding me into this phase. We continued with all the song and surprisingly ended with a song that acted like the necessary beginning for the next stage in our work...the opening and casting of the Circle. "Blessed be", I said, as I realized we had already Casted our sacred circle, even though it was nothing like I had originally planned. It was better and the "Divine" always has a better idea...doesn't "She"?

We began our Circle with the song that we ended our Chant workshop with. Then, because we had already invoked the elements in our meditation, that was not necessary, so the next thing was invoking Hathor.....but wait.... I felt strange. Hathor was with us ALL DAY long and I felt, more than anything, a sense of gratitude to her at that particular moment. One of the womyn agreed and encouraged me to go with that... so I did. We sang my original song composition to Hathor, while dancing. This essentially enforced the invocation to Hathor. Next the Working; I passed around the fragrant oil I made and they followed suit. "Dearest Syster, I adorn you as the Goddess that you are...." we each placed oil unto each other's neck and heart chakras as we said these words. It was a truly a very tender, memorable moment.

Then, as no Beltane is complete without celebrating with a Bonfire jump.... I played an inspirational, jumping fiery music CD. The Music was played, we raised energy with our clapping hands and we jumped the bonfire several times while speaking our goals, declaring it joyfully aloud!!! Mine was for Energy, pleasure and the Success of Grove of the Feminine Divine etc...We jumped happily at three different times and it was exuberant and so much Fun. I shared Ffiona Morgan's Wisdom on spell working and the requirement of this intense energy. We had a great time! Then it was time to Devoke....

I thanked the Goddess Hathor and each one of my systers present for their amazing energy contribution. The elements were devoked by singing "Return, return, return elemental song" as we went around the burning cauldron!!! That was also very magickal as we could all feel the energy ground and I literally brought them, physically down, to the floor, so that by the time the song was finished we were on the floor, rested, GROUNDED. "The Beauty Song" was the last suggestion and without missing a beat, it led them right into "The Circle is Open Song".... And there we ended... PERFECTLY!!!!! SEAMLESSLY!!!!! BRILLIANTLY!!! Low to the floor, grounded and blissful. Blessed be to the Goddess of Delight and Pleasure, All Hails Hathor!
So Mote it be!!!!

HATHOR GROVE GODDESS GATHERING CHANTS

LIVING TEMPLE....
My Body is a living Temple of Love....
My Body is a living Temple of Love....
    My body is the Body of a Goddess(3X)
    My body is the Body of a Goddess (low 1X)

MOTHER OF DARKNESS....
Mother of Darkness, Mother of Light
Earth beneath, the Soul in flight
Songs of Love and Love of Life
Guide us to our Heart....

BORN OF WATER...
Born of Water,
Cleansing, Powerful
Healing, Changing
We are... (continue to repeat to raise energy...)
By Delaney Johnson, Starhawk, Reclaiming Collective

A SONG FOR HATHOR... *by B.M.M.*
Dance Goddess, Dance!
Eroticism Rises...
Dance Goddess, Dance!
Eroticism Rises...
Hathor.... Hathor.....(vocalises on her name.)
Beauty and Pleasure,
We call at this Moment,
Mine and Hathor,
Mine and Yours (face the Woman near you) *(continue to repeat as you raise energy).....*

GODDESS INVOCATION SONG
Lady, Lady Lovely Lady,
Are you from an Ancient Star?
Lady, Lady, Blessed Lady,
Come to us, from where you are...
    Magick Sister, Mother, Daughter,
    Tell us what will come to pass...
    You are Moon, Earth and Water
    You are here with us at Last...
Lady, Join us in our Circle,
Lead us in the Spiral Dance,
When you speak, Your Magick words....
Will send us All into a Trance.... *From Starhawk Alive Mind DVD*

WE ARE A CIRCLE by Rick Hamouris
We are a Circle, within a Circle, with no Beginning and never ending....
You hear us Sing, You hear us Cry,
Now hear us Call you, Spirits of Earth and Sky
Within our Hearts, there goes a spark
Love and Desire, a burning Fire...
We are a Circle, within a Circle, with no Beginning and never ending....
Within our blood, within our tears,
There lies the offering, of living water...
Take our fears, take our pain
Take the Darkness, into the Earth again,
**
The Circle closes, between the Worlds
To mark the Sacred Space,
Where we come face to face...
We are a Circle, within a Circle, with no Beginning and never ending....

CHAPTER THIRTEEN

"I make mistakes, I am out of Control and at times hard to handle, but if you can't handle me at my worse, then you sure as hell don't deserve me at my best...."
Marilyn Monroe

"I love people who make me laugh. I honestly think it's the thing I like most, to laugh. It cures a multitude of ills. It's probably the most important thing in a person..."
Audrey Hepburn

WELCOME BAUBO

OUR ALTAR

Altar cloth: Green or brown altar cloths.
Image: Statue of this Goddess, or a semi nude woman, Shela-na-gigs are okay to incorporate as well, Yoni floral cavernous images.
Canvas art or photo of the Goddess and or photos of joyful women, paintings of our sacred womb and yoni.

Always present on the altar;
A cast iron cauldron, drums, speaking stick, a silver pentacle, athame, elemental representations.....

Air: Smudge wands, Incense type sticks, cones, charcoal brisket and fine powdered herbs or wind mobile and or feathers
Fire: candles, glass enclosed candles or pillars in yellow or pink and a women image candle, and vagina shaped candles.
Water: small glass bowl with Water or chalice of red wine
Earth: Platter of fruits, green lush plants, a small dish of soil and or herbs, Olive or laurel branches.

Other items pertinent to this particular gathering
Items that bring us joy, bag of jokes,
Textile, Fabric pieces, board and glue
Clay or artistic Symbols of our genitalia
Bunnies to represent frolicking energy
Red Roses lots of greenery
Bowls of consecrated Water
Rocks and Gemstone
Plate offering of Barley
Sarongs or gauzy textile
Writing pens and paper, safety pins,
Workshop items like; clay, photographs, yoga mats
Tarot-, "the Fool" or other oracular items

Offering example food, Baked vagina shaped Cookies, Barley, wine, Pork if you are not oppose to meat, breads.
Sacred objects from members:
Notes:

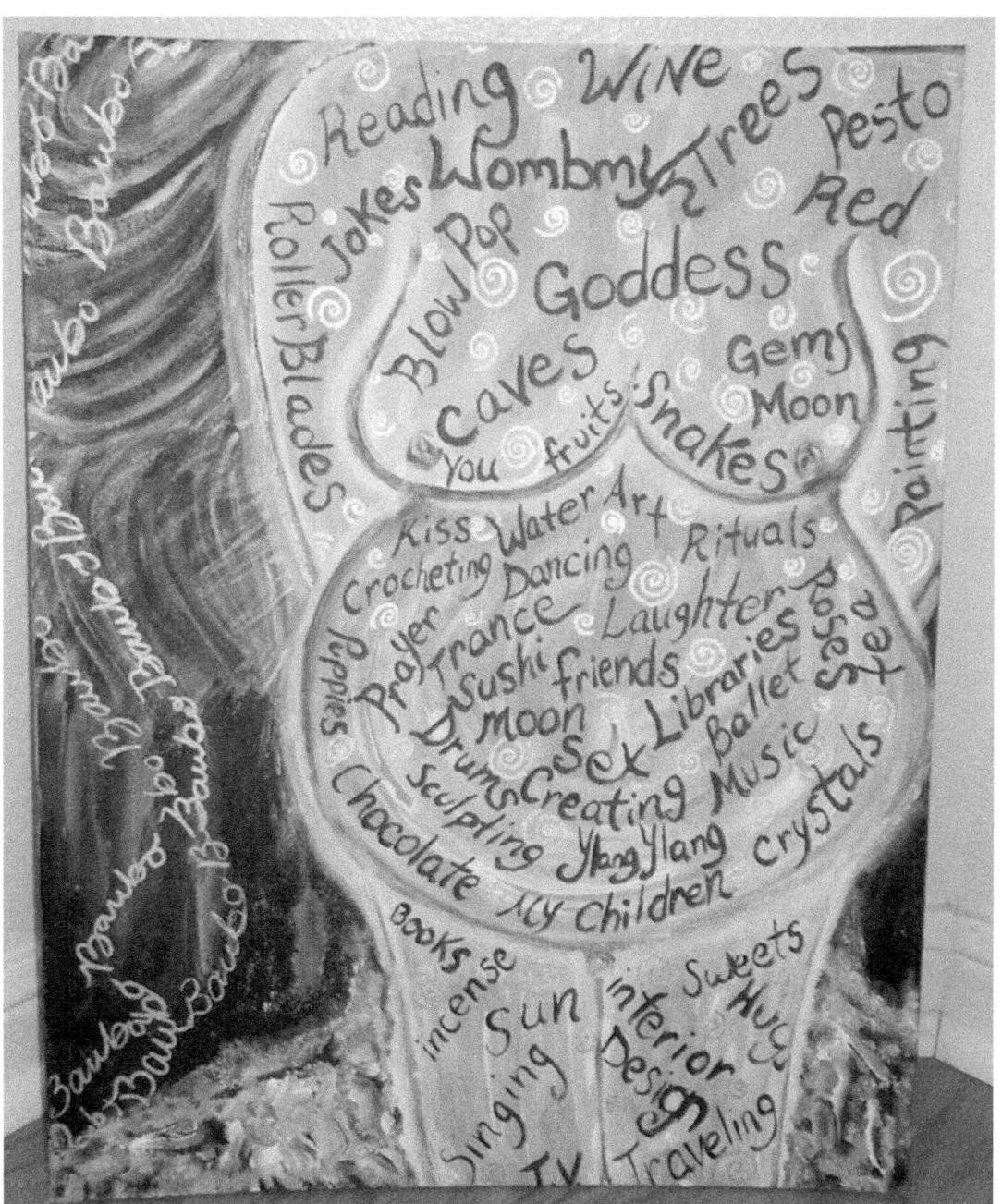

Baubo

Rebirth

Baubo Altars

Altar

Yoni Crafting

Aspecting Baubo

BAUBO

Baubo is the Greek Goddess of laughter and liberated sexuality. According to the Greek philosopher Homer, Baubo was born out of the union of Pan and Echo. Her name is believed to mean, *"belly"*. Other interpretation state that her name means, *"old crone."* We can understand this interpretation of her name because during her time, the word crone had a different meaning than it does today. The word crone, back then, was believed to be a Wise mature woman, not the old hag stereotype meaning it's become today. Thus Baubo, right from the start, appears to us as the wise matron who has something to teach us regarding our belly.

In mythology, we speculate that Baubo was married to a known Swine herder, as some of the writing of the time allude to this and this was consider quite a profitable occupation. During this time in history, a Swine Herder made a rather good salary and thus it was considered to be a desirous vocation for a man. She was believed to have had a son from this union and his name was Eumolpos. Eumolpos literally means *"Sweet Singer"* and often, the writing of the time reveals that many aspiring singers in folklore, were notorious for referring to him as their own original Singing teacher, to gain for themselves some credibility.

According to one of the popular, well known Greek lore, Baubo was employed as the nurse to the lame daughter of King Celeus, named Iambe, but she will forever be known in mythology as the one who succeeded in breaking through Demeter's sadness and lament. The Goddess Demeter, distraught by the disappearance of her daughter, Persephone, wandered the Earth aimlessly. In disguised, she came upon the King's abode and was welcomed to stay with their family. Everyone in the kingdom tried to cheer up this sorrowful old looking woman, but no one was able to reach her soul. Baubo offered her Barley and started to talk to the Grain Goddess, who at this point was disguised as an old woman. Still to no avail, Baubo was just not able to reach her and Demeter remained sad. In a moment of complete and utter silliness, Baubo lifted up her skirt to Demeter and reveal something that must have been strange and hilarious because it not only shocked Demeter, but also moved her to smile. That initial smile busted into a laughter that somehow helped her recover parts of her old forgotten Divine self. Somehow through this very act of her boisterous belly laughter, Demeter rediscover her brilliant self, once more. Because of this occurrence, she was able to move to action and eventually return to her post as Goddess of the Grain and consequently, was able to return the Earth to its natural cycle.

It is not clear what Baubo revealed under her skirt that made Demeter laugh so greatly, but some text allude to transgender genitalia, or a deformity or just an over exaggerated open vagina, like the Celtic, Shela-na-gig. Throughout history Baubo is often drawn and depicted with this exaggerated genitalia to reflect the sexual freedom she so expressed with Demeter in this tale. Sometimes she is also depicted with her face drawn or painted upon her belly, to reflect her connection to this sacred place in our body.

Unquestionably, Baubo is a Goddess that takes pleasure in bawdiness and unabashed light in her sexuality. She is the healing power of laughter and light heartedness. She is the Goddess of friendship because of her connection to Demeter and she wields the power of laughter. When she is invoked, She brings joyful mirth and fun, and thus helps connect us to the powerful healing nature of a good healthy laugh, the kind that emanates first from our core, cathartic laughter found in our sacred belly.

"Close friends contribute to our personal growth.
They also contribute to our personal pleasure, making the music sound sweeter,
the wine taste richer, the laughter ring louder because they are there..." Judith Viorst

BAUBO'S GIFT TO US

As with some ancient Deities there are always bound to be conflicting stories about their origins and their myths -Baubo is no exception. In this article, however, I would like to focus on Baubo's unquestionable attributes, her importance among the assemblage of Feminine divine deities and most importantly her gifts and relevance for us, as modern day wommin.

Baubo, is known as the Goddess of sexual liberation, bawdiness, a good hearty belly laugh and the healing power of joy, frindship and laughter. These are gifts that transcend time, as laughter has always been deemed magickal and alchemical in its ability to transform severe pain, spiritual malaise and heartache into something we don't need to die and cave into, but, quite possibly, can actually overcome and trascend.

There have been numerous scientific studies revealing the positive effects laughter and regular comedic relief has on our serotonin levels and our overall health and well-being. No one can deny the power of a good chuckle when we are feeling less than our best. It is also a well-known fact, among occultist, that laughter is the death of all maladies, awkwardness and even negativity is weakened by a joyful heart. The phenomenon of trolls, psychic vampires, dark entities and malign spirits are weakened and dissipate with the piercing sounds of jovial laughter -especially those of children, who can teach us a thing or two about surrendering to the joys of unabashed silliness and cackles. One of the best ways to raise the vibrations in a home plagued by strife, arguments and darkness, is to create multiple opportunities to laugh in that home. Thus a house warming party full of joviality has become a great customary ritual and an ideal way to bless a home and assure the grumbles will stay far away from the premises. These are just some spiritual remedies Baubo alludes to in her myths. Laughter can indeed heal, elevate and cure all temporarily weakened souls, as it did with Demeter.

The Greek Goddess of the Grain was in severe mourning and had suffered a great lost. Her sole, beloved daughter had been abducted and possibly raped by her own uncle, Hades. The tragedy of such a devastating occurrence appeared to have moved her to the brinks of her own death, as Demeter was no longer recognizable, no longer shone in her effervescence divine brilliance. And in her mourning, she willingly relinquish her duties and her authentic self. The story is very reminiscent of Amaterasu (The Japanese Sun Goddess) in that, both Divine Deities are so traumatized by the tragic occurrences in their respective lives that they surrender to great depression, retreat from their daily duties and their sadness almost seems to engulf, drown and overpower who they really are.

As the myth goes, Demeter was inconsolable and it appeared no one, nor anything, not even the multitude of decadent God offerings, could bring her back. I contemplate on how often unexpected tragedies have a way of traumatizing, shifting us into this dark realm where we too temporarily forget our inherent gifts and abilities to resurrect and regenerate ourselves. Yet as wommin, regenerating ourselves is clearly our domain and it is where we excel.

Everything about us, as wommin, points to this inherent gift and the exposure of our Yoni makes it undeniable because it's such a powerful ancient symbol of our Womynhood and our regenerative powers. In both Uzume's and Baubo's iconic stories, the liberation and exposure of the Yoni results in a necessary, personally transformative Global change. Both Amaterasu and Demeter experience a sort of death and rebirth, an awakening, through this unveiling of the naked Yoni.

We, as wommin, are truly regenerative creatures and Baubo chooses our yoni as the sacred vehicle to remind us of this vastly awe-inspiring detail. The gift of rebirthing and regeneration is ever exemplified in our blood, its monthly cycles, in the way we produce eggs every month and those that are not fertilized get discharged in our monthly menstrual blood. We are example of that power of regeneration in our ability to rebirth new eggs, a month later, and again repeat this same cycle of death and rebirth. Some of us even bleed (menstruate) in conjunction with the appearance of the full or new moon in the heavens and we're able to synchronize our menses together within a group of Systers. Our ability to birth new life within us, if we wish to, is another obvious example of wommin's ability to regenerate herself over and over again, if she chooses to.

We are regenerative in the way our breasts (as new mothers) knows just the right amount of milk to produce to feed our infants and after breast feeding, emptying the breast of milk, hours later, our body is able to reproduce even more milk than before, in order to meet the expanding, nutritional demands of a growing human being. That is the gift of creation and re-creation at its finest.

Our multi orgasmic nature compared to a man's lack thereof, also exemplifies this inherent gift of regeneration. In the way that we, as wommin, can be multi-orgasmic and after pouring out our juices of ecstasy, we can come again and again and again, whilst a man will ejaculate once and lose a great deal of his vital energy and life force in that one expulsion. Hence the reason men are more likely to fall asleep after an orgasm, while a womyn experiences a resurgence of energy.

It is in our very nature to continually regenerate ourselves and unearth our strengths and rebirthing skills, over and over again. The image of our Yoni is a powerful symbol and reminder of this gift. And because of this, birth, death and rebirth are closely linked to our gender's gift.

"Baubo's sudden exposure of her genitalia reminds Demeter (of who she is) that being a woman, having a yoni, gives her the power to endlessly create new life...." (page 61, "The Yoni...." by Rufus C. Camphausen)

I imagine that the sight of a middle aged woman, unexpectedly exposing her genitalia would shock anyone into a fit of laughter. Some speculate that what Baubo exposed was far more than just your average Yoni. There are some that suggest Baubo was a hermaphrodite, containing within her, both male and female genitalia. Still there are others that suggest that Baubo might have just had a very unusual, exaggerated large yoni. One will never really know what exactly Baubo exposed between her legs, but whatever it was, it held the antidote and remedy for Demeter's lament. The act of such an unexpected, some might say, crude gesture, was enough to shock the Goddess OUT of her despondent state and place her back on the road of remembering her authentic self and her divine capabilities. In Baubo's rather exhibitionistic display of her Yoni, she rather beckons the Fertile Grain Goddess to remember her inherent womanly gifts of rebirth, transformation and regeneration found within her own magickal cavernous yoni.

When greatly grieved and saddened, it is dangerous to forget that within us (more specifically our womanhood, our yoni) there is a capacity to regenerate, transform and re-connect with our inner joy, our sacred sanctum and the power of unabashed, belly laughs. These are the gifts of the Goddess Baubo. She introduces us to the healing powers found in our Yoni, our gender and the cathartic magick of laughter. Baubo shows us how our belly laughs, in particular, can move mountains, even those obstinate, self-destructive state of beings, like depression, while directing our attention to one of the most ancient powerful symbol of the Goddess- our Yoni.

BAUBO GROVE GODDESS GATHERING

PURPOSE: To honor and recognize our sacred Yoni, to honor the healing power of laughter, joy and merriment, to honor the Goddess Baubo.

CHANT WORKSHOP (see song Text sheet) *"I am Magick womyn, giving birth to myself"* and *"Spiraling into the Center"* and *"I am the Witches Daughter..."*

CHECK INS: with our Grove speaking stick we will go around the circle to Introduce ourselves, speak about how we are feeling and what we have been up to since our last gathering.

DRUMMING CIRCLE TRANCE: Participants are invited to grab a percussive instrument from our musical basket offering. Each womyn is encouraged to start making sounds with her instrument, until eventually, via listening to one another, we begin to synchronize and create a Cone of Power. This drumming circle will lead to our next exercise.

GENTLE BODY MOVEMENT AND DANCE: to connect us with our Earthly body, wommin are encourage to get into their bodies, shake it, let it loose, gyrate, get "jiggy" in our skin...

LESSON ON THE GODDESS BAUBO
learning of her etymology, and looking at her presence in Greek myths

GODDESS WORKSHOPS

WORKSHOP I: We begin this workshop by simply presenting an image or a photo from nature (or some other place) that for you, personally resembles a womyn's yoni. I usually like to go out venturing in the wild and take photo images of trees, caverns, patterns on rocks and of courses flowers, like roses, as these all remind me of my womanhood. It is always fascinating to see what captures our eyes in this workshop.

WORKSHOP II: Textile art of our Yoni. With various pieces of fabrics and glue we will be creating womyn's labyrinth/Yoni, gluing the various layers upon a canvas or wood board.

WORKSHOP III: Sculpting our own Yoni with Polymer clay or other air dry Clay. Polymer Clay will be handed out and attendants are asked to create an image or representation of what they think their vagina looks like. This will become a sacred reminder of our value as Goddess women and they will be used in our afternoon ritual. This might create a lot of laughter, joking around and merriment. Hopefully bonding and talking will ensue. It is all in the spirit of Baubo. As the Clay bakes and hardens we move onto the next work

WORKSHOP IV: Naming our Female parts. Men have been doing it for years, and in this workshop we will contemplate on our beautiful Yoni, especially after crafting with our Yoni art projects and polymer-clay, and we will give her a fun, appropriate, revealing name. Remember this is all cathartic but also loads of fun among your systers. So give her a name and share the reason why and have fun.

WORKSHOP V: Re-enactment of the story of Baubo and Demeter.... If two wommin are willing to entertain. They can re-enact what, we can only imagine, happened between the despondent grain Goddess and the merry Baubo on that faithful day in Eleusis.

WORKSHOP VI: Participants are asked to bring and share a single Photograph that instantaneously brings personal joy. …..My personal example tends to be puppies, my own children, Tuscany and Hawaiian landscapes…etc. To create bonds between participants we will share our own photos and placed them upon the altar as well.

WORKSHOP VII: A special meditation on the "Healing power of Laughter" and how to tap into joy will be played on the stereo for all to trance.

WORKSHOP VIII: Discussion on how we deal with sadness and the pitfalls of depression. Pre-conceiving solutions to the inevitable ups and downs of life. Creating a strategy for keeping ourselves healthy, balanced and happy. Making a list of at least five things that you know raise up your endorphin levels and bring you joy. _____, _____, _____, _____, _____.

WORKSHOP IX: Pantomiming or mirror exercise paired up with partners…. Music will be played in the background for added effects. Sometimes we don't realize the face we are presenting to the world and it can be quite astounding to learn that there might be discrepancies between how we think we are perceived and the reality. In sacred space, a partner, mirroring your facial expressions, can help reveal to you the face you are presenting to the world.

WORKSHOP X: We are reaching the end of the day and since we are celebrating Laughter, it only seems appropriate to have a presentation of "The Comedy hour". Bawdy jokes will be written on slips of paper and every woman will select a joke from the handbag and present it to her systers, front and Center stage, like the style of a comedian.

WORKSHOP XI: The day of Goddess Workshops can end nicely, just as it had begun, with some type of Body movement. I would suggest a short series of stretches and light Yoga poses, including the Lion pose. **Monkey face Exercise,** wonderful way to stretch our facial muscles, can be added, making a silly face for ourselves then turn to the woman next to you….shock her and make our Systers laugh aloud.

WORKSHOP XII: Creating a floral arrangement for our personal altar. It can be very therapeutic and meditative to do this after a rambunctious activity. Flowers are beautiful symbols of woman's sacred genitalia, thus they are appropriate to work with as we invoke Baubo's energy. This is also the perfect time of year for working with flowers and herbs. Together we can look for those flowers that resemble our womanhood and continue making merriment.

****

Images and statues of Sheela na gig,
<u>Book:</u> Femalia by Joani Blank an art book on Yoni, The Dinner Party by Judy Chicago, Vagina Monologue by Eve Ensler, The Metamorphosis of Baubo by Lubell, Georgia O' Keefe Floral Artworks ,
<u>Google:</u> Vulva Museum, Kirsten Anderberg.com
and check out Susun Weed's website she has lots with Marie Summerwood

REFLECTIONS ON BAUBO
She brings us the invaluable gift of friedship and laughter ….How it can heal and cure all pains, even if it's just temporarily, she lightens our burdens with a few jokes and a chuckle. Transparency and crudeness sometimes shock us into uncontrollable, cathartic laughter. Laughter is the best source for healing and our yoni also holds a great amount of delight and healing power, if we allow ourselves to look into its caverns -for the giggles of ecstasy are not far.

LAUGHTER MEDICINE
What raises your endorphins & serotonin levels?
What brings you Joy?

This was my own personal list that manifested after some thought. It is offered here merely as inspiration for you to create your own list of joys.... and "Laughter medicine."

I LOVE.....
Being in my Body
Dancing
Anything physical like running, skating, rollerblading, archery, riding a bike, walking on trails or on a treadmill.
Sex and climaxing
Dark, nutty chocolate
Traveling to new locals
Sleeping under the stars and the Fullmoon
Good soul-ful music (opera, folk, hip hop, rap, rock)
Watching ballet performances and ice skating
Museums-viewing breathtakingly expressive art
Architecture and interior designing
Creating; whether its crocheting a sweater, sewing a dress, painting an image on my canvas, sculpting with clay, handcrafting candles or soap or cake decorating. Anytime I am creating/giving birth to something I am in my element and happy!
Liking what I see in the mirror
Completing any task on my to do list.
Comedians (Omg!) I love a good comedian
Some Reality TV shows
My childhood shows and cartoons like Bugs Bunny, Jetsons and Bewitched
Fantasizing, imagining and positive daydreaming
Pictures of my mom and dad, they are both deceased now
Seeing an old Photo album of my past and my past family and travels
A well written, good book
A good positive movie or documentary
The sounds of drums, many drums-I loooove drums it sends me to ecstasy!
Animals, petting puppies especially and watching spiders at work and snakes
My children when they are getting along and exemplifying family love and harmony
Crystals and colorful gemstones
Chakra work
A good effective meditation
Knowledge, learning something new and interesting
Prayer, invocations, rituals and aspecting in trance
Communing with the Divine and my witchy systers
Yoga, if I can get past the initial uncomfortable stage
A platter of fresh Sushi and Miso soup
NYC Mister Softee ice-cream cone with sprinkle
NYC Pizza
NYC Valencia Cake
A good ol' used bookstore
Antique stores full of old stuff
Incense of sandalwood and patchouli
The scented oil of Gardenia, Frankincense, Ylang ylang
When I finally bleed after pmsing intensely
The feeling that I am not alone
The stillness of Dawn
Hearths and the flickering flames of a candle
The ocean

I encourage you to carve out a quiet moment for yourself now and make your own list of endorphin raising energy medicine....

BAUBO GROVE GODDESS GATHERING RITUAL

Purify by earth - the Soil, okay from a store, bought package or grounded Coffee to be used on attendant's forehead to **anoint and purify**.
Also an offering of Barley as they enter.

Attendants: *They should bring a photo, artwork or clay image or drawing of their Yoni/vagina and this collection will be placed on altar for all to see.*
Large Center **Alta***r, right on floor where they will all place their own clay creations over an altar cloth.*

Intent Purpose stated: to create merriment and honor Baubo and our womanhood.
Casting Circle: prose with wand or branch or a bouquet of flowers around the circle.

Quarters called
* Guardians of the Watchtowers of the **East**, Ye Powers of **Air**,
Place of new undertakings and new life, light air and the giggles of children, breezes that tickle our skin with rippling laughter,
We call on you to bring us your gifts
Guard and Hold our sacred space, Hail and welcome
(*attendants repeat*) Hail and Welcome!!!

*Hail Guardians of the Watchtowers of the **South**, Ye Powers of **Fire**,
Place of comforting heat that emanates from our Yoni, Heat that stirs our womanhood warmly welcoming us to play.
We call on you to lend us your gifts
Guard and Hold our sacred circle, Hail and Welcome
(*attendants repeat*) Hail and Welcome!!!

*Hail Guardians of the Watchtowers of the **West**, Ye powers of **Water**,
Place of our ebb and flow, our moon connection, waters of intimacy and life.
We call on you to bring us your gifts
Guard and Hold our sacred space, Hail and welcome
(*attendants repeat*) Hail and Welcome!!!

*Hail Guardians of the Watchtowers of the **North**, Ye powers of **Earth**,
Place of manifestation and regeneration, ancient caverns that hold sacred mysteries,
We call on you to bring us your gifts
Guard and Hold our sacred circle, Hail and welcome
(*attendants repeat*) Hail and Welcome.

Invoking Goddess Baubo: Let us call and invoke her with **loud laughter!**
Every participant is encouraged to reach deep inside their belly and let out a great big hearty laugh, and like a cone of power, create a series of laughter incorporating our belly.

She appears and speaks....
There is more to me than has been written
I am so much more than one story
but it's nice to be remembered in this way.
For Demeter and I had a good laugh that day
and I will forever be remembered
as the one who broke her sad spell,
her self-imposed exile...
The Earth finally was able to heal itself

and return to its fertile, lush state.
And the world could rejoice once more.. Everyone did!
Can I help you rejoice and heal with my silliness too?

Oh I'm happy to be a part of that story.
But there are many more tales untold.. yet...
can we create our own tale of laughter
amidst tragedy and uncertainty?
Shall I reveal to you the mysteries,
my gem, between my legs to bring you, also,
out of tragedy and lament?
Haa.. Haaa.. Haaa..
How silliness and laughter cures all ills...
See my dance and join me in the fun......

The Working:
Re-enactment: A woman to represent Baubo doing her silly dance and enticing every women there with laughter and giggles.
Baubo will hand out pieces of paper with pen and ask them to write. Woman will write on a small piece of paper; what annoys her now, what makes her feel like Demeter (sad). When all are ready, **Baubo** will invite them to speak, by speaking first herself.

> *"I wish to abolish Your sadness and thus I sit and crush the sadness of the world.*
> *What will you sit and crush with your "Booootyyy".*

Every woman around the circle, Takes her note, reads it aloud, and then SITS on it (along with a loud whoopy cushion) with laughter. Every womyn in the circle will encourage it with laughter and applause.
When all have done this, the Goddess will encourage silly physical movement as part of the magick to raise energy. Perhaps a spiral dance ensues as they reach for their Vagina altar representation and show it off within the dance.
Chant: *"I am Magick Womyn"*

Baubo then helps with the grounding by uniting our hands together and beginning the embrace offering - each sister will hug and thank her sister standing next to her by saying;.
> ****Thank you for the precious gift of friendship and laughter***

Chant: *"We all come from the Goddess"*

Hold hands as we begin **Devoking and Thank the Goddess**
Dearest Baubo,
we thank you for sharing with us,
through our Sister's giggles and effervescent cackles,
the healing gift of Laughter.
May we taste you and seek you,
more often in our lives
and may, remnants of this joyful day, linger in our hearts.
Go if you must, stay if you will...
Hail and farewell Baubo!

DEVOKING
Elements/Closing Chant: *"By the Earth that is her Body, By the air that is her Breath...."*
Final thoughts, hugs and giggles, before
Opening Circle with "Merry Meet Chant."

LECTURE ON YONI, LAUGHTER & BAUBO

PURPOSE OF LECTURE: 1.Meaning of YONI, herstorical evidence, 2.The power inherent in reshaping our thoughts and perception our Yoni. 3.The relevance of Baubo's gifts to us as wommin- Joy & embracing our sacred Yoni.

Yoni is a Sanskrit word that refers to a woman's genitalia, inside and out, it includes her outer vulva, labia, clitoris and her inner womb. It is a word that easily translates as *"womb"*, *"origins"*, *"source of all"*.

As Sanskrit was a holy language, intended for religious documentation, with many symbolisms in its sacred alphabet, it can reveal a deeper level, to help in understanding the meaning of certain words. In the case of the Sanskrit word, Yoni, it is interesting to note that, although the word is pronounced {YO-NEE}, it is however written as, YOIN. According to Rufus C. Camphausen, in his book, *"The Yoni, Sacred Symbol of Female Creative Power"*, he elucidates this theory even further, when he invites us to look at the meaning of each letter in the word Yoni.

> **"Y- the animated principle, the heart, the true self, union,**
> **O-Preservation, brightness**
> **I- Love, desire consciousness to shine to pervade pain and sorrow,**
> **N- Lotus motherhood, menstrual cycle, nakedness emptiness pearl...**
> (pg 3 -Rufus C. Camphausen,*"The Yoni, Sacred Symbol of Female Creative Power"*)

"The Eastern Tantrics and other ancient cultures worship the divine in the form of a Goddess, the term YONI has acquired another, more cosmic meaning, becoming a symbol of the Universal Womb, the Matrix of Generation, and Source of All..." (pg 2 -Rufus C. Camphausen,*"The Yoni, Sacred Symbol of Female Creative Power"*) As wommin, it is imperative that we are aware of this ancient definition of our womanhood because it adds a better understanding of our origins, who we are at the core and how we should perceive ourselves. It has the power to drastically change our perception of who we are or believed to be, when we are awaken to the truth of our own ancient divinity.

We are not some secondary gender and our genitalia is not some dirty, smelly sinful place, as so often derogatorily depicted in our modern day colloquialism. With pejorative words given to it like; black hole, man-trap, pussy, beaver, snatch, muff, ditch, pit of darkness, noose, fish market, etc.. It is not surprising, so many wommin have turned away from their source of power, not even able to befriend it, acknowledge it with love, close scrutiny nor worship. (*)*"...How in the name of all that is Holy, can anyone think that the place where all of us come from, the very place of our birth, is a place of shame? It is the most important, the most powerful, the most beautiful place on earth. Worship it with all your heart or you will be lost...."*
(Rufus C. Camphausen,*"The Yoni, Sacred Symbol of Female Creative Power"*)

I personally do not give much credence in the belief and ludicrous theories of Penis envy, championed and popularized by the beloved father of psychology, Sigmund Freud (1856-1939). Nor can I put too much value on the tales of Phallic worship, for long before the Penis/Lingham was worship, there was clearly the veneration of the Yoni, Wommin and thus the Goddess.

A multitude of archeological finds throughout history and ancient cave drawings all corroborate to the veneration of Yoni. When we consider the daily lives of cave people, primitive humanity, our ancestors and the lack of tools and sophisticated implements, it is astounding to realize that they would take such painstaking effort to commemorate and document what was clearly of utmost importance to them by consistently painting Yoni symbols. If that's not an expression and proof of love, then I don't know what is. Consider the hours it would take, to chisel, sculpt or paint these intricate symbols, in the darkest of caves, in less than ideal circumstances and all, as an expression of love and worship, to the one who was at the center of their devotion- Yoni, Wombyn, the Goddess.

As a modern day wommin coming to this realization, I can't help but be touched and honored that my ancestors would exalt a part of me and preserve and immortalize my gender in this way. Think of the influence and vast, positive impact this historical fact would have on the fragile developing self-esteems of the young. To say that it doesn't affect some part of my own psyche and self-esteem would be false and clearly, if young girls across this earth had this knowledge from an early age, I believe the effects on our society, as a whole, would be positively transformative.

Even more astounding is learning that many Yoni images were often found deep in the center of dark caves, suggesting that perhaps there were special journeys (one can only speculate of a spiritual kind) required before reaching the inner sanctum. Here too, is yet another proof of the importance of Yoni to primitive humanity, as it received the highest place of honor, the most respected locale, the core, the center. Throughout all of history and even in our present day, the center has always been regarded as the seat of power and this was the chosen place, worthy of our ancestor's spiritually crafted Yoni images and her worship. These ancient symbols and paintings (often done with red ochre to symbolize blood) found within the inner sanctum of caves, therefore reveal the potency and high regard of Yoni.

For our primitive ancestors, the Yoni was Divine, mysterious and clearly something to marvel. We must also consider that primitive humanity had no medical, biological or scientific knowledge about how the reproduction system worked. The genitals, both for men and for wommin, quite obviously was a source of pleasure and ecstasy, not related to reproduction. To primitive man there was no connection between sex and procreation.

It would have been nearly impossible for them to correlate man/sperm/eggs and the fertilization process necessary for human conception to take place. However, what WAS clearly evident to them was the way a female clan member could grow and swell her belly and maybe, nine full moons later, from her blood and her Yoni, give birth to another human being. And in these very non-secluded primitive, open communities, births would have been a public event, indeed, for all, in the clan, to witness and marvel, as the womyn's yoni open itself up to become the sacred passage way for new life to be born. Clearly, the veneration of Yoni and her blood, would have been very logical.

Both men and wommin in the clan, all observed that it was womyn, her Yoni and her blood, that had the capacity to bring forth new life and indeed this would have been deemed the ultimate sign of great divine power. And if from her blood and subsequently, her yoni, new precious life can be born, what else can she manifest with her great powers? Surely she can make the land and fields grow plentiful and turn them into fertile source of sustenance, as her own body effortlessly appears to be. Thus, important sacred rituals, where her blood was poured out into the fields, ensued, in the hopes that her creatrix powers would be transferred and be evident there too. She was nurturer, sustainer, preserver, teacher, creator and she was called, Goddess - worshipped and revered for her obvious numerous magickal gifts - Gifts much respected, necessary and sought after by primitive humanity.

Life and death were clearly under her domain as she bled for days on end, without any hint of expiration, pain, nor insurmountable discomfort and every time these blood episodes occurred, she survived and lived. For primitive man, blood was often associated with pain, illness, disease, and impending death, especially when we consider the brutal fighting and wars amongst various tribesmen. Yet, their female clan members were able to bleed like warrioress, from their yoni and they did not die. This too was an act of omnipotent Divine powers. It is no wonder that God was seen as feminine, and wommin; her Yoni, her blood, were the first to be worshipped, commemorated in sculptures and cave drawings, exalted in every important aspect of their lives through pottery, weapons, dwelling décor, walls, temples and caves. Clearly Yoni veneration has been in existence since the earliest of time and as wommin we benefit, by greatly acknowledging and reclaiming this practice and embracing the Divine aspect of our gender.

Hail to the Goddess that lives in all Wommin!

When the moon is waxing to Full, approach your altar and place images of the Goddess Baubo and if possible, a Yoni image. This spell can be done on the Equinox or Beltaine, preferably upon Sunrise on a Sunday or Friday. A candle wax image of a woman, in the color Green, is suggested. Charge and anoint candles with "blessing oil,"(see appendix) and also carve, charge and anoint the working candle in the suggested color of white or yellow. Create an offering plate of Barley, sweets and beer to the Goddess. Have fun with this working as Baubo delights in your laughter. Drum, sing, hum and even dance to raise energy while lighting your candles and invoking her essence to your spell.

SPRING VAGINA BLESSINGS
* This Sabbat arrives to bring good news
The sun grows strong
and spells comes true
And by its strength
I cast this spell
let good health reign
to make me well.

This image of me
A candle green,
is lit to awaken
good health in me.

Blessings be upon my warm spot
Where life springs forth
Where ecstasy is fully experienced,
Where pleasure will abound
Where life will be created,
Where precious humanity
Springs forth,
Where my children will be born…

And by the powers of the waxing Sun
With will and word,
this spell is done.

This spell is best done sky clad and during the Full moon or at least when the moon is waxing. On your altar, place images of the Goddess Baubo and if possible, a Yoni image. Decorate your altar with plants and things that are obviously alive, fertile and growing in good health. Have a mirror that you've deemed special for ritual work. You will use this mirror to study your yoni and gaze into your eyes as well. Light pleasing incense of jasmine and sandalwood and let the smoke rise, swirling and twirling around you, your candles and your altar. Acquire a red Yoni shaped candle which you can find at a botanica or occult shop. Charge and anoint this candle with Health oil or "Blessing Oil", (see appendix). Include a white or green working altar candle as well. As an offering, have a plate of honey, barley and spring water, which you will interchangeably pour in and out of your two altar chalices. Drum, sing, hum and even dance to raise energy while lighting your candles and invoking her essence to your spell. Baubo loves to hear your laughter and hearty belly laughs will truly invoke her presence.

HYGEIA-SACRED CAVERNS
*From you I draw my power,
My womanhood, My strength
My ecstasy, my pleasure
My gift to those let in

Moon bound,
Regenerative, giver of life,
Heal by sacred fire,
Heal by candlelight,

The various Rivers that meet in you
Flow through you,
since humanities birth,
I honor and value, My sacred Cavern
Reminder of the Great Mother Earth

POEM TO HONOR MY VAGINA

Dark, moist labyrinth
Place of great mystery
Beholder of great pleasure and pain

Through you my blood flows
Through you I birth life
Through you I regenerate
My waters flow through (you)

Muscle wrapper
that squeezes great ecstasy
A playful spot for a tongue

Folds upon folds
A mystical Cavern
I've yet to discover all your fun

But today, I will honour you
With these words I've penned
Your value and health are mine to tend.

The source of great power
Source of my womanhood
A place for the Goddess to rest

Hold you with high regard
Admire you NOT from a far
And know that I am truly blessed.

BAUBO
Laughter heard among good friends
Joy unearth and hearts begin to mend.
Belly Woman, Exposing herself
Demeters' Medicine who came to help.

Lift up your skirt
Shedding light on the truth,
"Immortal One,
Don't you recognize you?"

Baubo, bring your blessings,
Bring the cackles to singe pain,
Bring the friendships that are long lasting,
Let your visit hearken change.

Positive friendships
Of truth and love.
Of joy and laughter
From the immortal ones.

Bawdy Baubo,
Light hearted and kind,
We welcome your energy
and the gifts from the Divine.

In the darkest of sorrow,
May we recognize light,
In the cackles and silliness,
May we embrace our birth rights...

Hail and welcome, Baubo!

Journaling about Baubo Goddess Gathering

I must say that the last two Grove Gatherings for me have been wonderful, moving me to another level of comfort and confidence that indeed, this is what I am suppose to be doing and I am feeling quite positive about the direction we are going in. This last Gathering for me had to be one of the best, and part of that I will say, has to do with finally having within my group, dedicated, trusting amazing wommin. We have passed the two year mark and some have been with me since the very beginning. The quality and level of intimacy is beginning to reflect itself in our magick and it's an amazing thing to witness and I am blessed to be a part of it.

<u>LION POSE</u>
We came into the sanctuary with our usual effervescent, scattered womanly energy and I believed the remedy to this was synchronizing our breathing. Bringing us more focus on tranquil breath work, loosening up our jaw and face, connecting to our inner child, we did the Lion's pose. Lots of giggles ensued here but it loosened us up, got us focus and it was fun!

<u>SINGING CHANTS</u>
"Magick Woman," "We are a circle," "Do you remember", There were more songs on our list but because of time restraints I limited it to a few. Also, I felt we had successfully raised enough energy with the few songs we sang, so that was good.

<u>CHECK INS WITH NAME, INTRO AND ZODIAC</u>
This was short and gave new wommin a chance to speak, introduce themselves and be heard. Briefly reminded wommin of the speaking stick, our sovereign, Queenly rights, when it is held by a Grove Syster and all went nicely here.

<u>DRUMMING CIRCLE CONE OF POWER</u>
Typically we hear a drumming CD track and ground into this space in this manner, but I felt that the Goddess we were honoring, Baubo (being the Bawdy, earthy Goddess that she is) merits our physical energy and so an actual drumming circle ensued.

You know, drumming circles always scare me because they truly require a synchronicity, at the very least a willingness to open to that potential of blending in with your systers and homogenizing into ONE sound. Sometimes you can feel the resistance from some participants who will fight it, and don't quite get it and won't give up their individuality, they struggle with the beat until the surrounding energy of the drums picks up, starts to swell and overtakes the astral plane and "POW" they soften and surrender to the magick. Gosh, and when it happens.... it can be astounding, like sex... very climactic. I felt we reached that point after a few minutes and just as seamlessly brought it to a close as well. You could hear the buzzing, swirls that remained in the room, long after we were done drumming.

<u>YONI /Vulva image Sharing</u>
We each reached for our image, shared a story about it and passed it around the room for all to see and marvel. I was impressed with the beautiful images shared; red flowers, seashell, candle images, sculpture, artwork. It was a moment of genuine awe to view all these sacred reflections of our womynhood.

Then, sadly, two ladies had to catch a flight and needed to leave prematurely... I immediately became quite aware of the danger and disruption this potentially COULD cause to our group energy -especially when we had created it so wonderfully up till then. So I paused for a moment to take them to the door, went outside to feed dogs treats and water and returned to the group knowing full well I needed to keep our energy level up all the way up.

<u>YONI BAUBO LECTURE</u>
This part swirled and swirled for me and now in retrospect, I realize what I was intuitively doing and its necessity. I was successfully, attempting to keep energy levels elevated for the group. By instinctively choosing that very critical moment (after two members had just left) to speak on Baubo and her importance for us as wommin in my usual fiery, animated, passionate manner. It worked....with our energy. We did not miss a beat and all remained rather seamless and uninterrupted. At some point I also passed the Shee-la-na-gig <u>oracle card</u> and very briefly introduced her aspect, without taking away from our working with Goddess, Baubo.

MANIFESTING HAPPINESS
Right after the lecture, I reminded participants what this gathering and Baubo was all about- joy, merriment, our yoni and the healing power of laughter. With pen and paper and a gentle song playing in the background, I encouraged them to write a list of those things they knew could bring them joy and successfully gets them out of a depressive funk. Afterwards we shared some items from our personal list by reading them aloud.
This led quite smoothly to the next exercise... sharing our Joy with energy work.

SHARING OUR LAUGHTER and PARTNERING ENERGY WORK.
With Enya's celestial soft voice lingering in the background, we looked deeply into our partner's eyes and started this important cathartic work. Woah!!! I should not have been surprised by the level of intensity and the massive break-through. Not a single person with a dry eye, as we were all moved to tears and they were good tears, reflection of powerful break-throughs and, in my humblest opinion, the intimacy we experienced as group via the Goddess. I was also unable to contain my tears.
Energy work, is inherently very intimate in nature and something you only want to "practice" in a safe environment with those you can trust. I explained to them why I waited this long to introduce this type of work and why it was important, for me, that we as a group established now a deeper level of intimacy. Grove can then aspire to be a sort of "Witchlet" laboratory to acquire and practice important skills like these. After such an intense workshop, I felt that my new, unconventional type of ritual, would work out just fine for us as the next step.

THE RITUAL
Before starting our ritual, a sister had a special request to send energy for her young daughter and so we held hands for a few minutes beforehand to do just that....
To cast the circle, Oil was passed from syster to syster, placed upon the sacred third eye as we affirmed each other as daughters of the Goddess. Participants were invited to relax, ground in the moment and simply listen to the elemental invocation via this meditation I read. The vibrations of my golden bell was incorporated between each quarter call and candles were lit too, as elements were invoked.

We moved quite smoothly into our clay creation spell-work and I sensed, that worked beautifully with Soweto enraptured drumming playing in the background. We spoke our spell around the circle with our spell petition as we swirled the smoke of the incense around our red clay Yoni creation.

Then in a moment of enlightenment, I realized that although we were invoking a Goddess of belly laughs, we hadn't done much boisterous laughter, so I briefly explained the power of laughter and invited them to join me in creating a cone of power with laughter. Giggles, more giggles, laughter, belly engaged and more over the top laughter and then cackles, loud boisterous, bawdy, Baubo style witchy cackles..... And Woah... I took flight. For me, I felt myself soar higher and higher, almost as if my laughter and the energy we created, intoxicated me, put me in a state of intense ecstasy, making me feel light as a feather and buzzing. I instinctively reached for chocolate before attempting to devoke our beloved Goddess Baubo as I felt my entire body vibrating incessantly and euphorically flighty. As I devoked, the words just flowed right out of me and I felt her fully in my body at this point. I made sure to ask, if anyone had anything to add before we finished to make sure others were handling the energy well. We Devoked Elements, again letting intuition and spirit choose words...and they flowed right out. Candles snuffed and soon after, we were opening up the circle with song...."the Circle is open, but unbroken......"

Yummy feasting started right after and our day came to an end, boisterously. Hail and Welcome Laughing Queen, Baubo!!!

BAUBO GROVE GODDESS GATHERING CHANTS

ELEMENTAL GODDESS CHANT

Earth, Air Fire Water, I am the Witches daughter
Baubo is me and I am she
Earth Air Fire Water, I am the witches daughter
Pele is me and I am she,
Earth, Air Fire Water, I am the Witches daughter
Hathor is me and I am she,
Earth, Air Fire Water, I am the Witches daughter
Gaia is me and I am she.....

SPIRALING INTO THE CENTER

Spiraling into the Center, The center of the wheel,
Spiraling into the Center, The center of the wheel,
We are the weavers, We are the woven ones,
We are the dreamers, We are the Dream.
We are the weavers, We are the woven ones,
We are the dreamers, We are the Dream. *(repeat) by Starhawk*

WE AVE AND SPIN

Weave and spin,
Weave and Spin,
This is how our work begins,
Mend and Heal,
Mend and Heal,
take the Dream
and make it real *by Starhawk*

I AM MAGICK WOMAN (?) Shelley Graff

I am Magick /Sacred Woman, Giving Birth to myself
I am Magick /Sacred Woman
Giving Birth to myself
from deep inside the wells,
From your loving eyes and wisdom
My truth that I must tell,
I am Magick /Sacred Woman
Giving Birth to myself....

HUMBLE YOURSELF

Humble yourself in the arms of the wild,
You gotta lay down low
Humble yourself in the arms of the wild,
You gotta ask her what she knows and
we will lift each other Up,
Higher and higher,
We will lift each other Up,
Higher and Higher.....By unknown source

ROOTS GO DOWN

My Roots Go Down, Down to the Earth,
my roots go down, Down to the Earth,
my roots go down, down to the Earth
my roots go down

SWEET SURRENDER

We are Opening up in Sweet Surrender
to the Luminous Love light of the one
We are Opening up in Sweet Surrender
to the Luminous Love light of the one
We are Opening.....We are Opening (2X)*By Gladys Gray*

June

June is the sixth month in the Gregorian calendar and according to the Roman poet, Ovid, the Latin word for June was *"iuniores"* meaning *"younger one,"* alluding to the month being one that caters to the young. The Astrological sign for the month of June is Gemini, the twin. Gemini is ruled by the swift and crafty, divine messenger, Greek God of travel, science and communicator - Mercury (May 21-June 20). During this month we can see the influence of these mercurial attributes, revealing themselves quite subtly through summer.

There is one common theory attributed to the Roman poet, Ovid, that believes the month was named after the Roman Goddess Juno, who is wife of Jupiter, the Roman King of the Gods. Juno was the Goddess of marriages and the patron Goddess of all women's well-being. As a result, June became known as the traditional month of matrimonies. In ancient times, it was believed that marriages performed in June, would receive Juno's blessings for a long lasting union. This was also a respected time for all contractual agreements, and legal dealings. June, therefore appears to be a time of much celebrations with many types of unions, hand fasting, and weddings to attend. Even in today's modern age, June, remains to be the ideal, favorite month, among betrothed couples, to pledge their undying love and thus, all celebrations of merriments are common at this time of year.

Honeysuckle, strawberries and roses grew in abundance during this time of the year in some regions, therefore, the full moon in June is often referred to as Strawberry Moon or Rose Moon. It is also important to note that roses were sacred to the Deities of love and marriage and therefore it would correspond easily to one another. The Full moon of this month was also sometimes called Mead Moon, named for the fermenting drink made of honey. Honey was also sacred to the Goddess of love and marriage and it was often used in offerings to Juno, to endear her to bless nuptials and various other sacred rites. Honey has always been associated with solar sacred offerings to various deities from different pantheons, including Saraswati. This month's full moon was also sometimes known as Strong Moon due to the magnanimous, intense strength of the sun's power at this time. The daylight hours now are stretching and reaching to be at their longest, when by mid-month, we approach the sabbat of the Summer Solstice.

Interesting to note, that at this time, in the U.S.A., the patriarchal male energy is celebrated with the arrival of Father's Day on the second Sunday of June. Many of us take this opportunity to honor the men in our lives, whether they are our fathers, grandfather elders, brothers, uncles or even our own sons. We pay tribute to the role of fatherhood and those who have blessed our lives fulfilling this most auspicious role. For some Pagans, the masculine aspect of nature is venerated now, as well as, honoring the consort of the Goddess.

The waxing sun reaches its zenith and now, quite subtly, slowly it begins to shorten the days once more and this is celebrated with the Summer Solstice, also known as Litha and Midsummer. It's important to note that we are also smack in the middle of our calendar year and naturally concern ourselves with making the best of our time. Picnics, barbecues, vacations and beach outings with friend and family are common. June, more often than not, finds us enjoying the outdoors, warm bright, sunny days and numerous summer activities and we are more apt to be engaged (consciously and unconsciously) in the worship of nature and the Goddess.

This month we call upon the Celtic Solar Goddess, Aine, who will help us tap into our divine beautiful strong selves, our creativity and teach us how to manifest balance and honor, from both, fire and water. We will also work with the Hindu Goddess Saraswati, to awaken, in us, our creativity and make vows and agreements with ourselves, to unearth our gifts and lovingly offer these gifts back up to the Universe.

CHAPTER FOURTEEN

"Language is Magick, it has always been magick, since the time sorcerers uttered their first incantations, which steeped our human past in marvelous myths..."
Virginia Hamilton

"I have seen the Sea when it is stormy and wild, when it is quiet and serene, when it is dark and moody and in all its moods... I see myself..." Martin Buxbaum

WELCOME SARASWATI

OUR ALTAR

Altar cloth: Shades of blues and maybe a second white altar cloth underneath.
Image: Statue of this Hindi Sacred Goddess sitting on her Lotus also, Indian tapestries with her image, Canvas art or photo of the Goddess and or photos of the ocean/river and Musical items, music books/sheets, Large important books and of course, images from India, are all appropriate to display on your altar.

Always present on the altar;
A cast iron cauldron, drums, speaking stick, a silver pentacle, athame, elemental representations.....

Air: Bird statuaries, peacock feathers, Incense type sticks, cones, charcoal brisket and fine powdered herbs of Frankincense, Sandalwood and Jasmine.
Fire: Candles, glass enclosed candles or pillars in whites and or blues
Water: small glass vessel or bowl with Water, River Water is best.
Earth: Fresh flowers, dish of soil and or herbs. Surround your altar with growing lush, fertile plants and flowers; especially white and pink in color.

Other items pertinent to this particular gathering
An artistic offerings like music scores, books and art,
A curved genie filled bottle
Symbol of a Lotus flower
Figurine of a Peacock, Doves
Stringed instruments or a vibrating gong or bell
white Roses, lots of greenery
Bowls of consecrated Water
Mala Beads and Gemstone
Sarongs or Veils
Plate offering
Writing pens and paper, books
Light blue gauzy fabric to represent water
Workshop items
Tarot or other oracular items

Offering Honey, apples, rice, Palak Paneer (spinach & cottage cheese) Chickpea curry, Naan (leavened homemade Indian flat bread) Kaali Daal (Black Lentils)
Sacred objects from members:
Notes:

Saraswati

Saraswati Altar

Saraswati Mala Crafting

SARASWATI

Hindu Goddess of Learning, Wisdom, Music and Cosmic Knowledge. Saraswati is considered Supreme Knowledge herself. She is Mahavidya (holder of supreme knowledge), Maha-vani (the transcendent word), Smirtishakti (the power of memory), Maha-vidya (transcendent knowledge) and Arya (the noble one). She is the Goddess of the word, education and all Art forms; music, poetry, dance, writing, crafts, science, literature and because of this, she becomes a patron Goddess to students, teachers, scientist and those in the creative arts. Saraswati is also known as Vagishvari (mistress of speech), Jnanashakti (the power of knowledge), Bharati (eloquence). In Japan she is known as the Goddess Benzaiten. Subhaga (the bountiful one who provides immortality), as she is sometimes addressed, is also the Guardian of Truth. She is the representation of Sattua Guba which is; Goodness, Grace, and Purity. Born from Brahma, Saraswati is both daughter and wife of the creator of the universe and thus becomes known as Mother of the Universe.

In Hinduism, She is part of the Feminine Divine Trinity, also known as Trimurti, along with Durga and Lakshmi and she was one of the very first Deities in Hindu mythology addressed and revered as Mother. Long ago, it was believed that Vishnu had three wives that quarreled constantly. Vishnu, enamored by Lakshmi's brilliance, kept her as his wife and gave Ganga to the God Shiva. The Goddess Saraswati was bestowed upon the God Brahma. Her husband, Brahma, was the God of creation, creator of the Universe and she is considered his counterpart. Saraswati is the feminine aspect of the creator and thus, is revered as the Creatrix -overseeing all forms of creations in the Universe. Known also as Satarupa, Savitri Gayatri and Brahmi/Brahmani (related to Brahma), Saraswati, is a Goddess also called upon for Divine protection and spiritual enlightenment.

In Sanskrit, Sara means *"Essence"* and Swa means *"self."* Saraswati thus literally means; the *"essence of self."* In Hindu mythology, she is at times referred to as "dhaara-pravaah", a Sanskrit word meaning "The One who flows." This is more likely a reference to her role as a River Deity.

Aryan history presents her, first as the Saraswati River, a river that purifies and nourishes. She was known as the sacred river that imparts the flow of creativity, hence Saraswati becomes known as *"the One who flows"*. Though it does not exist today, it was a mighty river that once flowed from the West-End of the Aravalli Hills into the East- End of the Rann of Kutch, flowing into the Arabian Sea. Ancient text, like the Rig-Vedic Hymns, praise Saraswati, depicting her as a great, powerful river, bursting with energy, a fertile roaring invigorator, with strong flowing movement and able to break down mountains. It is in this sacred work that we get a strong descriptive image of this beloved Hindu Goddess.

As a River deity, she was associated with fertility, prosperity and the agricultural growth and productivity of her land and thus like the Greek Grain Goddess, Demeter, she becomes very much a Mother Goddess; protective and nurturing of her people.

There are numerous beautiful detailed images of Saraswati, but immediately, in all of them, we note that she is not heavily adorned, with heavy colors and jewels, the way Lakshmi is. Unquestionably, this reveals a strong symbolism, that knowledge is valued and more prominent than earthly riches for this deity. Saraswati's skin is often depicted as luminous white or light yellow. The predominance of the color white is quite evident, as she is often shown wearing a white sari and more often than not, sitting on a white lotus. The color white represents her purity, truth and her supreme knowledge. Sometimes she is depicted ridding a white swan as her vehicle and this is a symbol of her powers of discrimination. The Swan is a bird with the reputable gift of discrimination, known for its ability to separate milk from water, it represents one of Saraswati's powerful attributes- as she is able to discriminate between the good and the bad, falsehood and truth. In some depictions we sometimes see a beautiful peacock sitting by her side, gazing up at the Goddess, almost as if it is awaiting her gifts. Peacocks are birds associated with arrogance and pride. Traditionally known as a vain, temperamental, yet beautiful creature, the peacock becomes a symbol of the supreme beauty, possible through her powers of creations, but it also warns against vanities and the preoccupation on external beauties and appearances.

Saraswati is often portrayed with four arms and they reveal some of her most important divine gifts. They are a symbol of her omnipotence and the four human personality elements; mind, intellect, alertness and ego. Her two front arms, represent her engagement in the physical realm, and they are usually occupied playing the Vina/Lute. Her obvious connection to music and the arts is well represented in this pose. Her two back arms represent her connection to the spiritual realm, as one arm holds a book, the sacred Vedas/scriptures, also known as Pustaka. On her other arm she holds Akshamala, also known as mala or prayer beads.

Saraswati is sometimes worshipped as a purifier, an attribute directly related to her gift with fire; the fires of creativity and those found in our belly. The Navel Center region, sometimes depicted in the color gold, with 64 lotus petals or 64 sun fire flames, is often associated with the Goddess Saraswati. It was considered the center of transformation, the source of energy of creation and here we meet one of Saraswati's attributes as a blood purifier and healing Fire Goddess. In Vedic scripture, sometimes she is referred to as Shonapunya, which is a sankrit word meaning, "one who purified blood." In this case she is reminiscent of the Celtic Fire Goddess Bridgit, who was also closely associated with the elements of water and its purifying fires, both, for healing and creativity.

Her home was believed to be in the state of Kashmir, among the Himalayas. In many parts of the U.S.A. and in India today, Saraswati is still very much loved and revered. There are numerous festivals all across India that honor this beloved Mother Goddess. In the South, there is the Navaratri, a nine day festival honoring the feminine divine, it celebrates this Great Goddess and there is also the infamous PUJA-a three day Spring Festival in Bengal and North India which also honors Saraswati annually.

Kalpanashakti (the power of forming ideas), Sarada (giver of essence), and Dhaneshvari (the divinity of wealth) are among some of her other numerous titles. This beloved Goddess was also known as Kamadhenu, which means, *"wish fulfilling cow."* Reflected in this particular title is a deity that nurtures and provides sustenance for her people, much like the Egyptian Goddess Hathor, who was considered the Celestial Bovine of her people. Interesting to note that Apples, which have always been a symbol of supreme knowledge, are her favorite food and it is customary to leave offerings of honey, water and fruits upon your devotional altars to this iconic matriarchal Hindu Goddess. All Hail and welcome Divine Mother, Goddess Saraswati!

SARASWATI GROVE GODDESS GATHERING

Purpose: To ignite creativity within us and thus honor the Goddess Saraswati. To fertilize our own individual creativity.

CHECK INS: We gather around a circle, as we tend to do early on in our day, and we state our name, how we have been doing lately and a skill that we consider ourselves to be good at for example, *"I am Lulu and I can make people laugh...."*

CHANT WORKSHOP: "The River is Flowing," "Sister River giver, returning whole," "Born of water," "The Ocean is the beginning of the world." *(see song text sheet...)*

AGREEMENTS: Together, as a group, we read our list of Agreements regarding confidentiality and trust issues around our monthly gathering circle and add any pertinent bylaws necessary.

CHECK INS II: Sharing an image of the Goddess via the Goddess card oracles or her actual sculpture. Sharing our personal thoughts on this River Goddess.... How does she appear to us personally? What attributes seem to jump out at us most prominently. As we gaze into her image, we connect and begin to invoke her presence into our gathering.

LECTURE ON THE GODDESS SARASWATI
her etymology, her various names, myths and worship

GODDESS WORKSHOPS:
WORKSHOP I: The effective use of **Mantras**.
 Beginning with the simplest.... "Om..." for peace
   "Om Saraswatiye Namaha..." and *"Lokah Samastah Sukhino Bhavantu...."*
     (May everyone, everywhere be happy, May the whole world be joyous!)
In this workshop we will be learning numerous other effective mantras to connect with Saraswati. *(See special page in this chapter)*

WORKSHOP II: With gentle music in the background we present and offer an exhibition, **Artist Gallery**....Each attendant was asked to bring a creative work they are presently working on or have recently completed to share with the group in a gallery showing. They will be on display and we will write anonymous thoughts that the various art conjures up, as well as words of encouragement to our fellow Grove artist...

WORKSHOP III: **Mudra**, Hand Gestures and simple Yoga Poses, that align us with the Feminine Divine. Gentle music will be played in the background and we will engage our hands and body in a form of prayer, magick and divine connection.

WORKSHOP IV: **Chakras** and healing **Gemstones**. Talking briefly about our seven chakras and some healing gemstones that help restore and balance us. (see appendix on Chakras and Gemstones). There will be numerous stones on the altar to explore their attributes and experiment with their energy.

WORKSHOP V: **Mandala Creation.** Together we will learn of the cathartic use of mandalas and begin to outline our very own insightful creation, on a small canvas board or fabric. We might also experiment creating one on the ground, incorporating the use of dry beans, rice, pasta and other items.

WORKSHOP VI: **Beads and Mala**. Crafting and learning other common practices for beads, rosaries and malas. We gather our craft supplies to create a Mala bracelet from our crafting beads or a prayer necklace. As we are working we will chant to imbue our bracelet with the magick from this day.

WORKSHOP VII: What does Creativity means to you personally? Offerings and Sharing Creativity, **A Meditation**: that will lead right into communally creating an Art piece....

REFLECTIONS ON SARASWATI

Here is an ancient Hindu Goddess who is alive, breathing, still very much revered today; both in India and in the United States. And she is a tangible, very relevant deity to all wommin across the globe. She touches upon a deep, connective part in every womyn's journey, that sustains itself from ages to ages- it is our spirituality, knowledge, creativity and our role as mother to our creations. Saraswati teaches us to honor our skills, education, the wisdom we acquire and our inherent creative gifts.

According to Hindu cosmology in the begining was chaos, void, formlessness and disorder and the creator God Brahman searched for a solution to the perceived problem. It was then that Knowledge presented itself to him as Saraswati herself. She emerged with her vina/lute and the sacred scriptures, ridding her white swan. She was born from Brahma's mouth, again suggesting her jurisdiction over the realm of speech and sound. And it was believed that Mantras were thus born by her very presence and because of her introduction to mantras, all in the Universe began to take shape, with her gift of sound, knowledge, spirit and purity.

She calls you to contemplate on what feeds your spirit and asks you to value ALL your artistic longings, for they are a reflection of her essence and much needed in the world today. She is also a wonderful Goddess to call upon for blessings on your children, if you are a mother in need of guidance. As a nurturing mother deity and a Goddess of knowledge, wisdom, education and the arts, she is ideal to invoke when we wish for our own children to have artistic and or academic success.

She is not only the advocate of education and wisdom for children but also begs you not to run away from your own voice, intelligence, and creative gifts, rather, embrace them and let them be an offerings to the Divine.

Today, just as in ancient times, Saraswati is the one to call upon when we need to unearth the pure beauty and power of our own voice and tap into our wisdom and spirituality. Hindi cosmology reveals she was born from the essence of sound and she becomes an important Goddess to awaken us to the power of our intelligence, wisdom and our voices, especially in its creative expressions.

SARASWATI GROVE GODDESS GATHERING RITUAL

PURPOSE: To ignite creativity within us and thus honor the Goddess **Saraswati.** To fertilize our own individualize spirit of creativity.

Purification/anointing by Consecrated Herbed water.

Casting Circle with consecrated water sprinkled around the circle and prose. Also a very creative way of casting this circle would be with a musical instrument like a Flute/piccolo or the neck of a guitar in honor of her divine connection to music.

Quarters called

* Guardians of the Watchtowers of the **East**, Ye Powers of **Air,**
Place of awakenings, artistic conceptions, Winds that bring initial ideas and dreams
We call on you to bring us your gifts, those found in the stones of Turquoise, Sodalite and Lapis lazuli.
Guard and Hold our sacred space, Hail and welcome Air!
(*attendants repeat*) Hail and Welcome!!!

*Hail Guardians of the Watchtowers of the **South**, Ye Powers of **Fire,**
Place of tenacity and the drive to create, flames of desires to express your soul's vision
We call on you to lend us your gifts, those found in the stones of red jasper, fire agate, citrine and carnelians.
Guard and Hold our sacred circle, Hail and Welcome Fire!
(*attendants repeat*) Hail and Welcome!!!

*Hail Guardians of the Watchtowers of the **West**, Ye powers of **Water,**
Place of Saraswati's great river of creativity, fertility and nourisher, place of Harmony and the flow of artistic currents.
We call on you to bring us your gifts, those found in the rose quartz, the amazonite and aventurines.
Guard and Hold our sacred space, Hail and welcome Water!
(*attendants repeat*) Hail and Welcome!!!

*Hail Guardians of the Watchtowers of the **North**, Ye powers of **Earth,**
Place of manifestations, the art found in all of nature -reflecting the pulsating artistry of the Earth. We call on you to bring us your gifts, those found in the green malachite, the obsidian and grounding hematites.
Guard and Hold our sacred circle, Hail and welcome Earth!
(*attendants repeat*) Hail and Welcome.

Invocation: First with musical instruments like bells, tambourine, rattles, Lute.
Invoke with her mantra repeated several times....
Chanting: *Om eim Saraswatiye Namaha, Om...*

Saraswati Aspected appears... Speaks of her gifts and instructs...
I was once known as the mighty Saraswati river,
Its current so strong it could divide mountain's
My currents today move and conquer the soul to create.
Create works of Art, Paintings, Sculptures, Stories,
Songs, Speeches, Dances,
Poetry, Prayers, Music and more.

I am the inspirer,
the force behind that hunger to express.
expressing pieces of you,
expressing pieces of me,
I am the source of your late night crafting
and your endless pursuit of knowledge to create
and heal.

You can't deny me...and my Spirit of creativity.
Tap into its power...
Create!!! Express!!!
As the river's water swells and grows
needing an outlet to outpour...
Where will you pour out my Divine gifts?
Where will you release or express yourself?
I call to you - as you call to me.
Follow your bliss.
Honor me,
worship me by creating works of Art.
How will you express outwardly the manifestation of my presence
I am Saraswati and I breathe spirit and knowledge into your life?

"Creativity and Music are my domain. Listen to my (lute) music and let it now bring you inspiration, Use it to create an offering to me as I cherish all acts of creativity."
With music gently playing in the background, participants will have a chance to spell craft into their own personal **mandalas**. Small canvas boards will be made available for all to engage in. During the mandala creation, you are encouraged to chant a Mantra continuously over it.

Music begins....
Then With inspirational music heard in the background the attendants will take their canvas or sketch pad and draw, paint, sketch, creating art they personally choose to do, as they are moved by the Goddess music. The magick is your art creation at this moment for it will exemplify what you hope to magickally manifest.

Afterwards, Saraswati will deliver her personal message to you through this trance art work. When the Music ends, surrender the creation, Saraswati will invite the attendants to come up one at a time and make an offering. One by One, the attendants come to the center and present their creations upon the altar with these words:
"I offer you my creation and I dedicate myself to
creating:_____"

Saraswati takes the art offering, places it for All to see and then, giving a gift, she says:
" I Bless your dedication with these Beads (or another token gift) **let it serve as a reminder of our special day together.**

Her river, represented by a blue turquoise gauze fabric, will be placed by each attendants feet to cross over and return back to their place in the circle. Attendants crosses over, then returns to the circle...
Chants: *"Syster, River Giver, returning Whole,"*
A plate of Honey **offering** is passed around the circle; a time to ground but also to share any last thoughts before devoking... **Chants:** *"The River is flowing..."*

Thanking and Devoking Goddess...
Beloved River Goddess of the Sacred word,
We thank you for awakening
your gifts of creativity in each of us.
Your presence flowed within this space
and like the scent of Jasmine,
may it forever linger in our heart and soul.
With gratitude for your presence here today,
we bid thee adieu, most Holy one.
Hail and Farewell, Saraswati!

Devoking Quarters with Elemental Chant: *"The earth, the air, the fire, the water, return.."*
Open Circle: Merry meet Chant. ...

Cakes & Ales/Potluck meal shared

SARASWATI GUIDED MEDITATION

Find a comfortable spot- you can sit or lay down- Close your eyes and know that you will be safe. We are about to embark on a special journey. In this journey we will travel to India BUT we will also travel to other distant lands - wherever the river takes us... Join me! Come... We begin with deep restful sleep.... Close your eyes, rest and sleep, the best journeys begin with this sacred act...

With your mind's eyes, you awake from a dream, though you are not sure because there before you is a beautiful Hindi Woman. She appears ridding on a white elegant Swan, wearing a long white Sari covered from head to toe. She emanates celestial light and her Golden beauty is indescribable. By her feet is a long stringed musical instrument and a greenish blue, small peacock. In her hands she holds what looks like a rosary beaded necklace -a Mala, and in her other hand she holds a golden book. You study her closely trying to retain every detail of her appearance. Imagine your surprise when she extends two additional arms before you and draws you closer for an embrace. You melt into her bosoms, the way a child does unto his mother's breast, and you take in a deep breath. Can you smell the sweet honey scent coming out of her pores? **Who are you?** ...You naively ask but Before you can continue she places her lips upon yours.... *(pause)*
Knowledge has been passed on to you with this act and now you KNOW who she is.
"Greet her, tell her of your endeavors and your personal creative goals" *(pause)*

She takes you by the hand and you follow. Together you walk down a winding road, down a path where you begin to see a trail of water. You walk and notice your feet begin to feel the trickle of a stream. You keep walking with her until you reach the open landscape that holds the grand River. Her fruitful, fertile river that magically connects to all other bodies of water from around the world.
Can you see her glistening River? *(pause)*
You stand together, side by side, and study the water. Silently you watch the ebb and flow of this River. Sometimes strong waves of currents... and sometimes so calm and tranquil. She enjoys watching you, as you admire the hypnotic movement of this water. *(pause)*
"Breathe" She says
**"Breathe, for in every breath is a spark of
my Divine light
Breathe, your breath is the soul of creation
Breathe, for in your breath you honor me"**

She holds up a bottle and says;
"With your breath, place All of your creative visions in this bottle and together we will manifest a precious "Message in a Bottle" that in the end, will be your most valuable gift to me." *(pause)*
You follow her directions and the bottle (sealed with your breath) is tossed into the river. The Goddess enters the water too, as she endeavors to guide it and guarantees its safety. She follows after it until you can't see her, nor your bottle, anymore. Still you can't take your eyes away from the waters and you fall into a deeper trance.... deeply absorbed in the ebb and flow of her river. *(pause)*

Quite suddenly you detect the sound of music in the air. There is drumming and chanting. You follow the rhythmic sounds and find a group of children, one of them holding an open bottle that looks a lot like the one Saraswati gave you earlier. They have all sorts of musical instruments and together they are making music, jamming happily and dancing. They don't have much clothing and they appear skinny and malnourished but they are unquestionably happy- consumed in their music making. One of the children sees you, he bows down to you, places his breath in the bottle and tosses it back into the river. They all disappear just as quickly as they came and now there is only silence as you watch the bottle travel farther away on the water.

You decide to walk along the edge of the river and try to make sense of all of this. Was that whole scene real or just a mirage? *(pause)*

As you walk you notice someone sitting alone sobbing near the river. Instantly you want to run to this Raven haired, older woman, to comfort her and to try to help. As you speed up your step, her sobbing stops and to your surprise, you notice the message in the bottle has now reached her. She wipes the tears from her eyes and pulls a large book out of her purse. Tossing her reddish hair, she begins to write. She writes and writes and writes and is so absorbed in her writing she doesn't even notice you, as you observe her and proceed to walk right passed her. *(pause)*

"**She's Okay**" you say to yourself and just as you do, you notice she picks up the message in a bottle, bows down to you, breathes into it and tosses the sealed bottle back into the water. **Can you see the bottle floating in the river again?** *(pause)*
Soon you won't, as it disappears along with the aspiring writer.

You continue now to walk along the edge of the river. And after a few steps you notice there appears to be an easel and a blank Art canvas resting on it. No one is around for miles and it is quiet. *(pause)* All of a sudden you hear the splish splash of a swimmer enjoying herself in the river. She comes out of the water, with her long dark curly hair soaking wet, holding in her hands the message in a bottle. She dries off her wet olive skin and after opening the bottle, she runs excitedly to her paint palette and her brushes. You stand aside unnoticed, behind a rock where you think she can't see you and you watch. Joyfully she approaches her easel and you observe how she begins mixing the colors. Her wrist, twirling, doing a hypnotic dance with her paint brushes to acquire just the right brush strokes. You are as enchanted with her, as she is with her Artistic creation and move in for a closer look. *(pause)*

Some time passes, or so it seems. When she appears to be satisfied with her art, she turns in your direction, bows down to you and whispers *"namaste."* Then she too breathes into the bottle and runs back down into the river where she tosses it. Slowly her image fades from your sight and so does the bottle.

The sun is setting now and as you continue to walk along the edge of the river.
It gets darker as you reflect on the last few scenes, wondering if it was all just a dream. The Full moon is providing all the light that you'll need now. You smell a sweet scent of incense; patchouli, jasmine, sandalwood ......then you hear the resonating strong voices chanting, **OooooM.** In the dark of night it is hard to see clearly but you feel compelled to search for this "**Om**". As you begin to walk, the first thing you see is a makeshift altar, with all sorts of items. And you see it again, the Message in a Bottle, **open**, among the sacred objects on the altar. You are stunned but pleased at its long journey. *(pause)*

A group of Wommin, begin to surround you and the altar. They continue chanting **OM**, while creating a circle with their bodies, surrounding you. **OooooM... OoooooM...**
A ritual is just beginning and you are now part of it, among the circle and you are there...listen to the strong, **Ooooom....**
Can you smell the scent of sandalwood, jasmine and patchouli ?
Listen...OM
Listen to the **OM... OM...SARASWATIYE NAMAHA (repeat)**
Can You hear its resonance.? **Om,** Ringing, Vibrating in your head, in your body, in your heart ...
Om Saraswatiye namaha *(repeat continually)*
You hear her name...She's being called,
In this ritual she's being invoked, **You are There...**
Where she is being honored and revered with the celestial bell chimes and the **"OM"**
- the continuance "OM"
You are There...
OM...
And now (**OM**)...**You are Here...**
Where she is being honored and revered with the celestial bell chimes and the "**OM**"
-the continuance "OM"
you are Here... "O M"
and now –"Om"- You are Here....

*The breath of creativity has been in you from your first encounter with her....
It serves to connect you to the Divine source with encouragement, healing, acknowledgement, refinement of skills, passion and inspiration. The greatest gift you can give to her is in sharing this breath of creativity. See how Saraswati's River connects us all, to one another. See how the message in the bottle reached many lands, see how it **Now Returns** to you as we call on Saraswati and return... return... return... return....

Return...Om Saraswatiye Namaha
OM Saraswatiye Namaha
Om Saraswatiye Namaha..... *(repeat until they come out of meditation)*
Return, return..... *(repeat until a whisper)*

PROJECT: ******What gifts do you have for Saraswati?**

******What talents will you share and offer to others In her honor?**
Attendants will write their answers with colorful markers on A large decorated art canvas thus their answer will become part of an artwork in itself for the Goddess..

Another project idea is to hand out small bottles and just like in the meditation, have them breathe into the bottles their creative goals and cork this bottle. If participants choose to, they can decorate this bottle with glass paint, markers and decoupage clippings.

All Hail to Saraswati!!!!

MANTRAS AND CHANTS FOR GODDESS SARASWATI

1. Lokah Samastah Sukhino Bhavantu....
Meaning: May everyone, everywhere be happy, May the whole world be joyous!

2. OM Eim saraswaaaatyei Swaha --------In the Rig-Veda

3. Ambitambe, Naditambe, Devitambe Saraswati...
Meaning: The best of Mothers, best of Rivers, best of Goddesses, Oh Saraswati.

4. Saraswati saaram vaati iti
Meaning: she who flows towards the absolute is Saraswati *according* to the Veda's Pada Paathat (etymology)

5. A prayer to Goddess Saraswati (*Saraswati Vandana Mantra*)
Yaa Kundendu tushaara haaradhavalaa
Yaa shubhravastraavritha
Yaa veenavara dandamanditakara,
Yaa shwetha padmaasana
Yaa brahmaachyutha shankara prabhutibhir Devaisadaa Vanditha
Saa Maam Paatu Saraswatee Bhagavatee Nihshesha jaadyaapahaa

Meaning: "May Goddess Saraswati, Who is fair like the jasmine -colored moon and whose pure white garland is like frosty dew drops; who is adorned in radiant White attire, on whose beautiful arm rest the veena and whose throne is a white Lotus, Who is surrounded and respected by the Gods, protect me. May you fully remove; lethargy sluggishness and ignorance..."

6. GAYATRI MANTRA
OM Bhur-Bhurvah- Svah
Tat savitur varenyam
Bhargo devasva dhimahi
Dhiyo yo nah pracodayat

Meaning: "We meditate on the glory of the Creator; Who has created the Universe; Who is worthy of Worship, Who is the embodiment of Knowledge and Light; Who is the remover of all Sin and Ignorance; May She Enlighten our Intellect."

Resources: Sarsawati; the Goddess of learning
By Stephen-Knapp.com and Riversaraswati,gsbkerala.com Wikipedia.org..

Some additional Helpful Mantras
Source: Mirabaihelperyoutube channel and http://Sanskrit mantra.com, LilaSakuraYoutube Channel, Book-"Healing Mantras, using Sound Affirmations for Personal Power, Creativity, and Healing," by Thomas Ashley-Farrand, published in 1999 by Ballantine Wellspring Book, New York

1.	Om Vaj ra Sattwa Hung	To Remove negativity
2.	Om Chandra Meeli, Soorya Meeli, Kuru Kuru Swaha...	Evil Eye Remover
3.	Om Shar avana Bhavaya Namaha	Attracting positivity and all good things
4.	Om Thiru Neela Kantam	For Karmic Resolution
5.	Om Hraum Mitraya Namaha	To attract true Friendship
6.	Om BhasKaraya Namaha	Brilliance intelligence awakener
7.	Om Gum Ganapatayei Namaha	Obstacle Remover calling Ganesh
8.	Om Shrim Maha Lakshmiyei Swaha	To invoke Feminine Divine abundance
9.	Om Shring Hring Kleeng MahaLakshmi Namaha	To invoke Lakshmi prosperity Blessings
10.	Om Shreem Kalikaye Namaha	Invoking She who is dark and powerful-Kali
11.	Om dum Durgayei Namaha	Calling on the Feminine Divine essence -Durga
12.	Om Kala Vide Namaha	Om and salutation to the knower of the right time
13.	Om Eim Saraswatiyei Namaha	Invoking Saraswati Blessings

MANDALAS

The *"essence of having," "containing," "circle-circumference," "completion,"* these are all various translations of the Sanskrit word, mandala. A mandala, in my opinion, is a sort of, revealing artistic chart or map of our inner journey. Crafted in a free flowing trance like state, it can unearth where our spiritual, emotional and present state of mind is and possibly where it yearns to go.

Through-out the ages mandalas, can be found utilized in numerous cultures from Hinduism, Buddhism, to Christianity. You can find them on the floors of entrances to significant places of worship, stained glass windows of churches, and the outer décor of secular monumental architecture. Of course, we see them in numerous illustrations found in both secular and sacred books of the past. If you look carefully, you will find them reflected amidst nature herself, think of seashells, flowers, tree groves, caves, rocks and crystals.

Mandalas have traditionally been utilize to establish sacred space, as is evident in the way we sometimes see them on the floor entrances of significant historical monuments, but they are also used as a form of concentrated focus and an effective form of meditation. In some cultures like the Navajo Indians and Tibetans, they are created from sand paintings and released in sacred rituals that reinforce the teachings of impermanence.

A mandala and a yantra are similar, with the latter being more geometrical in design. The two terms are sometimes used interchangeably, however, yantras are often described as being a living, tangible representation of the Goddess/Gods and as a tool to invoke the respective deity. Mandalas are often crafted in a circular fashion, with a repetitive motif and powerful symbols that communicate with the subconscious mind, taking it on a journey that eventually leads one to the awe transformative, holistic center. The colors and patterns combine to evoke a different plane of reality that transcends time and space and thus they are perfect to incorporate in our rituals to the Divine.

The world renown psychoanalyst, psychiatrist, Carl Jung described Mandalas as the ideal world represented and depicted within this circular imagery. He believed Mandalas functioned to help a person with integration of the scattered parts of oneself. It was his belief that humans became disintegrated when their internal realities did not match those exterior ones created by outside influences, such as families, friends, environment. He often encouraged his clients to tap into their unconsciousness by creating mandalas, as this was a successful method to unearth hidden parts of oneself. Dreams, active imagining and creation of mandalas were just some of the various methods he advocated to connect with the forgotten pieces of ourselves, lodged deep in our subconscious mind. Jung believed Mandalas were Universal Archetypes that revealed our personal inner journey and self-development. (*Pg 14 "Mandalas and Meditations" by Cassandra Lorius*)

Crafted alone, mandalas can bring about an intimate moment of deep self-reflection, but mandalas can also be a powerful tool of magick when done in rituals and created in sacred space among our systers. Everyone present lends their energy to its manifestation and that can be quite an amazing, magickal experience. Engaging our senses in the process can add many powerful layers to our mandalas. Humming, together creating a cone of power, while we work out our design, can be an effective way to incorporate sound- as is playing soft music in the background to engage our auditory senses. Scented oils and the smoke of incense can tap into our sense of smell and encouraging body movement as we paint our mandalas, engages our kinesthetic senses.

Of course, our sense of sight is engaged with surrounding altar décor and the various colors and patterns utilize in the creation of our unique mandala. In gatherings, encourage one another to trust your instincts and freely create what the soul needs expressed, on this piece of cloth, paper or canvas. Afterwards, we can share them with each other around the room and even talk about what they successfully reveal and conjure up.

MUDRAS

Mudra is a Sanskrit word, meaning "seal". Mudra are sacred hand, fingers and body gestures that are used to effect the healthy flow of prana- breath/life force. Often used in conjunction with yogic breathing exercises, meditation and chakra works to harmonize prana energy. There are numerous poses documented in various sources, but for our workshop we will limit it to the few mentioned below.

THE ELEMENTS REPRESENTED BY OUR FIVE FINGERS

Thumb	Ruled by Fire
Index finger	Ruled by Air
Middle finger	Ruled by Spirit
Ring finger	Ruled by Earth
Little finger	Ruled by Water

Gyan Mudra is achieved by joining the tip of your index finger and your thumb, while holding up the other three fingers joined. This is believed to impart happiness, sharpens memory and intellectual development.

Apaan Mudra is created by joining the tip of your middle and ring finger to the tip of your thumb, while holding the other remaining fingers straight. This is believed to reduce constipation and helps your body release waste.

Prana Mudra is done by pressing the tip of your thumb with the tip of your pinky/little finger and your ring finger, while simultaneously holding the remaining fingers straight. This Mudra helps distribute life force energy throughout your body and is believed to help with your vision.

Prithvi Mudra is achieved by joining the tip of your thumb with the tip of your ring finger, while holding the remaining finger straight. This Mudra is believed to impart happiness and a stronger body.

Ling Mudra involves interlocking the fingers of both hands together and keeping the left thumb up while the right thumb encircles, around the left thumb. It is believed to produce heat in your body and help cure coughs and cold ailments.

<u>**Suggested Book for further studies on Mudra**</u>
Mudras; Yoga in Your Hands by Gertrud Hirschi.
Healing Mudras: Yoga for your Hands by Sabrina Mesko.
Power Mudras: Yoga hand Postures for Women by Sabrina Mesko.
The Healing Power of Mudras by Rajendra Menen.
Yoga of Light-Meditations, Mudras and Expressions of the Divine Feminine, DVD, Featuring Sharron Rose

THOUGHTS ON CREATIVITY AND SARASWATI

Creativity? There has never been a time I wasn't engulfed by it. Creativity has always been the breath in my soul, my literal heart beat and an integral part of my own genetic make-up. Whether it was singing and ballet dancing as a small child right into adulthood, or as a teenage *"fashionista,"* sewing up one of a kind outfits to intrigue my peers, while heavily invested in my aspiring acting and musical career - expressing myself creatively has always been a large part of who I am. My life has known no other way of existence.

As a young womyn, I continued to immerse myself in various forms of creative expressions, which led to my degrees, music conservatory education and ultimately the pursuit of an Opera singing career. In this genre, I was consistently called upon to embrace my creativity, but I didn't limited it to just music. I was fascinated by all kinds of expressive arts and they've always had quite an obsessive hold on my soul. Today I continue to fulfill this need to create, by engaging in paintings, creative writing, interior decorating homes and Goddess altars. I also do quite a bit of sewing and have crocheted my own personal collection of groovy fashion knit wear. Then there is also cake decorating for my young boys, jewelry making, sculpting with clay, crafting various genres and creating rituals for the Feminine Divine.

I have an Artist soul and undoubtedly it requires me to create daily, less I, literally, sense myself wither away. There have been few, rare moments, when I've experienced the wilting demise of my soul, due to an absence of a creative outlet. It is not a pretty episode. It is excruciatingly painful for me to endure and almost always puts me in danger of severe depression. In this case, creativity has functioned as my savior, for when I have been at my lowest, it has become my therapy, my antibiotic and my magick cure. Whether it's mine own creative works or the pleasure of experiencing some one else's creativity, via an art gallery, concert, book creation...I am healed by the transformative powers of creativity, rendered through the human heart, spirit, mind and hands.

It might sound strange for some, but for me, I experience Creativity as a strong ocean current wave, that almost always engulfs me, but in a positive way. When it surges, it takes over and demands all of me and will literally consume me and my every waking moment- taking me to a place where there are no clocks, no judgments, no pause, no human needs (like meals or bathroom breaks). It takes me to a bright, transcendent realm that is both a compulsion and orgasmic because it feels like nothing else in this world matters as much and it literally feeds my soul. An intoxicated, heated intimate bond between artist and art subject becomes blurred into this seductive trance state of mind. When it is just me and the particular project I'm working on, I experience attributes of the subconscious, watery womb Goddesses like Aphrodite, Ix Chel and yes, Saraswati. Through my creativity I collect healing. Through my creativity I touch upon the Divine.

In the midst of really intense moments of creativity, I trance easily, journeying as if I disconnect temporarily from my body, it sometimes does not even feel like me, but someone or something else, surging like an energy volt, working through me. I have recently learned this is what they refer to as *"the Zone"*. Well, I experience *"the Zone"* a lot in creativity and almost always crave it daily, like an unusual obsession to spiritual ecstasy. It is then that I comprehend the essence of Saraswati and Aphrodite and the enchanting, hypnotic powers of these all-consuming creative water Deities.

My creativity might never bring me the fame and fortune I naively thought it would in my youth, but it serves a greater purpose now-it is my therapy, it is the breath in my soul. I create now out of pure love and this deep rooted desire to express what is lurking in the pools of my watery subconsciousness. I create to express & experience the Feminine Divine. I invite you too delve into creativity to taste what she has to offer you.

As Saraswati is the Goddess of Knowledge and Education, she was often invoked, in particular, for children's protection and academic blessings. This invocation was created especially for this purpose. Prepare a bright yellow candle, or light blue, with children's astrological symbols. Charge the wax with Student oil, concentration oil or blessing oil (see appendix). On your altar have photos of the children and relevant, important academic books. Place upon your altar a statue or photo image of Saraswati and offer the Goddess a bowl of honey and a chalice of Spring Water. Decorate this sacred space with colorful flowers, like roses, lotus, daisies and tulips. Best to perform this spell when the moon is waxing to Full. On a Sunday, at the first hour of sunrise call upon the Goddess, invoking Saraswati's benevolent powers, to you and your children.

SARASWATI

For my children and myself
Saraswati, come to our help,

Goddess of learning
Open our minds,
Acquiring knowledge
Connecting with the Divine

Books read quickly
Memorized with ease,
Understanding fully
all the words we read.

Goddess of Creativity
Awaken us to our gifts
Fertile River Deity
Inaugurate our soul's shift,

Flow into our lives,
Most ancient Holy Mother
That together we may daily
Learn to Bless one another.

Saraswati, Mahadevi
On your lotus may we dwell
Let thy Rivers of enlightenment
Within our soul,
ebb and swell

Hindi Mother, receive our Gratitude
Herein this work,
Saraswati, we invoke you!
Hail and welcome!

SARASWATI
*Intellect and wisdom
Educational pursuit
Goddess Saraswati
I invoke your attributes

Bring your Blessings
To my children
that they may succeed
Do well in their schools
Be recognize and be seen.

Let them grow smarter and wiser
With each passing day
Protect them, bless them
Enlighten their way

Acquiring and applying
the knowledge they receive
Good health and intellect
to all your children.
Blessed Be.)o(

On a Sunday, Wednesday or Friday and best if it is the first hour of sunrise -as we are utilizing Sun's energy, perform this spell with confidence. The moon's position should always be considered and in this case it would be best if it was a waxing Moon. A White or Yellow pillar candle, carved with your initials and a sign of the sun carved in its wax. Asperge it with Frankincense and Myrrh as your incense and use Sun or blessing, anointing oil(see appendix). Acquire a moonstone, an opal or a quartz crystal to accompany the working candle, later on you will want to place these stones under your pillow to induce special dreams. Include your tarot deck near your candles and recite this invocation for three consecutive days as your candle burns. By the third night endeavor to consult your cards and pay close attention to the messages you receive from them and from the dreams you have in the coming weeks.

ILLUMINATION
*Illuminating hour of the sun
Light the way for me
Open up my mind to find
my life's destiny

Help me to regain
Passion and insight
Goddess I invoke you thru
this sacred Rite

In Tarot and in Dreams
help me to hear
Your words of wisdom
warming my receptive ears

As I say goodbye
My rhyme I know you've heard
This spell is cast
By my will and word.
So mote it be…

SARASWATI GROVE GODDESS GATHERING CHANTS

The River is Flowing,
The river is flowing, flowing and growing,
The river She is flowing, Down to the Sea.
Mother carry me; your child I will always be.
Mother carry me down to the Sea.
The Moon she is changing, waxing and waning,
The Moon She is changing, high, above me,
Sister, challenge me, your child I'll forever be,
Sister, wait for me, till I am free. *By Diana Hildebrand-Hull*

Syster, River, Giver...Returning Whole
From Victorian Christian's creation, Elijah The band of Light
Syster, River, Giver...Returning Whole,
Syster, River, Giver...Returning Whole,
    Open up, To receive
    We are what we Believe. *(REPEAT)*
    Syster, River, Giver...Returning Whole,
    Syster, River, Giver...Returning Whole
Growing Roots like the Trees,
We are planting seeds. *(REPEAT)*
Syster, River, Giver...Returning Whole,
Syster, River, Giver...Returning Whole,
    Stored in Deep, Stories Sleep,
    Within Us, These Tales we Keep. *(REPEAT)*
    Syster, River, Giver...Returning Whole,
    Syster, River, Giver...Returning Whole

Closing Chant
By the Earth that is her Body
By the Air that is her Breath
By the Fire that is her bright Spirit
By the Living waters of her womb
May the Peace of the Goddess
Be forever in our Hearts
The circle is open but unbroken
Merry Meet and merry Part
The circle is open but unbroken
Merry Meet and merry Part *(continue from the beginning)*
by Elaine Silver

Let it in, Let it flow
Let it in, Let it flow
Round and Round we Go
Weaving the Web of Women,
Let it in, Let it flow
Round and Round we Go
Weaving the web of life... *by Marie Summerwood*

***The Ocean is the beginning of the Earth
The Ocean is the beginning of the Earth (2x)
All Life comes from the Sea
All Life comes from the Sea....
    The Sun is a reflection of her Light (2x)
    All thing grow with her love.
    All things grow with her love...
The mirror is a reflection of our heart (2X)
    See the Goddess rest in us.
    See the Goddess rest in us....*By Delaney Johnson, Starhawk and Reclaiming*

When we are Gone, they will remain
When we are Gone, they will remain
Wind and Rock.....Fire and Rain
They will remain, when we return
The winds will blow and the fire will burn. *By Starhawk*

CHAPTER FIFTEEN

"Life is not about waiting for the storms to pass, it's about learning how to dance in the rain...." anonymous

"In order to stay healthy, give your heart a reason to keep beating..." Lisa Oz

WELCOME AINE

OUR ALTAR

Altar cloth : Dress your altar with a purple velvet altar cloth, add a Silver or Gold cloth to overlay it. Although your altar colors will always vary if you're commemorating the season.

Image: Statue of the Celtic beautiful red haired Goddess
Canvas art or photo of the Goddess, Images of the Sun, a flag of Ireland is also appropriate, photos or images of Faeries and the landscape of the Forest. Images of the Sun since this is a celebration of Midsummer.

Always present on the altar;
A cast iron cauldron, speaking stick, drums, bell chimes, notes, a silver pentacle, athame, elemental representations.....

Air: Smudge wands, Incense type sticks, cones, charcoal brisket and fine powdered herbs in Cinnamon, frankincense, myrrh and orange or lemon peels.
Fire: Carved Yellow Pillar candles or glass enclosed candles in yellow or red. A sun or star shaped candle is also wonderful to use.
Water: Chalice or small glass bowl with Spring or rain water
Earth: display lots of freshly cut, colorful flowers like roses, carnations, sunflowers. A small dish of soil and or meadowsweet herbs is also suggested.

Other items pertinent to this particular gathering
Rocks and Gemstones like Citrine, Peridot, Mooonstone and Yellow Jasper
Witches Cloak or Scarf
Images of Red Mare, rabbits and Swans
Round mirror
Workshop items like paper mache' or other clay product
Raw wax and candle making mold kits
Mini personal altar shrine Box
Bag of Rune for oracular usage
Four Elemental Dragon figurines
Tarot- "The Sun"
Writing paper and pen
Bell chimes

Offering Honey, Bread and Milk, Barley beer and other fruits, vegetables and meats.
Sacred objects from members:
Notes:

Aine

Aine Altars

AINE-pronounced [AW-NE]

The Lady of the Lake, Aine is also known as Aine Marina, Aine Cliach, Cnoc Aine, Aine of Knockaine. She is a much beloved Celtic Goddess whose name appears throughout several regions in Ireland where she is most revered to this day. The Knock Aine of Ireland, Dun Aine and Aines Hills in the province of Munster are most reflective of the worship of this Goddess. Three miles South West of Lough Gur is the region of Cnoc Aine or KnockAiny and this is the reputed Hill of Aine. She is also most celebrated and revered in Dunany point, which is lovingly referred to as Dun Aine, in honor of the Goddess.

The etymology of her name reveals a lot about the character of this Goddess. Her name means; *delight, pleasure, agility and melody.* In Gaelic, Aine means *"radiance"* and this would be a fitting name for a Goddess believed to be both a Solar and a Lunar deity. The Celtic Goddess, Aine was also often known as the Irish Red Mare that no one could outrun, because this was her chosen form to shape shift. Like most ancient, Celtic Goddesses, there are a number of various attributes linked to her myths.

At some point she was solely revered as a Sun Goddess and held to high esteems during the holy day of Midsummer, Litha (or Summer Solstice, as is better known to some). Burnt offerings of straw and flowers were made to this Solar Goddess in order to insure favorable blessings on love, crops and homes. There are some documented prose and rituals that support this belief and reveal her significant worship at this time of the year, with torch-lit processions through-out the fields to insure a prosperous, fertile crop. Lughnasadh (August 1st) is also a holy day traditionally associated with this Solar Goddess and most notably sacred to her are the three days (Friday, Saturday, Sunday) following Lughnasadh.

Yet Aine is also very much known as a legendary enchantress, a Moon Goddess and a Goddess of Love- She was known to have numerous divine, royal and human lovers, with a preference for the latter. She was a goddess called upon for fertility magick (whether it was fertility for a woman or the Celtic land itself) and thus, she became a patron Goddess for wommin, agricultural magick and the proliferation of animals and crops. Most notably she is identified as the Faery Queen of Munster and is an appropriate Goddess to call upon when working with Faery magick.

She was believed to be the Daughter of King Egobagal, one of the Tuatha de Danann and there is even some confusion regarding her possible assimilation with other Goddesses like Grainne and the Morrighan. There are some that sometimes view Aine as simply an aspect of Grainne, as both Solar Goddesses, respectively, reflected the waxing and waning Solar year. Still there are other myths that depict her as a Goddess and daughter, even possibly a wife, of the Sea God, Manannan. Thus here, we see a connection to the element of water, hence the South-West cardinal points are sacred to her, as they are to two other well-known Goddesses like; Saraswati and Brigit.

There are some of the opinion that Aine was an absolutely beautiful, human woman, from the Leanan Sidhe, meaning, *"Sweetheart of the Sidhe"* and a direct connection to those people with the surname O'Corra. It was believed, she possessed a magickal ring that could unearth faeries and some alleged she became enchanted by the Fae, and taken in by this magickal realm. Subsequently, she became the Faery Queen of Munster and was forever connected, lovingly, with faeries. As a Faery Queen, she was very fond of mortal men, consorting and mating with numerous lovers and thus she is often attributed for creating a magickal Faery race, called the Dinnshenchas [Din- sheen-k'has]. These were believed to be, more specifically, shape shifting, fire dwarf faeries that came to strengthen and assist wommin in danger of being harmed by men and they undoubtedly served their Queen, Goddess Aine.

Many of the beloved Celtic myths that survive today reveal a great deal about Aine's character and her attributes. According to one Celtic story of the time, she once made a quirky, strange vow not to sleep with a gray-haired man and this tale exemplifies her serious commitment to promises and magickal vows. When Aine's lover, Fionnis, was sadly enchanted by her jealous sister-Miluchrach, and his hair turned gray, Aine kept her vow. In yet another infamous tale we see glimmers of the strong character of this beloved Irish Goddess as she is credited for killing The King of Munster, Aillil Olom, after he had attempted to rape her. In yet another revealing Irish tale of Aine we learn of a stone, known as Cathair Aine. It clearly was an enchanted stone that belonged to the Goddess and it was believed that anyone who sat on it was susceptible to losing their wits. If anyone dared sit on her rock for more than three times they were doomed to loose themselves forever. In this tale, we again see Aine's character as a Goddess not to offend, for her fiery, red wrath through-out various myths has proven to be severe. There are, however, also tales that reflect her generous powers of creativity bestowed upon bards and writer, yet if they failed to meet her high demands and expectations she would not hesitate to severely punish them.

Most of the myths agree that Aine became the wife of Gerald, The Earl of Desmond, although it is not clear how that union came about. There are numerous conflicting tales of how they first met and fell in love. According to some legends, The Earl of Desmond came across the enchanting beauty, while she bathed in a river and he was instantly smitten. He spied upon her magick cloak, the one that was so often used by Aine to enchant men into lovers, and he saw her scattered clothes set upon a nearby boulder and essentially, he blackmailed her into matrimony, refusing to give back her prized possessions until she agreed to the union. Another version of this story, tells of how he saw her combing her hair by the river and upon discovering her unsupervised clothes, he stole her legendary magickal cloak. Wearing the enchanted cloak himself, he used her very own magick powers against her, to ensnare and enchant her into love and marriage. Still another version tells of how she herself, having a reputation for being a beautiful enchantress and acquiring numerous lovers, wore the magick cloak and ensnared The Earl of Desmond into marriage.

Married to the Earl of Desmond, together they had one known son; Geroid Iarla, Earl Fitzgerald- although here too there might be conflicting mysterious stories. In some of the writings of the time he is addressed as "The Magician". Some believed he is indeed Merlin, or an archetype of Lancelot in Arthurian mythology. According to one famous tale, upon the birth of their son, Aine warned her husband not to ever be surprised at what their son could do. It was a type of taboo The Earl of Desmond needed to agree and adhere to, but one day he witness his beloved flesh and blood, jump in and out of a tiny bottle, a very non-human act and the poor man could not contain his utter shock. This very act resulted in Geroid turning himself into a wild Goose and Aine fleeing her marriage and the husband who failed to keep his critical vow.

Some believe their son, the Magician, still lives today under the Lake, inside Lough Fur, in county Limerick and one myth claims that he will one day return to remove all foreigners from his beloved Ireland. The immortal Goddess Aine is still very much revered today by the Irish and the name itself is quite common in certain regions of Ireland. There is great pride in this beloved Goddess, some even feeling an ancestral connection to her and many believe she still lives today in Knock Aine, in a Faery Castle.

Call upon the Goddess Aine for Faery magick, solar and lunar spells, fertility and prosperity rituals, love magick, creativity spells -especially for writing. She can also be called upon when needing to flee an unsuitable mate, when endeavoring to give birth to wizards and magickal offspring, and when making oaths and vows. She will be very sympathetic and prove to be helpful when doing work to punish rapist as well. The (Lair Derg)Red Mare, Rabbits and Swans are her sacred animals and she was often called upon when blessing cattles and herd, especially during her feast day on Midsummer's day. The Meadowsweet is associated with Aine but also the Yew tree, which reflects her connection with life and death.

AINE - GODDESS GROVE GATHERING

Purpose: We gather to connect with Aine in her Solar aspect and endeavor to celebrate the season of Fire, with the arrival of Summer Solstice, and connect with this sacred element.

Check Ins: Speaking stick will be passed around the room so that each womyn, while holding the stick, has a chance to be heard fully, as she introduces herself and what brings her to our Goddess gathering this day.

Chant: A Song text sheet will be offered as we begin creating sacred space with our voices through singing. Songs offered that honor the season at this time like *"Spirits of fire Come to us......"* and *"The Ocean is the beginning of the Earth...."* and *"I am the Witches Daughter"*

Sharing Images: This moment we can each share our own personal image of the Sun, but it's also wonderful to have an Image of the Sun Tarot Card. Let this Sun card be passed around the circle of wommin, so that each womyn has a chance to reflect and invoke her image of the Sun to our space.

Drumming and Dance/Movement: To connect our earthly bodies to this divine process we will each grab a percussive instrument and begin to gently raise a cone of power with sound. It can begin with a single rattle and increase with more instruments and then our voices humming entering the sphere and through-out we can add swinging movement, whatever feels comfortable and freeing.... **Grounding** the energy that we raised we can now begin....

LECTURE ON THE CELTIC GODDESS AINE,

her myths and various attributes and how this immortal Goddess is relevant to us today..

GODDESS WORKSHOPS

WORKSHOP I: Handcrafting homemade candles but in particular- Bright Yellow candles. This might be messy and time consuming (which is why it is best to do it early on in the day) but it can be quite fulfilling and a bonding experience, as wommin get into a sort of meditative groove while mixing and pouring and through-out every step, focusing on intention for these tools of magick. Wax, wick, molds and detail instructions on crafting candles can be attained from any craft shop or even the internet. It is really quite easy to do once you have supplies.

WORKSHOP II: With soft Celtic Music playing in the background, wommin are invited to relax, trance for a moment and contemplate on the Sun at this time of the year. Together we will conjure up the images that came to us collectively during this trance journey.

WORKSHOP III: If at all possible, participants are encouraged to go outdoors for this workshop, which will involve painting an image of the Sun using only five colors (Red, Yellow, Black, Orange and Blue). With nature and music in the background transcending us, painting can become quite cathartic and revealing.

WORKSHOP IV: The Goddess Aine was reputed to own a very powerful cloak of Enchantment, which she used quite often. In this workshop wommin can either create their own cloaks (or even a simple scarf)of Enchantment and consider the potential for this textile to be utilize as a powerful tool of Glamour Magick, in the same fashion that

Aine would employ it herself. If sewing machines are available, wommin can gather together to sew a cloak or scarf. At the very least, they can utilize this workshop to embellish a store bought cloak or scarf and imbue it with her positive energy.

WORKSHOP V: Energy work with crystals, in particular those crystals and gemstones that relate to our Third Chakra -the **Solar Plexus chakra.** Stones like; citrine, yellow jade, yellow mookanite, Jasper and carnelian are perfect to use at this workshop to stimulate and awaken this chakra. We will experiment with stonework energy.

WORKSHOP VI: Another alternative, if gemstones are not available, is rock painting. Rune symbols can be drawn on a series of simple rock which will act as our sun talisman for the meditation. These painted rocks are also excellent altar décor and can become your own personal oracle.

WORKSHOP VII: With Paper Mache we will be creating a Sun ornament for our Altar. We can use pre- fabricated Paper Mache' kits from the Arts and Craft store or handmade with glue, flour, paper pulps and some soap. Creation of a Large Sun for altar.

WORKSHOP VIII: a workshop dedicated to the discussion on energy, what is it? and why do we need it? Exploring where we might need more **Fire energy**. Redirecting energy, in whatever area we see it needed... Areas to consider for more Fire energy:
1. Creativity
2. Finances
3. Mind, Education
4. Home life
5. Health
6. Primary love relationships
7. Community social
8. Physical body, Sexual

WORKSHOP IX: At this point we can carve or charge our handcrafted candles and light them while reciting this invocation. During Ritual another candle spell will be offered as well.

****SPELLWORKING******

Sun Reaches its Zenith Height,
Blazing Flames, that shed insight,
We welcome you
In formal ways
By Will and word in Ritual today,
With Chants and Prose
and much Respect,
We call your Sacred element,
We light this flame,
Internalize your gifts
Thinking upon our Solstice wish.
Season of healing, energy and strength
Come now,
Make your entrance
Season of Fire,
Hail to Thee
This Sabbat is kept,
so mote it be!

REFLECTIONS ON AINE:

Although Aine is consider both a lunar and solar Goddess, I personally see her very much linked to the element of Fire and the Sun. Judging from her numerous myths, she appears to also exemplify conventional characteristic of a Fire Goddess, in her short temper and fierce reaction to those who offend her. She was known to shape shift as a red-mare and this, for me, connotes the element of Fire and thus the Sun. She is known as the Queen of the faeries, attributed with creating a special race of faeries known as Dinnshenchas and this too supports the belief that she is very much linked with fire and its Solar correspondence. According to Celtic mythology, the Dinnshenchas are known as Fire Dwarf faeries that protect wommin in danger of being harmed by men. Also important to note that the meaning of "Aine" in Gaelic is, "radiance", and here too we have a strong reference to fire. I suspect that indeed at one point she was probably a Lunar Goddess but almost all of my research depicted her more as a Solar Deity.

For us modern day wommin, Aine is a beloved patron Goddess to call upon when we find ourselves in danger of being harmed, harassed or mistreated by men. She is known to be quite sympathetic to wommin struggling in this arena and being a fierce Goddess, whose known to quickly execute justice, she will come to your aid. Any spells related to just retribution towards rapist (or those that defile and degrade wommin) would work best invoking this Goddess. In these incidences she does appear to also exemplify Lunar deity qualities and is almost reminiscent of Goddesses like Artemis and Hekate, who are staunch protectors and defenders of wommin. When she abandons her marriage to The Earl because he breaks an important taboo oath, she, again, appears to take on a quality that reminds me of yet another Moon deity, the Mayan Goddess, Ix Chel. And her strength and autonomy are consistently reflected and exhibited in most of her Irish folklore.

The Celtics called on her during the Solar Holy days like, Midsummer and Lughnasadh, to bring about fertility and abundance to their land, but despite the modernization of our worlds we can still do the same today. Aine can be invoked to manifest abundance in whatever form that personally means to us and she can help make our work (be that in a farm field, an art studio or an office building somewhere) fertile and prosperous.

Most importantly, Aine becomes a wonderful Goddess to work with when endeavoring "Glamour" or "Love spells" as she was known to have numerous lovers by choice.

Whether we are living in the Middle ages or the Twenty-first Century, the pursuit of love is always of great value and concern, sought by everyone, regardless of century. Aine, thus, is timeless as a Celtic Goddess of Love. Call on Aine with sincerity and she will show you how to best honor her. She has numerous dimensions to her personality and she will reward your devotion by unveiling them to you, along with the secrets of a beloved Enchantress.

AINE GODDESS GROVE GATHERING RITUAL

Purpose: We gather to connect with Aine in her Solar aspect and endeavor to connect with Fire and celebrate the arrival of the Summer Solstice.

Asperge/Smudge: Greeter will ask each womyn, *"How will you enter this sacred space?"* Participants will answer, *"In Perfect Love and Perfect Trust"*.
Each participant will then enter through the watery blue or fiery red colored veil
Music is played in background as we gather, formulating our circle.

CIRCLE IS CAST with flowers scattered around the perimeter of the circle and anointing oil passed from syster to syster, the circle is cast. *(see suggested circle castings)*

QUARTERS CALLED:
Incorporating Dragons, to Shield and Protect among the four corners N,E,S,W. Representing the elements.
***

Hail and welcome Deep soil, rich brown, <u>Earth Dragon</u>, you the teacher that grounds us to this plane and helps us manifest abundance in our lives, we call you today to guard our sacred space, come from deep below the earth,
Hail and Welcome, Earth Dragon.

Hail and welcome Blue, white, billowy <u>Air Dragon</u>, you who stirs within our minds, filling them with insight and awakening our intellect, we call you today to guard our sacred space, come from high above the lofty planes,
Hail and Welcome, Air Dragon.

Hail and welcome Fiercely passionate, Red <u>Fire Dragon</u>, you the protector and invigorator, who teaches us mastery and leadership, we call you today to guard our sacred space, come from the rising yellow flames,
Hail and Welcome, Fire Dragon.

Hail and welcome Overflowing, aquatic <u>Water Dragon</u>, you who reaches the depths of our soul to touch our hearts and remind us of what is really important, we call you today to guard our sacred space, come from the surge and the waves of the healing waters,
Hail and Welcome, Water Dragon.

CHANT: *"Earth, Air Fire Water I am the Witches Daughter*
(Aine/ Nike/Hathor/Gaia) is me and I am she.... 4x

SUN GODDESS/SEASONAL INVOCATION *(see suggestion)*
CHANT: Invoking Aine further with a special Song
Wommin are then invited to gather around closely in a tight knit circle with their Yellow candles and Oil to anoint them. Each womyn will **Charge and Anoint Candle** by saying:
"By Stem, By Bud, By Leaf, By Flower,
I charge this Candle with Solar Power...."

INVOKING FIRE:
Going around the Circle each participants states what Fire is personally to them and we will keep going around the circle, now overlapping our voices and getting louder and more intense as we keep raising the cone of power, saying ***"Fire is... Fire is... etc...."***
Keep it going until you sense the Cone of power is raised and we have clearly invoked

Fire. *How will you know you've invoke fire? You will feel much hotter and many of the other attributes declare will be felt. Most noticeably the energy levels in the room will be quite obviously elevated.... And it is this ingredient that is vital to our working...*

THE SPELL: Now with the Fiery energy raised, each wommin takes her candle and lights it with these words....
      "I invoke the sacred energy of Fire for_____"
        (state your spell for example; to find a new lover, to improve health etc...)

When all candles are lit,
CHANT: *"Spirits of Fire Come to us, we will kindle the Fire..."*

SECOND PART: (*We return our lit candles to the altar, set them around the bowl of Water*).
With our Yellow Gemstone held firmly within our fist, focus now on the ocean and the earth and her dear waters.... Take this moment to Ground the excess Fire energy into this stone, which will become a tool of healing.

    "The Healing Powers of the Sun is within me
    and I extend this gift of healing to her Divine womb,
    our waters and all sacred marine life, Blessed Be..."

All wommin drop their gemstone into the bowl of water, one by one, calmly sending their best of intentions to heal our Global waters.
CHANT: *"We all come from the Goddess and to her we shall return....."*

Begin Devoking, the Goddess
Red Mare, Queen,
Goddess of Moon and Sun,
you came when called into our sacred space.
We thank you, Enchantress of the Fiery Realm,
for sharing your gifts
and blessing us with your presence here today.
With much gratitude, we bid thee Adieu.
Go if you must, Stay if you will,
Hail and Farewell Aine!

Devoking the Quarters.
Dragons of the Earth, Dragons of the Flame,
Dragons of the Sea and Dragons of the Sky,
when called, you came, to guard our space,
and for this, loving, act we humbly do pray.
May you know our gratitude comes deep within our hearts,
but now as we merry meet, so must we merry part.
Hail and Farewell Elemental Dragons!

Thanking one another for participating in the ritual and adding their energy. As we open the circle, turn to your syster look into her eyes and say, "You are the light and I am glad you shined here, thank you"

    CLOSING CHANT: *"The Circle is open but unbroken....."*

Potluck to follow

AINE POEM INVOCATION

Sun Goddess, Moon Goddess,
Red-haired mare,
Queen of the Faeries,
Enter our Lair.

Beautiful Aine,
We honor you this day,
With the flames of our heart,
And the words that we pray.

In your Magickal ring
Let us find a **place**,
Where we may receive
The Blessings of the **Fae.**

Hear us dear One,
You who knows what we feel
Woman, Enchantress,
By your flames let us heal.

Breaking away
from that which degrades,
Manifesting all
the loves that we may crave,

Prosperity builder,
Enchantress and fierce,
Thy skills and thy powers
We draw now here.

Come Aine, Goddess
We honor you this day
Hail and welcome
In our ritual today!!!

In honor of Aine, the Enchantress, this spell can be done on a Full Moon or the night of a waxing Moon. Suggested to do on a Friday or Sunday night, but anytime that you won't be disturbed is ideal. It is best to approach your altar, sky clad and after a special ritual bath of Jasmine oil, Lavender and Rose petals. Light your sweet scented incense and let the smoke permeate every part of your altar and your body. If you can go outside or to a nearby window, Draw Down the energy of the Moon by basking in her glow - enjoy the sacred Moonlight- for as long as you can. This incantation can be said while drawing down the Moon or before your altar, when lighting your spell working candles.

MY NAME
*Behold I embody the Earth and the sky
The Sun and the Moon
The flames and the Tides
Strong intelligent wise to the ways
Beautiful Enchantress like the Moon's rays

Priestess, Goddess,
Witch are my name
I am the weaver of mine own fate

Goddess of ol'
Who walked before me
Theirs is the strength
and the knowledge I seek
Caster of Spells,
Circles and brews
Awaken <u>Sister</u> to the Goddess in you

Aine Journaling -Grove Gathering

It had been a couple of months since our last gathering. The Memorial day holiday in May, the challenge of synchronizing our hectic schedules and, admittedly, my own insecurities and past disappointments, resulted in too many cancellations and yet, I knew I couldn't give up on Grove entirely. One of our grove systers had returned from a very long absence, due to a job abroad, and I was mortified to see that no one was commemorating her return to the states. Clearly this inspired me to get back, re-form our little community and acknowledge its importance. Meanwhile, wommin were also voicing their desire to come together again in fellowship and so I proceeded to return to my post, priestessing for the Feminine divine (not that I had ever stopped my own daily practice) but I returned to community and the sisterhood.

With the tragedy of the Gulf BP Oil spill and the Summer Solstice upon us, I felt compelled to do a healing ritual honoring both Fire and Water and the Fiery Celtic Goddess Aine came to me as the conduit for this work. I didn't know who would show up -since we hadn't gathered in a while I made it a point, not to over plan this particular day and this naturally made me uncomfortable- well, not having every detailed mapped out, the way I usually like to do so.... Still, I was pleasantly surprised overall at our day, especially our ritual. There were some new womyn, thanks to grove systers wanting to share our sacred space with their special friends and I met this unexpected surprise with much honor and excitement.

*As I anticipated, there was a lot of talking and catching up and we didn't even incorporate the use of our Grove speaking stick, so you can imagine the cocophony of wommin chatter. It was beautiful! There was sharing of our gemstones, sharing chakra knowledge and stories of the Goddess Aine. There was some singing like, "The Ocean is the beginning of the earth...."-which never seemed to hold as much weight, as it did **now**, in the midst of a catastrophic Oil spill killing our marine life. I offered a pre-recorded meditation and around the circle, I gifted each womyn with a crystal, glass butterfly to imbue their energy into while listening to the meditation. This glass butterfly was given as an alternate object used for the following water ritual. Wommin enjoyed the meditation and expressed their approval.*

While the day morphed, ebbing and flowing...the ritual I had planned out carefully was beautifully structured and quite effective. A threshold priestess, welcomed wommin with oil upon the third eye. The Circle was cast with prose and percussive sounds, Aine was invoked and the elements were called with "We are the Witches' daughter Song". Then began our work.

We raised a cone of power whilst invoking Fire. Around the circle each womyn stated a word to reflect what Fire meant to her personally and we went around the circle numerous times(yes numerous) as we slowly built a strong image of this powerful element. The conjuring of Fire started small and it too ebbed and flowed, sometimes it sputtered, but when it finally got going, it was magnanimous, volcanic, explosive and indeed powerful!!! We took all of that Fire energy and placed it in our respective personal, Yellow candles for our spell and sealed it with our collective-So Mote it be!

Then we went outside, in sacred nature, under the hot sun, to feel Aine's solar gifts and begin the second part of the ritual -sending healing to the Earth's waters. This was truly a powerful current that worked its way quietly, but intensely and it truly astounded me. When we re-entered the altar room, Watery sounding music was playing in the background, as we quietly focused and unified our magickal intentions for healing to our marine life. One by one, womyn placed their special gemstone (some citrine, some carnelian, rose quartz and various forms of crystals) gingerly, thoughtfully, into the large glass bowl of water to send healing to sea creatures. It was quiet, intense and for me, another memorable aspect of our beautiful day together. Two days later, a lot of positive news was heard from the media about marine life getting help by the proper channels and advocacy groups. Weeks later the capping of the oil spill was completed and successfully done. I'd like to think that we added to the global collective consciousness that had been praying along for a resolution to this catastrophe.

We were nearing the end of our ritual with devocations, when all of a sudden, one of our systers felt herself light headed, dizzy, and highly effected by our ritual work. Immediately we all came together, like the family that we are, to assist her and surrounded her with healing hugs and earthly grounding energy that she needed. It helped and we proceeded to open the circle and then go out afterwards to enjoy our potluck. Food has always been known as the best vehicle for grounding and that is why it is our natural way of ending our Gatherings.

GROVE OF THE FEMININE DIVINE CHANTS

I AM MAGICK WOMAN (?) DOD-Shelley Graff
I am Magick Woman, Giving Birth to myself
I am Magick Woman
Giving Birth to myself
from deep inside the wells,
From your loving eyes and wisdom
My truth that I must tell,
I am Magick Woman
Giving Birth to myself....

I AM THE WITCHES DAUGHTER
Earth Air fire water,
I am the Witches daughter Aine is me and I am she
Earth Air fire water,
I am the Witches daughter Nike is me and I am she
Earth Air fire water,
I am the Witches daughter Ix Chel is me and I am she
Earth Air fire water,
I am the Witches daughter Gaia is me and I am she

FIRE CHANT by Moving Breath
Spirits of Fire Come to us
We will kindle the Fire....
Spirits of Fire, Come to us
We will kindle the Fire...

We will kindle the fire
Dance the Magick circle round
We will kindle the Fire
Dance the Circle Around *(repeat)*

PROTECTION SONG By Lisa Thiel
I invoke the protector,
Divine Mother's embrace
I invoke the Protector
Divine mother's embrace...

With the arms of the Great Mother,
ever surround me, -With the arm of the Great
Mother ever surround me. (repeat)

MY BODY
My Body is a living Temple of Love
My Body is a living Temple of Love
My Body is the Body of a Goddess (3X)
(lower)My Body is the Body of a Goddess

BORN OF WATERS
Born of Waters,
Cleansing Powerful.
Healing , Changing,
We are...   *by Starhawk*

THE RIVER IS FLOWING
The river is flowing,
Flowing and Growing,
The River is flowing,
down to the sea,
Mother carry me
a child I will always be,
Mother carry me down to the Sea. *by: Diana Hildebrand-Hull*

GODDESS NAMES
Do you remember,
When God was a woman,
She had many, many names,
They called her Isis, Astarte, Diana, Hecate,
Demeter, Kali, Inanna...

THE OCEAN
The Ocean is the beginning of the world
The Ocean is the beginning of the world
All life comes from the sea
All life comes from the sea.
By Delaney Johnson, Starhawk and Reclaiming collective

WE ALL COME FROM THE GODDESS
We all come from the Goddess
And to her we shall return,
Like a Drop of Rain,
Flowing to the Ocean *By Z. Budapest*

July

The astrological sign for the month of July is Cancer, the Crab. Cancer is ruled by the watery, feminine, intuitive powers of the Moon (June 21-July 20) and this is an energy that will be experienced throughout the month. July is the seventh month of the Gregorian calendar, but in the Roman calendar it was the fifth month and was known by its Latin name, *"Quintilis,"* meaning fifth. Some speculate the month was probably named after the Roman ruler, Julius Ceasar around 46BC.

The Full moon was often called Blessing Moon, for indeed we feel the blessings of the Goddess, during this time of year, through the Earth's fertile transformation. Last month, we celebrated the height of the sun's power on the Summer Solstice at Midsummer and the solar energy of Fire continues to be prevalent this month. With this fiery, combustible energy felt everywhere, there are also the occasional lightning and massive thunderstorms. Together, we see how, fire and water influence the energy of July. According to the Farmer's Almanac, it is this reason why the Native Americans called June's full moon, the Thunder Moon.

The Chinese were the first to invent fireworks. With the combination of sulfur, charcoal and saltpeter, placed in bamboo pieces, and then set aflame, they created one of the most important ingredients to the customs of our U.S.A. holiday of Independence. Originally however, these colorful, loud fireworks were meant to drive evil away, but by the middle of the sixteenth century they were being used as a form of entertainment by many Europeans. It is therefore not surprising that upon migrating to the United States, many immigrants brought their traditions, like firework, with them to the new land.

With Independence Day celebrated through-out the U.S.A. on July 4th, this is undoubtedly a time of spectacular fireworks, both figuratively and literally and there is much warmth found among friends, family and community. Picnics and barbecues amongst loved ones are not that uncommon and travels to short and long distant locales are also prevalent. Romantic cavorting and liaisons permeate the warm breezes, perhaps indebted to the shorter outfits and the lack of heavy clothing covering us all up. There is a light casualness to July that encourages one to relax and enjoy all of nature.

July, is notorious for wrapping us in its warm bright light and conjuring up suppressed inner joys and childhood nostalgia. Warm days on sandy beaches, roller skating, bike riding, frisbee playing, with so many of our activities taking us outdoor, nature indeed beckons you to stop, look and adore her at every angle. Much like November, there are a great many opportunities for lots of family gatherings and get together among friends. The warm sun during this month is inviting and because we find ourselves outdoors, we might seem to be more in tuned with the elements, fae and nature spirits. The waters at our beaches and lakes, the gentle breezes that inaugurates our cooler evening hours, all help to connect us more to the elements. And the moon and the stars garner our love and admiration, when we turn our attention towards the heavens to enjoy the fireworks on the 4th of July. Our connection to the earth is magnified even more, simply by sitting near a lush, full tree and as we survey the bright scenery of green grass and colorful flowers, which by now have bloomed everywhere.

In some parts of the world the heat is unquestionably strong now as we find ourselves smack in the middle of Summer. The sun reminds us that fire is emanating from within and all around us. We are in the throes of the Summer season and the Goddess is adorned in her passionate, finest greenery. Enjoy this moment and the magick it affords to you.

This month we quench any thirst we might have, by invoking the watery energy of Erzulie Freda, a Voodoo Loa of luxury, opulence and romantic love and a Goddess who clearly advocates the enjoyment of life. As we are approaching the month of August, and, subsequently, our first Harvest, this month, we also will find ourselves inviting the primordial Goddess of the Earth, Gaia. With her, we acknowledge the beautiful blessings and abundance that are already prevalent in our lives and tap into her gifts of proliferation and creativity.

CHAPTER SIXTEEN

"Life is not measured by the number of breaths we take, but by the moments that take our breath away....." anonymous

"First realize that your world is only a reflection of yourself and then stop finding fault with that reflection" Nisargadatta

WELCOME ERZULIE-FREDA

OUR ALTAR

Altar cloth: Pink and white and maybe a second light blue altar cloth underneath.
Image: Statue of this Haitian Voodoo Loa/Goddess and her special Veve
Canvas art or photo of the Goddess and or photos of her special veve/sigils. Images that conjure up the ideals of Romantic Love, such as heart shaped items, flowers and idealistic scenes.

Always present on the altar;
A cast iron cauldron, drums, speaking stick, a silver pentacle, athame, elemental representations.....

Air: Feathers, Dove statuaries, Incense type sticks, cones or charcoal brisket and fine powdered herbs like sandalwood, jasmine, rose, honeysuckle can be incorporated into your working.
Fire: candles, glass enclosed candles or pillars, in pink and white, as many as possible. Women shaped image candles. Seven day saint candles are okay as well and your local botanicas can sometimes create special devotional candles for your Voodoo loa.
Water: Chalice or small glass bowl with Fresh Spring Water or a blush Sweet Wine
Earth: Lush tropical Green Plants and beautiful flowers like roses as your Northern representation. A small dish of rose petals or herbs can also be used. A platter of fruits and vegetable also represents the Earth.

Other items pertinent to this particular gathering
Scented consecrated Water
Scented oil and lotions
Sparking beads, necklaces and jewelry
Mirrors
Sacred Sigil and Veve
Chalice with pink Champagne
white and pink flowers and Roses, lots of greenery
Bowl of coins/money
Crystals, Gemstones and Three gold ring bands
Plate offering with decadent foods and sweets
French soaps and Chantilly Lingerie
Herbal plackets and Poppets
Writing pens and papers, safety pins,
Light blue gauzy fabric to represent water
Workshop items
Tarot -"Queen of Cups" or Voodoo Oracle cards

Offering scented perfumes, all things French, Sweet chocolates, melons, light or blush wines, like Muscato.
Sacred objects from members:
Notes:

Erzulie

Erzulie Altars

Erzulie Veve

Placket & Gemstones

Erzulie Altars

ERZULIE FREDA

Erzulie Freda, with her penchant for lounging around, is the Haitian Voodoo loa Spirit, or (most appropriately termed) Mystere of Love and Beauty, like the Greek Goddess of love, Aphrodite. She is the watery, Feminine mystere or Goddess (as I like to use these terms interchangeably) of all things that bring you pleasure, including decadent sweets, jewelry, cosmetics, fragrances, lacy feminine textiles, soft music, and affection. She is the benevolent spirit of sensual pleasures and sweet scents like the Egyptian Goddess, Hathor. Erzulie has also been compared to the Hindu Goddess, Lakshmi, as she is also the Voodoo loa Spirit of luxury, opulence and abundance.

Maitresse Erzulie Freda can be seen as a Goddess of Romantic ideals. She is the beloved feminine supreme archetype in the Haitian Voodoo pantheon and rules over all matters concerning relationships, flirtations, sensuality as well as prosperity and her worshippers' wellbeing but she is also known to have another darker side. There are some conflicting stories about her depiction, as some sources claim she was often portrayed, in New Orleans, as a light skin mulatto, sometimes almost white, with long, dark straight hair, while another aspect of her, more specifically, Erzulie Dantor, was depicted as the dark skinned Loa with a scar from her husband, upon her face. Milo Rigaud, in his reputable book, "Secrets of Voodoo", states that Erzulie was considered a very dark skinned Ethiopian and that the notorious, Queen of Sheba, was often identified with her. Because in Voodoo, the bright Sun was the Masculine spirit, known as Damballah/Danbhalah Wedo (also known as Legba), Aida Wedo (his wife), was his opposite, the night, the Moon and the Feminine Spirit, known in Haiti as Erzulie. It would make sense that in Haiti she would be represented as the dark skinned loa while in New Orleans, with the influence of colonialism, a lighter version emerged. Erzulie is the Mystere of eloquence, refinery, French culture, opulence and good fortune and, as can be expected, a very much beloved, powerful loa for all who practice Voodoo. She is so important to the culture, that she is considered the Heart of Voodoo.

Her catholic counterpart is the Virgin Mary, Mater Dellorosa (suffering Mother) as she is often depicted crying towards the end of Voodoo ceremonies, while in possession of her serviteur. Some believe she cries because she is never quite able to attain enough of what she wants. Others feel that she cries lamenting for those who are hurt by poverty or unrequited love and her tears symbolically take on the pain of the world so that others do not need to cry. In this compassionate role, she begins to resemble the Buddhist Goddess of Human Compassion, Kwan Yin, carrying the weight of human suffering upon her own heart.

Originally, the name Erzulie referred to a river in Benin and her worship comes from the West coast of Africa, but soon it traveled to New Orleans and Haiti and all across the Americas with the advent of slavery. There are many names given to this loa depending on the role that she is fulfilling. She is also known as Ezili and some Haitian literature claim that there are several aspects of this one Spirit such as; the older Grande Erzulie, Erzulie-Mapiangueh, Freda Dahoumin, Negresse Imanou Ladeh, Negresse Miroi-Ze, Erzulie Dantor, to name just a few. Here we will focus on Erzulie Freda as one spirit.

In Voodoo, a loa was seen as a powerful spirit, a mystere, and not as an archetype or Goddess aspects, the way we are accustomed to hearing about in Wicca and other earth based religions. A Voodoo loa, like Erzulie, was revered, honored and seen as an actual living person, who might even live near you and possess the same complex, yet tangible personality as any family member would. These spirits were not ethereal beings up in the sky, but were rather viewed as real, here on earth, and they were appeased and given flattery and various offerings.

Even the practice of Voodoo, in general, utilizes common every day household items and ceremonial rites, are not restricted to just church edifices. In this way the practice of Voodoo is appealing to all kinds of people, regardless of class or financial status. The name for a Voodoo temple is an Oum'phors and it contains a partly enclosed area in the middle called a peristyle. In the center of the peristyle is the Poteau-mitan, which is a most significant center post that plays an integral part in almost all Voodoo rites. Among its many meanings, it acts like a cosmic axis and connects earth to sky.

Two ways that this Voodoo Loa communicates with "Her" worshippers were through dreams and possession. Possession is when the human body becomes a vessel or container for the loa to act and speak from. It is reminiscent of evocations and aspecting in traditional Wicca and, often time, it is also referred to as "ridding the loa", for indeed, the worshipper appears to be taken on a wild ride, as the mystere incarnates into its worshipper, completely taking over the body and ridding it like a horse. When Erzulie is in full possession of a serviteur (worshipper), they will often speak French, even if they have only spoken in the Creole language all of their life. For this opulent feminine spirit is all about status and class, something that the French culture and language exudes, *that is*, according to popular Haitian belief. It is quite a phenomenon to witness someone who may never even have had proper education, as is the case within impoverish countries, and to see them quite suddenly start speaking in French as a result of a possession. It only serves to confirm that the loa do exist. Along with crying lamentation for the world, you can expect to see her serviteurs dance with sensual movements (girating and slithering their hips) and flirt incessantly with the male gender. It goes without saying that a man possessed by Erzulie Freda is going to express very frilly, feminine mannerism and have eyes only for his gender, therefore uptight heterosexual men might want to steer clear of her, for she is a lover of men.

Erzulie Freda can also be seen as a spirit of promiscuity. It was quite obvious that she relished and loved men. She enjoyed giving as well as being lavished with affection and was quite skilled at flirting. Her views on women were very different however. As Erzulie Dantor she was defender and very protective of women, but as Erzulie Freda, she was indifferent. Often depicted wearing three rings, which symbolize her three husbands, but interesting to note, her role with them appears to be more of a mistress than sole wife. Her Consorts were; Met Agwe (Lord of the Ocean), Ogou Ferraile (The Bold Warrior), and Damballah (The Wise White Serpent). Yet these three Voodoo loa were heavily invested in other prominent romantic relationships. For example, Agne was said to have another wife in, La Sirene and, according to some Haitian writings, Damballah really loved Aida Wedo, (The rainbow Spirit). Erzulie's third husband Ogou, had a strong attraction to Erzulie Dantor, who some considered Erzulie Freda's actual sister and not just an aspect of her.

This strong, iconic, Voodoo Feminine Spirit, is known to be very generous, but extremely demanding, with high expectation from her worshippers. It is not taboo to bargain with this Mystere, but be sure you remember your promise to her, for she will wreak havoc if you forget. When creating a shrine or altar for Erzulie, one is advised to use her favorite colors like baby pink and white. Never offer anything in the color black or red, as red is the color for her warrior sister, Erzulie Dantor.

An offering to Erzulie would not be complete without some kind of bouquet of flowers, like roses, and champagne, sweets; like chocolate, honey and candies. Generously court her and offer Erzulie Freda all the romantic accoutrements you would, to a new love in your life. She wouldn't expect any less from her worshippers. During Voodoo ceremonies, mirrors (one of her sacred symbols), fine clothing and fancy jewelry was made available to the serviteurs, who would come down with this spirit. At all cost, one is discouraged from exposing her to dust, dirt or any kind of smoke for she detested these things. She loves cleanliness and order, so you would be wise to provide a clean altar for this Voodoo loa. Because she is known to be very jealous, it is also best not to share her altar with the worship of other deities or spirits. It is best not to offend her by having a shrine in her honor, in your bedroom, where intimate relations are expected to take place. Strangely, this might offend her or stir-up her powerful jealous streak. Remember that the loa are real spirits, with strong human-like personalies and that includes some sticky ones like, jealousy and spite. If these demands seem too intimidating, know that it is okay to make the occasional offerings to Erzulie without a permanent, established shrine to her. Also, according to Haitian folklore, you cannot invoke Erzulie without first getting a pass from Legba, for Legba is the door opener to the spirit realm. Connecting with Legba will allow you to worship and invoke any Voodoo loa you choose.

    Another way to connect with Erzulie is through her Veve. Veves were sacred symbols drawn to invoke the Voodoo loa spirits and they were usually drawn over the floor with corn flour, spread across the ground or walls in special ceremonies. They were also drawn on doors and painted on ceilings and walls. It is quite a magickal act to re-draw one yourself, as you prepare to work with Erzulie. Redrawing a veve is quite meditative and almost becomes a sacred ritual to honor her, by its very nature. In this very simple act you will begin to feel her energy transpire. Another way to work with Erzulie and invoke her energy is through the common practice of ritual baths called *"Lave tet."* Since she is a spirit that loves fragrances, creating a ritual bath of clean rain water with basil, sugar and rose petals is a wonderful way to purify yourself before beginning a ritual for her, or as a ritual on its own. It is often suggested to bathe beforehand with a French fragranced soap and then create this sacred bath to soak in, while offering flattery to this beloved Voodoo Goddess. When you are finished, allow yourself to air dry.

    Voodoo is an oral tradition but also initiatory, as some believe you cannot declare yourself a priestess of a Loa without proper initiation from a Hougan or Mambo. Finally, it is also highly recommended to study, respect and support the Haitian Culture of your chosen Voodoo Loa spirit, to receive the utmost blessings from them. Voodoo is not a textbook religion but rather a spiritual practice that can be understood and appreciated best when, experienced. To benefit and work positively with a spirit requires you to build a respectful, loving relationship, slowly, cautiously and with a sincere commitment. I suppose the same rules apply for any solid relationship, whether human or spiritual. All relationships require time, patience, nurturance and careful cultivation, and above all, love.

    Take the time to get to know your loa and if you can, create a shrine for her. Spending time meditating and conversing with Erzulie Freda, daily, can open you up to the beauty of Voodoo and its intricate pantheon. In this way you build a personal relationship with your chosen Loa and will soon be gifted with their message(s).

    Make special note, however, that there are times when a Loa spirit will just not be drawn to you. According to Hougan and author, Kenaz Filan, if you have been invoking a spirit for some time, with petitions and offerings and making special shrines while praying to a loa and nothing seems to change for you, perhaps this is not the right loa for you to work with or perhaps, just not the right time for you to connect. Remember the Loa are real, with complex personalities, and they will either genuinely like you and attach themselves to you and your cause, or show no interest... but rest assure you will know when they are at work in your life. Voodoo loa make themselves very well-known and very obviously so, and you will know, without a shadow of a doubt, when you are being blessed by them.

    All Hails to you and Welcome Maitresse Erzulie Freda!

ERZULIE GROVE GODDESS GATHERING

Purpose: To honor Erzulie Freda, the Voodoo Goddess of love, luxury and beauty and learn about the Voodoo Loa and common practices.

Beginning with a Drumming Circle: Participants are invited to grab a percussive instrument (rattles, marracas, tambourine, drums, chimes, symbals etc..) from our musical basket offering. Each womyn is encouraged to start making sounds with her instrument, until eventually, via listening to one another, one by one we join in, adding to the circle. We continue to synchronize until we create a shamanic cone of Power.

Check Ins: Introductions and sharing our present emotional states with speaking stick. Around the circle we will share how we personally experienced the last esbats (Full Moon) and what we hope to manifest this month.

Chanting: Singing Old songs and learning new Haitian song too. (*see song text sheet*)

Altar Creation: Presenting our altar items to the group, sharing its personal significance and adding it to the Communal altar for Erzulie.

Drumming Circle and trance: African Drumming Musical CD recording can be used, but most effective if you have actual drumming among your systers.

Check ins: Image of the Voodoo Loa, Mystere, Erzulie Freda, will be shared around the Circle. How does she appear to us personally? We begin to invoke her communally in this process.

GODDESS LECTURE
Erzulie Freda's meaning, cultural context and common worship and Voodoo practice

GODDESS WORKSHOPS

WORKSHOP I: Redrawing Erzulie's traditional Veve, her sacred Sigil, on canvas or in our journals. See Photos in this chapter, try to recreate Erzulie-Freda's traditional Voodoo veve, while reflecting on the Loa's gifts. Music will be played in the background to help transcend us to Ife and connect us to the energy of the Mystere.

WORKSHOP II: Creation of a traveling altar or a small Shrine Box, dedicated to Erzulie with all her favorite special trinkets and treasures. You can use a specified craft box or even a simple shoe box, decorated and decoupage it with her image. Inside, add items that remind you of Erzulie's various gifts and attributes like; miniature fragrance bottles, heart shaped pendants, seashells, photos, magazine clippings, pink or white lace and gold wedding bands to name a few.

WORKSHOP III: Crafting handmade Poppets made out of felt or paper-mache' or wax images with an opening to allow for the insertion of blessed herbs during spell working.

WORKSHOP IV: Altar Ritual Bottle dedicated to Erzulie-Freda, hand painted and decoupage with her image on the outside and sweet floral scented ingredients added inside like; Hyacinth oil, carnation oil, honey suckle oil, Rose or Floridian water, Crushed pink Roses and a spritz of a French perfume. This delicious concoction can be incorporated in your next, "lave tet," love bath or Esbat shower.

WORKSHOP V: Creation of a special Glamour hand mirror or mirrored box for your magick altar. You can decorate the mirror with sea shells or beads and pearls or anything else Spirit moves you to use and dedicate this mirror, exclusively to Ezulie Freda and her worship.

WORKSHOP VI: In a meditative state (with trance drumming) we will connect with spirit and endeavor to also **innovate** and re-create a new Veve images for Erzulie Freda. Creating a special communal Veve, with inspiring music in the background, on a large canvas or altar cloth that may be utilized during our ritual to Erzulie.

WORKSHOP VII: Handcrafting paper rose flowers for Altar décor. Sketch out an image of a circular swirl on drawing art paper, which tends to be a little heavier than ordinary writing paper. Cut this swirl image and create a paper coil, roll the paper tightly starting from the outside end to create a spiral rose, then hot glue the ends to maintain that spiral flower shape. Now you can use these as altar décor created with the intention of your spell.

WORKSHOP VIII: Organizing awareness of political unrest in Haiti and brainstorming on how we, here in the U.S.A., can help the places where Voodoo is practiced like Haiti and New Orleans etc... Familiarizing ourselves with the lands where Voodoo is practiced. Sharing images, movies and or books to help us with our journey.

WORKSHOP IX: Creating an aromatic scented oil in her name. See the appendix for Scented Oil suggestions, but it's also a lot of fun experimenting with a few essential oils and combining 2-3 of them, to create your very own anointing oil, dedicated to Erzulie.

WORKSHOP X: Blessing and charging a Seven day glass Candle for her altar or shrine. After creating an anointing oil, now would be a perfect time to put it to good use, by charging your candles with it. In this workshop you will first carve sigils on your candle then bless it with incense and oil.

WORKSHOP XI: Erzulie Meditation offering... **Check ins-** Afterwards a discussion on our personal journey via the meditation.

We end the workshops by discussing the upcoming ritual for Erzulie.

REFLECTIONS ON ERZULIE-FREDA

Aw... Romance... how can anyone declare it dead? From the beginning of time and forever more, romance and love will always have an imperial, highly esteemed place in our universe. Erzulie-Freda swirls her watery energy of love for those beautiful, finer things in life and awakens in you the Universal coquettish spirit and the strong desire for exquisite living. She teaches us to adorn ourselves and bestow generously, great luxuries upon ourselves. She teaches us to value riches and long for fine beauteous possessions. She teaches us to see its value and invite a multitude of loves in our lives, as well as embracing the finest things money can buy. She is a catalyst for love, beauty and romance in your life and beckons you to acknowledge, you are indeed worthy of these things or better. Fine wine, French scents, delicious meals, mouthwatering sweets and exquisite lacey lingerie, pursue your heart's desire and share these delights and sweet luxuries with her and abundance will always be yours, these are her gifts.

ERZULIE GROVE GODDESS GATHERING RITUAL

Prepare altar: *Pink altar cloth, Roses/flowers in vase, Art canvas of Erzulie's Veve, French Bar of Soap, French Perfume like Coco Channel or Rose Water, lacy pinkish panties or head cloth, gold coins, Godiva or mon cherie chocolate, cotton candy or other sweets, honey, seven day Pink or white glass candle, A statue or image of Erzulie Freda.*

Purpose: To honor Erzulie Freda, the Haitian Goddess of love, luxury and feminine beauty and invite her spirit to attain our heart's desire.

Anointing and Purifying: Light gentle sweet Incense first. Then with Rose Scented oil on our Heart Chakra welcome each participant.
Let African Drumming Music Permeate the Ritual Space to begin.

Cast Circle (with Pink Rose Petals scattered around perimeter of circle)
This Circle is Cast with Love and Peace
Above, below on ground we meet,
The circle is cast with our intent
Love anchored here
And joy dispensed....

QUARTERS HONORED AND INVOKED
Winds to Sweep and stir Renewed,
Eastern Realm we call on you.
(light the Yellow Altar candle)
Welcome Air!

Flames to move us to our Cause,
Passion guide us when we are lost.
(light the Red Altar candle)
Welcome Fire!

Water flows, Express our Hearts,
Unify our broken parts.
(light the Blue or White altar candle)
Welcome Water!

Fertile Earth, that Births and Forms,
In your realm we are Transformed.
(light the Brown or Green altar candle)
Welcome Earth!

GUARDIANS: **Calling on Legba,** the Gate Opener to help us connect to our chosen Spirit. Light a white glass enclosed candle, to honor Legba and if you can, pour a bit of rum unto the earth as an offering to Legba.
Papa Legba, Join us to the Beloved Mystere,
Erzulie Freda, we Welcome Her here!

INVOKING ERZULIE
With song and prose dedicated to Erzulie, Call her.
A special **Dance Offering to Erzulie** should ensued.

Veve: Her veve, art Sigil, is passed around the circle as we futher invoke her stating:
"Come Erzulie-Freda be here now...."

Offerings will be made. Priestess begins with a bowl of golden Honey, passed around the Circle so that we may partake of her Sweet blessings. Each person is then encourage to make their own offering to Erzulie, bringing their item to her altar, saying;

"Beloved Beautiful Mystere, Erzulie,
I offer you_____, that you may sweeten my life
and hear our call today in this ritual"

African music CD drumming track will be played, to help align us with her energy.
As we listen to it, think about your request to Erzulie, how may she help you and make this into a special dance to her as you move to the rhythm. When the music has ended and we have clearly raised the energy- acquire and light your seven day **Candle,** in pink or white, or the specially made **Shrine Box** to her and now around the circle we will state aloud what we hope to manifest with Erzulie's assistance- this can be in prose or a simple statement....Everyone is encouraged to speak from their heart.
"May this Candle/Shrine to you, Erzulie, serve to remind me
of your precious gifts of love, abundance, beauty
and luxury, wherever I go..." So Mote it be...! Ashe!

Chanting: Voodoo Mahi Songs and
"....I am Magick Woman giving birth to myself"
Check Ins and Allowing a special moment
for divination and oracular consultation and guidance.

DEVOKING
Holding hands and gather around as we begin to ground (communal hum....) Begin to devoke, first Thanking the Mysteres, Erzulie Freda and then Legba, releasing their energy, in the best way we see fit. Let Spirit guide you and Speak your gratitude from your heart.

DEVOKING ERZULIE
When called Sweet Lady you came to us,
Maitresse Erzulie Goddess of Abundance,
Of Love and luxury of all your many gifts,
We sought to know you and present you our wish.
Thank you for your presence, receive our thank yous
but for now Dear Voodoo Loa we bid thee Adieu,
Hail and Farewell Erzulie Freda!!!

GUARDIANS:
Gate Opener Papa Legba,
we thank you for allowing us the passage way,
into this sacred realm
to visit with the feminine mystere, Erzulie.
You who opened the gate to let us in,
now open the gate to let us out,
Receive our sincere gratitude for your help on this day.
Hail and farewell Legba!
DEVOKING ELEMENTS: *Extinguish candles and releasing the Quarter/Elements.*
CHANT:"Elemental Return song,"

DEVOKING: YE-KE, MAR-CH-ALLAH, KU M BHA-LAH DYA
The ensemble of the loas, Peace be unto you!
Withdraw into the Light...

Release and Open circle, with: *"the Circle is open, but unbroken may the peace of the Orishas be ever in our heart, merry meet and merry part and merry meet again...."*

***Potluck feasting and merriment to follow*

MEDITATION JOURNEY WITH ERZULIE FREDA

Find a comfortable spot, you are invited to release and leave the mundane behind. Surrender to this sacred moment in time. This is your moment.....(pause) Close your eyes, breathe, breathe deeply. Follow my voice and let the sound of the drums sweep you into this land.(pause) Spiraling down we go. Spiraling to a land very different from what you may be accustomed to. Spiraling down into a land you welcome in your mind's eye, a green luscious land that beholds all of the beauty, comforts and luxuries you could ever imagine. (pause) Conjure now this magickal safe place. And spiral down, further down to the core of this space, spiraling with your mind's eye like through a tunnel or a birth canal, spiraling down, further to find all that is beautiful, all that is rich and luxuries...deep in the earth there are many treasures to behold. Spiral down to this land, the core of the earth. Feel its magnetic pull, as it draws you down.... Spiraling further... breathe. You are here, Ife... Abundance is here and with your mind's eye, you have arrived. Open your soul's eye now to view what's before you. (pause)

Note, what's ahead of you? What do you see?_____

Now walk further, explore. (pause) There are others gathered here. Some are dancing, some are in prayers and you follow them to see what they are seeing....
Before you now, is a beautiful, golden skinned lady with flowing dark hair, her full lips glistening from the droplets of what she has just tasted. Her bountiful curves rise up from the chaise, she is lounging on, the way hills and mountains rise up from the horizon. She glistens and sparkles from head to toe, like a gem crystal, left out for the sun to caress. She shines like water does, when the midmorning's strong sun, lowers to its surface like her desired lover. She is brilliance. She is abundance, for all around her, there are a multitude of precious items; coins, money, jewels, sweets and foods overflowing all from **their** gifts to her. These are offerings left to our beloved Mystere, Voodoo Loa, Erzulie Freda...She loves and lives off of them. (pause)

She survives all these years in this sacred realm because of our veneration, love and devotion to her. She cries if you forget her or replace her with others, for the pain is too much for her to bear. Did you know our offerings and invitations to her, sustain her breath and keep her steeped in reality? Like all immortal Goddesses, ancestors and spirits, they feed from our love and devotion to them and remain tangible from ages to ages, due to our remembrance and reverence.

The beautiful one appears to be sleeping. You cast your eyes all around her and you study the various gifts left to her...(pause) Some have notes attached with their supplications and wishes to the Voodoo Loa, some notes are of thanksgiving with gratitude for what she has already bestowed and some notes plead with special request for something new to manifest. You look around now....

What offering do you have for her? _____ *(pause)*
What will you write on your note? _____ *(pause)*

Approaching her as She sleeps, you whisper...
"...With my offering, I breathe life into your spirit, that you may awaken and in turn, may breathe life into mine and Bless me. .."

Ask her for what you need now_____ *(pause)*

What area in your life can you use Erzulie's blessing? _____
_____ ***(pause)***

Gently, she opens her almond shaped eyes and happily awakes from slumber. Stretching ever so gently, her slow body movement, graceful, like that of a Golden luscious serpent. You notice her long hands reaching. From the inside of her womb, deep within, she pushes, then with her hands searches and she reaches deep within, then out she pulls, and births a Golden box. Offering it to you she says;

> "...this Golden box contains your heart's desire,
> open it only when you are ready,
> open it when you feel worthy of this treasure,
> open it when you feel ready to attain your wish,
> open it when you have finally awaken too, as I have now,
> open it when you can recognize me, in you...."

Cautiously, you reach your hands out to behold her gift within your fingers. Studying the box in awe, you realize the great value in what you now hold and her words echo in your head, like a hypnotic, trance inducing chant...

> "...open it when you can recognize me, in you"

Your eyes, adjusting to the light, searches for the path back home, and with your sacred box in hand, you begin to walk towards the road, retracing your steps to the entrance of this realm. With your mind's eye, see the dark tunnel and once again journey. Walk the spiral that brought you here. Walk it back to where it all began. Walk up the spiral and follow my voice. Spiraling, <u>you</u> return. Spiraling upward now. Inhale and exhale. Return now to your home state of mind. Spiral now up, walk up this spiral like a ladder leading you up. Return to the feeling of your body on this earthly plane, return to your flesh, the seat, the floor, the grass, the cushion right under you. Return to your breath, as I count from five to one, backwards; five, four, three, (breathe and return) two, one....
Return now to this room and when you are ready, open your eyes, to join us here.
Welcome!

Perform this spell when the moon is waxing and growing to Full and preferably on a Friday or Sunday -in the first hour of sunrise. Set up your altar with an image of Erzulie-Freda, a photograph, artistic canvas art or an actual sculpture of the Mystere will suffice. Lay out your pink or white altar cloth and items that conjure up the ideals of romantic love. Include offerings to the loa of French champagne, dark chocolates, a dish of honey and sweet melons. Place exquisite laces in pink and silk textiles, as this Mystere, adores only the finest. Flank your altar with two sets of pink and white floral arrangements and candles of matching colors, as these are her beloved hues-not reds or black. Carve and bless your petition candle as you concentrate on your very detailed request to the loa. Use an oil that corresponds with your wish and complete the candle with sparkling glitter -which draws her attention to your working. Light a Rose scented incense and let the smoke permeate your candle, your body and all offerings. Boldly adorn your altar to Erzulie as best as you can for this spells effectiveness and recite the incantation sweetly and with sincerity.

ERZULIE-FREDA GLAMOUR SPELL

Erzulie Queen, Erzulie-Freda,
I call you forth, To sit on this throne
Let me honor you,
in this seat of Reverence,
Let me lavish on you, words that melt stones.

Queenly and Beautiful,
desired by All,
Your French scent alluring,
Will you come,
when you are called?

Sweet like Nectar,
You cry for the weak,
Your tears bring on healing,
And the change that we seek.

Bless me with Love,
Beauty and grace,
And in return
I offer you pink lace,

Bless me with cash,
Moncy in hand,
And a shrine, for you,
I'll place on my land.

Luxuries overflow,
in your presence
only the best.
Manifest in me your
Alluring essence.

Ashe! So Mote it be!
Welcome Erzulie!

Authentic Voodoo Chants
From Milo Rigaud's book, "Secrets of Voodoo"
City lights Books, San Francisco publishing, (1985, 1969,1914)

Page 41 From Milo Rigaud's book, "Secrets of Voodoo"
Beginning Voodoo ritual Chant

Come together, family, en e o;	La Fanmi semble'; en e' o
Come together, now, family;	la Fanmi semble', non;
E Agoueto, that's the call;	E Agoueto, ca hin'de;
We shall call, O;	na'pe', hin'de', o;
Come together, family, en e o;	la fanmi semble'; en e' o;
We shall call Papa Loko Atisou.	Na'pe' hin'de'PapaLoko Atisou.
Come together, family, en e o;	La Fanmi semble'; en e' o
We shall call Grande Aizan Velekete.	Na' pe'hin'de Grande Aizan Velekete.
Come together, family, en e o;	La Fanmi semble'; en e' o
Come together, now, family,	la Fanmi semble', non;
E Agoueto, Goueto, that's the call;	E Agoueto, Goueto, ca hin'de';
We shall call the Marassah Dosou,	na hin'de' Marassah Dosou,
Do-sah and Do-goueh.	Do-sah and Do-goueh.
E Agoueto! you can really call them!	E Agoueto! Ou ca hin de' you vrai!

Page 128-129 From Milo Rigaud's book, "Secrets of Voodoo"
YANVALOU

Legba-Highway, we are going	Legba-Grand-Chemin, nous pr'alle'
Ago, Ago yey	Ago, Ago ye!
Legba-Highway, we are going	Legba-Grand-Chemin, nous pr'alle'
To see if we shall pass;	oue' si n'a passe';
Legba-Highway, we are going	Legba-Grand-Chemin, nous pr'alle'
To see Papa if we shall pass	oue', Papa, si n'a passe',
If we shall pass the highway, my King!	Si n'a passe' Grand-Chemin, mon roi!
Ago! Highway, we are going	Ago! Grande-Chemin, nous pr'alle'
To see, Papa, if we shall pass.	oue, Papa, si n'a passe'.
Oh Ago! Ago yey.	Oh Ago! Ago ye!

Page 129 From Milo Rigaud's book, "Secrets of Voodoo"
YANVALOU Chant for Danbhalah and Aida Wedo

Danbhalah Wedo,	Danbhalah Wedo,
Behold your children, hey!	Gade' pitite ou yo, he!
Aida wedo, here are your children, hey!	Aida Wedo, min pitites ou yo, he'!
Danbhalah Wedo,	Danbhalah Wedo,
Behold your children, oh!	Gade' pitites ou yo oh!
A yey, a yey, oh!	A yey, a yey, oh!
Danbhalah, here are your children.	Danbhalah, min L'Enfants ou la.

page 130 From Milo Rigaud's book, "Secrets of Voodoo"
MAHI Chant for Erzulie Freda

It is luck, oh! O, it is Luck, oh!	Ce' chance oh! O, ce' chance oh!
It is not a magick charm that you have;	Ce' pas wanga ou gangnin;
It is Luck, Oh!	Ce' chance oh!
Grande Erzulie Freda,	Grande Erzulie Freda
It is luck that you have.	Ce' chance ou gangnin.
It is not a magick charm that you have;	Ce' pas wanga ou gangnin;
It is luck, O Mistress	Ce' chance, O Maitresse.

ENDINGS and DEVOKING

The ensemble of the lwas...	Ye-Ke
Peace be unto you!	Mar-Ch-Allah!
Withdraw into the Light...	Ku m Bha-Lah Dya

ERZULIE - GROVE GODDESS GATHERING CHANTS

*GODDESS CHANT
Isis, Astarte, Diana, Hecate, Demeter, Kali, Inanna.... *By: Deena Metzger & Caitlin Mullin*

*THE RIVER IS FLOWING
The River is Flowing
flowing and growing
The river is flowing
Down to the Sea
Mother carry me
A child I will always be
Mother carry me
Down to the Sea. (*Hold & Repeat*)
Down to the Sea (repeats...) *By: Diana Hildebrand Hull*

*MOTHER I FEEL YOU UNDER MY FEET
Mother I feel you under my feet, Mother I feel your Heart Beat 2X
Heya Heya Heya, Heya Heya Ho 2X
Mother I hear you in the Rivers Sound, Eternal Waters going on and on 2X
Heya heya heya heya heya ho 2X
Mother I see you in when the Eagles fly, Flight of the Spirit gonna take our time 2X
Heya Heya Heya, Heya Heya Ho ......By; Unknown source

I AM MAGICK WOMAN (?) Shelley Graff
I am Magick /Sacred Woman, Giving Birth to myself
I am Magick /Sacred Woman
Giving Birth to myself
from deep inside the wells,
From your loving eyes and wisdom
My truth that I must tell,
I am Magick /Sacred Woman
Giving Birth to myself....

***THE OCEAN IS THE BEGINNING
The Ocean is the beginning of the Earth (2x)
All Life comes from the Sea
All Life comes from the Sea....
    The Sun is a reflection of her Light (2x)
    All thing grow with her love.
    All things grow with her love...
The mirror is a reflection of our heart (2X)
    See the Goddess rest in us. See the *Goddess rest in us.*
(Texts embellished by B.M.M) By Delaney Johnson, Starhawk Reclaiming Collective

DON'T YOU KNOW
Don't you know
Your body is a temple,
And don't you know ,your spirit is a shine,
The other side of fear is a never ending love
Don't you know you and I are both divine
    You won't know what it means to really grow
    If you don't open up, to who's inside
    The other side of fear is a never ending love
    Don't you know you and I are both divine
And I lift up my glass and drink a toast
To all the women in me, I hold them so close
The other side of fear is a never ending love
Don't you know you and I are both divine
    I'm Part Princess, Part Witch, Part Goddess,
    Part Bitch, Part Spirit and
    I am Divine....
The other side of fear is a never ending love
Don't you know you and I are both divine
You and I, are both Divine ....by Elaine Silver

*ELEMENTAL SONG
The Earth, The Air, The Fire, The Water, Return, Return, Return
Below, Above , the Center is Love, Return, Return, Return...*By; Robin Rose Benne, Origins unknown*

CHAPTER SEVENTEEN

"When I dare to be powerful, to use my strength in the service of my vision, then it becomes less and less important whether I am afraid..." Aundre Lorde

"When you live your life with an appreciation for coincidences and their meanings, you connect with the underlying field of infinite.." Deepak Chopra

WELCOME GAIA

OUR ALTAR

Altar cloth: Brown, rust or green altar cloth with leaves or flower pattern.
Image: Statue of Mother Earth Bountiful Goddes
Canvas art or photo of Gaia and or photos of Greece, the Parthenon, the Globe, the Earth, flowers blooming, large fertile fields and the Earth's beautiful landscape. Round Pregnant Mamas, Mother's with their children, Wild Animals, also with their offspring.

Always present on the altar;
A cast iron cauldron, drums, speaking stick, a silver pentacle, athame, elemental representations.....

Air: bird statuaries, smudge wands, Incense type sticks, cones, charcoal brisket and fine powdered herbs like Angelica, Hawthorn, Mistletoe, Patchouli, Vervain, Yarrow. Crush and burn these herbs, allowing their smoke to be your Eastern representation.
Fire: candles, glass enclosed candles or pillars in greens and browns, women shaped, vagina shaped candles work.
Water: Chalice or small glass bowl with Water or red wine or Retsina.
Earth: For this altar it is best to have many green lush lively Plants and flowers. You may also offer a small dish of soil and or herbs, like the ones mentioned above, to stand as your Northern representation. Photos or actual statuaries of animals also work best.

Other items pertinent to this particular gathering
Our personal creative work offerings
Glass bowl of Soil
Plants and herbs, grass, potted trees
Green plackets and coins
Rocks, Crystals and colorful gemstones
An abundance of Snakes, they can be toy rubber snakes
Figurines of various animals they can be toys as well
A globe or map of our Earth
Pregnant figurines clay or other
Plate offering with lots of fruits, vegetables and rich foods
Writing pens and paper, safety pins,
Light green gauzy fabric to represent fertile earth
Workshop items
Tarot "The Empress" and "The Queen of Pentacles"

Offering example foods; fruits and vegetables grown from the earth, fresh homemade breads
Sacred objects from members:
Notes:

Gaia

GAIA

The name of this chthonic Greek Goddess is a compound word. The first part of her name, "Ge" means land or Earth, in pre-Greek substrate, while the second half, "Aia" refers to, grandmother, and has origins in the Indo-European language.

Primordial Goddess of the Earth, Gaia is maternal archetype, who was the personification of the Earth itself. Gaia whose powers created all living creature and beings on this planet, the sea and the sky. Gaia who was from the beginning, before the existence of Time, for Time was an actual child of hers. She was born from the dark, formlessness of Chaos and wasted no time in producing numerous beings on the Earth. Ancient Greek Goddess Gaia, whose origins and worship has been absorbed by numerous cultures and probably originated from Attica. Even today, Pagans and Non-Pagans alike see the Earth, and all of its intricacies, as Gaia herself, still breathing and living today, thousands of years later.

Gaia Theory and Gaia Hypothesis was documented in 1976 by James Lovelock. Here the Earth's living, producing, self-regulating system, is seen as Gaia herself, a living tangible Goddess. On April 22nd we celebrate "Her" via Earth day, which has become her modern day holiday, as we honor the Earth and concern ourselves with its survival and wellbeing.

According to Hesiod's Theogony, in the beginning was dark, formless, open, vast space known as Chaos. There was also desire, known as Eros. From the union between Chaos and Eros our beloved Gaia was born. One can view this delicate beginning described by Hesiod as very similar to the beginning of all life. The vast, dark, empty womb, mysterious and yet so full of potential, un-manifested until Desire comes into play. The joining of the two gives birth to our Primordial Mother Earth and from her all living creatures proceed.

According to the Greek myths, after Gaia manifested herself, she gave birth to her son, Uranus, who soon became her consort. With him, but also via parthenogenesis, she produced a multitude of beings, some monstrous and some Gods and Goddesses and not all anthropomorphic. She gave birth to Nymphs, the Sea, the Sun, Themis, Phoebe, the Cyclopes, One eye giants, Multi headed creatures, Memory (who would birth the Muses), Time, Cronos (who would later birth Zeus) and a multitude more. Her awe striking powers of fertility, procreation and abundance were evident in her ability and desire to populate the grand universe. Unquestionably, She is the raw power of fertility and creation- multiplying herself with and without a partner.

Uranus, as her son and lover, became very jealous, scared and angered at Gaia's obvious powers of creation- birthing and multiplying as continuously as she did. I suppose bearing witness to all those magnificent and monstrous creatures was probably quite intimidating for Uranus. Cunningly and with alterior motives, he noted her birth canal and decide he would block her sacred passageway, with his own genitals, to prevent any more monstrous offsprings' from being born. Daily, Uranus would enter Gaia, causing her much pain and blocking the birth of any further creations from being born. As can be expected, her womb, which served to procreate, grew and grew and expanded with each creation she manifested and retained, inside of her. Her fertile womb continued to grow and expand, holding in all of her multitude of creations. With her blocked passageway she keeps them inside, a painful, selfless act to protect them, but eventually she knew she had to devise a plan.

According to one myth, she crafted and constructed a sickle which was to be used specifically on Uranus himself. She called upon her first born, Cronos, and enlisted his help to end her agonizing pain by castrating his very own father. Carefully, Cronos followed his mother's detailed instructions. Upon approaching his father, he held the sickle and chopped off his father's genitals, tossing them into the Sea. From this act, his severed penis brought forth the sea foam Goddess of Love-Aphrodite. It also put an end to Gaia's labor and safely, she was able to release all of her contained children from her crowded womb. She became the grandmother of the first generation of Gods and Goddesses, and in her, we can see that we too are direct descendants of her lineage and intimately connected to this ancient deity. She is indeed our benevolent immortal, Mother Earth, who has garnered great respect and reverence through-out the ages by all.

Gaia is seen as the Goddess of creation, abundance, multiplicity and fertility. In her ability to create numerous children with and without partnership, we see her autonomy and her wholeness. We can tap into any one of her numerous Goddess gifts but also, we can call upon her as our Great grandmother to guide and protect us, as she's been known to do, for her beloved children of the Earth. She is a living, breathing relevant Goddess that was, is and ever shall be, long after we are gone.
Blessed Gaia, Hail to you Earth Mother!!!!

GAIA GROVE GODDESS GATHERING

Purpose: To connect with Mother Earth, Gaia and her powers of fertility, abundance, proliferation and creativity.

Check ins: With our Grove speaking stick in hand, one by one, we go around the circle to introduce ourselves and share one thing that we have mothered, nurtured and grown recently.

Chanting: *"Gaia Song", "The Earth is a woman..."* and *"She gathers her Daughters"* and *"There is healing in the Earth"* (see song sheet).

Drumming Circle: Participants are encourage to pick up a percussion instrument from the musical basket offering. We will separate, spreading out across the sanctuary and listen closely to one another as we slowly begin to raise the cone of power. One by one we will add our sounds of maracas, tambourines, bells, drums etc...and now slowly walk towards the center -meeting place- while all along listening to our systers drumming and contributing our own sounds to the sacred Earth. It is a walking drumming circle and it is an effective form of shamanic work. When we reach the center, we now add our voices, dropping the instruments, and replacing them with our own fertile, strong voices. Our heads ringing in this act, as the cone of power has been raised.

Check Ins: Sharing our thoughts. How do we personally view Gaia? There are numerous views on this ancient Deity and as a result everyone has their own personal perspective. In this special moment, we want to invoke her, in ALL of her guises, respecting and honoring everyone's view.

LECTURE ON THE GODDESS, GAIA
her attributes, myths and relevance for modern Goddess wommin.

GODESS WORKSHOPS
WORKSHOP I: Crystal therapy and studies of **Gemstone** properties. These gemstone treasures are found and grown by Mother Earth herself and it is only appropriate to study them now in relation to her. Handouts will be given (see Appendix) and samples will be made available, so that wommin can connect and experiment, feeling the various attributes from each stone. We will learn how to cleanse, charge and utilize these treasure in our magick making and healing practices.

WORKSHOP II: Plant Magick and mini indoor **herb garden**. Outdoors the weather might not be conducive to growing much , but that shouldn't stop you from creating and tending to your own inner herb garden. We will set up mini clay pots, with soil and plant some common herbs to begin an indoor witch garden. Some of the most popular herbs that we may grow are rosemary, thyme, lavender and sage.

WORKSHOP III: **Fertility Spell** workings. Fertility does not only related to biological birthing of our children, but also includes our creative works, for they too, require us to birth them and give them life. In this workshop we will discuss some ways to promote our own fertility -whether biological or creatively. Exploring Fertlity Spells.

WORKSHOP IV: The **tarot** card of "The Queen of Pentacles" or "The Empress" will be passed around the room so that participants may reflect on this card, its attributes and meaning, and how it may relate to a personified, Goddess like Gaia.

WORKSHOP V: Putting our mortar and pestle to good use. exploring **herbal use** in craft workings like; in poppets, plackets, and most commonly in handmade incense creations. Experimenting with various dry herbs and creating herbal incenses for our charcoal briskets.

WORKSHOP VI: Magick with our Animals and our Familiars. Discussing our beloved pets (Familiars and Totems), how they come into our lives and unearthing the various ways they are endeavoring to help us in our spiritual journeys. What are our animals teaching us? And are we receptive to their lessons for us? We will explore *"Animal Magick"* by D.J. Conway and utilze, Steven D. Farmer's, *"Messages from your Animal Spirit Guides, Oracle Cards"* for further insight into our **Totem animals**.

Discussion of our upcoming prosperity ritual to Gaia, to follow

REFLECTIONS ON GAIA
Gaia is a wonderful Goddess for ancient, as well as modern day wommin, to tap into their inherent fertile capabilities. She brings to us proliferation and the ability to birth numerous creations in our lives. She reminds us that as wommin, we do have this gift to multiply and procreate. She begs you to embrace the same Creatrix capacities she beholds, after all, she is your Earth Mother, great grandmother, and the apple doesn't fall far from the tree. You do share the same genetic make up. We are the daughters of the Earth, with the inherent abilities, as witches, to manifest that which we will. From child birthing to the birthing of a creative projects, she brings to our realm, proliferation, and teaches the value of our own fertility, as it extends into numerous areas in our lives.

GAIA GROVE GODDESS GATHERING RITUAL

Purpose: Inviting Gaia and her gifts of proliferation, creativity, prosperity and abundance.
Altar: Set up altar ahead of time as participants will need to have their herbs and special items ready and accessible. An image of Gaia, whether a sculpture or a Canvas art, should be prominently displayed, along with many plants. See description at start of chapter for more altar ideas.

Purifying and anointing: With a smudge of Copal and Sage, Participants are invited to enter the Ritual space. Priestess will anoint each womyn with a Blessing oil (see appendix) as she is lovingly welcomed inside the sanctuary.

CASTING
Circle is Cast with a Clear Crystal wand and words....

From East to West this circle is Cast,
Below, above, only good can pass.
I call upon good spirits and Gods,
To shield this circle and be our Guard.

QUARTERS CALLED
Earth my body, Water my blood,
Air my breath, and Fire my spirit... (sung/spoken)

Corresponding colored candles will be lit for each Quarter invoked and an Elemental representation preferably animal figurines; fish, eagle, lion, bear, snake, etc... These will be passed around the circle so that participants can personally connect with each of the sacred Elements, as we sing...

Intent spoken: Priestess will declare aloud our intention for the ritual.
"We are seeking to honor Gaia and also to tap into the powers of Prosperity and blessings of abundance in our lives through this Sacred rite"
Chant: *"She gathers her daughters"*

INVOKING The GODDESS, GAIA,
with prose or Orphic Hymns

Chant: *"Mother I feel you under my feet....."*

***Each participant was asked ahead of time to please bring one item from the list of Prosperity items and herbs.... They can acquire herbs from herbal shops, their grocery store, their gardens even tea bags. The important thing here is that the item comes from their hands and represents their energy and efforts in manifesting this prosperity communal working for all.

CREATION OF A PROSPERITY HERBAL PLACKET OF GREEN SPELL INGREDIENTS:

Ginger, Chamomile, Cinnamon and Cinnamon stick,
Patchouli, Hyssop, Other herbs....
Prosperity Oil
3X Dimes
Shredded Dollar bill
Gold and silver fairy dust
Green felt placket square
with gold/yellow thread........
Our personal spell wish written on slip of paper.......

Each Syster will come forward to the altar, where the large cauldron sits, and they will place their herb/item inside, grind it with the mortar and pestle and place inside the womb of the Goddess, the cauldron, while saying:

I enchant and add this sacred herb/item of (_____)
May it be blessed and be used for my intended purpose.....

***When all have finished adding their herbs we psychically cook it and enchant it with our energy and songs. *Dance, raise energy now for those herbs, singing;* **CHANT:** *"Gaia Song"*

Afterwards, back to our place in the circle (catch our breath) for a moment of silence, as we reflect on prosperity and what it means to us personally. With music playing in the background we will have a chance to consider what prosperity means to us personally. On a small slip of paper, which will be added inside the placket, write exactly what this Green Herbal placket will manifest for you personally. Green felt square placket will have already three sides pre-sewn and offered to the wommin....

Together wommin will gather around the Cauldron and one by one they take a small scoop of the communal herb prosperity mixture, whilst reading their slip of enchanted paper and declaring what they hope to manifest....

THE SPELL: *With this placket of Green I manifest (for example) "money"_____, So mote it be!***

When all have finished, together as a group, we will hand sew/close and seal the last side of the green plackets, whilst still visualizing how abundance and prosperity will appears. Say aloud as we stitch, what we envision and manifest through this act of magick. For example say aloud; *"... I see bills paid, I see lots of money overflowing, I see my wallet with lots of "Benjamins"/cash, I see a well- stocked pantry, refrigerators filled with food, I see new employment, I see children well fed and clothes, I see feasting and celebrations, I see many of us happy and blessed with more money than we can count.... Etc..."* Weave and stitch as we hold that vision in our mind's eye. We'll continue raising energy, chanting aloud our vision and saying positive affirmations as the spell is manifesting.

To seal the energy sing Closing Chant:
*"Earth, Air, Fire, Water, I am the Witches daughter,
Gaia is me, and I am She...."*

Final Check in before Devoking...
Prepare to Thank and Devoke the Goddess
Divine Mother, nurturer, protector,
your sustenance felt throughout our rites.
When called, you came and blessed us with your gifts.
Though we hope to remain forever in your embrace,
The time has arrived when we must depart this place.
Most Holy one, receive our gratitude
As we bid you, Dear Godess, adieu. adieu, adieu...
Hail and Farewell Gaia!

Thanking and Devoking Quarters & energy,
Thank you **Earth,** the Mother, the sustainer, fertile transformer,
With gratitude for guarding our sacred space, we bid you adieu.
As Ye arrived in peace, Depart in peace, Hail and Farewell Earth....

Thank you **Water,** the realm of our emotions and the Moon,
With gratitude for guarding our sacred space, we bid you adieu.
As Ye arrived in peace, Depart in peace, Hail and Farewell Water....

Thank you **Fire,** the realm of our inner flames, ambition and desire,
With gratitude for guarding our sacred space, we bid you adieu.
As Ye arrived in peace, Depart in peace, Hail and Farewell Fire....

Thank you **Air,** where we always begin ALL creative rites,
in our visions, intellect, new hope, and our receptive minds,
With gratitude for guarding our sacred space, we bid you adieu.
As Ye arrived in peace, Depart in peace, Hail and Farewell Air....

Opening the Circle with song, *"The circle is open, but unbroken, may the peace of the Goddess be ever in our hearts..Merry meet and merry part and merry meet again."*)O(

Cakes and Ale, Potluck feasting

Orphic Hymn to Gaia,
as translated and interpreted by Virginia Stewart, M.Ed

Oh Goddess,
Source of Gods and Mortals,
All-Fertile,
All Destroying Gaia,
Mother of All,
Who brings forth,
the bounteous fruits and flowers,
All variety, Maiden,
who anchors the eternal world in our own,
Immortal, Blessed,
Crowned with every grace,
Deep bosomed Earth,
sweet plains and fields,
fragrant grasses in the nurturing rains,
Around you fly the beauteous stars,
eternal and divine,
Come, Blessed Goddess,
And hear the prayers of your Children.
And make the increase of the fruits and grains
your constant care,
with the fertile seasons
Your handmaidens, draw near
and bless your supplicants.... *Trans & Int by Virginia Stewart, .Ed. M.*

This poem resulted after a transformative visit and communion in a nearby earth caverns and an intense connection and meditation with Gaia.....This poem may be used as an invocation to Gaia....

A LIVING GODDESS

Living breathing shifting Goddess
Quaking, bursting flowing with life
You who was since time began,
live today in all the land.
Look across this wide landscape,
See you in tree roots, water and caves.

See you in mountains
and continents and new formed lands,
see you birthing, creating
With immortal hands.

See you exploding in volcanoes,
and rustling in the breeze
How can anyone deny
your sacred energy?

In the animals; wild and tamed
In our food source you are contained
In every seed and living tree,
You are the pulse in everything.

We are conceived in reflections of you
Held by the threads of ancestral spool
You are the womb that holds us at birth
Nourish our souls and bodies on this Earth

Living now as in ancient times
How can anyone not see Earth Mother Divine?
You shift and expand and continue to grow
Your powers un-weakened by those who just don't know.

Feel her sighs, feel her breath
Feel her hold your earthly form,
Feel her trembles and her strength
as with seasons she Transforms.

Holder of life, of seeds, of bones
From you we emerged to make our temples and homes
Not dead on a cross, but present and alive
know her in **your** body, feel her from inside.

Believer in truths, secure in her powers,
she'll even allow you to worship whom you desire,
But know without question whom she truly is
For you'll meet her in the beginning as you will in the end

She is your Mother, divine, the Earth
Living Goddess who has sustained you since birth
Requiring nothing but your love and respect
Hail to Gaia,
Hail and Goddess Bless.........

I woke up one morning singing these words and it was during a time that I was working with the mother archetype. As someone who lost her mother at an early age, this is how Gaia Called me...

TRAVELS TO HER

***Motherless child
You've shed enough tears
Take your first step now,
And approach me dear.

Motherless child
Step into my arms
I am the shelter
to remove all harm

Motherless child
Hold what you feel
I am the love
that will mend and heal

Motherless child
Step into me
I am the circle
that will set you free

Motherless child
open your eyes
Here in my arms
Divine mother you'll find.

Motherless child
Come follow me
I am the warmth
that the child needs

Motherless Child
You are no more
Here in my bossom
I am eternally yours....

This poem manifested itself, one night, after a ritual in which the wheel of the year was embodied by Sabbat Priestesses. Each womyn embodied a sabbat and presented it to me, as I visited with each, while traveling down the spiral. It was very moving and I found myself connecting with the element of Fire through-out the entire time. In parentheses I have noted which sabbat is being referred to. This would also work as a solitary ritual, if you use something that represents each of the eight sabbats in the wheel or Goddess statues/images, to represent the different stops on the wheel of the year. It is a wonderful way to connect with the seasons of the year and inspire you to project and think ahead.

THE WHEEL OF THE YEAR

(Imbolc)   Fires, Quietly observe,
sensing which way to turn,
(Ostara)   Springing forth sparks
revealing what I yearn.

(Beltane)   Fires from my Yoni,
wanting to explode.
(Litha)   Fires from my heart,
which seems to always know.

(Lammas)   Giving birth, Giving life,
Fruition at last.
(Mabon)   Fires from my mind,
goes hand in hand.

(Samhain)   Those that walked before me,
Now next to me, Beside me,
Fires from their Souls,
I feel on Our journey

(Solstice)   And I travel further,
into the Spiral of Time,
To face the mirror,
which blurs the lines,

Between the now and tomorrow
I've yet to see.....
The now and tomorrow
I am manifesting,

Tomorrow is celebrated
Right here,
Right now,
In Sacred spaces,
as We circle around...

Personification of Gaia

Here is an Ancient Goddess beloved by Pagans and Non-Pagans alike. A living Goddess who is loved and seen in so many different distinct ways. Some view her as the Earth itself, some view her as the Universe, the cosmos and the far beyond. Some view her as the elements; Earth, Air, Fire and Water, all in one. Some view her as the quintessential image of motherhood -the always fertile, pregnant mother, life giver. Some view her as the infamous image of the Venus of Willendorf sculpture. Some view her an ancient spirit and some, as simply an energy present today, as it has always been. In this article I will personify Gaia for this is simply one of the ways she comes to me personally.

Reading the ancient Greek myths of the her time and learning of how she manifested, I began to see elements of Gaia and her mythos that resonated deeply with me now and some aspects of her that I find many womyn, in today's modern society, can identify with. As always I have a penchant for taking ancient Goddesses and feminine archetypes and relating them to our present day lives.

One of the most notable aspects of Gaia that draws me to her is her gifts of creation, multiplicity, abundance and wholeness. She appears as autonomous, procreating with and without a partner and effortlessly birthing life -almost exclusively dedicated to bringing forth her creations. This creation is not relegated nor restricted to just birthing infants, for Gaia created many wonders - from Goddesses and Gods, humans, ghastly monsters, time, nature etc, the list goes on.... This is a Goddess that, we as womyn, can call upon when we are endeavoring to birth anything that comes from the depths of our souls.

Her very nature is to grow, produce, multiply, create and yet, when Uranus, her son and consort, became bewildered, jealous and horrified, witnessing her astounding abilities, he was immediately compelled to put an end to it. As the myth goes, nightly, Uranus penetrated her, to obstruct her sacred birth passageway, but this did not put an end to her very nature. She continued to procreate, expand and nurse within her growing womb all her creations, because **that is** her very nature. Imagine the pain and discomfort of not being able to release your creations. Imagine the back log of all these little precious beings coming to life in the dark abyss of Gaia's sacred fertile womb - crowded -pressuring her insides, needing to be expelled out into the world. Imagine the pain of labor never finding the relief that birthing to light brings and yet, she needed to do this in order to protect her offspring. Her precious creations were at risk of being destroyed, if brought to light and so, she held them in her dark womb, for as long as she could, until finally the pain was too much to bear. According to the ancient myths, She constructed a sickle and asked her son Cronos to intercede and cut off that which was obstructing her ability to bring forth her creations. He did as was instructed and a myriad of creatures were thus born and unleashed and Gaia's gifts restored to the world.

Uranus and his need to "*squash*", dominate and destroy that which makes him feel inferior, scared and that which overwhelms him, is a symbol continually seen throughout history. In researching Gaia through her stories and myths, they seem to ignite, for me, a recollections of a distant, but relevant personal history. I reflect back on the Medieval Witch craze that began in the 1200 in Europe, but continued hundreds of years later across the new land, in Salem, Massachusetts, with the apparent sole intention of targeting and eradicating womyn who were **just being**...like Gaia...**just being**. Unjust accusations, excruciating, experimental tortures, thousands of wommin persecuted, destroyed and killed for the sake of the church and state, according to the oppressors- the Uranus of the time.

I think about Ancient matriarchal societies, wommin living, perhaps, peacefully, among themselves, harmoniously thriving and civilized. Wommin tapping into their powers....like Gaia, **just being**, whole unto themselves... and lo... how something outside of them...fearful, intimidated and wretched with violence, came to be that Uranus. Men feeling bewildered, inferior, emasculated, no longer wanting to rule with, but rather rule **over**. Now fueling patriarchy with violence, rapes, killings, and the cruel destruction of matriarchy and wommin-Goddess wommin. Patriarchy....a curse we still struggle with as modern wommin in the 21st century.....

I think about the Rise of Feminism even before the pivotal 1970's. I think of the struggles of every womyn, as she tries to free herself and unearth, and embrace and give birth to her deeply embedded ancient powers, even amidst oppressors and less than ideal circumstances.

The collection of Gaia mythos, and her tales with Uranus are timeless and as womyn, there is much we can reflect on. For me, the symbolisms in this myth are astounding, for how often, we as womyn in our most natural elements are not able to shine due to some extraneous situation or some imposed law brought about to oppress, manipulate or regulate our Goddess given gifts. And how often fear of destroying even our most fragile of creative ideas, keeps us from bringing them to light. We hide our talents, our dreams, our creations. We hide our endless potential for fear that they'll be destroyed even before having a chance to take in that first breath of life...like Gaia, we guarantee their safety by maintaining them stifled, hidden in our dark caverns. And yet, it is all still within us, still expanding, scratching at our insides begging to be unleashed. Can we see that Gaia runs parallel to us and our Goddess given gifts? For as descendants of Gaia our very nature **too**, is to create and if we look closer we can see that all those creations, regardless of extraneous circumstances, are still nursing within our dark fertile wombs, pressing up against our insides, maybe making it painful to deny, begging to be born and released unto the world.

Gaia is proliferation, autonomous being, abundance, multiplicity, and thus perfect to call upon when you are seeking to manifest abundance and a myriad of projects or creations. She is the very essence of fertility and reproduction and thus, quite obviously, perfect to call upon for any type of fertility workings, be they actual human babies or creative babies, like ideas we wish to birth to life. Gaia offers numerous ways to work with her energies in spell works and rituals. Ultimately though, She is that which holds us when we are born and supports us as we walk onward on her fertile Earthly realm. She is our ancient mother and has much to teach us, if we just quiet down enough to hear her exemplary tales, in the rocks, the soil, in her waters, the stars, the trees, the mountains and deep in the earth's caverns. For in all of nature she can be seen and heard, but her voice stands more powerfully when we hear it stirring, unquestionably, from within the depths of our very own souls. Blessed be!

Tapping into the Mother Archetype,
A Journal entry at the Harvest

Funny, back in December I remember now, how I sat among my systers in our sacred space and I contemplate on who and what I would dedicate myself to in the upcoming new year. The theme for our Goddess gathering that month was "our personal deities and renewed dedications." I remember sharing with my systers a recent dream I had of the Ocean mother Goddess, Yemaja and how, although all along I was strictly devoted to the maiden, virginal archetype, her appearance in my dream made it clear that the tides were bringing in something new and necessary. It appeared to me that the time had come when the Mother archetype would surface, making herself known to me in every way. Believing that all three powerful archetypes exist in every womyn, it seemed that up till then, I favored Artemis and Athena, even after marriage and giving birth to three boys. I was still genuinely committed to nurturing and sustaining the young maiden within myself...never wanting to lose myself to motherhood and refusing to play into the stereotypical role of sacrificial mother. But, lo and behold..... how the tides were quietly stirring and shifting within me , changing its course, sculpting me into an archetype I had long feared would swallow me whole. Here I found myself finally heeding the call, finally listening to her messages in numerous dreams and unable to escape the role she was placing before me to fulfill.

As we approach the sabbat of Lammas, the season of the First Harvest, I am compelled to examine the last few months and with awe and astounding amazement, I see how the Goddess indeed is alive and working her wonders. For at the last Winter Solstice, I had dedicated myself to slowly surrendering my virgin archetype goddesses, to slowly open myself up to the creatrix, the nurturer, the Mother Goddess.

This past year has placed me in a most auspicious position, as it has found me in the role of fertile "creatress," nurturer, teacher, caretaker, life giver, producer. Birthing new lives from the numerous projects running rampart, like a fertile field, in my soul.

On this Lammas, I examine my life and see how this was the year I truly tapped into the Mother. Although I have had my children for the past nine years now, this is the first year that I have felt the forge compressing and sculpting me and fully connecting to "She" who surrenders herself gladly for her creations.

A mother to my Group-Grove of the Feminine Divine- and all the blessed wommin attending our temple. This has been our first whole year together and indeed it has forged and anchored the mother archetype in me.

A mother to my numerous dogs and namely to Roxy, who just entered motherhood herself, by giving birth to six puppies. The mother energy I have experienced in the midst of caring for these tiny newborn, helpless pups and my bitch, has been astronomically intense and sheer overwhelming.

Even my physical body is reflecting a change, as my breast have grown plumper, my once sculpted boyish physique and six pack abdomen have soften. My hips and thighs, while not "Rubennesque", have new fuller curves and unquestionably my body is reflecting the changes in my inner landscape. I have had a metamorphosis to curvaceous, sultry mama. Even the temporal predominance of sexual thoughts and explorations also seems to hint at the manifestation of the creative mother archetype. As I peruse through my journal writings this year, I see many different references to sex;

getting it, needing it, dreaming of it, being grateful of it, wanting more, exploring ways of greater satisfaction in this realm…more so, than any other time in my life, sex has demanded my attention now. The maiden in me didn't quite feel a <u>need</u> to explore this issue much (as it just was) or at least not in the same way and yet, here its been another side of "Her" outpouring, results from the mother archetype, I suspect.

Mothering myself seems to be another way she has manifested, as I delve into my very own mother's story, her life and thus my lineage. My mom died at too young of an age and I never quite had a chance to get to know her, nor know what a mother and daughter relationship entails. Through research, prayers, and very intense detail dreams, I feel like we (deceased mother and I) have been nurturing and sustaining our relationship, even if it is while we are in two vastly different realms. I am most aware of her presence now more than ever and experience periods of deep empathy for the road she traveled on and the short life she lived. I am connecting back to her and thus, I am cultivating a much needed daughter, mother relationship with her, through spirit. It's been quite cathartic to learn, via the distant memories of my mother, about my own self, as I settle myself more comfortably in this matriarchal role.

In the painful, laborious creation of this beloved book , I am writing, I have experienced all the stages of motherhood, from conception to gestation, to finally giving birth to its manifestation. The numerous art works and crafty creations I have been submerged in, these past few year, have also felt like I was birthing them from the depths of my Gaian soul… Each and every art canvas, clay sculpture, collage creation, vocal composition….each and every creative expression, giving voice to the Goddess, has (for me) been experienced like a Gaian birth of some sort. Yes, I have been Mother this year!

In my encounters with different women, I find myself needing to understand their own personal journey, for they echo my own. I sense myself softening to them, as if they were my very own daughters, unlike previous years, where I might've sensed myself more sisterly, competitive and demanding. Here I find myself wanting to nurture, guide, feed, teach, support, protect and hold all wommin and children.

Watching television, I have cried endlessly this year at the numerous sad and devastating news reports on child abductions…. My heart wretched with anger and sadness for our beloved daughter and sons of the world. How devastating that the world is plagued with such evil and our precious children, our future heirs, are in jeopardy of being nearly extinct as they continually are being kidnapped, murdered, abused and silenced. Our birth rights and liberties to walk safely and freely among our own land, as womyn, is becoming fragile for our daughters & sons and ourselves -for how easily those liberties can be threatened, destroyed, snatched up from right under our noses and eliminated. The mother in me cannot even fathom one child going through this and laments for the adverse negative effects such trauma causes to society as a whole. A Universe that does not honor or place wommin in high regards is in danger of corrupting itself, for as Z. Budapest states so lovely in her book, "The Holy Book of Women's Mysteries", *"…To deny motherhood, is to deny women and there are two kinds of people; Mothers and their children."*

I will end this journal entry my making a commitment to further travel on this Gaia journey, with confidence, tapping into the mother archetype, but also at some point, returning to somehow find a balance between the Maiden, the Queen and the Mother…something I will look to Persephone to teach me. Blessed Be!

Anniversary Celebration, Bringing in much needed Prosperity and the powers of fruition with Gaia

Despite the fact that my life in the past few weeks has been very harried and chaotic, I somehow allowed this energy to be utilize in the most productive way possible for this gathering. It was our One year anniversary and although I contemplated rescheduling it, due to challenging planetary aspects and my own personal struggles, I persevered. I thought about the womyn and how my canceling might have a negative effect on them and how sometimes we commit ourselves to doing something and despite our own fatigue and feelings of reservations, we must come forward and face the challenge, knowing full well that the Goddess uses us as she sees fit. By the end of the day I felt good, renewed and the fatigue I was feeling took on a different hue. It was fatigue with a sense of well worth accomplishment, for a test had been met and passed. I was happy with our Goddess gathering and the Gaia Prosperity Ritual truly rocked!!!

By 12:30pm all the wommin had arrived and were finally settled in. Since we were already in our usual chattinesss, I thought we could start off with one chant and then move on to our formal check ins. As usual, check ins can be pretty scary for a facilitator because, while you want to encourage every womyn to fearlessly speak her truth confidently, without care, you also must think of the group as a whole and protect its core energy. Sometimes with check ins, womyn can lose a sense of boundary and begin talking randomly, nonstop, without clear purpose as they sort through their powerful emotions and it can almost become vampiric sometimes because it sucks the energy right out of the whole group. Sadly, I had to assert myself and move one syster along. I hated doing this, but in the end, I had to make a judgment call and as I looked around the room and read faces, energies and reactions, I felt it was direly necessary to move her along. I also remember when my beloved foremother, darling Ffiona Morgan, had to do this with me and as weird as I felt, I quickly got over it, knowing she was looking at the group's best interest of time. There was a suspecting troll-y cloud, I could see it, beginning to hover over, to drain the group's energy and I couldn't just let that happen. I am glad I bravely followed my instincts and nipped it in the bud right then and there because it could've turned ugly.

When it came time for me to check in, I found myself already talking much about Gaia, which seems to be a typical occurrence. The Goddess we are presently working on becomes so imbedded in us that she permeates everything in our lives, including conversations. I find that when I am working with a Goddess I begin to see her in EVERYTHING, from the mundane to the celestial forces around me. She becomes visible, tangible, and very prevalent in all facets of my life and almost everywhere I turn, is a reflection of her. Naturally talking about her during my own personal check in, was to be expected.

We sang more songs after our check ins and then moved on to our Group Agreements. I introduced a new way to approach our drumming circle. I asked the womyn to grab a percussion instrument and from the far corners of the space we would begin to Drum and then walk, slowly journeying eventually, to the center of our circle. During this time we connect to our neighboring systers through the language of the drums (like I imagine our ancestors would do) while essentially partaking alone in our own personal spiritual quest. It was very shamanic, experimental, but extremely meditative and moving.

Afterwards we shared our various images of Gaia and slowly brought her presence into our space. We talked about her myths, her origins and symbols, best times to call upon her and how she, as a living breathing Ancient Goddess, relates to us today.

To move us into the next stage of our day, I talked a bit about the season before us and our theme of prosperity during our first harvest. I talked about Lammas and the tenets of prosperity and how gratitude is a necessary first step for us, before any prosperity ritual. With drumming CD track, rubber stamped paper and pen at hand, we started to write all of our accomplishments from December till now. From the Winter Solstice to this very moment in time, what have we accomplished? For it is time to take stock of what we have done. Like, attracts like, and **we can't even begin to think of prosperity without first thinking about gratitude**, *for somehow counting our blessings changes ones state of hopelessness and need, into abundance. From here, we moved into our Sabbat ritual.*

I asked one of the newest members to take on the role of welcoming and anointing us as we entered sacred space. She was fabulous! The chiming of my bells around the room was the sign that we would begin. When everyone was anointed and present, I immediately started us in the song; " Air I am, Fire I am, Water, Earth and Spirit I am," as the elemental representation was passed around the room. Then I asked them to gather in, closely knit, as I would cast our circle. With athame raised, I felt the blue sphere and energy swirl around us. Assisted with their gentle rattling the circle was cast. Now we would call the elements more personally into our space by making the sound we individually think that element would make. With our voices we hissed, crackled, lilted and thumped, as everyone tried to embody the elements and welcome them respectively to our circle. I had not prepared anything to say for this, but when I started to feel the surge of these elements come into our space, I felt indeed inspired to speak up. Immediately afterwards, we sang, " Mother I feel you under my feet.." This was a perfect segue to invoke Mother Earth. I stood at the altar with poetry in hand. I asked a nearby sister to also invoke her with me. Together we read our poem and brought her energy to our circle. Gaia was invoked.

We sat around the large cast iron cauldron, one by one we placed our offering into the pot while enchanting our items and herbs. We sang the "Gaia song..." with much vigor as we circled around the cauldron in true witchy style. Then we stood silent for a minute, looking over this collection of sacred offerings and all of us engaged our psyche to see what it would produce. Aloud we spoke of what we saw, the results of this magick. "....money in surplus, womyn being able to prosper and make money, jobs security, wages and promotions coming in, children having plenty to eat, Bills being paid and mortgages being paid off, money everywhere, refrigerators full, more clients to our businesses, books being written, publishers calling on us, art and creativity flourishing, end of recession, companies being born, providing more employment, money, money in surplus for luxury and need, flowers just because, travels just because we can, money in surplus that now we can openly share with others, U.S.A currency, wallets filled, bank accounts with funds...etc...etc...etc..." The energy was being intensely raised communally into new heights and this was, by far, my favorite moment of the day....together we collectively saw the need of every woman in our circle, but also in the world and how we can play a part in bringing prosperity to ourselves and womankind....

Afterwards we sat down and began to fill our green plackets. We enchanted our placket and took the time to write our wish on the accompanied parchment paper inside of it. We sang; "Do you remember when God was a woman she had many, many names....." As we passed the prosperity oil around the room to bless our plackets. One new syster very much inspired, generously shared her patchouli oil as well and our magick was set and Done!

We prepared to devoke the elements, going counter clockwise, singing an Elemental Return song. With eyes closed and feeling the energy begin to ground and wane, I thanked Gaia and all the womyn present and completed devoking by opening the circle from hand to hand. Our Merry meet song was sung three times around the room, bringing the energy up, just enough to bid adieu and then it was done!

Potluck followed afterwards and that was just lovely. Lots of talk and yummy eating and with two new members lots of chit chatting and the creation of bonds. My only disappointment of the day was seeing that the ones who this day and ritual was most catered to and meant for, were Not there. I tried not to dwell on this feeling of let down that ensued, for again, it is not about me, nor should it be about ego, but rather what the Goddess has in mind for each of us, individually, as we all have our own personal spiritual journeys to make. We all have our ownrespective journeys and while I may hope to provide something of value to these wommin, the Goddess always has her own ways to deliver her messages as she sees fit.

All Hail to the Divine spirit of Prosperity, All Hail to Mother Gaia, Blessed Be....!

GAIA GROVE GODDESS GATHERING CHANTS

The Earth is a woman: The Earth is a woman and she shall Rises. By Z. Budapest

SPIRALING INTO THE CENTER
Spiraling into the Center, The center of the wheel,
Spiraling into the Center, The center of the wheel,
We are the weavers, We are the woven ones,
We are the dreamers, We are the Dream.
We are the weavers, We are the woven ones,
We are the dreamers, We are the Dream. *(rpt) by Starhawk*

SONG FOR GAIA *by B.M.M.*
Gaia, Gaia, Gaia, Gaia (beatX , beatX)
Gaia Gaia Gaia Gaia Come to me
Gaia Gaia Gaia Gaia (beat X, beatX)
Gaia Gaia Gaia Gaia Come to me
Strength of The Mother Earth, Whole unto Me
Pulsating Earth Right under my Feet
Now I draw your energy
Grounding me,
Now I draw your energy,
Grounding me....
(I said) Gaia, Gaia, Gaia, Gaia (beatX , beatX)
Gaia Gaia Gaia Gaia Come to me
Gaia Gaia Gaia Gaia (beat X, beatX)
Gaia Gaia Gaia Gaia Come to me ,*(back to beginning -repeat in rnd)*

SHE GATHERS *By Ruth Rhiannon Barrett*
She gathers her daughters by Moon and by Sun,
She gathers her daughters it has begun.
She gathers her daughters to turn the wheel,
She gathers her daughters to learn and heal.
She gathers her daughters by night and by day,
She gathers her daughters to lead the way
(Counter Melody) *By Moon and Sun, We have Begun, To turn the wheel, to learn and heal......*

EARTH, MOON,MAGICK by *by B.M.M.*
In the Earth, deep within,
There is A Magick,
I draw it in.
    In her Caves, in the Trees
    Hear her Heartbeat,
    Pulsing thru me.
When I Rise, I feel her Love
With feet Grounded
I'm soaring high above,
    In the Earth, deep within,
    There is A Magick,
    I draw it in
Ancient Moon, my Soul reveres
With my Singing,
I call you here.
    When this flame, ignites tonight,
    Priestess dancing,
    Under the moonlit night....
In the Earth, deep within,
There is A Magick
I draw it in....
    There is A Magick, I draw it in }3x

EIGHT BEADS CHANTS *by Carolyn Hillyer*
Girlseed
Bloodflower
(dip it)Fruitmother
Spinmother,
raise it) Midwoman
Earthcrone
Stonecrone
Bone .....

HEAR ME MOTHER
by *B.M.M.*
Mother, Mother, Mother, I call you,
Deep within my soul, you' re stirring my womb.
Mother, Mother, Mother, Hear my Cries,
In this Sacred Circle I Call you tonight.
Light the inner Flame, as I light the candle wick,
Call your sacred name and embrace myself as Witch.
Sky-clad I approach, to Elemental thrones,
Hear me, Mother hear me,
Through these words I wrote.

August

On the Roman calendar when March (the first month of Spring) was considered the first month of the year, August was better known by its Latin name, *Sextilis,* meaning sixth. August then, was the sixth month in the year but by around 700BC, it became the eighth month, thanks to King Numa Pompillius. By 8BC it was given the name August in honor of Augustus Caesar, who preferred to have his name sake bestowed on this month, rather than his birth month of February.

The Fiery sign of Leo is the month's astrological sign and its symbol is the fierce king of the jungle, the Lion. This sign is ruled by the sunny, jovial showman, ring leader, the Sun (July 21-August 20) and many of these attributes, and the deities that exemplify them, are celebrated in numerous festivals this month.

Its important to note that in some parts of the world, August brings oppressive heat, lazy, hazy, days of summer. Heat so strong that it slows us down. It might appear that all we want to do is lounge around or escape the strong heat, in some air conditioned room somewhere. Much like Winter, nature, once again, shows us who is boss and forces us to slow down, just enough to make notice that these are the final days of the season of warm weather and we should relish the gifts of the earth, found in her bounty. For August is merely a pause before autumnal winds of change come through. Although outdoors we are subjected to the brightest and warmest Summer days, I often see this month as a time of preparing to bid Summer adieu, for we can begin to anticipate what is about to unfold in the coming months. The following month brings the season of Fall, a great shift in our cosmic atmosphere with the beginning of the school year for most children across America. Some students are preparing to go off to college and inaugurate a great change in their world and in August, most summer vacations are coming to a complete end. Life will return back to serious business after this month, but for now, we acknowledge the spin in the wheel of the year while lingering and enjoying the final days of Summer and honoring the bounty of the earth.

According to the Farmer's Almanac, the Full moon in August was known as Grain Moon. It was also known as Barley Moon and sometimes Corn Moon as these were, traditionally, the grains harvested during this month. Corn, rice, millet, rye, barley, oats wheat, were all commonly harvested during this season. The Native Americans would sometimes call this full moon, Green Corn Moon, in reference to the long rows of sweet corn stalk abundantly blessing the fields in August.

This is the time when the earth seems pulsating with vigor and life. It's bursting with succulent, ripe gifts and she appears in her grand role of Mother, nurturer and sustainer, as we are fed and nourish by her incredible bounty. Tomatoes ripen, rows of corn stalk grace the fields, apples (beginning to redden) abundantly grow in orchard and the Dionysian grapes, though still slightly green, begin to clusters and hang from the vines. All of nature and Mother Earth is alive, juicy and brimming with vitality. It is living, breathing via its creations, plants and animals, breeding abundantly with mouthwatering fruits and vegetables - offering her enormous bounty to her children.

Since ancient times, Grain has always been the staff of life for numerous cultures and for agrarian societies, the power of the Grain and the power of the Gods was closely interconnected. From Greece, to Egypt, to the Americas and for the Romans and the Celts alike, grain from the harvest provided sustenance for the people in various ways, most significantly the production of beer, rice, and bread. A good harvest was unquestionably imperative and assuring its fertile success was a matter of life and death for a people who lived so close to the land. Therefore various cultures from different parts of the world would offer numerous traditional rites and agricultural festivals to appease the Gods in the hopes of securing sound blessings upon their crops.

There was a common belief that harvest spirits, lived among the grain fields and performing certain rites would entreat them to bless the harvest. Sabbats and Festivals like Lughnassadh and Lammas are surviving ancient Celtic rites that were initially meant to honor the agricultural gods and beseech their continued blessings upon their crops. The Witches Sabbat of Lammas comes to us on the very first day of August and it commemorates the first harvest. The word Lammas, comes from the Anglo-Saxon word meaning "Loaf mass" and here again, reflected in its title, is the importance of the Grain.

In Ireland, the Celts celebrated the festival of Lughnassadh, which honored the ancient Sun God, Lugh and his foster mother Tailtiu. This Celtic God resembles the Greek Sun God, Apollo, as both were considered powerful Solar deities, patron gods of beauty, prophesies, medicine, music and the arts. Interesting to note, these are the fiery qualities found in the astrological sign of Leo which rules the month of August. In some parts of the Americas today, farmers have Harvest dances where a Harvest Queen is appointed, and music, eating, merriment and various fun competitions are incorporated in the festivities. They also hold county fairs, both of which resemble some of the earlier Pagan practices of our ancestors.

Grain has always been closely linked with the gifts of the Gods. Inherent in them is the sacred cycle of life, death and rebirth and the theme of sacrifice and gratitude. Every culture, from antiquity to our modern day, recognized the importance of the first harvest at this time of year, as it would determine the kind of livelihood we would face in the coming winter.

This month we remember the Greek Matriarchal Goddess of the Grain, Demeter, to help us connect with the energy of the first harvest and find acceptance of the initial subtle changes of the season. We will also honor our role as daughter to our Mothers with the Maiden Goddess Kore-Persephone, who teaches us the art of balancing our maiden selves with our numerous other titles and roles as wommin.

CHAPTER EIGHTEEN

"Giving up doesn't always mean that you are weak, sometimes it means that you are strong enough to let go..." anonymous

"The real religion of the World comes from women much more than from men- from Mothers, most of all, who carry the key of our souls in their bossoms..." Oliver Wendell Holmes

WELCOME DEMETER

OUR ALTAR

Altar cloth: Orange, golden saffron colored altar cloth and maybe a second brown altar cloth underneath.
Image: Statue of this Greek Matron Goddess, Corn husk is also appropriate to display, Canvas art or photo of the Grain Goddess and or photos of Greece, Parthenon, corn fields, also images of fields, mothers and daughters.

Always present on the altar;
A cast iron cauldron, drums, speaking stick, a silver pentacle, athame, elemental representations.....

Air: Smudge wands, Incense type sticks, cones, charcoal brisket and fine powdered herbs, barley, large sweeping feather, or a simple bell.
Fire: candles, glass enclosed candles or pillars in yellows, oranges, browns.
Water: Chalice or small glass bowl with Fresh Spring Water or Red wine.
Earth: Pots of greenery in plants and colorful flowers, a small dish of soil and or herbs. A bowl of fruits and vegetables like corn husks, tomatoes, potatoes, apples and peaches are all appropriate to display.

Other items pertinent to this particular gathering
Plate offering of Corn husk
Plate of Barley
Flowers with plants and greenery
Gemstone
Writing pens and paper, safety pins,
Light gauzy fabric
Workshop items
Tarot- "The Empress"

Offering example of Greek Culinary; Orzo, feta cheeses, Spanikopitas, pita, Barley, Corn Bread, sweet baklava etc..
Sacred objects from members:
Notes:

Demeter & Kore

Grain Mothers Altar

Demeter & Kore's Altar

DEMETER

Demeter is the Greek Goddess of the Grain, also known as Deo and Chloe. Her Roman counterpart was Ceres. She was the most generous of the Greek Goddesses, representing the bounty of the fertile Earth. She was depicted as warm, altruistic and beautiful, with long luscious golden hair. Wearing a blue robe, wherever she was present, there was divine light and growing crops sprouting abundantly by her feet. Often seen as very matronly in a seated position, her presence brought celestial lights and a most wonderful fragrance, according to the writings of her time. She was responsible for the fruitfulness of nature and the fertility of the Earth. Her gifts to humanity were the harvest and agriculture. Interesting to note, the last part of her name, "meter", translates as Mother, revealing her other significant role as a Maternal Deity. She was a mother Goddess, with a most emblematic role as Persephone's mother.

Demeter was the granddaughter of Uranus and the primordial Earth Goddess - Gaia. She was the second daughter of the Goddess Rhea and the God Cronos. Rhea was mother of the first generation of Olympians and thus she was also mother to Hades (God of the Underworld and Maiden abductor) and Zeus (Husband and Father to Persephone). According to mythology, Demeter's father swallowed up his children and as the second child to her mother, she too was swallowed, then later released and saved by her sibling.

According to Greek mythology, Demeter married her brother, Zeus, and became his fourth wife before Hera, who was ultimately wife number seven, and the last of Zeus' wives. Her union with Zeus produced their only child, the beautiful maiden, Persephone, also known as Kore. One day Persephone and her maiden friends were out picking flowers. Attracted by a beautiful Narcissus flower, the young girl reached out her arms to pick it and it was then that Hades, God of the underworld, abducted the beautiful Maiden. According to one legend, he opened up the Earth and snatched her up and only two Deities heard her cry; Hekate and Helios. As the myth reveals, for nine days and nine nights, the once brilliant, benevolent Goddess Demeter, now roamed the Earth, sadly searching endlessly for her daughter. It was on the tenth day that Hekate, Goddess of the Crossroads, finally came to Demeter and told her she had indeed heard Persephone's cries and the sympathetic Crone now tried to help and console the despondent Goddess.

Upon hearing that Hades had abducted her daughter to become his unwilling bride and that Zeus, sanctioned this horrid act, she was angered and infuriated. To add insult to injury, Demeter (who at times, appeared to exist solely for her daughter) was made to feel as if she had no power over this situation and was suppose to simply accept the abduction and disappearance of her beloved child. Demeter was beyond grief and anger and would not accept this fate. Betrayed and full of grief, she withdrew her divine gifts from the Earth and left Mount Olympus. Inconsolable and terribly distraught, she wandered the Earth, in a stuporous haze of sadness and misery, as if her very soul had been stripped and her inner divine light snuffed completely. Disguised as a very old lady, in dark veils, concealing any hint of her previous Divine golden essence, she traveled through-out the cities and countryside and then came upon the city of Eleusis.

According to the Homeric Hymn, the despondently dark, unrecognizable Demeter found herself sitting by a well, on the outskirts of the city, when four bright maidens, endeavoring to draw water from the well, approached her. Callidice, Cleisidice, Demo, Callithoe were the daughters of Celeus, King of Eleusis and they approached the old lady, before them, with much intrigue and curiosity. After introducing themselves, they asked Demeter where whe came from and tried to understand why a woman of her suspecting age, was alone, outside of the city center and not already employed as a nurse by a house family. Demeter introduced herself as a woman from Crete, by the name of

"Doso" and claimed to have escaped the capture of pirates, who were going to sell her off. She weaved a convincingly good, yet, sad tale that captured the sympathy of the King's children. The maiden, Callidice, who was described as the "godliest" in the Homeric Hymn, suggested that the old lady follow them home. She convinced Demeter that their father, the King, would surely welcome her services in their household and that their younger brother would benefit from a nurse of her caliber. Upon meeting the disguised Demeter, the King Celeus, and his wife, sensed that indeed she would be a welcomed addition to their Kingdom and a fine nurse for their young son Demophoon, although in some text he was also known as Triptolemus. There is also some conflicting stories about Iambe as yet another daughter of the Queen or perhaps another name for the bawdy, jovial Baubo herself, who was the nursemaid who ultimately helped end Demeter's lament.

And thus Demeter, still in disguise, was employed by the Queen, Metaeira, to become nursemaid to the baby boy. She raised this baby as if he was her very own and indeed she grew quite fond of this child. In Demeter's care, Demophoon was raised like a God and her love for him, inspired her to bless him with the fires of immortality. The child was about to become immortal in her arms, when his mother, the Queen, intercepted the frightful traditional fire ritual. Imagine her surprise to discover the old nursemaid they had hired, was actually the Goddess of the Grain- Demeter. Immediately, Demeter's divine luminescence manifested, upon being caught by the Queen. And Metaneira was no sooner, harshly berated by the Fertile Grain Goddess for her interference in the will of the Gods. In her anger, the Goddess, demanded that a temple be built in her honor, immediately.

Once built there, in the city of Eleusis, in this temple dedicated to her greatness, the Goddess Demeter planted herself until the return of her daughter. She vowed she would not step foot on Mount Olympus, or allow anything to grow or be born on the Earth, until her daughter was returned to her. And this was a most tragic state for the earth and humanity's wellbeing. Zeus tried to implore her to return to her post. Other Gods and Goddesses also came to her, bearing gifts and supplications. The people of the land also left numerous offerings to the Goddess to entreat her to return. Demeter was unmoved and refused to give into their demands. In one myth, Zeus finally sends the messenger God, Hermes, to retrieve Persephone from the underworld and bring her back to her mother. He does and finally, Mother and daughter are reunited.

Their overdue reunion was full of intense heartwarming emotions but in the end, bittersweet. Demeter, learns then that Persephone had eaten the fruit of the dead, pomegranate seeds, while in the underworld and must now come to accept that her daughter will only be with her part of the year and return to her husband, Hades, in the underworld, for the remainder of the year.

The Homeric Hymn to Demeter focused on Demeter's response to Persephone being abducted by Hades and this was the basis of the Eleusinian Mysteries - the most powerful religious and sacred rites of ancient Greece. Held in secret for over two thousand years, these sacred rites ended with the destruction of the Eleusis Temples by the Goths around fifth century A.D. More recently there has been a resurgeance and interest in ancient mythology, anthropology, Paganism and Goddess spirituality. And research into these archaic, longstanding Greek rites, reveal a great deal about our ancestors and their spiritual practices - knowledge that can enrich our own present day beliefs and religious practices.

DEMETER GROVE GODDESS GATHERING

PURPOSE: to commune with the Greek, Goddess of The Grain, Demeter, and connect with the seasonal changes approaching.

CHECK INS I: With our Grove speaking stick in hand we introduce ourselves with our name, how we are faring at this time of year and briefly share our own experience with the Grain Goddess.

CHANTING: (*Song text Sheet available*)
"Thanksgiving Song", "Remember God was a womyn...", "We all come from the Goddess..."

DRUMMING: A Musical CD Drumming track is played to help Ground us in this moment and connect us to the energy of our circle. Trance and movement is encouraged.

CHECK INS II: a second check in, only this time we asks, "What changes do you foresee now for the coming Fall? Is this a welcomed change or do we meet it reluctantly?

CONE OF POWER: Together softly buzzing, humming and then rising up through the chakras, continually opening up to a stronger, louder, "Ma" sound. We should stagger our breath, so that it is one continuous tone and invocation to the Universal Mother..."Ma".

AGREEMENTS: Our Agreement Sheet is passed around and we each read a bylaw and discuss it, adding to it as necessary. It is signed, dated and submitted.

Together we will actually **create a Drumming Circle,** with every participant holding a percussion instrument and slowly building up a meditative rhythm.

SHARING: Pass around an image of Demeter, a sculpture or the Empress card in our Tarot Deck. Connecting with this image and slowly invoking her presence into our space. Each participant speaks aloud of what they see and considers the question, what does her image personally reveal?

GODDESS LECTURE
Begin by reading the story of Demeter and Persephone

GODDESS WORKSHOP
WORKSHOP I: Creating an Autumnal House blessing wreath. As we gather silk faux floral pieces, and glue/tie them to our wreaths, we contemplate on the Autumnal season and what we aspire to create.

WORKSHOP II: Musing thoughts
Read the musing and meditation to consider what this Goddess has to offer us and how we may best utilize her energy in our personal lives. ... an open Discussion can follow.

WORKSHOP III: Broom Making or Blessings our existing Besoms. Gathering ribbons, wires, a long staff and a straw bundles to fashion our own personal besoms. Participants can also simply bring their existing brooms and decorate them with various colorful ribbons and bless them by all the elements.

WORKSHOP VI: Kitchen Magick, Baking the Goddess, either making cookies or small cakes. Imbuing the dough with our intention and creating a Goddess figure to ingest its vital magick, within our core.

WORKSHOP V: Herbal and Poppet magick. Attain either two plain square pieces of felt or two human/doll shaped cut outs, sewn together, leaving the the top opening so that you may place all of your charged herbs inside of this figure. Then sew the top and seal it with your intention.

WORKSHOP VI: A Discussion on the sabbat of Lammas, its origins and various ways it is celebrated. Discussing Our upcoming Ritual....

WORKSHOP VII: A letter of Thanksgiving to the one who has nursed us and provided for us, could be our mothers, aunt, lovers or bestfriend etc...

REFLECTIONS ON DEMETER

Demeter arrives in our lives and awakens in us the powerful mother archetype. She is the energy of the doting mother and has much to teach us about the powers inherent in this role as nurturer and protector. This is sadly a role seldom valued by our modern day society, yet something transformative happens to a womyn when she becomes a mother, nurturer or a caretaker of another. Her entire world changes the moment she is placed in the role of mother and her inner landscape shifts into terrains of fierce protector and sacrificial planes.

Whether it is a helpless infant, a young awry child, a rebellious teenager or even a fragile elderly -caring and loving another human being evolves our world drastically in ways inconceivable by the maiden. And if we let it, it can sculpt our souls to astounding measures and it is this force that can bring great, positive changes to ourselves and our universe.

This Goddess helps us tap into that matrilineal power and yet, she is also a lesson on sacrifices, releasing and surrendering when necessary, to inevitable changes, whether they are seasonal or otherwise. She comes into our lives to makes us aware that the wheel of the year brings an internal and external shift and every season births something new. And thus, we are constantly adjusting to new stages in the cycle of our personal lives. Demeter asks you to value the vicissitudes found in nature, as it reflect the inner changes we must sometimes undergo concurrently.

Demeter Musing, Grove Goddess Gathering

Though I have often considered myself to be quite intimate with the maiden archetype, there have been times in my life when a mother Goddess, like Demeter, has swooped me under her realm and claimed me as her priestess. Her presence in my life becomes undeniable to those who are closest to me. Through-out the years, as a result, I have learned a thing or two about Demeter and her legendary myths in Greek Mythology. She has quite a lot to say and has always been very generous and all too eager to share herself with me as well. Here I'd like to explore her value and relevance for today's modern womyn and why she is a Goddess whose energy we could all benefit from studying and working with.

Demeter falls under the category of Mother Goddess, the nurturer, the one who comforts and can bring about healing because of her own compassion and understanding for human suffering. Her altruistic ability to connect and empathize with another and yet, derive great pleasure in that function is one of the most well-known and common characteristic of the Mother archetype. Demeter thus, has a lot in common with Deities like; Kwan yin, Selu, Cere, Gaia, Rhea, Brid, Amaterasu, Yemaja and the Christianized Virgin Mary, to name a few, as they all emanate the cherished aspects of the Goddess as Mother.

In Greek mythology, Demeter garnered the reputation as always being benevolent, giving generously and being devoted exclusively to the productivity of her land. Bestowing on humanity the ability to harvest, plant seeds, tend to, reap, grow and thus ultimately provide nourishment and sustenance to humanity. Isn't this the role that all mothers are called to fulfill? The dependable provider who assures the sustenance of her people. Thus this make Demeter a deity that was of the land, and closely linked to humanity and in many ways directly involved with the day to day life of the Greeks.

In the Eleusinian Mysteries, the most famous of Greek Mythology, we get a glimpse into Demeter's character and it is through her intensely close relationship with her daughter, Persephone, that we truly begin to understand this ancient beloved, Hellenic Goddess.

Here was a Goddess who was revered as the fertile, growing one, whose benevolence fed humanity. A Goddess whose generosity and happy disposition made the Earth lush, ripe and so full -reflective of her blissful insides. Yet, one wretched tragedy, the abduction of her daughter and thus the theft of her own sole role as Mother, resulted in devastation for the Earth. The Earth, yet again, reflected this Deities' insides -only this time it wasn't lush, pretty, nor fertile, it was gruesome, painful and deathly. Her sense of loss and devastation poured out into the barren fields, and now was reflected in the inhospitable, desolate Earth. Until her daughter was returned to her, all would know of her pain.

What must that feel like?
To love someone so much that you cease to be productive, you cease to be yourself, you cease to return to your role or job, until that person returns. Have you ever felt this aspect of the Goddess?
What must that feel like to always be known by a certain name, a role, a certain title and have that identity stripped from you without warning- leaving you nameless, jobless, with no identity.... Grasping... loss... trying to regain what was yours?

The Goddess Demeter does not take her daughter's abduction lightly, she does not take things sitting down. And while the Sun God, Helios and other Deities tried to convince her to just accept this fate, she refuses....

When have you refused to take things sitting down?
How does that experience change your inner landscape in moments of devastations and great tragedies?

    In true Goddess mode, Demeter refuses to let someone else manipulate her and trivialize the most important aspect in her life. She refuses to allow someone else (and in this particular case, the Male Gods symbols of Patriarchy) to strip her of her cherished crown as mother to her beloved Persephone- via this tragic abduction. NO!!! She will not just roll over and let it be. This once known pleasant, brilliant, patron, benevolent Deity, metamorphically transformed and tapped into her suppressed aspect. And the world would now be a witness to the dark side of this Mother Goddess. For indeed every benevolent, sweet Mother Goddess has within her, a Dark warrior aspect that would make a grown man cry like a baby. Nothing would grow on the Earth until her daughter was returned to her. Nothing would prosper until her role as mother was implemented once more.

Have you ever touched upon that other side...that darker side of the Mother archetype? Journal your experience...

    Here is where Demeter becomes a useful archetype for us as womyn who are constantly being told to turn the other cheek, get over things, accept certain situations... She awaken to her own bargaining powers, the one who will not take her loss lightly. And Demeter unearths her own gifts of stubbornness and fierce tenacity. She is the one who grieves and allows herself- to truly feel pain, loss and tears. Demeter is the Goddess who does not suffer silently, meekly in some corner of a room, but rather somberly, deeply feeling, outwardly expressing, and lets the whole world know of her displeasure and inconsolable grief. She is the one, who even in her state of depression, doesn't lose hope. She is the one who negotiates and barters and does whatever she has to do, until she gets her way. She is the energy of the stubborn one, who does not succumb to external pressures.

What do you stand for steadfast in your desire?

    We call on her, the Mother, when it appears we have loss something of great importance and we need her relentless tenacity for hope, that all is not lost.
We call on her, the Mother, to sustain us, to stay vigilant when it appears the whole world would prefer for us to give up.
    She is the one who retreats, as a result of her grief, but from this great pain she manages to manifest monumental changes and a transformation for all, in the midst of her sadness. In the end, She, Mother Goddess, is the one who helps us see what our persistence produces and then, only as a last resort, finding an appropriate agreement for the greater good of all. She facilitates finding a compromise that might end up serving a greater purpose. Typical of a Mother deity, She inaugurates a sacrifice for the greater good. In the end, Demeter came to accept and relinquish her beloved daughter for one third of the year and restored Humanity's Crops and Land.

What must we negotiate and finally compromise, for the greater good?
What will return your landscape to fertile ground?
What pain, grief, and loss, must be addressed and relinquished to bring about balance and to restore yourself back to you?
   ****Has anyone ever felt the presence of Demeter in their lives? (open discussion -share)

DEMETER GROVE GODDESS GATHERING RITUAL

Purpose: to commune with the Greek, Goddess of The Grain, Demeter, and connect with the seasonal changes approaching, Lammas Celebration.

Music/ **Altar** set up

Purification with smudge incense, scented herb water, or loud rattle:

Oil **Anointing** of third eye... line formation or sister to sister, to one another within circle

Circle cast: *(with rattle; All wommin rattle gently as priestess speaks casting circle with athame...)*
*Upon this Sphere, this Circle is cast,
Keep evil at bay, let kind spirits pass.
No more a room, but your Holy Space,
To worship and invoke, your essence and grace.
The Circle is Cast!

Quarters called Communally:

Holding each element, priestess speaks and presents; a lit candle, a chalice of water and a plant is passed around to each womyn so that each could feel and invoke the element aloud in her own way, thus it is done all together...
Air- We begin holding hands, inhaling, exhaling etc.. until we are one breath inviting air in our circle....
Fire - a lit candle is passed, Water -a blue water chalice, Earth -a potted plant (no cut flower)

QUARTER CALLS

Air *(hold hands)*
Breathe...Audibly Breathe..... Inhale.. Exhale... we call on Air...We Breathe collectively, to call on the Powers of Air found within our very own breath, ancient symbol of life force, of Prana. We breathe together... and invoke the powers of Air in our circle tonight.
Air, Guard and hold our sacred space, be here now with your gifts in place.
Hail and welcome Air...

Fire *(pass around the candle)*
This flame that flickers, a source of warmth and light and sometimes burning desire, we each behold within our own souls this very flame of justice and tenacity. Together we call on the powers of Fire. Be here now...
Fire, Guard and hold our sacred space, be here now with your gifts in place.
Hail and welcome Fire...

Water *(pass around a chalice of water)*
Water... your mysteries found within our own "wombmynhood." How we too ebb and flow and behold your magick in our tears and mourning. Come -as we call you Water to enter our circle.
Water, Guard and hold our sacred space, be here now with your gifts in place.
Hail and welcome Water...

Earth *(holding a potted plant -no cut flowers)*
Hail Earth, manifestor of our visions on the physical plane, transformer and nurturer. Healer, we invoke you Earth, through the bounty of thy first Harvest, we call you, through the beauty of our own Physical form and bodies. We call you, embracing our syster next to us, as we invite Earth and say,
Earth, Guard and hold our sacred space, be here now with your gifts in place.
Hail and welcome Earth...

******

INTENT: Invite them to sit as priestess speaks on the season of Lammas
The wheel turns once more and we stand among our systers in hallowed space to commemorate this special time of the year. Herein this moment, we celebrate the Season of Lammas, also known as Lughnasadh. Lammas is the first Harvest, a time when traditionally the very first grains were Harvested and people had much to celebrate. They would feast joyously and make bread from these first grains and they would offer them up to the Gods in sincere thanksgiving. They were mindful of this time, as the last few days before the change in season and they anticipated the dark of the year, potential fierce cold weather that could leave

some hungry, even dead.

For us, we might not have farms or tend to crops, or live as close to the land as our ancestors, but, it is at this moment in time, that we do consider what our past efforts have wielded and if our seeds and branches are providing evidence of first fruits. This can be seen as a time of our Spiritual Harvest, when we take stock of our efforts and what they have produced. From the Spring and through-out the year our seeds were planted and tended and now we're able to reap the rewards of our labor. It is truly a time of Thanksgiving, a time to celebrate the Harvest (whether small or large. This is a time to begin to look ahead as the wheel of the year turns once more. Please join me in this ancient rite....

Chant: "*I circle around the boundaries of the Earth....*"
Or "*Thanksgiving song*"

Ritual Statement: We have dedicated our afternoon to learning about **DEMETER**, We seek now to connect with her energy, invoke her and honor her in this ritual today.
Hold hands in tight knit circle and breathe again to connect:

Syster Invocation: "*We invoke you, Demeter-Mother, nourisher, Great Goddess of the Grain, Queen of all Harvest, Bountiful Mother who provides us with nourishment for our souls. We honor you. Be with us now in this ritual as we celebrate the first Harvest and your gifts. Hail and welcome..*"

THE WORKING:
Aspected Demeter Speaks of the Season of Lammas & instructs... (*A Corn Stalk search, like the egg hunt in the Spring, Re-enact the work that must be done in order to reap what we sow*)

"*Here do I stand your beloved Matriarchal Goddess, Queen of the growing & ripening, Goddess of the Grain, I am your Demeter... Abundance and Blessings I bestow upon you on this sabbat but it doesn't come without some hard work and effort... Go out into the fields and search to find your reward within the grains of the First Harvest... a corn stalk awaits you and it has a message only for you... When you have done your work, attained your corn, and read your message, return to me... Return as you always **should** and as its been done since the beginning of time, Maintain your ancestral traditions and make me the offering of your first Harvest... and Lammas will be just the beginning of many more blessings to come....Go now But return.. return... return....*"

***They go and they return holding their corn stalk...

Chant: "*Thanksgiving song*"

Goddess says: I ask you...*What has come to pass? What are you most grateful for? Come to my altar with thanksgiving!!!*
Each woman states what she is grateful for: "*I am thankful for _____ receive this offering Goddess from our Harvest as a gesture of my gratitude......*" *(they each bring their corn to the altar in a moment of thanksgiving and then return to their place in the circle...)*

Chant: "*Do you remember when God was a woman she had many names...*"

II. Demeter will speak of the dark month ahead,
what grieves her so, saying goodbye and what's to come...
"*Ah... I see you have much to be thankful for now...During the winter months, when I am separated from my beloved daughter Persephone...you may ask.. what sustains me during these (sad) dark months? It is the sweet memories of our Spring and Summer reunions and the knowledge and Hope that we will meet again as the wheel turns...*"

*** Candles are handed out now***

"*I share this, my glimmer of hope with you in this light (the candle).*
**May it light your way during the dark season...*
**May it remind you of the experiences we've shared in the Spring and Summer.*
**May it remind you of our light and our feasting today.*

**May it give you that flicker of hope when it is needed during the season of the waning Sun. As your candle is lit, in this magickal moment when time stands still,
State aloud what you hope for in the coming months. _____"*

Each candle gets lit, as they each recite one thing they hope for in the coming season. While holding candles - **Chant**: *"We all come from the Goddess..."*

Thanking the Goddess

"Great Goddess Demeter, we thank you for your presence here today. We thank you for evidence of your divine powers in every grain we have harvested thus far. Know that we are always ever grateful for the gifts that you bring into our lives. Bountiful Mother who comes to our aid when called, receive our most sincere thanks as we bid thee adieu. Hail and Farewell and blessed be."

As a symbol that priestess is no longer Demeter, take off the crown or whatever was worn, that symbolized this change.
We've invoked Demeter and we've commemorated the sabbat let us give our thanks and open our circle... *(keep your candles lit as we begin..)*

DEVOKING QUARTERS
We thank you Earth, Water, Fire and Air for your presence in this ritual affair.
As ye arrived in peace depart in peace- We bid thee adieu, Hail and Farewell.

OPENING CIRCLE
each womyn following the lead... Going counterclockwise, snuffing/pinching out the candle of neighboring sister to her right as each says;
"The circle is open, the Dark season approaches..."

We should be in the dark by the end of ritual singing...
"... the circle is open, but unbroken may the peace of the Goddess be ever in our hearts... Merry meet and Merry part and Merry meet again......"

The Sabbat has been kept, Go in peace, So mote it be!!!

ASPECTING DEMETER

Here do I stand your beloved Mother Goddess,
Queen of the growing & ripening,
Goddess of the Grain,
I am your Demeter...
Abundance and Blessings,
I bestow upon you on this sabbat
but it doesn't come without some hard work and effort...
Go out into the fields
and find your reward
within the grains of the First Harvest...
A corn stalk awaits you
and it has a message only for you...
When you have done your work,
attained your corn and read your message,
return to me...
Return as you always **should**
and as its been done since the beginning of time,
Maintain your ancestral traditions
and make me the offering of your first Harvest...
and Lammas will be just the beginning
of many more blessings to come....
Go now, But return.. return... return....

***participants go out and they return holding their corn stalk, which should have a personal message for them like a Chinese fortune cookie...

For this spell, gather numerous photos and magazine clipping of your ideal home, as well as classified (house for sale) Ads. Place these near the statue or photo of the goddess, Demeter. Also add a few dollars to represent the money in abundance available to purchase your home. Fumigate the area with Frankincense and Myrrh, for your incense. Create an offering plate for Demeter, with Barley, Corn and Bread and offer this outdoor, on the earth, to the Goddess. Acquire a brown or green candle, carve it with the symbol of a home and anoint it with blessing oil, Demeter oil or "wish come true oil" (see appendix). Then, on a night of the waxing moon, preferably on a Sunday or Monday, when the moon is in her ideal astrological sign of cancer, recite this incantation. Cancer rules the home and all domestic concerns and will lend its energy harmoniously to your spell.

A CALL TO THE EMPRESS & AN IDEAL HOME
*Demeter, Empress, Queen of her Dome
I call upon thee to find me a home
Where (mate/name/lover) and I
can live happily
And there begin our family

And by the elements I make it so
I conjure now our ideal home:

In a neighborhood that's safe and clean
A pleasant home that's Dog friendly
A lively, warm community
Where we can raise our family

Affordable and safe
A warm loving home
A library, a den,
and four rooms of our own

A kitchen, a bathroom and living room
A garden that faces the heavenly moon
Safely I ask, Let this work fast
And with these words this spell is cast

I manifest now
the home of our dreams
these things or better
so mote it be.

The start: How courage and inspiration began....
Journaling Demeter's First Gathering.

    I found myself very dissatisfied with the way things were going, especially with the present open spiritual group I was working with. I had devoted myself to the Priestess path and had spent a year facilitating and priestessing for this organization, but found myself frustrated with some of the catty, political nonsense and back stabbing, I both, witnessed and personally encountered. It was the group's June ritual, at this particular Solstice ritual, I noticed it was very chaotic, loose, unstructured and like most of their previous rituals, it seemed to lack some vital components of magick, in my humblest opinion. It served however to inspire me, bringing conviction and the realization that, indeed, I needed to create a Sisterhood, with the ideals and wisdom I had acquired, after over twenty years of experience in this realm. With courage, I proceeded to follow a vision that persistently demanded execution. Quietly, I listened to that little gnawing voice inside me. Slowly I began the outline and proposal, which helped give birth to "Grove of The Feminine Divine."

    What I remember most about this first gathering, aside from feeling nervous, was feeling so honored that these womyn took the time, out of their busy lives to lend support. They came to share fellowship with me and with love, they entrusted me to lead them into sacred space. I felt great support imbued in their collective energy and it was a moving experience to witness the manifestation of a vision and dream come true. It went rather smoothly, considering it was our first gathering together, but I also saw how I had over planned with much more activities than could fit in our time allotment. We naturally went over our time but it was great. My initial nervousness and concerns quickly simmered as soon as the Divine was called upon into our work and I felt confident that there would be many more opportunities for us to gather in the future. When I heard womyn sharing their stories it became clear to me why I was being called to do this work and I felt validated in birthing "Grove of the Feminine Divine".

JOURNAL ENTRY RE: DEMETER GROVE GATHERING

    It is now 5:22pm, about an hour after the last friendly faces left my home. Our first gathering? Not too bad... actually quite wonderful. Dare I say, a SUCCESS!!

    I should be proud as I sensed all the wommin were thrilled to have experienced this first Grove gathering. They all seemed genuinely happy that they came, communed with other wommin and linked to the Goddess and as a result received some valuable healing, knowledge and fellowship from it. In my mind, I think it went quite well, as 80% of what I had planned went accordingly. Then other times, I surprised myself in my ability to adjust and go with the flow, smoothly and effortlessly. Naturally some things changed spontaneously and I had to be respectful of energies and time restraints, but for the most part, it was well structured.

    The first woman arrived unexpectedly very early, while I was still in my mother role, getting my little ones and husband out of the house, which would later become our Goddess Temple. While I was very happy to see her, it also caused me some unanticipated stress, as I didn't have the Temple completely set up. I still needed to go the backyard to lay the corn husks on the grass for our harvest offering. I still needed to set up the smudging altar at the entrance and I still needed to light candles and ground my own scattered, nervous energy. Some day I will gladly welcome a right-hand assistant in this vision, but for today, I was offering this Womyn's gathering all on my very own. Needless to say, I was a bit stressed to see her here so early, as I had not even finished setting up our altars. Then the darling sweetheart, was talking so incessantly, that her chatter added to the nervous buzzing I was already experiencing. Being a Scorpio, with my moon is Pisces, does NOT help matters, as I'm an empath, and instantaneously always seem to absorb other people's energy. She was being sooooo friendly, trying to get to know me better at a precarious time when I was going to step into a monumental, yet nerve-racking role, in my life. Note to self; "getting to known you better" is a game best played long before a first time gathering. Needless to say, it was probably not the best time to "chit-chat" with me, as my mind desperately needed to focus, ground and relax into this pivotal moment. Funny, I reflected on my early days in the craft and felt like, I suspected my old High Priestess probably felt, all those times I was so damn chatty with her at the start of rituals, back in the old days. Imagine my stress trying to be cordial and friendly, while also trying to tap into the grounded, calm, "all knowing", wise facilitator, ha! I know, that's hilarious and certaintly, such crazy thoughts would add to anyone's stress level. Thankfully, as overly organize as I usually am, I managed to pre-prepared some stuff the night beforehand, so getting ready now, even with such an adorable distracting, was not a giant hurdle.

Two more wommin came next, arriving together on time. Though I had never met one of them, I was happy to welcome them both. Many more wommin arrived in pairs, minutes later to my delightful surprise. All who came that day shimmered in my eyes with a beauty that brought so much to our group's ritual. I made sure to thanked them very much, recognizing their efforts -especially with the high cost of gas and our hectic crazy lives. For me, it was important that I conveyed to them an appreciation, especially in these hard times we are in. I also felt their presence in my home was helping me birth and manifest a dream come true and was greatly indebted to them.

We began with a chanting workshop, and that was nice, but a bit choppy as I felt disconnected and unsure if they were feeling their inner songstress. Admittedly, for a retired opera singer like myself, facilitating a chant workshop is a lot more challenging, when you realize not everyone takes pleasure in the expressive genre and the art of the bard. We sang holding our song sheets and then we checked in with names several times. Then we Sang some more and had a check in with our own personal Goddess. I heard women claim for themselves; Demeter, Artemis, Saraswati, Isis, Crone, Hecate, Frigga/Freya... It was wonderful to hear them connect with their chosen Deity and the reasons behind it. Afterwards we followed it up with our Grove's bylaws and Agreements and all of the womyn agreed it was important to establish this now, while we are still in our embryonic stage as a group. Their encouragement validated my vision and it affirmed initial decision for this list of agreements. We went around the circle and read two bylaws each and this, in a sense, created our sacred circle. Afterwards, We had a moment of trance work with only the drums. It appeared we were drumming for a while and we had raised some intense energy because at one point, I remember looking into their faces as they came out of that drumming trance and it was so incredible. The face of Awe!!! We were all speechless, since this was our first time meeting.

I broke the sacred silence after our trance by suggesting a song to chant and then, the Goddess Lecture part of our day began. With a simple image of Demeter (reflected in the Tarot card of the Empress from "The Mythic Tarot" by Juliet Sharman-Burke and Liz Greene) passed around the room, each womyn was asked to say something that stands out from that image. "What qualities of Demeter, stand out for you?" This was insightful, as everyone had a similar, yet interesting, perspective on the image of Demeter and it was nice to begin to invoke her in this special way. When we were done, feeling her presence, I declared "She" is here! We had brought Demeter here, for indeed her presence was felt. I presented the beloved myth of Demeter and her daughter, Persephone and talked about her lineage and heritage. I continued tapping into Demeter's energy, piling layers upon layers of this sacred Goddess. Persephone's abduction, Demeter's Lament and the whole story rolled off my tongue like it happened in my very own family history and it surprised me at how effortlessly the story of her abduction came out. I suppose I was already aspecting the Goddess by this point. Then afterwards, I talked about its relevance to us, as womyn now and how this is a living Goddess that we can now certainly tap into.

The next part, for me was surprising, yet the most fulfilling, as I read my commentary and personal meditative musing on Demeter. It helped every womyn in that room reflect, relate and tap into Demeter's energy even further. Some were moved to tears, they shared intimate deep experiences during the check in that followed and I think we were all moved and strengthened. The check ins afterwards started to take a long time as some womyn now began to unearth overwhelming emotions and we started to connect with one another at a deeper level. For a split second I wondered, how I would get them out into the next stage of our gathering. Somehow I did...with the offering of our yummy potluck.... Unlike subsequent gatherings, this first one, we opted to do the ritual towards the end, after feasting. Since this gathering, we have opted to do our potluck feasting at the end of our day, personally, I learned rather quickly that I prefer doing rituals on an empty stomach. At this moment, I watched with pleasure, my systers enjoying their meal and being careful about not monopolizing their energy, simply stepping back every now and then, to let them socialize, like a mother taking pleasure in watching her children eating and being well behaved-ha. I was clearly already feeling Demeter's energy then, for I am not normally so invested in these mothering traits, as a bona fide Maiden.

For our subsequent ritual I was hoping for it to be truly communal and full of participation and so I encouraged everyone to take on a role. One syster helped with the anointing and entry to our sacred space, another syster helped invoking Demeter and during circle casting, I invited them all to gently rattle as I cast the circle with my Athame. Together we called on all the elements, by first breathing to welcome Air. A candle was passed around and they were asked to invite Fire with one word. I could tell some were a bit surprised and nervous to be so involved, but I encourage them to go on and know that all would be well. For community, I felt strongly about every person adding their energy to this first ritual. The chalice of water was passed around next and again they were invited to say something about the element of water, Lastly, a plant was sent around the circle, to call upon the element of Earth. It was truly a very tender moment for all of us to actively participate in this way, communally, creating sacred space.

The next stage felt a bit more improvised. After the elements were called the energy seemed weird to me. They were invited to sit and I quickly talked about Lammas and its meaning. I think I followed through with what I originally wanted to say but, the energy felt awkward and I still did not feel ready to bring Demeter and so, I had us stand now and breathe together once more. Breath always seems to help connect us to one another and the Divine. Then when the invoker locked eyes with me, she proceeded with her invocation and called upon the Demeter in me. The words from her lips were beautiful and moving and when she finished, I turned around, cloaked myself with the Golden robe and with soft eyes, looking at each one of them, I felt Demeter. Demeter then sent them outside, to contemplated gratitude and nature and to pick their own corn harvest with their special message. When we returned, we sang; " Do you remember, when God was a woman she had many names..." As I looked at the image of Demeter on our beautiful altar, I invited them to share thanksgiving and they each came with reverence making their own offering at the communal altar. At one point, still in aspecting trance, I erroneously started lighting their candles too soon, now their candles were lit and dripping. Quickly, I invited them to go around the circle and speak of what they hope to acquire or release for the season of darkness. With hot dripping wax, we quickly shared our hopes and followed it with two singing verses of "We all come from the Goddess". Yes!!! Even with hot dripping wax we braved it and continued onward, while the candles burned and drip. Devoking followed soon after, with simple heartfelt words. Prior to opening our circle, they were invited to pinch their candles wicks and snuff them out - an ancient tradition taught to me by a hereditary witch many moons ago. To my surprise there were womyn present, who had never heard of the taboo about not blowing out your flame. Snuffing out a candle and its flame, was downright scary for some of them. Still the very act of all of us doing this together, in sacred space to open our circle, was magickal. After the ritual they lingered and talked with each other for a long time and we all bonded nicely. We successfully tapped into the Goddess Demeter and I felt a glimmer of hope and great potential for our newly born Goddess Group.

The Altar never looked more beautiful. It was just breathtaking with all of their contributions, the many lit candles, statuaries and sacred items. There was a moment, when I looked at it from afar and it evoked such a warm tingling sensation within me.
We commemorated the sabbat of Lammas and brought Demeter's energy into our first Grove circle and I felt blessed to find myself at the inception of our Goddess group-Grove of the Feminine Divine.

Thank you Goddess... you have set me on a beautiful journey.....

DEMETER GROVE GODDESS GATHERING CHANTS

SONG OF THANKSGIVING
I thank the moon
and the stars
and the fertile Earth
for the lessons I've learned
and the way I'm nursed
(Part II A vocalize/harmonize on her name):
      Deeemeter... Deeeemeter........*By B.M.M.*

ARAPAHO SONG
I circle around, I circle around,
The boundaries of the Earth 2X
      Heyana Heyana, Heyana Heyana
Wearing my long wing feathers as I fly
Wearing my long winged feathers as I fly. *(repeat) by Arapaho Ghost Dance Song*

DO YOU REMEMBER
Do you remember, When God was a woman she had many, many names. (2X)
They called her Isis, Astarte, Diana, Hecate, Demeter, Kali, Innana.... *repeat*

WE ALL COME FROM THE GODDESS
We all come from the Goddess
and to her we shall return
like a drop of rain,
flowing to the Ocean.   By: *Z.Budapest*

MY ROOTS GO DOWN
My roots go Down, Down to the Earth
My Roots go down,
Down to the Earth
My roots Go down, Down to the Earth
My roots go down.... *by Sarah Pirtle*

WE ARE A CIRCLE
We are a circle, within a circle,
With no beginning and never ending(2X) *by Rick Hamouris*

ELEMENTAL CHANTS
***The Earth, the Air, the Fire, The water,
return, return, return
Below, above, The center is love
Return, return, return

EIGHT BEADS CHANTS
Girlseed
Bloodflower
(dip it)Fruitmother
Spinmother,
(raise it) Midwoman
Earthcrone
Stonecrone
Bone........ *by Carolyn Hillyer*

***The Earth is a woman and she shall rise... *by Z. Budapest*

CHAPTER NINETEEN
"The Flower that Grows in adversity is the most rare and beautiful of all..." Emperor

"Death is not the greatest loss in life, the greatest loss is what dies inside us, while we live...." Norman Cousins

WELCOME PERSEPHONE

OUR ALTAR

Altar cloth: Black and maybe a second dark pomegranate red altar cloth underneath.
Image: Statue of this Maiden Goddess with dark, long flowing hair.
Canvas art or photo of the Maiden Goddess and or photos of Greece, the Parthenon, caves, Groves, the dark of night. Dark Hooded Maidens. Caverns even a simple pomegranate suffices.

Always present on the altar;
A cast iron cauldron, drums, speaking stick, a silver pentacle, athame, elemental representations......

Air: A large feather to sweep the energy. Smudge wands, Incense type sticks, cones, charcoal brisket and fine powdered herbs like Mugwort, Anise, Benzoin, Patchouli, Sandalwood.
Fire: candles, glass enclosed candles or pillars in white and black at least three.
Water: Chalice or small glass bowl with Water or red wine
Earth: Plants, a small dish of soil and or herbs. Best to present on your altar, at this time of year, bare branches and a single flower (a White Rose or Narcissus).

Other items pertinent to this particular gathering
Robe and Circlet
Bare Branches in a vase
Pomegranate and seeds
Journals
Bowls of consecrated Water
A mini personal altar shrine box
Rocks and Gemstone
A lantern
cemetery hedge stone
photos
Writing pens and paper , safety pins,
Black Light gauzy fabric /Veil
Workshop items
Tarot -"The High Priestess"

Offering Water, Pomegranate or Cranberry Juice, a platter of Fruits, corn husk and Breads, Molloi -which were cakes/bread made in the shapes of vagina
Sacred objects from members:
Notes:

Persephone

Persephone's Altars

PERSEPHONE

Persephone or Proserpine (in Latin) is the Greek Maiden Goddess of Spring and Queen of the Underworld. Persephone has been immortalized as the beloved daughter of the Goddess of the Grain-Demeter. The ancient myths associated with her and her mother, place her as an important integral part of the renowned, Great Eleusinian mysteries.

The name Persephone has been anglicized but to begin our study of this Goddess it's best to first begin etymologically. As a young girl and daughter to her mother, she was first known, most popularly as "Kore", (variations of this name include Koura, Cora, Koure) which translates as *"the Maiden, young girl"*. This became almost a sort of nick name when referring to her in Eleusis. Some scholars also claimed that another connotation to this name alludes to *"young bride"*. This would mean that right from the start, her name reflects the role and path she would inevitably take.

Many discovered ancient vases and art work of the time, show depictions of her and her name noted as *"Pherophata," "Phersephata",* and *"Pherephassa."* This would appear to be her accurate, more formal name, as her actual Temple at Eleusis was called, *"Pherephation"*.

The first part of the name Persephone, erroneously is linked with light and if we look at the second part of her anglicized name, *"phone,"* derivative of *"phonos," "phoneme,"* it roughly means *"to slaughter or sacrifice."* Therefore, upon a closer look at her name, Persephone is normally translated as *"destroyer of the light,"* a rather unusual title for the Spring maiden Goddess but perhaps not so unusual for the Queen of the Underworld.

Upon closer inspection of her more authentic name, *"Pherophata,"* we get a different meaning and a more revealing insight into this ancient deity. Her name takes on a different hue if we consider the meaning of the first half of her ancient name, *"pheros"*, this word roughly means *"to bear, offer, carry, to bring."* Yet the second part of her original name *"phattas"* derived from *"phatos"* means *"the unspeakable, unutterable, incommunicable."* After much research, it would appear then that the name of this Goddess means, *"She who brings or conveys the unspeakable."* Thus as Queen of the Underworld, the Greeks believed her to be a bringer of the indescribable, of that experience that goes beyond words. She is the "Maiden of the ineffable" and a vastly crucial component of the Eleusinian Rites, which were responsible for teaching initiates, the secrets of life and death.

The Eleusinian mysteries and the Greek myths tightly associated with this epic have forever immortalized, Persephone as the Maiden Goddess of Spring and the Underworld. The ancient writings of the time like; Hesiod's Theogony (c700BCE), Homer's Iliad (written c 750-725BCE) The Odyssey (written c743-713BCE) and the Homeric hymn to Demeter, set in Eleusis,(written around 650-550-BCE) by an unknown author, all have contributed greatly to our knowledge of this Goddess.

As a child, Kore was extremely close to her mother, one of the twelve original Olympian Deities - Goddess of the Grain, Demeter. Her birth came about as a result of typical trickery played by the Gods. In one tale, Zeus turned himself into a Bull and with his sister, fathered Persephone. There is another more obscure myth that comes from Greek scholar, Appolodorus (180-120BCE) it places Persephone as daughter of Zeus and the underworld Goddess River Styx, born already in the realm of Hades, but this version is rarely mentioned and used typically to explain how Persephone becomes the Queen of the Underworld.

Demeter and Persephone had a very close intimately relationship and some speculate that perhaps the Gods, like Aphrodite and Zeus himself, did not completely understand nor approve. In one tale it is Aphrodite who is credited for arousing in Hades desire for his niece.

One day the beloved Kore was out in the flower fields near Enna, with her young virginal cousins, like Artemis, Pallas and numerous other maidens friends like; Galaxyria, Acaste, Calypso etc... She was not alone, as some artistic depictions might lead you to believe. She was actually in great company, plucking an array of beautiful fragrant flowers and engaging in the typical games that young girls play. When behold, the most beautiful flower she had ever seen, captivated her. Some described it as a three-petalled, blue fleur-de-lys, but the Homeric hymn described it as the one hundred bloom, white, sweet Narcissus flower. Enamored by its celestial beauty, the impetuous girl stretched her arm and reached to pull it out and upon doing so, the earth split open from below her feet, and, abruptly a chariot of black stallions came forth with Hades snatching the young maiden- disappearing from the scene. She let out one yell, but it all happened so fast, no one could claim that they saw or heard anything...no one, except for the all-seeing Sun God, Helios and the Wise Crone- Hekate.

For nine days and nine nights, distraught Demeter searched everywhere for her beloved daughter, but could not find her anywhere. On the tenth day, Hekate comes to her aid, shares what she knows and then takes her to Helios, for further information on the matter. To her astonishment and devastation, she learns of her daughter's abduction and horrid fate, as Bride of Hades. And to make matters worse, she learns that this arrangement was made and approved, behind her back, by Zeus himself. According to the popularized Greek myth, the despondent and enraged Demeter abandoned her post on Mount Olympus immediately and refused to let anything grow upon the earth until her daughter was returned to her. She spent her sad days traveling the earth, in disguised as an old woman and pledged the earth would witness a horrid famine that would destroy both mortals and immortals alike, until she was reunited with her beloved Kore.

Meanwhile, Kore was in the underworld now, as Persephone, Wife to her uncle, Aidoneus Hades. Imagine her confusion and her own lamentation- youthful flowering bright maiden, finding herself in the abysmal dark caverns of the underworld, greeted by the stench of death and the overwhelming sadness of loss souls. On the earth, she was brightness, frivolity, growing the flowers and the corn and as a girl she knew love only via her devoted mother. Here, so abruptly, she finds herself in this new realm, alone, in a foreign new role, as wife. The myth tells she would not eat nor drink anything in the underworld, during this time. Yet time went by and upon receiving word from the messenger God, Lord Hermes, that she would be allowed to leave the underworld and return to her mother, she partook of the food of the dead- seeds of the Pomegranate. Some conflicting stories state that she was offered 4-6 pomegranate seeds, by Hades himself and some state that someone else tricked her into taking them, in any case, she was now obligated to this realm. Her heartwarming reunion with her mother was bittersweet, as Demeter learned she would have to sacrifice her daughter to Hades and his underworld, one third of the year, due to the pomegranate seeds the maiden had ingested. During this time, the earth would be barren and cold and Demeter committed herself to forbidding anything to grow upon the earth while she mourned the absence of her daughter. This myth, on the surface, would serve to explain the Winter season and the agricultural sacred cycles so important to the Greeks and most civilizations at this time.

Persephone was sometimes depicted holding a torch flame or a sheath of Corn. She is often described as youthful, beautiful, trimmed ankle, bright minded, the one who makes the corn grow, and the one who has sympathy over the dead. One myth even tells of how she was not abducted but rather willingly sacrificed herself to the underworld upon learning of the sadness and confusion plaguing lost souls. She wanted to be their hope and guide. In this case she would be very reminiscent of many sacrificial Deities like Selu, the Native American Corn Goddess. As the Queen of the underworld she mothers and consoles the dead and it is through the entry of her bright aura, that THEIR hope is renewed. She appears supportive and much needed and yet, as can be expected, there are some conflicting tales of Persephone in her role as Queen of the Underworld. Some of the writing of the time make her just as fearsome and mistrustful as her husband, Hades and this is quite logical when we view unions between Gods(in other cultures and other time periods) and how they typically begin to share similar attributes. But in her, we see a consistent duality and it is this duality that intrigues me the most about Persephone.

Here is a Goddess who is required to live in two vastly contrasting worlds. Two third of the year she is among the living, under the bright sun, amidst the fertile and all that grows. One third of the year she is in the abysmal darkness among the dead, the hopeless, the stagnant, hidden away from the brightness of the sun. Yet when she goes from one realm to another, it is as if she never knew the other... It seems like no trace of darkness follows her when she returns to her mother's arms and her warm, carefree, Maiden brilliance seems tempered in the underworld. It appears as if she surrenders herself to whatever realm she is in and locks the door, and perhaps the memories, of the realm she just came from.

Thus, she appear to me to be a patron Goddess for those who walk in two worlds. Witches, psychics, priestesses and seers also intimately know Persephone, as they too are somehow required to live in the mundane world while simultaneously, having extrasensory, spiritual experiences. I reflect on the mother who is answering her toddlers question about the spilt milk, while concurrently seeing the ghost of her deceased father hovering nearby- she is present and answering the call of two opposing realms. In my own life I think of how often I have been active in an intense community ritual, in a trance floating, priestessing for the Divine and clearly in a completely different space, then at the end of it, having to ground, pack up my stuff, catch the local bus or subway and travel through a vastly different realm to get back home, after communing with the Divine.

Goddess of the twofolds indeed, we all touch upon Persephone at some point in our lives. Initially, I think about those who suffer with schizophrenia, Bi- polar disease, depression, but perhaps less obvious are those among us who are forced to live in two realms in the exact way Persephone must. I reflect on the multitude of coal miners in our world and how they are required to live and work an inordinate amount of time under the earth, in deep caves, separated from their families and friends and then, when mining season is over, they return to the upper part of the earth's surface, rejoin their families and routines, until they are called back to mine again. I reflect deeply on our Military and how they too touch upon Persephone's journey. Countless of men and women are called to duty and get deployed to places that probably make Hade's realm look like "Candy land." The things that these men and women of service are exposed to when they are deployed in war zone, places like Iraq and Afghanistan, is horribly astounding. Death and its gruesome stench is ever prevalent for the military and while they are in service, they are subject to a world vastly different than the ones they originated from. When their tour of duty is over, somehow they are required to put all those gruesome, bloody war memories behind them and come back to their families and loved ones, assimilate into their respective community and resign themselves to civilian living again....or at least, until they are called back again. This is Persephone's experience. She teaches us how to reconcile living in two opposing realms and as wommin, in particular, with so many roles we are obligated to take on, she is an ideal Goddess to work with.

Persephone, the Maiden, is often seen as part of the well revered Greek trinity, with Demeter as Mother, Hekate as Crone, but she is not only a part of the trinity, Persephone herself IS the Trinity. For me, Persephone comes across as really emulating the three most important feminine archetypes; Maiden, Mother, Crone. Some might say, she embodies four archetype, the last one being the Queen. When she is Kore, her Mother's daughter, she is the Maiden and when she is in the realm of the dead, she is touching upon the Crone archetype, but also the Mother, as she is compelled to mother the loss souls. As Hade's wife she is called Queen, which is a newly adopted archetype in the 20th century. Upon her return to the fields, she again seems to touch upon the attributes of the Mother archetype in her ability to do exactly as **her** very own mother does, make the Grain grow. She is Kore and while her mother, Demeter, was closely linked with Barley, the Corn, was made to sprout from the earth and grow because of her. As Kore (whose name resembles the word corn)she had the ability to make things grow from above and below the earth.

I believe Persephone also has much to teach us regarding our relationships with our mother and consequently all wommin. As the first womyn in our lives, our relationship with our mother can have a positive or negative effect on how we relate to all other, future wommin. The Maiden Goddess had a uniquely strong relationship with her mother, but so strong was her mother's love for her that Persephone's whole identity was mostly that of "daughter" and only after Hades enters the picture does she take on another, new role. Yet she vacillated between these two very strong roles as wife and daughter (belonging to her mother, belonging to her husband) and yet even as daughter she now exemplified the same gifts as her mother, thus becoming wife bestowed upon her a crown that had only been reserved for her own mother. I think for many of us, who do have trouble with our mothers, it stems from a lot of sources, but certainly not recognizing the thread that runs through both, mother and daughter, can contribute to some strife. When we can't acknowledge or embrace the attributes (good or bad)of our mothers' we fail to see those same attributes inherent in our own selves. And its not just our mother, dare I say, it also includes other wommin as well. When we try to separate ourselves from something or someone that we don't like, it's sometimes because, before us, they are reflecting back, something in us we are unwilling to face. Working with Persephone might help us unearth better ways to interact with our mothers and consequently all wommin and this is yet another reason why she is a wonderful Goddess for our gender to connect with.

PERSEPHONE GROVE GODDESS GATHERING

PURPOSE:
I. Healing Mother -daughter relationship,
Seeing our connection to our very own mothers, Empathize and connect with our mother, who is essentially a vast part of our own persona.
II. Recognizing the Maiden still lives in us. As Persephone is called upon to live in both worlds fulfilling two roles...we can call upon her with help to do the same.
Like Springtime, if we allow it, our maiden can come out to play every now and then, despite demanding new roles and even amidst largre responsibilities.

CHECK INS: With our Grove speaking stick, we will pass it around the room to introduce ourselves and share how we are feeling this month.

CHANTING *"Mother of darkness Mother of light", "Maiden, Mother and Crone" "Maiden sprightly" (see song text sheets)*

DRUMMING TRANCE: A deep low toned Musical Drumming Track (CD) will be played to help participants trance and then connect to this sacred moment. Grounding into the moment.

CHECK INS: With our Grove speaking stick, we will pass it around the room to honor the wommin in our lives, state our name, our mothers name and our Grandmothers name. Also maybe share a photo if they are available.

LESSON ON THE GODDESS PERSEPHONE
Learning of her etymology, her Greek myths and her relevance for today's womyn

GODDESS WORKSHOPS

WORKSHOP I: Discussion on the Goddess and how she appears to us personally. A photo of Kore/Persephone will be passed around the circle so that each womyn can reflect on her attributes.

WORKSHOP II: Two face Aboriginal Mask creation. Created with Plaster of Paris and a mold. One half of the face we will paint our image of *"She who is the daughter, the Maiden"* and then the other half of the mask we will paint, *"She who is the Queen of the underworld."* In this way we acknowledge and merge the power of these two archetypes.

WORKSHOP III: Gather photos and items of things that remind you of your youth/maiden years (past or present). Cut out clips from magazines of items that you enjoyed as a Maiden or words that trigger a memory. On a large Canvas or Glass frame, arrange your Maiden memorabilia to create a Collage.
This can be preserved for someone special like your future daughters or keep and display for yourself. It will serve to remind you of the maiden's journey and Persephone's delicate balance between her various aspects.

WORKSHOP VI: Set up a mother/ancestress altar (or travel shrine box)and honor the feminine spirits of the dead. Each shrine, for every syster will be quite unique. Share what you would include on this altar.

WORKSHOP V: Write a letter of thanksgiving to your mother but also a goodbye, as you will depart to journey with Persephone to the underworld and it will be a long time before you see each other again.

WORKSHOP VI: Sitting with our Darkness... With eyes shut, masked and or with a Veil over our entire face, we create a place of utter darkness and silence, to contemplate on the dark realm Persephone journeyed to. Could we endure part of the year away from the sun, in darkness, the way she does? What does this very act, under the dark veil, conjure you for you personally.

WORKSHOP VII: An Exercise to connect us to our Mothers

What are three things you love most about your mother?
_____
_____
_____

What three things did you inherit from your mother?
_____
_____
_____

What three things make your skin crawl about your mother?
_____
_____
_____

Look at these things, do they resonate within you as well?
Do you hold, or have the potential to hold these annoying characteristics?

What is her Sun sign and what is yours? How do the ruling elements of these signs mix? _____

Attain and study a photo of your mom as a young child. If you don't have a photo, close your eyes and envision what she might have looked like back then. Study the child's features and general disposition. If you saw her today, what words of wisdom would you need to tell this child? _____

Think back now at the years prior to your birth. See your mom as the maiden that she was prior to becoming your mother. If you can, find a photograph to reflect on. Can you rewrite her story and would it be vastly different from what it actually was/is? What would you tell your mother, as the maiden, before embarking on motherhood?
_____

Now, whether you are a crone, mother or maiden, see your mother at the age that you are right at this moment. If you can, attain a photo of her at your present age that might help in the visualization. What choices have you made in your life that are similar to hers?
How has your life differed from hers'?
Are you living the way she would chose to, if given the chance? Would she be someone you could hang out with as a close friend?
_____

The answers to these questions might begin to bring healing to mother-daughter relations.
It will help connect you to this womyn, we call mother, and help tap into an important part within your own persona.

REFLECTIONS ON PERSEPHONE

She teaches us to walk in multiple realms, particularly the earthly planes and the spiritual and consequently, the delicate balance of a witch and priestess in our industrial modern world. For wommin, it is always a delicate balance between our various roles- for we always manage, simultaneously, more than one role. Whether we are daughter, wife, mother and passionate lover, career woman, homemaker or witch and layperson, astral traveler and grounder, teacher and student , living in the past and present, or bi-polar, juggling with highs and lows, we are Persephone. It is always a delicate balancing act and She teaches us to walk the fine line with acceptance and grace. We also begin to heal mother daughter relationships with her energy.

PERSEPHONE SPEAKS
GROVE GODDESS GATHERING

I have been the frolicking maiden, without a care in the world. Living for my own merriment and delight. Relishing the bountiful love bestowed to me by my protective mother. I took great pleasure in coming and going as I pleased, never once worrying about a thing, because I knew her divine protective embrace was never too far. She was my watchful eye, when I blindly stepped forward, as youthful maidens often do, without looking. Mother's love for me was whole and so complete. I had no need to wonder, nor seek for another. I couldn't even fathom that there was another. But Lo..... How one day...something strangely awakened in me....and my world changed forever.

In one of my frolicking Maiden adventures, I traveled too far.... Much too far away from my adoring mother....so far, that I was no longer recognized as Daughter. So far, that I no longer was under her beloved watchful eye. I had crossed into an unknown landscape, so mysterious and yet so enticing. I arrived into a dark realm where the sun was not known, where light and life no longer breathes. I traveled too far into a realm where I was now wife and lover. My days of living carefree and simply for my own pleasure were brought to an end. Those days of personal merriment took a back seat to the role I would now have to fulfill... as wife, as lover, consoler of the dead, Queen of this dark domain.

Mother....oh dearest mother, how I always assumed it would always be me and you. How I took it for granted that you would always be there for me...and that we would always be together. Your precious gifts I failed to notice and acknowledge, until I arrived to this dark Queen-Dom....until the Heavy crown was placed upon my soul...

I am mother... heavy in my concerns for the dead and many others, heavy in my numerous obligations and sacrifices. I am Heavy in my relentless responsibilities and the expectations others have of me.

On this side, in this dark place, I am caregiver, nurturer, sustainer....
I am both student and teacher, supporter and helper. I touch love in its multifaceted infinite guises.
I am now your Watchful eyes....
I am now escort and protector, charioteer, law enforcer and Queen.

The most delicate of frail skeletal flowers have now been placed in my hands to nurture, teach, sustain and tend to...as I was a flower nursed to fruition. It is for me a privilege and an honor to be in such a sacred role as Queen and Mother.

Yes.... I can see that I am mother now, but I must remember that I once was that flower, young, light, carefree daughter and maiden. Though it feels as if she is suffocating and drying up here underneath the Earth, she is still alive...breathing faintly within me. Artemis, Diana joining hands with Gaia and mother Demeter to walk Persephone's journey of balance. I am Mother, I am Queen, balancing it all externally, internally, as I unearth... and still embrace, even in dark locales, the maiden within me.
So mote it be!

PERSEPHONE GROVE GODDESS GATHERING RITUAL

Purpose: To call upon Persephone, Find balance between two strong archetypes and honor our mother.
At the Entrance, Purification with smudge:
With Clove, allspice and frankincense incense in the cauldron
Anointing oil at the entrance by volunteered Priestess.

Circle cast

With a crystal wand or athame, Cast Circle with prose, also scatter the perimeters of the circle with grain and white flowers. *(See suggestions in appendix)*

Speaker proclaims our Intent for the Day....

Quarters called

* Guardians of the Watchtowers of the **East**, Ye Powers of **Air**,
Place of sudden winds that hearken to endings and beginnings, new stirrings and visions, Breath..... that inaugurates journeys, air that announces new realms....
We call on you to bring us your enlightening gifts
Guard and Hold our sacred space, Hail and welcome
(attendants repeat) Hail and welcome!!!

*Hail Guardians of the Watchtowers of the **South**, Ye Powers of **Fire**,
Place of August heat, ripening our first harvest and our loins, preparing us for seasonal changes.. Heat that emanates from deep within ALL sacred caverns; our heart, our womb, our earth...We call on you to lend us your feverish gifts....
Guard and Hold our sacred circle, Hail and Welcome
(attendants repeat) Hail and Welcome!!!

*Hail Guardians of the Watchtowers of the **West**, Ye powers of **Water**,
Place of the Grain Mother's lament and tears of longing, place of welcomed rain to feed and nurture of our fields....forbidden sweet nectars that drip from Persephone's lips....
We call on you to bring us your quenching gifts
Guard and Hold our sacred space, Hail and welcome
(attendants repeat) Hail and Welcome!!!

*Hail Guardians of the Watchtowers of the **North**, Ye powers of **Earth**,
Place of the Earth's powers of creation, place of the Harvest and the Grain, origins of roots and seeds. Deep within this realm there are mysteries to unearth. Earth teacher be here now. We call on you to bring us your gestating gifts
Guard and Hold our sacred circle, Hail and welcome
(attendants repeat) Hail and Welcome.
  Chant: *"Invoking Mother Song"* and *"Persephone's Song"*

INVOKING PERSEPHONE *(see suggested prose)*

Musical CD: *"Snake Woman"*
Enchanted Pomegranate seeds will be passed around the room to share
"With these seeds
That I now eat
Queen and Maiden
sings in me..."

Spell Working *(With music playing in background for ambiance...)*
We will write our mother a letter of "sacrifice-recognition" and "gratitude." Whether she is dead or alive, we will take this sacred moment within our circle of wommin, to consider one kernel of corn your mother has bestowed upon you, that you will now nurture and help grow and manifest. What legacy has she left within you? What gift has she passed down to you, whether conscious or unconscious.... Some of you might find this easy and some might not be able to think of one thing. Take this time to really reflect, not just on her role as Mother, but her role as an example of "Womynhood" in your life and how this plays a part in your own choices today as a womyn. Positive or negatively, our mothers have a great impact on our lives and how we interact with other wommin. Reflect now on the gifts passed down to you from your mother. At the very least she birthed you into this world and for that we can be grateful. Thank her in this letter. Consider the sacrifice it took for her to bestow this gift upon you.

When you are done, gather her photo or an object that was hers or personally meaningful to you, hold it near your heart and when you are ready light the flame with gratitude, sending her love saying:

"I thank you (mother's name) for _____,
I send healing to this relationship
with this flame..."

Wommin light candle and place it on altar.....

When she returns, priestess will be near, to place a flower or a maiden's crown- wreath on her head saying these words...

"The Maiden in you has returned once more
Persephone's Crown, Your head will adorn..."

Songs and Chants: *"We all come from the Goddess...."*

Final Check ins, Holding hands begin to devoke

Thanking and Devoking Persephone
Dearest Bright Maiden,
Daughter and Bride
When called you came,
to bless us with your presence
and teach us your wisdom and gifts.
We thank you Proserpina, beloved daughter Kore,
With gratitude we bid thee adieu,
Hail and Farewell Persephone!

Thanking and Devoking the Quarters thru Song:
"The Earth, the Air, the Fire, the Water, return, return, return, return..."

Opening up the Circle:
"The Circle is open, but unbroken may the Peace of the Goddess, be ever in our hearts...
Merry meet and merry part and merry meet again...."

****

Potluck/ Cakes and ales following

A SHORT RITUAL FOR PERSEPHONE (for solitary or group working)
Cast the Circle as formal or as informal as you choose.

Invoking the Elements with a traditional Elemental Chant:
"....Air I am, Fire I am, Water, Earth and Spirit I am..." while holding the elemental representation and briefly connecting with it as you sing.

Offer Pomegranate seeds, or its juice, to the Goddess at the altar and then offer it to yourself and others present, to touch upon Persephone's essence. You can do this either from a freshly opened pomegranate, store bought organic pomegranate juice (now readily available in stores) or you can also use Cranberry-pomegranate Craisins, which are like raisins.
"We offer and partake of your sacred pomegranate to touch ever deeper who you are Persephone. May we know you with this act. May we honor you on this day..."

Invocation of Persephone (reciting Prose and or calling her, from your heart)
Singing Chant: *"Eight Bead song"* or *"Mother of Darkness Mother of Night"*

Working: At this time we will be coloring an image of the High Priestess Tarot card, to personally connect with this obvious aspect of the Goddess, as Priestess, Queen and Maiden and allow her subtle personal message to come through for us via this working.

Persephone Meditation...
With a black veil over your head, contemplate on the Goddess of Spring now, as she finds herself, in the underworld. Amidst the stench of death and sorrow, by the side of her dark, powerful feared husband. In the dark of the underworld, there, she finds herself and you journey with her under your veil... Walk the long corridors with her, walk silently through the winding narrow pathway, unlit and damp. Walk through the strange whispers of inaudible words, in archaic languages, yet unknown to you. Walk with her further down, deep down into the place she is forced to call home, for one third of the year. In the realm of darkness, the bright maiden takes you to experience her moment of resignation into Hade's realm. This is her Queen-Dom, as much as his now. Take this moment to survey the room, look (as much as you can) all around you and make note of what you see. In this deep mystical darkness, you will be required to engage your third eye, to fully see what is before you. (pause).
    Consider for a moment that life is cyclical and this darkness, with the possible uncomfortable state of this moment, is not meant to last forever. You find yourself with Persephone, in the stillness and paralysis of night, quietly listen to your inner guide and the message Persephone has for you in this dark realm. (pause).
    Your eyes have adjusted to the darkness, but soon you note Persephone's own silhouette becoming more pronounced. Her lines coming into focus clearer and the haze of her aura becoming brighter and brighter... As if someone has discovered the window to this place and is letting in the rays of light from the sun, now cascading before you. Persephone turns away from you to face this light and you feel her intense joyful anticipation deep within your own soul. It is an indistinguishable joyful anticipation and hopefulness, that now stems from YOU, it belongs to you. Feel this sense of great anticipation and hope, rising, filling you up (pause).
    The light has grown stronger and it awakens and stirs in you, memories of childhood games, running, skipping, playing tag and first kisses and treasured tender moments from your past. For that brief moment of reflection you lost track of time, but time does not exist here and you turn to look for the Queen. You look up as Persephone disappears into the bright light and beckons you to join her and her mother, Demeter. (pause) Come be reborn with me she says and sprout with the seeds and blooming flowers. You take her hand and join her, returning to the fertile earth above and the caresses of the warm sun.
    When you are ready, consider what you will surrender and give birth to in the coming months and join us in this time and place. Follow my voice to help you transition back to this room. Remove the veil from your head, when you are ready and ignite your spell candle. State aloud what you hope to manifest in the light of your inner and outer flame. And end with, "So mote it be... It is done!"

By the light of Persephone's return to her mother,
I too am revived and vow to manifest by this flame_____

Final check in, when you are ready to end ritual,
Devoke Goddess, Devoke Quarters/Elements, and
Open the Circle.

INVOKING PERSEPHONE

Queen of the Underworld,
Mother of lost souls,
Bride to Lord Hades,
Return as was foretold.

Bright Minded Kore,
Demeter's Sole Love,
Daughter, Spring Maiden
Call the Corn to grow above.

Now in the Springtime,
Return to your place,
Flowering the Earth,
With your beautiful face

Come as we call you,
As we seek to know you well,
Come Proserpina,
Goddess of two realms.

We invoke you Queen of Erebos,
Bride of the Dark haired Lord,
Flowering young Maiden
Come now thru these doors.

Thanking and Devoking Persephone

Dearest Bright Maiden,
Daughter and Bride
When called you came,
to bless us with your presence
and teach us your wisdom and gifts.
We thank you Proserpina, beloved daughter Kore,
With gratitude we bid thee adieu,
Hail and Farewell Persephone!

On the night of a dark moon perform this spell. Gather an images of Persephone in statue, photo or artistic form. Include on your altar, a pomegranate, devoted for the Goddess herself, a black veil and purple or silver candles. Carve your wax and anoint it with "Kore's Oil" or "Priestess oil" (see appendix). Surround your altar with numerous gemstones from the earth, like crystals, garnets, malachite, agate, hematite, red jasper, rose quartz, onyx, amethyst etc... and offer incense of frankincense, myrrh, cypress, patchouli, hyssop crushed herbs. Let your chalice hold Spring water- no salt. Begin this spell with a ritual bath. Cleanse your body with consecrated salt and a lightly scented oil and approach your mirror, upon the altar, sky clad. Gaze deeply into the reflection as you begin to speak.....

INNER PRIESTESS
*By the light of the dark
The candles aflame
Reflection are seen
through the scented haze

A glimmer into
What daylight hides
Lineage- ancestry
Magick from inside

The strength of the Goddess
The beauty of the Moon
Sky clad forms
Illuminating rooms

I look deep, ever deeper
Through the mirror to find
A Priestess has returned
from Ancient times

Daughter of the Moon
Temple of her domain
We are now and ever more
one the same....

HER JOURNEY AT SAMHAIN

Three months I'll rest,
In deep Magick sleep,
Arrive in a realm
Whose passage comes thru dreams.

And play with limitless,
No boundaries to fear,
Like shadows, formless,
Receptive to hear...

The whispers of grains,
Of tiny hopes and seeds,
In darkness they form,
A ray of light for me...

Surrender to slumber,
To gather my strength,
For Spring will come soon,
And I'll dream until then.

Partake of the Pomegranate,
And wander through the Halls,
Of Death and Darkness
As I greet the Fall....

PERSEPHONE GROVE GODDESS GATHERING CHANTS

MOTHER OF DARKNESS
Mother of darkness, Mother of Light,
Earth beneath the soul in flight,
Songs of Love and Love of Light,
Guide us to our Heart

I AM MAGICK WOMAN (?) Shelley Graff
I am Magick /Sacred Woman, Giving Birth to myself
I am Magick /Sacred Woman
Giving Birth to myself
from deep inside the wells,
From your loving eyes and wisdom
My truth that I must tell,
I am Magick /Sacred Woman
Giving Birth to myself....

BY THE EARTH
By the earth that is her body,
By the air that is her breath,
By the fire that is her bright spirit,
By the living waters of her womb,
May the peace of the Goddess,
Be forever in our hearts,
The circle is open but unbroken,
Merry meet and merry part (repeat)

SWEET SURRENDER by Gladys Gray
We are opening up in sweet surrender,
To the luminous love light of the one,
We are opening up in sweet surrender,
To the luminous love light of the one,
We are Opening ...We are Opening .....
We are opening.... We are Opening....

EARTH, MOON, MAGICK by B.M.M.
In the Earth, deep within,
There is A Magick,
I draw it in.
    In her Caves, in the Trees
    Hear her Heartbeat,
    Pulsing thru me.
When I Rise, I feel her Love
With feet Grounded
I'm soaring high above,
    In the Earth, deep within,
    There is A Magick,
    I draw it in
Ancient Moon, my Soul reveres
With my Singing,
I call you here.
    When this flame, ignites tonight,
    Priestess dancing,
    Under the moonlit night....
In the Earth, deep within,
There is A Magick
I draw it in....
    There is A Magick, I draw it in }3x

MAIDEN DANCING by B.M.M.
Spiraling Dancing, Up and Down
Reaching the Center with Floral Crown
Laughing Maiden, Giggles are free
I've awaken the Maiden in me.

See me Jump, Jump, Jump,
Cross the meadow Field
See me Fearless and Beautiful
and dancing the Wheel.

INVOKING MOTHER
by B.M.M.
Mother, Mother, Mother, I call you,
Deep within my soul, you're stirring my womb.
Mother, Mother, Mother, Hear my Cries,
In this Sacred Circle I Call you tonight.
Light the inner Flame, as I light the candle wick,
Call your sacred name and embrace myself as Witch
Sky-clad I approach, to Elemental thrones,
Hear me, Mother hear me,
Through these words I wrote.

GROVE GODDESS GATHERING CHANTS

SPARKS
Sparks from the Hearth
Of the Queen
Of Death and Light
Swarm through the dark,
Dance through the night
By J. Robin Gall For Starhawk', Reclaiming Tradition

SHE GATHERS *By Ruth Rhiannon Barrett*
She gathers her daughters by Moon and by Sun,
She gathers her daughters it has begun.
She gathers her daughters to turn the wheel,
She gathers her daughters to learn and heal.
She gathers her daughters by night and by day,
She gathers her daughters to lead the way
> **(Counter Melody)**
> ***By Moon and Sun, We have Begun***
> ***To turn the wheel, to learn and heal......***

WINGS
Wings wandering in the deep of night
A thousand Birds take flight
And our dreams are born
On the wings of Change
We are weaving the World tonight.
By Suzanne Sterling and Starhawk, Reclaiming Tradition

DON'T YOU KNOW by Elaine Silver
Don't you know
Your body is a temple,
And don't you know ,your spirit is a shine,
The other side of fear is a never ending love
Don't you know you and I are both divine
> You won't know what it means to really grow
> If you don't open up, to who's inside
> The other side of fear is a never ending love
> Don't you know you and I are both divine

And I lift up my glass and drink a toast
To all the women in me, I hold them so close
The other side of fear is a never ending love
Don't you know you and I are both divine
> I'm Part Princess,
> Part Witch,
> Part Goddess,
> Part Bitch,
> Part Spirit and
> I am Divine....

The other side of fear is a never ending love
Don't you know you and I are both divine
You and I, are both Divine by Elaine Silver

ELEMENTAL CHANT by anonymous
Earth my Body, Water my Blood,
Air my Breath and Fire my Spirit.

WE ALL COME FROM THE GODDESS by Z. Budapest
We all come from the Goddess
And to her we shall return,
like a drop of rain, Flowing to the ocean

September

The name of this month is derived from the Latin word "*Septum,*" meaning seventh, as this was the seventh month in the Roman Calendar. The astrological sign for September is Virgo, the maiden, ruled by the crafty, messenger of the gods, Mercury (August 21- Sept 20). Virgo is considered an earth sign and as we approach the second harvest with Mabon, it's easy to see how its energy will influence the entire month.

September has always been a month about getting back to business and adjusting to this seasonal change. The cosmic atmosphere is really about re-adjusting to changes in our climate, our roles and our routine. Sometimes it literally feels like the start of a new year as everything seems to shift- this holds even more weight for school age children, as they prepare for a new school year with new school supplies, shoes and scholastic wardrobe. The summer days have clearly ended -gone are the hot, sweaty days of August. For most of us, our vacations are over, our chances to visit and sunbathe on sandy beaches, in some parts of the world, are gone and family barbecues or picnic opportunities have lessen. Perhaps stemming from childhood and the educational system, this month always beholds that energy of returning back to work. Our ancestors, who lived so close to the land, would've also experienced this urgency to work, prepare diligently for winter and gather the harvest.

Now we return to our learning institutions or our employment and life just has that busy feeling once more. It is a time to take stock of your accomplishments and assess where you might need to make up for lost time. Even among the critters in nature, there is busy work being done, as they prepare to stock up, before the arrival of winter.

September, for most agrarian cultures, brings the second Harvest, only this time we are much closer to the cold, dark winter season. While we might want to rest and celebrate the new crops, we realize we can't stop there. We can't avoid the work load before us any longer and it is time, once more, to harvest and prepare for the changing wheel of the year. In ancient times, the effort and hard work at this point would assure a more pleasant viable winter. Harvesting and storing food was obviously imperative and downright crucial in order to survive the cold months.

The Full moon of this month was sometimes known as the Harvest Moon but it was also known as Wine Moon, as this was the time to harvest grapes for wine making. This commemoration also reveals the sacredness of wines and spirits, especially during the cold winter months. Alcohol had many uses, but an important one, was helping our bodies feel warm in the midst of frigid low temperatures. The Wine Gods, Bacchus and Dionysius, were often the two Deities honored in Greece and Rome during this time of year and many Pagans today continue to revere them for the Sabbat of Mabon because of this connection.

Mabon (around September 20-22nd) celebrates the Autumnal Equinox of this month and honors the waning sun during this time of harvest. Day and Night stand in equal balance on the Equinox. Balancing work and play becomes a challenge, as we endeavor to leave the summer behind us and enter the fecundities of Fall. Did you play all summer long or did you take the time, every now and then, to work and put some efforts into future projects? As the air gets cooler you sense the changes in Mother Nature and it is this change that motivates our very own souls to go forward, find balance, work and plan ahead. If you've paced yourself during those summer months, this will be smooth sailing for you. If you played all summer long, then you have much work ahead of you before the dark season approaches. This month we call upon the nourishing Goddess, Corn Mother/Selu, who imparts her wisdom of sacrifices, forgiveness and proper relationship to our harvested food. We will also tap into the Goddess Aradia, who begins to prepare us for the Dark season with her Occult teachings on how to further empower ourselves through nature and the traditional mysteries of the Craft.

CHAPTER TWENTY

"The goal of life is to make your heartbeat match the beat of the Universe, to match your nature with nature..." Joseph Campbell

"I brought children into the dark world because it needed the light that only a child can bring..." Liz Armbruster

WELCOME SELU

OUR ALTAR

Altar cloth: *Yellow or Orange, golden corn colored altar cloth and maybe a second brown altar cloth underneath.*
Image: *Corn or a Statue of Native American Corn Mother....*
Canvas art or photo of the corn Mother, photos of corn fields and husk, also images of mothers.

Always present on the altar;
A cast iron cauldron, drums, speaking stick, a silver pentacle, athame, elemental representations.....

Air: *Feather and Smudge sage and copal wands, Incense type sticks, cones, charcoal brisket and fine powdered herbs, barley, large sweeping feather, or a simple bell.*
Fire: *candles, glass enclosed candles or pillars in yellows, oranges, browns.*
Water: *small glass vessel or bowl with Fresh Spring Water*
Earth: *fruits and vegetables, and things that grow from the earth. Lots of plants and sunflowers, a small dish of soil and or herbs. Lots Corn husks and grains.*

Other items pertinent to this particular gathering
Plate offering of Corn husk
Plate of Barley or other grains
Flowers with plants and greenery
Writing pens and paper , safety pins,
Light gauzy fabric
Workshop items
Goddess Oracle image of Corn Mother

Offering *breads, grains, meals made entire of Corn, corn bread, corn soups, corn chips, honey and fruits can also be offered*
Sacred objects from members:
Notes:

Selu

Corn Mother

Reclaiming self

Corn Mother Altars

Selu/Corn Mother

Corn, or Maize as it is known by most Native Americans, was first developed in Central Mexico over 7,000 years ago. It was not something that grew naturally on its own in the wild but rather needed to be cultivated. According to historians it was started from the wild grass known as teosinte and in the beginning it looked very different from our modern day corn husk. As the Native American Indians migrated, corn began to be introduced to Peruvian culture, further south, as well as further up North, in the Southwest region of the Americas. Eventually its consumption became wildly popular throughout the Americas and when Christopher Columbus returned to Europe, after his expedition, he introduced the comestible to Europeans.

Corn became an imperative source of food for native Americans, but also a significant part of their daily lives and culture. Various part of the corn was utilized to make sleeping mats, moccasins, ceremonial masks and games and baskets, which helped transporting many different vital items. The ability to feed a whole nation with the grains of corn made it one of the most important staples in aboriginal's diet. Today Corn is no less important than it was 7,000 years ago. Reflect, if you will now, on what our lives would be like without corn.

Today our dependence on corn goes beyond the obvious; bread, cake, tortilla chips, popcorn, corn-muffins, sweet corn on the cob, etc, etc. It might surprise you to know that corn is employed in our aspirins, glue, cosmetics, shoe polish, and in our books as corn starch, as well as our clothing. It is utilized as corn syrup in our soft drinks and often used to feed farm Chickens that provide for our eggs. Corn can be found in the ink that graces our books and newspapers and it's a key ingredient to Ethanol, which is found in automobile fuel. So it becomes clear that Corn is incredibly valuable to the sustenance of a nation today, as it was with its inception.

It is therefore not surprising that corn would receive such veneration from aboriginals. To indigenous cultures that practice animism and saw spirit in all things, one could easily see how something so crucial and important, like corn, can become deified. Studies into these native cultures reveal that it was customary to craft a puppet made of stalks of maize from the first corn husk in a harvest and great care was taken to preserve this puppet or corn dolly (as it was sometimes referred to) in order to guarantee a continuous fertile crop for the year. It was ceremonially dressed in woman's attire and it was well regarded, for the duration of the year, until it was ceremonially burned and replaced with the first corn of the next harvest.

Corn woman appears in numerous indigenous tribes by various names and with a multitude of myths and folklore traditions, intertwined into Native's culture and because they have been passed down, throughout generations, via oral tradition (through song and dance) we are blessed to have many surviving tales.

Mayan believed humans were actually fashioned out of corn and Penebscot Indians believed Corn mother to be the first mother of her people. The Lakota plains Indians correlated the existence of Corn mother with White Buffalo woman and for the Seneca Indians of the Northeast, they believed in a beautiful Woman who lived high above the mountains as their divine Maize Goddess. The Creeks, in Southeast Americas, viewed Corn Mother as a highly revered Old Woman, while the Zuni people of the Southwestern United States of America had a myth about eight corn maidens. To the Aztec and Mexico, Corn Mother was known as Chicomecoatl, the Goddess of Maize but to the Cherokee nation, she was known as Selu. She was also known as yellow woman and Iyatiku to the Keresan people of Southwest Americas.

In researching and becoming acquainted with many of Corn Mother's various myths, there is a similar thread running through all of them. Inherent in the corn, and the myths related to Selu, are the themes of sacrifice, forgiveness and the cycles of birth, growth, life, death and rebirth. I have elected to elucidate here and share one of the Cherokee tales of Corn Mother, also known as Selu.

Some claim Corn woman was a spirit that was sent down to earth once a year to help the crop grow tall and strong, others tell a different story. Cherokee folklore reveals she was sent down to earth to live and feed the people. In this tale Selu, living on the earth, gave birth to two sons, who were always hungry. Every time they complained of hunger and asked for food, she would instruct them to sit and wait patiently, while she would quickly disappear into a nearby hut and magickally always come back with a basket full of corn. This happened quite often and the boys, while dutifully relishing their meals and plumping up on corn, started to wonder where and how their mother was getting food. One night curiosity got the best of them and they defied their mother's instructions to wait patiently. Instead, on this night, they decide to follow, creep and spy on their mother, as she entered the small hut. What they saw was far beyond comprehensible for the minds of two small boys and needless to say quite traumatic. Inside the hut, they saw their mother squatting above the basket, producing a multitude of corn from her very own body, filling the basket with their next meal. There are some lore that state Corn Mother produced corn from scabs on her body and some say from her feces. In either case she is essentially producing corn from her very own body and it disgust the boys. That night at dinner time, the boys would not eat, they confronted their mother with what they had seen and here again, some myth vary claiming that the boys, horrified, threaten to tell the entire village. In this Cherokee lore, Corn Mother realizes that her children and her people are now in jeopardy of not being able to provide for themselves and sadly she realizes the sacrifice required of her. She tells her boys that now that they know the truth, they must kill her and drag her body through the fields to ensure that corn will continue to grow and sustain her people. Wherever droplets of her blood spill, there corn will grow and now the children will need to feed themselves from this point onward. Some other myths tell another version of this story, claiming that Corn Mother's body had to be cut up into tiny pieces and scattered around the various corners of the world to ensure the survival of corn for the Native American people.

In this popular folklore of Selu, we meet the universal archetype of fertile mother and her message of procreation, nourishment, death and rebirth and sacrifice, as she willingly sheds her body and blood, to save and secure a nation of people and the future generations of Native Americans to come. With her death, she ensures her children will not starve to death.

I find that tapping into the energy and lessons of Corn Mother makes perfect sense to me at this time of year. Mabon is the second harvest for most Wiccans and commemorating Selu at this time of the year seems most appropriate, although I have also called upon her during the first harvest, at Lammas as well. I find that this holiday of the Autumnal Equinox, presents the theme of equilibrium in our lives, as we stand, in perfect symmetry, between both night and day. It is a good time to reflect on what requires perfect balance in our own lives and because Selu touches upon the issue of food and nourishment, and this is the second harvest, I can't help but consider how food and our relationship to it, is not always in perfect balance.

Our society struggles greatly with issues related to food. Just perusing through a contemporary woman's magazine I can't help but notice the predominance of malnourished looking, skinny models and then walking outside my door and seeing the unusual amount of unhealthy, obese people. Clearly as a society, we struggle with finding a right relationship with food. We either abuse it and consume too much of it, WITHOUT regards to its sacred vital role, or we disrespect it and call it the enemy, avoiding it, to fulfill an unreal body image. In either case, food is not being respected, nor approached with the reverence it deserves. Yet, if like indigenous people and our ancestors, we too saw Corn as Goddess, wouldn't our approach to food be vastly different? Wouldn't our relationship to food be immeasurably different than what it appears to be today for millions of people?

On this Autumnal Equinox, as I endeavor to connect with Corn Woman and her numerous cathartic lessons, I will also consider the lessons she has to teach me, as a Goddess womyn, about nourishment, balance and proper alignment with food.

SEPTEMBER- CORN MOTHER -GODDESS GATHERING

Purpose: To learn of our Goddess for the month, Corn Mother and Commemorate the Second harvest with much celebrating, gratitude and feasting. Learning of ways to magickally protect ourselves with the use of Herbs.

Chant Workshop:
"Eight Bead Chant", "We are systers on a journey", " May all go as I will", " Earth my Body", "The Equinox Chant", " Humble Yourself", and more...

Check Ins: With our Speaking stick, we will go around the circle as each wommin introduces herself and shares her journey to know the Goddess.

Agreements read communally...There is always a sense of reflection and reverence that permeate the room as we each read two bylaws from our communal Agreements that reminds us of our vows to one another and how we create sacred space within our group. Agreement sheets are passed, signed and submitted before moving onward.

Drumming/Movement: Depending on the number of attendants, we will either hear a Native American drumming CD Track, to ground us in this moment and connect us to this aboriginal realm or create an actual drumming circle amongst our systers. Sometimes incorporating both a CD and actual drumming works effectively as well.

Check Ins II: With our trusty sacred Speaking stick, around the circle we will each share our culinary taste. Name **three** of your favorite foods that you consider so delicious, they are for you a gift from the gods.

Goddess Lecture

A discussion on Corn Mother as found in various tribes and cultures, her myths and ways to honor her best...

GODDESS WORKSHOPS
Workshops I:
A tarot image of Corn Mother and a reading from "*The Goddess Oracle*" will be shared around the circle. Wommin are encouraged to share their impressions of her image.

Workshop II:
A form of cleansing asperge- Vibrational work- Shaking off Debris as each womyn stands in the center of the circle, surrounded by her systers as all cleanse her with vibrations. Participants should focus on clearing energy from the person in the center of group.

Workshops III:
Mabon Meditation -Consider playing a gentle drumming track in the background while you read a meditation to the group or simply play a shamanic drumming track with no speech to allow participants to journey alone, at their own pace.

Workshops IV:
Anonymously, every participant will write on slips of paper any particular magickal needs, prayer or spell request and or remedy they need. We can all add our suggestions to help one another and maybe even discuss things that have worked for us personally in the past. Request will be placed in cauldron. Opening dialogue about our needs for safety and protection, boundaries and respecting one another's privacy.

Workshops V:
Learning about some ways to protect our environment and ourselves through magick, herbal plackets and incenses, Four Thieves vinegar, war water, witch's Protective Bottle

Workshops VI:
A discussion on the cathartic powers of offering forgiveness. Reciting together a powerful simple mantra to offer Universal forgiveness to others and ourselves.

Workshops VII:
To connect with Corn Mother even further we will endeavor to prepare a corn dish. If time permits, we will gather our ingredients around the kitchen counter and communally bake corn muffins or corn bread or a corn salad. Each participant will have a chance to add her energy to the dough, envisioning balance, good health and wellbeing to all wommin.

Workshops VIII:
The media is constantly bombarding us with distorted images of the female body. In this workshop we will go through several popular magazines with our clipping implements, to consciously point out those images that are unhealthy for us to internalize, as wommin. Then we will search for those images that are more realistic and plausible, everyone will have an opinion on this sensitive topic. We will have a very open and honest discussion about our diets and how we feel about our bodies. We will discuss what is healthy balance and define for ourselves, what a healthy female body looks like. Vows to become more conscious about how we are portrayed in the media and maybe even write letters to a few selected advertisement corporations and T.V. networks to educate them on their damaging campaigns.

Workshops IX:
Mortar and Pestle. Grinding and imbuing our sacred herbs with our best intentions for safety and protection. A Protective Black Herbal Placket filled with enchanted herbs for our protection during the dark season.
Protective herbs like: Rosemary, angelica, clove, cinnamon, sage and lavender, bay leaf, mugwort, basil, vervain, hyssop, mistletoe, ginger, lemon verbena, sarsaparilla etc...
PLACKET INVOCATION of Protection stated aloud:
"Herbs to Shield and Keep me Safe,
Placket I charged, to guard my place..."

REFLECTIONS ON CORN MOTHER/SELU

In Selu we encounter a Goddess who has much to teach us about balance, the sacredness of food and the importance of having the right relationship with it. Aspiring for balance and respect for our nutrional intake is one way she comes to me. As modern day wommin this is an extremely important, yet sentive subject, as many of us are inundated with unhealthy views on food, diets and body images. Whether we are consuming too much of it or whether we are making it the enemy, purging and avoiding it, Selu reminds you of the importance of food and its connection to life, as the Corn is the Goddess herself.

There is also a very important aspect to Corn Mother, that ties in perfectly to this time of year. The sacrificial Mother, who willingly allows her blood to be shed so that a nation of her offspring can survive is a theme pertinent to this time of year as well. As we are approaching the dark season many us will need to assess and willingly surrender goals that no longer serve our highest good, in order to be free to move onward in our spiritual journey. As life gets chaotic and we start to get really busy with a mundane of new responsibilities sometimes we need to consider what needs to be sacrificed for the greater good of all. Selu arrives to inaggurates balance, sacrifices and forgiveness, whether this is offered to others or directly to our own selves.

CORN MOTHER - GROVE GATHERING RITUAL

Purpose: To celebrate the Second Harvest and honor the season of Mabon, incorporating the precious attributes of our totems/animals and crafting a communal knot spell.

ASPERGE
with a gentle smudging of copal and sage, every wommin will smudge herself at Entrance.

CIRCLE CASTING
Standing up and Holding each other's hand, turn to the womyn next to you, look deeply into her eyes, breath and when ready...declare aloud:

"In Perfect Love and Perfect Trust, I Cast this sacred space For Us...."

(in this way, intimately, we pledge to one another, connect as systers and declare that it is OUR love and trust in each other that formulates the strongest of boundaries in our sacred circle.)

*****

CALLING QUARTERS: *Incorporating our sacred animals*

Sacred Spirit of the *****East**, Element of *****Air**
Herein we call you, represented in your Holy creatures,
Our feather friends, the eagle, the birds we see daily taking flight in our vicinity.
We invite and invoke its powers of rising above all hindrance and journeying to safe, ideal locale.
We bid thee, be here now, to guard and hold our sacred space.
Hail and Welcome, Air, **Response**: *Hail and welcome, Air*

Sacred Spirit of the *****South**, Element of *****Fire**
Herein we call you, represented in your Holy creatures,
Our Fiery friends, the Lion and the Jaguar.
We invite and invoke its powers of stamina, valor and courage.
We bid thee, be here now, to guard and hold our sacred space.
Hail and Welcome, Fire, **Response**: *Hail and welcome, Fire*

Sacred Spirit of the *****West**, Element of *****Water**
Herein we call you, represented in your Holy creatures,
Our Aquatic friends the Dolphin, the Mermaid, her Sea-Turtles.
We invite and invoke its powers of healthy fluidity, beauty and gracefulness.
We bid thee, be here now, to guard and hold our sacred space.
Hail and Welcome, Water, **Response**: *Hail and welcome, Water*

Sacred Spirit of the *****North**, Element of *****Earth**
Herein we call you, represented in your Holy creatures,
Our domestic pets and familiars, like our dogs and cats and the Hare
We invite and invoke its powers of steadfastness, unconditional love and grounding support.
We bid thee, be here now, to guard and hold our sacred space.
Hail and Welcome, Earth, **Response**: *Hail and welcome, Earth*

GODDESS INVOCATION TO CORN MOTHER:

Corn Mother, Yellow Woman,
Iyatiku and Selu,
Nourisher, Provider,
On this day, We honor you.
Come Brilliant Teacher,
On the Kernel of your Grain,
Connect us to your Life Force,
Bring your gifts to our Terrain....

CHANT and MOVE: *"Eight Bead Chant...."*
Speak of our impending knot spell, pass cords around the group as we prepare to raise energy and with **Native drum music CD playing,** invite them to move, dance, connect energetically with their selected yellow cords and consider what they hope to manifest with this spell. Immediately after music ends, we drop, gather in the center, holding our cords and begin;

NINE KNOT SPELL (see accompanied chant sheet for spell text)
Each womyn reciting one line as we knot, until all are done.....

1. By the Knot of One, this spell has begun
2. By the Knot of Two, it will come true
3. By the Knot of Three, I draw it to me
4. By the Knot of Four, it opens all doors
5. By the Knot of Five, it's radiating alive
6. By the Knot of Six, this spell is fixed
7. By the Knot of Seven, it connects with the heavens.
8. By the Knot of Eight, its power is great
9. By the Knot of Nine, It IS DONE and now MINE...
****An it Harm none, by the power of three,
these things or better,)O(So mote it be....

I created this particular knot spell, but must give credit to the inspiration I found long ago in Doreen Valiente. She documented one of these Knot spells in her book, "Witchcraft for Tomorrow" Phoenix Publishing, Washington- 1987edition, first published in 1978

CHANT: *"It is done, it is done, it is done, done, done..."*
CHECK INS: Final thoughts on our day and ritual. Make sure everyone is grounded and ready to devoke.
CHANT: *"She's been waiting, waiting..."*

Thanking and Devoking Goddess
You came when called into this sacred space,
to hold and sustain us
Nourish us with your gifts.
Though we hope to visit with you again,
for now we must bid thee adieu.
Receive our Gratitude, as we say,
Hail and Farewell, Selu.
****

Devoking Elements
Sacred Spirit of the ***East**, Element of ***Air**
Herein we called you, represented in your Holy creatures, Our feather friends,
Your presence felt in our ritual today, we thank you for guarding and witnessing our rites.
Depart in peace as we Thank you well,
Dearest Air, Hail and Farewell!!! **Response**: *Hail and Farewell, Air*

Sacred Spirit of the ***South**, Element of ***Fire**
Herein we called you, represented in your Holy creatures, Our Fiery friends.
Your presence felt in our ritual today, we thank you for guarding and witnessing our rites.
Depart in peace as we Thank you well,
Dearest Fire, Hail and Farewell!!! **Response**: *Hail and Farewell, Fire*

Sacred Spirit of the ***West**, Element of ***Water**
Herein we called you, represented in your Holy creatures, Our Aquatic friends,
Your presence felt in our ritual today, we thank you for guarding and witnessing our rites.
Depart in peace as we Thank you well,
Dearest Water, Hail and Farewell!!! **Response**: *Hail and Farewell, Water*

Sacred Spirit of the ***North**, Element of ***Earth**
Herein we called you, represented in your Holy creatures, Our domestic pets and familiars.
Your presence felt in our ritual today, we thank you for guarding and witnessing our rites.
Depart in peace as we Thank you well,
Dearest Earth, Hail and Farewell!!! **Response**: *Hail and Farewell Earth*

Opening the Circle
with these words recited to our neighboring syster, starting with your right...
"In Perfect Love and Perfect Trust, with Gratitude I release this Circle for us....."

)o(The Circle is open.....

****Remember to Gift them scroll of Selu's Words...
Extravagant Potluck and feasting to follow.....

CORN MOTHER

Corn Mother hearing,
Corn Mother nurturing,
Corn Mother sacrificing,
Returning again.

Corn Mother, feeding us Love
Corn Mother, pulsating in each stalk
Corn Mother, hearing the hungry child
Unearthing, ruminating,
from her human flesh, creating.

Daily in the hut, secretly you squat,
Bringing forth the grain, that they
Demanded and sought.
They could not believe,
Nor accept this way to feed,
Divine Mother forgave them and
Knew it was time to leave.

Corn Mother hearing
Corn Mother nurturing
Corn Mother sacrificing
Returning again.

Corn mother, shedding her blood,
Seeing past the present,
into the great beyond
Preservation of her people,
May the Corn help them live on.

Corn Mother's blood in each kernel we eat,
May we embrace all her rainbow parts.
Preservation of her children,
May we all return to her,
through our own awakened sacred heart.

Corn Mother hearing
Corn Mother nurturing
Corn mother sacrificing
Returning again.

SELU GODDESS INVOCATION

Corn Mother,
Yellow Woman,
Iyatiku and Selu,
Nourisher, Provider,
On this day, We honor you.

Come Brilliant Teacher,
On the Kernel of your Grain,
Connect us to your Life Force,
Bring your gifts to our Terrain....

SELU DEVOKING SELU

Corn Mother, Iyatiku,
You came when called
Into this sacred space,
To hold and sustain us
Nourish us with your gifts.
Though we hope to visit with you again,
For now we must bid thee adieu.
Receive our Gratitude, as we say,
Hail and Farewell, Selu.

JOURNALING- CORN MOTHER- GROVE GATHERING

Although, as Grove Goddess wommin, it seems we do most of our delicious chit-chatting and catching up, gathered around the kitchen counter, we still begin our Grove day, minutes later, with our traditional **Check Ins** : Lots of talking had already ensued beforehand as expected, so this was an opportunity to get in one last word or so...and also bring our focus to the goal and day at hand; namely connecting with Corn Mother. Each participant shared 1-3 foods that they are particularly fond of. What foods bring you comfort pleasure and nourishment? We briefly talked about issues with food and how Selu, being a Goddess of Nourishment and closely linked with food, brings a message about "food not being the enemy." In our society, where we are overloaded with the latest fad diets and frightening images of what we should look like, we have prostituted and degraded food by either taking in too much of it, disrespecting it, or completely not valuing it enough and depriving ourselves of its splendor and magick. Food is not the enemy, it is a source of great comfort and nourishment and absolutely necessary for our survival and it has always been like this since the beginning of time- Selu reminds you of this. It behooves us to get in the right relationship with food by honoring it; neither hoard nor reject it, but balance is needed. Respect and honor the food you come into contact with on a daily basis, we don't need to fear it or abhor it, just connect it with it in a healthier manner to manifest a healthy appearance and a better way of living. This lively discussion dominated the first part of our day together.

Next we reviewed our group's Agreements.
Each woman shared a couple of lines from our group agreement sheet and with its reflective nature, it naturally began casting our Sacred circle. This achieved, what it always seems to beautifully create, a reflective and very respectful state of being. The buzz of the room, that had started our day with the check ins, was now simmering, quieting, intensifying. Everyone around the circle read from the list of Agreements and in their voices, tenderness was expressed.

I next suggested an exercise to **vibrationally clear out our chakras and aura.** While standing in a circle, everyone would surround a volunteered Center womyn, as they chanted her name and rattled and shook percussive instruments all around and over the womyn's astral body, in an effort to bring balance to their aura- removing negativity. It was wonderfully executed, as each wommin expressed sensations, release and a cathartic exchange of energy in the room. For me, the most memorable moment was when my own heart chakra began to press and pulsate, linking itself empathetically with some of the wommin there. With each Wombmyn receptively standing in the middle of this circle I sensed their present state of being and the great healing taking place. As for my experience when it was my turn to stand in the center of this circle? It was electrifying and I felt rebooted and charged by their vibrational rattling.

Following this exercise was our Chanting singing workshop.... Indeed it was Fun and energetic as we sang Native American songs and other chants appropriate for the season. This was quite exciting because, among us, we had willing, very eager, wommin who wanted to tap into the power of their voices and it was clear they were enjoying themselves as we all sang in unison, then in beautiful harmony. We even danced a bit.

The next part of our day was touching as we connected with an Image of Selu (Oracle of the Goddess Tarot passed around). To help connect us to our purpose in this Grove gathering, her image was passed around the room. As we studied her, reflecting on her various powerful symbols, we then verbalized what she conjured up for us personally. This became a Check in and again, quite magickally began our introspective connection to Corn Mother.
Afterwards, the room felt serene and indeed a Temple had been erected. I proceed next, by offering a drumming track of Native American Music to help us go even deeper into Corn Mother.
(Drumming Track - Journeying deeper to Corn Mother, allowing us to ground into this moment and continue journeying to her, only now via her Native sounds...)

When we came out of the Drumming Trance I began talking about Corn Mother's numerous myths. **Commenced Lecture** on Selu, reading and sharing her various stories and attributes. Her relevance to us now. Her message of forgiveness, sacrifice and nurturance, as a critically important mother deity and one so often found in numerous cultures. I talked about Animism, where there is no mundane and everything has sacred spirit. The Corn itself was and is Selu and we contemplated on the significance of this for us as modern wommin now and our great -great- grandchildren and how She lives on, as an important deity to venerate. Musing on balance at this time of year and the reverence for Food, how its lost its proper respect. Corn Mother begs us to find a healthy relationship with food, as an important source of comfort and nurturance. Mabon, being a season of balance is a perfect time to contemplate on our relationship to food and what we need, to sustain us.

This month, one of our Spellworking is an Herbal placket: Selecting pre-made black felt plackets, taking an ear of corn, incense fumigation, and carnation oil to begin charging. We began our Herbal Placket Spell Work by each wommin, sharing with her sisters within the circle, the herb she has an affinity to. This became a sort of magickal Herbal check in, as each woman spoke, while crushing and placing her favorite herb inside the gathering vessel. Placing them, while charging with intent for protection for all and reciting invocation spell repeatedly until Cone of power manifested the right level of energy needed. It was awesome and I felt my heart chakra warm and my head spinning in that woozy intense, spinning feeling. After a period of stretching we prepared for the ritual, even though, we all agreed, we had been in a ritual state from the moment we started our day together....

SELU - MABON RITUAL: To begin, Invited them outdoors to **smudge** themselves with Copal and Sage. No High Priestess here, as we each are priestesses and this falls under the category of being empowered to take care of our needs..... after smudging, we then entered the room with good indigenous, Native American music already playing to set the mood.

CASTING CIRCLE, Syster to syster..... This was very intimate as we were required to look deeply into our neighboring systers eyes, recite the circle casting words and there was no bullshit here... You have to be sincere and indeed come from a place of trust and love to look at someone in the eye and make this pledge of a sacred circle for our craft and worship... I felt it was indeed very effective within a small group of wommin like us. We indeed created the circle by our will and word with our respect and promise to one another....

Calling Quarters and Invoking Selu:
incorporating animals, lighting elemental candles and passing the animal statuary representations.....then invocation of Corn Mother and passing the two husks of Corns/Selu. I read my short prose to invoke the elements and honor the creatures from each realm, while one syster helped in lighting the corresponding elemental candle. Then I passed an animal representation, so that each person in the circle can personally connect with the quarters being invoked. Invocation of Corn Mother and passing the two husks of Corns/Selu as her representation. I thought this went great and smoothly led right into the Mabon meditation. I invited them to find a comfortable spot and just listen for...the wheel has turned once more.....

MEDITATION: Inviting them to find a comfortable spot, relax, trance drumming played softly, as I read a meditation specially made for Mabon. All the wommin seemed to have fallen in a deep trance as I spoke. I mean I could feel them going deeper and deeper into the meditation, trancing ever so intently, going deep within... it was quite effective and amazing for me to witness. I only wish that I could've taken part in the trancing journey, more fully myself, but couldn't as the orator. As we came out of the Trance, I made sure to ask if everyone was okay or had anything to share,

Then **We sang**: "BeadChant" to slowly bring them out and prepare for our knot spell.
We sang; "Girlseed, bud flower fruit mother...." as we passed around the circle, the basket of Golden yellow yarn and elected our personal cords to work with.

CD Track- more heavy Native American drums in this track- beautifully pulsating to inspire them to move now and manifest their own personal energy to imbued in their cords. Talked about how it Helps with the connection and aligning your energy to the cord. They were encouraged to move around while listening to the heavy drumming, spirited music and move, move connecting with their cord. Then immediately after, when the energy was raised, we sat, poured all that sweat and energy into the cord and started the spell... "by the knot of one, by the knot of two....", until all had recited and finished NINE KNOTS. This worked fabulously and effortlessly. I felt good about our connection and the way we were able to transition from one activity to the next and it was all, coherent making perfect sense to me, every step having sacred purpose and leading naturally to the next.... And from what others have shared with me afterwards, the magick has been working superbly.

Afterwards we had a **final check in-** Devoked The Goddess and the Elements and added the 5th element.

FIFTH ELEMENT Devoking: Invited them to put their hands on their heart, as we acknowledge and give thanks to the fifth element, our spirit. We give thanks for one another's presence here, our communal contribution in our ritual today....

OPENING CIRCLE Then most touching part was we opened the circle the way we had opened it; with these words, "In perfect love and perfect trust with gratitude I release this circle for us...."
Merry meet song, three times sung as we walked windershinn around the circle to release....

***Potluck Feasting** right after and of course that was yummy and fun as we connected, on a more social level.*

This Grove Goddess Gathering was one of the most flawless, beautiful, harmonious ones ever. We had, among us, some of the most authentically Goddesss-like wommin and they lent a great deal of positive energy to make it a memorable day for all present. I felt that each one of us exemplified the priestess role without the painful challenges so often seen in groups where not every one wants to own their own power, so for me it was lovely to truly be among systers who understood the whole purpose of our Goddess Gathering. From the onset of our day, I really felt the presence of Corn Mother, ironing out, unifying and holding us in the goldenspun thread of her sacred blanket and it was magickal. Gatherings like these touch a deep part of my soul and leave me in a state of Divine euphoria. The wommin that came really gave a lot of themselves to contribute to that feeling and I am greatly indebted to them.

FINAL AFTER THOUGHTS

*****On** an even more personal note,*
I must say that in the days
and weeks following this Grove gathering,
I felt Selu's Magick most profoundly in my Heart Chakra.
For me this was surprising, as I somehow
expected to feel her most in my solar plexus Chakra,
which sometimes deals with stomach and
digestive issues.
I expected to feel her having more of
an effect on my dietary/nutritional
needs and IBS digestive struggles,
but that's not what transpired.
Instead, I felt her motherly attributes transfer
over to me and heard her expound incessantly
on the necessity to nurture my heart
and the cathartic and liberating powers of forgiveness....
Only through forgiveness,
can I begin to release the weight that has crept into
my body, mind, heart and soul....
Forgiveness.....
Forgiveness for those who have done me wrong in the past,
forgiveness to those who are presently trying to do me wrong,
forgiveness for those who I know will inevitably,
do me wrong in the future
and most importantly....
forgiveness offered to my own self,
when I fail to meet my own idealized expectations and criterions.
The more I listened to her, the lighter I felt
and the more room I made for real magick to show itself to me.....
It has been revealing itself to me beautifully
and I feel incredibly blessed.
Blessed Be Selu....
Thank you and Hail to thee beloved Corn Mother.

CORN MOTHER - GROVE GATHERING CHANTS

WE ARE THE FLOW
We are the flow, We are the ebb
We are the weaver, we are the web *(repeat)*
We are the spiders we are the thread
We are the witches back from the dead....
By: Shekhinah Mountainwater

Mother of Darkness
Mother of Darkness,
Mother of Light,
Earth Beneath the Soul in flight,
Songs of love and Love of life,
Guide us to our heart.....

EQUINOX CHANT
Onward we go round the Spiral
Touching darkness, touching light
Twice each year we rest in balance
Make choices on this night
Make choices on this night   *By: Marie Summerwood*

We are Sisters on a Journey
Singing in the Sun,
Singing thru the Darkest Night
The Healing has begun,
Begun.
The Healing has Begun... *by Susun Weed*

MOTHER I FEEL YOU UNDER MY FEET
Mother I feel you under my feet, Mother I feel your Heart Beat 2X
Heya Heya Heya, Heya Heya Ho 2X
Mother I hear you in the Rivers Sound, Eternal Waters going on and on 2X
Heya heya heya heya heya ho 2X
Mother I see you in when the Eagles fly, Flight of the Spirit gonna take our time 2X
Heya Heya Heya, Heya Heya Ho ......By; Unknown source

EIGHT BEADS CHANTS by Carolyn Hillyer
Girlseed
Bloodflower
(dip it)Fruitmother
Spinmother,
(raise it) Midwoman
Earthcrone
Stonecrone
Bone .....

SPINNING THE WEB OF LIFE
Let it in let it go,
Round and round we flow
Weaving the web of women
Let it in, let it flow,
Round and round we go
Spinning the web of life. *By: Marie Summerwood*

RATTLE MY BONE, unknown source
Old Woman Wrap your cloak around me,
Death Bringer rattle my Bones,
Old Woman Wrap your cloak around me,
Death Bringer rattle my Bones,
Rattle my Bone, Rattle my Bones,
Death bringer rattle my Bones

BY THE EARTH THAT IS HER BODY, unknown source
By the Earth that is her Body
By the Air that is her Breath
By the Fire that is her bright Spirit
By the Living waters of her womb
May the Peace of the Goddess
Be forever in our Hearts
The circle is open but unbroken
Merry Meet and merry Part
The circle is open but unbroken
Merry Meet and merry Part (continue from the beginning)

EARTH, MOON, MAGICK, *by B.M.M.*
In the Earth, deep within,
There is A Magick, I draw it in.
In her Caves, in the Trees
Hear her Heartbeat, Pulsing thru me.
When I Rise, I feel her Love
With feet Grounded, I'm soaring high above,
In the Earth, deep within,
There is A Magick,, I draw it in
Ancient Moon, my Soul reveres
With my Singing, I call you here.
When this flame, ignites tonight,
Priestess dancing, Under the moonlit night....
In the Earth, deep within,
There is A Magick
I draw it in....   There is A Magick, I draw it in }3x

CORN MOTHER
Sacred Corn Mother, come to me
Make my way sacred, fill me with beauty *(repeat)*
Sacred Corn Mother, come to me
Fill me with beauty(2x), Fill me with beauty, that I may bring others beauty...*By: Lisa Thiel*

CHAPTER TWENTY-ONE

"An intention is a quality of consciousness that you bring to an action.." Gary Zukav

"Only within yourself exist that reality for which you long. I can give you nothing that has not already its being, within yourself. I can throw open to you no picture gallery but your own soul.." Hermann Hesse

WELCOME ARADIA

OUR ALTAR

Altar cloth: Black altar cloth and maybe a second silver or purple altar cloth underneath.
Image: Statue of this Lunar maiden Goddess, black cat statuary, moon and sun images. Canvas art or photo of the Goddess and or photos of Florence, Tuscany landscape, the moon, Forest, night.

Always present on the altar;
A cast iron cauldron, drums, speaking stick, a silver pentacle, athame, elemental representations......

Air: Smudge wands, Incense type sticks, cones, charcoal brisket. Incorporate fine powdered herbs of Mugwort, Mandrake, Benzoin, Sarsaparilla, Rosemary and Bay Leaves, crushed and lit as incenses as your Eastern element.
Fire: pillar candles, glass enclosed candles or pillars in various colors, depending on personal workings, women shaped, or lunar shaped candles, skull or cat shaped, seven knob candles or pyramids.
Water: Chalice or small glass bowl with Water, or Red Sweet Wines.
Earth: Add lots of Green and purple colored plants, a small dish of soil and or herbs like the ones already mentioned above, as these are all appropriate for your Northern element.

Other items pertinent to this particular gathering
Hooded Robes and Circlets
Figure of a Black Cat
Scrolls of The Charge of the Goddess, tied with red ribbon
Books and Grimoires
Rubber stamps or wax seal
Lunar and Solar pendants
Candles, poppets, herbal plackets, magical craft workings
Oils and incense creations
Bowls of consecrated Water
Writing pens and paper , safety pins,
Light gauzy fabric/veil
Workshop items
Tarot -"The Hierophant" and "The High Priestess"

Offering example Roman Italian food; Bread, Foccacia, pasta dishes, tomatoes and garlic, moon cakes or cookies shaped as moon and stars.
Sacred objects from members:
Notes:

Aradia and her Altar

Aradia Altar

Protective Placket Crafting

Protective Witch Bottle Crafting

ARADIA

Etruscan Goddess of the oppressed; the poor and enslaved and those that lived on the margins and outskirts of society.... those who would later be called witches. Aradia is the Goddess of the Strega, or Stregheria (an old Italian tradition of witchcraft). Her manifestation is ornately rich with interesting folklore and conflicting stories and yet, she is one of the most important Deities for Pagans and modern day Witches.

She was known as the daughter of the Roman Moon Goddess Diana. According to Janet and Stewart Farrar's book, *"The Witches' Goddess, the Feminine Principle of Divinity"*, 1987, Phoenix Publishing Inc., Aradia was born out of the tempestuous union between sister and brother, the sun and the moon. Because she attained both of her parent's light bearing attributes, she can be seen as the Maiden who brings enlightenment and magick to her people. In the *"Vangelo, the Gospel of the Witches"*, which is attributed to being conceived by a Florentine hereditary witch named, Maddalena and later published by Charles Godfrey Leland, Diana was the first Goddess in the universe. This Tuscan Stregheria cosmology proselytize that in the beginning was darkness and this darkness was the Goddess Diana and from her, she divided herself between light and darkness. The light, that was a part of her and that she eventually birthed, was the Sun, known as Lucifer. He became both brother and son as he was a part of her divided self and a manifestation, born of her.

Lucifer was excruciatingly handsome and as the Sun God, in this Etruscan folklore, he was divinely beautiful. In the Moon Goddess Diana he stirred within her a passion that was a taboo and an overwhelming desire for him. Being her brother and son, this deity of sunlight wanted nothing to do with what she offered and thus, the Sun fled her sight, whenever she was present. This only made her long for him even more. According to one tale, Lucifer owned a very special, beautiful cat, which he loved dearly and kept by his side. It was a known fact that he frequently slept with this cat, as cat owners so often do. One night Diana overtaken by her desire for him, shape-shifted, taking on the form of this cat and it was then, in the night, that she was able to seduce her brother, the light, and with him conceived their daughter, Aradia. Aradia, she who beholds the divine heavenly attributes of both her radiant parents. It is from the sun and the moon that magick is born and thus Aradia is the Goddess of Magick.

As recounted by Janet and Stewart Farrar in their book, *"The Witches' Goddess, the Feminine Principle of Divinity."* The Sun God was enraged to discover this grave deception, but Diana, skilled in the art of enchantment, hummed him a melody that made him succumb to her love. This humming melody was described as reminiscent of the buzzing of bees, an incessant buzzing reverberation that was symbolic of the spinning wheel of life, she would ultimately weave and spin in man's life. From her all beings came to be and she ultimately controlled their destiny.

The myth goes on to tell of how oneday the Goddess Diana decided to live upon the earth with mortals and quickly she garnered a great reputation, as people learned of her numerous remarkable abilities. Her powers could no longer be concealed from the world and thus they made her into their Queen. She eventually revealed her true identity and returned to the heavens, to continue chasing after the light, Lucifer, but before leaving the earth she promised to continue to educate humanity on the art of magick and sorcery. Diana looked to her daughter, Aradia, to continue upon the earth, the work that she had started – educating the oppressed and spreading her teachings on witchcraft.

It's important to note that the earth, at this particular time in these folklores, had become a night-marish, dreadful place for those who were poor, uneducated or of the wrong class, culture, gender and religion. The climate in Europe, but in particular Italy at this time, catered to the church and the wealthy and they were brutal and tyraniccal against the poor. It was class warfare as the rich brazenly abused and degraded the uneducated and those that lived outside of the city, in the countryside. The powers that be were enforcing all kinds of new laws meant to destroy their existence. It was a tense time in our history as the church and the rich were uniting, asserting more power, demanding higher taxation, oppressing more people to enslave and rule over them, while demanding that they give up their Gods and replace them with new church saints.

Back in the 1300's, poor peasants were seen as the oppressed class and they were victimized by the wealthy feudal land owners. Sadly they were desperate, highly impoverished people and when they would finally escape their abusive masters, they often found themselves living like outlaws in the woods, ostracized vagabonds, living like scavengers. These marginalized people thus, became known as the first witches of the Stregheria tradition in Italy.

Naturally, if you (like most of our ancestors) lived close to the land, entrenched in your familial tradition, you would certainly have great reverence to the earth and nature, not the papacy. Praying to the spirits of the earth so that your small garden would produce food, or to the rain gods, so that your thirst could be quenched or to the fire sprits to keep your makeshift hearth and home ablazed with warmth, would seem logical. But this very act extracted power away from the growing church and state. Many were imprisoned, their lands overtaken when they failed to follow new societal rules or pay taxes, and they were treated horribly. A Goddess like Aradia then becomes necessary, almost compulsory as their personal saviouress. And her gifts of educating people on magick and witchcraft, and thus how to rule over their oppressors, becomes the factor that gives rise to her popularity, given the social conditions of the time period.

As instructed by her mother, the Moon Goddess Diana, Aradia was to teach the oppressed class how to free themselves from enslavement, how to poison and how to enchant. She taught them how to utilize the gift of magick found amidst nature and how to manipulate weather patterns to work and conjure rain, lightning and thunderstorms. Aradia taught how to bind and eradicate enemies and escape their persecution.

For many of us, who follow the traditional threefold and tenfold Wiccan law, we cringe at the thought of exercising or advocating such severe hexing measures but it is very important for us to understand the validity for a Goddess like Aradia, and her teachings, when we consider the social climate of the time.

The discovery of Aradia and this prominent beloved archetype in the pantheon of Goddess Spirituality, must be credited to nineteenth century author, Charles Godfrey Leland (1824-1903). He was an American journalist, anthropologist, folklorist, linguist, collector of myths and practices, and even a veteran of three wars. He was educated in Princeton Universiy, continued his studies in Heidelberg, in Munich and then the Sorbonne in Paris. Mr. Leland spent a great deal of time in Europe researching Gypsy lore, magick, mythology and witchcraft. In particular, he spent a vast amount of time in Tuscany researching Italian Folklore and through his research came across a woman he named, Maddalena. Maddalena, whose real name might have been Margharita Taluti, was a type of rare witch informant for Mr. Leland, who became close friends with him during this time. Also important to note, he was initiated into *"La Vecchia Religione"* (the Old Religion), which is another term for Italian witchcraft, in 1888, after becoming the first president of the Gypsy-Lore Society. According to Leland, his friend, Maddalena, claimed to be a real hereditary witch and part of an old dying tradition of witchcraft called Stregheria, in Tuscany. He met her in 1886 and according to the legend, it took her nearly eleven years to handwrite and finally submit her documentation of her witchcraft practices and folklores, to the author. In this manuscript we learn a great deal about Aradia and the ancient Cult of the Moon Goddess, Diana, as recounted by the hereditary witch.

Mr. Leland, who was by this time already in America, took her manuscript and tried to translate the Italian and decipher her fragmented handwriting as best as he could. It took him two years to finally get this work published but in 1899, his book, *"Aradia-Gospel of the Witches"* was finally published by David Nutt. It remained fairly unknown, until around the 1950's when other writers and practicing occultist unearthed it, recognizing its scholarly importance, at a time when there was an obvious resurgence of interest in witchcraft in the U.S.A. and abroad.

Today some of the beautiful invocations in this little book have become a sort of liturgy for all Wiccans. *"The Charge of the Goddess"* first found in Maddalena's handwriting, appeared in the Gardnerian witch, Raymond Buckland's book, in 1968. Doreen Valiente (1922-1999), another well-known witch during this enlightening revolutionary time period, later adopted it into her own writings and both, Starhawk and Z. Budapest have also rendered their own versions of this beloved adopted invocation. Today it continues to be a beautiful expressive prose, often recited and adopted by most Pagans as a part of traditional Wiccan liturgy.

The Goddess Aradia, though initially she was not viewed as a Goddess but rather as an avatar, appears to be very much like the Christian Messiah. Aradia, was her mother's messenger. She was imparting magickal wisdom that was to be shared while on Earth, to spread the word and teachings of her mother, the Moon Goddess. In this case she fulfilled the role of a teacher and messenger about Witchcraft to those who were sorely oppressed by the Catholic church. She becomes their heroiness and savioress and in Aradia we see the spirit of the Priestess, the teacher, the messiah and the spirit of the daughter (like Persephone with Demeter) because her identity was so strongly linked into her role as daughter and fulfilling her Mother's worship. Her value comes, when we remember her as a messenger of empowerment through the practice of witchcraft and as a divine messenger of the ancient Moon Goddess, Diana, sharing her mother's traditions and acting as a daughter and Priestess of the Moon.

ARADIA GROVE GODDESS GATHERING

PURPOSE: Learning about **ARADIA**, Witchcraft, Magick and Spellcasting.

Check ins: Introducing ourselves to one another and speaking about how we are feeling as the season changes once more. Wommin will share what element they feel more connected with and why.

Chanting:
Singing *"Aradia Song" and "Magick Woman" and "Mother of Darkness"(see the Song sheet)*

AGREEMENTS:
Our Group Agreement Sheet is passed around and we each read a bylaw and discuss it, adding to it as necessary. It is signed, dated and submitted. This is wonderful way to begin our day and gently reminds everyone of our rules to be loving and respectful.

Check ins II: Around the circle, with our speaking stick, we share our personal definition of magick and openly discuss our previous challenges and successes casting spells.

Drumming Circle: All participants select a percussion instrument from the musical basket offering and begin to shake rattle and roll. We begin to resonate, making musical rhythm until they we are synchronized and now energy is raised within our circle.

Check ins III: An image of Aradia will be shared around the circle to allow every wommin present to connect with this deity and speak aloud what attributes she is most connected with. Slowly invoking Aradia to our circle in this way.

GODDESS LECTURE
the Goddess Aradia, her birth and mythos and her gift offerings to modern day witches

GODDESS WORKSHOP
WORKSHOP I: The use of the word "Witch" and the term "Hereditary Witch."
This is a wonderful opportunity to have open dialogue about the term"Witch" and discuss its usage through out history. Is this a label we welcome for ourselves now or do we struggle with the word? What positive or negative images does this word conjure up for us personally? Can we find new ways of Globally shifting its meaning and usage to reflect a more positive quality for the word Witch? How do we feel about the term,"Hereditary Witch" and do we know our own lineage?

WORKSHOP II: Components of Magick.
In this workshop we will discuss and reveal the many important components and tools to be considered for a successful spell.
       1. Assortment of various candles to chose from.
       2. Planetary Hours and Days
       3. Color relevance
       4. Correspondences of the Moon and Astrological signs

WORKSHOP III: Spells and how they work.
We will discuss some vital, often neglected, forms of magick making. Raising energy, anointing, charging candles, the use of charms, poppets and plackets, squares and sigils.

WORKSHOP VI: Communal Spell
Preparing for our Grove communal spell working. Carving a candle, creating and sewing a poppet, grinding an herb in the mortar or just sitting down, writing a spell together among our systers in sacred space. This is a workshop to practice the "Art of the Strega" as we will compose a short communal spell to grow and enrich our group.

WORKSHOP V: Hexes and Ethics of Magick.
This is a very controversial topic and everyone will surely have an opinion about it but we will endeavor to have a respectful discussion on Hexes and consider when is it permissible and when is it not. We will also share our own personal experience with Hexerai practices, its success and pitfalls.

WORKSHOP VI: The Goddess Aradia and the tradition of Stregheria was believed to have originated from the Etruscan region in Italy. It is truly a beautiful province. To help us connect deeper to this beloved Goddess we will visit the area of Tuscanny, as well as other areas in Italy, via photographs, books and or a documentary DVD. Delving into the culture of a deity helps connect us more to her energy and thus we will briefly look at Italian culture, language, folklore and the land itself in this workshop.

WORKSHOP VII: Protective Witch Bottle creations
Into a small, empty glass bottle we are going to charge and add the ingredients traditionally used to create a Witches Protective spell bottle for your home.
Using rusty nails,
needles (prickly things),
egg shells,
cut up threads,
acetone, vinegar,
and a collection of potent, magickally charged herbs.
Appropriate herbs for your witch bottle are:
Garlic,
Bay leaves,
Rosemary,
Patchouli,
Black Peppers,
Mugwort,
Sage,
Mandrake,
Anise,
Mistletoe and any other herbs,
or combination of herbs, that you feel speak to you most. Add a little bit of your own blood or urine and a bit of red wine vinegar. While creating this spell bottle, concentrate on what you want it to do, example *"Protect my home," "keep my family safe", "stop infidelities"*, etc... Let your witch bottle stand under the light of the nearest Full moon outdoors for three nights, so that the magick is sealed. After this, you may seal your witch bottle with melted wax on the cap edge and place it, concealed, near the front door of your home for maximum protection. **The Magick is done!**

REFLECTIONS ON ARADIA

Mistress of magick, Maiden Queen of the Witches, how there is much to learn from you and your mother's ancient rites. Bella Pilligrina, who exemplifies the path of the devoted Priestess, we look to you for guidance as we too journey on the same path....

Aradia enters your life to teach you how to triumph over your oppressors, not in the bloody battlefield of wars, not in the collegiate debate halls, nor in the grain fields of the farms, nor in the cyclist marathons, but in the dark of the night... with the moon and the stars and all of nature as your powerful tools of magick.

She enters your life to awaken you to your lineage and long standing traditions, that if looked closely, will reveal a primal connection to all things in nature. She triggers memories of you secretly practicing the Craft in the dark of night, drawing down her silver rays, amidst the circle of a beloved family. Aradia teaches us the importance and self-empowering gift of magick and how, no matter how oppressed we think we might be, at our disposal are the gifts of the craft and our very own lineage as witches.

For us modern day wommin seeking spiritual enlightenment and more occult knowledge, Aradia is the finest teacher, for she unearths and connects you back to your clan family and a tradition steeped in your ancestry. And for those on the path of the priestess, and teacher of spiritual knowledge, she is our ideal Patron Goddess and guide. We are well supported and loved by the Goddess, and the powers inherently found in nature are available to us whenever we so choose to use, recognize and put them to practice. Magick exist to be a powerful, transformative tool in our lives and Aradia inaugurates the Prietsess path.

ARADIA GROVE GODDESS GATHERING RITUAL

PURPOSE: Honoring the Maiden, Queen of the Witches -**ARADIA**, and commemorating the upcoming sabbat.

Asperge
*We begin with incense, a smudge of copal and sage permeating our altar and sacred space. Each participant is blessed with oil upon their third eye as she is welcomed into the sanctuary.

Threshold Entry:
"It is better to rush upon my blade here, than to enter into this place with fear wrenching your heart….How do you enter this sacred space?
Participants are invite to reply as they see fit with these words:
In perfect Love and perfect trust"

CIRCLE CASTING
Priestess silently goes around the perimeter of the circle with athame pointed to the ground then to the sky, envision a bright blue light surrounding the space.
Each syster reaches for her neighboring syster's hand and says;
"From hand to hand this Circle is cast"

CALLING QUARTERS
With my breath, I call upon the Sylphs and invoke the powers of **Air**.
Come from your ethereal Eastern realm, Hearken to my call, spirits of the East.
Let thy gentle breezes, which inspires and awakens insight, penetrate the spheres to join us here in this sacred space.
Hail and Welcome Air!

With this red flame, I call upon the Salamanders and invoke the powers of **Fire**.
Come from your sweltering Southern realms, Hearken to my call spirits of the South.
Let thy bright energy, which ignites truth and mobility, penetrate the spheres to join us here in this sacred space.
Hail and Welcome, Fire!

With my blood, my sweat and tears, I call upon the Undines and invoke the powers of **Water**.
Come from your flowing Western realm, Hearken to my call spirits of the West. Let thy stream of authentic emotions, gently ebb and flow, cascading down all the way through the spheres to join us here in this hallowed space.
Hail and Welcome, Water!

With these stones, the soil beneath my feet and my earthly body, I call upon the Gnomes and invoke the powers of the **Earth**. Come from the solid mountainous Northern realm, Let thy transformer, regenerators, nurturer and Creatrix, pierce through the spheres to join us here in this sacred space.
Hail and Welcome, Earth!

With my heart which unites all, I call upon the Center and invoke the powers of **Spirit**. Hearken to my call, ye ancient Revered Ones. Let all thy gifts of wisdom and knowledge, cross the realms and celestial spheres to join us here in our sacred space.
Hail and Welcome Spirit!

CHANTING: "Earth my Body, Water my Blood, Air my Breath and Fire my Spirit…."
Intent Declared: Speaker shares what is about to unfold and our purpose for the day.
Together Singing *****Aradia song*****
Priestess gives a reading index card to each participant… Each syster present, will read **aloud** a section of the Star Goddess around the room, until it leads to the beginning, back to priestess who will then aspect…

Aspecting of ARADIA
Priestess Speaks The Charge of the Goddess/aspecting in trance...

When the last words are uttered...
Raise the cone of power: Hum and dance around to imbue the space with her energy. Begin with a low hum and let it grow into a full open mouth, open heart, "Aw". Feel your chakras vibrating as a result from this exercise. Send the enegy around the space.
      CHANTING: *"She's been waiting, waiting"*

*TRASURE HUNTING:
Taking a few minutes only, participants are now asked to retrieve four tools of magick that represent the four elements(or aspects of magick). They can find these outdoors or in their purses or personhood and prepare to charge these as an unsuspecting protective amulet. Some suggestions are small stone, feathers, seashells, metal coins, jewelry, paper drawing, herbal roots or flower etc...When they have found their items they should return to the circle to begin working.

*Around the circle we will gather our four items into a pre-sewn brown felt bag and bless it by all the element; Incense for **air**, Oil for **water**, Our rubbed heated hand for **fire**, And placed on our heart chakra for **earth***

Around the Circle each womyn states:
    "This amulet made by witches' hand
    To guard and shield me as I plan
    By earth, by water, by fire, by air
    Goddess bless this magick, I now wear.."
     (then hang or place on your body)

Chant: **Mother of Darkness, Mother of Light** Here it will be charged by all: Together we Dance around it. Chant, hum and raise the cone of power!

COMMUNAL SPELL
Wommin will retrieve their candles from the altar and they will now be lit with our intended purpose in mind. Around the circle each womyn will state aloud what she hopes to manifest and surrounding sisters affirm with a loud;
"An it harm none, it is Done, Done, Done..."
As all candles are lit we will begin to hum and sway raise up, and maintain the energy then end with **Chant:** **IT IS DONE SONG**

RITUAL GIFT
Aspected Aradia will Pick up **Cauldron** full of scrolls, tie with red ribbon and the words: *The Charge of the Goddess*... Ask them the question:
Do you vow to keep my mother's legacy, Do you promise to keep the Goddess alive within you.? They answer: ***I Do..***

DEVOKING:
Now holding each other's hand we close our eyes and breathe. Reflecting and visualizing what has taken place and then stepping back into this moment.

DEVOKING ARADIA
Aradia, Maiden Goddess of the Witches
Conceived of Night and Day.
Daughter of both the Sun and the Moon
Bringer of enlightenment.
Messenger and Priestess.
I thank you for your teachings,
Your gifts of sorcery, castings and Magick,
Magick, which in our moments of darkness,
gives us hope...
And thus your teachings become the lantern,
that guides us Out of despair.

Mistress of Hope...
Teacher of the Ancient Mysteries
and of our ancestral lineage,
Reminding us always of our
Long standing Heritage
and the Power that is within us...
Thank you, Aradia.
Stay if you will,
Go if you must,
Hail and Farewell   Aradia!

Devoking the Elements

We thank you Center for sharing your enlightening gifts and the energy of wisdom within our ritual today. Receive our gratitude as we bid thee adieu. Hail and Farewell powers of **Spirit.**

Northern Realms of mountaineous spirit, we thank you Sacred Gnomes for sharing your Creatrix gifts and transformational energy within our ritual today. Receive our gratitude as we bid thee adieu. Hail and Farewell powers of the **Earth**

Western Realms of flowing spirit, we thank you Sacred Undines for sharing your Watery gifts of the heart and harmonious energy within our ritual today. Receive our gratitude as we bid thee adieu. Hail and Farewell powers of **Water**.

Southern Realms of sweltering spirit, we thank you Sacred Salamanders for sharing your Fiery gifts and passionate driving energy within our ritual today. Receive our gratitude as we bid thee adieu. Hail and Farewell powers of **Fire.**

Eastern Realm of ethereal spirit, we thank you Sacred Sylphs for sharing your gifts of vision and the awakener's energy within our ritual today. Receive our gratitude as we bid thee adieu. Hail and Farewell powers of **Air**.

Elemental Chant: *"The Earth, the Air, the Fire, the Water, return, return, return, return..."*
Thanking each Syster present.

Opening up the Circle with Chant:
"The Circle is open, but unbroken may the Peace of the Goddess, be ever in our hearts... Merry meet and merry part and merry meet again...."
****
Potluck/ Cakes and ales following

STREGHERIA

"True Magick is neither black nor white. It is both, because Nature is both, loving and cruel...all at the same time. The only good or bad is in the heart of the Witch. Life gives a balance of its own..." The movie, "The Craft"

    Although Stregheria shares many similarities to Wicca, it is arguably not a form of Wicca. It prides itself in being a revival of an archaic religion that dates back, probably further than the once presumed fourteenth century. It is an ancient spiritual religion, akin to an early form of Shamanism, steeped in Tuscan cultural history and Italian folklore. Like most archaic religious practices, there are numerous, conflicting stories of its origins, but there is also much that confirms its validity, birth and existence.

    Etymologically, *"Stregheria"* is the archaic Italian word for witchcraft. It is sometimes referred to as *"La Vecchia Religione"* which means in English, "The Old Religion". The word, *"Strego,"* means to enchant and in Italy, the word *"Strega,"* refers to a female witch, while the word *"Strogone,"* refers to a male witch. Stregoneria is a common Italian word used now when referring to witchcraft, but you might also find the archaic Italian word, Stregheria, more commonly used.

    Two distinctly different authors are attributed for unearthing and devoting further research into this long, almost forgotten hidden religion; Charles Godfrey Leland (August 15th, 1824- March 20th, 1903)and Raven Grimassi (born 1951-). "**Aradia, Gospel of the Witches**" was published by Charles G. Leland in 1899 and in 1994 Raven Grimassi published, "**Ways of the Strega.**" Grimassi later published several more books on the fascinating subject; "**Italian Witchcraft**" in 2000 and in 2001 "**HeridataryWitchcraft.**"

    Charles Godfrey Leland claimed that this religion goes back farther than the 14th century, before Pre-Christian times. His writings reveals that this is actually an ancient Etruscan Religion that blended itself with the Tuscan peasant religious practices of the time. Charles Godfrey Leland, among his many professions, was an American writer, anthropologist, Linguist, Folklorist. Educated in Princeton University, he traveled a great deal and in the late 1800's lived in Italy, where he was studying and researching Gypsy and Italian folklores. In Tuscany, he formed a very close, special friendship with a woman by the name of Maddalena and from this relationship he acquired a great deal of knowledge about *"La Vecchia Religione..."* Maddalena proclaimed to be a Hereditary Witch with a vast knowledge of the ancient witch practices that had been passed down to her by her family. With her as his informant and her own Italian hand writings and documentations (which were later translated), Mr. Leland was able to publish with David Nutt, a small book. He had written numerous books before, but by far the one that gave him notoriety and has survived all these years was, "**Aradia; Gospel of the Witches,**" published in 1899- years after his initial meeting with Maddalena.

    The book revealed a number of incantations, spells, practices, incredibly beautiful and eloquent prose and the mythos of Aradia. It presented the Maiden Aradia as daughter of the great ancient moon Goddess, Diana, and told of how she was sent down to Earth, temporarily, as a messenger to teach the art of sorcery to those who were enslaved and oppressed by the wealthy, Feudal lords of the land. Life was very different back then and these spell workings and incantations reveal how necessary magick and the craft was to the poor. It was their only salvation, when Christianity was victimizing and abusing them and Aradia became their personal, spiritual avatar.

    According to Raven Grimassi, "Stregheria is the worship of the source of all things through the personification of the Goddess and God." *Raven Grimassi "Way of the Strega".* Grimassi believed that the Hereditary witch cult of Stregheria became widespread due to a type of Holy Strega (Aradia) and he believed she was not just an archetype, but an actual woman who was documented as living in Tuscany in the fourteenth century, teaching the old ways that had been taught to her, by her family.

Long ago in the Tuscan Hills of a town named Arida, a woman by the name of Aradia di Toscano was born. Some documents claim she was born on August thirteenth in the year 1313. Perhaps this date is given in an effort to connect her even further with witches and the revered thirteen moons in a year or perhaps indeed this is her precise date of birth. According to Grimassi, Aradia traveled from town to town in the Roman and Tuscan hillside to share, among the rustic Italians, her aunt's teachings of the *"La Vecchia Religione."* At a time when the poor and those that lived outside the margins of "civilized" society, were being oppressed and enslaved by the rich and privileged class, her teachings were the only source of empowerment and hope. It would seem to fit the bill in fulfilling the desperate hunger of an oppressed class.

The people that lived on the hillsides, in far away villages and quite far removed from the cosmopolitan city centers, could not relate to the lofty Gods and the growing, oppressive religions, like Catholicism and Christianity. For those who lived so close to their land, whose livelihood was dependent on the benevolence of nature, their reverence and worshipped was relegated to those they were in communion with on a daily basis. Hence, Stregheria with its proselytization of the old ways and the worship of agricultural Gods, elemental Spirits, forest faeries, the Moon and the stars was a religion they could easily identify with.

Aradia became affectionately known as *"La Bella Pilligrina"* for she traveled far and wide, teaching her family's ancient tradition of Italian witchcraft and as a result Stregheria became wide spread throughout rural villages, the Alban hill region, Etruscan villages, and in particular the town near Lake Nemi, as some documents of the time period reveals. The city of Benevento as well, became particularly instrumental in flourishing *"La Vecchia Religione"* and was even attributed for later inventing an alcoholic drink, appropriately named by them, *"Strega Liquore."*

According to Raven Grimassi, Aradia became known as the Holy Strega and accumulated quite a following. Consequently, to her devotees, she became known as a highly regarded avatar and the beloved daughter of her mother, the Moon Goddess - Diana. The worship of nature Gods and Goddesses (honoring both polarity of genders) was common; with their Moon Goddess, Diana and her Consort Dianus being the two most highly regarded. There were many others like Herodias, Tana and Tanus and of course; faeries, forest & tree spirits were also venerated.

Similar to Wicca, in their use of enchantments, incantations, amulets, talisman, hexes, poppets, oracles and divinations, theirs was an old tradition. They utilized herbalism, totem animal magick, fairies, magick of spell casting, rituals and they had sky clad meetings under the full moon in groves or Boschetto (forest) amidst nature -these are all part of Stregheria. Like Wicca, there are eight holy-days or sabbats traditionally celebrated and they coincide with the change in season and the honored Nature Deities.

Their Rites traditionally focused on the agriculture and fertility of the land, hexes and protection, as well as imbuing everyday objects like Keys, scissors, knives, horseshoes, pearls, gemstones, rocks, trees, salt, clove of garlic, herbs, roots, red ribbons, statues, (to name just a few), with the energy of the Divine. For sacred rites, a High Priestess assisted by her High Priest led the coven and this too is very similar to most Wiccan traditions. They also utilized a Maiden known, in Italian, as *"Dama D'onore"* and the traditional Gate keeper, known in Italian as *"La Guardia"*. Altars were normally placed in the highly venerated North Quarter because it was believed to be a place of great power. Their tools of magick were everyday items like feathers, sea shells, needles, rocks painted with a pentacles, crystals and wood branches as wands. Knives as athame, salt, sand, potions and herb concoctions, chalice or bowls of water, sometimes candles, bells and offerings of honey, milk, wine, and spirits like "Strega Liquore."

Interesting to note that Hebrew Mysticism in the Middle ages, undoubtedly, had a great influence on Stregheria rites and practices. Masonic Lodges in the 1800's, obviously, borrowed from various traditions, not excluding, *"La Vecchia Religione"*. The notorious protagonist and main contributors to Wiccan Religion; like Gerald Gardner, Doreen Valiente, Dion Fortune, Aleister Crowley are indebted to the teachings of Italian Witchcraft and *"La Vecchia Religione"*. According to Raven Grimassi in his Book "The Holy Strega," Aleister Crowley studied Italian occultism and lived in Italy from 1920-1923. He was attributed to forming the "Abbey of Thelema," with licentious mural paintings of the nature deities like the Horn God, Pan and the Goddess. When the city got word of his Pagan creation, he was booted out of Sicily. Yet another well-known contributor to Wicca, Gerald Gardner, borrowed much from Stregheria and initially had learned a great deal from Aleister Crowley himself. This would explain the coincidental similarities, Wicca and Stregheria share.

Witchcraft has always appealed largely to wommin, with its message of female empowerment and inherent feminine divinity. It appears more matriarchal than other religious faiths. In major cities, in the fourteenth century, men were the predominant rulers during this time and one can only presume how the practice of Stregheria and the sight of a large group of wommin gathering for any reason, could've been seen as suspicious, bothersome and possibly a threat to their own patriarchal religions. When Stregheria found itself in danger of being banned and extinct by the patriarch, it needed to transmute itself. According to Raven Grimassi, three witch clans, a Triad, sprung forth in an effort to preserve this ancient religion and safely pass down, Aradia's teachings, to future generations. The distinctly three traditions of Tanarra, Jannara, Fanarra, evolved from Aradia's ancient witchcraft teachings.

Fanarra was located mainly in Northern Italy and this was a witch tradition that was considered the keepers of the Earth mysteries. Their form of worship emphasized the land, sacred sites and places and objects found among the earth. They held true that Nature is filled with spirits that inhabits objects and places, making them sacred to witches and at our disposal for powerful magick.

Janarra, was a tradition mainly located in Central Italy and they were believed to be the keepers of the Lunar mysteries. Their form of witchcraft highly regarded the cycles of the moon and the powers inherent in our own connection to the moon. Drawing her down and regular gatherings (*Veglione*, Italian word for full moon rites) under the Full moon was part of their tradition. During this time there was also a common, indigenous belief that the souls of the dead dwelled in the moon awaiting their final resting place and in the Janarra tradition, the moon is honored as the sacred dwelling place of the feminine divine-the Goddess- as was Aradia's initial teachings.

Central Italy also became the home for the Tanarra Tradition, whose emphasis was on the Stellar Mysteries. In 1981, The Aridian Mysteries was born (named after Aradia's birthplace) and it was established in North America. The Aridian tradition is considered a direct extension of the Tanarra, Stellar mysteries. According to Raven Grimassi, it is a tradition dedicated to reviving the archaic teachings of Aradia, the Holy Strega.

There are numerous wonderful books on Italian Witchcraft, *"La Vecchia Religione"* and both the ancient and modern practices of Stregheria. I know that I have only touched the surface of this profoundly, fascinating subject here. To learn more, I encourage you to look into Charles Godfrey Leland's books and the multitude of books written by one of the leading, modern day protagonist of the Stregheria tradition, Raven Grimassi.

The Charge of The Goddess

I am the Beauty of the Green Earth,
And the White Moon among the stars,
And the Mysteries of the waters,
And the Desire found in Human hearts
Call unto your soul, Arise and come unto me,
For I am the Soul of Nature
that gives life to this Universe,
From me all things proceed and
Unto me all things shall return.
Before my face, Beloved of all,
Let thine inner most self
be enfolded in the rapture of the infinite.
Let my Worship be among the Heart that rejoices
For behold, all acts of love and pleasure are my rituals,
And therefore,
Let there be Beauty, Strength, Power and Compassion
Let there be Honor, Pride, Mirth and Reverence.
And you who thinks to seek me,
Know that your seeking and yearning
shall avail you not,
less you know the mystery,
For if that which you seek
you cannot find within yourself
you will never find without,
For behold,
I have been with you since the Beginning
And I am that which is attainned,
At the end of desire.

*Excerpt from the Charge of the Goddess by Doreen Valiente,
it has also been rewritten and modified by both Starhawk and Z. Budapest*
************This is a Scroll created and given to you with Love from: Grove of the Feminine Divine

SOME COMPONENTS OF A SPELL

When we endeavor to perform a spell there are a few important ingredients that would serve us well to become familiar with. After all, spells require an investment of energy, time and sometimes even money and why wouldn't we want to do everything possible to assure that it's not all wasted and in vain? Hence, it behooves us to familiarize ourselves with some helpful occult knowledge that have been utilized by both high magick wizards and witches since the old days. I know some of you might be thinking that all this information might be overwhelming or discouraging to the novice and frankly, magick does work in mysterious ways sometimes, but trust me when I tell you, knowledge is power and the more you know, the better your choices and your workings can only be improved by this knowledge.

Each day of the week is ruled by a planet and each astrological planet rules over a number of areas in our lives. This influence can lend itself positively or negatively in our workings. It is also not limited to the days of the week but also the hours in our days and night. There are numerous books on the subject of Planetary hours and daily correspondences, like Maria Kay Simms, "A Time for Magick" and Charmaine Dey, "The Magic Candle", but below I touch upon some basic information to get you started on this fascinating topic.

Sunday is ruled by the benevolent youthful **Sun** and therefore any workings having to do with healing, children, strength, clarity, abundance and growth, showmanship, attraction, audiences, light, social or and victorious workings are all well suited on this day.

Monday is ruled by the emotional, introspective **Moon** and any spells involving emotions, the home, protection, the mother, feminine, intuitive and psychic powers are all perfect to do on this day.

Tuesday is ruled by the aggressive, red planet **Mars** and this day is excellent for protection spells, vengeance, retribution, strong emotions, passionate sex workings, ambition and energy, physical feats, and spells for courage.

Wednesday is ruled by the renowned communicator, **Mercury**. This day is perfect for spells that have anything to do with communication (writing, singing, speaking), reconciliations. Travel spells and spells that have anything to do with learning, are ideal during this day.

Thursday is ruled by plentiful, growth expanding, benevolent **Jupiter** and that means anything that you already have, but want more of, will be positively influenced on this day. It is an ideal day for money and abundance spells, prosperity workings, weight related spells and any magick of a social nature.

Friday is ruled by the beauteous, harmonious **Venus** and you know what that means....love, attraction, beauty and romance. Any spells that have to do with love, relationships, friendships, beauty and glamour, bringing about harmonious relations, physical attraction, music, the arts –for they all fall under Venus' domain and therefore your spells will be influenced positively if done on this day.

Saturday is ruled by restrictive traditionalist **Saturn** and any spells having to do with the father, justice, law, endings, stubbornness, homes and houses and long standing and restrictive issues would benefit from the influence of this day.

CHART OF PLANETARY HOURS
from astrolabe.com but often attributed to Maria Kay Simms from her Book; "A Time for Magick" (Llewellyn 2001) also can be found in Charmaine Dey's, "The Magic Candle",

Sunday	Monday	Tuesday	Wednesday	Thursday	Friday	Saturday
1. Sun	Moon	Mars	Mercury	Jupiter	Venus	Saturn
2. Venus	Saturn	Sun	Moon	Mars	Mercury	Jupiter
3. Mercury	Jupiter	Venus	Saturn	Sun	Moon	Mars
4. Moon	Mars	Mercury	Jupiter	Venus	Saturn	Sun
5. Saturn	Sun	Moon	Mars	Mercury	Jupiter	Venus
6. Jupiter	Venus	Saturn	Sun	Moon	Mars	Mercury
7. Mars	Mercury	Jupiter	Venus	Saturn	Sun	Moon
8. Sun	Moon	Mars	Mercury	Jupiter	Venus	Saturn
9. Venus	Saturn	Sun	Moon	Mars	Mercury	Jupiter
10. Mercury	Jupiter	Venus	Saturn	Sun	Moon	Mars
11. Moon	Mars	Mercury	Jupiter	Venus	Saturn	Sun
12. Saturn	Sun	Moon	Mars	Mercury	Jupiter	Venus

*After Sunset/Hours of Night *

Sunday	Monday	Tuesday	Wednesday	Thursday	Friday	Saturday
1. Jupiter	Venus	Saturn	Sun	Moon	Mars	Mercury
2. Mars	Mercury	Jupiter	Venus	Saturn	Sun	Moon
3. Sun	Moon	Mars	Mercury	Jupiter	Venus	Saturn
4. Venus	Saturn	Sun	Moon	Mars	Mercury	Jupiter
5. Mercury	Jupiter	Venus	Saturn	Sun	Moon	Mars
6. Moon	Mars	Mercury	Jupiter	Venus	Saturn	Sun
7. Saturn	Sun	Moon	Mars	Mercury	Jupiter	Venus
8. Jupiter	Venus	Saturn	Sun	Moon	Mars	Mercury
9. Mars	Mercury	Jupiter	Venus	Saturn	Sun	Moon
10. Sun	Moon	Mars	Mercury	Jupiter	Venus	Saturn
11. Venus	Saturn	Sun	Moon	Mars	Mercury	Jupiter
12. Mercury	Jupiter	Venus	Saturn	Sun	Moon	Mars

PERSONAL IDEAS ON
HOW TO APPROACH ASPECTING

"Renounce all the faces in your Heart, so that the Face without a Face may come to you..." Rumi

When I am preparing to Aspect for an upcoming event I live with this Goddess for a long period of time, usually however long it takes me to fully get to know her better. I generally do not like aspecting "cold" on the spot, although I have felt myself trance rather unexpectedly into this form of worship. Generally, however, I prefer to establish a good solid relationship for a few months, sometimes a year and a day or at the very least a few weeks, before I attempt to embody a Goddess.

I begin by studying up on the Goddess historically, culturally, learning all about her ancestry and lineage. I make up a list of curious questions I ponder and muse on, that will give me a more intimate look into this Goddess and I answer them as I go about my research. Slowly, I create a very detailed picture of what this Goddess looks like and slowly internalize it for my own self. What she eats, how she would walk and talk, the timbre of her voice and inflections. Who are her friends, her lovers, her domain? Where does she live and work and how does she spend most of her time? I become an investigator who slowly takes on the identity of her subject.

Aspecting this Goddess I will hate what she hates, love what she loves, share in her passions and even her skills. I take on her interest and her passions. I begin addressing myself with her name and slowly adopt her history, her ancestry, and her experiences, as my very own. Prior to fully entering this transcendent state, I have been communing with her through meditation, mantras, all the while seeking to know her better. I will usually receive strong, vivid dreams that confirm our spiritual connection. All around me I will notice her various manifestations coming through, even in the most mundane of things, and slowly she permeates everything around me.

The most obvious evidence of this process is in my journal writing, where you'll see an obvious split from me to the Deity I am becoming or working on aspecting. My writing will take on a different hue and it becomes obvious that this Goddess is asserting herself fully in my life. This however cannot happen unless I open myself up to welcoming this rather disruptive energy and direct schism in my life.

By the time ritual night arrives I am already in that divine realm or at least not very far from it. When I begin, there is a sort of pop in my soul, mostly in my heart chakra, as if the pressure has been let out with her first uttered words in the very act of Aspecting. I feel an overflow of relief that what I've contained in me, has now the setting and "the Welcoming" to manifest itself through sacred ritual.

Afterwards I do experience some fatigue but that varies depending on the Goddess I've aspected. For the most part, I experience a sensation of being hazy and euphoric, like I'm inebriated... It is reminiscent of a dream state, not quite sleeping and not quite awake yet. Afterwards, I usually need a few days to come down and ground. After two days or so, I can then revisit, review the night and begin seeing glimmers through that haze, catching glimpses and passing images of the sacred rite.

With much awe and respect, I give my sincere thanks and show my Gratitude to the Goddess with a candle or some sort of personal ritual. This also helps me pull back and return to my own energy. Eventually, I do return to me and this moment becomes very obvious, as I begin to feel more in my body and more like myself.

The value of aspecting and the importance of this spiritual journey reveals itself to me when I have fully recovered and I can't help but feel honored then and quite appreciative that I was utilized as a Priestess by the Goddess, even if just for a short moment. This experience adds great depth to my spiritual practice and intimately connects me to Goddess in astounding ways.

POLARITIES & SHADES OF MAGICK

"Our mind is capable of passing beyond the dividing line we have drawn for it, beyond the pairs of opposites of what the world consists, other, new insights begins...." Hermann Hesse

We live in a world of polarities. There are those that would disagree with me and feverishly seek to eradicate the idea of dualism in our world, but for me, I recognize that we live in a multidimensional world, bequeathed with dualism and lots more in between.

Within one being, one soul, one creature, one place and one situation, there, you'll find the yin and yang, dark and light, left and right, positive and negative, good and evil. Just like Goddesses, elements have their classified negative and positive traits. When invoking or aspecting in group or solitary rituals, you must decide which specific characteristics you are seeking to invite to your circle and then, consequently, work with. Sometimes we do need those attributes typically considered negative - and as children of the earth, we have license to utilize them when necessary, but with great care.

As witches we must keep in mind that spells, magick and witchcraft in general, is NEVER good nor bad. It just is. Much like Nature itself, it just is! How we utilize the elements found in nature, the deities and forces surrounding us, is what determines the kind of Magick we are devoted to working with. And the more time you spend in this realm, the more you will find that indeed, not everything in the occult, or nature for that matter, can be defined so cut and dry. What I might consider negative you might be perfectly fine considering it positive. A spell meant for revenge and retribution on a rapist to some, might appear as a form of dark magick, while for others it's seen as just and a positive form of magick. A simple love spell for some, couldn't be further from being considered dark magick, while for others it might very well appear to be coercion and thus dark in nature.

I hate using the terms Black magick verses White magick, as this is a very erroneous classification reeking of racism and perpetuating a false stereotype. In my opinion, it is not right to associate the color black with negativity and white with all that is positive. In this case, I like to define "negative" as something you do not want in your magickal workings and "positive" as something you do want and desire, in your spells and rituals.

As we all know Black and Darkness can sometimes bring about healing, respite meditation and positive rest. Think of how nighttime can often be associated negatively with shadows, the unknown, ghost and creatures of the dark, scary, not so positive. Now think about how nighttime allows the whole world to heal itself, recharge, recuperate and gain strength and prepare for the next day - not so scary now, as it becomes associated with healing, rest and necessity.

The Sun, and the attributes of light, are often defined as positive and popularly desired. Yet have you ever driven with bright, white light of the sun, blinding you to the scary point that you fear your life is in danger. White light- not too positive in this case. Yet while in the cold, Northern countries, the sun and all of its brightness, is a welcomed element, in this wretched, relentless snowy region. Think of the Desert and how the sun's light, and its heat, can be your curse and ultimate death. This is just one, over simplified way of viewing polarities in the realms of magic and ritual creations.

Magick contains both dark and light attributes. We as humans contain both dark and light traits in our own persona. It is up to the witch and practioner to assess and decide what energy is needed, which Deity and attribute do we call upon, which spell and course of action would serve the situation best -while all along considering ethic and the magickal law of three folds. *"....For that which you weave returns to you times three..."* Also, the Wiccan rede states ... *"An it harm none, do what thou will..."* yet this longstanding beloved phase must receive careful thought and the utmost consideration, for again it's not so black and white and discrepancies are quite evident. How can we ever be so sure our will won't inavertently harm someone out there? And shouldn't we also consider ourselves as part of that equation when we vow not to harm anyone? But I digress here, my point is that magick has many shades of "white and black", negative and positive and when engaged in the art of spells and rituals we need to clearly define the exact attributes we seek in our circle. It is best to ponder which characteristics do we choose to tap into at that very moment. And most importantly, we need to meditate and give careful thought to our desired outcome and who will be effected by our will in the end. How we utilize our occult knowledge and what workings we choose to do with this knowledge, ultimately determines whether it is considered negative or positive magick.

Lastly I'd like to share a common way I end many workings to protect me from any manevolent will wielding....

"An it harm none, by the power of Three,
These things or Better,
So Mote it be...."

Prepare your body and soul for this work, by first engaging in a ritual cleansing bath. Use consecrated water and lightly scented Almond oil on your skin, when you come out of the bath water- allow yourself to air dry. This spell should be done on the night of the Full Moon and at a time when you know, you will not be disturbed. At your altar, gather the working candle, which can be any color, though purple/magenta is highly suggested. You can also use white or silver as an alternative. Carve your candle with your witch name and astrological sign and anoint with "Priestess oil", (see appendix). Fill your chalice with an offering of Red wine. Use incense of frankincense or sandalwood to fumigate the entire altar area, as well as your body. Approach your altar, sky clad or in your witches robe and take a few minutes to meditate and align yourself with the energy of Aradia. You may drum, hum, sing, all in the sincere effort to connect with the Divine. If you can do this while outdoors or facing a window open to the view of the Full Moon, all the better. Recite the incantation while gazing upon her beautiful enchanting beauty. Draw her down to your heart chakra, your head chakra and your 3rd Eye....

MOON MAGICK
* Silvery Moon, Full in Bloom
Hearken to this rhyme and tune
Yours is the power and magick I seek
Help me unleash the magick in me

I am your daughter
A Goddess by right
Charge me as such
on this Lunar night

Enchantress, Witch
Weaver of my fate
These are the names
I now embrace.

Like my sisters,
The Witches of ol'
I am yours to guard
and to behold

Illuminating Rays
of silvery light
Open my mind
to divine insights.

Bless this work
and my intent,
I draw down the Moon
embrace her Descent.

Journaling Grove Gathering- Invoking the Magick of Aradia,
After Attending The Goddess Gathering Festival, initiated by Z. Budapest-

I found myself approaching this month's gathering with much vigor, courage and a renewed sense of purpose. It was truly a rocket ship gathering where everything fell into place and the pace of our day went smoothly and fast. I felt more comfortable in my skin and sharing all of myself with these beloved wommin. My usual fears and insecurities seemed to have vanished after the previously attended Z. Budapest Goddess Festival, in California, and I felt stronger than ever, spiritually. I was indeed at the best place internally to lead the womyn of "Grove of the Feminine Divine." The Priestess lesson for me this month was how my own personal wellbeing could dramatically effect the way I gather and priestess my fellow systers. Having a healthy level of confidence is a necessary, vital component to serve Goddess, womyn and your community best.

JOURNALING ARADIA - GROVE GATHERING

WOW!!! It was so awesome, the best most gratifying Goddess gathering ever! Perhaps it is Aradia herself that elicits such excitement and euphoria in her priestess but I am still giddy, as I usually find myself after doing some intense, ritual work with this Goddess. I feel like.... yes, I was able to bring home some of what I learned at the Goddess Gathering in San Jose, California with Z. Budapest. I felt like I was indeed more on top of myself as Priestess and less hesitant. My brain at times was a little scattered, bursting with more information than I could transmit to them, but I also found myself not hiding, nor freaking out about it. I just let it flow as it needed to. I know that I was in the present moment, doing my very best and that was all that mattered. We didn't end until past 5:30pm. The ritual and workshops ended by 4:30 and then thankfully, the feasting was done towards the end. It felt good to eat with them and I felt less phobic about the socializing during our potluck. This was only our second meeting. We were all famished indeed at that late hour. I truly felt love and support from all the women there who made a commitment to join me once again. They expressed joy and thankfulness for being a part of the Grove and I, in turn felt much gratitude. It was special because just when I was feeling like my group would never fly, it starts to show off wings, pretty wings... and it was awesome!!! Gratifying indeed!! Blessed be to the Goddess!!!

    Everything went very smoothly. We really did not get going till after 12:30pm because we were all initially gathered in the kitchen preparing our melons and various foods. Instinctively I limited the songs we learned during Chant Workshop and that was a good idea because with only a few songs we raised just the right amount of energy we needed. It was a smashed when I invited them to get up to sing and really feel, "My Body is a living temple of Love". I invited them get into their physical bodies and I danced around too, and I shared my energy with them. You could see and feel their spirits raising up and up in this process. Another time the energy just skyrocketed was when we had ended our spell intent and we sang "It is done". It indeed was awesome! I also loved, when we used the drum CD track on the stereo. I felt that really synchronized us and put us into sacred space immediately after our check ins. It was apparent that some had stressors and challenges going on in their personal lives and that drumming moment, where we tapped into the rhythmic energy, was amazing!

    The Aradia lesson part for me was a little choppy. I felt I had sooo much to say, as usual and all of my thoughts were jumbled up, skyrocketing out of my mouth, unable to quite come out in a neat order. Still, I eventually got most of it out and I am glad I posted on the group's internet page information about Stregheria because it gave me a chance to at least get something scholarly out of my system in pristine order. The rest of my presentation about Aradia was a blur for me, wonder if I was then already aspecting.... I read a bit from Stewart and Janet Farrar's Book about how Aradia was conceived and that helped put me back into some pristine scholarly order, but I wondered if it was enough information for them, given our time restraint. In the end I believe it was fulfilling for them and just as I had hoped.

    It appeared that the spell workshop, was the most exciting part, as we all discussed openly certain practices and delved into ethics of Magick and hexing and stuff. It was a lot of fun and a lot of information to delve into as well. Maybe it was too much information for one sitting, but I was so glad to see my systers taking notes in their notebooks. This revealed that they took this as serious I as do. It was thrilling to share my knowledge and I even amazed myself with how much knowledge I indeed had acquired all these years. I shared some of my personal experiences with spells that the Universe did not approve of and it felt cathartic to actually admit to some of my ")o(working" mistakes and the lessons learned as a result. Overall I think we shared a wealth of information that I hope will inspire and help as we begin to work more with Aradia. The wommin were even taking photos of the altar and that is a definite sign indeed of their enthusiasm.

Three of them did not bring any working tools with them, so it was nice to have a few yellow tapers that I could offer them and oils, herbs and a pin to carve their symbols. In this way they applied what they had just learned to our spell work and I enjoyed helping them with this. We did not light our spell candles then but prepared to light them upon the upcoming new moon, which is tomorrow. So in this way we did POWERFUL prep work which is so often neglected, but so important and they had something like homework to take with them.

Because it was only a small group, our ritual was perfectly intimate. We sat on the floor most of the time and having removed the trunk table from the center, we gathered in a nice tight knit circle. It was wonderful when they added their voices with full heart and soul. Instead of having someone else do the purification I felt strongly about doing it myself because it was only our second gathering and I did it with the drum CD in the background and with the feathers- blowing away impurities, negativity all in the name of the Goddess. Then asking them the question that would welcome them into our space. They were invited to also bless themselves with the waters at the altar. It started quite nicely. Casting the Circle by hand was good, Calling Quarters, I had to read from my notes as I felt I was wearing entirely too many hats that day and for some reason, didn't trust I could deliver without a brain freeze at that pivotal moment. Opting not to risk an embarrasing injury to our ritual, I read from my notes and no one seemed bothered by it.

Priestessing, The Charge of the Goddess was from the heart, free flowing and no doubt, I was already aspecting. I believe it was intense, even for me- I felt it within every living cell of my body....and I looked out into their tearfilled eyes and I felt mine own also swell.... The song that followed was also heartfelt..."She's been waiting" –Then I realized only later that I forgot the cauldron scroll part of our ritual, which was supposed to happen after the "Charge of the Goddess" but I suppose at this point I probably wasn't all there and swept into the sacred moment, details like these get overlooked easily if I am aspecting. As they were leaving I elected to give them their scroll gifts and take the time to ask them by the door...about keeping the Goddess alive within them. So That was surprisingly a most ideal, beautiful way to end our day, while still maintaining part of the Ritual I had forgotten. I also found myself hugging them as they left, but realized, I neglected to welcome them in this way when they entered into sacred space at the beginning of our ritual. It's quite astounding when at the end you realize things actually worked out better than how you had planned. This was a wonderful group of great powerful wommin, with fantastic energy.

The women that were there, were the perfect blend of energy- a small number but a BIG Impact. Even more than the last time. One of the Systers is already talking about adding more days, maybe meeting more than once a month. I guess we'll see. If the interest is there -YES, I would be honored -but not if I have to pull teeth to wrestle with people's schedules. Nonetheless, I am very excited about how things are working out!!! Thank you Goddess....May I be forever in your service!

So Mote it Be....)O(

ARADIA GROVE GODDESS GATHERING CHANTS

Welcome, Welcome, Womyn…
Welcome, Welcome, Womyn…(2X)
Welcome, Welcome, Womyn to our Circle….*Presented By Ava*

Witch, Magick, Candle spells all that is you.
Witch, Magick, Candle spells all that is you
Born from the Sun and the Love of the Moon
Oh Aradia, Aradia keeping us safe
Magick Syster, teaching us the ancient ways… *By B.M.M.*

She Gathers *By Ruth Rhiannon Barrett*
She gathers her daughters by Moon and by Sun,
She gathers her daughters it has begun.
She gathers her daughters to turn the wheel,
She gathers her daughters to learn and heal.
She gathers her daughters by night and by day,
She gathers her daughters to lead the way.
(Counter Melody) *By Moon and Sun, We have Begun…..To turn the wheel, to learn and heal……*

My Body is a living temple of Love
My body is a living temple of Love (2X)
My body is the Body of a Goddess
My Body is the Body of a Goddess
My body is the Body of a Goddess
(Lower) My Body is the Body of a Goddess… *Presented By Rabbit Mathews*

She's been Waiting -Waiting
She's been Waiting -Waiting
She's been Waiting so long
She's been waiting for her children
To remember
To return…. *by Paula Walowitz*

Mother of Darkness.
Mother of Darkness
Mother of Light
Earth Beneath the Soul in flight
Songs of love and Love of life
Guide us to our heart…..

The Earth is our Mother
The Earth is our Mother
we must take care of her (repeat)
Heyana, heyana hey ya na (repeat)

Listen to my heart Song
Listen, Listen, Listen to my heart Song
Listen, Listen, Listen to my heart Song
I will never forget you
I will never forsake you
I will never forget you,
I will never Forsake you ….. *by Susun Weed*

EARTH, MOON,MAGICK by B.M.M.
In the Earth, deep within,
There is A Magick, I draw it in.
In her Caves, in the Trees,
Hear her Heartbeat, Pulsing thru me.
When I Rise, I feel her Love
With feet Grounded
I'm soaring high above,
In the Earth, deep within,
There is A Magick,, I draw it in
Ancient Moon, my Soul reveres
With my Singing, I call you here.
When this flame, ignites tonight,
Priestess dancing, Under the moonlit night….
In the Earth, deep within,
There is A Magick, I draw it in…. There is A Magick, I draw it in }3x

October

This month is believed to receive its name from the Latin word "*Octo,*" meaning "eight," as it was the eighth month in the Roman calendar. The astrological sign for the month is Libra, the balancing scales, ruled by beautifully, harmonious Venus (Sept 21-Oct 20). The Full Moon of this month was more commonly known as the Blood Moon. According to the Farmer's Almanac the Native Americans named it Hunter'sMoon.

Reds, Oranges and Yellows, are the prominent colors surrounding us in the Earth's landscape, and the beautiful foliage, in some parts of the world. Pumpkins and gourds are everywhere. Much like February, there is a sense of mystery in the air. A time when in the darkness and deep beneath the earth, you know that nature is working her magick once more. The Goddess, in her Crone aspect, is heavily invested in her work. In the air you begin to feel the change that inevitably takes us into a time of introspection. Change, is stirring the cauldron all around us. In the air and our climate; our inner and outer landscapes announces, to those of us connected to nature, that the season of darkness is clearly upon us now.

For Wiccans, this is the final harvest. Our work is considered done. And here, as the last harvest, is the reaping or the regretting, for what we sowed or forgot to sow. This month we are aware of the physical and spiritual planes. The Wiccan year comes to an end and we celebrate the weight of this in the Celtic holiday known as Samhain, an ancient Celtic word that translates as *"Summer's end."*

For non-pagan, this holiday is better known as Halloween, but interestingly enough, its name derives from a mixture of Pagan and Christian Lore. Saints and Christian Martyrs, who died for their faith, were honored on "All Saints Day" and the eve of this day was known as "All Hallows eve". Also known as "Hallowmas", this holy day literally translates as*, "Mass of the Holy Ones"* and it is directly connected to our modern day, Pagan sabbat - Samhain.

For Witches, this is considered the end of Celtic year. It stands between the balance of the old and the new, the living and the dead, autumn and the coming of winter. The end of the old year. For our ancestors living so close to the land, they would have stocked up their food pantries and welcomed their farm animals inside their home for this time in the season, in preparation for the cold winter. As indoor hibernation replaces the customary outdoor activities of the summer, it lends itself to the feeling of an annual cycle ending and the anticipation for the birth of the Sun, at the Winter Sols-tice. These are all influencing themes of this month. It is the quiet before the storms, as the subsequent months, for most people in our modern era, will bring a fair amount of stress, whether you are a farmer or a city dweller. With the mainstream holidays a few months away there will be a resurgence of excessive activities we won't be able to escape from and much of it, goes against what our bodies naturally wants to do in the winter.

Samhain and Halloween is the time to remember and honor those who have passed away, more specifically those who died during the year. We honor the dead and thus the spiritual realm commands our attention at this time. As is evident in all the Halloween costumes and ghostly stories, psychic related activities and haunting phenomenons, it truly is the time to remember the underworld and those who have crossed over to "Summerlands." We can honor the dead in the traditional dumb supper, in elaborate altars, in prayers, visits to graveyards and churches, in our own special rituals or even in just a single candle prayer. Some opt, at this time, to connect with the dead, via the talents of psychic mediums and oracle readings, but just admiring a simple photo of a lost loved one, can be the most profoundly, powerful remembrance ritual. At this time of year, the Cosmos will support any effort to contact your deceased loved ones, making it easier to connect.

Naturally, this is the month to call upon the ancient Greek Goddess Hekate and the Voodoo loa Maman Brigitte, as both deities, respectively, rule over the dead, cemeteries, mysteries of the craft and those sacred thresholds appearing before us now at this time of the year. With their help we will gain Divine insight, face our own mortality, journey to the underworld and connect with ancestors and beloved departed souls.

CHAPTER TWENTY-TWO

"The lighter we travel, freed of our own psychic encumbrances, attachments, expectations and ego control, the more magickal life becomes..." Sonia Choquette.

"People only see, what they are prepared to see..." Ralph Waldo Emerson.

WELCOME HEKATE

OUR ALTAR

Altar cloth: Black altar cloth, possibly a purple one underneath.
Image Statue of the Crone Goddess
Canvas art or photo of the triple formed Hekate, triple formed tree trunks, wise grandmothers, and or photos of Greece, Cemeteries, skulls, Caverns, and Caves, hounds and of course the Moon.

Always present on the altar;
A cast iron cauldron, drums, speaking stick, a silver pentacle, athame, elemental representations.....

Air: Smudge wands, Incense type sticks, cones, charcoal brisket and fine powdered herbs like; Cypress, Myrrh, Sandalwood, Patchouli, Pine, Mugwort, Angelica. These can be crushed and then burned as your Eastern representation.
Fire: candles of all kinds are appropriate to you, glass enclosed or pillars, preferably in black and or white. You may also incorporate witch, cat, knob or skull candles, easily found at this time of year and they can also be purchased at your local Occult shops.
Water: small vessel or glass bowl with Water or red wine/Retsina
Earth: A Floral arrangement of Bare branches, or purple colored Plants can be a lovely symbol for the element. Also a small dish of soil and herbs like; Yew berries, belladonna, mandrake, hemlock, opium poppy and the ones mentioned above, can all work wonderfully as your Northern representation.

Other items pertinent to this particular gathering
An Abundance of various Keys
Large Cast Iron Cauldron
Lantern
Photos of our Ancestors
Figurine images of Black Dogs
Figurine Images of owls and snakes
Skulls and hedge stones
Offerings of Herbs like Mugwort and mandrakes, belladonna, garlic and eggs
Writing pens and paper , safety pins,
Black Light gauzy fabric /veil
Workshop items
"Death Card" from the Tarot
Various Tarot Decks and other oracles

Offering eggs, garlic, onions, wine, Retsina, bread and water.
Sacred objects from members :
Notes:

Hekate

Hekate Altar

Altar

HEKATE

Hekate is Goddess of the Crossroads, Ancient chthonic Goddess of the Moon and the dark night, Goddess of the Gateway and beloved Goddess of the Witches. One later myth claims that she was a demon Mother to a clan of vampires, called Empusae and they would trap young men into bed and then kill them, feeding off their carcasses but we won't dwell on this obscure questionable aspect.

Hekate is better known as a Triple Goddess of the Crossroads and Goddess of magick and sorcery. Sometimes also seen as Goddess of Childbirth- as this too, is an entry way, of magickal significance, into the world of the living.

She was protector of entrances and homes. Most importantly, she is a patron Goddess for women in all stages of life. Her name means *"she who works from afar"* also interpreted as *"she who works her will"* and one of her primary roles was to guide the souls to the underworld. She was the only Goddess who could travel through all realms. Beloved by Zeus, she was given rule over the Underworld, but also the Earth and the Sky. She had a special relationship with Zeus because according to some, she was the only Titan that aided him during the battle of the Olympians against the Titans, but, as with all ancient deities, there are many conflicting stories about her early incarnations.

Some believe this ancient Goddess has origins in Mycenaen Greece, possibly originating in Carians of Anatolia. Though she had a very large cult following in Thrace. She is said to have been a native of ancient Thrace. In Asia Minor and Thrace she had numerous followers and a very large cult following among the Eunuchs, her servants. In many Greek homes, while the hearth was Hestia's domain, the entryway was Hekate's and altars with offerings were often dedicated to her here. Offerings to Hekate were also made at cemeteries and at three way fork roads with meat, honey, goat blood or actual black dogs, being sacrificed to her.

Hekate is often depicted with three heads and sometimes they were the heads of a snake, a dog and or a horse, other depictions portray her with just the heads of three dogs. The sound of barking dogs were said to warn you of her omnipotent presence and she was known to easily shape shift at will, into her beloved totem. Black female dogs, in particular, were sacred to her and were sometimes sacrificed in her name by her followers. Because black dogs were her totem animal she, herself, was also sometimes referred to as the "black bitch." The Frog was another animal connected to Hekate because its ability to cross between two elements.

There are some conflicting stories about her birth. She appears to be a Goddess of ancient origins with many myths regarding her manifestation. One theory, found in the Theogony, was that she was a child of the great Mother Earth, Gaia and Uranus or perhaps even a siblings of Zeus. A more accepted genealogy came from other writings by Hesiod who stated that Hekate was the daughter of the Pre-Olympian Titans, Perseus and the Star Goddess, Asteria. The sister of Star Goddess Asteria was the Goddess of Childbirth, Leto. Leto as we know gave birth to the twins; Apollo and Artemis. This would mean that Hekate was a cousin of the Maiden Moon Goddess, Artemis. Here we understand her connection as a Moon Deity and the geneology that intimately connects her to light, most notably, the Moon's. This would also imply that their Grandmother would have been Phoebe, the ancient Titaness Moon Goddess and their Great Grandmother, the Primordial Earth Goddess- Gaia.

Not much is known about Hekate's romantic life but we do know she had two daughters. Her union to Phorcys created her daughter, Scylla. With Hermes, the Messenger God and God of Magick and Science, she unites and gives birth to Circe. Circe later becomes Medea's aunt. Medea, according to the myths of her time, becomes a notoriously powerful Sorceress, Priestess and Queen of the Witches, due to the teachings from her extended family. She later becomes a devoted High priestess of her grandmother, Hekate.

Perhaps, Hekate will forever be most remember for her involvement with Demeter and Persephone and the Great Eleusinian Mysteries. Remember that it was Hekate who heard the Maiden's cries, when she was abducted by Hades and it was She, who tried to console the despondent mother and offer aid in regaining her beloved daughter. Thus Hekate became known as a Goddess who was very sympathetic to the universal cries of all wommin, most notably those in great distress and in danger. Women abused or mistreated by men received her utmost protection and she executed just retribution against those offensive men, when supplications were made by her worshippers. As a Goddess who could travel through all three realms, she was often invoked for safe journeys by those going to unknown, distant lands. In ancient times, she was often called upon by women in the midst of childbirth, a precarious delicate state for most women and as a Goddess of entryway, one can see how her presence would be compulsory for both, death and births alike. As a Goddess of the night, the dark moon and all things mysteries, she became a patron to witches and sorcerers, seeking divine occult knowledge.

Today there is a great resurgences in her cult and her worship remains strong among her growing followers. One trip to the library now will reveal an increase in the amount of books published on the fascinating subject of Hekate and her continuos worship.

One of Her festivals, in which she was honored, was held on August 13th and the 30th of November.There are many herbs associated with Hekate. Yew berries, Cypress, belladonna, mandrake, hemlock, opium poppy are all linked to the Goddess of the underworld. Not surprising, herbs that were hallucinogen or help alter states of consciousness are all appropriately associated with this ancient Greek Goddess.

Ancient Goddess -HEKATE LESSON NOTES

Hekate the name means: *SHE WHO WORKS FROM AFAR...*

GENEOLOGY:
1. Her Origins are in Mycenean Greece and possibly in Asia Minor -in Caria of Anatolia which is southwest area known now as Turkey.
2. The ELIADE -place her as a Pre-Olympian Goddess
3. Some liturgy states that she was a child of the primordial Earth Goddess Gaia and Uranus and thus a Sibling of Zeus.
4. This would explain why Zeus had a special fondness for her and why she had free rule over all the realms.. Earth Sky and Sea and was able to travel freely thru all the realm of the Dead and the living.

II. A more accepted geneology is found in HESIOD

1.- She was believed to be the only daughter of the Titan Perseus and the Star Goddess Asteria.
2. Her grandmother then would have been the ancient moon Goddess (light bearer)- Phoebe and then her Great Grandmother would have been Gaia.
3. In this geneology, Asteria was Sister of the Goddess of Childbirth, Leto,
4. Leto is Mother of Apollo and Artemis.
5. This would make them direct Cousins of Hekate. Not surprising they all share many of these light bearing attributes with one another.

HER FAMILY:
1. She was known to have had two daughters Circe and Scylla.
2. With her consort Phorcys she had Scylla and
3. When she joined the Messenger God of
Magic and Science, Hermes, She gave birth to Circe.
4. Scylla later gave birth to Medea, who, as many know, became a devotee and Priestess of her grandmother, Hekate and was known as one of the most powerful witches in Greek Mythology.

ATTRIBUTES:
1. Guardian of the entryways, threshold, crossroads gateways and keeper of the keys, three headed, Lady of the underworld,
2. Goddess of the Witches and thus those that live and practice their craft, outside the boundaries of Society.
3. Teacher and protector of Women and Guardian of the Soul, the Dead.
4. She Facilitated not only the soul's journey out into the underworld but also as a Goddess of gateway, assisted the soul's entry into the body upon birth-that is why she was often called upon in the role of midwife.
5. She rules the night, the dark moon and is considered part of that trinity with Demeter and Proserpina as mother and maiden but she's also a part of the trinity with Selene (mother) and Artemis (the Maiden). Thus, Hekate is viewed as the shadow/dark aspect of the maiden Moon Goddess-Artemis.
6. Associated also with Demeter's Lament, as the one who consoled her and helped locate her missing daughter in Hade's Realm.

TOTEM ANIMALS:
1. From the beginning we learn of her associated with Hounds, especially black dogs. Some literature refer to Hekate as the Black Bitch.
2. Dogs were sometimes sacrificed in her honor and often the sound or appearance of a black hound denotes her presence nearby. * Snake, because of their regenerative gifts,

shedding and growing new skin.
3. Frogs also associated with her because they could travel through both elements.

IMAGES:
1. In Classical mythology she was depicted as a mature woman, relatively young and NOT the old Hag we've been accustomed to seeing. She should be embraced as a beautiful very vital crone, not the ugly haggy image so often proselytized. She is a triple Goddess and in her you will find all three archetypes; The Maiden, Mother and Crone.

2. Hekate was also depicted with three heads and sometimes they were the heads of a snake, a dog and or a horse. Other depictions simply portrayed her with just the heads of three black dogs.

3. She was also, more often, portrayed with three women's heads, looking in three different directions, a possible reference to her ability to look at your past, present and future but also alluding to her three realms.

OFFERINGS:
Eggs, Barley, Garlic, onions, black plums or grapes, honey, Caviar, cedar or sage, myrrh Incense, Retsina Wine or dry Red Wine or berry juice

IN RITUAL:
1. Call on her during the Dark of the Moon
2. Pay close attention to the dreams you have after working with her.
3. She has been known to speak using her worshippers therefore aspecting with her is fairly easy. Wiccan and Trance Author Diana L. Paxson suggest, protecting your head Chakra with a veil if you do not wish to go into spontaneous trance or spirit possession. To come out of trance work you might try water over your head to help ground you.
4. To symbolize her torches it is best to have two flames/candles at her altars, along with food offerings and her fragrances....

"HEKAS, OH HEKAS, ESTE BEBELOI..."
"BE FAR FROM HERE ALL THAT IS PROFANE"

Sources
Diana L. Paxson -Article in Sage Woman Magazine issue #39-Autumn 1997

HEKATE GROVE GODDESS GATHERING

PURPOSE: To honor our beloved ancestors and Hekate, the Goddess of the thresholds and Entryways.

Check ins: With our speaking stick in hand, Introducing ourselves, within the circle and sharing how we feel at this very moment about the dark season. How do we experience the Dark of the Moon.

CHANTING: (see new songs and text sheet)
"Crone songs," "Going Down in the Cauldron," and "Hekate Song"

Drumming: raising energy within our circle with a powerful drumming musical track played for participants to enjoy, trance, move or simply absorb and be still -grounding in the moment. Greek music with the predominace of the Bouzouki sound can also be offered as a nice alternative.

Check ins *(part II)*: Introducing our deceased. Every participant will present and share a photo of their beloved deceased with a few lines to describe him/her.

Discussion: Hekate- Sharing her photo or an image of her from the Goddess Oracle, Goddess Tarot or any number of other depictions of Hekate. Unearthing what does her image mean to us personally. Pass around an image of the Goddess and let every womyn share what it conjures up.

THE GODDESS LECTURE:
Talking about Hekate, her etymology, lineage, history and myths

GODDESS WORKSHOPS
WORKSHOP I
Creation of a Hekate Sacred Lantern. Many images of Hekate depict her holding up a lantern, in the darkest realms, bringing light, like the image of "**The Hermit**" in the Tarot card. In this workshop we will create a lantern/luminaries, by poking a pattern of tiny holes into a frozen tin can. When we melt the ice within the can, dry it out, then place a votive within, the holes can be seen and they should reveal a nice pattern. A chain link is added to the top for easy transport.

WORKSHOP II
Oracular studies, Tarot reflections. In this workshop we will reflect on "The Hermit" and the tarot card of "Death" and consider how these card connect us with Hekate's energy.

WORKSHOP III
Making or adorning a Hooded Ritual Robe/Garb. Often at this time of year, when the weather gets a little nippier, we can all use a hooded robe for our outdoor rituals. In this workshop (time permitted), we will sew our own robes or at the very least, decorate and embellish already purchased robes. This would also be a wonderful time to bless your Witchrobes by all the elements, among your systers as well.

WORKSHOP IV
Since this is the month of Halloween and Gourds and Pumpkins are plentiful, we will carve our own pumpkins and with acrylic paints, decorate Gourds.

WORKSHOP V
Discussion on Astral Travel and Trance work. Tis the dark season and Samhain is the perfect time to reflect on the psychic arts, mysteries, trance and astral travel. Together we will discuss the practice and its origins.

WORKSHOP VI
Oftentimes Hekate, who opened all entryways, was depicted holding sacred keys. In this workshop we will experiment incorporating keys into various Craft projects like creating a large key for our altar or crafting a special amulet made of several found keys.

WORKSHOP VII
Ancestress Meditation or outdoor walking meditation offering and a discussion on its effectiveness. Also a brief discussion on Labyrinth workings and its traditional usage. If time permits we will create a simple Labyrinth on small canvas boards.

WORKSHOP VIII
Participants are asked to now present their ancestors/ deceased photo and Share One gift that their life and death has brought to them..._____*Photo should be released into the awaiting center cauldron.*

Afterward Chanting*: " Listen to my heart song, I will never forsake you, I will never forget you..."*

REFLECTIONS ON HEKATE

Hekate arrives with her lit lanterns when we find ourselves in our darkest hour. She is the friend, the elder, the wise grandmother with a sympathetic ear to our plight and struggles as womyn, for she knows first hand our deepest experiences as womyn. She also knows how invaluable you are already as a future ancestress and her arrival inaugurates an awareness of sacred thresholds, other realms, other ways of being, your ancestors and the journey through the veil, towards death.

She who can travel so effortlessly through all realms, invites you to cross the entryway and journey, if only for a moment, to your deceased loved ones; the ones who still love you, still influence the living and still have much to share with you. She tells you to come, for there are many who wish to speak with you, some from eons ago and some... from just yesterday, but death, with its lack of linear time, cannot keep them away from you any longer. She shares the mysteries of the Spirit, that Death cannot silence our loved ones, not when she's around.

By her gentle hand, she lead you to your ancestry and the realm of the dead. She teaches you to acknowledge the spirit world and sit comfortably with thresholds and the the unknown and confront your own mortality.

Hekate loves to take us on spiritual journeys and will always meet you at that pivotal crossroad when the gnawing in your stomach, heralds a change is impending, and you seek courage and support for the journey ahead.

HEKATE GROVE GODDESS GATHERING RITUAL

PURPOSE: To open ourselves up to The Goddess **Hekate** and her gifts. To travel with Hekate and reunite with our lost deceased, loved ones, on this Sabbat night when the veil between the worlds are thinnest.

Procession, Purification: with specially made Hekate Oil *(recipe given towards end of book)*

Entrance

SPEAKER: States why we are here... *"We have spent the afternoon in fellowship learning about Hekate and now we gather here to honor her and those who have passed and commemorate the sabbat of Samhain."*

Cast circle:

Cast circle by sweeping the circle with decorated, enchanted besom/broom

*I cast this consecrated space
to hold our circle, in love's embrace
I build and make this magic land
By will and word and blue shield sphere
let only good enter as I will
and block the rest from passage here, ,
Preserve and guard our sacred rites
And welcome Deities that I call
Outside of time, outside of space
We stand here now in sacred space, The circle is cast!!!

Elemental call

CHANT:*(Air I am, Fire I am etc....)* unison or suggested prose below

Quarters called

* Guardians of the Watchtowers of the **East**, Ye Powers of **Air**,
Realm of the spirit and beginnings, Breath of our ancestors that still lingers within our souls
We call on you to bring us your gifts.
Guard and Hold our sacred space, Hail and welcome Air!
(*attendants repeat*) Hail and Welcome!!!

*Hail Guardians of the Watchtowers of the **South**, Ye Powers of **Fire**,
Realm of fire that dwells in our spirit, runs through the pulsating blood of the living, flames of Hekate's twin torches. We call on you to lend us your gifts.
Guard and Hold our sacred circle, Hail and welcome Fire!
(*attendants repeat*) Hail and Welcome!!!

*Hail Guardians of the Watchtowers of the **West**, Ye powers of **Water**,
Realm of healing waters, tranquil oceans glistening in stillness, reflecting like diamonds the light of the full moon, We call on you to bring us your gifts.
Guard and Hold our sacred space, Hail and welcome Water!
(*attendants repeat*) Hail and Welcome!!!

*Hail Guardians of the Watchtowers of the **North**, Ye powers of **Earth**,
Realm of the living and tonight of the dead. Bones that sustain us, earth from above and from below us. Let thy hard wintry soil open to support us in our journey to Goddess. We call on you to bring us your gifts.
Guard and Hold our sacred circle, Hail and welcome Earth!
(*attendants repeat*) Hail and Welcome!!!

Invoker calls Hekate *(see suggested Hekate invocations)*

ASPECTING HEKATE*Hekate appears and speaks, allow her to speak thru priestess

HEKATE arrives & Speaks. *(see suggested Hekate Aspecting prose)*
She Introduces herself then instructs
I want you think of those you have lost either this year or in previous years. For I am the one that can travel through both realms. I can bring you to your loved ones and bring them to you. Just

as I brought Persephone from the underworld leaving Hades to reunite with her beloved Mother on this plane, I can do the same for you. Tonight the veil between our worlds are the thinnest and we can visit with our loved ones who have passed on to the other side, through that veil.

***MEDITATION OFFERING**

HEKATE'S REALM:
Visiting quietly with our ancestors in a separate room already pre-staged, in the land of the Dead. Room set up with photos of our ancestors and lit candles and altars set for each honored deceased member like cemetary.

Hekate will take them into her realm, it will be smelly, dingy, very dark and musty.. After all, we will be entering the land of the dead. You will hear dogs that will announce Hekate's presence. She was often known as the Black Bitch and the sound of barking dogs decree her arrival... Grove members will enter her realm and they will search for photos of their loved ones already there, awaiting them. For this ritual participants need to have the experience of <u>searching,</u> for in this realm, there are many deceased and they will need to search to find their beloved waiting.

Photos and a candle will be set up before hand

Earlier during the day, when we first gather for check ins part II, we will introduce our deceased beloved and afterwards enter their photos into Hekate's cauldron waiting in the center. At some point after, Hekate's realm will manifest itself....

In Hekate's Realm, participants will have some time to be still and commune with the dead and write one question they want answered from them.

There is sacred silence here

When they feel ready to leave, please invite them to come, one by one. Hekate stands at the entryway, where we always can expect her to be, with tarot and keys and she will offer it to them. The tarot they chose will answer their question.

They leave Hekate's Dark realm and now come into the light, the living where there is feasting set up......

The Silent Dinner of the Dead Begins

Quietly one by one they prepare meals, gather, find their way around the kitchen and table without saying a word- only with gestures and energy. Photo of their deceased will be at the table too. We eat in silence, in reverence....

***When it is over, a bell will be heard to signify
we are ready to move onward, open our sacred space and end our day with Hekate.

Final Check Ins: Now open it up to talk if necessary......Hugs and bid adieu......

Closing Chant: *"Listen, to my heart Song"*

Final Check In: Summary of our day and final thoughts.....

Devoking Goddess

Trioditis, Enodia, Propolos,
Queen of the Wise ones,
You who guides and holds the Sacred Lantern.
Dearest Hekate, Thank you for your presence here today.
Though forever more, you hold a place in our hearts,
at this time in our ritual we must depart..
We send our gratitude as we bid thee farewell.
Go if you must, stay if you will, Hail and Farewell Hekate!

<u>Quarters Devoked:</u>
Earth, Water, Fire and Air,
your presence was felt
as you Guarded us with care.
Received our thanks, as we bid thee Adieu.
Hail and Farewell with all of our Gratitude....

Circle is open with Chant: *"By the earth that is her Body....."*

**Cakes & Ales, Potluck follow **

REFLECTIONS ON DEATH WITH HEKATE

Late last Sunday night, as I sat on my porch with my newly adopted four month old Boston Terrier, I took some time to reflect and quieted down, after a very chaotic, emotionally draining weekend. I sat down, with the palms of my hands warmed by the womb of this living being and was calmed by the gentle breathing of a very fatigued, sleeping puppy. I listened to all the intangible sounds swaying gently around me. A hush lulled me into a strange place. I listened serenely and finally heard the sacred message of the night... I listened for a long time when finally I heard the breeze speak...
"Are you willing to be open to what is on the other side of the veil...?"

October for me has always been a time of transition. It sits between the very noticeable end of summer and the threshold of Winter. And while in the East Coast, this transitional month is quite literal and outwardly obvious in the foliage, as the leaves change colors and the temperatures drop, here in the South-West, I am starting to learn to be aware of the same changes -though with a lot more subtle exterior signs. Here I marvel at how different the autumnal breeze feels upon my skin, there is a strange hush feeling in the air at this time of year. Even the critters of the land, in their own language, announce the turning of the sacred wheel and the whispers of the midnight breeze affirm the same message. The whole month appears to be a thin, mystical veil to me, not just on the day of Samhain, but the entire month and it truly is represented in the Death Tarot Card.

When the Death card appears in a Tarot spread, it usually signifies a death of some sort. Most people freak out at the mere appearance of this card in a reading because of it formidable message but this card has much to teach us. Death can be literal or metaphorically, but rest assure, it signifies an ending. While our immediate reaction upon seeing this card, might be one of fear and trepidation, its presence in a tarot spread hearkens to so much more than just doom and gloom. This card might be representative of the discomfort and upheaval that comes as a result of an ending, but more importantly, we are reminded that Death brings a transformation and a necessary rebirth. The tarot card of Death announces something is dying, but as a result something is being born. As we say our goodbyes, on the sabbat of Samhain, we stand on Hekate's sacred threshold, where saying goodbye to the old year, simultaneously, leads to opening ourselves up to the new and unknown-the mysteries we've yet to touch, for the coming year. One year must end before the new one can begin. Although a rather simplistic observation, meditating on these words has always brought me healing and strength when facing death, the unknown, and a brand new undertaking. Something must die, something must be relinquished before experiencing rebirth and newness. The concept of death and rebirth being intrinsically linked seems to be a common belief through-out religious tenets and spiritual ideologies. And for Wiccans at this time of year, it holds a great significance.

This Samhain, what will you say goodbye to?
What will you freely relinquish knowing that in the end, it will lead you to "new skin"?
Are you ready to open yourself up to what awaits you on the other side of the veil?

As painful as Death is to experience and just as painful as it is bearing witness to someone physically leaving our side and exiting this earthly plane, there is a seed of life found amidst this pain and tragedy. When the immediate shock and sadness subsides and after a multitude of tears have been shed, there arrives an opportunity to look past our mourning, into the greater landscape of this cognizant, symbiotic Universe of ours and discover the unquestionable birth of something new.

Every life on this planet has purpose. Every life should be celebrated for its intrinsic value in our miraculous universe. Every life on this planet feeds and inspires another throughout its lifetime and upon its death. If we can truly open our hearts and mind to this reality then perhaps more reverence and celebration would be given to death, the way it so often is lavished upon birth.

Let us look at just a few examples of how the tragic death of a loved one or a stranger can bring about an unexpected cathartic birth.

Someone who dies in the hand of a drunk Driver their death inspires people to become more aware of DWI and pedestrian and driving safety...
Someone who dies in the hands of an abuser might inspire a generation to address these issues and become an advocate for the protection of women or children abused.
A dear one dying of disease like aids/cancer/or mysterious rare disease, results in a desire to learn more and push for more funding to research and find a cure for these diseases...
The gruesome discovery of a serial killer taking a life leads us to birth more police and civilian awareness and the research into the corrupt minds of these criminals, in order to protect society as a whole.

It puts our seemingly insurmountable pain and sorrowful confusion after death into perspective, the moment we view someone's life AND death as part of a cyclical greater plan -intrinsically they **DO** go hand to hand. Death and rebirth are inseparable. When we open ourselves to honoring life and death as one, the same, and unearth the birth that is deeply rooted in Death, we and the deceased can find healing.

Sometimes death arrives at our own door and we don't quite know if our life purpose has been well served. We exit this realm wondering if we've made a difference. Those who remain mourning in the physical form on earth, can take the opportunity to celebrate and validate the deceased person's life and thank them in spirit form, for their presence and existence in this universe. For indeed their life and their death becomes both equally necessary to value on the Sacred wheel. Even those whose death unearth a mixture of unresolved negative emotions within themselves and those they have left behind, can benefit from our rites of gratitude and validation. We have to seek and exalt this positive symbol of rebirth in order to give value to the person's now past existence, and life on this earthly plane. It is undoubtedly cathartic for us, who remain on the earth with unresolved issues, struggling to make sense of things, and I can only imagine, liberating, for the departed, as well.

As we stand amidst the Dark of the year and endeavor to invoke the Queen of the Crossroads, I ask you now to contemplate on your beloved deceased, or on those who have passed away this year.... Some of you may know the dead personally, some of you may not. Yet I ask you to consider and think about the attributes of the living, the myriads of components that make up **one** life.

Think about the threads that bind us to one another as human beings, those threads that are so apparent among our family and friends but also those, not so obvious; sacred invisible threads, that weave in and out of our Universal tapestry, connecting us to a far greater lineage than we can possibly imagine. Think about our connection that transcends space and time and those long expanding threads that go beyond the now and beyond what you can grasp intellectually, those long unwavering thread that go beyond our self- imposed borders of time and extend around the many, a past lives, kingdoms, queendoms, tribes, ancestries.... threads that reach farther than the eye can see, upward into the never ending spiral of the Universe. Reflect for a moment on these words and when you are ready, ruminate the following questions... If you are willing, think upon someone dear to you that has moved onward. Connect with them and their memory and use this special moment to validate their life. Search in your heart for the answers to these questions and send them love. Send gratitude to the deceased as you bid them adieu...

****

***You have died in the physical form and sad as it has been to lose you to death you have given me...

_____

_____

****I thank you....._____, your death, birth this in me...

_____

_____

***To me, Your life meant...

_____

_____

***I hope that you know now how much you continue to mean to me. _____

_____

_____

***You are no more in the physical form, but your life essence and spirit lives on. I will continue to honor you, your life and death, in this way...

_____

_____

_____

HONORING HEKATE: ANCESTRESS MEDITATION

***The journey begins here, now... Think of your beloved (as Demeter thought long and hard for many days for her Persephone), think of the deceased, see their face.. Do you remember how they smiled, their gaze, the timbre of their voice? *(Pause)*
See them... *(Pause)* What Day with them, still lingers on in your soul? Remember? *(Pause)*
Remember now, the details of that event that cradles this person deep in your memory...
Do you remember how you felt? *(Pause)*
Can you see them clearly in your mind? Can you feel them even now? *(Pause)*
Now call out their name. In your mind, call out loud their name and bring them closer here,
With your heart, with your mind, with your desire, bring them here... *(Pause)*
With your intention, with your energy, with your voice calling them now, bring them here...
Once a year, when the veil is the thinnest I bring them forth, today you have joined me on this journey and together we will travel to the land of the dead.

*Think for a moment, how their death affected you? How did it leave you feeling?
What did they leave behind in you?
Every life is sacred. *(Pause)*
Every being that breathes is part of the greater infinite sphere of life...Every life has purpose and meaning and their's was no different. What did their life mean to you? What has that life taught you now that it is no longer on the physical plane? *(Pause)*
Reflect now what gifts have been passed unto you as a result of their life and death? *(Pause)*
    **** You are sacred. You too are part of the infinite sphere of life. The Breath of the Divine lies within you, fueling you, giving you life and vitality.
    ***You are living now. Think for a moment...Breathe...Upon your last breath, what gifts will you release and pass down to the next generation?
Now it's you.. Now it's you exiting the physical realm...
What do you leave behind? *(Pause)* What gifts do you leave for the next generation to tap into... for indeed you will be called... and their voices will echo awakening you from your slumbers in the underworld. And they will call you. *(Pause)*
Hear them calling you....for you are already an ancestress...
You are already part of the sacred cycle of life and death and one day it will be you, who will be called upon on a night like this.
    ***From where you stand right now look behind you and see all that has come before you. See those that came before, all those who have paved the way for you, See all those whose hand forged your spirit to become what it is today. See their faces...some might be very familiar... hold their image in your mind's eye...
Bow down and Thank them.
    Now from where you stand look ahead of you, deeply look using your internal heart and eyes to see, far, far beyond you, look past, look ahead of you. Where you stand at this moment, see beyond the horizon.. See them before you.. Can you see them? Can you see those YOU have paved the way for? For your life has already impacted them. You are already their ancestor and your vital breath and existence was and is monumental for them.
    Ancestress that you are, recipient of your foremothers gifts...What do you leave now to those who are before you? What gifts will you leave for them?.. What Wisdom and counsel do you (Ancestress) leave now and freely give to Your Great great-grand daughters, sons and the ones who will call upon you?
    ****You stand on the Sacred threshold, between honoring your ancestors looking in the past and honoring yourselves as ancestresses and looking ahead into the future. You stand here now in My Realm -Hekate's Realm upon the sacred entryway. Welcome... and when you are ready...follow my voice as I count backwards from ten to one. Breathe, and with your exhalation allow yourself to float back into this room, to this time, to this space, 10, 9, 8, return hearing my voice, follow it back to this room, 7,6,5, Breathe in, 4,3, follow my voice, return to your body, 2, 1. Feel the weight of your body and when you are ready open your eyes. Give your body a gentle stretch, wiggle your feet and if you're woozy, pat down your body starting from your head crown, down to your feet. Welcome!

ORPHIC HYMN TO HEKATE

I Praise Lovely
three-formed Hekate,
Enodia,
Saffron-veiled,
of Sky, Earth, and Sea,
Who Celebrates
Bacchanalia at the tomb
With the souls of the dead,
Daughter of Perses,
Lover of Solitude,
Honored with cakes,
Nocturnal ones,
Protector of dogs,
Invincible Sovereign,
Heralded by the roar of wild
Beasts...
Keybearing Queen of the whole
Cosmos.
We honor you Hekate!

Sources: www.paganinstitute.org/t/hekate
www.theoi.com/khthonios/hekate
www.Hermeticfellowship.org

INVOCATION TO BELOVED HEKATE

Beloved Hekate
Protector and Midwife
While others have feared you
I have revered you

For, to me, you have been
(my) mother, grandmother and sister -all in One
You have been my shadow
to guide me in those times of darkness
My comforter assuring me I'm never totally alone

Allow me to honor you by invoking you tonight

When I did not know your sacred name
I called on you simply with my cries...
Oh Hekate...
You who have held the lantern for me
when in the dark I have stood, paralyzed at the crossroads
I honor you...

Allow me to revere you
by invoking you,
representing you tonight in our ritual.

It is not difficult to call upon you,
the one I know & love
As I was born under the sun sign of Scorpio.
I feel connected to you
Queen of the Witches
Queen of the Night

Tonight, I will honor you
Give thanks to you
and ask for your continued protection and guidance.
I call you, not as the crone,
but as the All Seeing Triple Goddess that you are.

Enlighten me..
Help me to see even amidst my dark consciousness,
Reveal to me those steps before me,
Those steps in front of me, that I must make
to fulfill our hearts' destiny.

ASPECTING HEKATE
Queen of the Witches
Queen of the crossroads
These are just some of the names I'm known as.

Those who don't know me
LOOOOVE to hate me
BUT
For those who are in the dark
Or those who have lost their way
Sooner or later you will encounter me.

For I am SHE
who guides you in your DARKEST hour.
(Pause)
      I LOOOOOOVE the dark,
      I love the night, and
      I loooove this time of year.

I am the one that can travel through both worlds
and I can take you from light to dark and
from dark to light.

Mine are the gifts of transformation
and Regeneration
      Come to me   Come to me

Place your Darkest Hour
in my cauldron and I will transform it
into my BANQUET.

See my gifts of regeneration
As they have already started tonight
within your souls.

Come let's begin.....

ASPECTING HEKATE

Tricephalus, Trimorphis, Enodia, Kleidouchos
Phosphoros, Propolos, Trioditis, Nyktipolos

Queen of the Witches,
Lady of the Moon,
Queen of the Crossroads,
Triple formed Goddess...
These are just some of my many names...

Come...closer...
Do not fear me...
do not avoid me
I am a part of life,
just as I am a part of death.

In your darkest hour,
I hold the Lantern to light your path...

I hold the keys to unlock
those tricky passageways
and open -closed doors

I stand at the threshold
and there await you.
when you are confronted
with a life altering choice.

Look unto me,
for on your last day on Earth,
I will be the one to guide your soul,
to the Land of the Dead.

Yes, I can travel thru the realms,
Night wandering Queen,
that can take you from light to dark
and from dark to light.

On this Magickal day,
when the veil between our worlds
is indistinguishable,

I will guide you to those you have loved & lost.
...Just as I guided
the beautiful maiden (Persephone) out of Hades arms
and back to her beloved Mother...

I will do that for you today...
Come...Follow me...
Follow me on this journey, into the land of the Dead... *(meditation to follow...)*

Find an image of Hekate; a statue, photo or an artistic canvas image of the Goddess. Decorate altar with her symbols, like Iron rod Keys, black hounds, lanterns, skulls and skeletons. Set up an Ancestral altar with photos of deceased loved ones and black and white votive candles. You may also have an offering plate with some of her well known beloved foods, like eggs, pomegranate and garlic. Let your working candle be a white, seven day glass candles, anointed with "Hekate's oil"(see appendix). It is also a good idea to have your tarot or other oracular cards handy on this altar.

SAMHAIN
*Veil between the worlds
Thinnest tonight
We call upon those
Who have taken flight

Their flesh has decayed
But their Spirit lives on
We call upon those
Who have long since gone

On Halloween night
When our worlds
Have merged
Their message to us
Is clearly heard

We bid them to speak
By any means
thru Tarot, our Candles
or even in Dreams

And after tonight
Peace unto them,
Until next year,
When we meet again.

On Halloween night, at midnight set up your altar with veils and black altar cloth. Decorate area with Gourds and pumpkins and special floral arrangements, of bare branches to represent the season of barrenness and darkness upon us.   Place skulls and skeletons on your altar and an image of the Darksome Goddess, whether it is Hekate or Maman Brigitte…. Attain a black or white skull candle, sold in many botanicas and witch shops, anoint it with Blessing oil. As your working candle use Red or black and carve it with the symbol of the spiral or snakes. Anointed the working candle with Hekate or sabbat oil, (see appendix) and include a simple bowl of water with bay leaf to be charged in the name of the Goddess. Gather herbs of mandrake, rosemary, patchouli, pine and sage, to be crushed and used on your charcoal brisket as incense.
Call upon the Goddess and honor her on this hallowed night.

WELCOMING SPIRITS ON SAMHAIN
*Hail and welcome to the sabbat of Samhain.
Herein this ritual we honor it today
The new year begins as the old one ends
We give our thanks for the cycle of change.

Our worlds are united
like lovers intertwined
Indistinguishable
on this holiest of nights

The spirits come join us
For one night of the year
We remember the deceased
Those we love and hold dear

We give honor to the dead
With this candle of Red
And by this flame –
-the Sabbat is now kept.

This is a good time to peruse through your journal from the previous year and assess your journey. Consider which spells have worked and which have not. Consider the life lessons afforded to you and what you need to relinquish now. Offer a black candle for this purpose-to banish what needs to be released. Prepare a white candle, carved and anointed with blessing oil (see appendix), and this will represent what you will now commit to manifesting in the coming new year. On your altar, let your chalice contain either wine or Spring water and use sandalwood for incense. Scry into a small bowl of dark, dry soil and imagine what great works will manifest from seeds placed upon it in the near future..... For now, spend time with Hekate, as she presents you with her Lantern of insight during the darkest season. Oracular readings are in favor at this time of year, document your Tarot readings for future reference.

VEIL BETWEEN THE WORLDS
*Samhain has come
A new year has begun
Reflect on what has past,
Amidst the veil
At year ends tail
In two world
I boldly stand.

Review the lessons that I've learned
as this Wheel now has turned,
What will I create
Give and take
And Next year fully earned....

I manifest _____

I relinquish_____

LIFE'S DESTINY
*All seeing Goddess reveal to me
How to fulfill my destiny
What is the path I must take
To manifest wealth and a happier state
Open the gates to great success
Using my skills and passing all test,
Help me improve on all my skills
Let it be by word and will,
Clear and focus let my mind be,
Ready and open for opportunities,
Here's a list of crafts I do
Reveal the path I should pursue....

I am _____(repeat)

Honoring Ancestors. Calling on our Spiritual guide-Hekate

I learned so much about myself as a priestess from this Gathering and I owe it all to Hekate, my ancestors and every womyn present. I get goose bumps just thinking about this day and the experiences I had days after this powerfully, intense gathering. I had no idea the impact our day would have on everyone present, including our beloved ancestors. Womyn were crying as they experienced the presence of their deceased loved ones. Some Womyn were overwhelmed at what they sensed. Womyn found themselves grateful for the opportunity created, so that they could quietly visit with their deceased. My family home, which is our Grove Temple, was immensely noisy and crowded with all of these invited ancestral spirits long after each syster left. I found myself indeed at Hekate's crossroads, in her spirit realm, and standing on her threshold indeed, in total awe and reverence.

By far, as scary as it felt at times, I learned to open myself up to the Divine with great reverence and respect. This is definitely not child's play, especially when working with powerful deities like Hekate. I learned to allow myself to open up like a vessel and go where the Goddess wants to take me, but also to set up precautions and be ready for anything. I learned to trust that the Divine's message overrides mine own and to practice reverence, awareness, trusting what She is brewing within me.

JOURNALING GROVE GATHERING -SAMHAIN -HEKATE

It is now 7:06pm and the last two ladies left about two hours ago and my family wasted no time coming back in and returning to their abode, while I scrambled to get everything organized -back to normal. I stressed putting everything exactly where it was so as not to disturb their daily routine. Frustrating, but immediately going from Priestess, syster and friend and hostess- to mother and wife and organized home maker is challenging.

All I can say about our day is Love.... LOVE.... Looooove... There was a lot of love in this house today. There were tears, heartfelt tears of joy, gratitude and excitement and sisterly love and true sisterhood. I felt Hekate's presence and felt extremely good about how we honored her today.

As usual we didn't get finished till after 5:00pm so forget about luncheon, we seem to be getting accustomed to dinners now, Wiccan potluck dinners, after our rituals and often very late. Initial check Ins? Well, it was past 12:30pm before we finally got down to actually starting because in our typical fashion, we hung out around the kitchen, talked about a lot of stuff, chit chatted like girlfriends do, updating each other on our lives. Although we always seem to begin late, this moment of initial chatting and bonding, I have learned, is quite valid, important and almost essential when conducting a womyn's Goddess group.

I must note that our Drumming trance was phenomenal!!! I could tell we were truly melding just from hearing how synchronized we finally became with our singing rattling and our drumming. It was obvious that we were having a wonderful experience. I explained the magick involved in this synchronization and how that vibrational quality, clears and cleans our chakras and helps with the grounding process. They were all in agreement and beaming brilliantly after this drumming.

Chanting and Singing workshop was bumpy at first, but as we continued again after that drumming trance, WOAH!!!! It was awesome...My original song to Hekate was sung so beautifully, as were the other great selections. Some of these wommin have beautiful singing voices and I had text sheets this time, which helped them immensely. I introduced some of our all-time favorite Pagan chants and of course, they loved these and really sang them well.

The lecture part was a little wonky, as I was nervous with much to say but finding it challenging to deliver it orderly without looking at some of my notes. Eventually, when I began to lift my head off of my distracting notes and started talking from my heart, things smoothed out quite nicely. Funny how trusting my intuition and speaking from the heart always flows much nicer than I expect. We all started to talk and added our own stories to the collective mythos. I ended by reading poetry, in the Homeric Style, to Hekate, and that felt good, like I was tapping into a long standing respected tradition via the auric fields. This led us into the ancestor presentation. This was long, a little hard to sit through, but so worth it, when you learned of everyone's grief and lament. Although it was long it was truly moving. We ended this part of our day by singing the "Listen to my heart Song" and that was quite an effective way to end. I felt myself get choked up. I then excused myself, played a meditative track, to let them relax into this moment. As I went to the other room that would become the land of the dead, to place the photos and altar candles to honor the decease. When I came back I was surprised they were quietly relaxing to the music....Then we took a pause and began the ritual to Hekate and our ancestors. All took place very smoothly as we transition from one part of our day to another. There were some womyn who joined us for the first time and some I hadn't seen in a long time, so their presence at the gathering was indeed a blessing and they added so much to our day.

    I was extremely shocked at how the aspecting turned out, for I didn't know what to expect. Hekate comes to me easily as I've aspected her several other times I remember holding that Large cast iron Key and closing my eyes, I felt Hekate's spirit swirl and twirl, speaking through me. Outside, the dogs started to bark and howl (no Freaking kidding...) as if they were on cue. My three dogs had been quiet for most of the day but in this very pivotal moment of aspecting Hekate, they decided to bark incessantly outside. I knew then, that Hekate was making herself known as I drew her down in me. I can't really remember all the exact details, but I remember my syster's eyes and how tear-filled they were as each was moved.

    "Come to the woman with the snakes in her Head" and then Hekate's song by Wendy Rule, played in the background after our ancestral meditation. Music has always played an important part in sacred rituals and here these songs were quite effective in helping us transition to the land of the dead with Hekate as our guide. One by one -Hekate awakened them and took them by the hand, leading them to the Land of the Dead. This part too was so overwhelming even for me, as I witness them connecting to their beloved and they were no longer in my Garage -they were in the place for the dead. This room, the altar, the cloth, the candles, their photo... it truly became the land of the dead.

    Silently, Hekate witnessed them commune with their loved ones. Then I invited them to come out of Hekate's realm when they felt ready. This part too left a lasting impression, at how transformational it truly was. We traveled from the land of the dead to the dark threshold (the laundry room) pitch black. Hekate held an open silk bag of Tarot and had them pick one tarot card in the dark...pitch darkness. Then she asked if they were ready to join the living in a feast for the dead, only after they replied, was the doorway opened, to let out a sliver of light and here, they were greeted by the light (the bright kitchen light) and the beginnings of the festivities...as womyn began to prepare the table and their foods. For me it was surreal.

    I had a very intense reaction to what I was seeing and experiencing that day, both as a participant and a priestess. If I had been there as just an attendant to this ritual, I too would be just as moved to tears as some of the womyn were. I know they were indeed moved by their words, by their tears, by our final check in, as we stood there in sacred space about to devoke. I checked to make sure everyone was grounded well and back on this plane and they all were. We shared our experiences from the ritual... and woah ...I was moved to tears upon hearing each and every one's personal experience as it mirrored mine own.

    One beloved grove syster felt another spirit come through. Her other Grandmother came in to remind her she was still watched over and she felt a swell of emotions and tears just overcame her. She hadn't realized how much she missed her until that moment. Another syster also had another deceased come through unexpectedly. And still one of the womyn was going to go to just walk arbitrarily to a candle, when suddenly she was pulled and led to the right candle where she unexpectedly caught a glimpse of her deceased baby sister in the photo. One syster talked about how she really valued this gathering because she has a particular affinity to ancestor worship and was especially moved to have a meal with a photo of her grandmother before her. One young member got the King of pentacles tarot card during the Tarot selection- it was a clear indication of her deceased Father -making it known that he was nearby, as usual. That was astounding because her Father was a Capricorn too, which is the sign represented by that card. We all had tears in our eyes throughout the day... but they were good, cathartic tears. I feel that we were all very much like a family by the end of the day... Don't know if the vibrational chime and bell ringing that I casted around the house prior to their arrival, set that loving tone, but I never felt so good among my syster in my life and in my very own home, that was a blessing for me personally. As a hermit, stay at home mom, I was touched by the loving feeling we shared for one another. Great love and appreciation for our Goddess group was expressed and that too touched me in ways I can't even begin to explain.

JOURNALING HEKATE'S DREAM

I have not slept much all night. Finding myself in and out of light hazy sleep...believing I am wide awake one minute when I am actually in a dream. I had one of those spiritual attacks... you know, the ones in the dream state. The ones where I am literally standing between the worlds, scary as shit... And then there is that flat line... Oh dear Goddess... that sound of the Flat line Buzzing, flat-line sound.... piercing, terrifying tone that warns me of its impending arrival..."*Ah crap... here it comes...*"

After the Hekate ritual I was fine, all was well. I felt playful with my mate, we even had sex, which always helps with grounding energy. I felt pretty good and uplifted after our gathering and felt that all in the world was good. The moment I got into bed that night something else began to churn. I could not really put my finger on it but it felt strange. I wondered, was it someone putting a hex or strain on me or was it my own paranoid self. I couldn't shake it off, but I felt this undeniable "presence" in my home, like very obvious "intruders" that did not belong there. My home was strangely hosting a number of trespassers and I could hear their numerous footsteps as they were pressing up against my heart now.

In and out of sleep, I still felt them near me but now in my dreams. Unable to sleep, I went down stairs to confront them. With consecrated sage water in hand, I sprinkled it around the house, asking them to return to their realm and to go in peace. I blessed myself and all the rooms with sage water, then returned to bed and all, at the time, seemed okay. In my bedroom again, I tried to go to sleep but I fell in and out of strange dreams. I saw and heard the sound of my spiritual alarms-my dogs. I think I started to dream of my dogs...black dogs, Hekate dogs, they needed me. I saw a small rat, annoying the dogs outside and they needed me to protect them and get them inside the house. I went outside to check on my dogs and their state of being. It all seemed so real. I could hear and feel someone in our backyard, around the pool area, no... this was still a dream...or was it real??? I saw and felt my own footsteps pressing upon the cold soil, the crisp cold grass, and I walked barefoot around the backyard making sure my dogs were okay. I walked outside to check several times though I still don't know if it was physically or astrally. I walked in the physical realm.... I walked in the spiritual realm, journeying... I journeyed outside in the cool, dark of night. I walked around the pool, felt the hard, spiky grass under my bare feet was I there spiritually or physically. The wind was blowing now faster and harder than I've ever heard before... it was so loud, almost deafening to my ears. This was in my dream, but no... indeed it was the howling winds, stirring louder than ever and it was piercing my dream state.... Then it happened, it must have been around 3:30-4:00am. As best as I can, I will try with my words here, to recreate the visuals of the attack.

Hekate's songs were playing all along, playing continuously in my head, they still are, even hours after our ritual. The songs we chanted during our gathering and the songs I played aloud on the stereo, continued to play in my head. I was still in and out of a dream state, reciting Hekate's Greek names.

I heard myself saying Kleidoushous (key holder) Kouroutrophos (caretaker) Enodia (crossroad) then I heard a stronger voice saying, firmly, in Spanish "Yo soy de la tierra..." "I am from the Earth" all the while I was saying, **"No... No...No..."** I kept repeating this, while also hearing myself adamantly stating *"I am from the Earth Realm,"* in Spanish and all the while I was grasping, pulling, violently grasping, to hold on for dear life, like quick sand, I felt myself being yanked and pulled, the way it must feel for someone to be buried alive. Oh Goddess, I was being pulled and buried alive... I was being dragged to the other side... With all my heart and at the top of my voice I screamed for my husband, until my voice was hoarse and inaudible, I was SCREAMING, **"J..., J.., J..."** and grasping for him, next to me in bed. Like a baby about to be dropped, clinging for dear life, my hands were frantically searching for him as I desperately grapple for an anchor, anything to keep me safe. It was so real and the familiar flat line sound, piercing resonance-that horrid sound that always heralds and announces this spiritual schism, was heard.

I was literally being dragged and I couldn't get a hold of my spouse to help. I felt myself clinging for dear life, trying to grab a hold of him, the blanket, anything, all the while hearing the Greek names of Hekate being recited matter-of-factly over and over and over again. And that Spanish, strong voice saying "...no I am from the "Tierra"/ Earth." Realizing I had just aspected and I needed to return to my body... I kept saying my own name over and over again and holding my head chakra, while declaring my name aloud.

I woke up startled… looked over at my husband, who was soundly sleeping, snoring, unmoved by all of this and couldn't believe that all of my yanking and screaming had not awaken him. It was as real as it gets!!! I was having convulsions, still shaking uncontrollably, in a cold sweat when I woke up. It was one of the most intense experiences of my life. I suppose having some familiarity with the spirit world helped me come out of it, but this was more intense than I had ever anticipated. It took me off guard because I just did not expect it.

Immediately I woke John up, asked if he was OK. *"..Yeah"* he said *"why?"* … I asked him if he heard my screams. *"No… what?…"* He was still half asleep and it took him awhile before he finally realized what was happening. I asked him to hug me as this is the quickest way for me to ground and reaffirm my physical reality. Then calmly I told him of what I went through. In mid sentenced I said, *"…listen to the howling winds"* as they were again wildly stirring. I said this at the beginning of the conversation, by the time I had purged all this out of me, the winds had eerily calmed down …Twenty minutes later, I said again at that point, *"…listen to the wind now.. Do you hear any?"* There was silence, nothing but silence and then as if by my cue, the winds started up again, howling. Needless to say **he** was spooked!!! We both were.

I started to tell him how I had not mentioned my dad during the ancestor honoring ceremony and how perhaps I had offended him and maybe he was trying to let me know. Could very well be…or maybe it was just from aspecting Hekate. I think though, it was Hekate who unquestionably was still lingering in my aura and trying to take me to her dark spirit realm because there was clearly a struggle. I was being pulled and I was saying "NO..I belong to the Earth!!!" So I don't know, maybe both were involved in this. We honored many deceased loved ones, and I know that there were a lot of intruders, new beings in my house long after the ritual was over. I could still feel them with every fiber of my body and they were not at all familiar to me. My dad was there too, but there were others I sensed here, that made me feel uncomfortable, as they lingered and created much spiritual chaos, noisy energy, lots of business and noise. My house felt like Grand central station at that point.

My original plans will of course remain that I will honor both of my parents, and my ancestral lineage, for Samhain in a few days- that will not change. I will create a special altar for them too as I always do at this time of year. I think however, my dad from the great beyond might've felt slighted and I regretted any errors on my part. Early this morning, I went on the chat-list and gave my reverence to him among my grove systers. It might not mean much to them but for me and my dad, it did.

As painful as this episode was, I suppose it is a part of the deal when you are working intensely in the Spirit Realm and especially at this auspicious time of the year. My poor husband is subjected to things he barely comprehends, but I thank Goddess he was and has always been near to hold me during these situations. I also learned a grave lesson. Exhausted after a long day, and feeling quite good about how it turned out, I made the mistake of falling asleep never having showered. This is not like me, after each ritual working I always make it a point to shower, knowing that this will cleanse me both psychically and physically but more importantly spiritually from any clinging vibrations. Well, I failed to do this and paid the price. I was also supposed to smudge the house after such an intense ritual for the dead, but that too slipped my mind. Big Mistake! I was feeling good about our gathering and it felt like the house was unaffected. In the dark of the night, the truth was revealed and like roaches they came out of their corners to make themselves known…not in any evil way, just in their usual disoriented, noisy manner. Spiritually boisterous visitors, that I appear to be very sensitive to and can easily be overwhelmed by. The following day, I wasted no time and I smudged this entire house from top to bottom sending, them back to their realms, thanking them and peacefully asking them to return to their realm. The house took on a completely different hue after that, feeling very peaceful and serene. The next day it felt like a completely different house and we were all well too. The baby also did not have that unusual crying episode like he had the night before and the dogs were a lot quieter, unlike the constant barking from that night. My Dreams returned to normal too. Smudging, bells, raising vibrations, fully devoking peacefully, showering and grounding are always a crucial final step, not to be overlooked ever again. Painful but necessary lessons for a Priestess.

HEKATE GROVE GODDESS GATHERING CHANTS

HEKATE SONG by B.M.M.
I meet you on this Crossroad
Hekate, my Queen
You hold the Sacred Lantern
Helping me to see
Hecate , Hekate
Guide me in the Dark,
Quietly, I listen for your Howl and Bark
Hekate, Hekate
Holder of the Key
To your Dark Realm now
I must go Traveling.... *Repeat continuously...*

DOWN IN THE CAULDRON
I am going down in the cauldron,
don't you worry and don't you moan.
I am gonna lay my body down,
in the Cauldron,
Crones are calling, gonna be reborn
I am going down ... repeat

SONG & TEXT BY ARTIST WENDY RULE
Gone are the leaves of the Hekate...
Trees....
Shed to the wind
Till her skeleton claws....The sky.
I am alone....In a Forest
Of Memories.
Dragging behind me
the howl of the Winter......Hekate..., Hekate...., Hekate..... *(repeats...)*

EARTH, MOON,MAGICK by B.M.M.
In the Earth, deep within,
There is A Magick,
I draw it in.
    In her Caves, in the Trees
    Hear her Heartbeat,
    Pulsing thru me.
When I Rise, I feel her Love
With feet Grounded
I'm soaring high above,
    In the Earth, deep within,
    There is A Magick,
    I draw it in
Ancient Moon, my Soul reveres
With my Singing,
I call you here.
    When this flame, ignites tonight,
    Priestess dancing,
    Under the moonlit night....
In the Earth, deep within,
There is A Magick
I draw it in....
    There is A Magick, I draw it in }3x

Hecate chant
Hecate- Cerridwen, Dark Mother takes us in
Hecate- Cerridwen, Let us be reborn
Hecate- Cerridwen, Dark Mother takes us in
Hecate- Cerridwen, Let us be reborn

Hekate...song & text by Kate West
Hekate, Hekate, Hearken one
Lend your powers to our spell
Hekate, Hekate, Darksome One
Help us weave our Magick well...*continue to repeat-add 2nd part with just her name -Chanting Hekate*

HEKATE GROVE GODDESS GATHERING CHANTS

In the Darkness of the Night *By B.M.M.*
Plaaaaant a Seed
Magick made by candlelight
Stirring Silently
Growing, Growing By my might
Words I speak and Charge tonight
_____Cast a Circle, Raise the Vibe
With my Energy
Magick made by Candlelight
Sing so mote it be....Sing So Mote it Be!!!

***Onward we go round the Spiral
Touching darkness, Touching light
Twice each year we rest in balance
Make choices on this night
Make choices on this night *by Marie Summerwood*

**Mother I Feel You Under My Feet.
Mother I feel your heartbeat
Mother I feel you under my feet, Mother I feel your Heartbeat
Heya, Heya, Heya, Heya, Heya Ho
Heya, Heya, Heya, Heya, Heya Ho...

**Listen, Listen, Listen to my heart Song
Listen, Listen, Listen to my heart Song
I will never forget you, I will never forsake you
I will never forget you, I will never Forsake you .....

**Mother of Darkness
Mother of Light
Earth Beneath the Soul in flight
Songs of love and Love of life
Guide us to our heart.....

**SHE GATHERS *By Ruth Rhiannon Barrett*
She gathers her daughters by Moon and by Sun,
She gathers her daughters it has begun.
She gathers her daughters to turn the wheel,
She gathers her daughters to learn and heal.
She gathers her daughters by night and by day,
She gathers her daughters to lead the way
(Counter Melody) By Moon and Sun, We have Begun, To turn the wheel, to learn and heal......

EIGHT BEADS CHANTS by Carolyn Hillyer
Girlseed
Bloodflower
(dip it) Fruitmother
Spinmother,
(raise it) Midwoman
Earthcrone
Stonecrone
Bone .....

****Let it in, Let it flow
Round and Round we go
Weaving the web of Womyn
Let it in, Let it Flow
Round and round we go
Weaving the web of life... *By Marie Summerwood*

GODDESS INVOKING SONG
Lady, Lady, lovely lady,
Are you from an ancient star?
Lady, lady Blessed lady,
Come to us from where you are
Magick Sister, Mother, Daughter
Tell us what will come to past.
You are moon Earth and Water,
You are here with us at last.
Lady join us
In our circle
Lead us in the spiral dance
When you speak your magick words
Send us all into a trance...... *From Starhawk Youtube ritual*

ELEMENTAL GODDESS CHANT
Earth, Air Fire Water, I am the Witches daughter
<u>Circe</u> is me and I am she
Earth Air Fire Water, I am the witches daughter
<u>Hekate</u> is me and I am she,
Earth, Air Fire Water, I am the Witches daughter
<u>Medea</u> is me and I am she,
Earth, Air Fire Water, I am the Witches daughter
<u>Gaia</u> is me and I am she.

CHAPTER TWENTY-THREE

"Have courage for the Great sorrows of life and Patience for the small ones, and when you have laboriously accomplished your daily task- go to sleep in peace...." Victor Hugo

"The positive thinker feels the intangible, sees the invisible and achieves the impossible...." Author unknown

WELCOME GRAND MAMAN BRIGITTE

OUR ALTAR*

Altar cloth: Black altar cloth under, some black lace, a purple altar cloth overlapping the others. Creation of a second altar area, with set up and black or purple cloth on the ground.
Image Bones, lots of skulls and skeletal, a statue of an elderly loving couple or of the Crone Goddess. Canvas art, Her sacred Veve or photo of Cemeteries, tombstones, skulls, Caverns, and Caves.

Always present on the altar;
A cast iron cauldron, drums, speaking stick, a silver pentacle, athame, elemental representations.....

Air: Smudge wands, Incense type sticks, cones, charcoal brisket and fine powdered herbs like; Allspice, Clove, Frankincense, Patchouli, Mugwort, Angelica. These can be crushed and then burned as your Eastern representation.
Fire: candles of all kinds are appropriate to you, glass enclosed or pillars, preferably in black, white, purple or gray. You may also incorporate knob and special skull candles, easily found at this time of year and they can also be purchased at your local Occult shops.
Water: Chalice or small glass bowl with Water, pomegranate juice or sweet red wine
Earth: A Floral arrangement of Bare branches, or purple colored Plants can be a lovely symbol for the element. Also a small dish of soil, actual bones, grave dirt, and or herbs can all work wonderfully as your Northern representation.

Other items pertinent to this particular gathering
Photos of Cemeteries, Tombstones, wrought iron and crypts,
Her special Veve, art invoking symbol,
A top hat to also acknowledge Baron -her spouse
Scales and crosses,
Masks to wear
Lots of Skulls of various material; ceramic, plastic, cement, paper mache, candle wax, red clay
Large Cast Iron Cauldron
Lantern
Gourds and some pumpkin of the season
A multitude of black votives
Photos of our Ancestors
Offerings like unfiltered cigarettes, cheese, honey, chocolate truffles, rum, coffee grains
Workshop items: Writing pens and paper, Mini paper crafted black Coffins,
Black Lace, gauzy fabric /veils
"Death Card" from the Tarot, Various Tarot Decks and other oracles

Offering bread, red hot peppers, water, honey, unsalted roasted peanuts, rum, truffles, clear fresh spring water, cigarettes and black coffee.
Sacred objects from members :
Notes:

Altars for Maman Brigitte

Grand Maman Brigitte Altars

MUSING ON VOODOO LOA GRANDE MAMAN BRIGITTE

How does Maman Brigitte appear to me...?

     Maman Brigitte is a Voodoo Loa who comes to us from New Orleans, though her origins surely begin in Haiti and quite possibly Africa. She is often referred to as a new World Loa/Goddess (I mean no disrespect to the culture, but I will use the term Goddess which is so ingrained in my own personal vernacular when referring to this beloved Voodoo loa). In Voodoo, as is in most spiritual theologies fully submersed in ancient indigenous practices, the Loa is more than just an archetype or lofty deity but a personification of a living breathing spirit. Since this too is my own personal definition of a Goddess I will respectively, use both terms interchangeably.

     Maman Brigitte is born as a result of the merging African slave and European influence in New Orleans, but most important to note is that she is born, like most Loa, out of a need. With the brutal rise of the African and Haitian slaves came the increase in senseless horrifying deaths. A multitude of vagrant, unidentified, displaced cadavers abound and for a people who venerated their land and their ancestors, this was a most tragic experience, to say the least. Back home, when death arrived, they were comforted in the knowledge that they would be bury in their homeland and reunited with their beloved sacred ancestors. Dragged to this new land, they couldn't even hope for this, as their customs and spiritual beliefs were challenged and nearly eradicated through the vile practice of slavery and assimilation. Clearly the need for a loa, like Maman Brigitte, becomes imperative... a fiercely protective mother who assures you, your death will not be in vain, your bones will be properly cared for upon your death and your spirit will be led to your homeland to reconnect with your sacred ancestors where you belong. This is the very least you can hope for and Maman Brigitte takes on this critical role for a people stripped of everything else.

     There is clear evidence that there was a lot of mingling of cultures in this new land, and the Irish and English undoubtedly influenced the manifestation of this Voodoo loa. Grande Maman Brigit (as she is also sometimes called) is often linked to the Celtic Goddess Brigit, who was attributed to inventing the art of keening (a special funerary howl of grief), hence the similarity in their names and attributes. There are some that believe Maman Brigitte is known as a healing, matron smith Goddess, just like St. Brigit. Sometimes this Loa is even depicted as being very light skin, possibly blue eyed with reddish or white hair- the obvious genetic attributes of someone from European descent.

     In some of the writings I have read about this Voodoo Loa there is sometimes reference to Maman Brigitte, as just being another aspect of the Yoruban African Goddess, Oya. I don't see this at all... I feel her in my body vastly different than Oya. I love both Goddesses and worked with Oya exclusively a few years ago and can honestly say that these two are respectively different deities. They might share in some of their well known attributes like; being strong willed, ruling over the cemetery, and patron Goddesses to our female gender, being particularly sympathetic to women's issues, but they must be respected and worshipped as two very distinctly different deities.

     Oya is a Yoruban African Orisha, an ancient Goddess very much connected to the Niger river. She is most known as a fierce elemental Goddess of drastic Change, thunderstorms, high winds, tornadoes, cyclones and the Elements; Air, Earth, Fire and Water are associated with her. She is a warrior Goddess, who often will join her consort, Chango, in battles. She appears to me very physical, willful and strong, dare I say lots of testosterone energy in a feminine package. Yet even with noted connections to various lovers and husbands, she is not terribly tied into them for she is known as fiercely independent, intelligent, autonomous, a shrewd business feminine leader and an inspirer to women to share in her gifts.

Grande Maman Brigitte, for me personally, comes as a sort of Corpse Bride. It is not surprising the Celtic Goddess Brigit(whom she is so often associated with) also has a connection with this aspect and was known as St. Bride. Maman Brigitte clearly has this very strong linked to her Spouse, Baron Samedi, together they rule the cemetery. Respectively, they are both known as father and mother to the (Ghede) dead and share many similar qualities. Writings, documenting spiritual possessions, claim that when she arrives, although she can first appear very proper, she will sometimes take on some of Baron Samedi's eccentricities. She might even choose to wear his black top hat and match his level of vulgarity with her own bawdiness and potty mouth.

For Maman Brigitte, the cemetery alone is her beloved realm. Unlike the Orisha Oya, who had originally been given dominion over the Oceans and who (as some myths reveal) through trickery, was given the cemetery to tend to forever after, (a duty she rightfully might not fully embrace). Maman Brigitte appears quite comfortable as Mistress of the Cemetery. This is in total contrast to Oya and Maman Brigitte happily appears to reside over bones and claims the cemetery as her home and here too is another reason why I strongly believe Oya and Maman Brigitte are two very distinct deities.

I don't recall reading anything that connects Maman Brigitte to Elemental energy like; Winds, Fire and Water, unlike the Orisha, Oya. I don't see Maman Brigitte having any link or correlations to fighting wars or wielding a "machete" or sword... but maybe a long phallic shaped wand or pole to ride on during her licentious banda dancing. To me she appears so much more bawdy and lighter, it seems, in her derelict humorous nature and much too interested in getting a good chuckle than in fighting wars. Perhaps after a life of various stressors and "war- like" challenges, battled in the flesh, while living on this earth, it is in death that we can finally be liberated from such nuisances. Maman Brigitte makes it a point to remind you of the liberating freedom from these human, earthly, trifling concerns. She is not a war deity perhaps, because in death the battle is already over and done with and all that remains is a resignation to tend to your spiritual peace and happiness.

Another interesting observation is that Oya is known as the mother of Nine but it is Maman Brigitte who is known as the mother of the Dead. With all the dead being her children, (an obvious multitude) you can imagine she is a fiercely strong Goddess with some amazing matriarchal skills and when someone needs the guidance and ardent protection of a mother, she becomes the best one to invoke.

Some of the writing reveals that there is also a connection to Maman Brigitte invoked by her worshippers as a judge, like the Egyptian Goddess Maat. She is called upon when there are extraneous, unfair circumstances that need to be mediated and here too the loving, righteous, protective nature of a mother is almost compulsory.

To me, Maman Brigitte is indeed a New World (U.S.A.) Goddess of the Cemetery, with origins from Africa and Europe. For practitioners of Voodoo, she is the Loa of the dead, mother of the Ghede, Corpse Bride, wife to Baron Samedi. She is keeper of the bones and the one who greets you upon your awakening. The first female buried in a cemetery is sacred to her and you will find Maman Brigitte nearby this tomb. It is my belief that she is not a Goddess of the underworld like Persephone, Ma'at, Erishgigal or so many other underworld Deities like Hades/Pluto, but rather she is ruler of entryway, doorways, transitions. Here she resembles the ancient Greek Goddess Hekate, in this role as gatekeeper and as the one who dwells in those sacred transitory junctures. Her home IS the cemetery and her role is to help you understand you are no longer in the flesh, but of bones and then, soon enough.... of ether. It is with her help that we transition from one realm to the next and the next.

Lover of Bones, she is the gate keeper of the Cemetery and this is her realm NOT the underworld, not what I envision to be the forever after. To me, and of course this is just my personal opinion, when we first die, there might be lots of confusion and an obvious period of adjustment. For some...that period might be longer than others, but this period of adjustment is where Maman Brigitte is most needed and called upon. I suppose that is why she is known as the Mother of the dead. When you die or... find yourself in a strange, unfamiliar place, in a uniquely different circumstances and situation and lacking all that was, previously, familiar to your personhood, it is precisely at this moment when we most need "Mother". It happens upon our birth, as it happens upon our death. Maman Brigitte is the Mother who helps and guides us as we figure out how to maneuver our way in this new realm and with these new, vastly different skills. As a growing embryo, floating and merging with uterine water, was your specialty. Upon leaving that realm, to enter into the living, you encounter a vast set of circumstances that require the nurturance and guidance of mother for your very own survival, such is the inception of every human's life. As a Corpse, I suspect you'll have a similar experience as you find yourself exiting one familiar realm to enter another, quite mysterious perhaps just as daunting and scary of a place, as this living realm first appeared to you. And with death comes different skills to experiment and familiarize yourself with, a metamorphosis, new form of being, a vast set of circumstances that, again, require the nurturance and guide of mother for your very own survival- it is Maman Brigitte who, according to popular Voodoo tenet, will be waiting there to help in this role.

    You've probably never actually watched a human body decompose. The concept of death and its grueling intricate process in our modern day society seems so shrouded in mystery. I think in particular, in the U.S.A. now, death is more often than not, handled very privately, almost concealed and beautified for us. The old and sick, nearing death, are separated by sterile hospitals and old age homes, sometimes devalued, pushed away from society long before their actual deaths takes place. Cadavers receive beautifications via the practice of embalming and then there are some funerals that opt for a closed casket. No one appears to want to talk about it and for many Westerners, it is either not given much thought or it is simply feared. Perhaps what makes it so frightening is the inexperience and lack of knowledge of what actually happens to us when we die. And so it seems, that the process of rigamortis appears hidden from us... and most of us go to our own graves never knowing what to expect at this junction in our journey.

    Unless you are in the medical field, mortuary business or a forensic scientist, you probably have little experience and knowledge in the process of a decomposing body or the process of death. Ignorance in the process of dying might make it easier to trivialize its value and sacredness, unlike in centuries past and in those indigenous cultures, where death was and still is exalted and commemorated on the same stratum, echelon as birth. I muse and wonder how vastly different our present day society would be, if there was more reverence and respect, expressed and understood, towards the process of death. Living and dying are so intrinsically linked that I imagine, a reverence for death, would naturally result in a more heightened way of living in harmony with nature and a deep rooted respect and need to live every minute aware of the Divine within and all around... When the "Tomb" is honored, the sacred "Womb" is honored and everything in between falls harmoniously into place.

    For these indigenous cultures, their religion and spiritual practices are linked to the "old ways." Death and its sacred process is highly esteemed and venerated and thus merits a Goddess dedicated dutifully to its provision. Voodoo loa, Maman Brigitte fits that role perfectly as Mistress of the cemetery, guardian of the bones and Mother to the dead.

    Long may she be respected, loved and worshipped... Hail Grande Maman Brigitte!!!

"...Life is not a problem to be solved but a mystery to be lived ..." Hugh Prather.....

MAMAN BRIGITTE -OCTOBER GROVE GATHERING

Purpose: To CELEBRATE the end of the Wiccan year with Pizzazz and Euphoria. To invoke and give honor to the Mother of the Cemetery, Maman Brigitte, our ancestresses and our sacred bones.

Check In: Introducing ourselves and where we are emotionally and Spiritual at this time of year.

Grove Business: We will speak on the hopes for the new year for our group, **Agreements** can be shared here- if necessary, other concerns and thoughts can be openly addressed now.

Check In: II. In preparation for the New Grove Year, taking stock of what we have accomplished as a group, but also trying to discern where we want to move, progress and the future direction of our Sisterhood. Questionnaire will be anonymously completed (see accompanied questionnaire) and together we can brainstorm ways to best manifest our goals...

Chanting workshop Singing our songs and learning our ritual music.
"Old Woman wrap your cloak," "Dark Mother," "Going down in the Cauldron..." "Ancient Mother," "Rattle my Bone," "Eight Bead Song," "Mother I Feel You," "Snake Woman"

Drumming: Invite them to connect with her, via a fierce music <u>CD Drumming track</u> - Fire Dance or Soweto Drumming CD track and together we can dance, drum, rattle and create a good drumming circle if there are enough wommin...

Check ins III: Since we all know each other's names at this point, it would be good to do a check in on the **Personal meaning of Samhain** this time of year... what does "Samhain/Halloween" personally mean to you....?

Goddess Lecture on Maman Brigitte
how she comes to us and what are her attributes and her relevance to us now. Exploring New Orleans Voodoo and the Mistress of the Cemetery, Maman Brigitte.

GODDESS WORKSHOP
Workshop I: Who do we honor?
Honoring a woman who has died this year or if needed it could be someone from the past... let it be a woman who is beloved to you, that you want to honor now, at this sacred time of year. You may have a photo and share... what do you celebrate about this person's life? What did they teach you or gift to you?

Workshop II: R.I.P.
Coffin creation, painting a wood or a little cardboard coffin box. Decorate it as a place to bury items in our lives that need to be put to death. It will be the place where we put things to rest in peace.... This can be utilized in the ritual with Maman Brigitte instead of or in addition to the bone skulls previously suggested.

Workshop III:
Death reflection. Meditation on the process of death and what we can expect our body's to experience. Reflections on our bodies <u>Decomposing</u>, held by the earth, and meeting her for the first time....

Workshop IV:
Witch Bottle creation for protection of the home and communally creating a Witch bottle of Four Thieve Vinegar to protect ourselves and bring blessings to our abode.
(See page 431, Aradia Chapter, for a Traditional Witch Bottle Recipe)

Workshop V:
Mask decorations, sculpting and crafting Mardi Grass/Carnival style ornate Masks.

Workshop VI: <u>Skull Meditation</u> (see suggested script to read, reflect and share)
Reviewing our entire Wiccan Year, what do we surrender from the previous year now. What aspect(s) of our personality are we willing and ready to surrender now. What do we now relinquish and metaphorically put to death now.

Workshop VII:
Looking ahead, trying to project and anticipate our upcoming year. With incense and our words, we will Bless our brand **new calendars** and together envision all the best for the coming new year.

Workshop VIII:
Frame-able Collage of what we hope to birth in the new year. Creating something that will automatically bring our mind into proper focus for our goals this upcoming new year. We will have a timed exercise to search quickly through magazines to cut out images that our subconscious are drawn to as reminders of what we hope to manifest in the coming months. Creating a collage under time restrictions to sharpen our focus on our goals and connect better with our subconscious.

Workshop IX:
Decorating Katrinas and actual Skulls as offerings for Maman Brigitte. Whether we have paper mache skulls or whether they are made out of clay, sugar, flour, plaster, glass or plastic, we will endeavor to decorate them as colorful and as creative as can be in her honor.

Workshop X:
Since Maman Brigitte is the New Orlean Voodoo Goddess of the Cemetery, this would be a wonderful time to view photograhs, artwork , a Book or a DVD Documentary on the numerous beautiful cemeteries and tombstone, not just in New Orleans, but from around the world.

A discussion about our upcoming
Samhain ritual, honoring
Maman Brigitte follows.

MAMAN BRIGITTE MEDITATION FOR SKULL WORKING

What part of past year, do I gladly surrender and put to death? Here in these bones, in this skull (I hold in my hand), I symbolize it...

What transpired in the year that you are now able to let go? Think back at the last **Winter Solstice** and your state of being then, as you began the Wiccan New year. Contemplate on maybe the most stressful part, you can recall, of the year. Go through the various seasons (last Winter..., last Spring..., last Summer..., this Fall....). Think upon the last Eight sabbats and esbats... Which time of the year found you happiest? Which found you at your saddest or most frustrated? Think about the lowest point, the challenge or challeng**es** of the year, for at this very moment you will have a chance to confront this experience and finally surrender it, so that you may move forward, into the New Year, free of this pain.

What was last **Imbolc** like for you? Were you feeling embryonic then? Were there **new** challenges brewing under the icy cold, wintry surface of your land or old ones, waiting to return for a long stay? Did you feel hopeful or trepidation? Did you feel regretful or a sense of potential freedom and renewal? Think upon last February and re-visit those feelings for a short moment before releasing them and moving onward.

Lets reflect now on the months of March and April. Think about this past Ostara..... **Your seeds**....what precious seeds did you hold dearly, in your hands? What were you planning then? How did you feel in the midst of **Spring**? Was there a feeling of great potential or unsuspecting havoc? Did you feel the pull and surge from the core of the Earth as its energies manifested a balanced axis? Go back, and try to remember your state of being at the commencement of Spring? Revisit your feelings for a short moment, then release and surrender them, before moving onward.

Think upon last **Beltane** and the start of Summer.... Colorful ribbons flowing from the beloved emblematic Maypole, spiral dances and fertile lush green fields. What was tugging at your heart then? Was your spirit as alive and fertile and productive as nature appeared to be all around you, at this time of year? What were you facing then? What were you celebrating or still hoping to celebrate soon? Allow yourself to travel back to this time and reflect on your state of being then. When you are ready, release and surrender any negative experiences from that period.

Travel back with me to the middle of the year, back in June... Think back about your situation and your state of being at the **Summer Solstice**. What entered or exited your life at this time of the year? What themes permeated your realm in the middle of the scorching Summer heat? How did you greet the height of the Sun? Were you energized and sunny or scorched drained? Were you exuberant or indifferent and complacent? Allow yourself to remember this time and reflect on your state of being then. When you are ready, release and surrender any negative experiences from that period before moving forward.

Now, think about the first of August, **Lammas** or **Lughnasadh.** Summer and it's heat, slowly appearing to wane away...loosening its grip. Were you ready for the change of season then? Or did it sneak up on you? Did you find yourself upset at how fast summer came and went? Or were you fully eager and ready for the seasonal change? What did the end of Summer bring or take away? Revisit your feelings for a short moment, then release and surrender them, before moving onward.

Contemplate on just a few months ago...how was your **Thanksgiving, at Mabon**? Was it well commemorated? Did you find yourself amidst a bountiful harvest? Or did you stress and lament about what you still lacked? What themes did you encountered at this time of year? What was your state of being at this last harvest? How did you feel as you reflected on the blessings from the year? Was there balance in your realm on this Autumnal Equinox? Were you able to see and appreciate much? Or were you overwhelmed by work and challenges requiring your attention? Allow yourself to travel back to this time and reflect on challenges and your state of being then. When you are ready, release and surrender any negative experiences from that period.

As we reflect on the old year and prepare ourselves for the new, consider for a moment if there was anything that happened or any goals that changed or didn't manifest... Were there any experiences that you gladly wish to surrender now and bury, hoping to forget, hoping they will not repeat, nor have any more hold on you from this day forward? The time has come to release experiences that have held you in a negative state...

Here at **Samhain**, contemplate on what part of the year do you gladly surrender and put to death? In these bones, in this skull, **symbolize** it....and offer it to beloved Voodoo Loa, Maman Brigitte; Lover of bones, Banda dancer, Gate keeper of the underworld, Fierce mother to her children-the dead, Corpse Bride, Mistress of the Cemetery, your spirit guide... She will gladly take these bones and compost them into her realm. Let this skull, you hold, be a symbol of that which has died in the old year ...Let it symbolize that which you can now willingly surrender and say goodbye to.

This is not something you need to mourn sadly, for as Maman Brigitte will reveal to you, we can sometimes rejoice in death and be happy to be DONE with something.... a situation... an old dream that does not serve us well anymore... a challenge met and won, something or someone or an old aspect of ourselves that needs to be surrendered... We can take this opportunity now to honor endings and our sacred old bones, surrendering them in a celebratory manner, to the Goddess, at this time of year, as we make room for the new in our lives. Maman Brigitte will meet you at the cemetery when you arrive and she will gladly take those bones as her own...and you no longer have to worry about them. She is a fierce Mother and judge and she will gladly alleviate your burdens and take good care of those painful bones from your past, lightening your load.

So what do you rejoice, in finally surrendering, in the new year?
What carcass has been laying around in your realm for far too long and now needs to be gladly relinquish to the Mother of the dead- Maman Brigitte?
Let it be symbolized in this skull and these bones and be ready to surrender and offer it to the Goddess.... And then join her in celebrating this death at Samhain and greeting the New Year lighter, with peace, in a celebratory state... Blessed be!

MAMAN BRIGITTE -SAMHAIN GROVE RITUAL

Purpose: Samhain Ritual. To CELEBRATE the end of the Wiccan year with Pizzazz and Euphoria. To invoke and give honor to the Voodoo, Mother of the Cemetery, Maman Brigitte, our ancestresses and our sacred bones.

RITUAL : Everyone in Masks/or Heavy make-up in Festive costumes, representing elements or deities....
Supplies: Incense, black/other candles, cauldrons, chalice, coffins, skulls, Glue, scissors, magazines, cardboards, paper strips, drums, collage boards, mask, offering, rum etc.

Communally Hearth Altar:
Her Veve, Black over velvet purple altar cloth, Maman Brigitte statue, Death skeletal figure, pentacle cauldrons 2-3x, center white candle, elemental 4xglass candles. Her symbols; the scale and the crosses, statue of her, masks like carnival, Mini handmade coffins, skulls, and bones, black or purple lace textiles, White and Black candles, Lanterns, images of cemeteries, graveyard dirt, tombstones, phallic symbols, Black top hat, Drums, For wommin-black votives to light upon entering ritual space for ancestral, they should have their calendars and collages and candles for altar as well.

Floor ALTAR: A separate black altar cloth on the floor, in the middle of the room....
This altar will have ALL the skulls, the coffins, rattles/drums needed for our circle casting etc...where we will sit and gather like an actual cemetery.

Offerings: Water libations, Please NO Salt, Various Sweet Wines, dark chocolates and truffles, unsalted roasted peanuts, Coins, unfiltered cigarettes, Block of cheese and appetizers for participants, Rum, red hot 21 peppers, bread, honey, black coffee.

Beginning purifying the space with Frankincense incense, cinnamon and allspice... and Bells for raising of vibrations all around the room.

Oil Anointing to welcome one another into the space. Each woman will anoint her syster sitting next to her with a welcoming message from the heart...(*no script, adlib here connect to source*)

In complete darkness, wommin are invite to scatter around, maybe lounge in the sitting room, they should talk and eat, enjoy music, laugh and carry on as normal... **"For when death comes we are almost never prepared for its arrival"**

Maman Brigitte will elect each person individually, awake them, and whisper in their ears.....
"For when death comes,
we are almost never prepared for its arrival....
And thus I call you now to death's realm,
stand and journey with me..."

Bring them to the entrance and smudge them or use Incense stick as you study them and circle around them hauntingly, Offer them a pomegranate seed and then Maman Brigitte will ask...
"What offering do you bring to me,
that I should let you into my realm....."
"Aw.. Bones, a skull????
Therefore, Come in... Light your flame
to honor those who came before you,
those whose shoulders you stand upon now"

(*black votives offered on altar*) She takes them unto floor altar and places their skull offering on the ground altar).
"Among the bones and coffins,
light your flame of gratitude,
think upon those who came before you,
to pave the way-Your Sacred Ancestors."

****

MUSIC: BUFFALO BEAT or FIREDRUMS
Participants sit, contemplate, quietly and wait for all to join in the circle. Priestess speaks:
**"Rise, stand up...Look around you,
we are no longer in the light of day,
but in the Dark of the year,
among tombstones, coffins, bones & spirits."**
Standing Facing inwardly now, a moment of silence.

**"In silence we cast our personal shield,
communally we cast this circle tonight."**

When all are facing outward Priestess says:
*"I conjure now this circle of power, by my will and word,
A meeting place between humanity, and all that is good, sacred and divine.
a place of safety and sacred boundaries
A container and preserver of the energy raise within thee
A place outside of time and space,
A repellent and shield against maligning energy
Where Sacred boundaries grant protection to all here today.
Be thou a place held sacred,
to the ones invoked here today.
I do so conjure thee, by my will and word... so mote it be!*
The circle is cast!

Afterwards, begin to drum/ rattle and invite them to do the same as we walk clockwise around the room. End with gallantly with **"So mote it be!"**

ELEMENTAL HONORING and INVOCATION
(Volunteer Participation encouraged as always, also see Quarter call suggestions in this chapter)

End with CHANT: *"Bones Come Dance with Me," "Old Woman Wrap your Cloak around me, Death bringer rattle my bone..."*

SHORT MEDITATION to further invoke the Goddess/Loa energy.
Hail and welcome Maman Brigitte!

Coming out of meditation with **CD Music: Dream Weaver Michelle Mays...**
Hand out their spell coffins as the song ends
*****
So what bones do you gladly surrender this time of year ...

"Death Brings a certain Freedom and lightness of the ethers. I invite you to unburden yourselves... Listen to your skull, listen to your bones, they will reveal so much wisdom and truth to you. What do they tell you, now that you need to release ? Listen to your bones, what do you gladly surrender at this time? Listen to your bones, what do you gladly release now, unburden yourself, write it on this parchment paper and place it in your coffin,... you will intuit whether you should bury, burn, drown, and how best to handle this magickal coffin."

CHANTING: As we release into these coffins sing; *"Mother of Darkness, Mother of Light..."* place box in large cauldron, as they say what they gladly release. (they can retrieve at the end. there will be a moment of silence afterwards.... Maybe mourning tears....the cauldron will be taken outside....)

allow silence, then a Bell will ring to signal a shift*
Each womyn will approach the altar, before her personal Collage, to light her "Hope candle"
Invitation to Remove our masks and dance and sing:
"I'm going down in the Cauldron" (body movement raising energy here and standing...)
Incense stick passed around,

Blessing our Calendars around the circle as we sing and **state aloud** what our visions for the new year will be. We go around in circle stating ALL of our wishes (lots stated) aloud.
(Collages should be on altar already for inspiration).
Systers support and affirm each other's wish with, **"So Mote it Be"** this should be, jovial, celebratory, comments should be blurted out bawdy and with love and joy and we should state for each other;
"I envision YOUR year with_____ as_____ etc.. repeating her wish."

CHANT: *"We all come from the Goddess..."*
THANKING AND DEVOKING ANCESTRAL SPIRITS
Hail and Farewell, Beloved ancestors who came,
To Legba and to you, all honor was given thru this flame.
With Gratitude we bid thee Adieu
Hail and Farewell to you!

DEVOKING MAMAN BRIGITTE
Mother of the Ghede
Bawdy Maman Brigitte,
Bone Keeper Goddess
Thank you for coming to our feast.

You led us to our Ancestor,
And fueled our Samhain spells,
Receive our Gratitude, Dear Mother,
As we bid thee, Hail and Farewell!!!!

THANKING AND DEVOKING ELEMENTS
CHANTING: *"The earth, the air, the fire, the water, return, return, return, return...."*

OPENING CIRCLE: *"The circle is open but unbroken, may the peace of the Goddess, be ever in our hearts, Merry meet and merry part and merry meet again...."*

Lavish Potluck to follow and sharing our ancestral dish

QUARTER CALLS & INVOCATION OF ELEMENTS

INVOKING EARTH:
Hail and Welcome Earth Gnomes of the Northern Realm.
Solid Transformer, manifestors, busy skilled workers, producers of that which sprouts and pierces through the Earth.
Competent, skillful, innovator,
lending courage and strength to our form.
Connect us to thy roots, that reach deep inside Earth's Core.
Hearken to our Call, Realm of Transformation and bear witness to our Rites.
In you may we surge, blossom, and thrive confidently,
taking our rightful place upon the Earth as we invoke your gifts tonight.
Hail and Welcome Earth!

INVOKING AIR:
Hail and Welcome Sylphs of the Eastern Realm.
Place of beginnings, Of rising Sun.
Of Dreams and visions yet Unmet.
Of Births initiated by Sacred Breath.
Of Winds that stir what once was Dead
Awaken and enliven us to your Depths.
Hearken to our Call "Inspirer" and bear witness to our Rites. In your presence nothing can remain stagnant and we invoke your gifts tonight.
Hail and Welcome Air!

INVOKING FIRE:
Hail and Welcome Salamanders of the Southern Fiery realm.
Of Blue and Bright Orange Embers,
Burning Charcoal, burning bright,
That Fire from a Dragon's breath,
fiercely protecting what is right.
Of Flames that envelop my Yoni and vibrate heat upon my heart….
Thy flames that seeks love's Passion, the fuel for any spark to start.
Hearken to our call Volcanic realm, bear witness to our Rites.
In you we taste Sex, ambition and drive and we invoke your gifts tonight.
Hail and Welcome Fire!

INVOKING WATER:
Hail and Welcome Undines of the Western Watery realm.
Of vast expanse Oceans and playful Aquatic friends. Of moisture upon the Parched and Dry and waves that swell our souls to feel. Of Melodious Songs, sung by doves and mermaids. Of all that dances on the waves of magick, Of all that is beautiful and Divinely Femme.
Hearken to our Call Moon Realm, Womb throne, Pearl maker….bear witness to our Rites. In you may we taste balance, truth and beauty as we invoke your gifts tonight.
Hail and Welcome Water!

JOURNALING - GROVE SAMHAIN GATHERING- HONORING MAMAN BRIGITTE

The energy for our day started off quite high, as we had agreed to come donning ritual attire, animated costumes and Halloween masks. With each womyn, coming through the entry doorway, was her electrified awakened, bright aura and clearly everyone was feeling charged, beautiful and Goddess-like. There was the usual chatter amongst Grove sisters and as expected, we were already starting off late. Somehow, even after a few years of meetings, I must remember to allot time for this predictable monthly occurrence. For us wommin, talking, sharing our tales and catching up with one another, seems indeed compulsory and I must remember to honor this aspect of our nature, more often.

Reflecting back on our day, everything appeared so seamless and effortless. I didn't feel the normal jitters that seem to invade me while facilitating our gatherings. It was important to me that I be sincere and respectful in my approach to Maman Brigitte and to this end, I had devoted myself to connecting with her energy as far back as last Samhain. Yet last year, insecurities and fear kept me from following my intuition to present her to Grove. This year, however, I felt the relentless gnawing surge to celebrate her with my sisters and thus, it should not surprise me that our Grove gathering turned out to be so spectacular as it was. Indeed I felt I honored "Her" with love and a genuine reverence that luminously permeated my home weeks after our magickal night together.

Our singing was awesome and full of enchanting Witchy energy, thanks to the number of songstresses that blessed us with their presence. Some chants were new to the wommin but they caught on beautifully and it felt good to harmonize and blend our voices the way we intuitively did.

The speaking stick was a new concept only for the new wommin in our midst and yet it was effective in getting us to focus, quietly listen to one another and really connect. Everyone had a chance to introduce themselves and share why this time of year is so special to them personally.

A black and white Xerox image of Maman Brigitte was shared around the circle. The results of this time honored practice never fails to astounds me, as each womyn gazes upon the image and, uncensored, speaks of what she sees. Some saw their own reflection in Maman Brigitte, some saw a Crone, some saw their own grandma, some saw a proper New Orleans woman, some shared... recognizing in "Her" image, an ancient wisdom that goes far beyond what we could ever know in human form. These revealing reflections from our group were powerful, especially when I purposefully had not yet started the lecture on Maman Brigitte.

Smoothly thereafter, I facilitated them right into Voodoo practices and my lecture on the Voodoo Loa, Grande Maman Brigitte. It was a very stimulating and yet cathartic, conversation on death, our societal issues with the death process, the Voodoo culture in New Orleans and the attributes that Maman Brigitte presents to our lives. I was most pleased that there were several in the group who expressed a deep understanding of the value of honoring a Loa/Goddesses like Maman Brigitte. We went from a anthropological lecture, to a beautiful enliven conversation on death and life and the ways our modern day society undervalues and conceals the process of dying. It was all so appropriate for this time of year as the veil grows thinnest and in our effort to really connect with the Mistress of the Cemetery.

After the lecture I offered the Skull Meditation. They were invited to sit, relax, hold their skull gently in their hands and listen to my words as I guided them through a reflective look at this past year via the eight sabbats. As you would expect, looking at a whole year via a meditation can be very lengthy, but the process was a must, and indeed it was cathartic for those that partook of it. Where else in our rushed, mundane, day to day living, do we have a moment to quietly reflect on days, months, seasons passed? It was a golden opportunity to really look at the last twelve months or so and consider what needs to now be surrendered at this auspicious time of the year. It was important and also helped facilitated our ritual work that much more because, by the time we found ourselves at the core of our ritual, we knew what our work was going to be about. The ritual spell really began with the taking in of this powerful meditation. Afterwards, I looked to see if they were okay. This then led right into a Drumming CD track, so that each woman could connect with Maman Brigitte in her own personal way.

For me, it ended up moving me so greatly that I started to gyrate and... before I knew it, I was dancing, I mean fiercely dancing in spirit ...I mean really dancing, all around the room spraying this ghostly powerful vapor of Maman Brigitte to the entire group and our space... I think I was the only one dancing too and I remember my vision felt hazy, compromised and altered. I felt like I was trancing in and out and yet, I couldn't quite let myself go fully there, well, because it was my responsibility to fulfill our day's work and later an intricate ritual for "Her." It was however enough to massively shift the energy in the room and transform it into our temple to honor Grande Maman Brigitte.

Right afterwards, I introduced the Collage art spell work. We had a limited amount of time to complete or at the very least begin it. I could tell some were snipped that they could not finish it but such is life... Later via email, I explained to them that this feeling of "urgency" was a part of our working with Maman Brigitte. She waits for no-one and when death comes you have no choice but to drop whatever it is you were doing or hoping to do. Life must be led with that realization and that urgency is to be honored. For me it is a harsh reminder that I need to stop procrastinating in my life and do my best to work in harmony with "time" and then, be ready for the day when I'm called into a different realm. That surrendering of harsh expectations and the embracing of fluidity and unexpected change, is a delicate balancing act, one I personally struggle with. In our "Hope Collage" creation I witness some other wommin sharing in this "time" struggle.

Right after the Collage, we prepared for the ritual. At this time it was wonderfully dark, pitch black in the house and this was the very first time we had a total nightfall upon one of our Grove gatherings. It was a SPECTACULAR SIGNIFICANT ELEMENT to our ritual and I can't rave about it enough. Working in the realm of death, cemetery and Maman Brigitte required this transition from day to night, dusk to sunset and it was truly effective. This was her vision for us.

Beginnings:

Now typically Pagans are told when venturing into a ritual space you are to quietly contemplate and reverently reflect on the sacred space you are about to enter. For this ritual, however, I felt very, strongly about doing the opposite. It was important that participants be engaged, deeply engrossed in the living; talking, laughing and carrying on, for that is exactly how death sometimes comes....

" For when death comes, we are almost never prepared and thus I ask you now to stand up and join me on this journey to my realm..."

Maman Brigitte wanted us to feel this shock, this regret, this interruption to our living and then the tug...a yank into her realm!

At the entry way, they were smudged, given a pomegranate with allspice and participants were required to a "pay the piper" with an offering. They were given a chance to surrender their bones or Skull in order to enter and they were instantly invited to light a candle to, their ancestors, those whose shoulders they stand upon, immediately upon entering the room. There, in silence they contemplated on their ancestors while waiting for the entire group to join.

*When all were seated around the floor's altar cloth, which by now resembled an actual cemetery with numerous bones, skulls and a myriad of coffins, we began. I made note aloud, that we no longer were in the light of day, we were now in "**Her**" realm and invited them to cast a personal circle of protection inwardly. The bell was rung and we were all now facing outwardly, casting the circle communally. A few words were stated in a call and response fashion and the circle was thus cast effectively. Quarters were called by volunteered Grove priestesses, although I had prepared mine own full elemental invocation just in case that original plan didn't happen. My elemental invocation script can be found in this chapter. I must note that, for some wommin it was their first time invoking and indeed it was beautiful. They really added a wonderful energy to our ritual and I am most grateful to share ritual space with such amazing wommin!*

Immediately following quarter calls, I invoked Maman Brigitte, but honestly, "She" had been with us since the beginning of our day, so in essence, I simply read a short meditation that connected us to her energy even deeper. It was sooooo very dark in the room by this point and I only had the light of the numerous candles on our altar, yet it was so hauntingly evocative, giving me the chills as I carefully struggled to read the words before me.

Maman Brigitte was invoked and I followed it with a very witchy song on our CD Stereo player. I passed around slips of paper, pen, and the handcrafted coffins and invited them to write what they gladly release this moment. I also encouraged them to listen to their intuition on the best way to dispose of these after the night is through. We dropped these coffins, one by one, into the large Cauldron, while stating what we were surrendering and sealed it with a "so mote it be". At this point it dawned on me that we had not sung any of the songs I had originally planned, so I started to sing "Mother of Darkness, Mother of light..." they joined me in the chant as we closed the dark part of our spell work.

Wommin were invited to take off their masks, as we were now entering the light part of our ritual spell work... the hope for the new year. Here again I came to a realization, we had not drummed and again this was something I had pre-planned into our day, so I passed around the percussive instrument and we had a short but (I must say) one of the most power drum circles ever. It was dark, we were in very close proximity to one another, low to ground nearest the Goddess and we were amidst candles, spirits, our ancestors and our powerful witch will....it was intense!!! I felt unusually liberated and free as I drummed, without any of my usual concerns of judgment and the rhythm just spiraled awesomely, all in "Her" honor...... It led to the next part of our ritual, "hoping" for the New Year.

Incense was passed around the circle as we smudged our New Calendars and one by one we began to speak our wish. Laughter and cackles, roared as we went around the room stating our hope for the new year while our Sisters chimed in with loud, bawdy, comments and expletives, all in an effort to support and envision for us the manifestation of that wish becoming real. It was spectacular!!! This method of spell work had Maman Brigitte's fingerprint all over it, her bawdy, "tell it like it is" energy was undeniably present and everyone was unquestionably highly charged and euphoric during and afterwards....it was great!

Being mindful of the time, we prepared to devoke and that went rather smoothly. The circle was open with our traditional song and our ritual successfully ended with the exuberant excitement as our day had begun. A lack of time prevented us from all sitting down at the dinner table and enjoying our delicious potluck together. This is the only part of our day I regret very much. Every one made great effort to bring great food that would honor their respected ancestors, sadly the lack of time prevented us from truly partaking in this most sacred act. So, I will need to work harder at making up for this next time. Food and the sharing of a meal, as we do in a potluck, is sacred work, not to be underestimated. Especially when we endeavor to honor our ancestors with the preparation and the actual digestion of the meal.

Ashe, to our ancestors... I do believe we honored them in various other way on this Samhain night and all together, we journeyed to the threshold, to Maman Brigitte, where we sat by her to receive her wisdom and blessings.

All and all it, was a great Samhain Ritual with my Grove Sister and I am beginning to see the manifestation of those dear tender seeds placed in the earth a long time ago.Blessed Be!!!
The Goddess is Alive and Magick is Afoot!!!!

***A powerful dream came to me the evening of all Souls day, after three nights of commemorating the sabbat of Samhain and honoring my ancestors. Written in a Trance, I believe this was a transmission on death...

Dreams, I realized, are like death....
Yes... Time is irrelevant...
One second may seem like eternity...
One moment seems to mesh
and blend imperceptibly between
time and space, into one another, like water.
It's so watery, so transparent, liquefied,
so dominated by the moon
and all that is Feminine and mystically lucid....
Dreams, like Death, leave you questioning....
Did you really hear that?
How? With what tools? Did I really see that???
What eyes receive such vision?
What senses receive these divine messages?
How? When eyes are closed
and body seems lifeless in sleep....
how could I see so vividly into Veils,
passed realms, I can hardly delineate?

SHARING A PERSONAL EXPERIENCE, AFTER WORKING WITH MAMAN BRIGITTE

Less than a week after our powerful Grove Ritual, honoring the process of Death and Maman Brigitte, the Tower in my world came tumbling down....a massive life altering occurrence took place and I'm still processing the entire gruesome situation, only weeks after. I asked for clarity, I asked for honesty, I asked to be free of painful, negative relationships that do not serve me well anymore. I asked to be liberated of illusions, delusions and complacency and lies, but little did I know the consequences of my request to the Divine.

Exactly six days after this ritual, my husband was hospitalized in a psychiatric ward. At his place of employment, unbeknownst to anyone, he had attempted to end his life rather than confront the reality of our relationship and the numerous years of lies about finances. With a collection of suffocating loans having confiscated his entire paycheck, a family of three little boys to feed and a zero balance in the bank account, the lies had finally caught up to him and he couldn't deny anymore the lie he was living and keeping from me. Having confided in no one and feeling alone and disconnected from reality, he saw death as his only option. In that dark, desperate, lonely instant, he proceeded with his fantasized plans, but thankfully it failed and that pivotal moment changed both of our lives forever. His boss learned of what transpired and my husband was immediately taken to the hospital for three days of observations and evaluations and thus began our journey through "Her" forge... and "Her" fires of Divine transformation. Exposing and peeling layers of illusions, brought to the brink to face the oozing raw skin, that begged for recognition, care and healing.

Conditions of his release from the hospital were; a commitment to outpatient therapy treatment, delving into his psyche(a frightful prospect for him) and the reasons for his numerous lies and pathologies, open honesty with his marriage partner and working to attain financial health. He is presently working hard on all of these and together, we are trying to salvage our marriage. Too soon to tell what will happen in the end but, without a doubt, I am convinced that this was a long awaited answer from the Divine. I called on "Her" when in my naivete and confusion, I needed answers and she heard my desperate plea and made "Herself" known. She fiercely pierced through my realm and his, like a lightning bolt, knocking out outworn facades, lies and edifices with no apologies, for honesty and "Her" will, shall be done, And so it came to be.

Never underestimate the power of magick and its ability to completely catapult your life. She shifts you into terrains you must travel on, but only to unblock you from your own sabotaging self and ignorance. It is a simple warning to always be mindful and careful of what you wish for because you just might get it, but not in the package you might've had in mind, for "She" ultimately will decide how her magick gets delivered.... And so it is, so mote it be!!!

MAMAN BRIGITTE- GROVE GATHERING CHANTS

WE ARE A CIRCLE by Rick Hamouris
We are a Circle, within a Circle, with no Beginning and never ending....
You hear us Sing, You hear us Cry,
Now hear us Call you, Spirits of Earth and Sky
Within our Hearts, there goes a spark
Love and Desire, a burning Fire...
We are a Circle, within a Circle, with no Beginning and never ending...(chorus)

RATTLE MY BONE
Old Woman Wrap your cloak around me, Death Bringer rattle my Bones,
Old Woman Wrap your cloak around me, Death Bringer rattle my Bones,
Rattle my Bone, Rattle my Bones, Death bringer rattle my Bones.

ANCIENT MOTHER
Ancient Mother, I hear you calling,
Ancient Mother, I hear your sound,
Ancient Mother, I hear your laughter,
Ancient Mother, I taste your tears... (rpt) *by Deena Metzger & Charlie Murphy*

EIGHT BEADS CHANTS *by Carolyn Hillyer*
Girlseed
Bloodflower
(dip it)Fruitmother
Spinmother,
raise it) Midwoman
Earthcrone
Stonecrone
Bone .....

GOING DOWN
I'm going Down in the Cauldron
don't you worry and don't you moan,
I'm gonna lay my body down, in the Cauldron
Crones are calling, gonna be reborn (rpt)

Mother of Darkness
Mother of Darkness,
Mother of Light,
Earth Beneath the Soul in flight,
Songs of love and Love of life,
Guide us to our heart.....

INVOKING MOTHER
by B.M.M.
Mother, Mother, Mother, I call you,
Deep within my soul, you' re stirring my womb.
Mother, Mother, Mother, Hear my Cries,
In this Sacred Circle I Call you tonight.
Light the inner Flame, as I light the candle wick,
Call your sacred name and embrace myself as Witch.
Sky-clad I approach, to Elemental thrones,
Hear me, Mother hear me,
Through these words I wrote.

SHE'S BEEN WAITING - by *Paula Walowitz*
She's been waiting, waiting
She's been waiting so long,
She's been waiting for her children
to remember to return (repeat)
Blessed be and blessed are the Lovers of the Lady,
Blessed be and blessed are, Maiden , Mother, Crone,
Blessed be and blessed are, The ones who dance together
Blessed be and blessed are, The ones who dance alone.......

MOTHER I FEEL YOU UNDER MY FEET
Mother I feel you under my feet, Mother I feel your Heart Beat 2X
Heya Heya Heya, Heya Heya Ho 2X
Mother I hear you in the Rivers Sound, Eternal Waters going on and on 2X
Heya heya heya heya heya ho 2X
Mother I see you in when the Eagles fly, Flight of the Spirit gonna take our time 2X
Heya Heya Heya, Heya Heya Ho ......By; Unknown source

EARTH, MOON, MAGICK, by B.M.M.
In the Earth, deep within,
There is A Magick, I draw it in.
   In her Caves, in the Trees
   Hear her Heartbeat, Pulsing thru me.
When I Rise, I feel her Love
With feet Grounded, I'm soaring high above,
   In the Earth, deep within,
   There is A Magick, I draw it in
Ancient Moon, my Soul reveres
With my Singing, I call you here.
   When this flame, ignites tonight,
   Priestess dancing, Under the moonlit night....
In the Earth, deep within,
There is A Magick
I draw it in.... There is A Magick, I draw it in }3x

BONES, *By "Flight of the Hawk"*
Bones, come Dance with me,(3x rept)
Dancing in the the desert, in the desert tonight (2Xrept)
Bones, Come Sing with me, (3X rept)
Dancing in the desert, in the desert tonight (2Xrept)
Bone dance know the Shaman dance
Bone dance hear the Raven cry
Bone dance see the Ancestors,
Dancing in the desert, in the desert tonight (2xrept)
Bones, Come fly with me, (3x rept)
Dancing in the desert, in the desert tonight (2Xrept)
Bones come die with me, (3Xrept)
Dancing in the desert, in the desert tonight (2X)*back to start*

November

November is the Eleventh month in the Gregorian calendar, yet this month probably attained its name after the Latin word *"novem"*, meaning "nine," as it was traditionally the ninth month in the Roman calendar. The astrological sign for November is intense, passionate Scorpio and the venomous scorpion is its symbol. Scorpio is ruled by fiery, aggressive Mars, but also by transformative, regenerative, dark Pluto (Oct 21-Nov 20). It is these significant elements that influence the energy of the month of November.

The Full moon of this month is sometimes called Frost Moon, as the first Frost usually arrives at this time, in some parts of the world. According to the Farmer's Almanac it was also known as Wind Moon, Oak Moon and Beaver Moon because, for the Native Americans, this was the best time to hunt for Beavers, as their fur was quite desired during the cold winter months. The swamps would not have been frozen yet and hunting for beavers would have proven successful.

The Anglo-Saxon often referred to this month's Full moon as Blood Moon because this was typically the time when animals were slaughtered and their blood spilled upon the earth. Keep in mind, that for our ancestors, the last Harvest would've been at the end of October, nothing will grow on the land from this point onward until the coming of spring. In preparation for the anticipated long Winter, food, including animal meat, would've been chopped up and prepared for storage. Food that they stored away now needed to last them for the entire winter season.

November's Full moon was also often known as the Mourning Moon and there are many obvious reasons for this name. At the end of October we traditionally honor our ancestors during one of the major witches sabbat- Samhain, but for other cultures, like Mexicans and South-Westerns, the season of honoring the dead continues right into the first week of November. November 2nd finds many Mexicans, non-Pagans and Pagan alike celebrating, *"El Dia de los Muertos,"* Day of the Dead. Interesting to note that the celebrations take on a much more festive, humorous hue, as people often dress up their skulls in bright colors or as celebrities. Parades (of both adults and children dressed up in skeletal outfits) are not that uncommon in Mexico. Their altars (to honor their beloved deceased) would typically have bright orange and yellow marigolds, sugar and elaborately painted skulls and beautifully dressed female skeletal figures called Katrinas. Altars to the dead would also include platters of their favorite tasty foods, along with the photos of the departed. You might also find many Mexicans, as well as Catholics, spending the days and nights at their local cemeteries with their beloved deceased. The Spanish Catholics observed this time to mourn the dead and pray for the departed souls on their traditional "All Souls Day" on November the 2nd.

Towards the end of the month many celebrate the U.S.A. holiday of Thanksgiving, which was originally conceived as the first harvest of Indian corn by the Pilgrims in 1621. Pilgrims and Native Americans sat down together and shared in the bounty of the Earth by feasting on all kinds of foods in the young, new land of America. The festivities lasted for three whole days and was originally commemorated sometime in the summer months, but the U.S.A. government later changed the date and today we honor this historical event by re-enacting it, with our own festivities, the fourth Thursday of the month.

Inherent in Thanksgiving are family gatherings, dinners, pumpkin pies, red and orange autumnal leaves, turkeys, corn and a cornucopia of all sorts of edibles. Towards the end of the month, this is the dominate theme. It has become, however, a peculiar time of overindulgences, whether its shopping too much and hoarding or being swayed by all the astronomical, unbeatable sales everywhere. A variety of indulgences at parties and dinners temps us all. In general, this marks the beginning of the holiday season and all that it entails; lots of gatherings, long and short voyages to family and friends, elated and stressful spirits, Dining room tables spread with decadence, football games and sweet nostalgic parades, and did I mention, shopping..... In the U.S.A., towards the end of November we are inducted into the Christmas shopping season, with the traditional 'Black Friday', massive insane sales offered the day after Thanksgiving.

Amidst all the chaotic and blurry festivities, it is a good time to contemplate on our own personal blessings. A time to truly look at what we have to be grateful for and set aside quietude, sanctuaries, creating moments of deep reflection and Gratitude.

This month we call upon the Polynesian Goddess of the Moon- Hina, to help us tap into our sacred sanctuaries. We honor ourselves as Goddess Womyn and embrace the healing powers of the Moon. We also take the time to invoke the Greek Goddess of the Hearth- Hestia. We call on her to express our gratitude, we honor this ancient beloved Goddess, that she may assist us in bringing fiery spirit blessings, peace and her divine energy to our sacred hearth and home and festive celebrations.

CHAPTER TWENTY-FOUR

"Some people, they grow up in a tunnel, with the only light inside themselves, And sometimes, when they finally get out of that tunnel, they shine that light for other people..." from the movie, "Precious"

"Those who make peaceful revolutions impossible, make violent revolutions inevitable..." John F. Kennedy

WELCOME HINA

OUR ALTAR

Altar cloth: White or Silver and maybe a second blue altar cloth underneath.
Image: Statue of this Lunar Polynesian Goddess, hula dancers, images of the Moon and rainbows. Canvas art or photo of the Polynesian Goddess and or photos of the ocean or the Moon, tropical Hawaiian landscapes and hula dancers, Tikis, Hawaiian images are all appropriate to display on your altar.

Always present on the altar;
A cast iron cauldron, drums, speaking stick, a silver pentacle, athame, elemental representations.....

Air: Smudge wands, Incense type sticks, cones, charcoal brisket and fine powdered herbs, of Jasmine, Frankincense, Sandalwood, Mugwort. Large feathers, wind chimes and or bells.
Fire: candles, glass enclosed candles or pillars in whites and or a women shaped, or lunar shaped candles.
Water: Coconut water offered in a small vessel or a glass bowl with fresh Spring Water, White Wine can also be offered in a chalice.
Earth: A bowl of fresh fruits like; pineapples, coconuts, bananas, peaches and mango are an excellent representation for the Earth. A small dish of soil and or herbs and Lavishly decorate your altar with a myriad of fresh vibrant, brightly colored flowers.

Other items pertinent to this particular gathering
Figurine of Colorful Rainbow
Lunar pendants
Bunnies to represent the moon's totem symbol of fertility
White or Red flowers, lots of greenery
Bowls of consecrated Water
Mini personal altar shrine box
Rocks and Gemstone
Plate offering of coconuts,
Writing pens and paper, safety pins,
Light blue gauzy fabric to represent water
Workshop items
Felt fabric, Tapa Cloth or Hawaiian textile
Tarot -"The Moon"

Offering Polynesian Culinary; pineapples, coconuts, Tuna sushi, pork, coconut rice, fruit salad
Sacred objects from members:
Notes:

Hina

Hina Altar

Lunar Water Connections

HINA

Hina is the Hawaiian Goddess of the Moon. Her name, translates as "girl" or "woman" and sometimes even more precisely as "woman in the moon." Hina, in Polynesian and Tahitian cultures, connotes the feminine spirit. According to Hawaiian cosmology, the first Gods to step foot on the great Island of Hawaii were Ku and Hina. Respectively male and female. Ku was viewed as the rising Sun, the East and Hina his opposite, the west and the setting sun. This links her directly to the Moon. Hina embodied all the attributes of a Moon Goddess. She ruled over Fertility and intuition and she ruled over the waters; the ebb and flow of life and procreation. Hina also reigned over planting, agriculture and the fishing cycle.

As the first female Goddess of Hawaii, she ruled over the procreation and population of her people. Much like the Greek Goddess Gaia, Hina is seen as the Creatrix. She created a number of impressive descendants, like the Pig God, Kamapua'a and Maui, the demigod. Hyphened and variations of her name can be found in several other Goddesses throughout Hawaiian mythology. There are also some references to Hina as a triple Goddess, much like many significant, ancient Goddesses throughout mythologies of various cultures. She was attributed for bringing numerous gift to the Hawaiian people including the revered coconut.

According to one myth, Hina, in the heavens, was so enamored by the lush landscape of Hawaii that she decide to descend upon it and make it her temporary home. Hina came down from the cosmos and made the island of Maui her abode and there, she fell in love with a mortal and married a man known as a great warrior. Together they lived in Ka'uiki, under the volcano called, Haleakala. As the Hawaiian lore reveals, most of her days were spent working hard, pounding the Kapa board to make fine craftsmanship textile and clothing. She was known to make magic with her extraordinary Tapa cloth and her contribution to Hawaiian Textile was significant.

Everyday Hina worked very hard, fetching water and fresh shrimp for her family. She also worked hard on her Tapa cloths but as time went on, her husband became very lazy expecting her to do everything because, after all, she was a divine Goddess. Her half-blood children, also became too much to handle, as they too adopted their father's laziness and arrogance. They were known to be quite mischievous and extremely demanding of their mother.

According to one popular Hawaiian lore, one day, when Hina was out by the river working, she caught sight of the most beautiful rainbow (although in some stories they say she had the ability to manifest rainbows herself). In this story she tried to climb up the rainbow to join the brilliant light of the Sun that called, but the heat of the mid-day sun was too much for her to handle and she could not bear it. After exhaustibly trying to climb it, she fell and slipped off the rainbow. Then, over heated and weakened, she fainted and passed out. Some time passed by before she finally woke up in the early evening hours to rush back home to her family. As one would suspect, when she returned home, her abusive husband, needless to say, was furious and he berated her stronger than usual. The children also added insults to their mother, angered that their precious dinner had not been prepared.

Late at night, when they had all fallen fast asleep, Hina longingly stared out at the window and there presented before her, was another brilliant light that once again captivated her heart- the light of the Full moon. She remembered the light of the sun beckoning her in the day time and yet, here was another brilliant light strongly urging her to come again. It was then that her heart stirred and she felt the strong urging to leave her misery behind and unite with the familiar divine light before her. She wasted no time and immediately packed her bag with her prized calabash and tapa cloth. Hina endeavor to take only her most cherished possessions with her. One look at the brilliant light of the moon and she was enamored by its comforting light. Enchanted by the glow, she was determined, more than ever, to leave her painful situation on earth, to go and join this beloved light, now beaming from the moon. This light was a spark of remembrance, a familiarity she had long forgotten that was now being restored to her via, the Moon.

    A rainbow appeared, as if by magic, she manifested this sacred vehicle to lead her to her Divine destination. As she began her climb, she was invigorated and renewed and felt great determination to reach the moon. Alas, she was getting closer when all of a sudden, she felt the sensation of her leg being pulled. It was him...her abusive, earthly husband caught sight of her trying to escape and he violently tugged and pulled on her leg. He threatened her and screamed at her, not to go...but this only made her more determined to leave. With all of her Divine strength she pushed onward, towards the Moon. But he had the strength of a warrior and he was strong. He pulled and yanked and with a mighty force he pulled her foot right off. He severed Hina's foot and, simultaneously, fell down to the ground, while she managed to muster up enough strength to continue onward on her journey, until she made it safely inside the moon.

    Within the moon Hina found rest, peace and eventually was able to heal, recuperate and grow a new foot. Legend says she still feels throbbing in her foot as a reminder of what she endured and left behind on earth. Hawaiians today still worship Hina and seek her reflection in the full moon She continues to be revered as the beautiful Lady of the Rainbow-Beloved Feminine Goddess of the Moon.

Hina Musing -Creating Sanctuaries

Our beloved Polynesian Goddess of the moon and her legends can be seen as a metaphors for women in need of safety. Whether it is a safe place in our own individual mind, inner soul or an actual physical place or room. Our safe space can be found in a number of places, like rituals (whether solitary or within a group) or a special meditation that transcends and transports us there. Even a simple prayer, as one envisions Hina recited to the light of the moon she saw from her window, can bless us with a sanctuary. In times of stress, we can utilize our imagination and simply visualize this sacred temple or we can actually create it physically. Either way, Hina and her most popular myth, teaches us the importance of this sacred space for wommin.

    When we are feeling hopeless, overwhelmed and confused in our daily living or when sadly, our own lives are compromised and threatened, a personal sanctuary becomes absolutely invaluable. It allows us a chance to regroup and rethink our personal situation. It allows us a chance to find healing and renew our sense of self-worth. Sometimes this sacred sanctuary, whether real or imagine, can make the difference between life and death for some women.

    Having endured so much abuse on earth, Hina reaches that pivotal point when she begins to long for an exodus. Hina's escape into the divine Moon and the very act of selecting it as her new home, is symbolic of this transformative phase in her life. The moon, which has always been a symbol of intuition and feminine spirituality, becomes her sanctuary and she looks upon it now, as her way out of her unhappiness –the Moon thus becomes her "savioress." Herein the Moon is Hina's safe place, to retreat from her troubles -in this case, her lazy human husband and half blood, mischievous children.

    Inside the Moon, she endeavors to heal, regroup, regain her sense of self and reconnect with something that goes so deep, far deeper into her lineage and ancestry than she could possibly begin to understand intellectually. But she comprehends it intuitively, and the call is to her soul, which has no boundaries, nor timelines and unquestionably, she can no longer deny the call. Hina follows her intuition and goes inside the nurturing, grandmother moon that calls unto her, leaving behind her stressors and those painful earthly trials and tribulations.

Also quite a powerful metaphor is when we get to the part of the lore when her leg is severed. At the most pivotal point, when she was approaching her sacred place, her scoundrel of a husband grabbed her leg, pulling and violently yanking it- not letting her go, not letting her take care of herself. He pulled her so hard that her foot comes off. Yet the Goddess perseveres, abandons her severed, bloody foot and continues on her journey towards the moon. There is a powerful message here, for we learn that sometimes, there are parts of us that must be cut off and severed, before beginning any journey of self-healing and self-discovery. As the cutting off of a foot is bloody and violently painful, it is what Hina must endure before reaching her sacred sanctuary within the Moon.

The husband tugging at her foot can be seen as a symbol of our obligations and our roles, making every effort to tug, break and defeat us. And sometimes this gruesome act, being fueled by selfishness, anger and volatility, is so intense, that indeed, parts of us are broken in the process of our healing. The husband here, is that which keeps us in the perpetual state of hopelessness, paralysis, keeping us where we are or where we have always been.

Sometimes our obligations and responsibilities keep us stagnant and, in the only place we've probably ever known, thus blocking us from any further growth. Opportunity for change and transformation are stunted. That tugging of the leg is symbolic of being blocked from what could essentially transform us… improve us and give us wings. Her foot is tugged and ripped like the clipping of a bird's wings (or an attempt to do so) right at the critical moment it's about to take flight. In this case, Hina did not let this sabotage her flight and, with mutilated "wings"(aka leg) she continued on her journey.

Sometimes those you least expect, those you believe love you the most, are the ones that can impede your progress in life. Sometimes those beloved people or situations try to stunt our own personal growth and transformation, like Hina's husband and family. It can be a brother or sister, a mother, father, relative, lover, boyfriend, girlfriend, professor, boss, even a mere acquaintance. Sometimes it's a deliberate action and sometimes it's on another unconscious level or dark part of our own psyche, but the intent remains the same, to keep you in your place.

In Hina's tales we learn of the importance to care for our own selves as womyn and the value in finding our own personal sanctuary, whether it's *"Calgon moment"* in our sudsy bathtubs, an elaborate candle light ritual or trance meditation or in severe cases, a woman's shelter or friend's home. Our sacred sanctuaries are important to define and possess, as we go through life's numerous trials and tribulations and endeavor to grow spiritually.

Hina Grove Goddess Gathering

Purpose: to Honor Hina-the Polynesian Goddess of the Moon, address our stressors and recreate our sanctuary and sacred place of rest and rejuvenation...

Check in I: with speaking stick in hand each woman will be given an opportunity to state her name, and what has led her to the group.

Agreements: Reciting aloud, one by one, our Group agreements, to insure a harmonious pleasant time, trust and understanding within our circle. We review the ones we already have and add any new ones that come to mind, ending with our signature and submission.

Chanting: *Singing, "Lady of he Moon," "Weave and Spin", "Sweet Surrender..." "I align my Desire...." (see song text sheet)*

Drumming for trance Work: *(Musical Drumming CD is played)* Authentic Polynesian style music will be played throughout the day. Here the sounds of Tahitian, "Bora, Bora" drumming will be heard to transcend us and begin our journey to Hina. Wommin are invited to close their eyes and let themselves trance & connect to the moment.

Check in II: What would you personally take with you If you had to leave the Earth and jump into the Moon, like Hina? What do you cherish and what would you take?

LECTURE ON THE GODDESS:
Hina and her myths and Hawaiian culture and folklore

GODDESS WORKSHOP

WORKSHOP I: Placing our stressors into our personal **Tapa Cloths** (felt fabric) Hammering it in the way she would.... Then binding this Stressor so that it can't get to us again. During the ritual relinquishing and offering it to Hina, placing it in her basket.

WORKSHOP II: Clay working-creating a protective **Moon pendant** (baking it in the oven) and afterwards passing it around so that each of us can enchant it with a collective good wish and energy for our systers.

WORKSHOP III: Endeavoring to pay homage to the Hawaiian culture and the Goddess, by learning a few key words in the Polynesian Language. Adding these words to our spells. Some of these words repeated continually can be use as powerful Mantras *(see page of suggested Hawaiian phrases in this chapter)* **Aloha**: Meaning Hello, goodbye, also means Love, **Aina**: Land Earth, **Akamai**: Smart Intelligent, **Hau'Oli**: Happy, **Mahalo**: Thank you, **Mele**: is a Song, **Nani**: beautiful enjoyable, **Niu**: coconut, **Wahine**: is woman

WORKSHOP IV: Breathing and adding Gentle **Hula** movements and reflecting on their meaning with Polynesian music playing in the background, participants will have a chance to connect to this aspect of the Goddess.

WORKSHOP V: Altar set up. Blue or green cloth, plant, cauldron, salt dish, lit candles, water chalice, athame, wand/branch, art canvas of Hina, other Moon image, Goddess statue, a basket, the Lei, note cards, add an actual pineapple or coconut and cranberry juice for toast...Have fun during this process, as this also is part of the magick.

WORKSHOP VI: Drawing Down the Moon. A discussion on this ancient practice and some ways we can incorporate it in our modern day spiritual practice.

WORKSHOP VII: Creating **travel altars** to encapsulate our spells. Utilizing a small box and Elemental representations, we will decorate it and decoupage magazine clippings to create a travel altar we can easily take with us anywhere we go.

WORKSHOP VIII:Coconut Crafting. The Coconut was very important to Hawaiian culinary and it was considered sacred to this deity. In this workshop, we will consider ways of crafting with it to better connect with Hina.

WORKSHOP IX: Exploring Moon Folklore and the important attributes of the **Moon in astrology**. Looking into our astrological charts to see where the Moon is located and what it reveals about us.

WORKSHOP X: Lastly, a wonderful way to connect with this beloved Hawaiian Deity is to connect with her home land. A Dvd or a Book dedicated to photos of Hawaii will be shared around the circle, allowing everyone a chance to connect with this Goddess via the images of her lush verdant landscape.

REFLECTIONS ON HINA

Womyn who lives in the light of the moon... you have much wisdom and strength to impart on us. Hina is seen as the Lady of Rainbows and the Lady of the Moon. She comes into your life to connect you to the spirit of this ancient symbol of Femininity. The moon has always been embraced as The Goddess herself and a powerful representation of Feminine spirituality..... She has been worshipped since the beginning of time and for many Pagans and Witches she is the core of their religion.

This immortal Hawaiian Goddess teaches us the importance of our sanctuaries, our place to repose, and our sacred altars -whether they are literal and physically tangible or whether they are simply internalize in our psyche. Hina introduces us to the importance of sacred space.

She asks us, to survey our lives and with a fine tooth comb, identify where our stress and obstacles are originating from. She beckons you to find safety and reconnection to your source of inner divine strength and spirituality. Where do we go to retreat and recharge? Where is our safe haven, away from chaos? Hina awakens us to our divine selves, and the sacred sanctuaries found within us, as well as connecting us to the ancient wisdom, of our mother, The sacred Moon.

HINA GROVE GODDESS GATHERING RITUAL

Purpose: to Honor Hina-the Polynesian Goddess of the Moon, address our stressors and recreate our sanctuary and sacred place of rest and rejuvenation...

BORA BORA DRUMMING CD
music heard throughout entire ritual

Asperge: Purify and Clear each womyn by air, through the Sacred bundle of Feathers...and a Smudge of copal and sage. Welcome each womyn with ***"Aloha"*** and a colorful Hawaiian Lei around her neck.

Let each womyn enter and **anoint** *(with Coconut Oil)* her syster next to her by saying...
"Welcome into our sacred space."

Intent Declared: As everyone is now gathered within the circle, Speaker announces our intention for the day; "We are here today to honor the Lunar Goddess, Hina."

Cast the circle: *With a long crystal wand recite suggested prose or you may also use vibrant colorful flowers to cast your circle with flower petals.*

From the ancient powers of the Moon
Spirits young and old hear own tune,
Aumakua, Sacred and Divine
Guard our Circle at this time.
Round and round your energy sphere,
Only the Good is welcomed here.
***
The Circle is cast, we stand between the realms
outside of time and space.
The immortal ones are here to guard our sacred place.
Blessed be!!!

Call Quarters:
Aloha Aumakua (ancestral spirits) of the **Earth**. Place of the Pohaku. Papa (rocks and stones), the beautiful Leilani (heavenly flowers) and the sacred Honu (turtle). Beloved Aina (land or earth), We bid you to come join us in our rites. Guard and hold our sacred space.
E Komo Mai (Welcome) Hail and Welcome **Earth.**

Aloha Aumakua (ancestral spirits) of the **Air.** Place of the sacred Lani (Sky/Heavens) and playful home of the soaring Manu (bird). We bid you to come join us in our rites. Guard and hold our sacred space.
E Komo Mai (Welcome) Hail and Welcome **Air**.

Aloha Aumakua (ancestral spirits) of **Fire**. Realm of our Pu'uwai (heart) and the Volcanic Goddess Pele and the brilliance of the Hoku (star). We bid you to come join us in our rites. Guard and hold our sacred space.
E Komo Mai (Welcome) Hail and Welcome **Fire**.

Aloha Aumakua (ancestral spirits) of the **Waters**. Place of the Moana (ocean), where the life giving Wai (fresh water) flows abundantly. Realm of Mahina (moon) and our beloved Goddess, Hina. We bid thee, join our rites. Guard and hold our sacred space.
E Komo Mai (Welcome) Hail and Welcome **Waters.**

Aloha Aumakua (ancestral **Spirits)**Kumu, makua, Ku. Place of our teachers, our lineage and protectors We bid you to join our rites. Guard and hold our sacred space.
E Komo Mai (Welcome) Hail and Welcome Sacred **Aumakua.**

GODDESS INVOCATION

*Hina, Rainbow Goddess of Tahitian land
Goddess of light, fertility and wombmyn
Your lore & tales live on today,
Ancient Aumakau we seek to know your ways.
  *Enamored by the Moon's divine light
  You heard the call and followed it one night
  climbed up the rainbow that always came,
  your vehicle of magick to inaugurate this change.
*No more a victim of earthly pain,
No more in shadows of abuse and hate,
The light exposed forgotten gifts,
Ancestral's hand in spiritual shifts
  *Another home awaits your return
  When earthly stress your stomach churns,
  When darkness falls and shrouds your life,
  Your saviouress is found in thy moonlight.
*That call as Wombmyn you hear so clear
The need to travel to her light to be near.
The need to fuse your souls as one
The Moon is Hina and she invites you to come.
  *"Repose and retreat and find healing in me
  I serve to be your blessed sanctuary,
  Awaken aumakua, that lives within you
  Hawaiian Goddess who lives in the sacred Moon."
*We invoke you Moon Goddess and call you to this place
Teach us your vision to make sacred space.
To find our sanctuary in moments of stress
To know that there is power in Goddess.
  *We call you Hina, and honor you today
  With coconuts and reflections of your ancient land
  May we find protection
  in your sacred Lunar hands
  Hail and Welcome Hina!!!!

Chanting: Goddess Songs, *"We are opening up to sweet Surrender," "Eight Bead Chant..."*
As an Offering to Hina, we shall engage in a simple **Hula dance** with Hawaiian Music playing in the background.

MEDITATION: Participants are invited to find a relaxing place to rest for the meditation offering.
  Afterwards Check Ins: Thoughts on our journey and experience via the meditation.

Raising the **Cone of power** with our intonations, vibrational hums while holding hands. When we have raised the energy now, around the circle of wommin we will go lighting our candles with our vows...
Womyn states aloud:
*"With this flame, I vow to care for myself and create sanctuaries via_____ (examples; music, prayers, crafting, meditations, jogging, personal rituals, sisterhood connection, etc..)
This I make true, So mote it be..."*

Candle will be brought unto the altar afterwards, where a **Lunar Pendant** or a **Hawaiian Lei**, will be placed around each participant's neck as a reminder of this special day now.
  Tahitian drumming and movement can be enjoyed at this time, followed by
    Chanting: Goddess Song *"Lady of the Moon"*
    Thanking and **Devoking the Goddess**
    Lady of the Rainbow,
    Beloved, Hawaiian Goddess of the Moon,
    Thank you for your presence in our ritual today,
    You came when called and shared your sacred gifts with us
    and we are forever transformed by your Divine light.
    With gratitude, we bid thee adieu.
    Stay if you will, Go if you must.
    Hail and farewell Hina!

Devoking the Elements,
Aumakua (ancestral **Spirits**) Kumu, Makua, Ku. Place of our teachers, our lineage, protectors and ancestors. We thank you for sharing your gifts and guarding our sacred space. As ye arrived in peace, depart in peace with our most sincere Gratitude. Mahalo,we bid thee **Hail and farewell, Spirit of the Center.**

Aumakua (ancestral spirits) of the **Waters**. Place of the Moana (ocean), realm of Mahina (moon) and our beloved Goddess. We thank you for sharing your gifts and guarding our sacred space. As ye arrived in peace, depart in peace with our most sincere Gratitude. Mahalo,we bid thee **Hail and farewell, Spirit of Water.**

Aumakua (ancestral spirits) of **Fire**. Realm of our Pu'uwai (heart) and the brilliance of the Hoku (star). We thank you for sharing your gifts and guarding our sacred space. As ye arrived in peace, depart in peace with our most sincere Gratitude. Mahalo,we bid thee **Hail and farewell, Fire.**

Aumakua (ancestral spirits) of the **Air.** Place of the sacred Lani (Sky/Heavens). We thank you for sharing your gifts and guarding our sacred space. As ye arrived in peace, depart in peace with our most sincere Gratitude. Mahalo,we bid thee **Hail and farewell, Spirit of Air**.

Aumakua (ancestral spirits) of the **Earth**. Place of the Pohaku (rocks and stones), We thank you for sharing your gifts and guarding our sacred space. As ye arrived in peace, depart in peace with our most sincere Gratitude. Mahalo,we bid thee **Hail and farewell, Spirit of Earth.**

Expression of Gratitude for ALL the womyn who are present helping create sacred space, **Mahalo Kaikuahine!!!**

Opening the Circle with Chant:
"By the earth that is her body, by the air that is her breath, by the fire that is her bright spirit, by the living waters of her womb..."

POTLUCK TO FOLLOW AFTER
POTLUCK Offering: Thai Chinese Rice with added Pineapples and onions and peppers, Coconut or lemon cake, Colada virgin smoothie, cheese and crackers, pineapples and coconuts...

HINA MEDITATION

Find a comfortable spot to sit or lay down in. Relax, close your eyes and when you are ready, take a deep breath counting to four and exhale counting again to four. Again, inhale- 1,2,3,4 and exhale-1,2,3,4. Take another deep breath to connect you to this very moment as we endeavor now to take a special journey.

As you follow my voice, I invite you at this moment to reflect on all of your stresses and stressors. List them, see them in your mind's eye. Sweep them up and form a pile or a mountain with all that is nagging at you at this very moment. Can you see the long list of your personal *"to dos"*? (pause) Can you hear all the demands placed on you now? Reflect on all of your various roles, some more pleasurable than others. Reflect on all of the people around you that expect things from you; your bosses, business associates, lovers, partners, husband, children, neighbors, friends, relatives, professors, teachers, mother, father, siblings... Allow yourself this moment to meet them face to face. You will be safe in this process and you simply observe. How does that make you feel? What does this do to your body and to your mind? What does your instinct tell you to do right now? How will you get through this? Listen to all of those voices, placing demands on you, the long "to do" list that others have made on your behalf. There might be things like *housework, laundry, dishes, papers to grade, car issues, job searches, event planning. Or you might have stress concerning time and money restraints, feeding the children, pets, relationship issues, bill payments, job presentations and deadlines, cooking, driving to and from, homework, tending to the garden, returning calls, getting back to old friends, resolving misunderstandings, gossipy neighbors or family issues, etc...* The list goes on and on, and although it is a very personalized list, it is one that every human being is confronted with. Take this time to hear the demanding voices all at once, listen to their demands trying to tug at you..... Allow the demands, stress and obligations to rise up to the surface. Risk the temporary discomfort and simply observe with your mind and make note of your body's reaction to it. You are safe in this process and are simply here to observe. (pause)

Now think about your obligations to yourself. Do you have any? How do these obligations conflict with those others have created for you? How do you reconcile this and how do you normally make it work? Does it overwhelm? Can you hear all of their voices, along with your own, placing innumerable demands on you? Just you. What does that bring up? Can you hear your own inner voice here or is it being drowned by theirs? Does it make you want to run? Does it make you feel overwhelmed, hopeless? Does it make you want to escape it all? (pause) Let the numerous voices and demands you hear, now blend, muddle, incomprehensible. (pause) Step back and away from the mountain of stressors and the now imperceptible voices. Move back and slowly detach yourself from them and see the scene diminishing before your eyes, with the rise of nighfall, the darkness swallows your stressors and obligations whole. Rest in the growing darkness of this nurturing womb, night has created for you now. (pause)

Your eyes search about and gaze up, looking upon the darkened night sky. With teary eyes still adjusting to the stark darkness you begin to discern something before you. You see trees, lots of tree, leaves and branches jutting out and through this... you can detect shimmer, a slight growing flicker of light appears. Amidst this blackened midnight sky, there are shimmering lights. Reflect on what might this shimmering light be representative of, in your life....(pause) It is hard to see where exactly this light is emanating from until you move a few tree branches apart. What in your life acts like the jutting out branches? Reflect now on what needs to be removed in order for you to have clearer sight?.... (pause)

You see now the source of these hypnotic lights... It is the beautiful Moon, inebriating you, enticing you now, like when a lover intends to seduce its target of affection. The light of the moon unearths in you a strange feeling of being in a lovers embrace, it consummes you, your every thought, every feeling and every being of you, making you forget anything that ever was or any concerns that might've been. It is only "the now" and this special embrace between you and your new love- the Moon. In its light you hear its enchantment and the call to join her and leave the stressors all behind. Only think of the now and this very moment of magick. Take this moment to consider what you would gladly leave behind to join her. (pause)

"*Come*" says the moon "*Come, I can take you away from all this. I can give you safety - Sanity- Your True Self.... I can give you what you need* now at this very moment..." You begin to hypnotically go up... In your mind's eye see yourself rising upward, climbing on the moon's rays of light. As you climb closer and closer you feel something on your leg. There is a strange heaviness upon your leg now. In the excitement of the moment, it almost went undetectable, but now its pain draws your attention.

Something is pulling you back down... What is it? What or Who is trying to keep you back down, hindering and obstructing your journey? As painful as it may be to confront, turn to see who or what is by your foot_____(pause).

Gather up ALL of your strength - for the need to unite and restore yourself within the moon is stronger than anything else at this moment. You manage to pull yourself away. In the process your leg is horribly severed, a piece of you is left behind but it is only a tiny piece and you are not destroyed by this. You still have most of you intact and the rest, has the potential for healing within the sacred place you are about to enter. Onward you continue on your journey to your sanctuary. Higher, higher you climb, higher to be close to your new love. Breathe and with the exhalation, see that you have arrived. (pause).

In the moon you feel the immediate coolness. The fresh air waste no time rejuvenating your lungs and it restores your enbattled spirit. Breathe this new exhilarating fresh air, breathe this hope of liberation within your lungs. Take in a good deep breath, feel its coolness awaken your lungs to this new state of being in this Lunar realm. With each breath you take now, you intimately connect deeper and deeper to the Moon. Breathe. (pause) Soon the Moon equips you with her very own strength via this breath. Her light and insight, her clarity, her energy, her magick, her restorative powers, all -now- within you. Feel her brilliant rays of light. They are like arms around you, within you, holding you up, keeping you steady afloat.

From up in your moon sanctuary you have sight and all is clearer now. What do you see? (pause)

From where you stand now, life is not overwhelming and there is nothing unsurmountable from this sacred Lunar realm. When you view all of life's obligations and those demanding inner voices from this distance, from here... in your safe sanctuary it all seems like tiny specks, trivial, insignificant in the wide landscape of the Universe. Can you now see what once stressed you so and tried to disempowered you? (pause)

With your mind's eye can you see and detect this advantageous perspective? Note how it makes you feel.... (pause) From your sacred moon sanctuary you are tickled with laughter to come to this dawning realization. Lighter, you laugh now, lighter, you begin to feel, less burdensome, lighter you experience yourself now. With each laughter weightless, lighter you feel... lighter you float at peace. Remember this feeling of weightlessness and allow yourself to float higher into the ether now. Daylight is breaking and a new day is about to begin, with vastly new opportunities upon us now. Your sacred sanctuary, internal or external, allows you the distance you need to rethink, regroup, reclaim, re-access, and re-gather your whole self.

Within the moon you find healing. You can come to her at will whenever you have need or desire. You can tap into her gifts and make your own personal healing sanctuary. You can come to this place in your heart, your mind and spirit, whenever you choose. You can tap into her strength and the gifts she has imbued in you. You can breathe, be validated and realize your self-worth and your beauty. You can go within and and, through her... find safety.

Whenever you need added strength, a new point of view or perspective, She's never far away from you, your sanctuary is never far, **it is within you**. The moon imbued you with this gift a long, long time ago and this sacred sanctuary is your gender's heritage, found always within.... So mote it be!

Rest with this knowledge for a moment and when you are ready, follow my voice back into this room, taking a deep breathe. Breathe, follow my voice, exhale, I will count backward from ten to one, with each heard number, return. Return to this space and this time, back to this room. 10, 9, 8, 7, 6, 5, 4, 3, 2, 1.....

INVOCATION TO THE GODDESS HINA

Hina, Rainbow Goddess of Tahitian land
Goddess of light, fertility and wombmyn
Your lore & tales live on today,
Ancient Aumakau we seek to know your ways.

Enamored by the Moon's divine light
You heard the call and followed it one night
climbed up the rainbow that always came,
your vehicle of magick to inaugurate this change.

No more a victim of earthly pain,
No more in shadows of abuse and hate,
The light exposed forgotten gifts,
Ancestral's hand in spiritual shifts

Another home awaits your return
When earthly stress your stomach churns,
When darkness falls and shrouds your life,
Your saviouress is found in thy moonlight.

That call as Wombmyn you hear so clear
The need to travel to her light to be near.
The need to fuse your souls as one
The Moon is Hina and she invites you to come.

"Repose and retreat and find healing in me
I serve to be your blessed sanctuary,
Awaken aumakua, that lives within you
Hawaiian Goddess who lives in the sacred Moon."

We invoke you Moon Goddess and call you to this place
Teach us your vision to make sacred space.
To find our sanctuary in moments of stress
To know that there is power in Goddess.

We call you Hina, and honor you today
With coconuts and reflections of your ancient land
May we find protection
in your sacred Lunar hands
Hail and Welcome Hina!!!!

POLYNESIAN HELPFUL WORDS AND PROVERBS

Source from "The Hawaiian Oracle, Animal Spirit Guides from the Land of Light," by Rima A. Morrell, PhD and the Hawaiian-Words.com internet dictionary. With these words we can begin to create our personal, short invocations to the Polynesian Gods. Another wonderful idea is to chant words like a mantra or affirmation.

Malamapono a hui hou	**Take care, until we merry meet again**
Kaikuahine	**Sister**
Ipo	**Lover**
Himeni	**Sing**
Ha' awina	**Lesson**
Papa	**Earth**
Mahalo	**Gratitude**
Ku	**Deity**
Makua	**Parent**
Kumu	**Teacher**
Mai Ka Po Mai ka 'oia i 'o	**Truth comes from the night.**
Kama 'ia ke aloha a pa 'a i loko	**Bind love that it may remain fast within**
Welo ke aloha I ka 'o no hi	**Love flutters to and from before the eyes**
I ho 'okahi ka umauma, Ho "okahi ke aloha	**All are united in harmony and love**
Heiau	**Ancient religious temple on lava rocks**
Kahuna	**A Hawaiian Priest**
Menehune	**original natives to Hawwaian land.**
He 'ike papalua	**Second Sight**
E ka na 'auao, e aloha 'oe	**Oh Wisdom, love to you**
Ko A	**Warrior**
A hui hou ka ou	**Until we meet again**
Makana	**Gift**
Wahine	**Woman/Lady**
Pule	**Prayer, worship incantation**
Malana	**To Protect**
Pu'uwai	**Heart**
Hoku	**Star**

An invocation to call upon the Moon Goddess. This spell can be used within a group or in solitary workings. Best to perform when the Moon is waxing or Full and of course in the evening when you can see her enchanting, divine light. Prepare a candle in your preferred color and begin by fumigating yourself and the altar area.

A DEDICATION MOON RITE

Magick reveal itself to me,
Let my life be exemplary.
The Goddess is alive,
And magick is afoot,
And ALL I will,
Manifest like a book...

Luck and fortune,
Good health and great things,
Bless me, Your Priestess,
With thy Goddess wings.

To soar to the Heights,
Of all that's I've dreamed,
To rise to fulfill
And, with courage, Achieve

To soar to the depth of
All that can be,
Connect to the Goddess
And her immortal energy,

I dedicate myself now
on this sacred night
Blessed Goddess,
Receive me in this Rite.....

On the night of the full Moon, prepare yourself with a ritual cleansing bath. Lightly scent your body with blessing oil and fumigate your altar with your preferred incense. Prepare your Silver, white or purple candle with moon carvings and mugwort or "Priestess oil" (see appendix). When you know you will not be disturbed, go outdoors, either robed or sky clad and study her luminous light. Let her luminescent light draw you in and then... draw her down as you recite these words.

NURTURING MY GIFTS
Mother of the Silvery Moon
Ancient Goddess,
I call unto you
Awaken now the Priestess in me
And with this flame begins my journey...

Goddess Creatrix,
Shimmering in full,
I honor your powers
On this night in June.

Thanksgiving, Awareness,
Peace and love,
Within me, around me,
Below me and above.

The words I speak now,
To worship and maintain,
Your powers within me
Now and always.

Hear me now,
Goddess of the Moon
For you are of Me,
And I am of you. (*Spend time under the light of the moon and when ready Draw "Her" down...*)

MOON GODDESS
*Goddess of the mighty Moon
Sun, Star, Sky and Sea
Beholder of our wild
femininity
      Ancient and new
      Like the cycle of the moon
      Worshipped by all
      When our species ruled
Holy Creatress,
Who painted our skies,
We see your beauty,
with each moonrise
      Here we call forth,
      The source of our power
Join us Goddess
In this sacred Hour.

Creating Altars for our Homes and Group Rituals

I have always considered my entire abode as my altar and any place I call home is always reflective of this belief. In my present home I continue the tradition of scattering Goddess images (Statues and Art) throughout my house. Thankfully, those I live with tolerate my sense of "Goddess décor".

In my personal office (Wicce library, craft room) I have a large altar that mainly holds and displays, with a lot of conscious intention, all of my witchy supplies and tools. It also displays my beloved collection of Goddess sculptures. This altar doesn't change much, except when I have to make room for something new I've picked up along the way. I suppose this area has become more of a shrine than an altar these days. On my bedroom nightstand, I have a special Water, mermaid altar, that surprisingly decided to manifested itself on a sand and seashell covered, white tray. Carefully placed upon this tray, there is a cast iron Serena Goddess sculpture, adorned with pebbles, blue glass gems, sea shells, crystals and yes... sand from special locales, I've vacationed to. The altar colors are white, peach and various hues of blues and it serves to honor the special Deities of the watery, feminine realm. It successfully reminds me often to relax, let life flow and honor the element of water.

At the entrance of my home is an unsuspecting altar for Peace and Harmony with Amaterasu and the Buddha as guardians of this sacred threshold. Occasionally, incense burns and a glass enclosed candle sits before these two figures to invoke their much sought after, peaceful energy in my home, but their appearance there is so unobtrusive that many who enter my home, never even notice their presence. My main altar, however, is on the mantle of my Fireplace. This beloved, "Hestian" sacred altar space, changes regularly according to my needs and the seasonal sabbats. At the present moment; Saraswati, Gaia and Nike are there, being honored with a flame but various beloved Goddesses pass through here, to stay for a while, be adored and worshipped with candles, incense, herbs, food offerings and other gifts. This sacred space is appropriately found in the center of my home, where it attracts the many adoring eyes of my family, grove sisters, and all that enter my home.

For the most part, my altars are fairly traditional with the four elements always represented, wine or scented oils for water/incense, bells & feathers for air/soil, herbs & salt for earth/a burning candle for fire, or any variation of this. In the center, you'll find an image of the Goddess energy I'm working with; like a statue, photo, art or object that represents that deity. These are the basic "bones" to my home altars. I add other things, depending on the mood and my own needs at any given moment. For example, I might add photos, collages, poetry, jewelry, image candles, inspirational quotes, jewelry, trigger words, letters and books. Other trinkets will find their way on my altar as they come into my life.

I think there is something inherently cathartic about the creation of altars and yet, each one is so unique and personal. I love visiting people's homes and observing how special, sentimental objects (and their prized knick knacks) seem to act like living, breathing magnets, that seem to gravitate to one another and congregate into these little pockets of sacred space. These makeshift altars indeed seem to formulate themselves unconsciously and whether their owners know it or not, they do hold a great deal of power. I love hearing about other people's creations and the magick found in every symbol they feel inspired to offer on their altar . What fascinates me the most is that altars can really be anything you want them to be, as long as it fulfills your individual spiritual, aesthetic and emotional needs. For me, altars serve as intentional reminders of the Divine and the Magick that lives within and all around me. It is all too often that a stressful day can be remedied and lightened with just a short visit to my sacred space and it is in those moments that I can truly relish and appreciate the purpose and magick of our altars.

An altar is indeed the place that holds a piece of you and your sacred tools but, when doing group rituals, it also encapsulates the intent of your ritual. It is one of the first things attendants see when they walk into the sanctuary. Before any words are uttered or invoked, the altar stands to state and invoke them first for you. In the quietude of those first few minutes, as people await for the start of the ritual, their eyes begin to wander about, surveying the room and finally resting their sights upon the altar. Your altar sets the tone and holds their focus through-out and reflects what will eventually unfold. Be mindful and considerate of this when creating altars for group rituals. What you place on the altar should therefore be reflective of what you intend your ritual to be. If you are invoking a Deity to your ritual you should have a sculpture/statue or some kind of visual image of that Goddess or, at the very least, something representative of that Deity. If it is a sabbat, you should have something representative of that sabbat. For example; Eggs for Ostara, Flowers and ribbons for Beltane, A large cast iron cauldron for Imbolc, Corn Husk for the First Harvest, Black Veils, Bones and Pumpkins for Samhain, or a Sun, Moon or the globe of the Earth, can also be used to represent the changing season during your sabbat altar creations.

In ritual you call on the elements to guard and hold your sacred space and it would be wise to have images and symbols of these sacred elements represented on your altar as well.

*A chalice containing water for the West.
*A candle, wand branch or something red representing the element of Fire.
*Soil, Salt, a plant, fresh flowers, herbs any one of these can represent Earth.
*A bell, feather bundle, incense, your sword or athame can stand to represent Air.
*In the center a simple pentacle or a pendant of the moon
can represent spirit as your last element.

These are just some suggestions but as with all art, use your imagination and trust your instincts. If you feel compelled to use something different to represent any of the Deities, Sabbats or elements please feel free to express your individual vision. Allow yourself to experiment, create and express what's in your heart. Often times when you've established a close relationship with a deity you will be guided with a whispered suggestion for how to create an effective altar.

There are some that might dispute the need for all of this on an altar, perhaps feeling it's too much work or not necessary. I will simply state that these are my own reflections and beliefs and that this is just another way to enhance your ritual work. These are merely suggestions and a starting point for those who might never have given much thought to the art of Altars and their great significance. Altars are like works of art and the degree of interest and investment in art, varies from person to person. Altars are indeed very subjective and while someone might feel a simple rose is plenty for their altar experience, others might go the more elaborate route –and really, both are deemed just fine. When performing rituals among many attendants we set up altars for the purpose of enhancing their spiritual experience and conveying the sacred long before a word is even uttered. Altars set the tone and they help express the ineffable.

Blessings on your solitary and group altar creations!

HINA GROVE GODDESS GATHERING: THE MOON

"...The Sun gives us our spirit, but it is the Moon that gives us our Soul..." unknown

This month we are going to be looking at Hina- the Polynesian Goddess of the Moon. I thought it would be most appropriate to begin by reflecting a little on her home, the Moon, since she is, first and foremost, known as, "the Lady in the Moon".

There are some cultures that view the sun as feminine and the moon as masculine but throughout many more ancient cultures, more often than not, we hear of the Lady of the moon and the undeniable connection between wommin and this divine celestial orb. Since the beginning of time, it appears, the moon has always been known as the ruler of tides, cycles, fertility, the oceans and consequently the emotional realm and all of these attributes are closely linked to our feminine gender. We, as wommin, are unquestionably connected to the Moon, as even our monthly menstrual cycles reflect this deep cyclical connection. For some of us, who closely observe the phases of the Moon and our menstrual cycle, we might even experience the Lunar magnetic pull that has us bleeding precisely with the (respective) Full or New Moon, every 28-32 days.

In astrology, the Moon is the dominant ruler of the astrological sign of Cancer. Cancer traditionally rules over domesticity, which includes our home life, children, nurturance and the mother archetype. Astrologers believe the Moon represents our deepest personal need, our habits, our unconscious and the rhythmic ebb and flow of activity and energy. The Moon thus, symbolizes the feminine yin principle of receptivity, nurturance, and our image of mother. Consequently, this includes the Goddess and our spiritual connection to the Feminine Divine.

The moon's position when you were born reflects your interior life and reveals a great deal about a person's emotional instincts, private life, subconscious emotions, past lives and the intimate self- since the moon is considered introspective, mysteries and intuitive. *"The Moon is said to be the unguarded you, that acts on instinct and comes out in moments of crisis...."* (Donna Cunningham, "Café Astrology Notes")

Just as the Moon reflects the Sun's light and circles the Sun, in a symbolically protective manner, the Moon in our astrological birth chart, shows how we protect ourselves. It also reveals how we make ourselves feel secure, comfortable and safe. Thus, how we "mother" ourselves is reflected in the position of the moon at the time of our birth. Interesting to note that while our sun sign is instantaneously known, our moon sign does not always receive the same veneration. Approximately, every two to three days, the Moon travels and enters a new astrological sign, while the Sun, stays comfortably put, in a sign for about a month. Hence, knowing our Sun sign, is a matter of knowing what month you were born, while figuring out your Moon sign, might require a bit more research, once you've gathered the exact time and day of your birth. Yet knowing your Sun (outer image) and your Moon sign (inner image), creates a more accurate astrological picture of who you are. There have been times when you might hear someone say, *"...but I don't feel like a passionate, intense Scorpion, I don't even like oceans."* Or *"I know I am supposed to be a Mar's ruled Aries, but I think I really feel like a peace maker Venusian Libra etc..."* Reflected in these kinds of statements are people who might have a stronger connection to their moon sign than their sun sign.

> *"...When we are "acting out" our Moon, we are imaginative, creative, intuitive, sentimental, adaptable, introspective, and protective.*
> *On the negative side, we can be moody, restless and irrational..."*
> (by Donna Cunningham, From "Café Astrology Notes)

The Moon also reveals how you handle your intimate life and how you interact with other wommin. Looking into your sun and moon sign is invaluable in understanding your inner and outer personality. In your daily life, the Moon is what you fall back on, to restore your sense of emotional security. It's the little private habits that are comforting to you personally. It is no wonder that the Goddess Hina, selected the Moon as her protective dwelling place. It certainly reveals a great deal about this Lunar Goddess.

The moon has always been viewed as the symbol of Feminine divinity. In Hina's story, after some time living upon the earth, the Goddess finds herself overwhelmed and life becomes painfully burdensome and joyless. Hina looks up at the moon one night and remarkably finds comfort and healing offered by the light of this ancient, incandescent orb and she willingly surrenders herself to its magick and restorative gifts. Subsequently, she becomes one with the moon and in a sense, she retreats into her own Divine self and finds her own Feminine spirituality and healing within the moon.

For me, lighting a candle, chanting a mantra, doing arts and crafts, painting or other creative projects are extremely cathartic. Engaging in music, singing, dancing, even priestessing and joining with a group of wommin, to celebrate the Goddess, are all my own personal canoodling with the moon. These are all activities of connecting and communing with the Feminine Divine. When I'm enthralled in these activities, I am in my inner sanctuary of healing, tapping into the Moon and thus my own feminine powers.

Hina began to look longingly at her old home, her aumaka, the moon, after the notably dissatisfaction in her life, she looks up at the heavens and sees a chance to escape it all... Something calls her to come, return to her roots and leave it all behind.

For me, I muse and ask, ...*isn't that Goddess Spirituality....?* How often, when **"it"** calls us, it always seems so familiar like an old friend. Wommin unexplainably finding ourselves at a crossroad and pivotal turning point in our lives, for whatever reason, and then realizing, through her, that there has to be something, or even someplace else, where we could go to find shelter, retreat and return to source. The moon calling Hina back is a metaphor for returning to your origins, returning to an ancestral heritage, returning to your roots....and undoubtedly, it is a call to return to your core divine self, the Goddess.

Hina listens to that inner yearning and hypnotically travels towards the moon, following her intuition and heart's desire. We can see this as a metaphor, as we can't be Neil Armstrong physically traveling to the moon, but we can spiritually, emotionally, mentally, astrally go to a place as comforting, as enlightening as the moon. Reposing in her light during those times when we feel overwhelmed, beat down, stressed and dissatisfied by our lives and the mundane.

The moon and I mingle and unite. On a full moon, in particular, we connect. She equips me with her strength, her light and insight. I am gifted with her clarity, her energy, her magic, her lunar powers. I can come to her at will, extend my arms out, open myself up to her surge of divine light and I draw her down. I draw her all the way down, into my molecular effervescent receptive cells. I draw her down, I draw her in, delighting in the ancient practice that has been performed by countless of wommin, my ancestresses, witches, priestesses of old. It brings me great comfort to know, I can come to her whenever I have need or desire. I can tap into her gifts and make my own sanctuary within her light. I can come to this place in my heart, my mind and my soul, whenever I chose. I can tap into the gifts she has imbued in me -her inner strength. I can breathe, be validated and realize my self-worth and my own divine beauty. I can go to her, through this place of safety, whenever I need a new point of view or a new perspective. She is never too far away from me. Our temple of worship is never too far away....it is within us. The moon imbued this gift within every womyn, our personal sanctuary, our sacred home... So mote it be!

What actions do you take in moments of great stress?
Where do you go to regroup and regain your strength?

HINA GROVE GODDESS GATHERING CHANTS

SPIRALING INTO THE CENTER
Spiraling into the Center, The center of the wheel,
Spiraling into the Center, The center of the wheel,
We are the weavers, We are the woven ones,
We are the dreamers, We are the Dream.
We are the weavers, We are the woven ones,
We are the dreamers, We are the Dream. *by Starhawk*

WE AVE AND SPIN
Weave and spin,
Weave and Spin,
This is how our work begins,
Mend and Heal,
Mend and Heal,
take the Dream
and make it real *by Starhawk*

*FIRE DANCE SONG
I align my desire with the spirit divine
Dive into the coils of the Serpent's mind
I rise from the depth
My roots to my wings
I open up my head and the Firebird sings

EIGHT BEADS CHANTS by Carolyn Hillyer
Girlseed
Bloodflower
(dip it)Fruitmother
Spinmother,
(raise it) Midwoman
Earthcrone
Stonecrone
Bone

WE ARE A CIRCLE
(Chorus)We are a circle within a circle
with no beginning and never ending
You hear us sing, you hear us cry
Now hear us call you, Spirits of Earth and sky
Within our heart there goes a spark
Love and desire is burning fire (repeat chorus)
    Within our blood, within our tears
    There lies the offer of living water
    Take our fears, take our pains
    Take the darkness into the earth again (repeat)
The circle closes, between the worlds
To mark the sacred space
where we come face to face   By: Rick Hamouris

EARTH, MOON,MAGICK by B.M.M.
In the Earth, deep within,
There is A Magick, I draw it in.
    In her Caves, in the Trees
    Hear her Heartbeat, Pulsing thru me.
When I Rise, I feel her Love
With feet Grounded, I'm soaring high above,
    In the Earth, deep within,
    There is A Magick, I draw it in
Ancient Moon, my Soul reveres
With my Singing, I call you here.
    When this flame, ignites tonight,
    Priestess dancing, Under the moonlit night....
In the Earth, deep within,
There is A Magick, I draw it in.... There is A Magick, I draw it in }3x

*We are connected, Sister, Mother Connected...*By B.M.M.*

RETURN TO ME
Come return to me
Come return to me
Come return to our old home
Our blessed Ancestry.

    Step into the Moon
She waits for me and you
Let her light transform
While we explore
our spirituality.

You were once in me,
part of Matriarchy,
See your lineage now
as it unfolds
and brings you back to me
    by B.M.M.

SWEET SURRENDER
We are Opening up in Sweet Surrender
to the Luminous Love light of the one
We are Opening up in Sweet Surrender
to the Luminous Love light of the one
We are Opening.....We are Opening
(2X)*By Gladys Gray*

ELEMENTAL CHANT
Air I am,
Fire I am
Water, Earth and
Spirit I am. *By Andreas Corbin Arthen*

LADY OF THE MOON
Lady of the Moon
Come to us, be with us,
Lady of the Moon, Lady of the Moon...
    by B.M.M.

CHAPTER TWENTY-FIVE

"Blessings come in all sorts of disguises, when we open our hearts and eyes to acknowledge them, we begin living in the spirit and light of abundance..."B. Melusine Mihaltses

"When you find Peace within yourself, you become the kind of person who can live at peace with others..." Peace Pilgrim

WELCOME HESTIA

OUR ALTAR

Altar cloth: Deep reds and oranges and maybe a second golden altar cloth underneath.
Image: Statue of this Hearth Goddess or an image of a fiery spiritual woman, or simply a hearth fire. Canvas art or photo of the Goddess and or photos of Greece, the Parthenon, Fires, Hearths, circles, temples, and beautiful Homes.

Always present on the altar;
A cast iron cauldron, drums, speaking stick, a silver pentacle, athame, elemental representations.....

Air: images of White birds Incense type sticks, cones, charcoal brisket and fine powdered herbs of Clove, Anise, Cinnamon, Frankincense and Myrrh can be burned as your Eastern offering.
Fire: numerous candles, glass enclosed candles or pillars in deep reds, rusts and oranges.
Water: Chalice or small glass bowl with Fresh Spring Water.
Earth: rich foods, a cornucopia, Plants and pleasing floral arrangements of sunflowers are appropriate, as is a bowl of herbs, like the ones mentioned above. A small dish of soil and seeds can also work as a Northern elemental representation.

Other items pertinent to this particular gathering
A Cornucopia of rich delicious foods
A beautifully dressed table
Lots of Candles everywhere
Gourds and Pumpkins
A simply lit Hearth/fireplace
Orange, yellow flowers and herbs
Notes of Gratitude
Photos of loved ones
Plate offerings of homemade bread loaves and mead
Writing pens and paper, safety pins,
Red Light gauzy fabric/Veil to represent her fire
Workshop items
Tarot -"Queen of Wands"

Offering the entire Day and ritual will be a cornucopia of food offerings to the Goddess
Sacred objects from members:
Notes:

Hestia

Hestia altar

Handmade Candle Crafting

HESTIA

Hestia was the keeper of the Sacred flames on Mount Olympus and was highly respected and regarded as one of the original twelve Olympian Gods/Goddesses. According to numerous ancient writings, first offerings were always offered up to Hestia and her flames were the first lit. She was revered and greatly cherished by all Gods and mortals alike.

Greek Goddess of the Hearth and Home. Hestia is the personification of Hearth Flames. Her Roman counterpart was the Goddess Vesta. She was a Fire Goddess and her name literally means "*heart.*" In Latin, the word is interpreted to mean "*Focus.*" The hearth, in a domicile, was indeed considered to be the focus and heart of all dwellings and thus she is embraced throughout the ages, as the patron Goddess of Hearth and Home. Her symbol is the infinite, sacred circle and in ancient Greece, a circular Hearth Fire was a place of reverence for this beloved deity.

Not much is known about this ancient Virginal Goddess, but what we DO know, we have learned mostly through her rituals, the Homeric invocations and her worship, documented in the writings of her time. For example; The hearth, in most Greek homes, was considered the center of the home. The architecture of the time reflected its importance as most homes were built around this important entity. One common documented rite that reveals Hestia's importance was the blessing of a newborn. When a baby was first born to a family and the child was five days old, they would walk around their hearth, the center of their home, presenting the child to Hestia for her divine blessings. Afterwards they would commemorate the event by having a huge feast in gratitude for her blessings.

Another documented rite, that has still survived the ages, involves the blessings of newlyweds. It was customary for the mother of the bride to light a torch from her hearth fires and bring that light into the newlyweds home, to reflect the undying flames of lineage, being passed down from one generation to the next. Here too, Hestia's blessings would be invoked for a happy marital home life. Today this tradition continues only more subtly, via the unity candles incorporated in many marriage ceremonies, as bride and groom light one flame from the joining of their own, two, respective candles.

Hestia was greatly adored as the oldest of the Olympian Gods. She was the first born child of the Goddess Rhea and the God Cronos and thus was the oldest sister to all the Olympian Gods and Goddesses. As a result she was also the beloved Aunt of the second generation of Olympian Gods. Hestia was one of the first Olympian Goddesses on Mount Olympus, but was later replaced, in Greek mythology, with the God of Wine, Dionysus. Sadly, some believe this is reflective of a society that was already starting to undervalue the importance of wisdom, traditions and spiritual enlightenment -attributes Hestia represented and defended.

As Vesta, in Rome, her fires were attended to by the Vestal virgins, who took vows of celibacy as part of their initiations and service to her. They were suppose to be human, living embodiments of Vesta/Hestia herself, who was often depicted as pure and bright, a living flame, and thus the Vestal virgins had strict rules to live by. They were severely punished if they dared deviate from their role as celibate priestesses. Young girls, no older than six, were recruited to Hestia's service and their hair and clothing were unified to create anonymity within the priestess-hood.

The Goddess Hestia was rarely depicted in female flesh form, but rather as a flame, a spirit, a feeling of warmth and comfort. Her immortal spirit continues to live on today as she transcends all time and space. As a Virgin Goddess, she was an advocate for wommin's spirituality and was sometimes compared to Sophia, the Gnostic Goddess of Wisdom.

Hestia is synonymous with purity, sincerity, and spiritual devotion. As the oldest of the Virgin Goddesses, Hestia was one of three Deities unaffected by Aphrodite's charms and love enchantments. However, Aphrodite did manage to arouse great love for the beautiful Hestia, in both the God of the Sea, Poseidon and in the Sun God, Apollo. The chaste Goddess refused both of their advances, choosing to dedicate herself to her role as Goddess of the Hearth and vowing to remain pure and unfettered by romantic love liaisons.

She espoused celibacy and valued Spirituality above sensuality and derived great pleasure and satisfaction simply being herself, honored in the home, and being of service to humanity and her Divine family. Many of the myths of the time, are all in a agreement that Zeus was quite supportive and respectful of his older sister, thus he willingly (according to patriarchal writings) gave her the honored place of the hearth in the center of the home, as the ultimate expression of reverence to this Goddess. At Mount Olympus, hers were the first sacred flames lit, always in her honor first and she was given dominion over the entire maintenance of this Divine home. Unlike other virginal deities, she really does appear fully whole unto herself, content with simply being and serving her Olympian family and the whole of humanity with her sacred flames. She was disinterested in the power, drama and notoriety her siblings were incessantly engaged in.

When I think of Hestia I think of calm, tranquility and a deep spiritual love and peace. I think of those things that bring about stability and serenity, as she was never documented being involved in any of the numerous quarrels or disputes between the Gods. Hestia is the comfort and safety of our hearth fire, our core, our heart, our spirit and thus, both our internal and external homes.

Goddess of the Hearth and home, today she is still venerated and tended to with great honor. Hestia still lives on in the flames we tend to - the flames of our hearth found in the core of our homes and the flames we tend to in the core of our spirits and souls.

HESTIA GROVE GODDESS GATHERING

PURPOSE: To give thanks and show our gratitude and proper respect to the Goddess Hestia and request her blessings on our home/hearth.

CHECK INS: Getting to know each other, passing the speaking stick and sharing what this month usually means to us personally.

CHANTING WORKSHOP:
"We can Rise with the Fires", "Do you remember..." and "We are the Power"
(see song text sheet)

DRUMMING TRANCE: A powerful drumming(CD)Greek music track will be played to give participants a chance to trance and connect with this moment. They are invited to find a comfortable spot to relax and let the music move them however they feel best.

CHECK INS: How does this Goddess come to us personally? Personifying Hestia. She is depicted as a flame but what would she look like, to us personally, if we painted her?

GODDESS LESSON
On HESTIA, her myths, lineage, etymology and her attributes

GODDESS WORKSHOPS

WORKSHOP I: Making homemade candles, carving and charging store bought candles. We will gather chunks of wax, scented oil and coloring, to create our very own homemade candle. As we are making it, we are already imbuing it with our intentions. Those that have brought candles can now carve them with sigils & intricate designs and charge them with scented oils as they are imbuing their witchy intentions into the wax.

WORKSHOP II: A discussion on how to magickally bless our hearth and home. We will discuss some traditional spells that can be done to make our home more harmonious and peaceful. We will also discuss spells to protect and bless our homes via herbal plackets, witch bottles, holy water and smudgings...

WORKSHOP III: Fire scrying with the dancing flames of our hearth or altar candles. Getting in touch with Hestia's element and her sacred domain. With soft gentle music in the background, participants are invited to simply gaze into Hestia's flames and record any images or messages that come forth. Art supply will be made available for those who wish to personify Her on canvas.

WORKSHOP IV: Writing a letter of thanksgiving to someone who has had an impact in our life, but probably doesn't know it. It could be anyone from our grandmother, a serviceman or a teacher, and older sibling or even an author whose books have made a strong impact in your life.

WORKSHOP V: Discussing the Kitchen Witch tradition and how we can make magick with our cooking. Together we will prepare a meal or bake fresh, homemade bread, while focusing on gratitude and positive intentions and the magick inherent in the Kitchen witch.

WORKSHOP VI: Carving and decorating gourds and pumpkins for our ritual decoration. At this time of year gourds and pumpkins are plentiful and very popular. We will utilize them for our home altars by decorating them with sacred symbols and incorporating them into our magick.

REFLECTIONS ON HESTIA

Hestia comes into your life to direct your attention to your spirit, your hearth and your inner flames. Without the entanglement of a consort or sexuality, she teaches us to quiet down and connect to ancient wisdom and our true, inner spiritual nature. She is a lesson on the value of old traditions and the importance of expressing gratitude for our ancestral lineage, with those immortal fires that continue to burn from ages to ages. She awakens us modern wommin to value our own inner sacred core; our heart and spirit, and the importance of our hearth and home.

HESTIA GROVE GODDESS GATHERING RITUAL

PURPOSE: To give thanks and show our gratitude and proper respect to Hestia, the ancient Greek Hearth Goddess and bring blessings to our home & hearth.

*****A large table(preferably round) is set in Center of the room. It is decorated with Autumnal color table cloths (orange, yellow, browns & reds), napkins and dishware etc.. Gourds, pumpkins, corns, apples and all sorts of edibles are set at the table but there is more to come as the attendants will each bring a food offering for this ritual.*

Purification/anointing: Wommin will apply scented sabbat oil placed on the third eye and the heart chakra to one another as we enter sacred space and welcome one another.

Intent speaker: Declaration of Intent for Today's Ritual is spoken aloud by the priestess.

Circle Cast:
with a flame and prose around the room or with a wand, as this too is representative of fire, the circle is cast. Perimeter of Circle will have numerous votive candles. Each one will be lit as the circle is cast with these words..

**Since ancient times these flames hold honor
and represent the Divine,
Ancestors, Gods and Good spirits we call you,
As this Circle is cast tonight!** (rpt)

Quarters called
* Guardians of the Watchtowers of the **East**, Ye Powers of **Air**,
Place of healing Breath, sighs, winds of change and the breath of our Deities upon us, beginnings.... We call on you to bring us your gifts
Guard and Hold our sacred space, Hail and welcome Air!
(*attendants repeat*) Hail and Welcome Air!!!

*Hail Guardians of the Watchtowers of the **South**, Ye Powers of **Fire**,
Place of the Hearth and the flames of Hestia, our warm comforting home and the meals of our spirits, We call on you to lend us your gifts...
Guard and Hold our sacred circle, Hail and Welcome Fire!
(*attendants repeat*) Hail and Welcome Fire!!!

*Hail Guardians of the Watchtowers of the **West**, Ye powers of **Water**,
Place of the healing waters, gratitude and the emotional harmony in our family gatherings... We call on you to bring us your gifts
Guard and Hold our sacred space, Hail and welcome Water!
(*attendants repeat*) Hail and Welcome Water!!!

*Hail Guardians of the Watchtowers of the **North**, Ye powers of **Earth**,
Place of the Earth's great bounty, gifts found all around us in nature, our body, and this feasting, harvest... We call on you to bring us your gifts
Guard and Hold our sacred circle, Hail and welcome Earth!
(*attendants repeat*) Hail and Welcome Earth!!!

Hestia Invoked (*see suggested Hestia invocations*)

Hestia *(Aspected will speak of herself, her fires, the hearth and the home and this season…)*
Long have I been worshipped…
I was the first bore to my parents,
Cronos and the Great Goddess Rhea.
My grandmother is the primordial
Earth Goddess Gaia.
Have you not heard of the
Great Goddess Gaia, whom all things came from?
Her immortal magnitude lives in me,
as immortal flames of spirituality.

First and last of Olympian Gods.
Revered and honored by all on land
Mortals and Gods, first fruits they shared
Offers and traditions to show they still cared.

My Hearth Fires remained
while traditions are maintained
Like yesterday, within us,
They burn still today

Brother Zeus has gifted me the honored place
in the core of the home,
But I didn't need him to ordained this so.
My flames command their own divine respect
Gaze deeply into my Hearth flames
And see what Spirit reflects…..

Watch and gaze deeply
In the flames of your hearth,
and there you will see me
In each flame and each spark.

Hail and Welcome Hestia!!!

Offering Declared: *"The world is like a beautiful Garden, made up of a myriad of sacred components and I offer myself to humanity and the universe via this _____ (ex; pumpkin, turkey, honey cakes, banana, oranges etc..) And offering_____ (brightness, joy, beauty, knowledge, compassion, nourishment, etc…)"*

All have joined in around the food banquet. We eat and enjoy ourselves but we also will talk and make **Magick** this way too.
****We will talk about those people who do not know us personally, perhaps strangers who we've encountered who have inspired us, someone who has entered your spiritual family for all the inspiration they've imparted and for the great impact they've had in your life. We give thanks. Here we take the time to also show gratitude for them and raise a toast to them. Go around the table and share the person and how they have impacted your life. Around the circle with a toasting goblet or with the rattle, we'll individually name (1-2+) Spiritual teachers, whether authors, friends, or our animal familiars. Aloud we honor them, by saying their name and why we personally are grateful to them…. Below is only a suggestion to start, but participants, around the feasting table, are encouraged to speak from their heart and follow their intuition…

*"I send gratitude for_____(ex; Gustav Mahler and Mozart)
they taught me_____ (ex; spirit of music)"*
When the feasting is over, all will leave the table, gather back in a circle if we didn't feast there…

Move and Chanting: *"Spirit of Fire Come to us"*
Small candles will be handed out to attendants.
*We will charge it (within our hands) with the good energy of the night. All that warm fuzzy feeling we, as a group, created with **Hestia**. All of that intimacy, bonding, harmony and love will be imbued in our candles between our hands. Contain within our candle all of that energy we experienced on this **Hestia***

Ritual. *For this candle the attendants will take back home and re-ignite **Hestia's** energy in their own abode. From our group flame taken back to their home, as was done in ancient times. This flame will serve to call on Hestia energy again whenever we wish to connect with her again.*

Now we will light the candle using Hestia's Altar flame while reciting the **spell** below, repeating after her words:

Candle - holder of my wish
Nurse this spell release when lit
Flames ignite the warmth and joy
Peace with her is now employed
Spirit of Hestia, we celebrate you
By Hearth and Flames of Gratitude
Receive our thanks and bring to us
Happy Homes with Goddess luck
These things or greater
So mote it be!!!

Snuff or Blow out candle
Singing our Closing Goddess Chant

Gather and hold hands as we begin to **Devoke and Release the Goddess**
Hearth Goddess.
Virginal Flames of heart and home.
Spirit born, your Sacred Fires we touched upon today.
Thank you for manifesting your gifts within our circle.
You came when called
and we were blessed by your immortal flames.
Let thy wisdom permeate our soul,
long after we have bid thee adieu.
Stay if you will, Go if you must. Hail and Farewell Hestia!

Devoking of Quarters

* Guardians of the Watchtowers of the **North**, Ye Powers of **Earth**, Abundance and fertility, the bounty of the Earth in multiplicity, and harvest feasting have bear witness to our rites today. We thank you for guarding our sacred space with your divine element. With gratitude we bid thee adieu. **Hail and Farewell Earth!**

* Guardians of the Watchtowers of the **West**, Ye Powers of **Water**, expressive healing waters of thanksgiving and Harmony, have bear witness to our rites today. We thank you for guarding our sacred space with your divine element. With gratitude we bid thee adieu. **Hail and Farewell Water!**

* Guardians of the Watchtowers of the **South**, Ye Powers of **Fire**, Warmth of heart and home, our kitchens and hearth- that which feeds us when we are hungry and gives us sustenance.... all in Hestia's realm, have bear witness to our rites today. We thank you for guarding our sacred space with your divine element. With gratitude we bid thee adieu. **Hail and Farewell Fire!**

* Guardians of the Watchtowers of the **East**, Ye Powers of **Air**, winds of change and divine Breath, have bear witness to our rites today. We thank you for guarding our sacred space with your divine element. With gratitude we bid thee adieu. **Hail and Farewell Air!**

Open Circle
"The Circle is open, but unbroken may the peace of the Goddess be ever in our heart, Merry meet and merry part and merry meet again..."

HOMERIC HYMNS TO HESTIA

Hestia,
You who have received the highest honor
to have your seat forever,
in the enormous houses of all the Gods,
And in all the men, who walk the earth.
It is a beautiful gift you have received,
It is a beautiful honor.

Without you,
Mankind would have no feast,
Since no one could begin the first
and last drink of honey-like wine,
Without an offering to Hestia

And you Argeiphontes,
son of Zeus and Maia,
Messenger of the Gods
With your gold wand,
Giver of good things, be good to me,
Protect me,
Along with the venerable and dear Hestia.

Come, both of you
Inhabit this beautiful house
With mutual feeling of friendship.
You accompany good work
with intelligence and youth

Hello daughter of Cronos
You too, Hermes
With your gold wand.
As for me, I will remember you in another song.

SECOND HOMERIC HYMNS TO HESTIA

Hestia you who take care of the Holy house of Apollo,
Who shoots so far,
the house at sacred Pytho,
A liquid oil flows forever from your hair,
Come on into this house of mine,
Come on it here with shrewd Zeus.
Be gracious to my song.

Excerpts from "The Homeric Hymns," trans. Charles Boer, Dallas: Spring Publications, 1979

Hestia *(Aspected...)*

Long have I been worshipped...
I was the first bore to my parents,
Cronos and the Great Goddess Rhea.
My grandmother is the primordial
Earth Goddess Gaia.
Have you not heard of the
Great Goddess Gaia, whom all things came from?
Her immortal magnitude lives in me,
as immortal flames of spirituality.

First and last of Olympian Gods.
Revered and honored by all on land
Mortals and Gods, first fruits they shared
Offers and traditions to show they still cared.

My Hearth Fires remained
while traditions are maintained
Like yesterday, within us,
They burn still today

Brother Zeus has gifted me the honored place
in the core of the home,
But I didn't need him to ordained this so.
My flames command their own divine respect
Gaze deeply into my Hearth flames
And see what Spirit reflects.....

Watch and gaze deeply
In the flames of your hearth,
and there you will see me
In each flame and each spark.

Hail and Welcome Hestia!!!

Create a beautiful, lavish altar and a special offering plate for the Goddess. Place this offering outdoors under the moon. On your altar, have a representation of the manifested spell, maybe a photo or the actual object that you are giving thanks for. Carve and charge a white candle, anointing it with "Gratitude oil"(see appendix), although any color candle will do. Use sandalwood and myrrh incense sticks and an image of Hestia or the Goddess in particular that helped you. Include moving music and drums to raise energy and send your thanks to the gods. Afterwards be sure to send that gratitude and good feeling into the universe, with an act of kindness towards humanity. This spell can be performed at any moon phase on any day.

THANKSGIVING
* With gratitude in my heart
And thanksgiving for your gifts
Hail to the Goddess
for bestowing my wish

My prayers you've answered
Sad tears turn to Joy
I Thank you Dear Goddess
For Love's precious envoy.

Grant me the chance
to nurture this love
teach me all that
a Goddess does

Strengthen my spirit
to trust what is worthy
make all relationships
loving and sturdy

Hail to the Goddess, Hail to thee,
This ritual is cast in thanksgiving.

Beloved Hestia
of revered ranks
Herein this offering
receive my thanks.

This spell can be performed at any moon phase. Have a representation of the manifested spell that you are giving thanks for. Carve and charge an orange candle, anointing it with "Gratitude oil"(see appendix). Use sandalwood and myrrh incense sticks and an image of Hestia. On your altar have elemental representations like; wind chimes, bells or your athame for air, a red candle for fire, A chalice with rain water for Water and a bowl of soil or dried herbs for earth. Include moving music and drums to raise energy and send your thanks to the gods. Lastly, go outdoors, under the moon, and leave a well thought out offering by the entrance of your home.

GRATITUDE
* With Gratitude I light this flame
And with my breath I graciously say;
All of my thanks I give to you
A spell I Casted,
has now come true

Earth, Water, Fire and Air
I exalt you now in this ritual affair
God & Goddess of Ten thousand names

I praise you in myself
For we are One - the same

I welcome more Blessings
As I thank thee
Hail to the Goddess
So mote it be!!!

Perform this spell any night, but it's suggested on a Sunday, while scrying into the fires of your hearth. If that is not possible gather numerous candles, in shades of orange and red, and surround your altar only by this candle light. Place an image of the Goddess Hestia if you can or create one yourself, by making a painting of the Goddess personified. Incense of frankincense and myrrh can be used on your hearth or cauldron. Present on your altar, your home blessing placket or a protective witches bottle. Carve and charge a yellow or brown candle with Home blessings anointing oil or shield/protection oil (see appendix). Walk around your home, entering every room of your house, with the working candle and holy water. Call on Hestia to guard and Bless your hearth and home.

HESTIA BLESSINGS
*Hestia Goddess of the Hearth
From ancient times worshipped on Earth
Your Fires watched and kept aflame
I honor here your sacred Name

As the Vestal virgins did
Mortals, Gods and Priestesses,
Here tonight, I honor thee
Sacred Goddess now join me.

Let your sacred fires burn
With these candles I have lit
Bring your blessings to my house
Harmony, joy, luck and bliss

All who live in this sweet home
Guard, protect as though your own
Bless with Peace and Harmony
Let this house have your blessings,

Hestia let your hearth flames burn,
warmth and love from you we learn,
Gifts of nectar in gratitude,
In this spell we honor you.

Hail and welcome Hestia!!!

SPIRIT OF GRATITUDE
Birthday Journaling

An unusual feeling came over me, as I was in my car driving back home after a little shopping excursion. With the baby in the back seat finally calm and done with his screaming fit tantrum, I could actually now hear my thoughts....and connect with my inner self serenely.

Now, I am not sure why these feeling surfaced and swelled over me the way they did nor why at this very particular time. Could it be PMS? That seems to always get the blame for anything unusually intense in the emotional terrain. Maybe it is residuals from working with Hekate last month and calling on my ancestors. Maybe it is the dawning realization that tomorrow, I will be just two years shy of entering my Forties, I will greet yet another birthday but this time something feels different. Don't know exactly what to attribute this magnanimous realization but all of a sudden I felt warm, good, content, accomplished, satisfied, like I have just been nominated for something....like the *"Publishing Clearing House"* just left a dooozie of a check in my name. A felt this feeling of having won something astronomical and the distinct feeling of achievement that accompanies such a prize.

Rather unexpectedly, the tears started to swell up and the more I fought them, the more they streamed down my cheeks. My attention went immediately to my chest, no... I wasn't having a heart attack but strangely I felt my heart weighted. My heart felt surrounded...strange, it felt occupied by more than just me -my deceased mom and dad, my deceased ancestors all took a corner inside my heart for a split second and I felt their weight.

I may not have won the Academy Award, nor became the next Jennifer Lopez.... No, I didn't make it to the Metropolitan Opera to sing one of Mozart's beloved soubrette roles. And no..., I didn't get signed to sing multi record deals with Columbia Records... I didn't win any Grammys, nor meet, the artist formely known as Prince... I didn't marry a multi-millionaire Italian conductor, I didn't get to sing at "La Scala", in Milan, Italy.... I didn't get to appear on T.V. with a skyrocketing performing arts career. And no, I didn't become rich and famous... but DAMMIT, I MADE IT!!!!...

Somehow, **I made it**!!!! I have my health; emotional and spiritual health and mental health. I am at peace with my inner self. I am blessed with the most amazing children. Three beautiful, smart boys and family. My **OWN** family, something I never dared aspire for, and a loving husband, and a beautiful house, **OUR** home and here I am -actually driving, DRIVING in my own freakin car, fearlessly, something I never dared venture to do for some weird, phobia entrenched reason. And I am HERE!!!! I am actually alive... ALIVE and WELL and HAPPY about it....and incredibly grateful!

There was a time when I couldn't even imagine this. And all I could easily imagine was my own lifeless corpse being found months later in my tiny, cramped Manhattan apartment, already decomposed.... I wanted out so badly then and I couldn't see past the pain that was in front of me, IN ME!!!!... I couldn't and didn't want to. I had embraced the tragedies of my past as the dramatic tragedy of my future and subsequent death. I couldn't even muster up hope and I never- ever- even imagined this life for myself. I was way too busy, chasing another life that was only bringing me pain, rejection, disillusions, and so much deceit... Things I couldn't even comprehend then but that chase, was taking my soul and taking my will to live......

Now in retrospect, I realize that what I was chasing back then, was such a waste.... It was so trivial and insignificant compare to what I have now.... This? I was never able to imagine this life, I was never even able to hope for it and here it is. And suddenly, I feel prized, crowned and blessed.

So, YES...even in the car while driving I felt my parents...(I feel them now), holding me, warmly embracing me saying, *"yes... you have made it and we are so proud of you, this -what you have NOW is YOUR Academy award, congratulations....Happy Birthday, 38th years old, you made it to see it, we love you and we are happy you persevered with life and the living..."*

So my life didn't quite turn out the way I had envisioned and I didn't become rich and famous but I have something more valuable than any of that Hollywood crap...I am well, I am happy and healthy. I am grateful, I am authentically living, I am honoring those that came before me by simply engaging in the act of conscious living. I have a deep rooted peace and I have my wellbeing...Blessed Be!!! Oh... and I see my Birthday Gift from the great beyond has arrived early this year. Thank you Honored Spirits....)O(Thank you, for the spirit of Gratitude!!!

HESTIA GROVE GODDESS GATHERING CHANTS

CALLING ALL DIRECTIONS *by Elaine Silver & Melora*
When I look to the East, I see sunrise
When I look to the East I see Light
With the Soft, golden gift of the morning
I am breathing you in, now revived
      As I turn to the South, Fires burning,
      With the warm true acceptance of love,
      I am open to the Earthly pleasure
      I can feel your caress, now alive
      Yes, I can feel your caress, now alive.
As I come to the West, arms outstretched,
Ride the crest of the flowing waters of life,
I am floating on the waves of intuition
Clarity comes to me, grants me sight,
And I see day is one with the night.
      As I turn to the North, fall to my knees
      And I feel the pulsating power of Earth.
      I am taking in your warm, sunlit amber,
      I am one with you, fragrant field,
      Yes, I am one with you now, mighty Oak.
Lift my head to the sky, I see moonlight,
I am taking in your pure white light,
I can feel your power gently falling,
As I dance between your moonbeam this night
Yes, I dance between your moonbeams this night

SPIRITS OF FIRE
Spirits of Fire Come to us, we will kindle the Fire,
Spirits of Fire Come to us, we will kindle the Fire,
We will Kindle the Fire,
Dance around the circle round
We will kindle the Fire, Dance the Circle around.

WE ARE THE POWER *by Starhawk*
We are the Power in everyone,
We are the dance of the Moon and the Sun
We are the Hope that will not hide,
We are the turning of the tide.

DON'T YOU KNOW
by Elaine Silver
Don't you know
Your body is a Temple
And Don't you know
Your Spirit is a Shrine
The other side of Fear
Is a never ending Love
Don't you know
You and I
Are both Divine

You won't know
What it means to really grow
If you don't open up
To whose inside
The other side of Fear
Is a never ending Love
Don't you know
You and I
Are both Divine.

Dedication

CHAPTER TWENTY-SIX

*The Melusine
Gathering for Goddess*

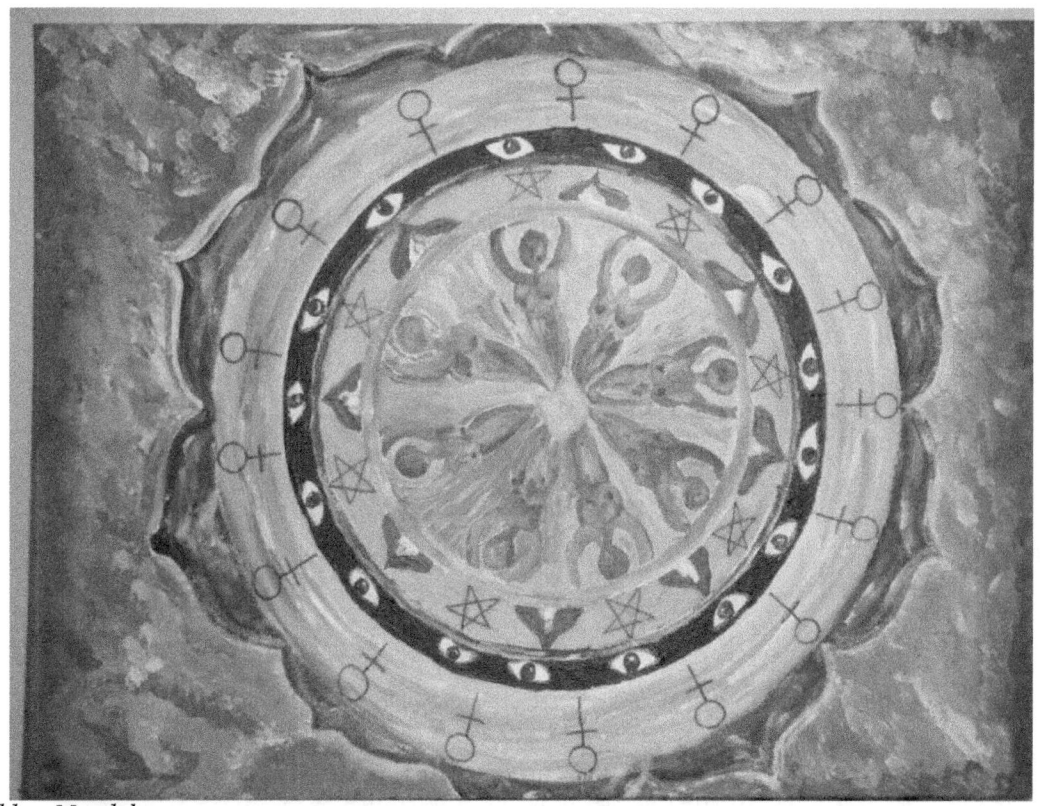

Goddess Mandala

Altar for Dedication

GROVE OF THE FEMININE DIVINE

We are a Goddess Study Group in San Antonio Texas,
which meets the last Sunday of every Month
to learn and discuss various deities
from different pantheons.
We meet to learn, share, talk, bond,
chant, make magick, have a meal together
and honor the Feminine Divine.

To join simply contact us
and complete the short registration form.
We welcome all womyn
with a serious interest and deep desire
to connect with
the Goddess within herself,
as we believe she is alive and Magick is afoot.

Our meeting places and times
are disclosed after registration
via post mail. This process is to
insure our safety and privacy.

We are a Sisterhood and
We All Come from the Goddess.
Come, Join us in
celebrating & honoring the Feminine Divine!

WELCOME TO OUR GROUP,
Grove of the Feminine Divine

This is a collaborative group in which we learn, grow, share, make magick, tap into our power and value ourselves and each other in this community.

We gather the last Sunday of the month to commune, bond, drum, learn and talk about a chosen deity, relate her divine energy into our modern daily lives and then celebrate that Feminine Divine through songs/chants, activities, sisterhood and powerful transformative rituals.

Please join us by completing this form and returning it back Either to group or privately to me: Groveofthefemininedivine@yahoo.com
All information is kept confidential and not shared.

Registration Form

*Yes I am interested _____ and I can come on Sundays _____
*BirthName: _____
*Name we should call you by _____
*Date of birth _____
*How did you learn about us: _____
*Mailing Address_____
*Phone number _____ Email: _____

*Your passions & hobbies: _____
_____

***How would you define yourself?
a. Searching for something not sure what
b. Just beginning your spiritual path
c. Some experience
d. Many years on your spiritual path
e. Declared Crone/Priestess

**Is there any particular Goddess(es) you would love to work with? please name:
_____

***What do you hope to attain from this group
(circle as many as apply)
*Social/friends   *Goddess history info   *ritual knowledge   *magick making
*spiritual support   *creativity   *nothing   *just curious   *priestess apprentice
*other_____   *specific spell working help: _____
***Meeting location and further pertinent information will follow after registration.

****GROVE OF THE FEMININE DIVINE AGREEMENTS

For Goddess and Magick study group dedicated to Wommin and the Goddess.

To make our time together pleasant, harmonious and free of pain and drama we agree as a group to the following guidelines.....

---To listen to one another.
---To respect the views and opinions of each person present and reserve judgment.
---To embrace and unconditionally support one another and honor our differences and our common ground.
---To speak from your heart and a place of truth.
---To bring up issues and conflicts as soon as it's permissible and not harbor ill feelings but address them a.s.a.p.
---To demonstrate willingness to resolve issues.
---To come from a place of love and good intentions and thus expect that others too also come from a place of love and good intentions.
---To work Positive magick for the greater good.
---To be open and aware that life and the Divine might have different plans than what we wish to will.
---To come ready to grow, learn, share and stand ground in sacred space.
___To keep the law of three, "...an it harm none, So mote it be..."
___To keep confidential some of what takes place within our group and those in attendance and trust that our privacy will be honored.
___To be empowered to choose for yourself when to speak and when to keep silent.
___To be empowered to ask for what you need
___To know that we come here from different paths as individuals but we are all respected as part of One Womyn Divine race.
---To know that you are A valued, important integral part in our community and thus will act in harmony with this.
(Together we'll add more as necessary...)

___

___

I have read and agree (Name) _____

Date _____

SOLITARY PRIESTESS DEDICATION

Purify smudge self with Copal and Sage. A special cleansing ritual bath should take place prior to this work.
Oil anointing with specially made Priestess Oil (see suggestion in book)
Casting Circle & Quarter Call (see suggestions but since this is a solitary ritual, do what feels best.)
Chant: *"Mother I call you," "Don't you know, you and I are both Divine..." "I align my Desire.."*
Music: Play a spirited drumming CD track to raise energy and dance.

When you have raised the energy, approach your altar, begin by lighting your Goddess candle...

Invocation

Here do I stand,
Dear Ancestors, Spirits, Deities of old,
Goddess and the great Feminine Divine...
Here do I stand to take up thy work,
to dedicate myself to you, now as always.
In this ritual, I dedicate myself as your Divine daughter,
always in thy service,
in the role of Priestess of the Goddess,
teaching womyn your sacred mysteries,
as they are revealed to me,
and sharing with them the expansive love,
that you've imbued in me, for magick, the craft
and the Goddess, the Sacred Feminine.
I dedicate myself to the advancement,
enrichment and fulfillment of this
newly formed Goddess study group called:

*Grove of the Feminine Divine....

(Light your second candle)
I do so dedicate myself to being Priestess to this Goddess Group of Womyn
and I ask that you bless my role and journey
in the sacred name of Aradia, Hekate & Artemis,
I ask that you help me attract the right members for this group.
I ask that you present, good honest sincere, positive wommin,
that will fit into our newly formed coven family,
...for it is indeed a family I'm birthing here
in the sacred name of Gaia, Athena, Oya and Brid,
I ask that there will be loyalty,
enthusiasm, harmony and
effortless commitment from all members.
Bless, guide and protect herein this Goddess group (*)
that it may flourish and strive,
with success and become an anchor
in the greater community of
Feminist Pagans -Dianics -Wiccans.
This I make true, by the law of three
and in the name of the Goddess,
these things or better, So mote it be!!!

*Herbal Placket Spell Working...

Consecrate tools of Magick that will be used; Athame, wand, cauldron, grimoire, jewelry, crown circlet, statues etc... and bless them by all the elements via incense, oil, herbs and the heat of your hands.

Meditate with Music/ Future Visualization
Grounding, Thanking Goddess,
Devoking quarters, Opening Circle, Tidy up.....

PRIESTESS DEDICATION
FOR OUR GROUP MEMBERS-GROVE OF THE FEMININE DIVINE

Purpose: To formally dedicate ourselves to the Goddess path and our Sisterhood.
Music will play in the background the entire time as we set up our communal Altar

Purification/Asperge: With smudge of copal and sage
Welcoming & anointing: Eye connections (our windows to the soul), Priestess Oil anointing for heart chakra and third eye -Ask them to anoint their sister next to them with a long, sisterly gaze of love, and a welcoming into the sacred space…. Connect with the spirit of love and sisterhood and open yourself up to gifting this energy to the womyn before you.

Cast Circle; Bell chimes vibrating tone as circle is cast with Athame
From earth to sky and elements around
keep safe this circle and all here on ground
Container, preserver this circle shall be,
And only allow good energy.
Through portals of light we bless this task
by will and by word
This Circle is now cast…..

Calling Quarters
*(see suggestions in appendix, though each participant should be encouraged to formulate **their own** personal invocation now to the elements)*
Elemental Chant: *"Air I am…fire I am, water, earth and spirit I am.."*

Intent spoken: *We have gathered today for the purpose of dedicating ourselves to the Goddess and to this Sisterhood….*

Priestess Invocation (light Goddess Altar Candle)
Great Goddess; Gaia, Aradia, Hekate, Oya,
Aphrodite, Artemis and a multitude of many more.
She of Ten Thousand Names revered since the beginning of time,
We call you, we lovingly invoke you to our sacred rites.
As we dedicate ourselves to our Sisterhood
and the Feminine Divine. *(light first candle)*

In the name of Themis, Skadi, Athena and Maat,
Bear witness to our vows and sacred rites
We call you Goddess as we link with you tonight. *(light second candle)*

We, your daughters come before you on this day__(date)__
Come- Lend us your wisdom,
your strength, your beauty and power…
We invoke you and call you on this holy hour,
to bear witness to this sacred rite,
as we dedicate ourselves to each other,
this group, further learning, to our craft and to you..
*Dear Goddess, Welcome and blessed be,
All Hails with Gratitude, Bless your daughters and Priestesses!
So mote it be!!!   **Wommin repeat:** *"So mote it be" (light third candle)*
**was facing altar now turn face them*
Participant all together recite **Charge of the Goddess**

Priestess will Declare
This rite formalizes our intent to work together as <u>"Grove of the Feminine Divine"</u>
as we follow the path of the Goddess and the Sacred Feminine and practice our craft to the best of our abilities. We state our intention to work together by our free will, in perfect love and perfect trust, for betterment of all…Are we all here so agreed?

All say: **We are**
(Signature with our witchname are collected on ritual parchment paper as candles are given in exchange.)

The Working: *Instructions are given to inscribe name on candle and anoint the candle all the while quietly visualizing yourself on this new path. When all are done begin spirited singing...*
Chanting: "*...Do you remember when God was a woman...*"

*Now priestesses, one by one, will approach the altar candle and incense stick to light their individual candles from it....Each womyn will light her candle from the center Goddess candle and state aloud **her personal dedication piece**. Each participant should have a few words prepared (personal invocation is fine) about their own hopes and vision as a newly dedicated priestess to this sisterhood.*
All support by saying: **So Mote it be!!!**

When candle are lit....

Together Recite Agreement created*
We are dedicants of the ancient, immortal Goddess
Worshipped since the beginning of time.
Seeking to work magick with her divine energy
Seeking higher knowledge and spiritual growth.
Tapping into our inherited Goddess given rights
And tapping into our own personal Womyn Power.
(each womyn will snip a piece of her hair to add to the Group's Cauldron as this is being recited)

From this moment on
We will not walk alone,
From this moment on
we will learn and grow.

Practicing our craft,
together we will worship
Build community
Rejoicing in the Divine
Celebrating ourselves as reflections of her light.

We vow to work from this day forward
in perfect love and perfect trust
According to the free will of all
and for the greater good.

Love is the law and the law is the bond.
In the name of the Goddess
and the Feminine Divine, we make it so...
With vows to thee
We are her Priestess,
So mote it be...!!!

Chant: "*We all come from the Goddess*"
Allow for a moment of silence, then begin humming and raising the Cone of power as our tone leads to an open mouth call to her, "Ma" and then ground this and begin to devoke.

Devoking Goddess
Great Goddess... We thank you for your presence in this special ritual of dedication to you. May your magick continue to guide and protect us, when we are together and when we are apart.
Hail and farewell!!!

Devoking Quarters
Sacred Earth, the transformer, manifesting the fertile creatress, We thank you for guarding our sacred space. As ye arrived in peace, depart in peace. **Hail and Farewell Earth.**

Sacred Water, the flow of balance and harmony in our expression, We thank you for guarding our sacred space. As ye arrived in peace, depart in peace. **Hail and Farewell Water.**

Sacred Fire, truth seeker, the drive and passion, We thank you for guarding our sacred space. As ye arrived in peace, depart in peace. **Hail and Farewell Fire.**

Sacred Air, wisdom and insight, divine vision and the gift of the mind, We thank you for guarding our sacred space. As ye arrived in peace, depart in peace. **Hail and Farewell Air**.

Open Circle, holding hands...
"...From hand to hand I open this space",
Chant:*"The circle is open but never unbroken... merry meet merry part and merry meet again"*

A short Blessing on the **Cakes & Ales** before distribution of moon cakes. As we are passing it, eating the food, we can go around make announcements or share anything we'd like to...

Final Thoughts: *Wommin are encouraged to create a more private moment for themselves at the communal altar if they wish to continue their working... The collection of hair offering will be kept in a Green or silver felt placket, which will be present for each and every sabbat, esbat and Goddess gathering to represent our Sisterhood. As more wommin join the group you may establish this Dedication ritually annually.*

ANONYMOUS END OF THE YEAR QUESTIONAIRE FOR GROVE OF THE FEMININE DIVINE

1. What areas in ")O(Craft" do you feel most competent in?
(examples But not limited; herbs, gemstones, spells, aromatherapy/oils, ritual wk, evocations, kitchen magick, sex-magick, warding, hexing, auras and chakras, candle magick, scrying, trance and visualizations, totem works, oracles, bard, dance and movement etc...)

_____

2. What subject (s) in the ")O(Craft" are you most curious to learn more about?
(See previous question for ideas...)

_____

3. If given One wish in the world, to be used for yourself, what would it be?

_____

_____

4. Name your three pet peeves or annoying characteristics about people....

_____

_____

_____

5. What would make this particular Group most appealing to you? What would you really like to see here?

_____

_____

_____

6. Name a Goddess you have worked with_____ and a Goddess or a spiritual practice, you know absolutely nothing about, but would like to?

_____

_____

7. Ask a question or a request of your Grove Systers, here, anonymously:

_____

_____

_____

Ways of Connecting to Divine

When we first encounter the Goddess and Feminine spirituality we open ourselves up to all types of new, unique experiences. It is not unusual to also unearth many strong emotions and spiritual callings; some very subtle, but others very startling and life altering.

The appearance of a particular Goddess might pierce through your realm, making herself known in your life through dreams, whispers, images, strange coincidences and even via friends and perfect strangers. Ordinary people and even animals might be among the numerous spiritual vehicles utilize by spirit, to get you to take notice of "Her" Divine call. If you find yourself being called to one particular deity or if you develop a persistent curiosity about a particular Goddess heed this as a sign to connect. Below are some suggestions on the various ways to link ourselves to Goddess, establish a positive respectful relationship to the Divine Feminine and connect even further to the particular Goddess tugging at your soul. Partaking in some of these suggestions will also facilitated easier connection for aspecting the Goddess, if you wish, in Sacred Rituals.

Prayer
A simple prayer or supplication, as has been practiced by all religions since the beginning of time, can begin to open up the channels of communications between you and spirit. Simply carve out a moment to speak in whispers or aloud about your intentions and believe that indeed you are being heard.

Imagery, Visual, Art
Acquire an image of the Goddess calling you and spend some time reflecting on her image and nuances. Allow yourself to even scry and trance while gazing deeply upon "Her." How does it speak to you? What is the message "She" is trying to convey to you personally? Does the image match with the message? In time you might want to keep your eyes open for anything that remind you of "Her" and maybe even acquire a sculpted statue. You can also handcraft one yourself and see how this, by its very nature, links you even further to her energy.

Meditation
Trance and Meditation, either experienced within a group or on your own, via a pre-recorded soundtrack or even by reading a script, can also begin to open up your consciousness. Be mindful of what transpires and document your experience (s).

Prose, Words stated, Invocations
After spending sometime meditating and in communion with the Divine you might feel inspire to pen a Prose or an Invocation to the "Her" as an offering, commitment or a pact of your union with "Her".

Historical Context/Cultural knowledge
It goes without saying, that learning as much as you can about the deity that is calling on you, is one of the first things you should engage in. Although some ancient deities have fragmented historical research, limited scholarly information and sometimes even conflicting stories, it is a good starting point for the new devotee. I would also suggest opening yourself up to any new, sometimes unorthodox, information spirit wants you to further look into, as a way to connect further into her Divine essence.

Sound, Music, Song, Melody creations and Rhythm
Music is another highly sacred language that can, not only reveal a lot about our deity, but keep us entranced and connected to her energy. Every Culture has its distinct sound; melodies, rhythms and favorable chosen musical instrument. We have a lot of historical information on the Goddess because of music, songs and prose, written in her honor and as special offerings to her in ancient times. Creating your own personal song in devotion to the Goddess is a wonderful, most cherished reflection, to honor her and even today it is well appreciated by Goddess. It will link and endear you to her, in much the same way as it did in Ancient times.

Culinary Foods/ Offering
What is "She" known for liking? Does "She" have a particular favorite meal, or fruit or vegetable, or a culinary preference with her offerings. Does her documented mythologies reveal a preference in food? As a devotee it will only behoove you to familiarize yourself with her taste in everything, including food and food can be used, not only as an offering but also to connect you even closer to a particular Goddess.

Language
Learning her native tongue or at least a few significant words in her language will endear you to her as well, in the same way that we are endeared and connected to someone upon learning they can speak our language, when we are traveling abroad.

Clothing Attire, Physical Body and Her Attributes
How does "She" appear to you? What is "She" wearing, when she comes to you in dreams and during meditations? In her mythologies, what did she often elect to wear? Consider if you can, what that felt like and how it directly affects her duties. If you can, acquire or sew an outfit that is similar to help you identify with this Goddess, even further. Consider what Her known attributes are and her distinct physical appearance, as they will help create a clearer image of "Her."

Activities beloved by that Deity
Familiarizing yourself with the activities your Goddess is known to love to partake in, can add another dimension to your sacred relationship. If your Goddess is a runner and likes to hunt in the forest, or if she loves swimming and lounging in the Oceans, or if she is known as an ecstatic dancer, taking an interest in her activities will open a better understanding of this deity and bond you to her, in the same way it so often bonds people into close relationships. Learning that she delights in growing a harvest, or surrounding herself with animals or that she is one who loves climbing mountaintops; all of these activities are a gateway to enhance your relationship with Goddess and further help your connection to "Her".

Totem/Animal
Sometimes Goddesses are known to have a strong affiliation with an animal and unearthing this connection will lead you to much valuable, hidden wisdom. Make every effort to connect with this sacred animal and they will reflect another important, yet often overlooked, aspect of "Her" essence.

Finally, I would encourage you to create a special journal, or utilize your Book of shadows, to document these thought-provoking findings and unique experiences with Goddess.

Blessings on your journey to "Her."

PERSONAL THOUGHTS ON ASPECTING

I have been a Wiccan for a number of years, both as a solitary and practicing within various open groups. At times, when preparing for rituals I have incorporated a technique called "Aspecting." Recently, I was asked to share my thoughts and personal experiences with this technique and here in this article I will attempt to do just that.

Aspecting is often a term used to describe when a priestess opens herself up to channeling a Goddess or an attribute of the Divine, in an effort to truly embody the Goddess, in physical form and present her living, breathing essence, into a ritual. When a woman avails herself to the art of aspecting, she is essentially invoking and calling into herself the Goddess. She is allowing herself to be a vessel for that Divine energy to enter and manifest itself, for all to witness in a ritual, through her speech, sight, action and movement, all via the body of the Priestess.

For me, aspecting is the Goddess bringing me even closer to her and her divine message and energy.... And it evolves quite naturally over the course of some time and with patience.

After spending some cerebral time learning about a particular Goddess academically, I will come to a point where I might crave to know her more intimately through my senses and this need becomes urgent if I am preparing for an upcoming sabbat or presentation. In my pursuit to invoke her, I will spend time meditating on the specific deity; reciting her name as a mantra, writing poetry and reciting prose as offerings to her. In my own personal practice I would set up a special altar for the Goddess and incorporate things that would personally endear her to me. Daily I will visit this altar and call her into me, and communicate with the Divine, night and day, the way a lover slowly but surely bonds with her target of affection. Daily the bond grows stronger until eventually the Divine feels ready to take me deeper and bring me even closer to her. And I begin to feel the tug and pull, and the surge, like that of being in the ebb and flow of "Her" waters. Slowly I float to the back and she floats to the front and She is welcomed into me and I allow this exchange. I surrender to this dance trusting her, as she is entrusting me with her essence.

When I am aspecting, I can feel the Goddess through my very pores, I do not entirely disappear, but it feels as if I am the background, the shadow, while She -the Goddess -becomes the foreground and we temporarily switch from our usual roles. The Goddess therefore becomes a forward manifestation. I am still there, but She is the dominant one before me and in this position she becomes living, breathing borrowing my physical form, while at the same time, allowing me to touch her essence and feel who she truly is, to the bone.

Some strange phenomenons happen when I am aspecting and I am not always aware of all of them at the moment that they are happening but I am enlightened by other's observations and by my own hands. For example; My art work and my journal writing will reveal the most obvious points of when I am aspecting. My penmanship changes, the language that I customarily will use changes to reflect the Divine's voice. My brush strokes and the subjects of my art, changes -reflecting her taste. Months later I'll find myself studying one of my old canvases and come to the surprising realization that, "oh..., it wasn't genuinely me creating that , where did that come from?" or "how and why did I paint that???.." It might seem sort of Sybil-like, but it's the only way I can explain the concept of aspecting for the Goddess.

Another phenomenon as a result of aspecting involves my body more intimately. For example; Sex, by other's account, might appear as if I've become more insatiable if I have been working with a Sex-Love Goddess like Aphrodite, Hathor or Pele. On the contrary, I can start to appear quite frigid and chaste if I am working with a Virginal Goddess like Athena or Hestia. When working with Artemis, I had a great need to be in the company of many women (my sisters) and I had a strong repulsion towards the male species, although they are quite normally the object of my affection. I also tend to be very defensive over my privacy, children and vigilant over women's rights, according to my journal writings. When aspecting Nike, I felt very competitive and became obsessed with lifting weights. Don't know if it was Nike or some kind of Amazonian Goddess, but my body became my temple , very sculpted, defined and running like a charioteer became a passion. A while back, I would crochet obsessively, non-stop, for hours on end. All day long without any breaks, I was fanatical with my crocheting projects. I literally felt like my hands were possessed during that time. My portfolio now reflects the wonderful accomplishment manifested through Brigit's hands and now I have a collection of knitwear and a whole large wardrobe completed via my crocheting. Thanks to the Celtic Goddess Brigit, I also took up jewelry making and tapped into the bard, writing many poems. When working with Saraswati I had a similar obsession with artistic expression; singing, painting circular works, writing and drinking lots of herbal infusions. Working with Athena I felt the pressure of her plate against my chest and a strange obsession for all things steel metal-like and this strong urgency to teach. I also felt very comfortable in the company of men like they were all, unquestionably my brothers. Judging from my writing, I appeared less emotional and more cerebral. According to family and those I share a home with, Demeter softens me and it is clearly a departure from my normal self. With her I cook more, living in the kitchen and garden and feeding everyone that comes along my way, like a Greek matriarch. I even found myself mothering strangers and of course, animals. I'd find myself weepy and indisputably my journal writings revealed a softer, more compassionate, emotional side. These are just some examples and personal notes from my own experiences aspecting the Divine, as I usually will chose to live with her for as long as she will have me. It could be a week, a month or just a few days but when I am ready to come back into my own I approach my home altar and with a small prepared ritual, I thank the Goddess and release the energy back. Sometimes it may take me a few days or so, to get fully grounded and back into my body, but I do eventually return to myself.

In the midst of sacred rituals, if I am aspecting I can feel my tongue and the formation of my words change and I can hear the timber of my voice alter. My stance and the way my body moves, also changes, as she takes over to make her presence known to the group and then she delivers her message and moves me through the ritual as she sees fit and all along I surrender...... surrender to her essence.

I am not an advocate of spontaneous Aspecting, as I feel this can be very tricky and rather dangerous to a novice. And in my humble opinion, I feel it's very important for a priestess to know how to shield, protect and ground oneself and block an unwelcome aspecting from occurring. There is quite obviously an intimate dance and relationship that you are undergoing when you are aspecting and needless to say, a great deal of trust necessary from both, you and the Divine. After all, you are lending out your physical form while she is lending out her essence and immortal spirit. And this is to be done with reverence and wisdom. Ideally you should not allow forces or Deities, to enter your sphere without your invite or consent. It is rather intrusive and for me, almost a violation to my well-being. Covering your crown chakra and holding on to some type of anchor like a talisman or a mantra repeated in your head, can help you stay grounded and avoid spontaneous aspecting. As you will soon learn, some Deities are easier to tap into while others are not and its important to remember to approach this practice with reverence.

In my experience, some Goddesses do not want to be aspected or contained, while others take great pleasure and reward your devotion with their presence. For safety reasons and for my own well-being there are some Deities I just wouldn't recommend aspecting, but that is simply a matter of personal choice and others might feel differently.

The skills and the wisdom that results from aspecting have been monumental for me and unquestionably enlightening. It takes patience and great desire to commune with Goddess in this way but the rewards are well worth it and your spiritual journey and rituals will benefit greatly. Happy aspecting!!!!

Things to consider when planning a Group Ritual

    I have been a Pagan most of my life and have attended numerous open sabbat celebrations and events of various sects. More recently I have been on the path of the Priestess, and as a result, my intuition and my inner third eye seems to have undergone a monumental rebirth and awakening, as I am seeing things I probably would've never noticed in years passed. These days when I attend open rituals and events, I am experiencing everything on a heighten sensitive, awareness level and from a very different sharpened perspective than I ever had before. When I am present at any Pagan event, I have one foot in as a participant, while the other is the critical Priestess eye, surveying the energy, noting what works and the things that don't for a group in worship and fellowship. Recently a series of, for lack of a better word, "wonky" rituals and Wiccan gatherings left me to ponder some important realizations.

    The most notable realization is that, the endings of rituals are just as important, if not more, than the middle and beginnings of these special events. Isn't that also the case with life in general?... How you leave this Earth is just as monumental as how you entered this life. Our last year at any learning institution has much more weight upon our graduation than those initial distant, awkward freshman years. And think about that timid introduction to a new partnership and the crucial ending of a first date which determines if another one is in the horizon. Yes, endings, in all areas of our lives are not to be underestimated. They connect and close the cycles in our world and since, in Wicca, we are very much aware of the cycles of life, death and rebirth, shouldn't we approach Ritual planning with this same reverence to cycles?

    Often when we plan a ritual we know what and or who we are honoring; specifying deities, sabbat holidays, or commemorating a special event. For the most part, this will lead into the core of your ritual and some type of activity, for example; candle magick, chanting, movement, oracular or meditation/trance work, to name just a few. In keeping with the traditional structure of Wiccan rituals we give thought to how we will cast a circle to delineate our sacred space. We give some thoughts to the guardians of that sacred space, by preparing to call the Elements. These can quite often be elaborately beautiful and often much thought is put into these two important components of a ritual's inception. However, devoking the Guardians, opening the circle and fusing the energy towards the end of a ritual is that important, yet often neglected threshold moment, that begins to brings us back to our point of origin and thus helps us complete the sacred cycle in our ritual. It brings our journey to a close. They call it "Grounding" but I'd like to call it, *"returning to source-bringing them back to where they started."*

    I would like to propose that when planning a group ritual more thought should be given to all aspects from beginning to end, but especially that delicate threshold towards the end. After all, as Priestesses we are the management of the Divine's energy, and we are entrusted to provide a powerful, transformational experience to those in attendance. In addition to a safe sacred space, we are to lead them through an internal journey that begins on the exterior, swells down the winding roads of the inner landscape and returns them (yes), return them carefully back to the exterior physical world, where it all started. It is not work to be taken lightly! It is a significantly, huge responsibility to accept the role of Priestess and I don't say this with arrogance or hierarchical grandiose belief, but rather with great responsibility, concern for attendees, and reverence for the Divine.

    I have attended group Rituals that were labeled "organic" when in fact they were dangerously chaotic and disorganized. I have witnessed the devastating melt downs of naïve innocent participants who, trusting for the best, were led and then abandoned metaphorically in the mist of poorly thought out rituals. I have watched, as so called leaders of groups have purposely manipulated energies and emotions from participants for their own disorganized, unmapped out rituals. I have literally seen energies being raised and then left to hang like a big smog over a group, with its leaders ill prepared to follow through and bring it to a close...grounding that energy. I have heard participants (including myself) wonder aloud the purpose of certain activities within a ritual, asking themselves afterwards, *"...what was **that** all about?"* And sadly, I have been in the presence of disoriented, (sobbing uncontrollably), participants after rituals. Sobbing is acceptable. Okay... *uncontrollably sobbing?* and clearly in grave distress?... not so much, in my humblest opinion.

    As a Priestess you are responsible for the beginning and ending of the journey but it's not a one way trip. That's for the participant to decide personally on their own. Our role as Priestesses is to take them on a spiritual journey, as their tourist guide, point out relevant sites and experiences (Ones that hopefully, when they feel called upon, will be revisited) and then bring them back to where they started. I mean, imagine if I convinced you to take an exciting trip with me to Mexico and you joined me in total trust, never having been there. In our drive, I point out all of these beautiful landmarks in this foreign country. We stop off at the edge of a cliff to admire the view. You are taking it all in, but then all of a sudden, I disappear and now you are left to figure out how to get out of this paradise or hell (that you were introduced to) all on your own. Gosh, I don't know about you, but that would be a nightmare!!! Nightmarish too, if there was no preparation for that pivotal moment. It would also unquestionably, negatively change and tamper my initial exciting experiences from the onset of this journey. Not to mention the obvious physical dangers when we fail to fully ground after an intense mind altering ritual.

    For me, I strongly believe that special thought needs to be given to what you want participants to leave with and performing experimental freeform rituals, just for the sake of variety is irresponsible, if done without these considerations. Acknowledging that the Divine always has the last word and our hopes and plans might need to be adjusted as we go along - our intention should be clear from beginning, to the middle, all the way to the end and even after. Connecting with each participant to make sure they are okay afterwards is crucial and making yourself available to them is part of a Priestess' duty. Sharing a meal, snack or simply talking, can help in the grounding process but also some type of physical contact can do wonders for bringing us back into our bodies and the Earthly plane. As a Priestess, consider how do you want them to feel weeks later? What kind of recollection do you want them to have of this day? How do you want them to remember this ritual?. Knowing of course, that we don't control what other's feel or their perspective, but taking full responsibility for setting the tray of an array of positive emotions and memories you want them to leave with. This is our role as Priestesses, offering ourselves as midwives in the whole, spiritual journey that rituals so often inaugurates.

PRIESTESS INVOCATION
Great Goddess; Gaia, Aradia, Hekate, Oya,
Aphrodite, Artemis and a multitude of many more.
She of Ten Thousand Names
Revered since the beginning of time,
We lovingly invoke you, to open portal doors.

As we dedicate ourselves
In this sacred rite
To our Sisterhood
And the great Feminine Divine.

In the name of Themis, Ma'at,
Athena, Skadi,
Bear witness to our vows
As we honor thee.

We call you Goddess
As we link with you tonight.
Receive us as your daughters
And Bless our sacred Rites.

Lend us your strength,
Awaken us from within
Unearth the powers
Of our Strega lineage.

In the forest, in the breeze,
In the oceans and the fields,
Through her celestial elements,
It is the way we Hex and Heal.

It is the way
of our ancient clan
and tonight we connect
with her immortal hands.

Bear witness to this rite,
As we dedicate ourselves to thee
Hail to the Primordial One,
As we chant, So mote it be!!!!

GROUP DEDICATION RECITE TOGETHER *
We are dedicants of the ancient, immortal Goddess
Worshipped since the beginning of time.
Seeking to work magick with her divine energy
Seeking higher knowledge and spiritual growth.
Tapping into our inherited Goddess given rights
And tapping into our own personal Womyn Power.

From this moment on
We will not walk alone,
From this moment on
we will learn and grow.

Practicing our craft,
together we will worship,
Build community
Rejoicing in the Divine
Celebrating ourselves as reflections of her light.

We vow to work from this day forward
in perfect love and perfect trust,
According to the free will of all
and for the greater good.

Love is the law and the law is the bond.
In the name of the Goddess
and the Feminine Divine, we make it so...
With vows to thee
We are her Priestess, So mote it be...!!!

CIRCLE CASTING PROSE
From earth to sky and elements around
keep safe this circle and all here on ground
Container, preserver this circle shall be,
And only allow good energy.
Through portals of light we bless this task
by will and by word
This Circle is now cast.....

PRIESTESS INVOCATION

Here do I stand,
Dear Ancestors, Spirits, Deities of old,
Goddess and the great Feminine Divine...
Here do I stand to take up thy work,
to dedicate myself to you, now as always.
In this ritual, I dedicate myself as your Divine daughter,
always in thy service,
in the role of Priestess of the Goddess,
teaching womyn your sacred mysteries,
as they are revealed to me,
and sharing with them the expansive love,
that you've imbued in me, for magick, the craft
and the Goddess, the Sacred Feminine.
I dedicate myself to the advancement,
enrichment and fulfillment of this
newly formed Goddess study group called:

_____*(Light your second candle)*

I do so dedicate myself to being Priestess to this coven group of Womyn
and I ask that you bless my role and journey
in the sacred name of Aradia, Hekate & Artemis,
I ask that you help me attract the right members for this group.
I ask that you present, good honest sincere, positive wommin,
that will fit into our newly formed coven family,
...for it is indeed a family I'm birthing here,
in the sacred name of Gaia, Athena, Oya and Brid,
I ask that there will be loyalty,
enthusiasm, harmony and
effortless commitment from all members.
Bless, guide and protect herein this Goddess group (*)
that it may flourish and strive,
with success and become an anchor
in the greater community of
Feminist Pagans -Dianics -Wiccans.
This I make true, by the law of three
and in the name of the Goddess,
these things or better, So mote it be!!!

PRIESTESS DEDICATION PROSE
Great Goddess as in ancient times,
Immortal ones,
Come as invoked here today.
We, your Daughters seek to know you,
To embrace you from within.

Awaken now our slumbered parts,
Those yet to be enlightened,
And let your love, light the dark corners,
So that they will be hidden no more.

Come sacred Maiden, Mother and Crone
Come Creatrix, life giver and keeper of Bones
Come Virgin, Amazon and Sacred whore
Come now as in ancient times before.

Come brightest star and darkest Moon
By air, by fire and earth's eternal tomb
By watery gifts found in our womb
Come Goddess we seek to worship you!!!

Lend us your wisdom, Your strength,
Your beauty and power...
We invoke you Dearest Goddess,
On this Sacred Hour.

We dedicate ourselves
To this ancient path,
Working as a sisterhood
Practicing our Craft.

We invoke you and call you,
To bear witness to our rite,
Hail and Welcome Goddess
On this Lunar Night...

GROVE GODDESS GATHERING CHANTS

DO YOU REMEMBER
Do you remember, When God was a woman she had many, many names. (2X)
They called her Isis, Astarte, Diana, Hecate, Demeter, Kali, Innana.... *repeat*

EARTH, MOON, MAGICK by B.M.M.
In the Earth, deep within,
There is A Magick, I draw it in.
      In her Caves, in the Trees
      Hear her Heartbeat, Pulsing thru me.
When I Rise, I feel her Love
With feet Grounded, I'm soaring high above,
      In the Earth, deep within,
      There is A Magick, I draw it in
Ancient Moon, my Soul reveres
With my Singing, I call you here.
      When this flame, ignites tonight,
      Priestess dancing, Under the moonlit night....
In the Earth, deep within,
There is A Magick, I draw it in.... There is A Magick, I draw it in }3x

LISTEN TO MY HEART SONG
Listen, Listen, Listen to my heart Song
Listen, Listen, Listen to my heart Song
I will never forget you
I will never forsake you
I will never forget you,
I will never Forsake you ..... *by Susun Weed*

(CREATING A CIRCLE) WE ARE A CIRCLE by Rick Hamouris
We are a Circle, within a Circle, with no Beginning and never ending....
You hear us Sing, You hear us Cry,
Now hear us Call you, Spirits of Earth and Sky
Within our Hearts, there goes a spark
Love and Desire, a burning Fire...
      We are a Circle, within a Circle, with no Beginning and never ending...(chorus)

(FACING NORTH) MOTHER I FEEL YOU UNDER MY FEET
Mother I feel you under my feet, Mother I feel your Heart Beat 2X
Heya Heya Heya, Heya Heya Ho 2X
Mother I hear you in the Rivers Sound, Eternal Waters going on and on 2X
Heya heya heya heya heya ho 2X
Mother I see you in when the Eagles fly, Flight of the Spirit gonna take our time 2X
Heya Heya Heya, Heya Heya Ho By: Unknown source

(FACING EAST) ARAPAHO SONG
I circle around, I circle around, The boundaries of the Earth
I circle around, I circle around, The boundaries of the Earth
      Heyana Heyana, Heyana Heyana
Wearing my long wing feathers as I fly
Wearing my long winged feathers as I fly. *(repeat) by Arapaho Ghost Dance Song*

(FACING SOUTH) SPIRITS OF FIRE
Spirits of Fire come to us
we will kindle the Fire,
Spirits of Fire come to us
we will kindle the Fire,
We will kindle the Fire
dance the magic circle round
We will kindle the fire dance the circle around

(FACING WEST) SISTER RIVER- *From Victorian Christian's creation , Elijah The band of Light*
Sister, River, Giver...Returning Whole,Sister, River, Giver...Returning Whole
      Open up, To receive
      We are what we Believe. *(REPEAT)*
      Sister, River, Giver...Returning Whole,
      Sister, River, Giver...Returning Whole
Growing Roots like the Trees,
Wee are planting seeds. *(REPEAT)*
Sister, River, Giver...Returning Whole,, Sister, River, Giver...Returning Whole,
      Stored in Deep, Stories Sleep,
      Within Us, These Tales we Keep. *(REPEAT)*
      Sister, River, Giver...Returning Whole,
Sister, River, Giver...Returning Whole....

CHAPTER TWENTY-SEVEN

Anahata Priestess Connection

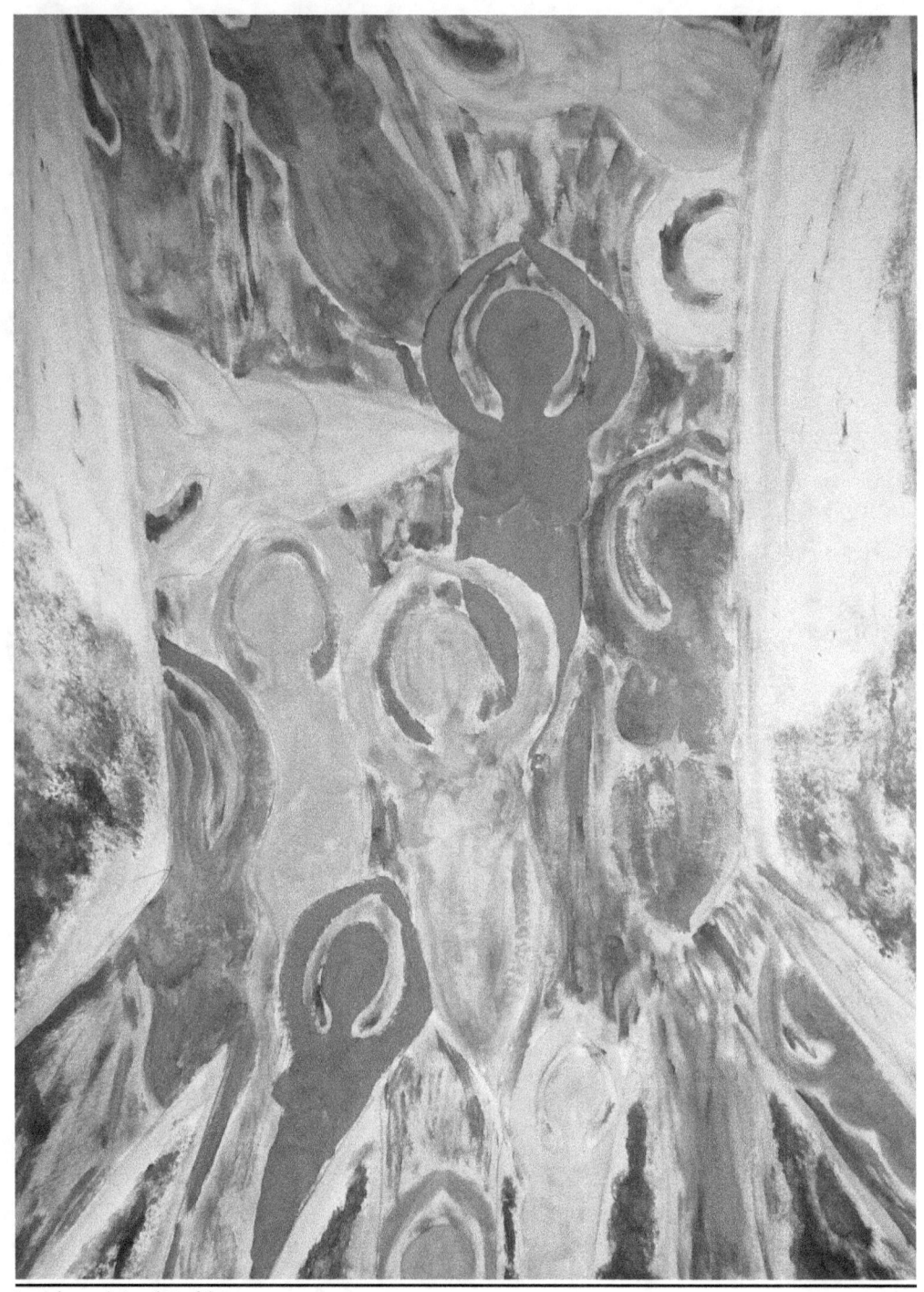
Growing the spirit of Goddess

"You have to leave the city of your comfort and go to the wilderness of your intuition, what you will discover will be wonderful...What you will discover is your true self..." *Alan Alda*

Helpful Tips and Observations When Gathering

Transparency and Clear Goals
One of the most important component when first preparing for a group gathering is having a clearly defined goal and purpose for the day. After all, wommin are carving out a precious moment from their extremely busy lives for fellowship and placing much faith in you, that it will be worthwhile. Reward them for their efforts to be present by, at the very least, having a concise objective for the day. Speak aloud what the purpose of this gathering is so that everyone's conscious, focus and intent can help contribute to its very own manifestation. In being transparent and open, it allows all participant to be on the same page, present and actively contributing to our mutual goal; namely and quite often, to connect with a particular deity, the seasonal sabbat and form sacred community.

Intimacy and Immediate Connection
In gatherings, it's to be expected that not everyone will know one another. In fact, you will have a larger percentage of the people attending being complete strangers, perhaps with vastly different personalities and lifestyle. Still, it is our similarities and common goal, to connect with the Divine, that becomes what we should ultimately hone into, as facilitators. The awkwardness of standing in a room full people you don't know can be daunting, both as a participant and as a facilitator and yet the kind of work and journey we are endeavoring to embark on together, at a Goddess gathering, is saturated and nursed in the arms of intimacy. Needless to say, it is incumbent on us to take on the challenge of building intimacy rather quickly in any group gathering. Many of the techniques below will aid in its ultimate fruition.

Removal of Barriers, Coziness and intimacy
Never underestimate the magickal effects of physical proximity and its ability to break (both, conscious and unconscious) psychological, emotional and physical barriers. Large rooms can be deathly cold, sterile and rather stalwart, inhospitable to intimacy. I have attended gatherings in large fancy rooms that made my jaw dropped in awe at their initial beauty but after and through-out the day-feeling cold, alone and uncomfortable, unsure if I even connected with anyone. On the contrary, I have attended gatherings in tiny closet like spaces, that initially made me cringe and worry if there was even enough room for all, and yet quite surprisingly, found myself feeling the warmth of kinship, love and yes....immediate intimacy, among those who were strangers just hours beforehand. The important lesson here is to prepare and plan accordingly. As we can't always elect the size of our gathering place, but we can be mindful of the potential pitfalls and how to make them work in the most positive way. In large rooms, I try to invite participants to stand or sit closer together and it invariably always forms a tight knit comfortable circle. The result? People soon find themselves at arms left, ready to receive or give a hug as needed and their initial reservations begins to slowly wane as the seeds of intimacy root themselves.

Atmosphere
Entering into an altered state of being, for some, can be more challenging than for others and while I like to think of the sacred permeating everything around us (including the mundane) I know that it helps when my environment supports and reflect images of the Divine. It is precisely why I take great care in decorating and altering the mundane environment to reflect "Her" Holy temple. To encourage and help shift wommin's consciousness as they enter the space of a Goddess gathering, I suggest bringing into the room many images from nature, statuaries, silken fabrics and tapestries. I also offer pillows, mats, rocks and crystals, lots of candles and incense and various colorful objects, like fruits and flowers to help set the tone of our day.

     Remember every time you gather you are erecting an ancient practice and a sacred sanctuary, and transcending the mundane by visually changing the space with appropriate Temple décor, will help participants tune out the stressful mundane and tune into the sacred.

Windows of Our Soul
In our fast paced, technologically driven world, we are sacrificing something of utmost importance and that is the power of human connection. Computerized customer service, online

shopping, take-out meals ordered through machines, cell-phones and emails ruling all forms of communications, computerized social network and so many other inventions that are meant to improve the quality of our lives and yet they divert us away from one of our most basic human need.... intimacy, human eye to eye connection.

I will say that personally this has always been a tough one for me to admit to, especially coming from New York City, where it appears in the mad rush and chaos of city life, no one ever looks at you. As a matter of fact, looking directly at someone for too long in the city is an invitation for trouble, so you grow up avoiding people's eyes and you learn from an early age not to invite trouble with your gaze.

However, I have discovered that there is something quite powerful and yes, magickal, about letting someone gaze deeply into your eyes and you in turn, doing the same. It is inherently vulnerable and yet, it the course and path of intimacy, one not traveled upon often enough in our so called "advanced" modern day society.

In our effort to create immediate intimacy within a group of wommin be sure to allow for a brief moment of connection through the eyes, for indeed, they are the windows to the Soul. When someone takes the time to look deeply into my own eyes, I feel affirmed as a human being. I feel recognized, supported, acknowledged and strangely...I feel valued, no longer just an invisible entity walking the earth in this carcass, but with the deep gaze upon me, I feel my soul is recognized, vouched by another fellow human being.... that is a powerful state of being and it births intimacy.

Loquacious, Garrulous, Chatty Gifts
There is no denying that as wommin one of our greatest gift is our ability to talk, empathize and gladly share everything that is going on in our lives. When we, wommin, get together it is only natural to want to talk up a storm and it's quite a powerful phenomenon to stand back and witness the intensity of our chatter. With this in mind, it is crucial that you honor and make the space for such a wonderful expression of womynhood. For gatherings, I like to offer a speaking stick which allows for each womyn holding it to take her turn speaking and also allows for others to practice fully listening in the most respectful, meditative way-without censoring or interruption. As long as she is holding the speaking stick, she is expressing a need to be heard and thus the space to be heard is created and we circumvent the potential for chatter chaos.

I also suggest offering a sort of icebreaker question, at the onset of every gathering so that wommin can begin to get to know one another better by sharing something more precisely about themselves. Depending on the question, this can also help in creating bonds and immediate intimacy among participants.

Awakening and Engaging the Body in our Journey
Honoring our physical body is just as important as our spiritual and in our gatherings it's always good to engage our heart, mind, spirit and body. In our quest to spend our day in fellowship and connecting with the Divine it's good to incorporate some type of movement and acknowledgement of that which houses our soul- the sacred body. I suggest incorporating an activity like; breathing exercises, stretching, yoga, tai-chi, mudras, handicrafts, even belly dancing to name just a few effective ways to engage our body in a Goddess gatherings.

Silence is Golden
You have planned your day with lecture talks, many workshops and a flurry of activities and all seems to be going well, but unexpectedly, there might be one or two moments when the awkwardness of silence rears its less than ideal, ugly head, into your gathering. Instinctively, you want to fill this, seemingly empty space with sound, **please don't**. There is something significant about the ebb and flow of a group gathering and silence is a part of that sacred cycle, even on this microcosmic level. Moments of silence are almost mandatory when endeavoring to connect with the Divine. Embrace all the ingredients of group gatherings, including this undervalued component amidst our journey to Goddess.

Silence and stillness is not something many of us excel at in our fast paced world and quite often, might make us feel very uncomfortable, even reaching to fix or eradicate it, but this is precisely where we are to find that much needed water fountain that quenches our dry throat before going on to the next leg of our journey. This is indeed a special aspect of the Divine, it is in a sense, a threshold. Between the talks, prayers, laughter, activities and chatter of wommin there will be some moments of silence… trust, that like all cycles, it will come and go and like all stages in our journey, it deserves our utmost respect and reverence. Allow silence to come and go as it pleases through out the day, sharing its gem of invaluable wisdom for all in the group to personally experience, for indeed silence is golden.

The Five Senses Must Always be Engaged in Any Group Gathering

The sense of touch, taste, sight, smell, and hearing, when honored and incorporated into our day, can truly have a most powerful effect and contribute greatly to a wonderful memorable Goddess gathering.

With the varying, sweet scents of burning incense and smudge bundles you can incorporate the sense of **smell.** Also living flower arrangements, herbs and scented oils can help connect us by way of our nose. Be sure to inquire if anyone has an aversion or allergies to any particular scents.

The sense of **taste** is incorporated rather easily with the inevitable tasty potluck held at the end of a ritual, cakes and ales or in a buffet, set out to be enjoyed throughout the day. Also, as part of our ritual, there are a number of food offerings like; honey, dark chocolate, fruits, water and or wine offerings that connect us by way of our taste buds.

The sense of **hearing** is activated with the appropriate, well thought out sequence of music, whether it is music offered on a CD sound track or music offered in a chant workshops at the beginning of our day together. When gathering, our sense of hearing should be actively scintillated with an assortment of pleasing sounds and that includes; the sound of our chatter and laughter, the sounds of drums and bells, the sound of a beautifully executed invocation to the Goddess, the sound of silence and meditations, the sound our beautiful voices weaving in and out fluidly and all coming together in **"Her"** honor.

Engaging the sense of **sight** with a feast of beautiful imagery that correlates to the Deity and season we are respectfully honoring, is quite easy to do and yet undervalued. While some in Wicca prefer to work without tools and eschew the use of elaborate paraphernalia and fancy accoutrements, I quite like to greatly engorge and arouse this sense the most.

With colorful ornate altar cloths (one or two) pedants and flags, Goddess sculptures or statues as representation of our beloved deities and various photographs and artwork, the sense of sight is engaged throughout our day and the images live on in wommin's mind, long after they have left the temple. Participants are encouraged to contribute to the visual feast by adding their own sacred tools and images, and the traditional tools of the trade like; our cauldron, athame, wands, flowers, bowls and chalices also grace our communal altar with their presence.

Lastly, the sense of **touch** is honored and incorporated with our various activities and handicraft creations. Yet most effective, the sense of touch is awaken, when the, scented anointing oil touches our skin, as we welcome one another into our sanctuary. It is also awaken when our hands join together as Sisters to cast the circle and when at the end of our day we embrace one another in the hopes that our exuberant, warm hugs will long last us, until we merry meet again.

Energy and the Art form of the Facilitator

One of the most important roles of a facilitator, besides disseminating important information on the Goddess, is managing and directing energy. In any given monthly, group gathering, you will find an array of different personalities, that come from all different walks of life and with various degrees of skills, regarding energy. Some womyn can be very quiet, low leveled energy, some can be, attention grabbers, very highly elevated, while still others, can drain and zap a room of vital energy within minutes. It's important, as a facilitator, to be aware of this and oversee the equal distribution of time and energy among ALL present in a group. That means if you sense someone is shy and not being heard, you need to make the way for them…a gentle platform for them, to get their needs met and be heard. If someone is rambunctiously being an obvious distraction, disrespectful or requiring an unusual amount attention, you'll need to divert it and find a way to shift the energy, gently, away from them, so that everyone in the group will feel more comfortable. If someone is standing distant, with their body language shielded and not saying much, you need to somehow pull them gently, energetically, into the orb of the group.

After a lecture or a certain group activity, sometimes one participant might display agitation and while another might even express fatigue, here too as a facilitator, you'll need to look for ways to neutralize, raise up the vibration in the room so that, the "one" person, doesn't bring everyone else spiraling down into that negative state of being. Spontaneous chanting or drumming might help, movement is also a great way to shake and shift the energy in a group, as is the act of simply addressing it to yourself and making your intention to remedy the situation.

When you stand as a facilitator, you have a vastly different perspective than as a participant and you have the wonderful advantage of looking out for the group's general well-being. Sort of like being in the driver's seat, redirecting energy when necessary will require you to be aware of energy at all times -your very own, the room's, nearby spirits and entities and the energy of all those around you.

Handling Trolls and Vampires Energy zappers and Manipulators

And speaking about energy, I need to briefly make note of the distasteful phenomenon of group trolls, vampires and troublemakers.

Occasionally, much to your surprise, you'll find yourself amidst one of these disruptive entities and perhaps (like I did) you'll ignore it, excuse it or simply try to dismiss it as just a figment of your imagination. **Don't!!!** These personalities are indeed real, and if left to go rampage, can cause a lot of unnecessary trouble within the group.

Be ever mindful of the power of energy and how easily manipulated it can be by maligned individuals; troll, vampires, sociopath and those with less than honorable intentions. Renowned and beloved witch, Z. Budapest, coined it as the *"Goddess of Discord,"* rest assure, there will invariably, always be someone who will, willingly, offer themselves in this nasty role, as the one who will attempt to throw off the balance and energy of the group. A lot of it has to do with power hungry, emotionally unbalanced individuals, who crave constant adoration and attention even at the unfortunate expense of everyone around them.

There are numerous books on the subject of psychic vampires, socio paths, malign people and trolls... how to recognize them, how to handle and banish them etc, etc... I will not go into these assorted, lengthy details here, for that is a book all unto itself, but I will strongly advocate being aware of them and taking necessary precautions when necessary.

If a regular participant in your group appears to balk, complain, whine and make more than your average negative comments, you might have a troll in your midst. If you have someone who appears to go out of their way to disagree with you publicly, appears indifferent to other's plight, gossips incessantly about many - be leery, this could be just the beginning tactics of a group troll. If you encounter a person in your group who appears to always have personal drama, takes every opportunity to voice their woes openly, often leaves early or arrives late - that might very well be a troll. If you meet a person that eagerly and often expresses an exorbitant amount of problems and yet when numerous solutions are offered by group members, they refuse to consider possible solutions, yes that just might be a troll, trying to monopolize the entire group's time and energy. Make a special note of how the energy of the room shifts when that particular person speaks aloud and note if you witness a low depressed or compressed drop in energy, a sort of sapping of vitality. If all of a sudden everyone around you begins to express melancholy, this is the pathetic work of a troll and psychic vampire in your midst. So what can you do, as a facilitator being subjected to this madness?

The first thing is to nip it in the bud as soon as you see it and this might require addressing the person in private, reminding them of our rules, group's modality and our efforts to look out for the group's best interest. In your conversation with them, make them aware of how they are coming across and ask if they are aware of this problem. If this doesn't help, the next step is to suggest that perhaps another group would suit them better and that they should not return. I would also suggest facilitators to follow this up with personal protection spells to shield themselves, the group as a whole, and its members. Early on, in the formation of Goddess gatherings, I strongly suggest crafting a spell to shield your temple's land, room and space from any and all troll, vampires or malign energy and, if necessary, adding a banishing spell, as both will lessen the likelihood of encountering one of these entities amidst your sacred Goddess group.

Extra curriculum activities and bonds
It is quite lovely when wommin start regularly attending these Goddess gatherings and begin connecting with one another on a more personal level. The bonds of true sisterhood and friendship begin to sprout even deeper when we start involving each other in our more private parts of our lives. Thus arranging for outside events, non- Goddess related, social get-togethers, at other times throughout the year, is perfectly natural and actually encouraged. As a facilitator I suggest having the occasional field trips scheduled like; visiting crystal shops, botanical gardens, bookstores, wine tasting, coffee shops, performances and variety shows, and natural trail hikes to name a few way to nurture stronger bonds with our Goddess systers.

Dependability, Reliability and Consistence
Just like when we begin any important courtship or relationship there is an initial period when we might not trust wholeheartedly and need reassurance that we're on the right track. Being present and available helps, but even more effective is being dependable, and every time you, as a leader, honor your commitment to host a Goddess gathering you are affirming this fact.

As a facilitator you might on occasion waver and question when and where to host gatherings. If the number of attendees unexpectedly fluctuates drastically, however, you might also get discouraged and carelessly even consider cancelling a date or two without much thought for its greater ramification. Let me, at this point, strongly advise against this choice of action.

People generally want to know and be assured that what they've invested their time and energy into, is going to stand the test of time and have longevity. Cancelling promised gatherings and or changing dates, place and time can be quite disturbing and deviates from the intimate, supportive, trustworthy and dependable group dynamic, you're trying to give birth to. To alternate these scheduled gatherings too often will promotes a feeling of insecurity and non-trustworthiness, so despite the occasional unexpected ebb and flow of attendance, you as a facilitator, must try to remain true and committed, if you expect wommin to do the same.

There are times when unforeseen circumstances prevent you from honoring your commitment, let it be obvious to the group the reasons why and do not under estimate the importance of making it up to them as well. Honoring the Divine and the Sisterhood is important work and missing it, just as hosting it, is not to be taken casually. Offering regular meetings at the same time each month as planned, reflects your true commitment to the group, its members and the Feminine Divine and you will find participants will soon eventually exemplify your model commitment.

CHECK-IN QUESTIONS TO HELP GROUP BONDING PROCESS

Share a pivotal point in your life when the Goddess called you, and you knew this was the spiritual path ordained for you?

Define for yourself what is a Priestess, a Witch, a Goddess Womyn?

What time of year (sabbats) do you most identify with?

If you could raise your magick wand and manifest anything, what would it be?

What kinds of spells have you performed successfully? Have you ever Hexed or asked someone else to do a special spell for you?

Do you recall dreams or use a dream journal? What was the weirdest or most vivid dream you've ever had?

What is your favorite color and why?

What do you personally feel happens when we die?
Do you talk to your ancestors or spirits that have passed?
In your next life how would you incarnate, if you had a choice? Do you believe in reincarnation?

What is your favorite form of oracular divination (rune, tarot, astrology etc...) and why?

What animals do you feel akin to? Do you work with Totem animals? Which have claimed you through-out the years?

What is your Zodiac -Sun Sign? And Moon sign? Which traits do you love most about your zodiac?

What deity(ies) are you dedicated/connected with?
What deity(ies) are you far removed from, fearful of or never expect to ever invoke?

If you could do anything what would it be? To the best of your recollection, what was your best age?

What is your favorite Witchcraft book and author?

Which archetype do you identify more; the Maiden, the Amazon, Mother, the Lover, the Magician, Queen or the Crone?

When you were nine years old, what did you hope to become?

How do you prefer to de-stress after a long day?

If you give birth to a Goddess what and who would she be the Goddess of?

What part of your body do you love the most? What part of your body do you like least?

Share something people are most surprised to learn about you.

What element (earth, air, fire, water) do you have an affinity to?
Do you work with Lunar energies and which phase of the Moon do you connect with best?

If you had only three things to take with you on a far removed island, what would they be?

In the Major Arcana of the Tarot card, which card speaks to you personally?

What vehicle (art, music, ritual, written words, prayers, sex, cooking etc...) helps you immediately touch Divine spirit?

What is your favorite scent? What smells repulses you?

When you meditate, where does your mind automatically take you to trance; a park, a mountain, the ocean, a cave, an old childhood home, where?

GODDESS GATHERING WORKSHOP SUGGESTIONS, Part I.

Amaterasu	Mirror work, scrying, mirror amulet in a beaded necklace, sushi creations
Athena	Shielded amulet, Warrior thinking cap creation, Crocheting, embroidery project, knot spell work, dream pillows, Grimoire creations and Blessings.
Skadi	Snow/Winter Magick, the Giant, our bodies, earth energy, wolf and other totems.
Nike	Chalice work, Head Laurel Wreath, medallion pendant creation
Brigit	Metal and glass creations, crocheting, bard creation, Candle making, carving, bread baking.
Oya	Sword work, Mask making creation, ancestral mini shrine, copper works
Pele	Root Chakra, Underwear painting, Volcanic mini altar creations, Black stone/lava rock artistic creation.
Artemis	Bow and Arrow work, Maiden Head Circlet, Forest Animal Totem work, amulet bag creation.
Aphrodite	Soap and lotion Making, scented Oil creation, Glamour casting, Bath and Love spells.
Ix Chel	Water works, Moon Amulet creations, Dragonfly protective pendant creation, painting our own rainbow art, Snake, Eagle and panther as a totem.
Hathor	Music work, Dance and movement (Belly Dancing), Cosmetic blessings, Scented oil creations, Sacred Altar Necklace, gemstones.
Baubo	Yoni Clay images, Painting our womb and power spot, red painting master piece, Vulva cut outs,
Saraswati	Water Works, Mantra works, Mudras, Mala Bead creations, Chakra work, Communal artistic creations, altar Cloth creations
Aine	Solar and Fire magick, Sun creations, fire energy, candle creations, candle charging and spell, Citrine and gemstone, hooded cloaks
Erzulie	Veve Art creations, Lingerie blessings, Scented oil creation, Cleansing Bath product creations, hearts crafting, mini shrines.
Gaia	Crystals and Gemstone works, plant magick, Fertility spells, mini Indoor herbal gardens, mortar and pestle working-Handmade incense creations, animal workings, baking.
Demeter	Herbal Plackets, poppets, Autumnal Blessings Wreaths, Broom making creations, Imbue dough creation, Baking the Goddess for ourselves to magickally ingest
Persephone	Two faced Mask creations, protective Beaded necklace, creations with pomegranate, veils, floral creation
Corn Mother	Corn Dollies and poppets, kitchen witchery; Baking and cooking with Corn, yellow cord weaving magick, home protective witch bottle.
Aradia	Spells and how they work, All components of magick, planetary hours and days, moon placement and color correspondence, ethics of magick and hexes, Witch Bottles, charms and candle magick.
Hekate	Oracular studies, Tarot reflections, Ancestral shrines, Gourd painting, pumpkin carving, lantern making, Trance and Astral travel discussion. Creation of Key craftings, Ritual Sacred Cape making.
Maman Brigitte	Skeletal, Bones magick, paper crafting Coffins, tombstones, candles, skull creations decorations, mask decorations, New Year's Hope Collages.
Hina	Moon amulets, rainbows, astrology exploring, travel altars, altar cloth, painting creations, coconut painting, Lei Creation.
Hestia	Hearth work, Scrying with Fire, homemade candle making, food as offerings
Living deity	Mask Creations, energy works, connecting with Goddess, choosing our magickal name

II. LIST OF CRAFT IDEAS FOR WORKSHOPS

*Herbal felt placket: Enchant a bowl of herbs communally and place in felt bag

*Seed Packets: Enchant the seed packet with what you wish to grow/manifest

*Tarot mystery in a Bag: Everyone picks a tarot card from a closed bag for divinatory purpose.

*Wreath creations various according to season; Place floral or other objects related to our ritual

*Decorate Plaster Goddess Statue pieces: bring them in and let them paint each statue

*Self Portrait or self-Photographs: Bring photo, place in cauldron, we enchant it, pass around

*Chocolate Goddess eating it to embody; Create and ingest her energy, enchant them, then we'll consume

*Rock Decorations; Paint or write a message on our rocks or a symbol, reminder of support

*Picking attributes Mystery in a bag; In a closed bag they will pick a paper or rock with a secret message

*Carving or Dressing a candle; Oil on our candles rubbing with our intent

*Floral Headbands; Glue flowers unto headbands

*Clay sculpting; Let the conscious take over to create a Goddess Symbol- ex; yoni pendant, moon or sun

*Enchanting our own body washing soap; Rub, imbue with intent like a candle

*Enchanting Notebook/Grimoire/journal; Place on Altar and enchant,
rubber stamp and seal within sacred circle .

*Breast Casting; Plaster of Paris strips do each other's Breast, Athena' shield

*Yoni Exaltation & admiration; Drawing or using clay to recreate our honorable spot

*Planting a seedling in a pot; Actually planting with intent

*Letter Writing to inner future self; Short writing within a sacred circle to remind us of our promises to our selves or a letter of gratitude.

*Creation of a Bio or Obituary. Begin writing it within a sacred circle after meditation

*Braiding and knot working weaving and spinning magick, crocheting a cord for a knot spell.

* Intuitive Hope Collages cutting and pasting images you are drawn to for an annual Hope collage.

* Blood Painting-using a little bit of our menstrual blood mixed with water or simply a deep red paint color, painting and abstract, intuit work of art on canvas. Reclaiming our Sacred Bloood mysteries.

*Baking a communal Bread imbued with positive intent

*Sewing a poppet or herbal placket container

*Altar cloth, mini travel altars, shrine box creation

* Utilizing natural materials like; sea shells, stones, bones, feathers, to create a special elemental amulet or a special altar mirror.

* ambitiously creating our own personal Oracle cards of 5-10 cards, hand painted or drawn.

* Ritual attire workshop; Creating special tunics, plaster elaborate masks, Gauzy faery wings and or traditional witches cape/cloak.

Below is a list of attributes associated with each quarter. It is just a short list of suggested images you can use when calling an element into your circle and ritual.

EAST AIR	SOUTH FIRE	WEST WATER	NORTH EARTH
Sword/Athame	Wand	Chalice	Salt
Feather	Candle	Water	Soil
Bells/Chimes	Hearth	Emotions	Plants
Birds	Lions	Swans	Snakes
Eagles	Dragons	Fishes	Rocks
Breath	Rubbing Hands	Body Fluids	Flowers
Panting	Heart	Tears	Animals
Fairies	Blood	Orgasms	Fertility
Intellect	Desire	Moist Kiss	Touch
Clouds/Sky	Underworld	Rain Forest	Earth
Airplanes	Forge	Harmony	Physical
Kites	Cauldron	Liquids	Regeneration
Gentle Breezes	Passion	Rain Mist	Mountains
Tornadoes	Obsession	Depth	Transformation
Twisters	Ambition	Ebb & Flow	Embrace
Conceptions	Cravings	Dew	Growth
Beginnings	Volatile	Menstrual	Change
Ideas	Consumption	Wine	Food
Inspiration	Persistence	Balance	Manifestation
Blue/White	Red/Orange	Turquoise/Bluegreen	Brown/Black
Knights Armor	Volcanoes	Singing	Human Flesh
Clarity	Tenacity	Music	Solidity
Nike	Brigit	Mermaids	Gnomes
Athena	Hestia	Yemaja	Demeter
Aradia	Pele	Aphrodite	Artemis
Hina	Amaterasu	Saraswati	Maia
Cool Air	Sun	Rain	Baubo
Libra	Aries	Pisces	Taurus
Aquarius	Leo	Cancer	Virgo
Gemini	Sagitarius	Scorpio	Capricorn
Incenses	Body Heat	Blood	Strength
Mind	Sex	Salamanders	Herbs
Air	Flames	Seashells	Pentacle

THE ELEMENTS/CALLING QUARTERS

When calling quarters we are embodying that particular element and inviting its attributes and characteristics in our ritual. We call on Quarters to guard and hold our sacred space. After casting our circle we call on the elements and the guardians of the Watchtowers for added protection and to guard the perimeters of the sacred space we've just created. Elements are very powerful and have often been described as being childlike and needing clear directions, less you want them to go rampart into your ritual - creating havoc. Clearly state which particular attributes you want present for your ritual as elements have a variation of different characteristics you can draw upon. Be clear with your needs. Call on them with confidence and assertion and be specific with how you want them to manifest in your ritual. Then be open to the incredible powers of Nature and the art of calling Quarters, it can be an electrifying experience.

Below are various suggestions for calling quarters.
1. Hail guardian of the watchtowers of the _____ ye powers of _____
   Lend us your gifts of _____
Come and bear witness to our rites. Hail and Welcome_____!

2. We invite you powers of the _____ Elemental forces of_____
   Bring to this circle _____
Guard and hold our sacred space, Hail and Welcome_____!

3. Hail ancient realm of the _____ powers of _____
   Appear to us as _____
And stand to guard our sacred circle, Hail and Welcome_____!

4. Hail place of _____ beholder of _____
   Bless us with your _____
Be here now to serve and protect, Hail and Welcome_____!

5. Welcome Spirit of _____ Sacred powers of _____
   Reveal your gifts of _____
Let thy energy dwell in our ritual tonight, Hail and Welcome_____!

Devoking is your opportunity to thank the deities and elementals forces that made themselves present during your ritual. Thank them for protecting you and guarding your sacred space. Kindly ask them to retrieve to their special realm and domain. Be a gracious hostess and they will make themselves available to you again and again in your future workings.

Some Circle Casting Suggestions

I. Circle Casting
*With Sword I conjure this magick sphere,
outside of space, outside of fear
For love is all that shields us here
Bright lights to quell, the baneful and weird.

II. Circle Casting
*Upon this Sphere, this Circle is cast,
Keep evil at bay, let kind spirits pass.
No more a room, but your Holy Space
To worship and invoke, your essence and grace

III. Circle Casting
*Container, Preserver, all within thee
this circle is cast, SO MOTE IT BE!

IV. Circle Casting
*I cast this circle from my core, from my spirit I call.. I call,
From above ,the light I use.
From below I see it bloom,
From the right it swirls across
Windershin in blue sphere frost
From the left it joins me now
feel the energy go round and round,
Feel the energy Go around (2X)
Go around, go around…

V. Circle Casting
*I cast this consecrated space
to hold our circle, in love's embrace
I build and make this magic land
By will and word and blue shield sphere
let only good enter as I will
and block the rest from passage here, ,
Preserve and guard our sacred rites
And welcome Deities that I call
Outside of time, outside of space
We stand here now in sacred space, The circle is cast!!!

VI. Circle Casting
*I cast this circle round and round
From root to stem
To leaf, to Crown
To guard and hold
Our sacred space
And with my words
I make it safe. The circle is cast!!!

CHAKRAS AND GEMSTONE WORKINGS
FOR GROVE OF THE FEMININE DIVINE

NAME	LOCATION	COLOR	GODDESS
1st Chakra	Base of Spine	Red/Brown/Blk	Kali/Pele/Gaia

MULADHARA/ROOT CHAKRA: Fire Agate, Red Jasper, Onyx, Obsidian, Hematite, Garnet.
Security, physical existence, stability, the self, earth grounding, home, basic human needs, sexuality, sex chakra for men.

2nd Chakra	Yoni/Belly	Orange	Sheela-na-gig/Baubo

SAVADISTHANA/SACRAL CHAKRA: Carnelian, Variegated Jasper, Tiger's Eye.
Sacral realm, sex chakra for women, Womb, water realm, creative expression, self-worth, emotions, energy.

3rd Chakra	Upper abdomen	Yellow	Amaterasu/Oshun

MANIPURA/NAVAL SOLAR PLEXUS CHAKRA: Citrine, Yellow Topaz, Yellow Jasper, Peridot, Serpentine.
Ego, willpower, impulses, anger, personal Power, our strength, desire, Confidence, interactions with others, realm of fire,

4th Chakra	Heart	Green/Pink	Aphrodite/Ix Chel

ANAHATA/HEART CHAKRA: Kunzite, Morganite, Rose Quartz, Green Quartz, Howlite, moonstone, Aquamarine, Bloodstone.
Love, compassion, trust, relationships and community.

5th Chakra	Throat	Blue	Saraswati/Hathor

VISUDDHA/THROAT CHAKRA: Turquoise, Malachite, Chrysocolla, Lapis lazuli.
Speaking, Singing, eloquence of speech, hearing and being heard, Creativity.

6th Chakra	Third Eye	Purple/Indigo	Athena/Hekate

AJNA/THIRD EYE CHAKRA: Sodalite, Lapis Lazuli, Amethyst.
Intuition and Psychic realm, Clarity and related to the Mind, Sight, Telepathy, Astral travel.

7th Chakra	Crown/Head	White	Hestia/Kwan Yin

SAHASRARA/CROWN CHAKRA: Quartz, Clear Crystals of various kinds, Single or double-terminated, rutilated, Moonstone, Zircon.
Enlightenment, Wisdom, Divine connection, receiving Divine insight.

OTHER STONES: *Emerald, jade, opal diamonds, Amber, ruby, sapphire, serpentine, tourmaline, fluorite, pearls, coral.*

Elemental Ways to Cleanse and Charge

<u>EARTH</u>: Burying in bowl of Salt or soil. Prefer to use a potted Herbal plant like Sage or Rosemary and bury the gem inside the soil for a few days.
<u>WATER</u>: Running them in lukewarm water then cold water rise and sometimes using rose water.
<u>FIRE</u>: Using Solar rays, Outdoors or by a windowsill, let it soak up the strength of the mid-day Sun.
<u>AIR</u>: Smudging with Copal and or Sage Wand Bundle. Let the smoke or an incense swirl around as you hold it up the swirling smoke
<u>SPIRIT</u>: On the night of the Full Moon, let the light of the Moon permeate and Charge your crystals and gemstones.

ALCHEMIST WICCAN OIL RECIPES BY THE AUTHOR

SEXY HATHOR LOVE OIL
Gardenia Oil
Jasmine Oil
Rose Oil
Orange Oil
Cinnamon Oil

AMBITION & FOCUS OIL
Pennyroyal (minty) Oil
Sandalwood Oil
Vanilla Oil
Lavender Oil
Lilac Oil
Pinch of Cinnamon

GET IT DONE/COURAGE OIL
Rosemary Oil
Lotus Oil
Lily Oil
Lilac Oil
Hyancinth oil
Tangerine Oil
A pinch of Frankincense powder

HEKATE OIL
Pine needle Oil
Myrrh Oil
Patchouli Oil
Patchouli herbs
Nutmeg Oil
Garlic herb powder
Vervain herbs

ENCHANTRESS OIL
Gardenia Oil
Coconut Oil
Lemon grass Oil
Ylang-Ylang Oil

SABBAT OIL
Lavender Oil
Jasmine Oil
Cinnamon Oil
Hyancinth Oil
Lilac Oil

MAIDEN GIFTS DEDICATION OIL
Honeysuckle Oil
Lotus Oil
Hyacinth Oil
Cinnamon Oil
Gardenia Blossom Oil
Damiana Leaves
White/Silver sparkles

DWELLING BLESSING
Carnation oil
Hyssop oil
Rosemary Oil
Pennyroyal oil
Black Cohosh herb

POSITIVITY & GRATITUDE
Jasmine Oil
Cinnamon Oil
Patchouli Oil
Yarrow herbs
Sparkle, a pearl, Peach coloring

SHIELD & PROTECT ME
Rosemary Oil
Myrrh Oil
Hyssop Oil
Sandalwood Oil
Vanilla Oil
Patchouli Oil

TRUTH REVEALER
Myrrh Oil
Lilac Oil
Hyssop Oil

CLARITY (dispel confusion)
Myrrh Oil
Lilac Oil
Cinnamon Oil
Tangerine Oil
Clove powder
Frankincense Granules
Blue/green color

SUCCESS OIL
Pennyroyal Oil
Hyssop Oil
Frankincense Oil
Myrrh Oil

SUN OIL
Frankincense Oil
Myrrh Oil
Sandalwood Oil

FIRE GODDESS OIL
Myrrh Oil
Orange/Tangerine Oil
Patchouli Oil
Nutmeg Oil
Cinnamon Oil
Ylang-Ylang Oil
Honeysuckle Oil

PRIESTESS OIL
Frankincense Oil
Ylang-Ylang Oil
Palmorosa Oil
Patchouli Oil
Tuber rose Oil

I Honor the Goddess of Ten Thousand names, She Who......

DECEMBER
Amaterasu — She who must come out of hiding, to shine her own light
Athena — She who must engage her mind, her skills and strategies
Living Goddess — She who creates "Her," today from need and vision

JANUARY
Skadi — She who must run with the wolves freely and seek justice
Nike — She who must be victorious

FEBRUARY
Brigit — She who must heal and transform in the fire
Oya — She who must destroy in order to rebuild

MARCH
Pele — She who unearths her roars and pursues her passions
Artemis — She who who is automous and leads her sisters

APRIL
Aphrodite — She who attracts beauty and love
Ix Chel — She who protects and heals thru her waters

MAY
Hathor — She who must delight in great pleasure
Baubo — She who cackles in freedom and friendship

JUNE
Saraswati — She who must learn, express with her voice and create
Aine — She who takes vows and enchants with her radiance

JULY
Erzulie Freda — She who must be loved and offered the best.
Gaia — She who must birth and procreate

AUGUST
Demeter — She who must mother and adjust to change
Persephone — She who balances roles and realms

SEPTEMBER
Selu — She who forgives and sacrifices
Aradia — She who practices Magick

OCTOBER
Hekate — She who opens the gateways to our Ancestors
Maman Brigitte — She who mothers the Dead

NOVEMBER
Hina — She who lives in the Moon
Hestia — She who honors the Spirit thru hearth flames
Dedications — She who begins the Priestess Path

A COMPLETELY BARDIC RITUAL, ADDITIONAL CHANTS

GODDESS CHANT
Isis, Astarte, Diana, Hecate, Demeter, Kali, Inanna.... *By: Deena Metzger & Caitlin Mullin*

WE ARE A CIRCLE
We are a circle within a circle
    with no beginning and never ending
You hear us sing, you hear us cry
Now hear us call you, Spirits of Earth and sky (chorus)
    Within our heart there goes a spark
    Love and desire is burning fire
    Within our blood, within our tears
    There lies the offer of living water
Take our fears, take our pains
Take the darkness into the earth again (chorus)
The circle closes, between the worlds
To mark the scared space
where we come face to face   By: Rick Hamouris

ELEMENTAL SONG
Earth my body, water my blood, air my breath, and fire my spirit

QUARTER INVOCATION SONG *By: Andras Corban Arthen*
*Air I am, Fire I am, Water, Earth and Spirit I am

WE ARE THE FLOW
We are the flow, We are the ebb
We are the weaver, we are the web *(repeat)*
We are the spiders we are the thread
We are the witches back from the dead....
By: Shekhinah Mountainwater

EQUINOX CHANT
Onward we go round the Spiral
Touching darkness, touching light
Twice each year we rest in balance
Make choices on this night
Make choices on this night *By: Marie Summerwood*

SHE WALKS WITH SNAKES
She walks with snakes, she stands on the moon
She walks with snakes, she stands on the moon
She walks with snakes, she stands on the moon
Mary, Mary, Mary Mary stands on the moon *(repeat)*
Touch me with your hands of light
Crown of stars to bless the night
Mother Mary give me sight, That I may see
She walks with snakes she stands on the moon
She walks with snakes she stands on the moon
She walks with snakes she stands on the moon
    Mary, Mary, Mary, Mary, Mary, Mary, Mary, Mary
    Mary, Mary, Mary, Mary, Mary, Mary, Mary, Mary
    Stands on the Moon..........................*By Marie Summerwood*

MOTHER I FEEL YOU UNDER MY FEET
    Mother I feel you under my feet, Mother I feel your Heart Beat 2X
        Heya Heya Heya, Heya Heya Ho 2X
    Mother I hear you in the Rivers Sound, Eternal Waters going on and on 2X
        Heya heya heya heya heya ho 2X
    Mother I see you in when the Eagles fly, Flight of the Spirit gonna take our time 2X
        Heya Heya Heya, Heya Heya Ho ......By; Unknown source

**WE ALL COME FROM THE GODDESS
We all come from the Goddess and to her we shall return
like a drop of rain flowing to the ocean.
    Huff and Horn,
    Huff and Horn, All that dies shall be Reborn
    Corn & Grain, Corn & Grain All that falls shall rise again
    We all come from the Goddess.......
    We all come from the Goddess.......
    And to her we shall return like a drop of rain flowing to the ocean
Sage & Crone, Sage & Crone Wisdom's gift s shall be our Own
Crone & Sage, Crone & Sage Wisdom is the gift of Age.
We all come from the Goddess...
and to her we shall return like a drop of rain flowing to the ocean.
    We all come from the Maiden
    and to her we shall return like a Bud-ding Flower
    Blooming in the Springtime. (repeat)
    We all come from the Goddess by Z. Budapest and Huff and Horn part by: Ian Corrigan

MY ROOTS
My roots go down, down to the earth, My roots go down, down to the earth (2X)
I am a tree, rooted in the earth (or any other option) (4x) or I am a gem sparkling in her light (4x) or *By: Sarah Pirtle*

I. AUTHOR'S ORIGINAL GODDESS CHANTS,

Created by B. Melusine Mihaltses- Some of these chants will be featured in upcoming Music CD.

A simple Chant for energy grounding
    We are connected Sister, Mother, Connected....
by (B.M.M.)

LAMMAS SONG OF GRATITUDE: for DEMETER
(Three part harmony) (Lower voice/ then higher to harmonize)
I thank the Moon
and the Stars
And the Fertile Earth
For the lessons I've learned
And the way I'm nursed... *(repeat to raise energy)*
(third part vocals on her name)
Deeeeemeter ....Deeeeemeter *By B.M.M.*

A SONG FOR HEKATE
I meet you on this Crossroad
Hekate, my Queen
You hold the Sacred Lantern
Helping me to see
Hecate , Hekate
Guide me in the Dark,
Quietly, I listen for your Howl and Bark
Hekate, Hekate
Holder of the Key
To your Dark Realm now
I must go Traveling.... *Repeat continuously... Creation by B.M.M.*

SONG TO AMATERASU
Out of darkness Comes the light
Amaterasu
Slowly growing to new heights
Take away our Blues
    Darkness Reign and soon will wane
    As you come to rule
    Sun reborn
    Hear us call Amaterasu....
    Amaterasu....Amaterasu....AMATERASU.....*(repeat) by B.M.M.*

SONGS FOR ARTEMIS
I feel her Powers,
running through me,
Artemis Blessing
I am you, you are me.
Queen of the Moonlight
Maiden and Free,
Lover of Women
Empower me, Empower me, Empower me....*By: B.M.M.*

SONGS FOR ARTEMIS
Lady of the Moon,
Be with us... Come to us....
Lady of the Moon,
Lady of the Moon.
Lady of the Hunt,
    Artemis, Artemis
Be with us.... Now be with us.... *By B.M.M.*

PELE'S SONG
Pele... Pele...
    Passion Fire burn in me
Pele... Pele....
I attract what my heart seeks
    Pele...Pele...
    Fire Stirs and stirs in me
Pele....Pele...
    What I will shall come to be *B.M.M.*

HINA RETURN TO ME
Come return to me
Come return to me
Come return to our old home
Our blessed Ancestry.
Step into the Moon
She waits for me and you
    Let her light transform
    While we explore
    our spirituality.
You were once in me,
part of Matriarchy,
See your lineage now
as it unfold
and brings you back to me............*by B.M.M.*

II. CONTINUATION-ORIGINAL SONGS

Created by B. Melusine Mihaltses- Some of these chants will be featured in upcoming Music CD.

A SONG FOR HATHOR...
Dance Goddess, Dance!
Eroticism Rises...
Dance Goddess, Dance!
Eroticism Rises...
Hathor.... Hathor.....(vocalises on her name.)
Beauty and Pleasure,
We call at this Moment,
Mine and Hathor,
Mine and Yours (face the Woman near you)
(continue to repeat as you raise energy), by B.M.M.

EARTH, MOON, MAGICK
In the Earth, deep within,
There is A Magick,, I draw it in.
    In her Caves, in the Trees
    Hear her Heartbeat, Pulsing thru me.
When I Rise, I feel her Love
With feet Grounded, I'm soaring high above,
    In the Earth, deep within,
    There is A Magick, I draw it in
Ancient Moon, my Soul reveres
With my Singing, I call you here.
    When this flame, ignites tonight,
    Priestess dancing, Under the moonlit night....
In the Earth, deep within,
There is A Magick
I draw it in.... There is A Magick, I draw it in }3x *by B.M.M.*

SONG to ARADIA
Witch, Magick, Candle spells
all that is you
Born from the Sun
and the Love of the Moon
Oh Aradia, Aradia
keeping us safe
Magick Syster,
teaching us the ancient ways... *by B.M.M.*

SONG FOR GAIA
Gaia, Gaia, Gaia, Gaia (beatX , beatX)
Gaia Gaia Gaia Gaia Come to me
Gaia Gaia Gaia Gaia (beat X, beatX)
Gaia Gaia Gaia Gaia Come to me

Strength of The Mother Earth, Whole unto Me
Pulsating Earth Right under my Feet
Now I draw your energy
Grounding me,
Now I draw your energy,
Grounding me...,
(I said) Gaia, Gaia, Gaia, Gaia (beatX , beatX)
Gaia Gaia Gaia Gaia Come to me
Gaia Gaia Gaia Gaia (beat X, beatX)
Gaia Gaia Gaia Gaia Come to me
(back to beginning con't to repeat in rnd) by by B.M.M..

ATHENA'S CHANT
Virgin Goddess
Sword and Shield,
Lend to us the gift to yield
Come when called into our lives
Bringing wisdom
Wise, bright Eyes. (rpt rnd)
Counter Melody: Come Athena,
Come Athena, Come Athena,
Wise one come (rpt2x).... *by B.M.M.*

MAIDEN DANCING
Spiraling Dancing, Up and Down
Reaching the Center with Floral Crown
Laughing Maiden, Giggles are free
I've awaken the Maiden in me.

See me Jump, Jump, Jump,
Cross the meadow Field
See me Fearless and Beautiful
and dancing the Wheel.
by B.M.M.

INVOKING MOTHER
by B.M.M.
Mother, Mother, Mother, I call you,
Deep within my soul, you're stirring my womb.
Mother, Mother, Mother, Hear my Cries,
In this Sacred Circle I Call you tonight.
Light the inner Flame, as I light the candle wick,
Call your sacred name and embrace myself as Witch
Sky-clad I approach, to Elemental thrones,
Hear me, Mother hear me,
Through these words I wrote.

III. CONTINUATION-ORIGINAL SONGS

Created by B. Melusine Mihaltses- Some of these chants will be featured in upcoming Music CD.

SONG TO MEDEA & ARADIA
In the Darkness of the Night
Plaaaaant a Seed
Magick made by candlelight
Stirring Silently
Growing, Growing By my might
Words I speak and Charge tonight
_____Cast a Circle, Raise the Vibe
With my Energy
Magick made by Candlelight
Sing so mote it be....Sing So Mote it Be!!! *By B.M.M.*

INVOKING MOTHER CHANT, *by B.M.M.*
Mother, Mother, Mother,
I call you,
Deep within my Soul,
You're stirring my womb.
    Mother, Mother, Mother,
    hear my cries,
    In this sacred Circle,
    I call you tonight.
Light the inner flame
As I light the candle wick!
Call your sacred names
and embrace myself as Witch!
    Sky-clad I approach, to
    Elemental Thrones...
    Hear me, Mother Hear me,
    Thru these words I wrote...*(rpt from beginning)*
Mother, Mother, Mother,
I call you
Deep within my Soul,
You're stirring my womb.
    Mother, Mother, Mother,
    hear my cries,
    In this sacred Circle,
    I call you tonight. *(con't to repeat in rdn)*

INVOCATION SONG TO OYA-YANSA
Hekua Hey, Yansa,
Hekua Hey, Yansa,
Oya, Oya
On Storms she comes,
Oya, Oya
Her Winds Transform,
Oya, Oya
We call on you,
Oya, Oya
Dance to this Tune....(con't *repeat*), *by B.M.M.*

Skadi Chant by B.M.M.
On High, above
In mountains,
I take pleasure alone
On my own,
Connecting with
The Soul of Nature
and the Animal's
expressive groans/moans.
I am One,
I am One with that Beast,
I am One,
I am One with the Leaf,
I am One,
I am One with the Breeze,
I am One,
I am One with the Flames of my Heart,
as it sways in the Trees...

REFERENCES AND BIBLIOGRAPHY

Amaterasu
Circle Round, Raising Children in Goddess Tradition by Starhawk, Diane Baker and Anne Hill
Goddess Mirror, Visions of the Divine From East and West by David Kinsley
The Book Of Goddesses, Past and Present: An Introduction to her Religion by Carl Olson
The Goddess Path, myths, invocations and rituals by Patricia Monaghan
The Goddess Oracle, A Way to Wholeness Through The Goddess and Ritual by Amy Sophia Marashinsky and Hrana Janto
Nihonghi -translated by W.G. Aston
SageWoman No.# 54 Summer 2001, Reclaim Your Power...and Find inner Peace, Too! by Lady Moondance
SageWoman No. #65 Truth and Beauty, Calligraphy lessons by Kela Vaeltaja
Wikipedia internet free encyclopedia

Athena
Ancient Mirrors of Womanhood, A Treasury of Goddess and Heroine Lore from Around the World by Merlin Stone
Grandmother of Time by Zsuzsanna E. Budapest
Goddess in Every Woman, a New Psychology of women by Jean Shinoda Bolen, MD.
Goddess Mirror, Visions of the Divine From East and West by David Kinsley
SageWoman No.# 35 Autumn 1996, 10th Anniversary, One of Ten Thousand; Goddess Lore and Ritual- Athene, The Reconciler of Opposites, Article by Diana L. Paxson
The Goddess Path, Myths, Invocations and Rituals by Patricia Monaghan
The Holy Book of Women's Mysteries by Zsuzsanna E. Budapest
Wikipedia.com a free Encyclopedia

Skadi
Ancient Mirrors of Womanhood, a Treasury of Goddess and Heroine Lore from Around the World by Merlin Stone
Llewellyn's 2005 Magical Almanac; Article; "Skadi, Norse Goddess of Winter" by Lily Gardner
pg 64-65 St. Paul Minnesota, Llewellyn Worldwide 2005
Norse Magic, by D.J. Conway, Llewellyn Publications
The Elder Edda, translated by Lee Hollander, Texas, USA, University of Texas, 1986
Skadi - Wikipedia.com free encyclopedia

Nike
GoddessGift.net
Hesiod's Theogony
Homeric Hymns
Loggia.com
Orphic Hymn 33 to Nike Translated by Taylor (Greek Hymns C3rd B.C. to 2nd A.D.)
Theoi.com Project
Wikipedia.com free encyclopedia

Brigid
Circle Round, Raising Children in Goddess Tradition by Starhawk, Diane Baker and Anne Hill
The Goddess Path, Myths, Invocations and Rituals by Patricia Monaghan
The Wheel of The Celtic Year.com chalice centre.net/imbolc
The Witches' Goddess, The Feminine Principle of Divinity by Janet and Stewart Farrar
Pan Gaia Exploring the Pagan World No #20 Summer 1999, Brigid in Ireland; Discovering the Magic by Diane Conn Darling
SageWoman No.#46 Summer 1999, One of Ten Thousand: Goddess Lore and Ritual article -Brigit, Inspiration Upwelling by Diana L. Paxson
Wikipedia.com a free Encyclopedia

Oya Yansa
A ritual for change, The tribal tradition Omnipresent Oya.com By Heathwitch
Carnival of the Spirit, Seasonal Celebrations and Rites of Passage by Luisah Teish
Jambalaya, The Natural Woman's Book of Personal Charms and Pracitical Rituals by Luisah Teish
Oya; in Praise of the African Goddess by Judith Gleason
Powers of the Orishas by Migenes Gonzalez-Wippler
The Blue Roebuck.com and A Primer in Dianic Witchcraft by Bendis also known as Deanne Quarrie founder of the Apple Branch
The Goddess Oracle, A Way to Wholeness Through The Goddess and Ritual by Amy Sophia Marashinsky and Hrana Janto
The New Book of Goddesses and Heroines by Patricia Monaghan
Paganwiki.com
SageWoman No. #47 Autumn 1999, Petition to Oya, a letter offering from a reader by Juniper in Colorado
SageWoman No.#55 Autumn 2001, One of Ten Thousand: Goddess Lore and Ritual article- Oya, Lady of Change by Diana L. Paxson
SageWoman No. #65 Truth and Beauty, Masks for the Goddess by Lauren Raine
Santeria, the Religion by Wippler, Migenes Gonzalez

Pele
Cofeetime.com by Betty Fullard-Leo
Goddess Mirror, Visions of the Divine From East and West by David Kinsley
MythicRealm.com
Pagan Anger Magic, Positive Transformations From Negative Energies by Tammy Sullivan
SageWoman No.# 54 Summer 2001, Reclaim Your Power...and Find inner Peace, Too! by Lady Moondance
Tales of Hina Online By Lana's Aumakua
The Goddess Oracle, A Way to Wholeness Through The Goddess and Ritual by Amy Sophia Marashinsky and Hrana Janto
365 Goddess, a daily guide to the magic and inspiration of the Goddess by Patricia Telesco
White Moon Gallery.com
Wikipedia.com free Encyclopedia

Artemis
An ABC of Witchcraft from Past and Present by Doreen Valiente
Ancient Mirrors of Womanhood, A Treasury of Goddess and Heroine Lore from Around the World by Merlin Stone
Ariadne's Thread, a workbook of Goddess Magic by Shekhinah Mountainwater
Goddess in Every Woman, a New Psychology of Women by Jean Shinoda Bolen, MD.
Grandmother Moon, Lunar Magic in our Lives by Zsuzsanna E. Budapest
Grandmother of Time by by Zsuzsanna E. Budapest
SageWoman No.#57 Spring 2002, One of Then Thousand: Goddess Lore and Ritual article-Artemis, Hunting The Moon by Diana L. Paxson
The GoddessGift.com Artemis
The Holy Book of Women's Mysteries by Zsuzsanna E. Budapest
The Mythic Image Moon Maiden: Young Diana by Wynter Rose Stiles
The Goddess Path, Myths, Invocations and Rituals by Patricia Monaghan
Witches, Investigating an Ancient Religion by T.C.Lethridge
Women's Mysteries Ancient and Modern by M. Esther Harding

Aphrodite
Ancient Mirrors of Womanhood, A Treasury of Goddess and Heroine Lore from Around the World by Merlin Stone
Ariadne's Thread, a Workbook of Goddess Magic by Shekhinah Mountainwater
Goddess in Every Woman, a New Psychology of women by Jean Shinoda Bolen, MD.
Goddess Mirror, Visions of the Divine From East and West by David Kinsley
Grandmother Moon, Lunar Magic in our Lives by Zsuzsanna E. Budapest
Grandmother of Time by Zsuzsanna E. Budapest
The Goddess Path, myths, invocations and rituals by Patricia Monaghan
The Witches' Goddess, The Feminine Principle of Divinity by Janet and Stewart Farrar
Wikipedia.com

Ix Chel
Ancient Mirrors of Womanhood, A Treasury of Goddess and Heroine Lore from Around the World by Merlin Stone
Grandmother Moon, Lunar Magic in our lives by Zsuzsanna E. Budapest
Librarythinkquest.org
Ix Chel Wisdom, Seven Teachings from the Mayan Sacred Feminine by Shonagh Home
Mayan Healers-Daughters of Ix Chel by Rozanna Herrera
365 Goddess, a daily guide to the magic and inspiration of the Goddess by Patricia Telesco
The Goddess Oracle, A Way to Wholeness Through The Goddess and Ritual by Amy Sophia Marashinsky and Hrana Janto
SageWoman No. #57 Spring 2002, Coming across The Great Goddess Ix Chel by Bethany Walsh Smith
Wikipedia.com the free Encyclopedia

Hathor
Ancient Mirrors of Womanhood, A Treasury of Goddess and Heroine Lore from Around the World by Merlin Stone
Egyptian Gods and Goddess- 4 from Ellie Cystalinks.com
Egyptian Mythology by Veronica Irons
Grandmother Moon, Lunar Magic in our lives by Zsuzsanna E. Budapest
Hathor, the Goddess of Love, Music, Beauty.com by Caroline Seawright
The Book Of Goddesses, Past and Present: An Introduction to her Religion by Carl Olson
The Goddess Oracle, A Way to Wholeness Through The Goddess and Ritual by Amy Sophia Marashinsky and Hrana Janto
The Goddess Path, myths, invocations and rituals by Patricia Monaghan
365 Goddess, a daily guide to the magic and inspiration of the Goddess by Patricia Telesco
Who is the Goddess Hathor? Pyramidcompany.com On the Internet by Rhiannon Barkemeijer de Wit
Wikipedia.com free Encyclppedia

Baubo
Goddess In World Mythology, a Biography Dictionary by Dorothy Myers Imel and Martha Ann
Goddessgift.com Article on the Greek Goddess of Mirth- Baubo
365 Goddess, a daily guide to the magic and inspiration of the Goddess by Patricia Telesco
Reconnect With Your Inner Goddess.com byAnita Ryan Revel-2000
The Yoni, Sacred Symbol of female creative Power by Rufus C. Camphausen
Wikipedia.com Free Encyclopedia

Saraswasti
Chakra Workout, Balancing your Energy with Yoga and Meditation by Mary Horsley
Goddess In World Mythology, a Biography Dictionary by Dorothy Myers Imel and Martha Ann
Grandmother Moon, Lunar Magic in our lives by Zsuzsanna E. Budapest
Healing Mantras, by Thomas Ashley-Farrand
Hindu Gods and Goddess by Swami Harshananda
SageWoman No.#46 Summer 1999, The Great Goddess Saraswati; Flowing River of Creativity, Inspiration and Joy by Suzin Green
SageWoman No. #64 Prayer and Invocation, One of Ten Thousand: Goddess Lore and Ritual- Article, Sarasvati, Word of Wisdom by Diana L. Paxson
The Book of Goddesses, Invoke the Powers of the Goddess to Improve Your Life by Roni Jay
365 Goddess, a daily guide to the magic and inspiration of the Goddess by Patricia Telesco

Aine
Aine - Wikipedia.com Free Encyclopedia
Ancient Mirrors of Womanhood, a Treasury of Goddess and Heroine Lore from Around the World by Merlin Stone
Love Magic, The Way To Love through Rituals, Spells, and the Magical life by Laurie Cabot
Goddess In World Mythology, a Biography Dictionary by Dorothy Myers Imel and Martha Ann
365 Goddess, a daily guide to the magic and inspiration of the Goddess by Patricia Telesco

Erzulie-Freda
Erzulie, Everyday better living.com by Judi Singleton
Pan Gaia, A Pagan Journal for Thinking People No. #36 Summer 2003 Erzulie Freda, Mistress of Love by Kevin Filan
Rituals and Spells of Santeria by Migenez, Gonzalez-Wippler
Secrets of Voodoo by Milo Rigaud
Spellmakererzulie.love.com
The Book of Goddesses, Invoke the Powers of the Goddess to Improve Your Life by Roni Jay
The Book Of Goddesses, Past and Present: An Introduction to her Religion by Carl Olson
The Haitian Voodoo Handbook, Protocols for Ridding with the Lwa by Kevin Filan
365 Goddess, a daily guide to the magic and inspiration of the Goddess by Patricia Telesco

Gaia
Ancient Mirrors of Womanhood, A Treasury of Goddess and Heroine Lore from Around the World by Merlin Stone
Circle Magazine, Celebrating Nature, Spirit and Magic Issue 87 Spring 2003 Earth and Spirit: Mother Gaia by Jesse Wolf Hardin
Gaia; A New Look At Life on Earth by J.E. Lovelock
Goddess In World Mythology, a Biography Dictionary by Dorothy Myers Imel and Martha Ann
Green Egg a Journal of the Awakening Earth Vol. 30 No #125 November-December 1998, Gaian Ministry; Reclaiming Earth and Spirit by Jesse Wolf Hardin
People of the Earth, The New Pagans Speak Out by Ellen Evert Hope and Lawrence Bond
Persephone Unveiled, Seeing the Goddess and Freeing Your Soul by Charles Stein
The Book Of Goddesses, Past and Present: An Introduction to her Religion by Carl Olson
The Goddess Path, myths, invocations and rituals
by Patricia Monaghan
The Encyclopedia of Magical Herbs by Scott Cunningham
Wikipedia.com a free Encyclopedia

Demeter
Ancient Mirrors of Womanhood, A Treasury of Goddess and Heroine Lore from Around the World by Merlin Stone
Circle Round, Raising Children in Goddess Tradition by Starhawk, Diane Baker and Anne Hill
Goddess in Every Woman, a New Psychology of women by Jean Shinoda Bolen, MD.
The Goddess Path, Myths, Invocations and Rituals by Patricia Monaghan
The Mythic Tarot, a New approach to the Tarot Cards by Juliet Sharman-Burke and Liz Greene
The Witches 'Goddess, The Feminine Principle of Divinity by Janet and Stewart Farrar

Persephone
Circle Round, Raising Children in Goddess Tradition by Starhawk, Diane Baker and Anne Hill
Goddess in Every Woman, a New Psychology of women by Jean Shinoda Bolen, MD.
Greek Goddess of innocence and Queen of the underworld. http://www.goddessgift.com/goddess-myhths/greek-goddess-peresphone.htm
Persephone Unveiled, Seeing the Goddess and Freeing Your Soul by Charles Stein
The Goddess Path, Myths, Invocations and Rituals by Patricia Monaghan
The Meaning of Persephone's name-m.anthony, http://quantum-witch.com/theos/w/p-name.htm
The Myth of Persephone- Greek Goddess of the Underworld by Laura Strong, PhD., http://www.mythicarts.com/writing/persephone.html
The Mythic Tarot, a New approach to the Tarot Cards by Juliet Sharman-Burke and Liz Greene
The Witches 'Goddess, The Feminine Principle of Divinity by Janet and Stewart Farrar
Wikipedia.com a free Encyclopedia

Corn Mother
365 Goddess, a daily guide to the magic and inspiration of the Goddess by Patricia Telesco
The Goddess Oracle, A Way to Wholeness Through The Goddess and Ritual by Amy Sophia Marashinsky and Hrana Janto
http://www.michellemays.com
Song: "Selu awa do li"
Corn - myth encyclopedia-mythology , god, story, names, world, creation, people, children, fire
http://www.mythencyclopedia.com/corn
http://www.abaxion.com/sz02.jpg
http://www.dovercards.com
http://www.rainewalker.com/selu.htm
Corn mother's gift by Chrity Salo
The story of Corn-History detective-in the beginning
http://www.campsilos.org/mod3/students/c-history.shtml
http://www.witcvox.com/music/bardic Circle-Michelle Mays;
The story of Selu, Michelle Mays

Aradia
Aradia; The Gospel of the Witches by Charles Godfrey Leland
Grandmother Moon, Lunar Magic in our lives by Zsuzsanna E. Budapest
Hereditary Witchcraft, Secrets of an Old Religion by Raven Grimassi
Italian Witchcraft -the old religion of Southern Europe by Raven Grimassi
The Book of the Holy Strega by Raven Grimassi
The Holy Book of Women's Mysteries by Zsuzsanna E. Budapest
The Witches 'Goddess, The Feminine Principle of Divinity by Janet and Stewart Farrar
Stregherie.com
Witchcraft for Tomorrow by Doreen Valiente

Hekate
Pagan Anger Magic, Positive Transformations From Negative Energies by Tammy Sullivan
The Witches' Goddess, The Feminine Principle of Divinity by Janet and Stewart Farrar
The Theogony by Hesiod
Homeric Hymn
Grandmother of Time by Zsuzsanna E. Budapest
The Holy Book of Women's Mysteries by Zsuzsanna E. Budapest
Hekate Soteira, a Study of Hekate's Role in the Chaldean Oracles by S.I. Johnston
Who is Hekate? from WitchVox.com by Helena Domenic
SageWoman No.# 39 Autumn 1997, One of Ten Thousand; Goddess Lore and Ritual Article by Diana L. Paxson Hekate Guide of the Soul

Maman Brigitte
http://members.aol.com/racine125/index1.html website by Bon Mambo Racine Sans Bout Sa Te La Daginen internet
www.Meta-Religion.com world religions/voodoo/ancestors.htm internet
SageWoman Magazine, Autumn 2008- issue 75 -Surrendering and Awakening-One of Ten Thousand; Goddess Lore and Ritual (page 31-37) Article- Maman Brigitte, Priestess of the Tomb, by Diana L. Paxson
www. Sosyetedumarche.com/html/b...te.html -internet
www.Thaliatook.com/AMGG/mamanbrijit- Thalia Took Oracle website
The magical buffet.com/blog½...cemetery internet
Secrets of Voodoo by Milo Rigaud
Wikipedia.com free Encyclopedia internet

Hina
Goddess In World Mythology, a Biography Dictionary by Dorothy Myers Imel and Martha Ann
Hawaiian Mythology by Martha Berkwith
Hina Adventures.com
Hina, the Woman in the Moon from Legends of Maui, a Demi-God of Polynesia
by W.D. Westervelt also on Sacred text.com
Many Moons, the Myth and Magic, Fact and Fantasy of our Nearest Heavenly Body,
by Diana Brueton
The Order of White Moon Gallery.com presents, The Goddess Hina by Leigh Hall
365 Goddess, a daily guide to the magic and inspiration of the Goddess by Patricia Telesco
The Hawaiian Oracle, Animal Spirit Guide from the Land of Light, by Rima A Morrell, PhD

Hestia
Ancient Mirrors of Womanhood, A Treasury of Goddess and Heroine Lore from Around the World by Merlin Stone
Goddess in Every Woman, a New Psychology of women by Jean Shinoda Bolen, MD.
Goddess In World Mythology, a Biography Dictionary by Dorothy Myers Imel and Martha Ann
The Goddess Oracle, A Way to Wholeness through The Goddess and Ritual by Amy Sophia Marashinsky and Hrana Janto
365 Goddess, a daily guide to the magic and inspiration of the Goddess by Patricia Telesco
Wikipedia.com free Encyclopedia

Other helpful and influential Books
A Book of Shadow by Tarostar The Circle of Star Meadow
New York, The Circle Of Star Meadow

An ABC of Witchcraft from Past and Present by Doreen Valiente
New York, St. Martin's Press inc., first edition 1973

Ancient Mirrors of Womanhood, A Treasury of Goddess and Heroine Lore from Around the World by Merlin Stone
Massachusetts, Beacon Press 1984

Aradia; The Gospel of the Witches by Charles Godfrey Leland
Great Britain, C.W. Daniel Co, 1974

Ariadne's Thread, A Workbook of Goddess Magic by Shekhinah Mountainwater
California, The Crossing Press , 1991- 4th printing edition of 1996

A Witches' Bible, The Complete Witches Handbook by Janet and Stewart Farrar
Washington, Phoenix Publishing inc., 1996 edition

Be a Goddess, A Guide to Celtic Spells and Wisdom for Self-Healing, Prosperity and Great Sex by Francesca De Grandis
California, Harper San Francisco a div of Harper Collins Publishers, first edition 1998

Book of Shadow, A Modern Woman's Journey into The Wisdom of Witchcraft and the
Magic of the Goddess by Phyllis Curott
New York, Broadway Books a div of Bantam Doubleday Dell Publishing Group, Inc. First edition 1998

Carnival of the Spirit, Seasonal Celebrations and Rites of Passage by Luisah Teish
New York, Harper Collins Publishers, first edition, 1994

Casting the Circle, A Women's Book of Ritual by Diane Stein
California, The Crossing Press, 1990 fourth printing of 1996

Chakra Workout, Balancing your Energy with Yoga and Meditation by Mary Horsley
New York, Sterling Publishing, 2007, first published in 2006 in UK by Gaia Books

Circle, Coven and Grove, a Year of Magickal Practice by Deborah Blake
Minnesota, Llewellyn Publications a div of Llewellyn Worldwide, Ltd. First edition 2007

Circle Round, Raising Children in Goddess Tradition by Starhawk , Diane Baker and Anne Hill
New York, Bantam Books a div of Bantam Double Day Publishing Group, Inc.1998

Creating Circles and Ceremonies Rituals for all Seasons and Reasons by Oberon Zell-Ravenheart and Morning Glory Zell-Ravenheart
New Jersey, New Page Books a div of The Career Press, inc., 2006

Crystal Handbook by Kevin Sullivan
New York, An Armadillo Press Book, A Signet book published by Penguin Publishing,1987

Devi: Goddesses of India by Donna Marie Wulff and John Stantton Hawley
California, University of California Press, 1996

Diary of a Witch by Sybil Leek
New Jersey, Prentice-Hall, Inc. First Edition 1968

Drawing Down the Moon, Witches, Druids, Goddess-Worshippers, and Other Pagans in America Today by Margot Adler
Massachusetts, Beacon Press 1981

Earth Magic, A Dianic Book of Shadows by Marion Weinstein
New York, Earth Magic Productions, 1980 the 4th edition 1998 printing

Egyptian Mythology by Veronica Irons
Paul Hamlyn, first edition 1973

Egyptian Paganism for Beginners: Bring the Gods and Goddesses of Ancient Egypt into Daily Life by Jocelyn Almond
Minnesota, Llewellyn Publications a div of Llewellyn Worldwide, Ltd. 2004 edition

Encyclopedia of Magical Herbs by Scott Cunningham
Minnesota, Llewellyn Publications a div of Llewellyn Worldwide, Ltd., 1985 the twenty-second printing -1997

From the Branch: A Primer in Dianic Witchcraft by Deanne Quarrie
Published by The Apple Branch 2008

Goddess in Every Woman-A New Psychology of Women by Jean Shinoda Bolen, MD
New York, First Harper Colophon a div of Harper and Row Publishing, 1985 edition

Goddess in World Mythology, A Biography Dictionary by Dorothy Myers Imel and Martha Ann
New York, Oxford University Press, 1993

Goddess Inspiration Oracle Guide by Kris Waldherr
Minnesota, Llewellyn Publications a div of Llewellyn Worldwide, Ltd. first edition 2007

Goddess Meditation by Barbara Ardinger, Phd
Minnesota, Llewellyn Publications a div of Llewellyn Worldwide, Ltd., First edition 1998

Goddess Spirituality Book, Rituals, Holydays and Moon Magick by Ffiona Morgan
California, Daughters of The Moon Publishing, 1992, the 1995 edition
Grandmother Moon, Lunar Magic in our Lives by Zsuzsanna E. Budapest
California, Harper San Francisco a div of Harper Collins Publishers, first edition 1991

Grandmother of Time, a Woman's Book of Celebrations, Spells and Sacred Objects for every Month of the Year by by Zsuzsanna E. Budapest
California, Harper San Francisco a div of Harper Collins Publishers, first edition 1989

Hawaiian Mythology by Martha Beckwith
Hawaii, University of Hawaii Press, 1970

Healing Mantras, using Sound Affirmations for Personal Power, Creativity, and Healing by Thomas Ashley-Farrand
New York, Ballantine Wellspring tm, a div of Ballantine Publishing Group, first ed.1999

Herbs in Magic and Alchemy, Techniques from Ancient Herbal Lore, by C.L. Zalewski
Great Britain, Prism Press, 1990

Hindu Gods and Goddess by Swami Harshanada
India, Mylapore Mandras, Sri Ramakrishna Math Printing Press, sixth edition- no year listed

Hereditary Witchcraft, Secrets of the Old Religion by Raven Grimassi
Minnesota, Llewellyn Publications a div of Llewellyn Worldwide, Ltd. Fourth printing 2003

Ix Chel Wisdom, Seven Teachings from the Mayan Sacred Feminine by Shonagh Home,
Redmond, WA, Ix Chel Publishing, 2010

Italian Witchcraft -the Old Religion of Southern Europe (previously titled, Way of the Strega) by Raven Grimassi
Minnesota, Llewellyn Publications a div of Llewellyn Worldwide, Ltd. Third edition 2003

Jambalaya, The Natural Woman's Book of Charms and Practical Rituals by Luisah Teish
New York, Harper and Row publishing, 1985

Llewellyn's 2005 Magical Almanac;
Article; "Skadi, Norse Goddess of Winter by Lily Gardner
pg 64-65 St. Paul Minnesota, Llewellyn Worldwide 2005

Love Magic, The Way To Love through Rituals, Spells, and the Magical life
by Laurie Cabot with Tom Cowan,
New York, USA, Delta Books a div of Dell Publishing, 1992

Many Moons, the Myth and Magic, Fact and Fantasy of our Nearest Heavenly Body,
by Diana Brueton
New York, Prentice Hall Press, 1991

Nihongi -translated by W.G. Aston
London, George Allen and Urwin, 1956

Norse Magic, by D.J. Conway,
St. Paul Minnesota, Llewellyn Publications 1997

Notion and Potion, a Safe Practical Guide to Creating Magic and Miracles by Susan Bowes
New York, Sterling Publishing Company, 1997

Oya, In Praise of an African Goddess by Judith Gleason
California, Harper San Francisco a div of Harper Collins Publishing,
1987 the 1992 edition

Pagan Anger Magic, Positive Transformations From Negative Energies by Tammy Sullivan
New York, Citadel Press a div of Kensington Publishing corp. 2005

People of the Earth, The New Pagans Speak Out by Ellen Evert Hopman and Lawrence Bond
Vermont, Destiny Books, 1996

Persephone Unveiled, Seeing the Goddess and freeing your Soul by Charles Stein
California, North Atlantic Books, 2006

Powers of the Orishas by Migene Gonzalez-Wippler
New York, Original Publications, 1992 edition

Rebirth of the Goddess, Finding Meaning in Feminist Spirituality by Carol P. Christ
New York, Routledge Publishing, 1997

Rituals and Spells of Santeria by Migene Gonzalez -Wippler
New York, Original Publications, 2007 edition

Santeria, The Religion by Migene Gonzalez-Wippler
Minnesota, Llewellyn Publications a div of Llewellyn Worldwide, Ltd. 2002 edition

Secrets of Voodoo by Milo Rigaud
California, City Lights Books, 1969, 1985 edition

Sexual Bewitchery and other Ancient Feminine Wiles by Barrie Dolnick, Julia Condon and Donna Limoges
New York, Avon Books a div of Hearst Corporation, 1998

Simple Spells for Love, Ancient Practices for emotional fulfillment by Barrie Dolnick
New York, Harmony Books a div of Crown Publishers, inc. First edition 1994

Spells and How they Work by Janet and Stewart Farrar
Washington, Phoenix Publishing, inc. 1990

The Book Of Goddesses, Invoke the Powers of The Goddess to Improve Your Life by Roni Jay
New York, A Quarto Book a div of Barron's Educational Series, 2000

The Book Of Goddesses, Past and Present: An Introduction to her Religion by Carl Olson
New York, Crossroad Press 1987 edition

The Book of Shadows by Lady Sheba
Minnesota, Llewellyn Publications, 1971 third edition 2000

The Elder Edda, translated by Lee Hollander,
Texas, USA, University of Texas, 1986

The Feminine Face Of God, The Unfolding Of The Sacred in Women by Sherry Ruth Anderson and Patricia Hopkins
New York, Bantam Books a div of Bantam Doubleday Dell Publishing Group, Inc., 1992

The Goddess Mirror, Visions of the Divine from East and West by David Kinsley
New York, State University of New York Press, 1989

The Goddess Oracle, a Way to Wholeness through the Goddess and Ritual
by Amy Sophia Marashinsky
Massachusetts, Element Books, 1997

The Goddess Path, Myth, Invocations, Rituals by Patricia Monaghan
Minnesota, Llewellyn Publications a div of Llewellyn Worldwide, Ltd.
1999 Seventh printing 2007

The Haitian Voodoo Handbook, Protocols for Ridding with the Lwa by Kenaz Filan
New York, Destiny Books Publishing, first edition 2006

The Hawaiian Oracle, Animal Spirit Guide from the Land of Light, by Rima A Morrell, PhD
New World Library, Novato, California 2006

The Holy Book of Women's Mysteries by Z. Budapest
California, Red Wheel /Weiser Books lnc, 2007 edition

The Holy Book of Women's Mysteries by Z. Budapest
California, Wingbow Press Books a div of Book people 1989 edition

The Homeric Hymn and Homerica/Loeb 57, by Hugh G. Evelyn-White
Connecticut, Harvard University Press, 1936

The New Book of Goddesses and Heroines by Patricia Monaghan
Minnesota, Llewellyn Publications a div of Llewellyn Worldwide, Ltd. 2002 edition

The Magick of Candle Burning by Gerina Dunwich
New York, A Citadel Press Book a div of Carol Publishing Group, edition 1992

The Magic Candle, Facts and Fundamental of Ritual Candle Burning by Charmaine Dey
New York, Original Publications, 1982

The Magic Shield, A Manual Defense Against the Dark Arts by Francis Melville
New York, A Quarto Book a div of Barron's Educational Series, inc. First edition 2004

The Magickal Formulary by Herman Slater
New York, Magickal Childe Inc., First edition 1981

The Mythic Tarot, a New Approach to the Tarot Cards by Juliet Sharman-Burke and Liz Greene
New York, A Fireside Book Publishing a div of Simon and Schuster Inc., 1986

The Politics of Women's Spirituality, Essays on the Rise of Spiritual Power Within the Feminist Movement Edited by Charlene Spretnak
New York, An Anchors Books, Published by Bantam Doubleday Dell Publishing Group, inc. 1982

The Sea Priestess by Dion Fortune
Maine, Samuel Weiser, inc, 1978, 1999 edition

The Spiral Dance, A Rebirth of the Ancient Religion of the Great Goddess by Starhawk
California, Harper and Row, Publishers, First edition 1979

The Witches' Goddess, the Feminine Principle of Divinity by Janet and Stewart Farrar
Washington, Phoenix Publishing, inc., 1987 edition

The Women's Spirituality Book by Diane Stein
Minnesota, Llewellyn Publications, 1987 second printing 1987

The Wiccan Rede, Couplets of the Law, Teachings and Enchantments by Mark Ventimiglia
New York, Citadel Press books a div of Kensington Publishing Corp. First edition 2003

The Yoni, Sacred Symbol of Female Creative Power by Rufus C. Camphausen
Rochester, Vermont, Inner Traditions International, 1996

365 Goddess, a Daily guide to the Magic and inspiration of the Goddess by Patricia Telesco
California, Harper San Francisco A div of Harper Collins Publishers, First edition 1998

To Ride a Silver Broomstick by Silver Raven Wolf
Minnesota, Llewellyn Publications, 1993 Ninth edition of 1996

Ways of the Strega: Italian Witchcraft: It's Legends, Lore and Spells by Raven Grimassi
Minnesota, Llewellyn Publications a div of Llewellyn Worldwide, Ltd. First edition 2000

What Witches Do, The Modern Coven Revealed by
Great Britain, Peter Davies Ltd. Morrison and Gibb Limited, first edition 1971

What Witches Do, The Modern Coven Revealed by
Washington, Phoenix Publishing Co., Revised U.S.A. edition 1983

Wicca, The Old Religion in the New Age by Vivianne Crowley
Great Britain and California, Aquarian Press an imprint of Harper Collins Publications, 1989

Witch Crafting, A Spiritual Guide To Making Magic by Phyllis Curott
New York, Broadway Books, first edition 2001

Witchcraft for Tomorrow by Doreen Valiente
Washington, Phoenix Publishing Co., 1978 the edition of 1987

Witches, Investigating an Ancient Religion by T.C. Lethridge
New York, Citadel Press inc. 1962, American edition of 1968

Women's Mysteries Ancient and Modern by M. Esther Harding

New York, Harper Colophon a div of Harper and Row, Publishers, first edition 1976

Magazines, Periodicals and Other Publications
Circle Magazine, Celebrating Nature, Spirit and Magic Issue 87 Spring 2003 Earth and Spirit: Mother Gaia by Jesse Wolf Hardin

Green Egg a Journal of the Awakening Earth Vol. 30 No #125 November-December 1998, Gaian Ministry; Reclaiming Earth and Spirit by Jesse Wolf Hardin
Green Egg a Journal of the Awakening Earth Vol. 30 No #125 November-December 1998, Ritual: Ancient and Modern by Ramfis S. Firethorn

Pan Gaia Exploring the Pagan World No #20 Summer 1999, Brigid in Ireland; Discovering the Magic by Diane Conn Darling
Pan Gaia, A Pagan Journal for Thinking People No. #36 Summer 2003 Erzulie Freda, Mistress of Love by Kevin Filan

Llewellyn's Annual Witches date book 1999
Llewellyn's 1999 Magical Almanac
Llewellyn's 2005 Magical Almanac
Llewellyn's Annual Witches Spell-a-Day Almanac 2003,
Llewellyn's Annual Witches Spell-a-Day Almanac 2008

SageWoman No.# 35 Autumn 1996, 10th Anniversary, Featured Column-One of Ten Thousand: Goddess Lore and Ritual.... Athene, The Reconciler of Opposites by Diana L. Paxson
SageWoman No.# 39 Autumn 1997, Featured Column-One of Ten Thousand: Goddess Lore and Ritual.... Hekate Guide of the Soul by Diana L. Paxson
SageWoman No.#46 Summer 1999, Featured Column-One of Ten Thousand: Goddess Lore and Ritual.... Brigid, Inspiration Upwelling by Diana L. Paxson
SageWoman No.#46 Summer 1999, Creating Ritual: A Guide to Design by Wendy Hunter Roberts
SageWoman No.#46 Summer 1999, The Great Goddess Saraswati; Flowing River of Creativity, Inspiration and Joy by Suzin Green
SageWoman No. #47 Autumn 1999, Petition to Oya, a letter offering from a reader by Juniper in Colorado
SageWoman No.# 54 Summer 2001, Reclaim Your Power...and Find inner Peace, Too! by Lady Moondance
SageWoman No.#55 Autumn 2001, Featured Column-One of Ten Thousand: Goddess Lore and Ritual.... Oya, Lady of Change by Diana L. Paxson

SageWoman No.#57 Spring 2002, Featured Column-One of Ten Thousand: Goddess Lore and Ritual.... Artemis, Hunting The Moon by Diana L. Paxson

SageWoman No. #57 Spring 2002, Coming Across The Great Goddess Ix Chel by Bethany Walsh Smith
SageWoman No. #64 Prayer and Invocation, Featured Column-One of Ten Thousand: Goddess Lore and Ritual.... Sarasvati, Word of Wisdom by Diana L. Paxson
SageWoman No. #65 Truth and Beauty, Masks for the Goddess by Lauren Raine
SageWoman No. #65 Truth and Beauty, Calligraphy lessons by Kela Vaeltaja
SageWoman No. 75 Autumn 2008, Awakening and Surrendering, Featured Column-One of Ten Thousand: Goddess Lore and Ritual.... Maman Brigitte Priestess of the Tomb by Diana L. Paxson

The Oracle from The Apple Branch Enzine
Susan Weed's Online Enzine
Zsuzsanna E. Budapest Online Goddess Enzine

Music and Recordings
Buffalo Beat (Trance Drumming) by Richard C. Schrei
Faerie Goddess by Elaine Silver
Lady of the Lake by Elaine Silver
Fire Drums by Music Mosaic
Music in Harmony with Nature by Earth Sings
Paint The Sky with Stars - the Best of Enya
Reclaiming Second Chants , More Ritual Music from Reclaiming and Friends
Sacred Drum Visions, The 20th anniversary collection, David & Steve Gordon-Sequoia records.com
Selu and Dream weaver from album "Fire Leap" By Michelle Mays
Shamanic Songs and Ritual Chants by Flight of the Hawk
She Changes, by Moving Breath
Sheila Foster, Meditations from a Women's Mystery School -Volume I- Invoking the Sacred Feminine...a wonderful collection of Feminine Meditations
Skin and Bone, Inanna, Sisters with Rhythm
Tales of the Drum, Soweto Percussion Ensemble
The Lotus Eaters, by Wendy Rule
Yoga Masters Meditation Series, Meditation for Emotional Freedom by Gael Chiarella founder of Yokobics
****

About the Author...

...She's supported by her ancestral lineage of strong, magickal, high priestesses'...

Great grand-daughter of a small town's renowned priestess, healer and advisor, B. Melusine was born and raised into a magickal, spiritual household. Her mother was an astrologer, dream analysis consultant, spiritualists and social worker, who dabbled in occult studies and B. Melusine was the recipient of the pool of spiritual knowledge shared by her ancestry. Her interest in the occult were nurtured and cultivated early on by extended family members and by those she surrounded herself with. By age 15, however, she faced the tragic unexpected loss of her mother and even more devastatingly, four years later, she would find herself mourning her father's death too, as he struggled and lost his battle with a liver disease. In the midst of tragedy, spiritual studies enlightened, comforted and guided her during this most difficult time of her life and her connection to spirit grew.

Music also, had always played a very important part in her life and, by its own accord, held a great deal of magick in her own self-healing. Continuing her education after High School, despite the grave loss of her parents, was compulsory and proved to be the right choice for her. In college she devoted herself to her music conservatory studies but continued her tarot and spiritual practice on her own. Her music conservatory disciplined garnered her a Bachelor's in Music, with summa cum laude distinction, from Westminster Choir College in Princeton, New Jersey. Pursuing her Master's Degree brought her back to her birthplace in New York City and in two years, she completed her Master's in Music in Voice Performance, at the prestigious Manhattan School of Music.

Time in New York City exposed her to numerous learning venues and greater opportunities to further her occult studies. At the New York Open Center she studied tarot with renowned psychic/tarot reader Patti Canova. She also participated in numerous lectures, seminars on spiritual matters, drumming circles and rituals. She participated in open Sabbat rituals held by thealogian Susan Marie Hellerer, DMIV. She also partook in lectures by Margot Adler, author of "Drawing Down the Moon" and Phyllis Currott, author of "Book of Shadows", "The Love Spell", "Witch Crafting" and HP of Temple of Ara, in New York City. Attending seminars by Kaitlynn, introduced her to the Fey Wiccan tradition, at The Source of Life in NYC. At the Learning Annex she took classes on traditional magick, tarot practice and participated in lectures and rituals held by Donna Limoge, co-author of "Sexual Bewitchery and other Ancient Feminine Wiles". Around this time B.Melusine had also joined a yearlong Pagan grove study with High Priest, Joe A. Zuchowski and his partner, distinguish High Priestess, Jezibell Anat, at New York City's emblematic "Enchantments, Inc.", where she learned the various disciplines of Witchcraft and Thelematic Wicca. She was later also handfasted in 1999, at this prestigious New York City Landmark.

At the Zodiac Lounge on the upper Westside in New York City, she was a member of The Zodiac Lounge Women's Circle -an all-female Goddess centered group led by High Priestess Jezibell. This, along with the numerous female centered Goddess literature she was being exposed to like; Z. Budapest, Shekhinah Mountainwater, Marion Weinstein, Ffiona Morgan, Diane Stein, all sparked a greater interest in Women's spirituality. B. Melusine, then added another spiritual women's group, when she learned of "Crystal Quilt Inc." in Manhattan, N.Y. They offered a weekly, all female circle, advocating the tradition of – "Wise-Woman Healing Ways" and it was facilitated by Robin Rose Bennett. Robin Rose Bennett is a well-known Herbologist, student of Susun Weed, Green-Witch and author of "Healing Magic; A Greenwitch's Guide Book" and it is in these numerous wommin circles that B. Melusine unearth great magick, empowerment, healing, sisterhood and an ancient way of being that resonated so close to her own ancestry. It was in these precious Wommin's circles, amongst some of the most amazing powerful sisters (*"all of us were hungry for wisdom, healing and knowledge,"* she remembers) that her life started to shift in ways she had not anticipated. These Goddess and wommin centered groups enriched her life greatly and in the presence of such great teachers, facilitators and priestesses, she was privileged to learn a great deal about the art-form and how to formulate groups and circles that nurture Women's spirituality.

Upon jumping the broom with her husband, she moved to Levittown, New York, in Long Island, where she continued her Goddess centered Wiccan practice, more now as a solitary, due to her new role as wife and mother. She immersed herself in informative books, the occasional Open group sabbat rituals and worked on creating her own Grimoires and invocations. She expanded on her artistry with numerous arts and craft projects and continued to raise her family. At this time also, she added Hinduism, mantra and yoga studies to her list of passions.

A change in climate and lifestyle lured her, and her family, to the South-West, in Texas, where she now resides with her three young boys, husband, two Boston Terriers, Luna- the malti-poo and a, rather aloof, mystical black cat. Just recently she was claimed by the newest member of her clan, a vivacious Corn snake affectionately called Nymphy-Lilith. Now in Schertz, Texas, she continues her eclectic Goddess spirituality practice and has included pagan art song compositions, spiritual crafting, intuitive arts, Goddess paintings, trance work and creative writing. Her first year in Texas found her immediately involved, facilitating and priestessing Goddess rituals for one of the few (at the time) established Goddess groups in the area. Seeing a need for more wommin centered sacred space and wanting to re-create the enriching sisterhood experiences from her past, in New York City, she started to consider formulating a Goddess group. It was only after a powerful series of visions, dreams and coincidences that she bravely took on the task. Being new to the area and not knowing many people was daunting at first, but her devotion to Goddess and Women Spirituality remained true and in that effort, she founded, **"Grove of the Feminine Divine,"** an all womyn's monthly Goddess Gathering group. Her first book, **"Gatherings for Goddess, a Complete Manual for Priestessing Women's Circles"**, holds her priestessing journey, invaluable lessons and precious experiences through-out the creation, nurturance and sustenance of this group. It is a treasure trove of insight for any dedicant heeding the call to promote community, wommin's Circles and Goddess Spirituality. It was also around this time she partook of several Goddess Gatherings sojourns, traveling to San Jose California, to attend the 2008 Goddess Gathering, where she finally met and was initiated by beloved founder of the feminist Wiccan Dianic tradition, Z. Budapest. The following year, she traveled to Madison, Wisconsin to attend yet another important Dianic event. This time, B. Melusine partook of Dianic Author and songstress, Ruth Barrett's Daughter of Diana, annual Goddess Gathering and here, she continued to expand her ritual experiences and knowledge of Goddess and Women Spirituality.

"Living Goddess Spirituality, a Feminine Divine Priestessing Handbook, " "Gatherings for Goddess, a Complete Manual for Priestessing Women's Circles", and "Goddess Grimoire Journal, a collection of Simple Prose and Spells," are now available on Amazon.com and at http://www.createspace.com /4002824, 3795965 and 3799105 or directly from the author's **website at http://www.Femininedivineworks.com**.

The author

"...But I being poor, have only my dreams;
I have spread my dreams under your feet;
Tread softly because you tread on my dreams...." Yeats

The End

Gathering for Goddess
A complete manual for Priestessing Women's Circles,
By B. Melusine Mihaltses

ISBN: 978-0-9851384-4-8   LCCN: 2012933200

Dear friends,

Thank you for your interest in our growing company and our various tools that facilitate spiritual growth. We have many more helpful products available for our wonderful patrons. Below we have provided an order form with some of our current offerings for sale. Please feel free to utilize this form to place orders or contact us; either by email, social networks, our blog or website, mailing address or Phone. Thank you again for your support, we look forward to being of service to you.

ORDER FORM:

	Price	Qty	Amount
1. Living Goddess Spirituality,	19.99		
2. Goddess Grimoire Journal,	15.99		
3. Gathering for Goddess Manual,	26.99		
4. Goddess Gathering T-Shirts (S, M, L)	11.99		
5. Artwork by the Author (please contact price varies accordingly)			
6. Meditation Recordings by author	11.99		
7. Goddess Songs Music CD Recording,	11.99		

Subtotal:

20% discount for purchases of 3 or more:
State Tax:
Shipping and Handling (3.95 per bk):
Total:

Enclosed Payment and this Order form in an envelope and Mail to:

FEMININE DIVINE WORKS,
B. MELUSINE MIHALTSES
P.O. Box 114
Schertz, Texas 78154-0114
Femininedivineworks@gmail.com
Groveofthefemininedivine@yahoo.com
Visit our WEBSITE at: http://www.Femininedivineworks.com

Your Name_____

Mailing Address _____

_____

Telephone _____
Payment Information: Check___   Money Order _____

Please allow 2-4 weeks for delivery

FEMININE DIVINE WORKS

FEMININE DIVINE WORKS, P.O.BOX 114, SCHERTZ, TEXAS 78154
www.Femininedivineworks.com

www.ingramcontent.com/pod-product-compliance
Lightning Source LLC
Chambersburg PA
CBHW081412230426
43668CB00016B/2213